SEX, DEATH AND PUNISHMENT

RICHARD DAVENPORT-HINES was born in 1953 and lives in London. His first book, *Dudley Docker*, was Joint Winner of the Wolfson Prize for History and Biography in 1985. He is a Fellow of the Royal Historical Society, and is married with two sons.

Extracts from the reviews of
Sex, Death and Punishment

'This is not a book to give to your lover.'

DAVID COHEN, *New Scientist*

'Davenport-Hines has assembled a fine collection of piquant opinions, that echo like grunts from the primaeval swamp, and he writes with wit, style and insight, as well as bracing indignation. This book is a real corker; it will annoy all the right people, and, I vouch, give much pleasure to everyone else.'

WALTER GRATZER, *Guardian*

'The reader of *Sex, Death and Punishment* will be entertained and appalled by the apoplectic fulminations of bishops, judges and editors. Davenport-Hines is a good hater in a good cause.'

ROY PORTER, *Times Literary Supplement*

'This timely, well-documented book brilliantly exposes the sham morality that lies beneath the stereotyping of "victims", the ostracism of the "infected", and the aggravated labelling of the "suffering".'

HAYDEN MURPHY, *Glasgow Herald*

'It is lively and fascinating, as well as timely.'

HILARY MANTEL, *Evening Standard*

'A disturbing look at intolerance.'

MICHAEL BROWN, *Yorkshire Post*

'Fascinating and vigorously argued.'

J. D. F. JONES, *Financial Times*

'Davenport-Hines' rage is full-throated and compelling.'

ANDREW MOTION, *Observer*

'Sweeps like a roller-coaster through a topical panorama of recurrent themes in the discussion of homosexuality and venereal disease.'

LESLEY HALL, *New Statesman and Society*

'A polemical, even a crusading book.'

DAVID SEXTON, *Listener*

'This is a heartfelt and stimulating book, a valuable contribution to an important debate.'

CHRISTOPHER HIBBERT, *Sunday Times*

'In this scholarly and well-argued book . . . Davenport-Hines spends a lot of time looking at the sexual habits of soldiers. A mucky job, if you ask me.'

PETER CHARLTON, *Brisbane Courier Mail*

SEX, DEATH AND PUNISHMENT

*Attitudes to sex and sexuality
in Britain since the Renaissance*

Richard Davenport-Hines

FontanaPress
An Imprint of HarperCollinsPublishers

First published by William Collins Sons & Co. Ltd, 1990

This Fontana Press edition published 1991

9 8 7 6 5 4 3 2 1

Fontana Press is an imprint of Fontana Paperbacks, a division of the
Collins Publishing Group, London

Copyright © Richard Davenport-Hines 1990

Printed and bound in Great Britain by
William Collins Sons & Co. Ltd, Glasgow

FOR JENNY

A perfect Woman, nobly planned,
To warn, to comfort, and command

WORDSWORTH

Acknowledgments

Many debts have accrued in writing this book. Jonathan Liebenau lent me his copy of Alan Brandt's history of syphilis in the United States and John Sturrock later suggested that I should review it for *The Times Literary Supplement*: without their intervention it might not have occurred to me to write a history of English sexuality from the standpoint of the AIDS crisis. I would have hesitated in this task but for the incitement of two friends, Jonathan Smith and Charlie Wilkinson, to whom I am grateful for much kindness and support. At a later stage I was given delightful encouragement by Robin Farquhar-Thomson and by Kate Jones. My agent Andrew Best of Curtis Brown and my editors at Collins, Stuart Proffitt and Philip Gwyn Jones, were marvels of sympathy. Others who have contributed to this book will forgive me if they are not particularized.

The resources of the London Library, the Wellcome Institutes for the History of Medicine at Euston and Oxford, and Gay's the Word bookshop in Bloomsbury were indispensable, and I remember with pleasure the friendliness of staff at each institution.

For the use of copyright material I am grateful to Lady Dalrymple-Champneys, to the Marchioness of Dufferin and Ava and the Deputy Keeper of Records at the Public Record Office of Northern Ireland, to the Countess of Longford and to Lord Monk Bretton. For permission to quote the poem 'Fire and Ice' I am grateful to the estate of Robert Frost, to Edward Connery Lathem and Messrs Jonathan Cape.

My wife found herself cast as my literary patron during the writing of this book. I owe much to her generosity and magnanimity which were seldom strained even long after my publisher's advance had been spent.

After some correspondence with me, the Home Office agreed to release the working papers of the Wolfenden Committee on Homosexuality and Prostitution, which had previously been withheld from the Public Record Office despite the lapse of more than thirty years which usually governs the public availability of official archives in Britain. This decision has enabled me to be the first historian to use some of Wolfenden's papers, but I should record that the Home Office did not release the verbatim minutes of oral evidence tendered to the Wolfenden Committee. This and other Crown copyright material in the Public Record Office is reproduced by permission of the Controller of Her Majesty's Stationery Office.

During the earlier stages of writing this book I worked at London Lighthouse, which provides hospice care for people with AIDS at a building in Notting Hill and is the nucleus of a network of professionals and volunteers providing care and counselling for people touched by HIV. Many of the ideas in this book were inspired by my experiences and conversations there, and in other respects my debt to those associated with London Lighthouse is immeasurable.

Kensington, September 1989

Contents

	Acknowledgments	vii
	List of plates	xi
	List of illustrations	xiii
1	Burning is Too Good for Them	1
2	The Secret Disease	16
3	Phoenix of Sodom	55
4	Dance as They Desire: the Construction and Criminalization of Homosexuality	105
5	Venus Decomposing: Sex, Disease and Punishment in the Nineteenth and Early Twentieth Centuries	156
6	Packets and Fanatics: the Royal Commission on Venereal Diseases	210
7	The Eaten Heart: Syphilis since the 1920s	245
8	Nights of Insult: Male Homosexuality since the 1940s	286
9	Hating Others: AIDS	330
	Select Bibliography	385
	Notes	391
	Index	427

List of Plates

The first visual representation of a syphilitic, from 1496, ascribed to Dürer *(courtesy of Wellcome Institute Library, London)*
Hogarth's depiction of venereal patients consulting a quack *(courtesy of Trustees of British Museum)*
An eighteenth-century male transvestite Governor of New York *(courtesy of New York Historical Society, New York)*
Lord George Germain (Viscount Sackville) *(courtesy of National Portrait Gallery)*
Sir Benjamin Thomson, Count von Rumford *(courtesy of National Portrait Gallery)*
'A Peep into the Blue Coat School' *(courtesy of Trustees of British Museum)*
'Arse Bishop Joslin and a Soldier' *(courtesy of Trustees of British Museum)*
'The Bishop of Sodom and his Fancy Gomorrah' *(courtesy of Trustees of British Museum)*
Lord Halsbury, the Victorian Lord Chancellor *(courtesy of Hulton Picture Library)*
Harry Quilter, the bullying Victorian critic *(courtesy of Hulton Picture Library)*

Oscar Wilde *(courtesy of Mary Evans Picture Library)*
Lord Alfred Douglas *(courtesy of Hulton Picture Library)*
Fred Barnes, gay music hall entertainer *(courtesy of Hulton Picture Library*
A Victorian prostitute 'Up in the World and Down on Her Luck' *(courtesy of Mary Evans Picture Library)*
'An Erring Daughter Cast Out into the Snow' *(courtesy of Mary Evans Picture Library*

Lord Meath, Christian philanthropist *(courtesy of National Portrait Gallery)*

Randall Davidson, Archbishop of Canterbury *(courtesy of Hulton Picture Library)*

Cosmo Lang, Archbishop of Canterbury *(courtesy of Hulton Picture Library*

Arthur Winnington-Ingram, Bishop of London *(courtesy of National Portrait Gallery)*

Soldiers receiving treatment for syphilis in 1916 *(courtesy of Établissement de Conception et de Production Audovisuelle des Armées, Fort d'Ivry)*

Philip Snowden *(courtesy of Hulton Picture Library)*

Revd John Scott Lidgett *(courtesy of Hulton Picture Library)*

Lord Willoughby de Broke *(courtesy of National Portrait Gallery)*

Sir Francis Champneys *(courtesy of Lady Dalrymple-Champneys)*

'Hello Boyfriend, Coming My Way?' *(courtesy of Public Record Office)*

'Here Comes the Bride' *(courtesy of Public Record Office)*

'A Shadow on His Future' *(courtesy of Public Record Office)*

Sir Alfred Mond *(courtesy of National Portrait Gallery)*

Earl Winterton *(courtesy of Hulton Picture Library)*

Sir David Maxwell Fyfe *(courtesy of Hulton Picture Library*

Rupert Croft-Cooke *(courtesy of Hulton Picture Library)*

'Every time you sleep with a girl' *(courtesy of Mates)*

'Women are only interested in men who are well equipped' *(courtesy of Mates)*

'They're awfully fiddly to put on' *(courtesy of Mates)*

List of Illustrations

Syphilis represented in a German pamphlet of 1496
(*courtesy of Wellcome Institute Library,*
   London)   27
The chapel of the London Lock Hospital in the
   eighteenth century
(*courtesy of Trustees of British Museum*)   36
A patient undergoing mercury treatment in the
   sixteenth century
(*courtesy of Mary Evans Picture Library*)   41
Advertisement for the treatment of venereal
   diseases in a London newspaper of 1820
(*courtesy of Trustees of British Museum*)   50
The face of a man who had engaged in oral sex
(*courtesy of Wellcome Institute Library, London*)   80
The face of a tertiary syphilitic
(*courtesy of Wellcome Institute Library, London*)   81
Broadsheet celebrating an execution for sodomy
   in the 1830s
(*courtesy of Mary Evans Picture Library*)   95
Broadsheet celebrating the pillorying of a
   sodomite in 1762
(*courtesy of British Museum*)   99
Miners dancing together in the late nineteenth
   century
(*courtesy of Mary Evans Picture Library*)   109
Henry Labouchere, framer of the infamous
   Amendment
(*courtesy of National Portrait Gallery*)   130
Charles Thickbroom, a rent boy of the 1880s
(*courtesy of Mary Evans Picture Library*)   136
A newspaper cartoon of 1929 stereotyping
   homosexuals
(*courtesy of Trustees of British Museum*)   150

Earl de Grey, one of the framers of the
    Contagious Diseases Acts
(courtesy of National Portrait Gallery)   168
Gay Ladies of London
(courtesy of Mary Evans Picture Library)   173
'Untreated Syphilis Deadly as a Bullet'
(courtesy of Public Record Office)   274
'VD is a Great Evil'
(courtesy of Public Record Office)   275
'VD can be cured'
(courtesy of Public Record Office)   276
A shrewd comment from Maudie Littlehampton
    on the humbug of the Wolfenden debates
*(courtesy of executors of Sir Osbert Lancaster
    and John Murray (Publishers) Ltd.)*   325
'The Scourge of the Eighties' in the *Sun*   334
The promoter of Mates condoms is attacked in the
    British press   355
British newspapers attack Pulpit Poofs in 1987   378

> the more I see
> Pleasures about me, so much more I feel
> Torment within me, as from the hateful siege
> Of contraries. JOHN MILTON

We of this kingdom have been repeatedly stigmatized by the other nations of Europe as a melancholy, dejected, gloomy people. The charge, I fear, is upon the whole but too well founded; and the proofs too visible, and sometimes too dreadful, to be evaded or denied. BISHOP BEILBY PORTEUS

Distrust all those in whom the urge to punish is strong. GOETHE

We hate the thing we fear, the thing we know may be true and may have a certain affinity with ourselves, for each man hates himself. The most interesting, most fertile qualities in every man are those he hates in himself and in others, for hatred includes every other feeling – love, envy, ignorance, mystery, the urge to know and to possess. It is hate that causes suffering. To overcome hatred is to take a step towards self-knowledge, self-mastery, self-justification and consequently towards an end of suffering. CESARE PAVESE

What concerns me is the harm you are doing to yourselves. I mean by perpetuating this talk of guilt and punishment, of banning and proscribing, of whitewashing and blackballing, of closing your eyes when convenient, of making scapegoats when there is no other way out. I ask you pointblank – does the pursuance of your limited role enable you to get the most out of life? HENRY MILLER

What is a history teacher? he asks. He's someone who teaches mistakes. While others say, here's how to do it, he says, and here's what goes wrong. While others tell you, this is the way, this is the path, he says, and here are a few bungles, botches, blunders and fiascos. GRAHAM SWIFT

CHAPTER ONE

Burning is Too Good for Them

> Yesterday an 89-year old grandmother from Solihull rang us . . . 'The homosexuals who have brought this plague upon us should be locked up. Burning is too good for them. Bury them in a pit and pour on quick-lime' . . . the majority of Britons would appear to be in agreement. *Daily Express* 13 December 1986

> Historians of every generation . . . unless they are pure antiquaries, see history against the background – the controlling background – of current events. They call upon it to explain the problems of their own time, to give to those problems a philosophical context, a *continuum* in which they may be reduced to proportion and perhaps made intelligible.
> HUGH TREVOR-ROPER

AIDS is a Copernican event in the history of sexuality. It will alter our view of the past as much as it will change conduct in the future. It needs to be considered calmly: instead, too often, it has been treated hysterically, unscrupulously or has generated a mindless rancour towards dying people. So I begin with solid facts, and a few sober predictions. The Human Immuno-Deficiency Virus (HIV) causes a viral infection of the blood which by damaging an individual's central nervous system and/or immunological defences can produce over seventy life-threatening but non-contagious conditions: in this ultimate manifestation, it is called Acquired Immune Deficiency Syndrome (AIDS). HIV is infectious (that is, transmitted by infection through bodily fluids), but the opposite of contagious, in the word's true meaning of communicable by social contact. AIDS will have a devastating effect on world health, on perceptions of sexuality, on sexual practice and on political life. The number of cases of AIDS reported worldwide increased by at least 1,500 per cent to 85,273 during the four years to April 1988; by the end of June 1989, 10,794 people in Britain were known to be infected with HIV, and a total of 2,372 people had developed AIDS, of whom 54 per cent had died. The World Health Organization estimated in 1986 that by 1990 it will be spending $1.5 billion annually to control HIV, and predicted in 1989 that the virus will have infected 40 million people by 2000. In African states such as Rwanda, Tanzania, Uganda, Zaire and Zambia the high mortality rate among young males trained to form the next administration cadre, or among professions such as medicine and engineering, is retarding national efficiency and changing the nature of political developments. The high incidence of the disease among Haitians led to a fall in the number of American tourists visiting the country from 70,000 in the winter of 1981–2 to 10,000 the following season. The resulting economic distress contributed to the overthrow of Jean-Claude Duvalier's presidency in 1986. Exasperation with the obtuse attitude to HIV of Queensland's Premier, Sir Joh Bjelke-Petersen, contributed to a Cabinet revolt and his enforced resignation in 1987. In some western countries, including Britain, the conceptualisation of and official responses to AIDS have been politicized.[1]

This is not a book about AIDS, but a book written in response to it. I recount social and medical perceptions of venereal diseases, especially syphilis, together with political or administrative responses, since the fifteenth century, and relate these to perceptions and treatment of homosexuals and bisexuals over the same period, with both themes placed within the context of modern British sexuality. Although it is important to recognize that the virus does not inherently or exclusively infect male homosexuals, 85 per cent of reported cases in Britain up to 1988 occurred in homosexual or bisexual men, 7 per cent involved haemophiliacs who were infected by contaminated blood products, with people who inject drugs comprising 2 per cent of reported AIDS cases. The reputation of AIDS as 'a gay plague' has been crucial to western reactions to the disease; indeed, as this book shows, this is the culmination of an enduring tradition – male homosexuals and people with venereal disease have long been treated as dirty, dangerous and contagious. A book could equally be written about the historical background to the ways in which AIDS has been depicted to the injury of drug users, or black people, or women; and indeed this book has implications for the experiences of all these people.[2]

It would be misleading to draw models for either public policy or private conduct regarding HIV too readily from the historic experience of syphilis or gonorrhoea. In some respects it is more comparable with hepatitis; the association with venereal disease is neither clinically accurate nor socially constructive. But AIDS *has* been saddled with 'a dismal cargo of appalling connotations', which draws on traditional perceptions of syphilis, of homosexuality and of social deviance. It is impossible to confront the stigma attached to AIDS, or the complexities that it raises, without a historical perspective. Because HIV is sexually transmissible, attitudes to it are governed by primitive, inchoate or unconscious anxieties with long historical antecedents. Historians, whose task is 'the study not of circumstances, but of man in circumstances', have a role in clearing some of this detritus.[3] It is in this spirit that this book is offered.

My themes are sex, dirt, fear and punishment. I examine some of the ways in which the British have imagined fearful dangers in what they deny or distrust in their own sexuality. I rely on the psychoanalytical concept of projection, whereby emotions, vices and qualities which an individual either rejects or refuses to recognize in himself are expelled from the self and relocated in another person or persons. The projector constructs a dark mirror of his own fears or desires in an image of a hateful Other whom he then persecutes. The blame he feels inside is projected out onto someone else: it is, to use a line of Shelley's,

the shade from his own soul upthrown.

Projection is a form of primitive self-defence which underlies many superstitions, and is seen in extreme form in the behaviour of paranoiacs. Impulses to exclude, isolate, purify and punish malefactors are characteristic of projection. Syphilitics and sodomites, I argue, have been objects of projection for centuries, and the appearance of a sexually transmissible virus identified with gay men has been a fatal conjunction in the history of projection.[4]

People become superstitious, as George Santayana noted, 'not because they have too much imagination, but because they are not aware that they have any'. Superstitions are the recourse of people who are full of nervous apprehension and lack self-knowledge. Sexual superstition and myth reflect the most oppressive anxieties or the more destructive crises in ordinary life, and project endemic sexual fears. Frequently the superstition takes the form of a fear of pollution. An individual whose behaviour or condition is found menacing by someone else is identified as dirty and dangerous – a pollutant. To attribute danger serves to place a subject above dispute, and helps to enforce conformity: to engender fear prevents people thinking in an open and unconfused way. Fears of pollution over-simplify and intimidate: they rely on the habit of thinking by chain of association rather than the process of reasoning. They involve a pre-logical, or even alogical, mentality which rejects scientific knowledge and depends upon pseudo-clinical observation. Often myths may be derided and seem to have been discredited in one era only to revive later. Myths such as that the size of men's nostrils was correlated to the size of their testicles, or that the breadth of a girl's mouth betrayed the breadth of her vagina, or that one could cleanse oneself of venereal infection by intercourse with a virgin, have waned and flourished even in the twentieth century. The ancient belief that the constitution of a child was determined by the condition of the parents during coitus – that early morning when parents were rested and vigorous was a propitious moment for conceiving a healthy child – or the superstition that a woman who had intercourse with her husband while thinking of the adulterer who usually fucked her would bear a child resembling her lover – find an echo in the belief of the twentieth-century moralist Mary Whitehouse that in some cases homosexuality 'is entirely precipitated by the abnormal (in terms of moral as well as physical norms) sexual behaviour of parents during pregnancy'. Such myths are as persistent as they are unpleasant.[5]

Pollution beliefs presuppose that inflexible, impersonal and inevitable punishment will smite transgressors: the very immutability of retribution reinforces the myth that there is an equally unchanging standard of behaviour, or an equally rigid code of morals. If punishment is personalized, if the circumstances and motives of the transgressor are considered, then the fantasy of unalterable moral law, or of timeless, unchanging natural morality, is exploded. Where situations are morally ambiguous, or where moral principles collide, fear of contagion can be used to hustle opinion into accepting that punishment or ostracism is an appropriate response. When an action offends a creed, or is held to be unvirtuous, yet does not provoke universal indignation, emphasis on the dangers of pollution can seem to aggravate the offence; opinion is marshalled against its perpetrator, who will be abused with all the rancour of simulated virtue. When there are no practical sanctions to support moral indignation, pollution beliefs may be mobilized to deter transgressors: fear of venereal disease, as we shall see, has been exploited to inhibit sexual desire. Hatred and vengeance are encouraged under the mask of social duty.[6]

Dirt can endanger physical health, but its threat to public salubrity is easily distorted by metaphors of disintegration. Let one example suffice. The Duke of Leeds' brother, the Revd Lord Sydney Godolphin Osborne, was a clergyman who toured the tenements of Glasgow in the company of policemen at night in the 1850s. He described them as a 'gully-hole' of human 'sewerage'. According to Osborne the tenements were 'deep dirt-pools of human life'; their inhabitants defiled and endangered the nation. Those who lived in such 'accumulated filth' were, he warned, 'creatures that in the days of revolution work out barbarisms and cruelties, with the language and demeanour of fiends. The horrors they commit become the marvels of history. We are much deceived if we argue that England knows no such element of evil.' In reality the Glaswegian tenements were filthy, vicious and diseased, but to Osborne dirt was not just a medical danger, it was an internalized metaphor for the decay he feared and an external metaphor for the political disorder that threatened the deference which kept his brother secure in Hornby Castle.[7]

Love and hate, Eros and death, are the adversaries which battle for supremacy over the human mind. The idea of death arising from sexual rapture holds a hideous thrill for those who are guilty or anxious about sexual expression. In the higher realms of art a picture like *The Climax* by Aubrey Beardsley (1894) identifies erotic consummation with extinction. A lower manifestation of this preoccupation is the genre of films including *Halloween* (1978) and *Friday the Thirteenth* (1981), in which a group of teenagers are murdered one by one by a maniac while they engage in naked romps, often in scenes of sylvan purity. The idea of an arbitrary and meaningless punishment abruptly inflicted on people cheerfully enjoying their bodies, the vision of death transmitted in ecstasy, the picture of violence destroying scenes of idealized innocence, all express an impulse in the human psyche which has been present throughout all ages. 'That the *Venereal Disease* was sent into the World by the Disposition of Providence, either to restrain, as with a Bridle, the unruly Passions of a Sensual Appetite, or as a Scourge to correct the Gratification of them, is an Opinion highly probable,' wrote one eighteenth-century physician. 'In the midst of sensual Pleasure there arises something bitter, nay very bitter, and we frequently meet with the Cause of Death in the very Fountain of Life.' [8]

Since the seventeenth century pollution beliefs have occasionally been united against both venereal patients and homosexuals. In a play of 1684, entitled *Sodom* and attributed to Lord Rochester, a court physician enjoins as the cure for an epidemic of gonorrhoea,

> To love and nature all their rights restore,
> Fuck women, and let buggery be no more,
> It doth the procreative end destroy,
> Which Nature gave with pleasure to enjoy,
> Please her, and she'll be kind – if you displease,
> She turns into corruption and disease.

By 1913 'the old view that syphilis is a divinely ordained penalty for illicit sexual indulgence, and that it is wrong therefore to seek to avert it' was 'seldom' formally expressed, according to a leading venereologist, Sir Malcolm Morris, but it persisted 'unconsciously' in the 'feeling of many'. In 1917, for example, a Cabinet minister, Austen Chamberlain, while discussing possible ways of regulating prostitution or reducing the incidence of venereal disease, commented that the British were a fundamentally puritanical race who resented 'legislation for making vice easy without the penalty which Providence attached to it'. More recently, following this cycle of sexual fear and mythology, there has been a recrudescence of concepts which regard illness as heavenly retribution. AIDS has been depicted as 'a sign from some wiser, greater authority than ourselves that we cannot continue spiralling downwards to the hell of totally indulging our baser appetites and survive without disease and anguish' by a leading British

newspaper columnist, Lynda Lee-Potter. 'Damnation is a consequence of evil,' she wrote in 1986: 'we are being damned by a
terrible disease caused by unmitigated sexual lust . . . both Nature
and God have devious ways of protecting us from the worst
aspects of our instinctive leanings towards destruction.'[9]

This view is as absurd as it is ugly. Sexually transmitted diseases
lack any of the essentials of retribution because they are capricious
in operation. Few more arbitrary or inefficient means of retribution could be devised. Syphilis 'attacks chiefly the ignorant, the
stupid and the poor: all those who do not understand how to look
after themselves', wrote a commentator in 1918. 'It singles out the
feebler and more incautious for its victims, while leaving the more
intelligent', or the more experienced, 'sinner' free to fornicate with
the impunity provided by prophylaxis. HIV has been contracted
by people with as few as one sexual partner in a lifetime; others
have escaped infection despite enjoying a high number of sexual
encounters.[10] Transmission of the virus depends far more upon
the nature of sexual couplings than upon their number or
multiplicity. HIV will tend to attack 'those who do not understand
how to look after themselves': in future, like syphilis seventy years
ago, it will reach the young, the ignorant and the incautious. It will
leave people experienced in practising 'safer sex' to do what they
choose, but will kill sexual novices.

In addition to the retributive superstition surrounding syphilis and gonorrhoea, HIV has been loaded with other stigmata. An
incurable disease is by definition mysterious and its contagion
must seem fearful. This is particularly true of any disease that can
be linked to homosexuality, which has itself so often been dubbed
a disease or discussed using the imagery of contagion. Homosexuality, according to the evangelical Bishop of Rochester in 1957,
was as 'contagious' as 'leprosy', while 'sodomy clubs' were
'plague-spots wherever they exist'.[11] In Britain and much of the
western world, HIV has been identified as primarily affecting gay
men, intravenous drug users and haemophiliacs. Its perception as,
above all, a homosexual contagion has brought a further burden
of social paranoia and political complexity to be borne by the
epidemic.

Venereal diseases and homosexuality have for centuries been
subject to stereotyping. We can only cope with the instabilities of
our world by categorizing it with stereotypical images onto which

we can project our most urgent fears. We defend ourselves when our integrity is threatened by acting as if the source of our anxieties and insecurities lies outside our control. Stereotyping occurs when we are too timid or lazy to think for ourselves about the details of our existence. As we grow older and experiences accumulate, we tend to rely still more heavily on our system of stereotype labelling. Facts which cannot be reconciled with the labels are ignored or twisted: self-censorship is unconsciously imposed upon our perceptions, so that we only admit sensations which confirm our presuppositions.[12] The reality of venereal disease has only been admissible when those with the disease could be depicted as wicked, rejected or deliquent. The existence of homosexuality, too, as we shall see, has been accommodated by invoking a caricature of effeminate titterers which ignores almost every fact of interest or significance concerning homosexual acts.

Centuries ago Montesquieu remarked 'that whatever is secret must be doubtful, and that our natural horror of vice may be abused as an engine of tyranny'. The apprehension that homosexuals constitute a Freemasonry of sorts, with arcane social codes and loyalties, whose secrecy spreads doubt and social disorder, is a theme of history which has been painfully revived by the spread of HIV. Homosexuality 'is not a quality which lies in behaviour itself, but in the action between the person who commits an act and those who respond to it'.[13]

One English bishop denounced homosexuality as 'morally evil and sinful in the highest degree' in 1954 because it violated 'natural law or, as the Christian would say . . . the purpose of the Creator who when He made man in His own image created them male and female'. He felt that 'the increase in unnatural offences is an ominous warning of something going radically wrong in . . . the social order'. Twenty-five years later another Protestant theologian defined the 'impurity' of homosexual activity as lying 'in the refusal of differences and the triumph of non-differentiation, i.e. disorder'. Sexual distinction, in this Christian belief, 'crowns the creative act of God' so that 'sexuality should be lived out by the man and woman as the very meaning of all differentiation, that is, recognized as a call to a relationship that is organized and creative, like a call to arms against the constant threat of disorder and chaos, whose most insidious form is the confusion of the sexes'. Such beliefs are millennial. Aretaeus the Cappodocian, writing in the second century AD, and using ideas centuries old, believed that males were foetuses which had grown to full potential and that women were lower in the natural hierarchy, failed foetuses, incapable of producing the hot semen which he identified with vitality and aggression. The Greek physician Galen, in the same era, believed that 'the Creator had purposely made one half of the whole race imperfect, and, as it were, mutilated'. In his treatise *On the Seed*, Galen warned that the male body would recede into a primary state of indifferentiation from women unless each man deliberately strove to maintain his virility, excluding 'softness' from his character, gait, physical bearing, cadences or acts. Elaborate codes of male deportment were maintained in Greek and Roman societies of Galen's time. Similar fears persist in the twentieth century. In the transition from childhood to adulthood characteristic of the modern world, it remains a condition of acceptance into the world of grown-ups that men are hard and aggressive, and that women are soft and passive. The fact that all men, in varying degrees and with vastly different levels of self-awareness, have tendencies which the world calls feminine – that they may wish to be sympathetic, demonstrative, gentle or creative – is potentially disruptive of social order. Contrary to such views, one of my themes is that the differentiation of men and women, and their allotment of antagonistic roles, their investment with rigidly separated desires or emotions, is not faithful to an underlying natural order, but largely a complex social artefact.[14]

There is nothing orderly about HIV. It neither defines nor recognizes social boundaries: in addition to spreading death and fear, it unmasks secrets and proves that the stereotypes which support social order are false. HIV can seem the enemy of differentiation. The most shocking aspect of Rock Hudson's death as a result of AIDS in 1985, judging from the press coverage, was that the actor belied his public image: despite his façade of heterosexual masculinity, he had practised homosexuality throughout his life. Journalists emphasized that social order was unreliable and 'must be constantly reaffirmed, examined and constructed'; assumptions about public heroes and masculine idols were chimeric. The death in 1985 of a chaplain at a British prison led to similar newspaper coverage which sought to stress that outward appearances can never be trusted. 'AIDS victim Gregory Richards led an amazing double life', according to the *Sunday Mirror*. 'After finishing work at Chelmsford Prison, Essex, he regularly slipped off to London for secret meetings with male companions.' The *Sun* also depicted 'the gay chaplain's amazing double-life' in which 'after work and church duties, a different Gregory Richards emerged'. The death from AIDS in 1987 of a London police constable was found deserving of similar coverage; it unsettled popular assumptions about the masculinity of uniformed men, cast doubt on the prevailing stereotypes of authority, and, among those in whom disorder fosters personal anxiety, raised a sense of imminent collapse. *The Times* noted that about eighty unmarried policemen and policewomen lived in the police housing block where Alan Douthwaite died, thus raising the spectre of further contagion undermining an institution thought to represent everything that is inviolable and orderly.[15]

Sexual desire is multiple: emotions are infinite in their variety and shading, yet society needs to classify and simplify them. What is called homosexuality in much of the modern industrialized world can cover not only erotic acts and thoughts, but also an illimitable range of acts and desires and sympathies which are not recognizably erotic. One can have homosexual feelings and yet not perceive oneself or be perceived by anyone else as homosexual. In other words, in the most unsettling and paradoxical manner, 'homosexuality exists and does not exist, at one and the same time.' This is horribly threatening to the authoritarian mind. It is often noted that those who articulate hostility to homosexuals or bisexuals are in a panic of anxiety about their own ambivalence or repressions. Violence against gays can be seen as a subterfuge which allows the aggressor to punish his own desire – but the wishes need not be immediately erotic. 'I cannot stand homosexuals. They are the most disgusting people in the world, and they are unfortunately on the increase,' ranted the Earl of Dudley in the House of Lords in 1966. 'I loathe them. Prison is too good for them.' Dudley was an energetic and aggressive man, 'lovable yet so moody and irritable' according to his homosexual friend Chips Channon. No one could know (probably least of all Dudley himself) what his outburst meant; his diatribe could easily be explained as that of a repressed homosexual, but it is probably more sensible to see it as the explosion of a man who had gone through life despising femininity in others and terrified about being in any way passive himself.[16]

Yet the reactions of all of society are surely based on more than a few individuals' terror about their own repressed wishes. The power and tenacity of homophobia derive from something more than an aggregation of individual neuroses. Western society would not have been so implacable in its behaviour to homosexuals if they were simply a threat to a few unfortunates blighted with confused sexual orientation. The State has never accepted the reduction of personal anxiety is numbered among its duties. For organized society to have reacted with such sustained hostility to homosexuals, it must be vulnerable in a deeper and wider sense. Homosexual desire is anomalous – in that it does not fit the stereotypes constructed for it – and ambiguous – because it is susceptible to so many interpretations. The slang word in north-east Brazil for a gay man is the synonym of 'doubtful'. Since medieval times at least western European homosexuals were classified with religious heretics for identification and destruction by the Inquisition. John Dryden's play *The Duke of Guise* (1682–3) carries several references to the threat posed by sodomites. 'Damned Neuters, in their middle way of Steering', he wrote, 'are Traitors, and assist by their Indifferency to the Destruction of the Government.' Gay men and lesbians cause doubt, confirm uncertainty, emphasize differentiation, symbolize contradiction, and confront normality. The vagrant impulse which characterizes homosexual desire, the insolent language and camp gestures, and above all *doubtfulness* are all horribly threatening to authority and authoritarian personalities.[17]

Fears of death and disintegration are everywhere in this subject. People have always lived in fear of the end of the world. Roman soothsayers like Haruspex who performed divination by sullying himself with entrails, Christian prophets and medieval schoolmen all predicted or calculated the end of life. The world would fall apart, humankind would disintegrate. Recently, for less than two centuries, in western industrializing nations, say from the late eighteenth century until the 1930s, one might profess to believe in progress: one could hope that the quality of human life was improving and that the world would not fall in. But the stench of Dachau, the blast from Hiroshima, the winds from Chernobyl, the din from Tehran have scattered the meliorists' camp. After a brief interlude, people are worrying about the death of the planet again, predicting human disintegration once more. This is not by chance.

Distintegration is what, individually and collectively, we fear most.

Excrement, anality and fear of death are inseparable. St Paul portrayed the human body as a holy vessel or temple, but it was a temple constantly producing waste products, that is human excreta, which so disturbingly evokes associations with a rotting corpse. Yeats marvelled that,

> Love has pitched his mansion
> In the place of excrement.

Freudians believe that the anus symbolizes all that must be expelled and dismissed from life; its repellent excreta symbolize the universal fate of death and decay. This evocation is especially strong in the case of HIV because one of the chief means of its transmission in the western world has been the act of sodomy, which thus forcibly emphasizes the disturbing links between excreta, decay and sexuality. The bowels of the earth, where men's rotting corpses were cast, were dreadful; anyone who enjoyed the bowels of living bodies was, by Christian standards, deviant. A popular poem of 1748 entitled 'Sodom's Catastrophe' conveyed this association:

> Where Sodom now lies buried in the deep:
> A stygian Lake, where stinking waters meet;
> To form a filthy Puddle, and complete,
> A *Mare Mortum* [sea of death], where the filthy stain
> Of Sodom's vices, do as yet remain:
> To warn Succeeding Ages to prevent
> The Efficient cause, and fatal Punishment.

Similarly 'a wretch in Newgate [prison], under sentence of three years for this abominable crime', who had 'been a common hack ever since he was twelve years old', was described in 1813 as 'this lump of excremental filth'. Oscar Wilde, protested a literary critic in 1912, 'slouchest out of the shameless slime . . . foul with perversities'. Sodomites, wrote another journalist in 1916, were 'intestinal worms'.[18]

This book is also a tribute to the power of language. Words are perhaps the most malignant and treacherous of mankind's possessions. They are saturated with all the sorrow and injustice of civilization. Rich in their potential to enhance the pleasure and meaning of life, they are used to prevent reflection or understanding, or as instruments of tyranny, or as ruses to separate people from their needs and instincts. The power of words usually results in the destruction rather than the enrichment of individuality. Their power is seldom wielded to achieve human elevation or fulfilment, but more often to deplete lives or eclipse personal experience. This book is about the consequences of centuries of verbal negativity and hate. A Dominican clergyman of the thirteenth century described homosexuality as 'evil filth'. 'It is yet without a Name: What then shall it be called?', asked an author at the start of the eighteenth century. 'There are not words in our Language expressive enough of the Horror of it.' In a poem of 1746, Charles Churchill wrote of 'monsters', 'vile pathics' and 'fiends'. In 1813 sodomy was described as 'this calamitous vice' and 'moral-blasting evil'; one practitioner was called a 'lump of diabolism' and another, more moderately, a 'vile old sodomite'. By 1890 'the hideous, and loathsome, and horrible details' of Lord Arthur Somerset's conduct with a young postal messenger were too 'odious' for the House of Commons to hear. A Conservative MP in 1921 spoke of 'this horrid grossness' and 'deep-seated evil' practised by 'abandoned' people who have 'forgotten all the dictates of Nature and morality'. In 1986 James Anderton, the chief constable of Greater Manchester, attacked the 'degenerate conduct' and 'obnoxious practices' of homosexuals, and implied a terror of excreta as the symbol of bodily decay, and an identification of excrement with sodomy, by denouncing people 'at risk' from AIDS as 'swirling around in a human cesspit of their own making'.[19]

Sexually transmitted diseases also collected an increasing weight of oppressive descriptions and verbal violence. Syphilitic prostitutes were identified as 'scatterers of pestilence' (to quote one doctor writing in 1857), but male phobia against syphilitics also 'drew on the guilty acknowledgment of a monstrous sexual self' to present the disease 'as the eruption of a repressed desire, the surfacing of a secret life'. Thus syphilis was described in 1869 as 'an ineradicable poison' tainting British blood, 'a pestilence whose march is so secret, and whose attacks are so insidious, that none can be certain of its escape ... its horrible and widespread loathsomeness ... continues to exercise its fatal power silently and secretly, its effects being inconceivably extensive and deadly, precisely because of the insidiousness with which these are achieved'.[20]

Dr Henry Maudsley, one of the founders of English psychiatry, saw tertiary syphilis as 'characterized by a virtually complete perversion of moral sense'. In Maudsley's description, 'A man who has been hitherto temperate in all his habits, prudent and industrious in business, and exemplary in the relations of life, undergoes a great change of character, gives way to dissipation of all sorts, launches into reckless speculation in business, and becomes indifferent to his wife, his family, the obligations of his position; his surprised friends see only the effects of vice, and . . . after a time, they hear that he is in the police court accused of assault or stealing.' Tertiary syphilitics, according to an early *Dictionary of Psychological Medicine*, 'cease to be guided, as formerly, by religion, altruism, sense of morality, or duty, patriotism, love of family, of truth, of friendship, of beauty'. Oscar Wilde, who was himself syphilitic, wrote his novel *The Picture of Dorian Gray* partly as an allegory of the disease. Gray is possessed by 'a horrible malady', and the 'leprosies of sin' turn his body into 'a monstrous and loathsome thing' with 'hideous face', 'misshapen body and failing limbs'; he develops 'warped lips' and 'coarse bloated hands'.[21]

Syphilis seemed so terrible a word that for years it was forbidden in French telegrams, and despite venereal diseases being debated in the House of Commons almost annually for twenty years, the word 'syphilis' was not uttered there until 1883. In which year St John Brodrick, a worldly young MP, in a private letter to his friend George Curzon, felt obliged to spell it 'Syp . . . is', as if it was a blasphemy or obscene curse. It was a disease whose physiological character was uniquely subordinated to other perceptions. Venereal infections were only 'in part a medical question', declared William Temple, Archbishop of Canterbury, in 1942, urging that their 'spiritual, moral, social and medical aspects should receive attention in that order'.[22]

One twentieth-century provincial gentleman of leisure, a retired lawyer, enunciated the attitudes which typified those surrounding syphilis. 'All the members of the family were accused, at one time or another, of having the disease; the circle broadened, my aunts had syphilis; it was written all over the letters of my remotest cousins; it was stamped on the handiwork of the gardener,' so his son recalled in 1972. 'Even a new housemaid would come under the ban . . . syphilis was never a pretty thing, not a pretty word, and from the lips of my father it sounded particularly foul, like the hiss of a snake. "Sshyphilis . . . sshyphilis . . . that's what the matter is with you my boy."'[23]

Both homosexuality and sexually transmitted diseases thus carry a long tradition of depiction as purveyors of disorder in western society. For centuries there have been calls for gay men and syphilitics to be identified, isolated and abused: they have been treated with similar revulsion, and have suffered the effects of the same compulsion to punish minorities and create scapegoats. People who denied their desire for sexual adventure or repressed their wish for multiple partners projected their fury and frustration at these unacknowledged desires out onto another group of people, syphilitics, who were reviled for having satisfied their desires. Similarly those who denied or did not recognize that they were sexually attracted to others of their own gender, or who were terrified of any relaxation in the rigid social and emotional differences that were attributed to or imposed on men and women, pitched their bad feelings about this denial into what they accordingly saw as a filthy dustbin for bad feelings, the community of practising homosexuals. Given this heritage, it is not surprising that the outbreak of AIDS, which in Europe and America has been insistently depicted as a sexual disease of homosexuals – a 'gay plague' – had occasioned a redoubled outburst of cruelty and has excited humankind's irrepressible urge to excoriate and to punish.

CHAPTER TWO

The Secret Disease

All men naturally hate each other. We have
used concupiscence as best we can to make it
serve the common good, but this is mere sham
and a false image of charity, for essentially it is
just hate.   BLAISE PASCAL

He that is Chast and Continent not to impair
his strength, or honest for fear of Contagion,
will hardly be Heroically virtuous.
                                    SIR THOMAS BROWNE

Is it just that with death cruel love should
    inspire,
And our tarses be burnt by our hearts taking
    fire?
There's an end to communion if humble
    believers
Are damned in the cup like unworthy
    receivers.   LORD ROCHESTER

The phrase 'venereal disease' was coined by Jacques de Bethercourt in 1527, but sexually transmitted diseases can be traced back
to biblical times. Until the 1490s there was no social perception or
medical identification of the disease which is now known as
syphilis, and until the nineteenth century it was often confused
with gonorrhoea. It is likely that gonorrhoea existed in Europe
and the Middle East before the fifteenth century, when syphilitic
infections probably first arrived from the New World.

Gonorrhoea, as is now known, is caused by a bacterium named
Neisseria gonorrheae, or gonococcus, which is usually sexually

transmitted, with an incubation period of between two and ten days which sometimes lasts as long as a month. Infection is often unaccompanied by symptoms, and is therefore hard to diagnose. The most common evidence is local genital discharge, and a burning pain when urinating; in women abnormal menstrual bleeding and anorectal discomfort are frequent. For men the most usual symptoms are urethral discharge with frequent and painful urination, sometimes attended by complications involving infected glands in or near the groin.

Syphilis, conversely, is caused by a microscopic, corkscrew-shaped bacterium, *Treponema pallidum*; in acquired syphilis, this bacterium enters the body through the skin or mucous membrane (usually during copulation) and has an incubation period of between five days and five weeks. Congenital syphilis is transmitted to the foetus inside the infected mother when the *Treponema pallidum* penetrates the placental barrier. Within days of an acquired infection, the spirochaetes (as the *Treponema pallidum* are also called) reach the lymph gland, where they swiftly multiply and enter the bloodstream. A small circular ulcer called a chancre may appear near the primary syphilitic lesion at this stage. If untreated during this primary stage, secondary lesions of syphilis appear on the body between three and six weeks later; there are a multiplicity of possible symptoms, which mimic a range of other skin disorders.

> Bones and joints often become painful, and circulatory disturbances such as cardiac palpitations may develop. Fever, indigestion, headaches or other nonspecific symptoms may accompany the rash. In some cases skin lesions develop into moist ulcers teeming with spirochetes, a condition that is especially severe when the rash appears in the mouth and causes open sores that are virulently infectious. Scalp hair may drop out in patches . . . The greatest proliferation and most widespread distribution of spirochetes throughout the body occurs in secondary syphilis.[1]

If not effectively treated, in anything from one to thirty years after the secondary infection has become latent, the third stage of the disease develops. In these cases of tertiary syphilis, rubbery tumours called gummas appear in soft tissues or viscera, followed by damage to the heart or other vital organs, or by various forms of spinal meningitis (progressing from weakness or numbness of the legs to paralysis), or neurological decline, manifest in blindness or deafness and perhaps culminating in a softening of the brain now called paresis but best known as general paralysis of the insane. But this summary of the two diseases is written with the benefit of hindsight, and cannot convey the protean nature of the symptoms which syphilis in particular presents.

References to venereal disease occur in the Bible, as do descriptions of leprous plagues which have some resemblance to syphilitic epidemics. Washing after copulation, particularly for men with urethral discharges, is recommended in Leviticus XV. An army of Israelites fighting the Midianites was held in quarantine to permit incubation of any infection and isolation of those diseased. An order intended to prevent sexual plagues demanded the execution of all Midianite women prisoners 'that have known man by lying with him'. Moses, who seems to have recognized the infectiousness of gonorrhoea, recommended cleanliness and segregation.[2]

There is little about gonorrhoea in the writings of ancient Greece and Rome, whose medical authorities such as Hippocrates or Galen mention it only casually to warn that constant loss of semen may vitiate physical strength. Aretaeus the Cappodocian, who lived two centuries after Christ, described gonorrhoea as 'not, indeed, a deadly affection, but one that is disagreeable and disgusting even to hear of'. He shared his contemporaries' concern at the loss of semen: 'if impotence and paralysis possess . . . the . . . genital organs, the semen runs as if through dead parts, nor can it be stopped even in deep sleep; for whether asleep or awake the discharge is irrestrainable.' Aretaeus betrayed the same fearful hostility to female sexual desire which characterized the outbursts of many later venereologists: 'Women also have this disease, but their semen is discharged with titillation of the parts, and with pleasure, and from immodest desires of connection with men. But men have not the same prurient feelings.' Even young patients with this disease, in the diagnosis of Aretaeus, 'necessarily become old in constitution, torpid, relaxed, spiritless, timid, stupid, enfeebled, shrivelled, inactive, pale, whitish, effeminate, loathe their food and become frigid; they have heaviness of the members, torpidity of the legs, are powerless and incapable of all exertion.'

In many cases the disease caused paralysis 'for how could the nervous system not suffer when nature has become frigid in regard to the generation of life? For it is the semen when possessed of vitality, which makes us to be men, hot, well braced in limbs, hairy, well voiced, spirited, strong to think and to act, as the characteristics of men prove.'[3]

Arab authors and those of the later Roman period began recommending specific therapies: Alzahavarius (Albucasis) prescribed seawater or salt water as a urethral injection, and this therapy continued for almost a millenium, with urethral injections of seawater still being recommended as a remedy for gonorrhoea in the nineteenth century, and sodium chloride being used until at least the 1930s. In the thirteenth century asses' or goats' milk mixed with the juice of plantago was recommended as a cure for urethral ulcers. Human milk mixed with barley water was used for urethral injections; other medieval physicians added sugar, oil of violets and milk of almonds to the mixture, or offered alternative recipes of barley water, honey water and an iris decoctum, or of antimony and acacia. Since patients demanded treatment, early physicians tried to satisfy them with innocuous prescriptions that would not leave them feeling that their case was hopeless. After the Norman invasion of England the French phrase for gonorrhoea '*la chaude pisse*' (hot piss) apparently led to the evolution of 'burning' or 'brenning' in English terminology in the fourteenth century. Other names for the disease were 'gleet', 'droeppert' and 'tripper', mostly references to the discharges from the penis or the burning sensation on urinating which characterize the disease.[4]

It seems that syphilis was introduced to Europe and the Orient by Christopher Columbus and his followers on their return from America in 1493, a transaction which is sometimes called the Columbian Exchange. Others argue that syphilis is merely a strain of treponematosis whose characteristics have been made more pronounced by social conditions, personal habits and climate, and which before the fifteenth century was often loosely identified under the generic name of 'leprosy'. The organism responsible for syphilis resembles those responsible for two tropical diseases, yaws and bejel, prompting speculation that syphilis acquired its present nature when man migrated to cool areas of the earth and began to wear clothes. The validity of the theory of 'the

Columbian Exchange' is irrelevant to the themes of this book. What matters is that at the end of the fifteenth century Europe experienced an epidemic of syphilis, which attracted a congeries of social and medical perceptions which differed from that attached to any other disease. Contemporaries saw it as a new infection which imposed new demands. Patients were prostrated with acute fever, severe headache, intense osteocopic pains and delirium, with death the common sequel. As there was no acquired immunity in the population, the symptoms in this early period were ferocious, and the disease virulent.[5]

The great stimulus to the epidemic was the invasion of the kingdom of Naples by King Charles VIII of France, the first stage of his campaign to be crowned Emperor of the East at Constantinople. In 1494 he mustered a nondescript army numbering about 30,000, including English, Hungarian, Italian, Spanish, Slav and Swiss mercenaries, together with French civilian drivers, ostlers and waggoners, German technicians and some 800 camp followers. As King Ferdinand V of Castile sent soldiers to help his kinsman King Ferdinand II of Naples, Spaniards who had had contact with the men of Columbus's expedition were present both in the offensive and defensive armies. Before Charles's army occupied Naples in February 1495, the Spanish defenders infected the Neapolitan women; in the revelry that followed the lifting of the siege, these women gratified the French soldiery, while infected Neapolitan men used prostitutes in the French camp. The disease was widely and quickly disseminated. Charles and his courtiers were great voluptuaries and it is possible that the king himself became infected, for all four of his children died in infancy, and the dynasty of Valois which had ruled France for almost two centuries expired with him. When Charles left Naples in July 1495, his mercenaries dispersed throughout Europe, returning to their homes where they spread the disease.

By 1495 Spain and Italy were ravaged by syphilis, which then spread to France, Germany, the Netherlands and Greece in 1496, to the British Isles in 1497 and to Russia and Hungary by 1499. Henceforth syphilis was endemic in Europe. An Italian described the appearance of this new infection in his country in 1495 and its swift transmission to Germany, east Europe and the Balkans. 'Almost the twentieth part of mankind suffered its malignity,' he wrote before his own death of the disease in 1500. A surgeon who had been present at the siege of Naples similarly described how in Italy in 1495 'owing to celestial influences, a disease appeared among the soldiers characterized by a small pustule on or under the prepuce about the size of a millet seed and later the patient developed aching of the extremities and pustules may appear over the entire body'.[6]

Syphilis became rampant, with the first case reported in India as early as 1498, and another at the Chinese port of Canton in 1505. Each nationality blamed another for the epidemic, reflecting the rapid international nature of its transmission and the instant need for easily identifiable bogeys. Portuguese who were infected by Spaniards called syphilis the 'Castilian' disease, the French called it the 'Italian' or 'Neapolitan' disease, the English called it the 'French pox', the Germans similarly dubbed it the '*Malade Frantzos*' in Poland it was known as the 'German' disease, in Russia as the 'Polish' disease, in Persia as the 'Turkish' disease and in Tahiti as the 'English' disease. The role of Vasco da Gama and other Portuguese navigators in infecting the Orient after 1497 is indicated by the Japanese word '*mankabassam*' for syphilis, literally meaning 'the Portuguese sickness'.

Many other names, of which the most popular was *Morbus Gallicus*, associated the disease with the French. Indeed the fact that the patron saint of France and of Paris, St Denis, was adopted by 1497 as the patron saint of syphilitics suggests that France, or at least its capital, was a focal source of infection after Charles VIII's Neapolitan campaign. (In due course Rue St Denis in Paris became a celebrated centre of prostitution.) The French attribution was equally common in literature. 'Nell is dead . . . of the malady of France,' declares Pistol of Mistress Quickly in Shakespeare's *Henry V*. Within a decade there were several hundred names in Europe for syphilis, although it is notable that in England it often was known as 'the occult disease' or 'the secret disease'.

Ruy Diaz de Isla (1462–1542), a physician working in Barcelona, gave the first published account of syphilis in 1497. He described his treatment of Columbus' sailors immediately after their return from Haiti for 'Indian measles', 'a disease, previously unknown, unseen and undescribed which' according to Diaz de Isla 'spread thence throughout the world'. His treatise was entitled *Tractado contra el Mal Serpentina* (literally the *Treatise against the Evil Snake*): 'the reason I call it serpentine', he explained, 'is because one cannot find a more horrible comparison, for as this animal is hideous, dangerous and terrible so the malady is hideous, dangerous and terrible.' Snakes carry a phallic association, and it is likely that Diaz de Isla at some level of consciousness equated the poison of a syphilitic's penis with the 'dangerous and terrible' venom of a snake.[7]

The word 'syphilis' was first used by the Italian physician Hieronymus Fracastor (otherwise Girolamo Fracastoro, 1478–1553), who in 1521 began writing a Latin medical poem *Syphilis sive Morbi Gallicus* as part of a preventive health campaign to emphasize the sexual basis of infection. He coined the word syphilis for the disease contracted by his fictional shepherd Syphilus who was 'smitten because he raised forbidden altars on the hill' instead of worshipping Apollo, and the name perhaps persisted because in its novelty it traduced the morality of no nationality and stigmatized no minority. Fracastor may have derived the name Syphilus from Greek words meaning either 'lover of swine' or 'companion in love', but certainly over the course of a century 'syphilis' supplanted other names such as *Morbus Gallicus*. There has been much speculation about Fracastor's derivation of syphilis; all that can be usefully said is that just as Diaz de Isla compared the disease to an 'evil snake', the sibilance of the word evokes viperous and venomous associations.

Fracastor's description of the disease was acute and accurate. He stressed that syphilis after its primary and easily removable symptoms simmered in its victim, sometimes without pain or inconvenience of any kind. 'When it has once been received into the body it does not immediately declare itself; rather it lies dormant for a certain time and gradually gains strength as it feeds. Meanwhile, however, the sufferers, weighed down by strange heaviness and irresistible languor, are going through life with increasing weakness, moving sluggishly in every limb. Their eyes, too, have lost their natural keenness; the colour is driven from their faces and deserts their unhappy brows. By slow degrees the corruption, arising in the generative organs, consumes the whole body here and there, or eats away the groin in its triumphant course. Then the symptoms of the disease reveal themselves more clearly ... the arms, the shoulder blades and the calves of the legs are racked with pain ... throughout the body unsightly scabs break forth, and foully defile the face and breast. The malady now takes a new form: a pustule resembling the top of an acorn, and rotting with thick phlegm, opens and soon splits apart flowing copiously with corrupted blood and matter . . . eating deeply in, it hides in the innermost parts and feeds dreadfully upon the body; and often we see joints stripped of their very flesh, bones rotting, and foully gaping mouths gnawed away, the lips and throats producing faint sounds . . . a mouldiness is want to spread through the body, and thence at length condense into a foul thickening of the skin. So one whose age has the air of spring and comely youth, looking with wild eyes on his distorted limbs, on his loathsome joints and swollen face, has often in his misery denounced the cruelty of heaven and of fate.' Fracastor sympathized with syphilitics in their despair and torment: 'to the sufferers no peace came . . . for them the Day was hostile – and hostile, too, the phantom of the Night.'[8]

Early clinical descriptions suggest that the disease was virulent in the first century of its observation in Europe, but diminished in severity at its primary stage after 1600. This may mean that the medical response was more self-assured or competent, or that popular repulsion and panic declined as syphilis became a more familiar part of social experience. The earliest sufferers with primary infections had rashes, frequently ulcerative and invading the mouth and nose to affect the palate and throat, often accompanied by bone pains and fever. By the seventeenth century these rashes seem to have been less prominent in early infections, but there were more reports of tumours containing gummy material, baldness and loss of teeth. Bone pains, especially nocturnally, continued. Physicians were bewildered as to suitable treatment: ancient medical authorities like Hippocrates or Galen offered no guidance. 'This frightful disease', Gasparo Torrella wrote, 'was absolutely unknown to the physicians of the day: none of them had ever encountered it.' When the public realized that not even the most experienced practitioners could suggest a cure they

> began to decry the art of medicine and to accuse it of impotence. 'A fine science', people said, 'that does not know how to cure the sick!' These reproaches . . . were not without foundation, for trained physicians avoided treating the disease, openly avowing that they understood nothing about it.

Doctors, according to Ulrich von Hutten in 1519, 'fled from the presence of the sick; above all, they took extreme care not to touch them . . . Their consternation was so great that they forwent their professional privileges, and left the barber-surgeons to prescribe remedies for the disease.'⁹

Until the nineteenth century gonorrhoea, chancroid and syphilis were not distinguished, but were treated as manifestations of the same disease. Physicians who saw patients with the old disease of gonorrhoea and the new disease of syphilis in association, or whose patients initially had gonorrhoeal symptoms but later developed chancres, assumed that the two diseases were identical. Others claimed credit for relieving the symptoms of gonorrhoea without identifying or treating concurrent syphilis. Paracelsus, the drunken professor of physic and surgery at Basle University who publicly burnt the books of Galen and Avicenna and commanded an overpowering reputation among contemporaries, extinguished doubts by declaring himself for the single identity of the two diseases. Joannes de Vigo in 1513 was the last practitioner for about three centuries to insist that gonorrhoea and syphilis were separate conditions, and gonorrhoea all but vanished from medical literature. As syphilitic symptoms became more lenient in the seventeenth century, practitioners felt obliged to address gonorrhoeal symptoms, which however remained classified as syphilitic, with many ingenious explanations advanced to explain the connection between early gonorrhoeal symptoms and later syphilitic symptoms.¹⁰

Nevertheless steady advances were made in understanding syphilis. The ease in relieving symptoms but difficulty in eradicating the infection were notorious. 'The sad consequences that attend its seeming declension, when it is left imperfectly Cured' were clear: 'in progress of time the matter fermenteth . . . and becometh much more acrid and malign,' as Richard Wiseman (1622?–76) wrote. The protean nature of its symptoms was equally established. 'The disease it's certain of itself kills no man, but after a long and tedious peregrination fires at last upon one symptom,' wrote Gideon Harvey, who identified tinnitis, deafness, blindness, or speechlessness as evidence of tertiary infection, and whose copious and vivid writings had considerable influence in the seventeenth century. It was recognized that infection, in addition to sexual transmission, could be conveyed by kissing, by sharing drinking vessels, and by breast-feeding. Medical and lay opinion held that syphilis and gonorrhoea were transmitted by sharing beds, clothes, or in Harvey's words, 'by kissing, shaking of hands, trying of gloves, [or] succeeding a pocky comrade upon a close-stool [lavatory]'. Wiseman was more sceptical: he averred, 'these are all such convenient excuses for the more shy and coy Patients who will not otherwise be brought to confess their distempers, that it is a pity to discountenance them.' There was equal recognition of the hereditary transmission of syphilis. 'How many Fathers have entailed Misery on their Progeny from ill-cured Poxes!' exclaimed the quack Joseph Cam, who warned that where parents were infected, babies received 'a taint in their Blood in their Mothers' Wombs.'[11]

Although most symptoms of syphilis were understood in the sixteenth century, scientific advances occurred in the following two hundred years. Giovanni Maria Lancisi (1654–1720) identified the connection between syphilis and aneurysm of the heart, for example. William Cockburn, a naval physician, advanced understanding of the character and development of gonorrhoea, although his methods of treatment scarcely differed from those of his contemporaries. An Anglo-Indian medical officer in 1767 and an apothecary in 1771 both contended that the two diseases were distinct: the latter, although the most despised in status of writers on the subject, emphasized that gonorrhoea, unlike syphilis, could be cured without mercury, and proved that chancre did not follow inoculation experiments with gonorrhoeal pus.

These advances were obliterated by the misinterpretation of an experiment conducted in 1767 by the celebrated John Hunter (1728–93). He inoculated himself on the glans and foreskin with pus from a virulent gonorrhoea without realizing that the patient from whom he inoculated himself also had syphilis. As a result Hunter developed both chancre and syphilis, which almost certainly caused the heart disease that killed him and perhaps also caused the infertility of his children; but worse than this personal tragedy, he deduced that gonorrhoea and syphilis had an identical virus. Further experiments led him to conclude that the blood and secretions of syphilitics were incapable of infecting recipients: by implication he denied both the heredity of syphilis and the possibility of extra-genital inoculation. Just as the pronouncement of Paracelsus had been decisive in the sixteenth century in suppressing the view that gonorrhoea and syphilis were separate diseases, by dint of the great reputation enjoyed by Paracelsus, so the personal authority of Hunter overbore scientific objectivity with disastrous results, which included the revival of the use of mercury as a treatment for gonorrhoea. In the words of an expert writing in 1913,

> Hunter dealt the most terrible blow to the doctrine of the involvement of the internal organs of syphilis. With a few calmly written lines he annihilated a doctrine which for three centuries had been proved upon countless bodies, and accepted by all the physicians in the world. Hunter merely said superficially: 'I have not seen that the brain, heart, stomach, liver, kidneys and other viscera have been attacked by syphilis, although such cases have been described by authors'; but this dictum was sufficient to cause visceral syphilis almost completely to disappear for more than half a century from the textbooks upon venereal disease.[12]

For two generations the scientific study of venereal disease was inhibited by the festoon of cobwebs spun around it by Hunter.

Despite the clarity and accuracy of many of the early medical observations of syphilis, the epidemic quickly provoked social and political responses which were as complex as they were confused. The first official reference to syphilis was made in August 1495 by Maximilian the Holy Roman Emperor, a man of gloomy piety. 'Formerly, as the result of blasphemy, famine, earthquakes, pestilence and other plagues fell upon the earth,' he instructed the Diet of Worms. 'But in these days of ours, as is evident, grievous and sundry sicknesses and scourges have ensued. Notably in our time there have been severe diseases and plagues of the people, to wit the evil pocks which has never occurred before nor been heard of within the memory of man.' From the outset, then, the disease was presented by the morbid and pious as a 'plague' which was retribution for blasphemy. This belief that the epidemic was divine punishment, or '*Flagellum Dei*', was depicted in a verse broadsheet published at Basle in Switzerland entitled *De pestilentiali scorra sive mala de Franzos. Eulogium* (1496) (see illustration below). An accompanying woodcut depicted the Virgin and Child enthroned on a cloud, with the Virgin offering a crown to Emperor Maximilian who holds a Crusader's flag and the Child Christ hurling darts at a woman and three men (one a dead soldier) beneath Him. Foul ulcers have erupted wherever the darts have fallen, indicating that the disease is a visitation from God. Such imagery may have gratified imperial vanity, or belauded the piety of the Church, but the public to whom this broadsheet was addressed apparently found the woodcut both merciless and unjust, for when it was republished at Augsburg in 1496 the woodcut was regraven to show the Child Christ sending healing rays to a woman and girl, with a man lying dead nearby.[13]

The title page of a pamphlet on syphilis published in 1496. Its author Sebastian Brandt was a jurist who also wrote the famed *Ship of Fools*

Although 'the foul scab and horrible sickness called the french pox' reached the English town of Shrewsbury soon after the siege of Naples, another military adventure was responsible for quickening the spread of syphilis in Britain. Perkin Warbeck, pretender to the throne of England, after peregrinations around Europe gathering political support from rulers such as Emperor Maximilian, was welcomed to Scotland in 1495 by King James IV, and was encouraged to make excursions over the English frontier during the following two years. Warbeck collected some 1,400 followers, 'valient Captains of all nations', 'some bankrupt, some false English sanctuary men, some thieves, robbers and vagabonds, which leaving their bodily labours, desiring only to live of robbery and raping, became his servants and soldiers'. Many of these mercenaries, who were garrisoned at Aberdeen, had also served in the siege of Naples, and by 1497 an epidemic had erupted in Scotland. In that year the first case of compulsory notification and isolation of syphilis in the British Isles occurred, when King James decreed that all syphilitics should leave his capital, Edinburgh, for treatment on the island of Inch Keith in the Firth of Forth. Anyone infected who had not reached Inch Keith by dusk on the next Monday 'shall be burnt on the cheek with the marking iron'. (Although this was the first legislative response in the British Isles to the syphilitic epidemic, there had been earlier enactments against sexually transmitted disease: a law of 1161 prohibited the brothel keepers of Southwark in London from harbouring 'women suffering from the perilous infirmity of burning', whilst an order of 1430 forbade London brothel keepers from serving men with '*infirmitas nefanda*', the hidden disease). Following King James's example at Edinburgh, the Aberdonian authorities in 1497 also introduced regulations to combat 'the infirmity come out of France and strange parts, that all light women to desist from their vices and sin of venerie' with the threat of branding on the cheek with a hot iron and banishment if the diseased did not conform to regulations. Ten years later, in 1507, the burghers of Aberdeen issued a further order 'that diligent inquisition be taken of all infected persons with this strange sickness of Naples' and imposed quarantine restrictions 'for the safety of the town'.[14]

In London around 1506 there was an attempt to suppress the brothels known as the Winchester stews which had provided syphilis with the popular name of 'Winchester goose'. The stews were wood structures south-west of London Bridge each with a stair giving access to the river Thames and enjoying picturesque names like the Cardinal's Hat. Their closure was a consequence of the epidemic, but was not uniformly enforced. The disease was also invoked by the State against dissidents or to discredit those who compromised political orthodoxy. After King Henry VIII determined to break his former adviser Cardinal Wolsey in 1529, his foe was accused of 'knowing himself to have the foul and contagious disease of the great pox, broken out upon him in divers places of his body', but to have daily visited the king, 'rowning in your ear, and blowing upon your most noble Grace with his perilous and infective breath, in marvellous danger of your Highness . . . if God of His infinite goodness had not better provided for your Highness'. This accusation against Wolsey was a classic example of isolating a hated opponent by depicting him as a dangerous and contagious defiler. Similarly a diatribe against lazy and luxurious clergy read to King Henry in 1524 identified them as notorious disseminators of the French pox: 'these be they that have made a hundred thousand idle whores in your realm, which would have gotten their living honestly in the sweat of their faces had not their superfluous riches elicited them to unclean lust and idleness. These be they that corrupt the whole generation of mankind in your realm, that catch the pox off one woman and bear it to another, ye some of them will boast among his fellows that he hath meddled with a hundred women.' Subsequently, after Henry's break with the papacy in the 1530s, 'the scandalous lives of priests, monks and friars made the strongest argument for the policy which the king had adopted towards Rome; and it so happened in those very years that a scandalous life was betrayed, and made odious in more than sentiment, by bearing an outward and visible sign.'[15]

Patients met social as well as medical rejection or political persecution. Many became outcasts, as lamented in a sermon of 1509 by Cardinal John Fisher, the Bishop of Rochester: men 'vexed with the French pox, poor and needy', were, he said, 'lying by the highways stinking and almost rotten above the ground, having intolerable ache in their bones'. The first recorded case of job loss occurred in 1511 when John Friendship, Fellow of Merton College, Oxford, was ordered to leave his work because he was infected with French pox. The people of sixteenth- and seventeenth-century England attached high importance to physical blemishes or ugliness as guides to an individual's inner state: the devil's mark on a woman could lead to her execution for witchcraft; not for nothing did Shakespeare depict the arch-villain of Tudor England, King Richard III, as a hunchback. Deformity or blemish was not only a pointer to wrongdoing, but its punishment. Just as criminals and beggars were branded by the iron, or had their ears lopped, syphilitic pox-marks were the distinguishing sign of other transgressors: the pollutants and the sexually defiled. Particularly if they were poor they were treated accordingly.[16]

The earliest known British venereologist was William Clowes (1543–1604). After practising as a surgeon in both the Army and the Navy, he was appointed to the household of Queen Elizabeth and surgeon at St Bartholomew's Hospital, publishing in 1579 the first major account of syphilis to be written in English. His essay, which was reprinted several times during the sixteenth century and enjoyed considerable influence, deserves scrutiny. Clowes was keen to establish that he did not pander to the laxity of his patients, whom he regarded with robust intolerance. 'I protest that the very cause that moved me to let forth this book, is not to encourage those wretches that wallow in the sin' of fornication, he declared, but 'to admonish them speedily to amend their lives, lest the Lord God in His just wrath do one day make the disease to be incurable'. This 'pestilent infection of filthy lust', he insisted ('I must speak boldly, because I speak truly: and yet I speak it with very grief of heart'), was 'a sickness very loathsome, odious, troublesome and dangerous, which spreadeth itself throughout all England and overfloweth as I think the whole world'. It was 'testimony of the just wrath of God against that filthy sin' of fornication, 'the original cause of this infection, that breedeth it, that nurseth it, that disperseth it'. Clowes estimated that within a period of five years, he and three other surgeons at Bart's Hospital had treated over a thousand syphilitics, and that between half and three-quarters of general admissions 'have the pocks'. His attitude to such patients was punitive and abusive: they were 'vile creatures' or 'lewd and wicked beasts'. Syphilis was 'the licentious and beastly disorder of a great number of rogues and vagabonds . . . forasmuch as the best avoiding and curing of every disease consisteth in shunning and removing the cause thereof, I wish all men generally, especially those which be infected, to loathe, detest, hate and abhor that stinking sin.' He wanted the magistrates of England to identify 'the offenders', and 'execute upon them such condign punishment as may be a terror to the wicked, the rather to abstain . . . from such abominable wicked-ness'; the 'huge multitudes' of syphilitics were a 'great danger' staining 'the whole nation'. The terms in which Clowes blamed 'idle persons' and 'lewd alehouses, which are the very nests and harbourers of such filthy creatures' resemble those of the royal charter of 1553 which was intended to enable the authorities to drain the 'filthy puddle of idleness' in London by seizing 'idle ruffians, tavern haunters, beggars and all persons of evil name and fame' and forcing them to work at the newly constituted Bridewell Royal Hospital. By the sixteenth century the English poor had been unyoked from personal servitude, and bridewells were new punitive institutions to instil laborious habits and correct the idle instincts of rogue members of the servant class. Clowes, encouraged by the spirit which produced bridewells to cleanse 'filthy puddles', thought the idle poor, freed from the discipline of their forefathers, were particularly syphilitic.[17]

Clowes did not condemn all syphilitics, but acknowledged that there were some 'good poor people that be infected by unwary eating or drinking or keeping company with these lewd beasts and which either for shame will not betray it, or for lack of good surgeons know not how to remedy it, or for lack of ability are not able otherwise to provide for the cure of it'. Already in Clowes' era a distinction was being drawn between 'guilty' and 'innocent' transmission of syphilis, as is shown by his description of treating a girl aged twelve with advanced syphilis which he diagnosed must have been conveyed to her by her parents or wetnurse. He also knew of a family whose 'poor silly Infants, which else had all died most pitifully' were put out by their mother to wetnursing, and thus 'infected five sundry good and honest women'.[18]

Previously writers like Fracastor had depicted syphilis as horrific and distressing, but in England by the late sixteenth century a new element of disgust or contempt for the syphilitic was intruding. Since the fourth century AD, Christianity had 'gradually assumed a very sombre hue' as it struggled for 'the absolute suppression of the whole sensual side of our nature', as Lecky described in his *History of European Morals*.

> The business of the saint was to eradicate a natural appetite, to attain a condition that was emphatically abnormal. The depravity of human nature, especially the essential evil of the body, was felt with a degree of intensity that could never have been attained by moralists who were occupied mainly with transient or exceptional vices, such as envy, anger or cruelty ... The consequences of this was first of all a very deep sense of

the habitual and innate depravity of human nature; and, in the next place, a very strong association of the idea of pleasure with that of vice. All this necessarily flowed from the supreme value placed upon virginity.

Now, in the sixteenth century, new refinements were added to medieval theology. The English Reformation begun by Henry VIII in the 1530s, and consolidated by his daughter Elizabeth after 1558, repudiated pagan beliefs and Roman Catholic superstition while it emphasized God as the Sovereign Creator. Lutheran Protestantism eliminated intermediaries between God and the individual's soul: God became at once more awesomely distant and yet more awesomely close. Providentialism – the intervention of Divine power – was seen in everything from a change in direction of the wind to the fall of kings. This concept of Providence denied that events were random or that justice was arbitrary. Everything happened because it had a reason, God's reason. With the rise of puritanism, the idea of a wrathful God taking vengeance on sinners through the workings of Providence became ubiquitous. To English Puritans, the reformation of the individual was a prerequisite to reformation of the world. Yet if one convinced oneself that one was the Elect of God, it was necessary to believe that many other people were the Rejects of Heaven – a belief which could only strengthen projective hostility against syphilitics. This was a time when even politics, to quote Blair Worden, became 'a public projection of the struggle which lust, will and passion wage against God's grace for the dominion of the soul': so it was not surprising that the impulses to create culprits and maltreat sinners which puritanism excited were, when coupled with the instinctive dread of defilement, the source of new punitive attitudes.[19]

The sense of sin is essentially apprehensive. A person who feels that he has sinned is above all convinced that he has performed an act which will bring misfortune on him in the future. Syphilis was often transmitted during fornication or adultery – acts surrounded by apprehension in themselves – and this gave it a specific association with sin, although many adulterers or fornicators escaped infection. Moreover, unlike most diseases, to which the ill-fed, ill-housed and ill-clad were usually more vulnerable, syphilis infected every class and often struck the most robust of the young. 'When it emerged from its hiding place in the body, pox often betrayed the difference between appearance and reality, between bravado and pretended distinction and the common rottenness inside.' It gave new and literal meaning to the threat that the sins of fathers were visited upon their children. The arbitrariness of transmission and the horrible course of the disease increased the sense of retribution. If some people were singled out, it must be, under Puritan reasoning, by God's will. Some historians have indeed suggested that the rise of Puritanism and diffusion of puritanism in the sixteenth and seventeenth centuries were stimulated by the sexual guilt and anxiety which the epidemic had engendered. If puritanism is defined as an intense sense of responsibility for one's own conscience, then the fearful conscience and retributive superstitions that syphilis provoked in some people, created a sympathetic environment in which purita-nism might spread. Nevertheless, it is significant that by the 1580s, when Cornish Puritans supplicated Parliament about 'the miser-ies, the ruins, decays and desolations of the Church', they took pains to stigmatize sinful clergy 'spotted with whoredom': those marked with syphilitic poxes were amongst those whose 'infect-ious breath, which savoureth of carrion, maketh God's children to abhor them, and the uncleanness and filthiness of their hands maketh them unfit ministers to wait at the Lord's table'. Puritan imagery like this, emphasizing both the sin and the contagious danger of syphilitics, preyed on primitive fears, and reinforced tendencies to ostracize venereal patients.[20]

Most of the seventeenth-century English bore feelings not of spontaneous rapture but of suspicion and guilt about their bodies in an era when popular religion associated sensuality with Adam's Fall from Divine Grace. For families surviving near subsistence level, it was essential not to be overburdened with children, so abstinence, *coitus interruptus* and buggery were practised within marriage. Filth, illness and poverty meant that copulation 'was neither the incarnation of love nor an *ars erotica*, but rather infrequent, functional, perfunctory and repetitive', providing the physical relief of orgasm as a matter of routine rather than as an act of imagination or fantasy. Even the sensuality of King Charles II's courtiers was defiant and self-conscious: despite libertine pos-tures they were inhibited sniggerers rather than joyous celebrants. Shame spoiled the delights of orgasm for writers as different as

Rochester and Pepys. 'The pleasure past, a threatening doubt remains,' Rochester wrote in one fit of post-coital gloom. In another poem he described how

> In liquid raptures I dissolve all o'er,
> Melt into sperm, and spend at every pore

– only a few lines later to rail in self-disgust against his prick:

> Worst part of me, and henceforth hated most,
> Through all the town a common fucking post,
> On whom each whore relieves her tingling cunt
> As hogs on gates do rub themselves and grunt.

Pepys often concluded descriptions of his orgasms with the same penitent phrase, 'God forgive me.' A diary entry of 1664 in which he describes taking a woman twice on a chair, 'the last to my great pleasure', is typical in its remose. 'So home to supper and to bed – with my mind un peu troublé pour ce que j'ai fait today. But I hope it will be la dernière de toute ma vie.' Rochester and Pepys alike were prey to what their contemporary John Oldham described in himself as 'the gnawing Remorse of a rash unguarded unconsidering Sinner'.[21]

Just as initial responses to syphilis were much influenced by the puritan movement, so in the eighteenth century some of the key influences on the institutional treatment of syphilitics came from Calvinistic evangelical preachers like George Whitefield, whose emphasis on the personal experience of conversion to Christian faith offered a model for the penitent transformation of sinners. Several of those most critically involved were part of the Countess of Huntingdon's Connection, a sect of Calvinistic Methodist clergy under the protection of a formidable aristocratic patroness. Their ascendancy in the treatment of syphilitics partly came about as the result of changing patterns of health care. By the mid sixteenth century the two royal hospitals in London, St Bartholomew's and St Thomas's, maintained sweat wards for treating patients with mercury (described in more detail on pages 40 to 42). Treatment facilities also developed at the lazar houses or leper colonies which were underutilized as leprosy declined (the word 'lock' given to these wards perhaps derived from the French word *loques* signifying rags, bandages or lints worn by people suffering from leprosy). In the seventeenth century London had two lock hospitals for syphilitics at Hackney and Southwark. Their emphasis on penitence and redemption was shown by an inscription on a sundial at the Hackney premises, 'significant of sin and sorrow' in the words of a Victorian antiquary: '*Post voluptatem, misericordia*'. During the eighteenth century general hospitals started excluding various types of patients from their wards, including maternity cases, children, those with infectious fevers or mental disorders and venereal patients. This was intended to protect the health and moral welfare of other patients: the rejected categories became the responsibility of the poor law authorities, with specialist hospitals opening to treat cases. It also provided an opportunity for Calvinistic Methodists to increase their influence and respectability in the metropolis.[22]

A new London Lock Hospital for venereal cases was opened around 1746 at the corner of Chapel Street and Grosvenor Place. The red-brick building (demolished on its centenary) was very plain; the chapel added in 1764 was equally grim-looking. The institution emphasized Christian repentance: typically Martin Madan, its first chaplain, had been a rich and rakish lawyer 'of a very gay and volatile Turn' before suddenly taking holy orders. 'Being in company one evening with some of his gay companions at a coffee house', Madan was commissioned by his fellow debauchees to attend a sermon of John Wesley's in order that the preacher's manner and discourse could be parodied for fun. Wesley's words on the text 'Prepare to meet thy doom' impressed Madan so deeply as to transform his life: he joined Lady Huntingdon's Connection in the late 1740s, and became an itinerant preacher accompanying men like the Revd John Berridge ('There was nothing particular in his Discourse, which was on *Repentance*, except that it was delivered extempore with a great Deal of *Tautology*, & Abundance of *Grimace*,' wrote a fellow member of the clergy of an open-air sermon given by Berridge with Madan in attendance: 'He is a droll kind of Man . . . till of late exceedingly eat up with the vapours & Lowness of spirits: but ever since he turned *Methodist* & *Field Preacher* had enjoyed a good state of health'). As chaplain to the Lock Hospital, Madan drew large attendances by preaching sermons on repentance and redemption which emphasized the sins not only of whores but of supposedly respectable society. He was author of *An Account of the Triumphant Death of F.S., A Converted Prostitute, Who Died*

View *of the* LOCK CHAPEL . *Hyde Park Corner...where a* Gospel Ministry

The grim and undecorated chapel where Madan and Dodd preached penitence and self-loathing.

April 1763, aged Twenty Six years. This described the 'interesting and delightful' deathbed repentance of a tubercular whore, who gratified Madan just before she died by declaring 'O Sir, I abhor myself – I abhor my polluted body, and my polluted soul – I am the filthiest wretch upon this earth – but there is mercy – that holy and immaculate Jesus knows my sorrows.' This was the best state of mind, Madan judged, for a sinner to meet her Maker. He himself was no stranger to the snares of lust, and had to resign as chaplain after publishing a book advocating polygamy in 1780.[23]

For a time one of Madan's closest associates was Dr William Dodd, who preached at the Lock Hospital and was chaplain to Magdalen House, an institution opened in 1758 for the reception of penitent prostitutes. 'The greatest part of those who have taken to this dreadful life', wrote the charity's promoter Charles Dingley, 'from those pampered in private stews, to the common dregs infesting our streets' were doomed to 'disease, death and eternal destruction, not through choice but necessity . . . The same necessity obliging them to prey on the unwary, diffuses the contagion; propagating profligacy, and spreading ruin, disease and death, almost through the whole human species.' Just over a thousand women were admitted to the institution in its first decade, of whom 23 died there 'with all the marks of unfeigned contrition', while others were expelled for 'petulance of temper, and refractoriness of behaviour' and still more were apparently restored to respectability. Dodd was a fashionable and eloquent sermonizer whose congregations wept buckets as he dilated on their sins; members of the public were encouraged to attend chapel at Magdalen House, to admire the evidence of the whores' repentance and then to search their own consciences. Like Madan, Dodd preached self-hate. 'Reflect upon yourself,' he told the whores on one occasion, 'abhorred by the thinking and the virtuous, despised and hated even by the most abject and vicious . . . an alien and an out-cast.' They had been 'enslaved to the abominable service of the devil, whose only joy is the misery of the human race; and who, for the most faithful service, hath only flames of hell and never-ending anguish to bestow'. He preached the primacy of paternal hierarchies: whores should 'settle it in their hearts, that no love can be equal to the parental; and that whenever the siren voice of seduction wooes them to forsake a tender father's roof, however sweet and sound, however alluring the promises, Destruction awaits the fatal step, and Ruin stands ready to close her gloomy doors upon them.' Just as Madan was forced into retirement by his belief in polygamy, so Dodd too was ruined: his social ambitions led him into debt, his wife's attempt to buy preferment in the Church led to scandalous charges of simony, and in 1777 he was hanged for forgery. The tortuous position of men like Berridge, Dodd and Madan is well conveyed by a description by V. S. Pritchett of a different sect in a different century which nevertheless contains the essence of their motives. 'Outwardly the extreme Puritan appears narrow, crabbed, fanatical, gloomy and dull, but from the inside what a series of dramatic climaxes his life is, what a fascinating casuitry beguiles him, how he is amused by the comedies of duplicity, sharpened by the ingenious puzzles of the conscience and carried away by the eloquence of hypocrisy,' wrote Pritchett, 'however much he may bore others he never suffers from boredom himself.' Madan and Dodd found not only spiritual fulfilment but other forms of excitement and emotional enrichment in their work: savouring the hidden motives of prurience, gloating and hypocrisy of some of the congregants who came to gawp at the humiliation of the whores in their chapels, relishing the furtive gratification which 'respectable' men and women took in mixing with 'wretched instruments of passion, the unhappy women assigned to this base service'.[24]

The influence of Calvinistic Methodism persisted at both the Lock Hospital and Magdalen House long after Dodd and Madan had left. Not all of the clergy involved can be censured for the complexity of their motives. The evangelical preacher Thomas Haweis (also part of Lady Huntingdon's Connection) who was assistant chaplain in the 1760s, the Calvinistic preachers Charles de Coetlogon and Thomas Scott who were appointed joint chaplains in 1785, were each more simple in their devotions, but still practised 'a Gospel Ministry' of non-conformist tendencies which stressed repentance of sin. Their approach, and the pietist assumptions that underlay their Christianity, became the convention for institutional treatment of nineteenth century syphilitics.[25]

Outside the introspective little world which Dodd and Madan orbited, in circles where young men were admired for sexual exuberance, it has been suggested that venereal infections carried little stigma, and were gaily known as the 'cavalier's disease' or 'the gentleman's disease'. An observer of 1738 asserted, 'It is hardly one in ten that a Town Spark of that age has not been clapt', but there is little evidence (and it is hard to believe) that syphilitics celebrated their condition (although it may be that cavaliers and Town Sparks, as groups at high risk of infection, regarded the illness as a misfortune rather than a sin, and as a subject for candour and affectionate consolation rather than tense and anguished secrecy). There was certainly a tendency to understate the disease's incidence. In 1662 the statisticians Sir William Petty and John Graunt analysed the causes of death given in London bills of mortality (approximating to death certificates), and found that only 392 individuals out of 229,250 were recorded as dying of 'the French pox'. 'It is not good to let the World be lulled into a security and belief of Impunity by our Bills, which we intend shall not be only as Deathsheads to put Men in mind of their Mortality, but also as Mercurial Statues to point out the most dangerous ways that lead us into it and misery,' wrote Graunt. 'Forasmuch as by the ordinary discourse of the World it seems a great part of Men have at one time or other had some species of this Disease, I wondering why so few died of it, especially as I could not take that to be so harmless whereof so many complained very fiercely',

Graunt found upon enquiry that those who died of it in hospital were recorded as dying of 'Ulcers and Sores', and that all mentions of the 'French Pox' were returned by the registrars of only two parishes, St Giles's and St Martin's in the Fields, 'in which places I understood that most of the vilest and most miserable Houses of Uncleanness were: from which I concluded that only hated persons and such whose very Noses were eaten off were reported . . . to have died of this too frequent malady'. This reluctance to record death from syphilis probably derived from a desire to protect the memory of the dead or the feelings of survivors.[26]

There is other evidence that syphilitics regarded their condition with remorse rather than rakish jauntiness. One venereal patient wrote to a medical adviser in 1706: 'my own unhappy Circumstances . . . being in my imagination as miserable as may be, and attended with anxious Thoughts, frightful Dreams, such as present nothing but Ruin and Destruction inevitable . . . for help in these my Straits, I have no other recourse but to you, humbly imploring you for my Deliverer, to retrieve me from the jaws of Despair.' All sorts of anxieties, guilts and obsessions were excited in patients. John Marten described in the early eighteenth century how he 'had a Woman in Cure, who received the infection from her Husband, and being but of a melancholic Disposition, would not for a long time be persuaded but that her Nose was coming off, and was in such Frights concerning it, that she would often feel of it, and rise up in the night to look in a Glass; but she at length found it was more her Fears than anything else, she and her Nose too remaining in a very good condition.' Feelings of remorse or guilt created in some syphilitics a desperate need for anonymity, or discreet treatment. Paul Chamberlen (1635–1717) found it profitable to advertize that his 'Lotions will be Privately Sent', under discreet covers, to syphilitics who were too shy to apply to him in person. Marten recorded a woman patient who repeatedly insisted that her source of infection was 'the common easing place' (lavatory) and denied that she had extra-marital sex, but that he was later told by a midshipman that he had infected the woman.[27]

By the seventeenth century surgeons and physicians were familiar with phobias about venereal disease among patients. 'These dreadful Symptoms have frequently possessed the imagination of some people, who having taken the way to get the Pox are soon persuaded that they have it,' Wiseman wrote in 1676. 'These men will strangely imagine all the pains and other symptoms they have read of, or have heard other men talk of', and importune physicians, surgeons and quacks in turn to cure their imaginary ailments until 'many of these hypochrondiacs' had 'ruined both their Bodies and Purses' with unnecessary treatment. Marten was also familiar with 'dismal apprehensions' surrounding syphilis and with cases where hypochondriacal patients had committed suicide. Such 'desperation' was not reported with other diseases: the sexual nature of transmission set it apart.[28]

Syphilis was widespread at the Court of King Charles II after 1660 and was discussed with less inhibition, it is true. One courtier, Sir Alexander Frazier, an amateur abortionist and venereologist, was 'so great' with royal mistresses like the Duchess of Cleveland 'and all the ladies at Court in helping them slip their calves [embryos] when there is occasion and the great men in curing them of their claps, that he can do what he pleases with them'. The treatment for syphilis of one member of the Royal family is recorded. 'Prince Rupert is in very bad state and so bad that he do now yield to be trepanned,' Pepys wrote in 1666. 'It is a clap of the pox which he got about twelve years ago, and has eaten to his head and come through his skull, so that his skull must be opened, and there is great fear for him.' Trepanning was performed on the prince 'without any pain, he not knowing when it was done. Having cut the outward table, as they call it, they found the inner all corrupted, so as it come out without any force; and their fear is, that the whole inside of his head is corrupted like that, which do yet make them afeard of him.' Despite the apprehensions of his surgeons, Prince Rupert was back at Court within a few months, 'pretty well as he used to be, only something appears to be under his periwig or the crown of his head', and survived another fifteen years. Whatever the inanities of Restoration courtiers, in this and other cases they did not commit the folly of turning away from other men in contempt.[29]

From the late fifteenth century onwards mercurial compounds and salves were used as specifics for syphilis, although their therapeutic efficacy was questionable. An Arab ointment containing a ninth part of mercury had been introduced to medieval Europe for treating scabies. Because syphilitic ulcers resembled the sores of scabies, this ointment was applied in the 1490s to treat syphilis; mercury was adopted as a cure for syphilis shortly afterwards. However, the risks involved in prolonged or heavy use of mercury were underestimated, and it was administered in heavy doses which, though they sometimes forced rapid results, also caused gangrene. In the fifteenth and sixteenth centuries mercury was applied as ointment, by plaster applied to the body, by fumigation and in pill form. It was given not only to syphilitics but to gonorrheics, and as urethral discharges were interpreted as Nature's means of purging contagion, they were encouraged rather than treated.

A sixteenth-century illustration of a syphilitic undergoing mercurial treatment.

Barber shops were dens of male comradeship, where a man was likely to admit to his friends that he had received an infection and perhaps ask for advice. Consequently, from an early date, mercury was used by barbers on syphilitic customers, and soon cobblers, vagabonds, mountebanks and quacks were jostling to exploit human desperation by offering mercurial treatment. Patients were confined half-starved for up to a month in a hot room where they were smeared with mercury, plunged into vapour baths and laden with clothes to produce sweat. Saliva spat out by patients was thought to be the syphilitic poison expelled by mercury. Dosages of mercury were so high that jaws, tongues and palates ulcerated, gums swelled, teeth loosened while 'saliva dribbled incessantly from the mouth and soon grew intolerably foetid, and so infectious that it tainted and polluted whatever it fell upon', according to Ulrich von Hutten who took the treatment but died of the disease in the 1520s. 'The lips being touched by it became ulcerated, and the inside of the cheeks excoriated. The whole apartment stank; and this method of cure was so hard to suffer that a great many chose to die of the disease rather than submit to it.'[30] It was to the endurance of this mercurial treatment that Shakespeare referred in *Timon of Athens*:

> Be a whore still; they love thee not that use thee.
> Give them diseases, leaving them with their
> lust.
>   . . . bring down rose-cheek'd youth
> To the tub-fast and the diet.

The pain of mercury treatment meant that it was considered an appropriately punitive treatment for syphilitics: persistence in using mercury long after outward manifestations of syphilis had receded was sometimes 'Calvinistic sadism' intended to deter patients from further sexual ventures. It was seen as such by John Dryden, whose poem 'The Medal' (1682) likened mercurial treatment to fanatical clergymen who were so vindictive as to have forgotten all Christian precepts:

> Religion thou hast none; thy mercury
> Has past through every sect, or theirs through thee,
> But what thou givest that venom still remains
> And the poxed nation feels thee in their brains,
> What else inspires the tongue and swells the breasts
> Of all thy bellowing renegado priests.

The cauterization of gonorrheics of both sexes had equally punitive and deterrent motives. Authority was asserted by medical practitioners over patients whom they regarded as reprobate. Venereal disease was harder to cure because of 'the ungovernable disposition of the Patients', Wiseman wrote in 1676. He preached submission and sexual continence as part of the cure, equating

continence with obedience to authority. Harvey similarly opposed
'Excess of Venery'.[31]

As a counter-reaction to mercury treatment, after about 1515,
some physicians and quacks commended preparations such as
china root, sarsaparilla, sassafras and guaiacum. The latter was
particularly important. Spanish visitors to Haiti had previously
noticed that the therapy applied there was based on decoctions
from guaiacum trees, and after 1508 this ineffectual treatment
gathered many adherents. The publication of Fracastor's poem
was even delayed for five years while, at the suggestion of his
patron, he added a new section extolling guaiacum. It survived in
the British Pharmacopoeia for four centuries, like china root
which was retained there until 1932 or sarsaparilla which,
although deleted from the British Pharmacopoeia in 1914, was an
ingredient of Zittmann's Decoction still used at the London Lock
Hospital in the late 1930s to treat tertiary syphilitics with chronic
ulcers, and named after its inventor, Johann Friedrich Zittman
(1671–1757). These nostrums were commemorated in the epitaph
of Thomas Bamford, a seventeenth-century musician who died of
venereal disease:

> No Marble Monument shall cover
> The Grave of this poor Martyr'd Lover.
> Here lie no Bones nor Flesh, but rather
> *Guaiacum*, and *Sassaphras*,
> and *Turpentine*, the Quacks' disgrace,
> Have sent Tom Bamford God knows whither.[32]

Other remedies were tried such as the blue flower *Lobelia
siphilitica*, which seems to have been recommended as a specific by
Iroquois Indians to an eighteenth-century British administrator of
colonial America, Sir William Johnson.

Syphilis penetrated literature within two decades of the siege of
Naples. It reached political satire and utopian politics in the Latin
edition of More's *Utopia* (1516; first translated into English
1551). In Utopia affianced couples display themselves naked to
one another before marriage so as to prevent ignorance or
deception about each other's venereal health. In *Timon of Athens*
Shakespeare described the syphilitic ravages caused by prostitutes
whose faked orgasms he described as 'strong shudders' and
'heavenly agues':

Consumptions sow
In hollow bones of man: strike their sharp shins,
And mar men's spurring. Crack the lawyer's voice,
That he may never more false title plead,
Nor sound his quillets shrilly: hoar the flamen,
That scolds against the quality of flesh
And not believes himself: down with the nose,
Down with it flat; take the bridge quite away
Of him that, his particular to forsee,
Smells from the general weal: make curl'd-pate ruffians bald;
And let the unscarr'd braggarts of the war
Derive some pain from you: plague all;
That your activity may defeat and quell
The source of all erection. There's more gold:
Do you damn others, and let this damn you,
And ditches grave you all!

The penile skin decay that occurred in some syphilitics meant that they had to be circumcised: Hudibras, as described by Samuel Butler in 1663,

> had such plenty as sufficed
> To make some think him circumcised.
> And truly so he was perhaps
> Not as a proselyte but for claps.

One bawdy of the 1680s described how lechery 'frequently brings the lascivious Prodigal more than Circumcised from the Surgeon, and sends him Noseless to the Grave'. Addison was to write a more elegant essay on false noses in 1710.[33]

The origins of syphilis were much discussed and were often used to stigmatize vulnerable minorities. The summary of attributed origins made by Gideon Harvey included several which are familiar. Black people were blamed; hostile foreigners were seen as sources of syphilis, so that one popular celebration of the defeat of the Spanish Armada in 1588 assured its readers that the fish which devoured the bodies of drowned Spanish sailors, or feasted on their blood, could not transmit the venereal diseases acquired thereby to Englishmen who subsequently ate the fishes' flesh. Women became the object of hostile projection: it would be hard to overestimate the importance of syphilis in legitimizing men's fear of the dangerous sex. 'Venereal disease extends its influence much further than might appear at first glance,' as Schopenhauer noted in 1851. 'Since Cupid's quiver also contains poisoned arrows, the relations between the sexes have assumed a strange, hostile and even diabolical element.'[34]

Syphilis was attributed to Caribbean cannibals: it was 'brought us from the West Indies . . . but particularly [from] those *Anthropagi* that sustain themselves by feeding upon men's flesh'. Interracial sexuality was suspected. Whores accommodating in quick succession men from different nations, whose genitals 'differing in temperament, and impelled into one womb, might engender a strange sort of putrefaction, like variety of meats causes putrid crudities in the stomach', it was supposed. There was distrust of foreigners which was not surprising given that epidemiology recognized the importance of international transmission. Harvey recommended medical examination and quarantine at ports: 'part of the Custom House must be converted into a Lazaretto [quarantine building, a word derived from leper colonies], to search all Foreigners before they set foot on shore.'[35]

But above all, the anxiety about syphilis revivified the male myth of Feminine Evil. The malefic mystery of menstruation was invoked: Paracelsus believed 'this malady to be engendered between a *French* leper, and a *Neapolitan* whore, whilst she had her courses upon her'. Another attribution was similarly hostile to women, while acknowledging the role of the French invasion of Italy in 1495 in the epidemiology of syphilis. 'An Italian witch of indifferent beauty, being extremely provoked by some French soldiers, that had pillaged her house, seated within sight of Naples, for revenge (others imagine she was hired by the Spanish) plotted the ruin of the whole Army, by spreading a diabolical disease among them, and to that purpose prostrated her body to the very next comers.' Harvey, who was appointed physician to King William III in 1688, disbelieved tales of diabolical magic: syphilis, he explained, was transmitted 'not supernaturally, or by Witchcraft, but by ejaculating Venereal Seeds' within women's bodies. Male terror of what is hidden away inside female genitals was rampant in venereological writings.[36]

Sexuality in modern western Europe has been characterized by the persistence of a crude defence against anxiety which psychoanalysts now designate as 'splitting'. Under this process, objects or instincts which have both erotic and destructive possibilities are split into polarities of 'good' and 'bad'. There follows idealization of what is perceived to be good, while the other extreme is anathematized. Syphilis, or anxiety about it, contributed to this process. Lubricity has been depicted as the antithesis of domestic purity: whores, pimps and deceivers swive, cheat and wrangle in an underworld where actions and words have multiple layers of meaning, and everything is presumed to end in degradation and dirt. One example of splitting took the form of the denigration of women who found exuberant pleasure in sex. Both desired and feared, they came to seem the incarnation of badness, and were represented as filthy. Rochester in the seventeenth century wrote of Mistress Willis,

> Bawdy in thoughts, precise in Words,
> Ill natur'd though a Whore,
> Her Belly is a Bag of Turds,
> And her Cunt a Common shore.

Hence the prostitute came to seem 'the perpetual symbol of the degradation and the sinfulness of man', as Lecky wrote in his *History of European Morals*, on whose 'ignoble form' was 'concentrated the passions that might have filled the world'.[37]

In a development of paramount importance, the epidemic affected sexual technique to the detriment of women. The Pox was most infectious when it had been 'excited through the excess of heat caused by a vigorous execution', wrote Gideon Harvey in his popular textbook *Great Venus Unmask'd* (1672). 'Contagious clots . . . diseased with a triplicated manginess and conceived in foul Scorbutick wombs, scattering with filthy and infectious menstrues, do now unite, and are violently baked . . . like bricks in a Furnace.' Women's sexuality was feared and misunderstood as well as desired: their bodies were the objects of male appetite, but also dangerous incomprehensible objects containing 'foul Scorbutick wombs' which could poison or emasculate the men who penetrated them. Cunts could give men ecstasy, but they could also seem voracious holes, with powers to suck or ingest fingers and penises. Female passion was suspect and the female orgasm distrusted. Harvey recounted 'a curiosity of twelve students, who to try the insatiableness of a woman, all one after the other, aggressed a filthy whore, whereof three only retreated with a blast'. From this incident he drew somewhat phallocentric conclusions. The causes of 'contagion inhere sometimes in the passive female, otherwise in the active male', he wrote. 'The virulent female possibly is frigid, and the virulency deeply latent, so that the first aggressor shall only heat her a little, and scarce reach the contagious Miasmus, and so prepares the way for his successor, and escapes; the second coming on fresh, promotes the preceding work, and stirs her to the quick, by which means he gets more than he brought, but perhaps a Wench may be so frigid, that a dozen Hectors shall scarce heat her . . . and though she may be lustily clapt, yet none of them shall be tainted with the evil; and so it's possible a hundred may negotiate with the same malign whore, and all evade, provide she be frigid, as generally they are: in short, whores prove most contagious, when they are impelled to a satisfaction; for then they are apt to vent showers of Miasms, with their genitures that were dormant in their frigidity.' In other words, there was nothing so dangerous as women who *enjoyed* sexual intercourse.[38]

Half a century later the quack John Marten offered similar advice to men equally calculated to reduce women's sexual pleasure. He warned that if 'the Man made long stay in the Woman's Body, and through the excessive Ecstasy, Heat and Satiety, welter and indulge himself in that Coition, [that] is much the sooner way to attract the *Venom*, than quickly withdrawing'. One result of the popular treatises on syphilis which proliferated after 1660 may have been that men became more negligent of female sexual satisfaction, or more frightened by it. The advice they were receiving was to make penetration as hasty as possible, and the weight of this advice must have increased male anxiety and precipitated ejaculation. It was not only the preservation of female health that was ignored in literature on syphilis, but also the satisfaction of female desire was banished from the seventeenth century on the basis of medical supposition. As Rochester wrote in 'The Debauchee',

> I send for my whore, when for fear of a clap,
> I dally about her, and spew in her lap.

The meanings of this advice, and its consequences on sexual behaviour, are so far unimagined by historians: for sexual trust generally and women in particular the results were surely devastating.[39]

There was an element of sexual envy in these counsels of

disappointment, or perhaps the self-exculpation of men who had long failed to stir their women partners 'to the quick'. 'If perhazard she trades with a handsome fellow she likes, her fancy having the command of her uterine spirits, oves her appetite, and be sure his lot will prove unfortunate,' Harvey noted almost with relish. 'Whence extract the reason, why the Pox is fatal to most handsome men.' Who will suppose that Harvey was handsome?[40]

The value of circumcision was debated. Some physicians recommended circumcision to stop 'the virulency otherwise being hidden under the prepuce' and 'insinuating' itself into the body; for this reason it was asserted 'that the Jews, because they are circumcised, may venture with less danger: a gross mistake certainly', rebuked Harvey, who regarded Jews as so repellent that few people would have sex with them. 'We grant them less pockified for want of occasion,' wrote Harvey. 'The prepuce is rather a defence since those, whose glans is well covered, come off with less harm.'[41]

The fact that syphilis was one of the few diseases for which medical practitioners offered a specific remedy in the form of mercury might be expected to have marginalized quack venereology, but quacks were sly enough to exploit even this. For example Paul Chamberlen, in advertising his 'Great Venereal Specifick Remedy, and Elixir for the Secret Disease', took the discomfort of mercurial treatment as one of his main selling points. The cure offered by Chamberlen was 'without Salivating, Purging, Vomiting, Confinement, Hindrance from Business, or Disorder to the Patient', he advertised in 1728–30: indeed his elixir was 'an utter Enemy to Mercury'. According to Chamberlen, a venereal infection at primary stage was ' a mere Local Injury' comparable to 'a Cut Finger, or a Broken Shin'. Chamberlen's advertisements protected him against the inevitable failure of his concoction. 'It may sometimes happen, that after Persons have had even a GOOD Cure of the Venereal Distemper, there may still remain some little Dripping or Oozing, proceeding not from any Infection in the Body, but purely from a Weakness in the Parts, that will sometimes be after the BEST of cures.' When this occurred, Chamberlen urged his customers to buy more of his elixir. Under the most extreme form of mercurial salivation treatment, patients were expected to spit out three pints of saliva daily, and even milder therapeutic regimes were so vile to the sight and smell, and so degrading, that many patients preferred the emollient lies and futile nostrums of men like Chamberlen and John Spinke. Quackery may not have cured anyone, and often created dependency in patients, but it left some of them feeling less discouraged and humiliated.[42]

Medical students and younger physicians made money treating venereal disease by avoiding the expense of a regular consulting room. In the 1720s, for example, the landlord of the Royal Oak on the corner of Pall Mall and St James's Square lent the back room of his alehouse to 'several young surgeons, who used to have their Injection and Syringes' there for 'patients who were clapped'. Other qualified physicians, practising as venereologists, advertised in the personal columns of early nineteenth-century newspapers like the *Morning Chronicle*: so too did the London Lock Hospital in language that is eloquent testimony to prevailing attitudes (see illustration on page 50). But although venereal disease was not the domain solely of fringe practitioners, they were important in the development of social perceptions. Their advertisements and handbooks were intended to make them as much money as possible, and it served this end to maximize anxiety and distress, so as to panic patients into putting themselves quickly and unreservedly into the quacks' money-clutching hands. Quacks, even more than physicians or surgeons, used language intended to ensure that patients consulted them as soon as possible after infection, and then unconditionally submitted to their authority. Marten described the cautionary cases of patients 'who from . . . trivial Symptoms neglected, were plunged into those desperate, too often irretrievable, and sometimes ignominious conditions, to the Reproach and Disgrace, as well as Discomfort and Dissatisfaction, both of themselves and Relations'. Such neglect had ended with a 'disgraceful' deformed appearance, the cause of which all neighbours and friends could surmise:

> When *Honour's* Lost, 'tis a relief to die;
> Death's but a sure retreat from Infamy.[43]

Hogarth's representation of the libertine Viscount Squanderfield consulting a venereologist in *Marriage à la Mode* (1743) (see plate) provides an eloquent representation of eighteenth-century venereology. Here was a demi-monde of cruelty, duplicity and exploitation, in which hopes were often cheats and patients were often

Advertisement for the treatment of venereal diseases in a London newspaper of 1820.

dupes. The pillbox lid, placed between the viscount's legs, draws attention to his groin, and suggests that he has a venereal disease. His jaunty manner and erect cane suggest that he is far less distressed by his infection than his young mistress, who dabs at her face with a handkerchief as she thinks her life ruined. The facial expression of the purveyor of venereal pills mixes deference with cunning: he glowers and yet smiles with false encouragement. The consulting room is full of phallic symbols, including the tusk (whose grains would be used as an aphrodisiac) which is aligned to the wall like a barber's pole so that Hogarth can hint at the man's kinship with barber-surgeons. The skull on the table is marked with syphilitic erosion; a bleeding dish and urine bottle are also displayed. His female assistant is marked with syphilitic spots, and there are other suggestions that she is a procuress. Overall the impression given is of meanness: the venereologist and procuress look hypocritical, predatory and self-assured; the attitude of the viscount seems reckless and self- deceitful; while the only person genuine in her emotions or expression – the sad and frightened girl – is ignored by everyone.[44]

The perils of self-treatment and the risks run by impoverished syphilitics were exemplified by Thomas Chatterton, the precocious boy-poet who died aged 18 in 1770. He is often said to have committed suicide in despair at his poverty, but it is as likely that he died from arsenical poisoning while trying to treat his own syphilis. After contracting the disease in 1769, Chatterton could not afford Greek Water, sold at half a guinea per bottle under a patent granted to its devisor by King George II, so he tried several futile quack remedies and a course of mercurial salivation lasting three weeks which brought only temporary respite. Rather than repeat the ordeal of salivation, he followed Paracelsus's advice by adopting a meagre diet of fruit while taking increasing doses of arsenical water together with opium to cope with the vomiting. Within a month this treatment had killed him.[45]

Quacks were masters of mutual denigration. 'Many thousand unfortunate persons (wounded in the wars of *Venus*) . . . have been cheated of their Money, chased of their Lives, and died in Ignominy and Disgrace, unpitied by their best of Friends and nearest Relations,' wrote Marten, 'which Tragical Scene is totally owing to a Gang of *Empirical Rogues, Villainous Quacks, Devil's Emissaries, Impostors* [and] *Ignorant Pretenders.*' His contemporary Joseph Cam lamented in 1719: 'This Business is now become a Refuge to every little Bankrupt', who pirated other people's nostrums and drew 'the Unthinking Populace into their Ruin'.[46]

Critics of quackery alleged that it encouraged lechery. 'You advise all Mankind, which is prompt enough of itself to offend, to use *Machinery*, and to fight in *Armour*,' one quack who advertised and sold sheathes was told in 1737; 'If so, you are . . . the *Propagator* of Wickedness.' The sheath was originally intended not as a contraceptive but as a preventive against venereal infection. Made of animal gut, it had to be moistened and tied at the end with ribbon before use, and was a luxury which could only be afforded by the rich. It was first described in an account of syphilis by Gabriello Fallopio entitled *De morbo gallico*, published in 1564; the earliest known description in English occurred in 1704. Its author John Marten referred to an ointment, the recipe 'of which I purposely omit inserting', ostensibly 'lest it should give too much encouragement to the Lewds', but in reality to dupe syphilitics into buying his own anti-venereal remedy. Nevertheless he did reveal to his readers, 'if Lint or Linen Rags be divers times wet in it, and dried in the Shade, of a sufficient bigness to involve the *Glans* or Nut of the Man's Yard, or to cover the inner parts of the *Privity* of the Woman, and applied and kept on for a while before Engagement, will so harden the *Members*, dry up the superfluous Moistnesses, and resist Putrefaction, as that no one that uses them, shall ever be afflicted with the *Pox*.'[47]

The earliest parliamentary reference to sheaths dates from 1705, when in a debate on the proposed Union of England and Scotland, the Duke of Argyll (described as 'sober, thoughtful, a good husband . . . whose loftiness of mind did not prevent his harbouring the most illiberal contempt of women') produced from London, which he had recently visited, 'a certain instrument called a Quondam, which occasioned the debauching of a great number of Ladies of quality, and other young gentlewomen'. Colonel Cundum, or Condom, the reputed inventor of the sheath, seems to have been a mythical figure. Opponents of the Union such as Lord Belhaven and Stenton ('a rough, fat, black, noisy man, more like a Butcher than a Lord') regarded Argyll's instrument as symbolizing the excesses which would occur after Anglo-Scottish union. Belhaven even wrote a verse against Argyll, which included the couplets

> The Syringe and Condum
> Come both in request,
> While Virtuous Quondam,
> Is treated in Jest.

The praise of sheaths which occurs in early eighteenth-century poetry suggests that it was during the reigns of the first two Georges that these 'Master-strokes of Art', as John Gay called them, became widely used by those who could afford them.[48]

Some people found sheaths to be passion-killers. 'The *Condum* being the best, if not the only Preservative our Libertines have found out at present,' it was noted in 1717, 'yet, by reason of its blunting the Sensation, I have heard some of them acknowledge, that they had often to choose to risk a *Clap*, rather than engage with spears thus sheathed.' James Boswell in 1763 'picked up a fresh, agreeable young girl' who when he took out his 'armour' (that is, sheath) 'begged that I might not put it on, as the sport was much pleasanter without it, and as she was quite safe'.[49]

Syphilis, as we have seen, was a disease which was defined by powerful social perceptions that influenced clinical medicine and often dominated the treatment which patients received not only from qualified practitioners or quacks, but also from lay society. From at least the late sixteenth century syphilitics were often (but not invariably) presented as the epitome of sexual corruption and social degradation: they were sources of pollution whose carnal desires and physical ruin seemed to symbolize decaying social order. Their disease was seen as an affliction of sinners, the vengeance of a wrathful God for sexual exuberance. The ways in which mercury was applied show how therapeutic treatment could be subordinated to the desire to punish the afflicted. Syphilitics were stigmatized, and made to suffer. Unless they were socially privileged, they were at risk of becoming outcasts, degraded and despised, self-hating and self-destructive, shunned and abused as defilers. The multitude of people, who largely found their sense of social cohesion in their fear of life, expanded, intensified and systematized their hostility to syphilitics. As lazar colonies became venereal hospitals, and leper's *loques* or bandages gave such institutions the name of lock, so syphilis supplanted leprosy as *the* dreaded contagion, and the prostitute was allotted the new role of social leper. Whores became a new category of untouchable upon whom fears could be projected and violent language could be hurled. A treatise on venereal diseases of 1737 for example fastened on 'the filthy gulph of a Harlot' as the source of infection: a tone not only of repugnance but of hatred rang out.[50]

The archetype of this fate is a whore in Tobias Smollett's novel *Roderick Random* (1748). Her description deserves full quotation because it reports every anxiety and stigma that the more unfortunate syphilitics had borne for two and a half centuries.

Smollett's whore recounts that 'she found herself dangerously infected with a distemper to which all women of the town are particularly subject; that her malady gaining ground every day she became loathsome to herself and offensive to others; that she had accordingly put herself into the hands of an advertising doctor, who, having fleeced her of all the money she had or could procure, left her in a worse condition than in which he had found her'. Smollett was a physician as well as a writer; with this expertise, he made his character describe how she had often seen, as she 'strolled about the streets at midnight, a number of naked wretches reduced to rags and filth, huddled together like swine, in the corner of a dark alley; some of whom, but eighteen months before, I had known as the favourites of the town, rolling in affluence and glittering in all the pomp of equipage and dress. And indeed the gradation is easily conceived; the most fashionable woman of the town is as liable to contagion as one in a much humbler sphere; she infects her admirers; her situation is public; she is avoided, neglected, unable to support her usual appearance, which, however, she strives to maintain as long as possible; her credit fails, she is obliged to retrench and become a nightwalker; her malady gains ground; she tampers with her constitution and ruins it; her complexion fades; she grows nauseous to everybody; finds herself reduced to a starving condition; is tempted to pick pockets; is detected, committed to Newgate [prison], where she remains in a miserable condition until she is discharged. Nobody will afford her lodging; the symptoms of her distemper have grown outrageous; she sues to be admitted into a hospital, where she is cured at the expense of her nose; she is turned out naked into the streets, depends upon the addresses of the lowest class, is feign to allay the rage of hunger and cold with gin; degenerates into a brutal insensibility, rots and dies upon a dunghill.'[51]

CHAPTER THREE

The Phoenix of Sodom

Sir J. Mennes and Mr Batten both say that buggery is now almost as common among our gallants as in Italy, and that the very pages of the town begin to complain of their masters for it. But blessed be God, I do not to this day know what is the meaning of this sin, nor which is the agent nor which the patient.

SAMUEL PEPYS, diary 1 July 1663

It takes all sorts to make a sex.   SAKI

There is nothing like desire for preventing the things one says from bearing any resemblance to what one has in one's mind.

MARCEL PROUST

The relationships between individual sexual acts and society – the ways in which perceptions of intercourse reflect their social context – are one of the governing themes of this book. Sexuality is not an unchanging and immutable fact of nature, but a humanly constructed artefact open to many and changing interpretations. The ways in which sexual acts are perceived and treated derive from the societies in which they occur; if they change it is because these societies have changed. If, for example, a society discards St Paul's view of marriage as no more than a defence against lust, and sees it instead as engaging the affections or providing companionship, then perceptions of intercourse will move too. There will be less disposition to see women as inferior vessels whose only purpose is to receive semen. The objects of male lust, and the ways they are treated, will be seen from different perspectives. The new outlook will affect not only relations between the opposite sexes, but the interaction of men with men and women with women. Thus until the eighteenth century sexual relations between men were usually treated as a commonplace method of achieving physical pleasure. It was seldom an exclusive sexual taste and was untouched by ecclesiastical fulminations against corrupters of the Natural Order. Sodomy was confused with bestiality or subsumed in a general whirl of debauchery, often treated as less sinful than blasphemy, and subject to less disapproval or legal intervention than rape or the seduction of minors. But after 1700 the imagery and social labelling pertaining to sodomy in England were transformed.

But some explanations are required. What is meant by the phrase 'social labelling'? What should be understood by words like 'sodomite'?

Social labelling is the process which creates deviant roles, like those attributed to the homosexual or the addict or the homeless and jobless. It erects an unmistakable and fortified frontier between the realms of permissible and impermissible conduct to stop people from drifting casually across the border into deviant behaviour. Labelling frightens off the drifters with an enfilade of sanctions better suited to the outright defector: the first move towards the borderland of deviance immediately raises the issue of total defection into a deviant role. Labelling is an imperfect way of preserving purity or social order because it tends to preclude changes of behaviour, reducing individuals' emotional flexibility or their power to change their lives. Stereotyping segregates the deviants or defectors, isolates their behaviour, and thereby bestows on them unsolicited loyalty to a narrow group. If rigid categorization deters some people from drifting into deviancy, it also forecloses on the possibility of some drifting back. Stereotypes are never random, personal or isolated from their historical context: they are among the defences which societies need in order to feel that they have control over their world. They are also the consolation of people who feel that the mental images which they have created and internalized are disintegrating. Stereotypes blur or exaggerate differences, and imply that the social order is secure. They offer simple images and explanations instead of unsettling ambiguities; their concern is less with accuracy than with containing human disorder.[1]

The modern labelling of a male homosexual presumes that he will be exclusively or predominantly homosexual in feelings and behaviour, effeminate in manner, passive in personality and in bed; it assumes that sexual desire will be a component of all his relations with other men, and that he always pursues and seduces boys and youths. But it was not always so. Until the nineteenth century different nouns were used to describe what is now called a homosexual: they evoked different images which were part of a different set of mental representations of the world. The *Oxford English Dictionary* records the phrases 'I am afraid thou wilt make me thy *ingle*' in 1592, 'smooth-chinned, plump-thighed *catamite*' in 1593, and 'young beardless *ganymede*' in 1603. The nineteenth-century neologism of 'homosexual' has connotations which were alien to nouns like ingle, or sodomite, or bugger. 'It is by the power of names, of signs originally arbitrary and insignificant, that the course of imagination has in great measure been guided,' Jeremy Bentham wrote of homosexuality in 1814. How was the power of names exerted? How did these originally arbitrary constructions develop into such significant imaginative forces?[2]

All men and women are drawn, in varying degrees, and with a differing measure of self-awareness, to members of their own sex; but in the seventeenth century neither they themselves, nor anyone else, believed that this attraction encapsulated their identity, or revealed all that it was necessary to know about their being. The word 'homosexual' was not coined until 1869, and had no equivalent two or three centuries earlier. Words like 'sodomy' and 'buggery' involved broader activities than what is now called homosexuality: they denoted general debauchery. Thus a Puritan writing in the reign of Queen Elizabeth denounced 'games of Sodom' played on Sundays such as 'heathenish dancing', bull-baiting 'or else the jackanapes do ride on horseback'; later, in the 1660s, 'Sodom' was the name given to heterosexual brothels in London. An ode addressed to King Charles II by John Oldham warned that he was called 'Effeminate' because

> Cunt was the Star that rul'd thy Fate,
> Cunt thy sole Bus'ness, and Affair of State.

Debauchery was identified almost as much with the luxury and plenitude that demoralized Sodom and Gomorrah as with sexual vice: the jurist Sir Edward Coke affirmed in 1644 that sodomy originated in 'pride, excess of diet, idleness, and contempt of the poor'.[3]

Early biblical proscription of homosexuality is not surprising among wandering desert tribes whose survival in a hostile environment depended upon their procreative power. The first relevant biblical condemnation of sodomy occurs in Genesis (chs 18–19), 'when the Lord rained upon Sodom and upon Gomorrah brimstone and fire'; although the most notable feature of the story is that after Lot had escaped from Sodom, but had seen his wife transformed into salt, he enjoyed sexual relations with his daughters, who both bore him sons. Leviticus (20:13) stigmatized sodomy as an 'abomination' in a list of ordinances directed against adultery, fornication, incest and nakedness. St Paul lambasted the 'vile affectations' of paganism: 'their women did change the natural use into that which is against nature: And likewise also the men, leaving the natural use of the woman, burned in their lust one toward another, men with men working that which is unseemly, and receiving in themselves that recompence of their error which was meet.' (Romans 1: 26–27)

The early Christian Church identified erotic relations with the same sex as illicit lust (*luxuria*) which was liable to result in damnation and it was not until the eleventh and twelfth centuries that the new penitentials, biblical commentaries and canon law which were revitalizing Christianity began to emphasize sins against nature, although there was a respite of several centuries before sodomites were widely burnt at the stake. The medieval Church often stigmatized heretics alongside sexual deviants, and the Spanish Inquisition, with its terror of deviance or disorder, classed heretics and sodomites together as a group to be identifed and destroyed. During the twelfth century the Albigensian sect of southern France and northern Italy were known as *bougres* or *bougeron* because their religious beliefs were supposed to derive from Bulgaria, and the word *bougre* (bugger) became a synonym for sodomite. Other sects suffered from similar slurs, and a persistent tradition arose. By the Renaissance, charges of sodomy and charges of heresy were almost interchangeable: allegations of witchcraft and lesbianism were sometimes equally muddled or consolidated. So wise a man as Coke believed that the Lombards 'brought into the Realm the shameful sin of Sodomy' and treated 'sorcerers, sodomites and heretics' as if they were identical in committing 'a sin horrible . . . either against the King Celestial or Terrestial . . . by heresy [or] by buggery'.[4]

Christian and Jewish traditions stressed sexual acts as procreative acts necessary for the renewal and survival of the race. Sexual activity for pleasure was sometimes represented as perverse, although in the medieval era the Church tended to more severity in banning sexual acts that might result in extra-marital conception than those without the risk of producing children. In seventeenth-century England too there is evidence that local authorities were more concerned to prevent the birth of bastards who might have to be supported by the parish than in preventing other forms of illicit sex.

In England sexual acts like sodomy, bestiality or incest fell within the purview of Church rather than criminal courts in the medieval period. An ecclesiastical law of 1290 ordered sodomites to be buried alive, but this sentence seems never to have been imposed, and the few sodomites who were convicted by Church courts were hanged by the secular authorities. Hanging was introduced by King Henry VIII in 1533 to punish 'the detestable and abominable Vice of Buggery committed with mankind or beast' and had no counterpart elsewhere in Europe. The great historians of English law, Pollock and Maitland, conclude that Henry's statute of 1533 'affords an almost sufficient proof that the temporal courts had not punished' sodomy, 'and that no one had been put to death for it for a very long time past'. At the time the king was divorcing his wife Catherine of Aragon so as to be free to marry Anne Boleyn, which course had separated him from the Church of Rome and led to the dissolution of the monasteries. Beyond the seizure of Church property, Henry wanted to limit the jurisdiction of ecclesiastical courts by redesignating certain offences as temporal crimes for trial in ordinary courts. The statute of 1533 was part of this process: it was not occasioned by any strong urge to repress sodomy, but partly derived from Henry's paranoia, which led him to kill two of his wives and persecute his subjects. In contrast with sodomy, incest, which was a sensitive issue to Henry (as Catherine of Aragon had previously been married to his brother), remained punishable only under ecclesiastical law; having escaped recodification in his reign, it was not made a criminal offence until 1908 in England. Tudor definitions of sexual criminality were arbitrary.[5]

Coke claimed in his *Institutes of the Laws of England* (1628), which gives the first detailed treatment of the statute, 'that somewhat before the making of this Act, a great Lady had committed buggery with a Baboon and conceived by it'. Fanciful though this is, Henry VIII's original legislation was directed against buggery 'committed with mankind or beast' and bore only a loose construction of what sodomy meant: only in 1718, it seems, was the law applied to cover anal penetration of women as well as of men in England. This vagueness was reflected across Europe: a penal code of 1532, which was promulgated by Charles V, the Holy Roman Emperor, interdicted crimes against nature, including intercourse between men, between women and between humans and animals, but was not more specific. Coke's reference to the great lady and her baboon typified the sixteenth century's identification of buggery with bestiality; anal penetration was seen as the action of beasts. This attitude is conveyed by a lampoon on Lord Hunsdon, reputedly a sodomite as well as a syphilitic, a cousin of Queen Elizabeth who acted as her Lord Chamberlain 1597–1603:

> at Hoxton, now, his monstrous love he feasts:
> for there he keeps a bawdy house of beasts.

John Donne, also writing of the Elizabethan Court in the 1590s, speculated as to 'who love whores, who boys and who goats'. Sir Volvptvovs Beast, a character created by Ben Jonson (?1573–1637), taunted his wife with tales of his infidelities with mistresses, boys and beasts:

> Telling the motions of each petticoat,
> And how his Ganymede moved and how his goat.

This association with bestiality persisted in the legal mind, so that a barrister was speaking under the influence of Tudor and Stuart jurists when he referred during a trial of 1893 to 'the acts of beasts in human form who had striven to degrade' his client. In the 1960s Lord Chancellor Dilhorne was still talking about bestiality and buggery in the language of his ancestor Coke.[6]

All this suggests a set of attitudes in which more emphasis was put on a man achieving sexual satisfaction than on the identity of his partner. It was a hierarchical society ruled by men in which children were to be well disciplined and women were expected to be submissive. The phallus was supreme, and carefree indeterminacy about the objects of its pleasure was permissible. Given this outlook, sodomy by teachers of those in their power was tolerated. Headmasters who in 1541 and 1594 were found to have sexually enjoyed male pupils survived with their reputations scarcely tarnished. Throughout the sixteenth and seventeenth centuries it was customary in Oxford and Cambridge colleges for a tutor – always a bachelor, and often in his twenties – to share his bedroom with several undergraduates of fifteen to eighteen years of age. 'Had I some snout-fair brats', wrote John Marston, who had some experience of homoeroticism, it would be better that they endure burning than that

> some pedant tutor in his bed
> Should use my fry like Phrygian Ganymede;

but the youths' parents seem not to have realized the temptations presented to tutors and boys, all at an age of strong sexual urges, by collegiate sleeping arrangements, or else not to have thought that it mattered. These attitudes – whether originating in innocence, indifference or tolerance it is hard to judge – were not modified until the early eighteenth century.[7]

Henry VIII's legislation of 1533 was seldom enforced, although it was re-enacted by him in 1536, 1539 and 1541, as well as revised during the reigns of his three children. The predilections of King James I, who succeeded to the throne of Scotland in 1567 and to that of England in 1603, perhaps resulted in a more lenient approach to the laws. As a youth he was infatuated with his cousin Esmé, Duke of Lennox, and at the English Court James showed marked preference for handsome young men, such as Robert Carr, whom he created Earl of Somerset, or George Villiers, whom he created Duke of Buckingham. As Richard Savage later wrote,

> Queens, with their Ladies, work unseemly things,
> And Boys grow Dukes, when Catamites to Kings.

It is sometimes suggested that there was a double standard based on class: that male homosexual desire was tolerated among the powerful, or was exclusive to royalty and aristocrats. The implication that rich lords practised with impunity pleasures for which poor men were put to the stake is unjustifiable. English court records show the rarity of prosecutions for sodomy in the sixteenth and seventeenth centuries. Between 1559 and 1625, for example, there were only four indictments for sodomy in four counties near London combined (Essex, Hertfordshire, Kent, Sussex). This low level of accusations is the more striking because in just one of those counties, Essex, with a population of about 40,000 adults, some 15,000 people were summoned to court for sex offences between 1558 and 1603. Such an average of 330 summonses annually, involving about 1 per cent of the sexually mature population, suggests an inquisitorial society where people were quick to denounce each other's transgressions. In the few prosecutions for sodomy that occurred, the primary issue was the preservation of social order, more particularly the maintenance of paternal rights, rather than the suppression of sexual acts or affections between men. Those indicted tended to be yeomen or labourers who forced their attentions on others, or a man surprised with the son of a neighbour, or a stranger to the vicinity. The law was seldom invoked if sodomy occurred in institutions like schools ('Give him no tutor – throw him to a punk/ Rather than trust his morals to a monk,' warned one poet), brothels or private households. Given the level of summonses for other sexual transgressions like bestiality, bigamy or incest, this indifference to sodomy was not a sign of national tolerance, but suggests either that there was little sodomy in Renaissance England, or indicates a reluctance to denounce men as sodomites, or a failure to relate sexual exchanges between men to the provisions of law.[8]

Until the eighteenth century even humble households contained servants, who were employed to help the master in his trade or business. They were not necessarily apprentices and, like the children of the household, left when they could afford to marry and start a household of their own. Consequently many unmarried young people lived in their workplace, either as children or servants of the householder: such confinement limited opportunities for external sexual contacts, and sexual relations between master and servant, or between servants, whether heterosexual or otherwise, were common. The absence of prosecutions for sodomy between masters and servants can be interpreted to mean that such relationships did not occur, or that there was reluctance to intervene in relationships conducted inside private households, especially where one of the men was subservient to the other. There is corroboration of the latter explanation, with some types of manservant apparently more sexually complaisant than others. Around 1680 Rochester declared in his cheerful 'Song':

> There's a sweet, soft page of mine
> Does the trick worth forty wenches.

In 1748 Smollett depicted a lord whose 'favourite pathic' was his valet; but in 1765 a 'drunken riot' erupted after two young men, Sir Thomas Gascoigne and the future Lord Dorchester, made sexual overtures to their manservant. 'Exacting such offices from their coachman as the *valets de place* only are used to render, and meeting with an opposition that wine and lust could not bear, a violent skirmish ensued.' What valets were expected to take this coachman would not endure.[9]

The exception to this complaisance was the execution in 1631 of the Earl of Castlehaven. His conduct had exceptional features without which he might have escaped prosecution: but, like Oscar Wilde two and a half centuries later, his ruin raised awareness of existing legislation and stimulated punitive urges, although after the case in 1640 of the Bishop of Waterford (which had political implications) no man is known to have been hanged for sodomy in Britain during the rest of the seventeenth century.

Castlehaven was found guilty by his fellow peers of crimes 'so heinous and so horrible that a Christian man ought scarce to name them'. His worst offence against social order was not the sadism with which he treated his wife (whom he held down while she was raped by his catamite), nor his voyeurism, nor even his sexual acts with young pages. His fatal indiscretion was his wish for his favourite youth, Henry Skipwith, rather than his son, to father his daughter-in-law's children, so that Skipwith's descendants would inherit his peerages and land. 'My Lord said he would rather have a boy of my own getting than any other,' testified Skipwith; and to this end the girl was from the age of twelve forced to submit to Skipwith, without however conceiving. This abuse of the hereditary system outraged peers like the Lord Keeper, Lord Coventry of Aylesborough, who admonished Castlehaven that 'having honour and fortune to leave behind you, you would have the impious and spurious offspring of a harlot to inherit.' (This preoccupation with stopping a man's property being inherited by children fathered by his wife's lover was the most pronounced feature in the development of English divorce laws from the Duke of Rutland's divorce of 1688 until the Divorce Act of 1857.)[10]

The Attorney-General, Sir Robert Heath, described Castlehaven's rape of his wife and sodomy with his servants as crimes 'of that rarity that we seldom know of the like'; they were so 'pestiferous and pestilential [in] nature that if they be not punished they will draw from heaven heavy judgments upon this kingdom'. Heath warned the peers who were trying Castlehaven to 'be cautious how you give the least mitigation to such abominable sins; for when once a man indulges his lust, and prevaricates with his religion, as my Lord [Castlehaven] has done, by being a Protestant in the morning and a Papist in the afternoon, no wonder if he commits the most abominable impieties; for when men forsake their God, tis no wonder he leaves them to themselves.' Once again religious inconstancy and theological unorthodoxy – and the anxieties they aroused regarding personal or social disintegration – were tangled up with fears of sexual deviance in a confused and complex way.[11]

The disparity between the language used by Heath to denounce Castlehaven's lusts and the reality of everyday experience of men's attraction to one another was irreconcilable. It is doubtful that the men who customarily shared beds in the crowded little houses of the early modern period, who fumbled with one another or sodomized one another, saw themselves as indulging in those practices which were so scarifyingly proscribed in the language of criminal indictments. (Defendants were accused of 'wickedly, devilishly, feloniously, and against the Order of Nature' committing that 'sodomitical, detestable, and abominable Sin called Buggery (not to be named among Christians) to the Great Displeasure of Almighty God, and to the Disgrace of all Mankind'). The verbal violence that surrounded sodomy concealed the extent of sexual activity between men. Vehement but imprecise censure of such activity coexisted with modes of sexual conduct which required no heights of self-awareness or depths of self-analysis. Except in immediate sexual encounters, there was no reason for anyone to define their sexuality. While homoeroticism lacked any distinct social characteristic and was just another way of getting sexual relief, it was rarely noticed or prosecuted. Just as the eighteenth-century author of *Onania* claimed of masturbation, 'a great many Offenders would never be guilty of it, if they had been thoroughly acquainted with the Heinousness of the Crime', so it was not until the eighteenth century that homoerotics became 'thoroughly acquainted' with what they were doing, or conscious that it might have implications that were not purely personal. This condition is summarized by the bewildered exclamation of a man who was arrested in a police trap of 1726 for intent to commit sodomy. As a constable testified, 'We asked the Prisoner why he took such indecent Liberties . . . and he was not ashamed to answer, *I did it because I . . . knew him, and I think there is no Crime in making what Use I please of my own Body*.'[12]

Outside the Puritan tradition, the existence of pansexual or bisexual libertines was well attested in the seventeenth century. Men who were able to satisfy their wish to enjoy a variety of sexual experience and roles did not feel constrained to take only women as partners, although the bisexuality of such men was often cited as evidence of a jaded sexual appetite. Restoration rakes, such as Rochester, celebrated anal penetration, of either sex, as a defiant act: and there was no supposition that a man's taste for fucking other men excluded a taste for fucking women. John Donne wrote of those who

> in rank itchy lust, desire, and love
> the nakedness and bareness to enjoy
> Of thy plump, muddy whore, or prostitute boy.

John Oldham wrote in 1683 of 'how cheap you may a Harlot, or an Ingle keep', as if these were unexceptional and non-exclusive alternatives. Men who enjoyed both harlots and ingles were thought heavily preoccupied with sex, but not unimaginably deviant.[13]

There are many interpretations, but few absolutely ascertainable explanations, in the history of sexuality. A mixture of hard evidence and gentle nuance does however suggest that the labelling of sodomy altered in eighteenth-century England as elsewhere in Europe. An account of Castlehaven's trial published in 1699 explained that an 'abomination that shocks our Natures, and puts our Modesty to the Blush, to see it so commonly perpetrated, is the *Devilish and Unnatural Sin of Buggery*, a Crime that sinks a Man below the *Basest* Epithet, is so Foul that it admits of no Aggravation, and cannot be expressed in its Horror, but by the *Doleful Shrieks and Groans of the Damned*'. Such denunciations seem to have little sense of sodomy as anything but 'devilish and unnatural'. Yet a little over thirty years later Paris police reports began substituting the word '*pédéraste*' for '*sodomite*': the biblical term, with its over-tones of divine prohibition of sin, was replaced by a more neutral term, not signifying love of boys, but denoting a man who directed his sexual desire at other men. In England men who acknowledged the taste increasingly found that it carried a disturbing reputation. By 1816, as Lord Byron exclaimed 'in an agony' when his bisexual behaviour was bruited by a former mistress, 'even to have such a thing *said* is utter destruction and ruin to a man . . . from which he can never recover.'[14]

There was increasing self-awareness about carnality during the seventeenth century concomitant with the developing sense of the Self. A line of poetry written by Traherne in 1674 – 'A secret self I had enclos'd within' – is recorded by the *Oxford English Dictionary* as the first instance in which the word 'self' took its modern meaning of 'a permanent subject of successive and varying states of consciousness'. The *OED*'s earliest dates of usage for words suggest that a new, more tense and introspective spirit was abroad among the English. Self-knowledge and self-lashing are both cited for 1613, followed by such words as self-humiliation (1634), self-denial (1640), self-fearing and self-suspicion (1646), self-examination (1647), self-destructive (1654), self-wronging (1656), self-contradiction (1658), self-torturing (1668), self-determination (1683), self-conscious (1687), self-betraying (1698), self-condemnation (1703) and self-comprehending (1711). Diaries reflected the change in people's awareness of themselves as individuals: a new taste for self-scrutiny becomes discernible. The few diarists of sixteenth-century England were not introspective. During the thirteen years after 1550 in which the London undertaker Henry Machyn kept a diary he made only two references to himself: both were to record his birthday, and significantly neither the dates nor ages tally. Sir Francis Walsing-ham's diary is an aide-memoire of journeys or conferences, Sir Thomas Coningsby's journal graphically describes military opera-tions, but both men typically excluded all references personal to themselves. A great change occurred later in the seventeenth century. In 1667 John Thoresby for example told his twenty-year-old son to start keeping a diary as 'a good method for one to keep a tolerable decorum in actions because he is accountable to himself as well as to God': and from then until 1724 Ralph Thoresby kept a daily journal 'chiefly designed for my daily direction and reproof', as he recorded. It became an exercise in self-examination and self-reproach ('By reason of the quivering and dithering of my body and the depravedness of my heart I could not understand anything to purpose'). Thoresby began his journal in the same decade as did Pepys, whose favourite maxim that 'what a man's mind is, that is what he is' encapsulated this new sense of personal identity. By the mid eighteenth century diaries were an established form of introspection, emphasizing a new and stronger sense among some people of themselves as individuals. Once people began to think harder about their inner selves and motives, in the manner of Thoresby or Pepys, they became more self-aware regarding sexual desire.[15]

This new consciousness of individuality took several forms. Marriage had mostly been seen as little more than the institution within which men could appease their lust: the purpose of marital sex, moralists and theologians agreed, was procreation. Idealized love or affection were all but irrelevant. The hold of this orthodoxy over the upper bourgeoisie and nobility was loosened however in the late seventeenth century. As people became more preoccupied with the Self in themselves, so their interest grew in the possibility of the Self in others. Some men had an increasing sense not only of their own inner identity, but that intimate attachments with women – such as mutual respect, trust and confidence between husband and wife – could give a man the strength and pleasure which hitherto had mainly been attributed to (male) boon companions. Women began to be perceived not just as apparatus for procreation, but as individuals with whom men could find it agreeable to work and play. Not coincidentally it was in the mid seventeenth century, so Lawrence Stone suggests, that more wives escaped the tyranny of constant pregnancies by convincing husbands to practise *coitus interruptus*. This exercise of marital consideration was one of many signs noticed by Stone indicating a new ideal of affectionate, child-oriented marriage which in turn inspired a revision of hopes and expectations between the two sexes, at least amongst the propertied classes. The widower brother of Lord Peterborough and Monmouth who in 1714 recorded 'losing his double comfort, wife and friend' showed the developing sense of marriage as companionate and of family life as gratifying. Wives, it was realized almost for the first time, could also be friends. But simultaneously the economic, social and psychological forces which traditionally had supported the family weakened. Among propertied people the advice and intervention of kin in the domestic arrangements of the nuclear family were much reduced though not eliminated: hopes of personal happiness reduced the importance of property exchange, patrimony and dowry in all but the most artistocratic marriages. More private hopes and deeper emotional needs were invested in marriage just at the moment when marital life was becoming riskier – when the optimistic lover who aspired to a lifetime's fulfilment was courting lifelong disappointment. Personal insecurity about infidelities intensified. Ribald versifiers of the eighteenth century remind the historian that it was a period obsessed with adultery: it ought perhaps to be called not the Age of Reason, but the Age of Cuckold Anxiety. Married men had never been more vulnerable and sore.[16]

Amongst the English propertied class there was a reconceptualization of sexuality during the early eighteenth century which formed part of wider changes in philosophical belief and social organization. 'One truth is clear, Whatever is, is right,' wrote Alexander Pope in 1733, confident like his contemporaries that under God's natural order everything in the world was in harmony and tended to universal good. The Enlightenment view of sexuality as integral to human nature stands in contrast to seventeenth- or nineteenth-century opinions. In 1895, for example, one critic contested Henry James's comment, apropos of sexual passion, that 'half of life is a sealed book to young unmarried women', and questioned if even one-tenth of the lives of most adults was concerned with sexual passion. 'Life has to contain manual and mental labour, buying and selling, travel, sport, personal ambition, public interests, private friendships, and these . . . must be terribly crowded if they are to be packed into one moiety of life, that sexuality may disport itself in the other.' The more open and easy modes of the eighteenth century were contrasted by their practitioners with the deadly continence of monasteries and nunneries, or with the double-faced, self-deceiving behaviour of the puritans. Evangelical moralists were mocked as dissemblers: Sir Henry Englefield, for example, described Lord Bloomfield as 'a canting, methodistical hypocrite, always talking religion and morality, but living, though a married man, in barefaced adultery with Lady Downshire'.[17]

The behaviour of the aristocracy would have been thought dangerously ungovernable if replicated in the lower orders. The following description by Lord Glenbervie in 1807 of aristocratic marital intrigues is so complicated that it is hard to tell who is cuckolding whom. 'Lady Sutherland, now Marchioness of Stafford, had the reputation for several years of having an intrigue with her husband's brother-in-law, Lord Carlisle, (long the *amant en titre* of Lady Jersey, with whom he had replaced William Fawkener, when he discarded her to marry Miss Poyntz and to be treated afterwards by her as he had treated Lord Jersey and many other husbands).' To Glenbervie, who was an affectionate husband and father, these affairs might be scandalous, but they were more a matter of fun than outrage.[18]

By contrast plebeian sexuality caused alarm: eroticism was as unsuitable for servants as atheism, and likely to lead not only to social disorder, but to overpopulation, a menace which haunted eighteenth-century thinkers. The populace was required to respect the discipline of family, workplace and religious taboos, and to practise a prudential morality. The difference between acknowledging community pressure and keeping to the routines of work, or of flouting authority and moral precepts, often proved to be the difference between living well and dying in despair and poverty. Nevertheless the Society for the Reformation of Manners, founded in 1691 by puritanical Christians to prosecute prostitutes, pornographers, sodomites, sabbath-breakers, swearers and the lewd, was despised for employing tawdry snoopers and harassing the poor in their pleasures. Some of its activists were excited into repression to punish their own desires: Charles Hitchin, Under-Marshal in the City of London, who was fined £20, condemned to the pillory and imprisoned for six months in 1727 for attempted sodomy, previously 'had taken a World of Pains and spent a great deal of Money in discouraging the Profaneness, curbing the Vices, and reforming the Manners of the present Age'. The Society provoked riots when it tried to shut brothels but (before being disbanded in 1738) enjoyed some credit for denouncing sodomites, several of whom were arrested or hanged in 1725–6 through its efforts, at a time when the labels that were being fixed to sodomites made them seem conspicuously at odds with the prevailing discipline based on prudential morality.[19]

Later the Society for Enforcing the King's Proclamation Against Immorality and Profaneness was formed in 1787. Its members included two archbishops and seventeen bishops; its first president was the Duke of Montagu, 'one of the weakest and most ignorant men living' known for his 'formal coldness of character'. The other four dukes on its council included a former prime minister, Grafton, who had espoused the Unitarian religion after many years in which 'openly . . . daringly and with repeated effrontery, [he] insulted the virtue and decency of mankind' by consorting with whores and pimps. This repentant rake keenly supported an organization intended to encourage morality and virtue amongst the rich and powerful and to influence the character of national government by removing the lingering taint of puritanism and social subversion from the cause of moral reform. It was a small organization, dominated by MPs, peers and ecclesiastics, including Beilby Porteus, Bishop of London from 1787 until his death in 1808. He was a generous, imaginative man, who fought long and hard against the slave trade, detested corruption inside and outside the Church, and although an evangelical, favoured toleration of Roman Catholics. His life was animated throughout by devotion to Christ: the prospect of lost souls afforded him the utmost distress. For him the greatest of the commandments was to love God, and the chief test of this love was obedience. Sensuality was a dangerous adversary of Obedience. The apostolic admonition 'to flee youthful lusts' (2 Timothy, ii 22) was, Porteus preached, 'so indispensably requisite both to temporal and eternal happiness, that it must, at all events, and by every possible means, be inculcated and enforced'. Most of 'the vice and misery that desolate mankind' ('murders, frauds, breaches of trust, violations of the marriage bed, the ruin of the unguarded and of unsuspecting innocence, the distress and disgrace of worthy families, the corruption and subversion of whole kingdoms') sprang from 'irregular desires' which 'burst through all restraints of decency, justice, honour, humanity, gratitude; and throw down every barrier, however sacred'. This was the authentic voice of Christian moralism, fighting sin and demanding obedience, which was to swell to such resonance in the nineteenth and early twentieth centuries.[20]

The cause of moral improvement was transformed by the blood

and tumbrils of the French Revolution. In Britain the threat of social strife or national ruin became exigent after 1793: the propertied classes felt a new need to assert the primacy of hierarchy and the duty of deference among the lower orders. One manifestation of this sharper fear of social indiscipline and licentiousness was the projection of fears about disintegrating social cohesion in London onto sexual deviants which by 1810 resulted in so many men going to the pillory (see below, pp. 98–101). Another consequence of these fears was the formation in 1802 of the Society for the Reformation of Vice, later derided by the Revd Sydney Smith as 'a society for suppressing the vices of persons whose income does not exceed £500 per annum'. Its middle-class promoters defined vice in terms of social indiscipline and their early activities were imbued with patriotic wartime conservatism, although they increasingly concentrated on prosecuting blasphemy and obscenity.[21]

A regard for privacy developed over the same period. From the late seventeenth century the plans for larger houses incorporated corridors, which allowed servants and others to move about buildings without intruding on the occupants of reception rooms or bedrooms (houses previously had comprised interlocking suites of rooms). The middle classes, in smaller houses, began to complain about prying servants, while aristocrats ensnared in divorce cases usually found that the most telling evidence against them came from servants. Reflecting this desire for privacy, the physical distance between people increased in the eighteenth century. Householder and visitor, master and servant, or servants together often shared one bed early in the century, but such trust was increasingly poisoned as the idea gained strength in all but the lowest classes that physical intimacy was 'uncivilized'. The pleasantness or convenience of bed-sharing was overborne by the new decorum requiring privacy and physical distance. English attitudes to kissing by men altered. Gentlemen in the late seventeenth century embraced or kissed one another freely, but by 1749 the author of *Satan's Harvest Home* identified male kissing as an example of Italian effeminacy liable to culminate in sodomy. Foreign visitors to England were increasingly warned against demonstrativeness. 'The kiss of friendship between men is strictly avoided as inclining towards the sin regarded in England as more abominable than any other,' warned a German travel book of 1819. English travellers abroad were revolted by Continental affections. 'I find it is the custom for Men to kiss each other at parting,' an Englishwoman confided to her travel journal in 1814. 'The Canaille take advantage of this and kiss each other all day which with their horrid leers . . . has a loathesome effect.' Once physical privacy had become emblematic of social progress, male kissing was so inhibited, and physical demonstrativeness so severely restricted, even within the family, that in 1879, when warm-hearted Lady Dufferin saw the German Chancellor, Bismarck, kiss his adult sons, she thought it 'a pretty and unsophisticated custom'.[22]

It was against this background that the labels of Sodom were transformed. A new and stricter code of private words, physical gestures, clothing, vocal mimicry and other rituals developed and came to characterize a new sodomite subculture. The London taverns which were the centres of male prostitution in the seventeenth century were superseded by 'molly houses', backrooms in a private house or tavern, where prostitution had a smaller role. There were perhaps twenty London molly houses in the 1720s, although over the following ninety years such places either declined in number, or became harder to identify. These molly houses were occasionally raided – for example in 1707 and 1726 – and the group arrests that ensued were novel. Hitherto prosecutions for sodomy had usually been directed at isolated individuals in specific circumstances, as when parental rights were violated, or when a man had made himself vulnerable by bad neighbourliness. Prosecutions became an international phenomenon too. The paroxysm of arrests in England in 1726 occurred just after two hundred Frenchmen were implicated in an '*école et bordel de sodomie*', the leader of which was burnt alive in May 1726, with the majority of the accused receiving sentences of between three and six months (although a bishop and other clergy involved were banished, and a painter cut his throat while awaiting trial). The example of the Paris investigations stimulated the Society for the Reformation of Manners to action in London. In the same period there was a mass persecution of Dutch sodomites (aristocrats, diplomats, physicians, lawyers, clergy and lower-class youths) of whom two hundred were executed by drowning, hanging or burning. These events fascinated western Europe: one scholar has traced over two thousand different British newspaper reports of the Dutch trials over the course of two years.

To find the causes of this outburst of morbidity and hate one has to examine the distinctive features of molly houses, and relate them to more general cultural changes.[23]

The important new factor in provoking semi-official harassment of molly houses was that their congregants revelled in feminine mimicry and in acting out (with a mixture of mockery and envy) scenes from heterosexual family life. As a police spy testified at the trial of a molly house keeper: 'Sometimes they would sit in one another's Laps, kissing in a lewd Manner and using their Hand indecently. Then they would get up, Dance and make Curtsies, and Mimick the Voices of Women . . . Then they'd hug, and play, and toy.' The mollies had their own 'dialect', to use his word: they would ape coy, flirtatious girls, crying, '*O Fie, Sir! – Pray, Sir – Dear, Sir – Lord, how can you serve me so? – I swear I'll cry out – You're a wicked Devil – and you're a bold Face – Eh! ye little dear Toad! Come, buss!*' The back room in molly houses to which men retired for sex was known as the 'chapel'; sexual acts performed there were known as 'marrying'; the first sexual conjunction between two men was known as 'a Wedding Night'. Some mollies not only assumed female nicknames, or adopted feminine language, but created pregnancy rituals, culminating in mock lying-ins where a 'pregnant' man gave birth to a doll, or some other such object, like a Cheshire cheese or a pair of bellows. In short the mollies were not only 'kissing and hugging, and making Love (as they called it)', to quote a witness of 1726 – enacting the sexual rites of husbands and wives on 'Beds in every Room in the House' – but were playing out the other domestic roles of men and women. Whether facetious or otherwise, the notion that male pairing can be cheerfully promoted as a comparable alternative to male-female domesticity has disturbed the authorities more recently than the 1720s.[24]

Some unhappily married men resorted to the molly houses. Bitter at heterosexual marriages from which they had hoped for more than their grandparents' generation but which had proved arid, they derided the institution of marriage and ridiculed their wives. It is not coincidental that in an era when, to quote Lawrence Stone, 'the institution of marriage was undergoing very severe stresses – perhaps even a major crisis – as a result of the profound changes in domestic relationships that were taking place', the dialect and acts inside the molly houses became explicitly imitative of heterosexual marriages. This in turn stimulated the raids and mass arrests because, despite the disappointed misogyny of some mollies, other husbands remained more susceptible to outrage. They saw that some couples found matrimony to be the greatest pleasure of their lives, but that for them it had proved one of the 'torments of the world', to quote Lord Chesterfield: the strains of companionate marriage resulted in 'many very uneasy' days. Such men were angry, grieving and confused – and then they heard about the mollies with their mock chapel, their parody Wedding Nights and their false pregnancies where a pair of bellows was delivered. What an opportunity for projective hatred! The ensuing raids of molly clubs and group arrests in turn stimulated the labelling process which enforced stereotypes and tried to apply absolute standards of differentiation. There were new tensions, new constraints and new risks as a result of redelineations of sexual desire.[25]

In this era of marital crisis, when some members of the nobility, gentry and bourgeoisie were struggling to assess themselves as individuals, we begin to find people who were openly unhappy with some of the social expectations of their gender – for example the first-known English transvestite. Edward Hyde, Viscount Cornbury, afterwards Earl of Clarendon, was Governor of New York and New Jersey in 1701–8, where in the words of a later moralist he 'earned a most unenviable reputation, which he appears to have fully deserved, and his character and conduct were equally abhorred in both hemispheres'. According to Glenbervie, Clarendon 'was a clever man' whose 'great insanity' was showing himself in women's clothes (see plate). When New Yorkers complained that he opened their legislative assembly dressed as a woman, he retorted, 'You are very stupid not to see the propriety of it. In this place and particularly on this occasion I represent a woman (Queen Anne) and ought in all respects to represent her as faithfully as I can.' Effeminacy and male transvestism were not clearly distinguished at this time, and there is no evidence that Clarendon was a molly. He was undeniably, though, a man who felt false when he dressed and behaved as men were expected to do (it was probably relevant to the acting-out of his fantasy that the Queen whom he imitated was his first cousin, to whom he bore some facial resemblance).[26]

The links between early English male transvestites like Clarendon and the development of effeminacy and those other special traits which became identified as signs of homoeroticism were a great deal more complex than a common basis in epicene behaviour. Nevertheless, as the eighteenth century wore on, there were increasing efforts to depict sodomites as effeminate, and general incredulity followed when this caricature was disproved. Gibbon regarded all sodomites as epicene: he wrote of 'the voluntary and effeminate deserter of his sex' whose 'unmanly lust' was an 'indelible stain of manhood'. In 1810, when thirty men were arrested in a raid, it was generally believed that 'this passion has for its object effeminate delicate beings only', and there was astonishment when this proved to be 'a mistaken notion'. Those detained included a coal merchant renowned as Kitty Cambrie, a police runner known as Miss Selina, a drummer with the soubriquet Black-Eyed Leonora, a butcher ('Pretty Harriet'), a blacksmith known as the Duchess of Devonshire, a grocer called Sweet Lips, 'an athletic bargeman' dubbed Fanny Murray, 'an Herculean coalheaver' who liked to be called Lucy Cooper and a man nicknamed Kitty Fisher, 'a deaf tyre smith: the latter of these monsters has two sons, both very handsome young men, whom he boasts are full as depraved as himself'. (These campy nicknames were partly taken out of fear of entrapment by blackmailers and policemen: the grocer called Sweet Lips would be harder to trace outside his club if casual visitors did not know his real name).[27]

Earlier it had not been thought bizarre if a libertine attested the variety of his inclinations by using both women and ingles. If one could afford it, bisexuality had been as normal as Freudians now claim it to be. But once marriage was seen not as a way of containing men's lust, but as a way of finding empathy or romance, the deliberate rejection of women of one's own class became a much more 'offensive' act. With the onset of the Romantic movement in Britain after 1770, womanhood and the prospect of enduring emotional love inside marriage were subject to increasing idealization (the reality of course was often far more dreary). But according to this outlook it seemed 'abominable' when 'men of rank, and respectable situations in life' were 'wallowing either in or on beds with wretches of the lowest description', to use Robert Holloway's description of one molly house in 1810. Although men might take mistresses from any class, it became incomprehensible that 'a man of fortune and fashion' could enjoy sex with 'grenadiers, footmen, waiters, drummers and all the Catamite brood'.[28]

With the sharpened sense of individuality, it became less respectable for a man to prove his sexual prowess without regard for the identity of the partner on whom he worked off his lust. In the early eighteenth century we find an emergent new protectiveness towards male adolescents. 'Among the chief men in some of the colleges, sodomy is very usual,' it was reported in 1715 by Sir Dudley Ryder. 'It is dangerous sending a young man who is beautiful to Oxford.' Fifteen years later, when the Warden of Wadham College, Oxford made sexual overtures to an undergraduate, parental protectivenss or awareness of male seduction had sufficiently increased for the boy's father to complain so distinctly that the Warden had to flee to France. Magistrates concurrently developed a sense that teachers who had sex with their pupils might be corrupters. When the Court heard that Charles Banner, who was indicted at the Old Bailey in 1723 'with an Intent to commit the unnatural and detestable Sin of Sodomy' with a lad aged fifteen, kept a school at Smithfield, the judge exclaimed: 'A School! Does any Body trust their children with him?' The fact that many parents in the neighbourhood did trust Banner in this way helped facilitate his acquittal. Until the late eighteenth century parents were content for boys in boarding schools to sleep two in a bed, and it was only around the time of the French and Napoleonic Wars that voices were raised against the practice. 'What nasty indecent tricks do they not also learn from each other, when a number of them pig together in the same bed-chamber, not to speak of the vices which render the body weak?' Mary Wollstonecraft exclaimed in 1792; and General Sir Eyre Coote was ruined when his sado-masochistic romps with pupils at Christ's Hospital School were publicized in 1815 (see plate). There was also a growing inhibition among men about their early fun with other schoolboys. 'I have been thinking of the great hold I have given you over me', said the eighteenth-century politician William Windham miserably, 'by telling you that my school name was "Tricks and Fancies".'[29]

A liking for male sodomy was not pursued to the exclusion of other pleasures. Married men constituted about one-third of those arrested in Paris for soliciting other men during the eighteenth century. In the same period Londoners who enjoyed sex with other men were often husbands and fathers: of eleven male defendants on charges of sodomy or attempted sodomy whose cases are reported in *Select Trials at the Old Bailey* (1742), at least six had married. A description of London sodomites sixty years later concedes the same point: 'many of these wretches are married; and frequently, when they come together, make their wives, who they call *Tommies*, topics of ridicule.' Nevertheless it was crucial to the process of stereotying that occurred during the eighteenth century that the existence of bisexuality was denied, and that the myth of polarized desires was created. 'My ignorance is great on such subjects,' wrote the sister of a married man suspected of affairs with men in 1817, 'but I believed always that the one was incompatible with the other.' This belief would have been difficult to sustain in the earlier period when sodomy was seen as a practice of the sexually exuberant and bore few if any other connotations: but by the early nineteenth century the false labels were fastened.[30]

For many people sodomy was not what one's friends and neighbours did, still less what one did oneself. It was what outsiders did, or it was a foreign habit, or an evil committed by people one never met. It was an imported vice: sodomites and foreigners were equally suitable as objects for people to project their bad feelings and hostility onto. 'Let not England forget her precedence of teaching nations how to live,' Milton adjured in the seventeenth century, and within decades there was a strong tradition that English morals were sterner than those of foreigners, particularly the French and Italians. Dryden, in the 1680s, wrote of 'a damned love-trick new brought over from France'. Daniel Defoe, in *The True Born Englishman* (1701), wrote that

> Lust chose the torrid zone of Italy,
> Where blood ferments in rapes and sodomy.

Churchill, in 1746, attributed the source of 'sins of the blackest character, sins worse than all her plagues' to 'the soft luxurious East, where man, his soul degraded', was no better than a 'beast'.[31]

Yet despite the sharper definitions that developed, it is wrong to assume that men were labelled as sodomites exclusively on the basis that they performed sexual acts with other men: lots of men engaged in such activities without being identified in this way. The crucial mediation was their social behaviour and sexual role.

What men did with their partners' bodies, or had done to their own, was decisive. W. H. Auden once classified three types of homosexual act, each of which he considered to be a symbolic rite: he suggested that the relationship between two men is best comprehended in terms of the symbolic role which each expects the other to play. Some men prefer oral sex as a way of playing out the fantasy of Son and/or Mother; others practise anal sex and play at Wife and/or Husband or Mother and/or Father; while the third category 'daydream of an Innocent Eden where children play "Doctor"' and engage in quasi-fraternal acts like mutual masturbation or intercrural sex (slicklegging), which Auden dubbed 'Plain-Sewing' and 'Princeton First-Year'.[32]

Auden's symbolic rites – the questions of whether a man penetrated or was penetrated, or avoided penetration of any sort – have been crucial to the processes of labelling. Comradely acts in Auden's last category – of randy or lonely men rubbing their bodies together, or handling one another's penises – seem to have upset few people through the centuries, to have been exempt from labelling and, in England, to have avoided effective legal sanctions until the 1890s. Other rites have always evoked more complex responses. In many cultures adult men, so long as they were the active partners in sodomy, were not stigmatized for enjoying sex with other men or assumed to be sexually indifferent to women – but men who were passive sodomites were traduced unless they were youths or transvestites. Ancient Greece provides an example of this. By contrast in Renaissance Venice anal penetration was the object of severe legal intervention, but because masturbation was so common among sexually active youths, mutual masturbation among men was thought natural enough to be largely disregarded. In turn the eighteenth-century English were preoccupied with sexual passivity. Pornographic pictures, such as those by Rowlandson, often showed the woman as naked or almost naked, but the man as clothed, with his breeches open or down. This was not because of coyness about depicting an erect penis, but reflected the identification of males as sexually dominant beings who need not undress when they used women as passive objects to assuage their appetite. These assumptions about passivity had important implications for anal intercourse between men: the act of sodomy was a rite which replayed those pertaining to husband and wife, or father and mother. It confronted and mocked the roles taken in heterosexual partnerships, and when this was coupled with more visible effeminacy, or new sensitivities about the institution of marriage, profound adjustments of attitudes ensued.[33]

The trials of men indicted with sodomy or attempted sodomy recounted in *Select Trials at the Old Bailey* (1742) provide some guide to the preferred acts of the period, with the proviso that all defendants were anxious to prove that there had not been emission during anal intercourse because they were more likely to be treated leniently. Fellatio is not described in any instance; of the cases where the charge is not malicious, and the sexual act is identifiable, two involved mutual masturbation; two others were of slicklegging; and one was of anal intercourse. Anal penetration is difficult unless one of the men carries a lubricant; and this requires a premeditation and perhaps an affluence which did not characterize most of the defendants. Typically, in 1721, a prosecution witness testified that George Duffus 'forcibly entered my Body about an Inch, as near as I can guess; but in struggling, I threw him off once more, before he had made an Emission, and having thus forced him to withdraw, he emitted in his own Hand, and clapping it on the Tail of my Shirt, said, *Now you have it!*' Paris police archives in the same decade show that men importuning one another either specified active sodomy, or sodomy which was active or passive without preference. Mutual masturbation by men did not raise problems, but the shame of passivity, derived from notions of male and female roles, meant that it was harder to accept being sodomized than to be the active partner.[34]

Oral acts were seen as wanton. In a period when circumcision was rare, except as the result of venereal infection, the smell from accumulated bodily secretions, fecal and urinary traces, perspiration, bacteria, dust and dirt under the foreskin restricted forms of sexual gratification. Perfumes, lotions, unguents and scented aphrodisiacs were used in late seventeenth-century England by the rich, among whom oral-genital contact may have been more attractive; but the urban and rural poor never used body cosmetics and seldom even soap and water. Fellatio or cunnilingus was doubtless enhanced for some people by such odours, but for many others they were objectionable. The bidet, which was known in Britain by 1752, was unpopular more from moral than hygienic considerations, thereby confirming that oral sex was generally considered debased.[35]

The portrait of a man who had engaged in oral sex, as illustrated in Sir Alexander Morison's *Physiognomy of Mental Diseases*, a medical textbook published in 1843 which tried to identify the different categories of mental illness by picturing the faces of typical patients. The caption to this picture read: 'Portrait of J. T. D. aged 40 . . . he was a day labourer, he had been insane four years before his death, and was so much addicted to this unnatural vice that it was necessary to seclude him from other patients, whom he continually annoyed: on one occasion the mouth of an idiot boy was the recipient: he died a few months ago of phthisis pulmonalis'.

Another illustration from Sir Alexander Morison's treatise on *The Physiognomy of Mental Diseases* shows a painter aged 36 with tertiary syphilis. Morison's caption stands as a case-history of general paralysis of insanity:

'This portrait exhibits a man of considerable eminence as an artist, in the last stages of a general paralysis, five weeks before his death. He is in a state of complete dementia, has scarcely any ideas, and remembers nothing – repeats a few words with little connection, such as "I am a Prince of the Ionian Islands, – I was a beautiful artist".

'He cannot walk without assistance, and it is necessary to secure his hands to prevent him tearing his clothes – His urine flows involuntarily, still his appetite continues good. His disorder existed thirteen months from its commencement to its termination in death, which was preceded by extensive gangrene of those parts of his body subjected to pressure.

'He is represented with the leather sleeves made use of in the Hanwell Asylum'.

John Marten was not only the first to publish in English a description of prophylactic sheathes in 1704, but gave the earliest account of all-male fellatio. His tone reveals the strength of taboos against oral sex. If buggery was 'an abominable, beastly, sodomit-ical and shameful Action' which was 'too commonly practised in this dissolute Age', still worse, so Marten explained, was 'a Man's putting his erected *Penis*, into another Person's (Man or Woman's) Mouth, using Friction between the Lips; a way so very Beastly and so much to be abhorred, as to cause at the mentioning, or but thinking of it, the utmost detestation and loathing'. He had treated 'a Man so infected' who admitted 'that the Person from whom he got it (being a Man) had . . . several Pocky Ulcerations in his Mouth; but in such a woeful pickle was this Patient of mine, and indeed (as I told him) very deservedly, that I never in my Life before, saw one . . . worse.' Marten's curiosity outstripped his disapproval, and 'being desirous to know the cause of this abominable Encounter (having never known, tho' before had heard, that such beastly Abominations were practised)' he asked 'if twas any Pleasure to him, and how he disposed of his *Semen*? he told me twas great Pleasure, and that he ejected it into the Person's Mouth he had to do with, who both willingly received it, and assisted, as he said, in this foul Act, by sucking his *Penis*. O monstrous! thought I, that Men, otherwise sensible Men, should so vilely debase themselves, and become so degenerate; should provoke God so highly, contemn the Laws of Man so openly, wrong their own Bodies so fearfully; and which is worse (without sincere Repentance) ruin their own Souls eternally.' A century later the repulsion excited by fellatio was equally strong. Fellatio performed by men was judged to be a revolting and extreme act: in the patient (see illustration on page 80) described in Sir Alexander Morison's *Physiognomy of Mental Disease* (1843), it was judged a symptom of insanity.[36]

The small forensic sample from the Old Bailey trials suggests that it was possible in the early eighteenth century to proposition another man for mutual masturbation or slicklegging without worrying oneself too much about anything other than the im-mediate personal involvement and physical consequences. As has often been remarked in the case of twentieth-century sailors or soldiers or labourers who have denied being homosexuals while persistently having sex with other men whom they call 'queers', it was possible for an eighteenth-century Londoner to avoid thinking of his homoerotic experiences as special or nameable if emotional intimacy was limited and certain sexual acts excluded as extremist. Distinctions between sexual acts were vital and at the heart of the labelling process which created the London subculture.

Of course male susceptibility to the male sex was not the exclusive prerogative of libertines, nor was its expression always sexual, or permanently sexual. The experience of three eighteenth-century politicians – Lord George Germain, John Wilkes and George Selwyn – demonstrates how sexual passion for one's own sex seldom debarred desire for the opposite sex, and that affections flourished without culminating in sodomy.

One prominent man who met violent abuse as a sodomite was Lord George Germain (1716–85), son of the first and father of the last Dukes of Dorset. Germain was susceptible to young men, and reached the rank of commander-in-chief before being dismissed from the Army in 1759 for disobeying an order from Prince Ferdinand at the Battle of Minden. Attacked as 'Coward and Catamite' and as a 'Minden buggering hero', he suffered disgrace and ostracism before becoming an ill-fated Secretary of State for America (1775–82) during the War of Independence. When 'the pederastical American Secretary' was raised to the peerage as Viscount Sackville in 1782, there was a storm of protest: according to the 5th Duke of Leeds, who became Foreign Secretary in the following year, Germain was 'stamped by an indelible brand', while Lord Abingdon called him 'the greatest criminal his country had ever known' with whom 'every soldier as a man in honour is forbid to associate'. This hostility is not simply explicable as a result of the controversy over his strategy at Minden or because he was the politician responsible when the American rebels forced Lord Cornwallis' forces to capitulate at Yorktown: his 'homosexual reputation', declares his biographer, 'was his Achilles heel'. His most celebrated youth was Benjamin Thompson (1753–1814), the American inventor who was afterwards knighted by King George III and created Count von Rumford by Charles Theodore, the Elector of Bavaria. Thompson married a rich older woman when aged nineteen, but three years later was sent with despatches to Germain, whose favourite he remained for about five years. 'When he was first introduced to

Lord George, he was ... a very pretty boy and master of a hundred skills,' wrote their contemporary Lord Glenbervie, who described Thompson 'going about with Lady George and her daughters to balls as a sort of humble dependent and dancing with the young ladies when they could get no other partner'. For several years Thompson was 'the favourite, at once, of the father, mother and daughters, and the ill-fame of the father then, and the conduct of the daughters since, have served to keep the scandal alive' (see plate). Just as Castlehaven outraged his peers by trying to alienate his ancestral wealth to the descendants of his lover, so the 'extremely incautious' way in which Sackville patronized an ill-connected young man outside his family provoked the indignation of his class: the future Marquess Wellesley derided 'Sir *Sodom* Thompson, Lord Sackville's *under* Secretary'.[37]

A different example is provided by the radical MP John Wilkes (1727–97): as one male admirer said of him when young, his 'pleasure was made up of twenty different ingredients', including other men. The details of one such relationship survive. At the age of about twenty, when studying at Leiden, he met Andrew Baxter and his permanent companion, called Hay, in an inn. Baxter had a wife and children living in Scotland, but was settled at Utrecht, where he dabbled in philosophy and acted as private tutor to youths such as Sir Thomas Stapleton and Lord Blantyre ('free from all manner of vice, and has the sweetest disposition in the world', according to a description of 1747). Baxter conceived 'a passionate love' for Wilkes, whom he called 'my Dear' and who reciprocated his affection. 'Never man was thought so much upon by another, I dare say: tho' a woman perhaps may,' wrote Baxter in his earliest surviving letter to Wilkes of 1745. 'This is all a Riddle ... Let us keep our secret until it betrays itself.' Baxter used Wilkes to send loving intimacies from himself and Hay to other youths who, like Wilkes, had returned to England: 'pray be so good as to present both our services to Mr Dick ... a pleasant merry young fellow,' Baxter enjoined Wilkes from Utrecht, adding to an obscure message: 'Ye will not understand this language: but he'll know very well what it means.' Baxter always recognized that Wilkes desired women as well as loving his own sex, and after the latter had sent forewarning of his marriage, replied with generous congratulations, in a discreet but touching letter intended to be seen by the bride. Baxter was an affectionate, generous, sententious man, who showed serenity and courage in his letters to Wilkes during the agony of his last illness in 1750. He had been struggling to write a critique of Newtonian theory which he could dedicate to Wilkes, and almost with his last breath sent a letter appointing his protégé literary executor. Baxter died with his family, but was mourned by Blantyre and others, and seems to have been a man of great sweetness.[38]

Apart from men like Germain and Wilkes who acted on their sexual desires, there were others who, even if not homoerotic in practice, were devoted to other men in a way which Glenbervie in 1793 called 'sentimental sodomy', and which in the twentieth century is sometimes called homosocial behaviour by its aficionados. George Selwyn (1719–91), a political gossip whose sexual desires tended towards necrophilia also 'had a fondness for the Duke of Queensberry . . . and Lord Carlisle, which had all the extravagance and blindness of passion', wrote Glenbervie. 'His attachment to them has been called a sort of sentimental sodomy.'[39]

Both Germain and Wilkes were in privileged positions, and it remains to look more closely at the fate of other men as social labelling became more adhesive during the course of the century. The choice for men who had sexual relations with other men was increasingly either to hide in an anonymous world of casual pick-ups and quick fumbles while retaining a masculine social manner, or to practise certain acts while furiously denying their social or emotional implications, or to succumb to the pressures of labelling by joining the molly subculture. The latter's effeminate argot and self-parodying rituals at least gave adherents a facile but pleasant sense of belonging which mitigated their sense of being hate objects and their own self-hatred. The alternatives, then, were to be so discreet as to be invisible, or to practise self-deception in a way that sometimes could only by maintained by acts of violence against one's sexual partners, or to conform to a stereotype (quaintly dressed, physically weak, giggly) that satisfied outsiders that one was powerless. The visibility of the subculture, the arbitrariness and inaccuracies which surrounded the way it was defined, its consequent meaninglessness and irrelevance – these were all reasons why sodomites made such wonderful objects to hate.

Molly houses were not owned or managed by sodomites, but by

heterosexual entrepreneurs, if two of the most famous prosecutions (Margaret Clap in 1726; James Cook in 1810) are representative. 'I participated in all the guilt except the final completion of it, which is abhorrent to my nature,' Cook (who bought his premises for £150) insisted after his trial, 'I had no unnatural inclinations to gratify – I was prompt[ed] by *Avarice* only, and not by the indulgence of vicious propensities.'[40] Although contemporary accounts emphasized debauchery, molly houses were above all places of refuge, often clandestine, sometimes inward-looking and claustrophobic, at other times comforting, in which congregants could forget the perplexities, hazards or isolation of their lives or the embattled loneliness of their marriages. The sexual desires of habitués were as much expressed in drinking, flirting, gossiping and discarding inhibitions as in copulation itself.

Molly effeminacy increased the isolation of the inhabitants of the subculture. Many men who felt sexual desire for other men shied away from molly clubs, rejected effeminacy, disliked camp mannerisms and were bored by men assuming female soubriquets. They felt no need for a female role, and found no comfort in assuming one. The consequence of social labelling was to drive such men into positions of greater isolation, where they sought secretive relationships, or anonymous sex with men who sold themselves in parks, alleys and under arches. Rochester had in the 1680s described the bushes of St James's Park, where

> nightly now beneath their shade
> Are buggeries, rapes and incest made.

These pick-up spots became more sharply identified with the passage of time. Lord Hawkesbury the Home Secretary recorded in 1808 that 'many persons' had 'been found lately, loitering about St James's [and Hyde] Park[s] every evening after Dark who are known to have unnatural propensities; and to meet there for the purpose of making assignations with each other.' Parisian police archives between 1700 and 1750 show how methods of pick-up varied according to place, time, and other conditions. During the day, in such parks as the Tuileries or the Luxembourg, men approached one another on the pretext of asking the time or for a pinch of tobacco, and prefaced their sexual propositions with smalltalk. On river embankments, in *pissoirs* or on the streets at dusk the approach was more direct, with little speech: repeated *public urination and ostentatious display of the genitals and buttocks were common. The evidence is less clear for London, but the author of Hell upon earth: or the town in an uproar* (1729) described 'nocturnal Assemblies of great Numbers of the like vile persons, what they call the *Markets*, which are the *Royal Exchange, Lincolns-Inn Bog-Houses*, the South-side of *St James's Park*, the Piazzas of *Covent Garden, St Clement's Church-Yard*, &c'. The word 'markets' was argot equivalent to the twentieth-century phrase 'meat-racks' where men, especially the young or poor, paraded themselves to be carried off for sex. The lavatories at Lincoln's Inn were what is now known as a 'cottage', where men loitered or exhibited themselves in the hope of getting sexual favours.[41]

The early seventeenth-century social grouping of sodomites had been inchoate and unobtrusive: even more than prostitution or lewd conduct, homoerotic acts were only prosecuted if their context outraged local community feeling. Yet this was changed by the raids of the early eighteenth century. Although the suppression of molly houses was spasmodic, and most of their habitués escaped arrest, mollies could not avoid realizing that they too might be arrested, abused, pilloried or hanged in the aftermath of a raid. Defendants on charges of sodomy ceased to be the solitary and astonished men found in earlier legal records. With the onset of random persecution superseding the specific prosecution of provocative neighbours, a sodomite was forced to acknowledge his affinities with men whom others wished to exterminate. As a result a sodomite faced a profound decision regarding his identity. If he made sexual contacts with other men, this choice was surrounded by anxiety, and affected non-sexual aspects of his life; the choice might prove to be one of life or death, and was recognized as such. 'We must risk our necks,' wrote a young sodomite in 1811, at a time of mass arrests, 'and are content to risk them.' Despite these occasional outbursts of hostility against molly houses, the authorities made no effort at their absolute suppression precisely because they seemed to stop sexual infiltrators. To don the identity of a molly or sodomite, to join and conform to the rules of a subculture, was a formidable decision. The homosexual experiences of Lord Byron in the early nineteenth century 'left him frightened, excited, perplexed and, on occasion, exalted', his biographer judges; but they also forced him into exile in 1816, and left him prey to 'hidden desires, alienation, paranoia, and a sense of solidarity with others with similar natures'. For many men this demanded too much. The reasons which drove some men to seek emotional surcease and safety in molly houses were exactly the reasons which stopped other men from going that far. Ultimately molly houses were an expedient which, by over- simplifying choices, levelling experience and restricting the diversity of human needs, satisfied persecutor and persecuted alike.[42]

The simplest explanation of molly effeminacy – that some men enjoyed it – should not be forgotten. For younger men, the tattling and wriggling of mollies became the more obvious role model available: effeminacy became the first stage in signifying their sexuality, and sometimes, as they grew more experienced, they found other roles or mannerisms better suited to their sense of themselves. At another level molly effeminacy gave cohesion to the subculture and seemed like the semblance of defiance. Yet mollies were colluding with their persecutors by offering a more distinctive and distinguishable minority than had previously existed. The new belief in a distinctly demarcated group, which was visible and pleased with itself, was conveyed by Charles Churchill in 1746:

> So public in their crimes, so daring grown,
> They almost take a pride to have them known,
> And each unnatural villain scarce endures
> To make a secret of his vile amours.
> Go where we will at every time and place,
> Sodom confronts, and stares us in the face;
> They ply in public at our very doors,
> And take the bread from much more honest whores.[43]

Specialized dress was one feature of this *demi-monde*. Bisexual Restoration rakes had been foppish, but three generations later a certain type of man was thought recognizable by the length of his hair, the brightness of his clothes, the precision of their cut and the details of his personal jewellery. Tobias Smollett in his autobiographical novel *Roderick Random* (1748) depicted a stylized sodomite called Whiffle. He was 'a tall, thin young man' (a captain in the Royal Navy) with hair flowing to his shoulders 'in ringlets, tied behind with a ribbon', and wore 'a white hat, garnished with a red feather' and a pink silk coat, which 'by the elegance of the cut retired backward, as it were to discover a white satin waistcoat embroidered with gold, unbuttoned at the upper part to display a brooch set with garnets, that glittered in the breast of his shirt, which was of the finest cambric'. The backward cut of the coat seems to have held some sexual nuance. Whiffle's 'crimson velvet breeches scarcely descended so low as to meet his silk stockings, which rose without spot or wrinkle on his meagre legs, from shoes of blue Meroquin, studded with diamond buckles, that flamed forth rivals to the sun! A steel-hilted sword, inlaid with gold, and decked with a knot of ribbon which fell down in a rich tassel, equipped his side; and an amber-headed cane hang dangling from his wrist. But the most remarkable parts of his furniture were, a mask on his face, and white gloves on his hands, which did not seem to be put on with an intention to be pulled off occasionally, but were fixed with a curious ring on the little finger of each hand.' Whiffle was attended by a valet called Vergette (whose surname was a pun on a French word meaning tiny penis), and a surgeon named Simper, 'a young man gaily dressed, of a very delicate complexion, with a kind of languid smile on his face, which seemed to have been rendered habitual by a long course of affectation'. The captain was suspected 'of maintaining a correspondence with the surgeon not fit to be named'.[44]

In addition to foppery, there were other dress-codes. Some youths signalled their sexual availability to other men, or tried to increase their attraction, by wearing artfully torn trousers: 'one of the lowest attendants' at one raided tavern was a youth 'whose breeches, from the superfluous apertures, gave manifestation of rapturous attacks upon his virtue'.[45]

Another episode in *Roderick Random* depicts a middle-aged earl called Strutwell exploring the sexual availability of the young narrator. Strutwell talks at such length about the toleration of sexual relations between men that exists abroad that Random wonders if the earl, 'finding I had travelled, was afraid I might have been infected with this spurious and sordid desire abroad, and took this method of sounding my sentiments'. Provoked by this suspicion, Random argued against sodomy 'with great warmth, as an appetite unnatural, absurd and of pernicious consequence; and declared my utter detestation and abhorrence of it' by quoting some verses:

Eternal infamy the wretch confound
Who first planted that vice on English ground.
A vice that 'spite of sense and nature reigns
And poisons genial love, and manhood stains.

Strutwell smiled at this indignation, 'told me he was glad to find my opinion in the matter so conformable to his own, and that what he had advanced was only to provoke me to an answer'. This scene resembles others re-enacted many thousands of times a year more than two centuries later and shows the ways in which sodomites fell into disavowing their own desires, and, by coming to believe in their own denunciations, slid imperceptibly into self-hatred. With the need for sexual overtures to be cautious, or for flirtation to be surreptitious or ambiguous, men had to be quick and ready in their denials of what they wanted most. It is not surprising that their behaviour became confused, or that they covered themselves by acting in complicity with their oppressors. Such processes account for the behaviour of a man like the Duke of Cumberland ('a mixture of narrow-mindedness, selfishness, truckling, blustering and duplicity, with no object but self, his own ease and the satisfaction of his own fancies') who was investigated in 1810 on suspicion of having slit the throat of one of his valets to prevent him disclosing the duke's 'improper and unnatural' relations with another servant, but who nevertheless attended the public execution in 1811 of a young army ensign and his sixteen-year-old drummer-boy lover.[46]

The shame, self-hatred or fear which accompanied stricter social labelling meant that sodomy increasingly became the cause of malicious charges or blackmail attempts. In 1722 Henry Clayton, 'a scandalous Villain', after quarrelling with his landlady over his debts to her for gin, accused her of being 'a bawd' and another tenant ('a poor, honest, ignorant Man') of being 'a Pickpocket and Sodomite Dog'. Ned Courtney, a spiteful and unstable young sodomite who described himself as 'saucy', was also prone to making mischievous allegations against men with whom he wanted to get even. As early as 1728 men were said to solicit in London streets solely with the intention of blackmailing those men who responded to their overtures.[47]

There were more sophisticated forms of extortion. One source for this chapter is a book entitled *Phoenix of Sodom, or the Vere*

Street coterie (1813), produced in collaboration by James Cook, the illiterate landlord of the White Swan in Vere Street which was raided in 1810, and Robert Holloway, who loaned him money while he was in Newgate prison. Decades previously Holloway had published a polemic accusing the London magistrate who had convicted him of obtaining candlesticks by false pretences of having started life as a pimp, and his new literary effort was no less scurrilous. Holloway conceived a plan to recover the money which he had advanced Cook by letting it be known that they were collaborating on a book, and then extorting those who feared being named. 'Peers, Footmen and Foot-soldiers will be held up to the indignation of mankind,' they threatened. 'That the reader may form some idea of the uncontrollable rage of this dreadful passion Cook states that a person in a respectable [business] house in the City, frequently came to his sink of filth and iniquity, and stayed several days and nights together; during which time he generally amused himself with eight, ten and sometimes a dozen different boys and men!' recorded Holloway. Cook visited the man's office demanding money which had previously been refused, and ruined his reputation by describing the circumstances 'before some of the parties connected with him in business'. Less sturdy victims paid the rascals in order to ensure suppression of their names.[48]

The early eighteenth century saw the first use in England by the authorities of *agents provocateurs* or police spies to trap men. In general there was more recourse to the 'thief-taker', freelances who pursued criminals in the hope of reward, whose practice was to lure offenders into committing a crime for which they could be arrested; but there was only one sort of sexual offence in which the police trap was used. Previously the authorities had acted against sodomites who caused outrage without taking the tactics of active intervention, presumably because transgressors were seldom sufficiently distinguishable. But the emotional ambushes and revenges of the companionate marriage, the hostility that could be focused on the distinctive molly culture, the fact that what we hate most is in ourselves – these all stimulated a new vindictiveness and aggression against men who exemplified the disintegration of the family. In one of the earliest examples, Thomas Newton, a visitor to Mother Clap's house who stood bail for her after her arrest in 1726, was forced into the thrall of the police as an informer and *agent provocateur.* When he went to offer bail for Mother Clap, as he testified, two constables called Willis and Williams, connected with the Society for the Reformation of Manners, 'told me they believed I could give Information which I promised to do'; but he avoided doing so for several weeks, until he was himself arrested. There then followed some bargaining in which Newton was promised his freedom in return for co-operating with the authorities: as Willis testified, 'in March, Newton was set at Liberty, but he came the next Day, and made a voluntary information . . . against several of the Sodomites', at least one of whom was later executed.[49]

Newton continued to be used by the police. In July 1726 he testified at the Old Bailey: 'Willis and Stevenson the Constables, having a Warrant to apprehend Sodomites, I went with them to an Alehouse in Moorfields, where we agreed that I should go and pick up one, and that they should wait at a convenient Distance.' He knew a path which 'was frequented by Sodomites, and was no Stranger to the Methods they used in picking one another up'. He loitered in the area: 'In a little Time the Prisoner passes by, and looks hard at me, and at a small Distance from me, stands up against the Wall, as if he was going to make Water. Then by Degrees he sidles nearer and nearer to where I stood, 'till at last he comes close to me. *'Tis a very fine Night,* says he; *Aye* says I, *and so it is.* Then he takes me by the Hand, and after squeezing and playing with it a little (to which I showed no dislike) he conveys it to his Breeches, and puts — into it. I took fast hold, and called out to Willis and Stephenson, who coming up to my Assistance, we carried him to the Watch-house. I had seen the Prisoner before, at the House of Thomas Wright, who was hanged for Sodomy.' Moorfields remained a cruising area to which the police sent *agents provocateurs.* Eighty-four years after Newton's lethal visit, two men were charged 'with the intent to commit an abominable crime'. The prosecution described how 'a *posse* of Officers' had gone to Moorfields one night 'for the purpose of apprehending wretches of so debased a cast'. Both defendants 'set up a plea of drunkenness, but it was overruled'.[50]

Statistics on prosecutions for sodomy are imperfect. Between 1760 and 1772 there are only two known trials in which a sodomist was sentenced to death, and on both occasions King George III pardoned the men. Conviction rates fell after a legal decision of 1781 that both penetration and emission of semen had to be proved (Castlehaven in 1631 had been convicted on proof of emission, not penetration). As in many other areas, the severity of the letter of the criminal law was often mitigated by the mildness of its application by judge or jury. The figures for London and Middlesex, which exist from 1749, suggest that although there was less than one execution on average every decade from 1750, after 1804 executions for sodomy in Middlesex averaged one annually. Prosecutions for 'assault with intent to commit sodomy, and other unnatural misdemeanours' also increased, with a peak of 29 convictions for England and Wales in 1810 and 22 in 1813. Once a conviction had been secured, punishment was severe, with 80 per cent of those convicted being hanged in 1810, a much higher level of deaths than for most capital offences; 28 out of a total of 42 convicted sodomites were hanged in 1805–15. Excluding 1818–19, for which figures are unobtainable, there were 1,920 executions in total between 1805 and 1835, of which 53 were for sodomy and 400 for murder. The evidence therefore suggests not a sustained campaign against sodomites, but the existence of sharper awareness and more focused hostility as the result of social labelling.[51]

Neighbourhood was important; with few exceptions, the different districts in cities like London, Paris or the Hague were like contiguous villages, in which everyone knew their neighbours, and where the neighbourhood regulated the behaviour of individuals. Early in the century sexual deviants were subject to the informal sanction of their neighbours, but remained in neighbourly contact: sodomites did not incur general hostility, but rather discreet reproach, because they were not seen as slavish in their passions or markedly distinguishable. The exceptions proved the rule. John Dicks in London in 1722 outraged feelings by plying the boy whom he had picked up with alcohol until he was too fuddled to realize what was happening, and irritated people by calling the boy 'his Dear, and his Jewel, and his precious little Rogue'. A mason who, in 1723, was denounced to the Paris police had a 'bad reputation, having always in his company young men of the neighbourhood whom he would lure to his home'. If he had respected his neighbours and enticed the sons of people from a different district he might have been safe. The formation of a milieu reserved exclusively for mollies altered the boundaries between sodomites and neighbourly jurisdiction as the century progressed: once homoerotic men were consigned to subcultural isolation, they ceased to be part of other communities which might protect them or keep their chastisement out of the hands of law officers.[52]

Eighteenth-century England was localized in its organization. Power and loyalties were fragmented; reliance on prudential morality was normative. But by the early nineteenth century, when the nation was undergoing the social and demographic changes associated with industrialization, there was a move towards administrative centralization and procedural codification, and a new attitude to the role of law prevailed. 'He would fain make the penal laws of his country the representative of the public conscience, and would array it with the awful authority to be derived from such a consideration,' it was recorded of a speech of one MP in 1823. 'He would fain make it the fruit of moral sentiment, in order to render it the school of public discipline.' Morality enforced by parliamentary acts was partially to replace morality enforced by community pressure: civilization was to be bolstered by fines and punishments. 'The office of the nation is by stern and righteous punishment to restrain man's self-will when it breaks out into acts,' the Christian social reformer F. D. Maurice believed. 'The duty of a legislature is to make vice criminal,' wrote the head of the Criminal Investigation Department at Scotland Yard in 1891: 'a man's acts are governed, and his character is moulded, by incentives to virtue, and the checks which hold him back from vice.' This change of outlook led to increased prosecution of sodomites by the 1840s, and to a more vengeful policy of ostracism. 'The wretch, who stood in little fear of imprisonment, pillory or death, might perhaps be affected by the terror of perpetual disgrace and scorn,' as one MP told Parliament in 1816 in the aftermath of Sir Eyre Coote's scandal.[53]

In 1828 the need to prove penetration or emission was removed under new legislation, which kept buggery as a capital offence, although both legislators and the judiciary used the term to indicate any form of non-procreative sex, including oral sex or heterosexual coitus using contraception. During 1842–9 only murder exceeded sodomy as a cause of capital convictions in Britain: indeed in 1846 more death sentences were pronounced for sodomy than for murder, but it seems that after 1836 all capital sentences for sodomy were commuted. This increase in capital

THE TRIAL AND

EXECUTION

OF

CAPT. HENRY NICHOLS,

Who Suffered this Morning,

AT

My thoughts on awful subjects roll,
Damnation and the dead ;
What horrors seize the guilty soul
Upon a dying bed !
Lingering about these mortal shores,
She makes a long delay,
Till, like a flood, with rapid force
Death sweeps the wretch away

This suit and steahan he descends
Down to the fiery coast,
Amongst abominable fiends,
Himself a frightful ghost.
There endless crowds of sinners lie,
And darkness makes their chains ;
Tortur'd with keen despair they cry,
Yet wait for fiercer pains.

HORSEMONGER LANE GOAL, SOUTHWARK.

HEINOUS, horribly frightful, and disgusting was the crime for which the above poor Wretched Culprit suffered the severe penalty of the law this morning, Monday, August 12, 1833, at the top of Horsemonger Lane Goal. His name became known to the public during the investigation relative to the death of the unfortunate boy Paviour, who was lately, it is suspected, so inhumanely murdered by a Gang of Miscreants. He was also spoken of, as being concerned with a Captain Beauclerk, who destroyed himself while in Horsemonger Lane Goal, some months ago.

Thank Heavens, the public Gallows of Justice in England is very rarely disgraced by the Execution of such Wretches ; but, every person must have observed, with dismay, how greatly the number of diabolical assaults of a similar nature, have lately multiplied in this country.

His TRIAL took place at Croydon, on Friday, August 2, before the Honourable Sir James Parke, when the Jury returned a Verdict of GUILTY, on the clearest possible evidence : the statement of the boy Lawrence, with whom the offence was committed, was very clear. It was confirmed by the testimony of a person connected with Capt. Beauclerk.

The Judge immediately pronounced the dreadful sentence of the Law, advising him to make all the atonement in his power to an offended GOD, the few days he had to live ; for, he might rest assured, the sentence would not be mitigated.

Captain Nichols displayed the greatest calmness, and was unmoved throughout the Trial, and even when the dreadful sentence was passed, he remained perfectly collected.

At nine o'clock this morning the full penalty of the law was carried into effect upon the above individual. Upon being brought back from Croydon to Horsemonger-lane he devoted nearly the whole of the time left him in making his peace with his Creator. On the sheriff going to demand his body he was in the chapel with the Rev. Mr. Mann, the chaplain of the goal, and in a firm voice he informed that gentleman that he was satisfied with his sentence, and was fully prepared to die. He trusted that he had found mercy in his God, and that his crime would be forgiven. So firm was his faith, that he did wish to live another hour. In the course of these observations, the rev. gentleman happened to sigh, on which the culprit said, " Do not sigh." Upon seeing Mr. Walters, the governor, he took that gentleman by the hand, and said, " Although an unfavourable impression existed against him in the prison, he had to thank him and the goalers for their tenderness and humanity towards him." He then turned round, and said, " I am ready." On walking along, the bell was being tolled, when he begged that it might be stopped. He then walked with a remarkably firm step to the drop, and in a few minutes he ceased to exist. He apparently died instantaneously. The culprit, who is fifty years of age, was a remarkably fine looking man, and we understand had served in the Peninsular war, and was of a very respectable family. Since his apprehension not a single member of his family ever visited him, and we understand that it is not their intention to demand the corpse. Under these circumstances the body will be sent to one of the hospitals.

Emerson Printer, Tooley Street.

Broadsheet celebrating an execution for sodomy in the 1830s

sentencing partly reflected the new attitude to parliamentary laws as schools of moral sentiment and public discipline. Possibly also it was the result of long-term peer pressure among lawyers. Back in 1810, for example, two men appeared before Sir John Eames at London Sessions after being arrested by policemen posing as pick-ups. 'The evidence adduced against these prisoners was of so black a hue, of so abominable a nature, that we cannot pretend to give any report of it; but much credit is due to those who presided, for listening so patiently as they did to such disgusting details,' a journalist wrote. 'So anxious was the Court to do justice, that they were occupied by the above trials till a very late hour.' Sir John Eames was fascinated, and perhaps resembled the judge whom Jeremy Bentham saw moments after 'consigning two wretches to the gallows' for sodomy. 'Delight and exultation glistened in his countenance; his looks called for applause and congratulations at the hands of the surrounding audience.'[54] Magistrates and judges acquired the habit of seeking admiration in this way. An attempt in 1841 to abolish the death penalty for sodomy failed, and it was not until 1861 that it was replaced in England and Wales by penal servitude of between ten years and life (Scotland followed suit in 1889). In other European countries, such as Austria, Prussia, Russia and Tuscany, equivalent laws were relaxed in the eighteenth century, and in 1791 a new legal code in revolutionary France decriminalized sexual relations between men altogether. The last known Dutch use of the death penalty for sodomy occurred in 1803; the French criminal code, which was imposed by Napoleon upon the Dutch in 1811, did not penalize consenting homosexual acts so long as minors were not seduced. At least one German state, Bavaria, imitated the Code Napoléon, but Prussia, in its hostility to Napoleon, did not (although the death penalty was abolished there in 1851).

The early-Victorian attitude to homosexual acts and the criminal law is ill-documented, but the case of Sir Felix Booth gives a rare insight into official attitudes of the 1840s. Booth was a distiller who gave his name to Booth's Gin and munificent subsidies to Arctic exploration (the magnetic North Pole was discovered on an expedition financed by him in 1829–30). For his role in seeking a Northwest Passage he was rewarded in 1835 with a baronetcy, which because he was then a bachelor aged sixty was created with a special remainder to his brother and nephews. Sir

Felix had a younger cousin and namesake who in 1842 wrote to the Prime Minister, Peel, and to other authorities, alleging that the baronet had committed a 'most serious' offence nine years earlier which, if necessary, he would publicize in the *Weekly Despatch*. Peel forwarded young Booth's letter to the Home Secretary, Sir James Graham, asking if Sir Felix should be prosecuted. 'I suspect that it is the result of an attempt to extort money,' Graham replied of the allegation in a letter to Peel which shows the official attitude to homosexual crime to have been cautious and not vengeful. 'The Police never prosecute except on Charges preferred by their own Officers, and on evidence which they have tested and believe,' Graham wrote. 'It has not been the rule to investigate accusations of this kind, which do not rest on official information: and I see danger even in the first Step of an Enquiry, which may do an irreparable injury to an innocent Man, and may serve the purpose and gratify the revenge of a malignant miscreant.' In short the Home Secretary deprecated indiscreet or impulsive intervention: 'I am afraid of any step which may aggravate the mischief', he told Peel, in 'horrible affairs of this nature'. The past scrapes of Sir Felix were left uninvestigated. Graham's decision was doubtless influenced by the fact that Booth was a rich man, who had lately received a baronetcy – public revelations about his private vices would only be a social and political embarrassment. Graham's decision had nothing to do with tolerance: capital convictions, secured by *agents provocateurs* or on other first-hand police evidence, were at their highest level in the 1840s.[55]

Scrutiny of naval courts martial between 1700 and 1861 shows that although sodomy was regarded as a serious crime, comparable with mutiny or murder, there was reluctance to convict the accused of offences for which he would be executed. For this reason, as is shown by a recent study of naval discipline on the Leeward Islands station between 1784 and 1812, sailors accused of sodomy were usually punished summarily by order of their commanding officer, rather than court-martialled, which in two out of three cases resulted in execution. Summary punishment on board ship usually comprised either a long flogging, or 'running the gauntlet', in which the culprit marched slowly backwards and forwards between two lines of all other hands on board, who flailed him with short, knotted ropes, to the sounds of the Rogue's March. More generally, beyond the Leeward Islands, only 30% of those tried for sodomy in 1756–1806 were acquitted entirely: courts martial tended to find them guilty of a lesser offence, such as indecency, which carried a lighter punishment. There were eleven naval courts martial for sodomy during the Seven Years War of 1756–63: during 1761–2, for example, there were two sentences of a thousand lashes and three executions. Thereafter there were no naval courts martial for sodomy until the outbreak of war with revolutionary France in 1793. During 1797, which was a year of naval mutinies, some naval officers associated sexual revolt against authorized values with rebellion against the hierarchy of command: three men were sentenced to death for sodomy by a court martial, followed by two in 1798, two in 1800 and others in the period to 1805. After the Napoleonic Wars, accusations of sodomy almost vanished, and in 1816–29 there were no naval courts martial for sodomy at all. The last time a British sailor was executed for sodomy was in 1829.[56]

Arrests were the occasion for mob violence. 'A man of about 60 years of age stood on a pillory in *Cheapside* for a detestable crime,' a magazine reported in 1762 of an incident which inspired the illustration opposite. 'The population fell upon the wretch, tore off his coat, waistcoat, shirt, hat, wig and breeches, and then pelted and whipped him till he had scarcely any signs of life left, but hung by his arms until he was set up again, and stood in that naked condition, covered with mud, till ... he was carried back to *Newgate* [prison].' When Cook's house in Vere Street was raided in 1810, its occupants were taken to Bow Street police station, where a mob gathered. 'Such was the fury of the crowd assembled', reported the *Morning Herald*, 'that it was with the utmost difficulty the prisoners could be saved from destruction.' All the defendants pleaded not guilty, but offered no defence, and were found guilty as charged. They received sentences of either two or three years, preceded by an hour in the pillory, and were taken in an open cart to the pillory guarded by 100 mounted and 100 unmounted police. Businesses from Ludgate Hill to Haymarket closed for the event and a tumult of abuse and missiles pursued the transgressors through the streets. A new pillory had been erected, and fifty women were given privileged places from which to pelt the men with offal, blood and dung donated by local butchers. Money was collected to supply the women with drink to fire their fury. Cook was knocked almost insensible, and was afterwards whipped by a coachman.[57]

This is not the THING:

OR,

MOLLY EXALTED.

Tune, *Ye Commons and Peers.*

Broadsheet celebrating the pillorying of a sodomite in 1762

The pillory had always been vicious, and the streets of eighteenth-century London spasmodically erupted into tumult against imagined conspirators and scapegoats (notably Roman Catholics in 1780). While the social labels on sodomites were still tenuous, such men were at less risk of being taken as the hate objects of low rioters. But as stereotyping was more strictly enforced, and fears of defilement found a focus, so the victimization became more concentrated. The foundations were laid for centuries of cruelty and oppression. Although legal sanctions were not invariably draconian, the pillory and rituals of verbal abuse established a tradition of community violence sanctified by lawyers and social usage of which vestiges remain today. Mob excitement ignited more quickly and furiously in the first decade of the nineteenth century than in previous epochs, fuelled, apparently, by the distress and hatred of wartime. In one explanation, sodomy was thought to deprive women of husbands and children, and thus Britain of fighting men. It smacked of masculine enervation, which seemed a source of danger during the war with France which alternately smouldered and raged from 1793 until 1815. It was revealing that Holloway, writing in wartime, found it 'excruciating' to consider 'that a fine, elegant, perhaps beautiful woman, should be doomed to have her bed encumbered with a wretch, who loathes her person . . . and treats her with criminal contempt, to indulge his damnable propensities'. Unless the sodomite's wife resorted to adultery, Holloway (although he knew that homosexualism was not an exclusive taste) pretended that she was 'doomed to pine out her life in the most aggravated species of celibacy'.[58]

It was significant too that when sodomites were pilloried, the position from which missiles could be hurled with greater accuracy was reserved for the women whose kind the offenders seemed to have spurned. When Joshua Viguers was blinded in the pillory in 1810, 'the spectators loudly applauded the vengeance of the weaker sex, who showed the offender no mercy', and the hostility between mollies and wives was reciprocal, although not expressed in the same way. Dislike of companionate marriage and a frightened contempt for women seem to have been two of the themes of molly house chatter. But in addition to their role as sexual deserters, sodomites were mutineers whose deviance symbolized the cataclysm that was threatening Europe. The diabolical figure of Napoleon Bonaparte was thought to sympathize with 'unnatural acts' because sodomy was excluded from the list of criminal offences in the Code Napoléon of 1805, and the hostility and insecurity felt towards the Frenchies was turned on the sodomites. Indeed London in 1810 was seized not only by wartime tension, but by economic distress and social disorder which was stirred by radical politicians such as Sir Francis Burdett and William Cobbett. To persecute sodomites was both patriotic and cathartic, and offered a twisted form of social unity. Public participation in punishment of sodomites by the pillory enabled a community riven by political dissent and economic distress to unite for a brief moment against scapegoats who were convenient enemies precisely because they were so irrelevant to all political and social disagreements.[59]

It was for cognate reasons that God's furious destruction of Sodom was constantly evoked in references to men's sexual desire for one another. It was a tenacious image which long survived the Middle Ages. As late as 1750, when London was shaken by earthquakes, Thomas Sherlock, the Bishop of London, published a pastoral letter (of which 10,000 copies were sold within two days) attributing the tremors to the 'Wickedness and Corruption that abound'. Among several vices he specified, 'the unnatural Lewdness, of which we have heard so much of late, [which] is something more than brutish, and can scarcely be mentioned without offending chaste Ears; and yet cannot be passed over entirely in Silence, because of the particular Mark of Divine Vengeance set upon it in the Destruction of *Sodom* by Fire from Heaven, Dreadful Example!' Several needs were satisfied by attributing responsibility for divine wrath to sodomy. By blaming sodomites it was possible to project God's rage entirely outside His Creation, in a way that strengthened the image of a Divine universal order, and in turn strengthened the social hierarchy which claimed to be the worldly reflection of that order. It was attractive to blame the sodomites precisely because they were so irrelevant.[60]

By other projection, criminals were hostile to those convicted of sodomy. Bad as the convicts might feel, it was consoling to have another category of prisoner who everyone could agree was immutably more reprehensible. Prisoners on the hulks at Portsmouth were denounced – often anonymously – by one another as sodomites; while a clergyman attached to one London prison reported in 1819, 'for unnatural offences the other prisoners themselves feel detestation, and I have continually heard them say, that the sufferers [those executed] richly deserved it.' Once incarcerated in prison, men with little if any homoerotic experience often turned for sexual relief to other inmates. Their realization that the conditions of imprisonment had robbed them of control in their choice of sexual partners only made them angrier and more anxious about the small and distinctive category of Sodomite Prisoner.[61]

Sodomy was a crime 'not to be named among Christians'. At the same time that a public sense of it developed, inhibitions on public discourse were imposed. It was crucial to the process of labelling – of creating models of specialized and segregated deviance which would survive – that discussion of those very labels was discouraged. If there had been open conversation, rather than the employment of stereotyped phrases and proceedings, the process might not have survived commonsense questioning. The crucial idea that certain sexual acts were an exclusive and extreme speciality could not have been sustained. Consequently, when twenty men were tried at Warrington for sodomy in 1806, the judge, who sentenced five of them to hang, 'lamented that such a subject should come before the public as it must do, and above all, that the untaught and unsuspecting minds of youth should be liable to be tainted by hearing such horrid facts'. Hawkesbury, the Home Secretary (afterwards Prime Minister as Lord Liverpool), wrote in 1808 to Lord Sydney, the ranger of Hyde Park and St James's Park, urging that both places should be locked at night to stop men picking one another up there, and concluded that it was desirable in taking measures 'to prevent these scandalous practices' that 'they should be done as much as possible without divulging to the Public the disgraceful occasion of them'.[62]

Edward Gibbon regarded sexual desire between men as a contagion which was spread by luxury to the ruin of natural simplicity, and therefore believed that 'negroes, in their own country, were exempt from this moral pestilence'. Sodomites in privileged places were not only contagious, but conspired to protect those whom they had corrupted. 'The rich screen the guilty poor,' Charles Churchill complained in 1746: 'those who practise it [are] too great for law.' There was an appetite for vengeful humiliation of the proud. Investigations, so a newspaper advised in 1810, should concentrate on 'those in *high life* guilty of such abominations . . . One example in high life would be better than fifty in low.' Lawyers and politicians as well as newspaper moralists took this view. 'The hanging of one rogue in *ruffles* was of more public benefit than hanging a hundred in *brogues*,' one judge declared; similarly a member of Parliament adjured in 1816, 'if such crimes were effectually checked in upper life, it would have a great effect.' Sodomy challenged the notion that people would respect uniform and predictable private etiquette for all time, and therefore caused ineradicable anxiety about social disintegration. 'No event . . . is to be more lamented both on public and private grounds,' wrote a member of the Home Office after the arrest of the Bishop of Clogher with his trousers down in the company of a Guardsman in 1822 (see plate): 'It will sap the very foundations of society, it will raise up the lower orders against the higher, and in the present temper of the public mind against the Church it will do more to injure the Establishment than all the united efforts of its enemies could have effected in a century.'[63]

Such views survived throughout the nineteenth century: Lord Desart, who joined the Directorate of Public Prosecutions in 1877, believed that 'the mere discussion of subjects of this sort tends, in the minds of unbalanced people, of whom there are many, to create the idea of an offence of which the enormous majority of them have never even heard.' It was unthinkable to men like Desart that an illimitable number of homosexual acts were constantly passing undetected, and they attributed the increase in the number of prosecutions to the imitative instincts of the weak- minded; but as we have seen, the mass arrests of sodomites in Paris excited similar investigations and prosecutions in both London and the Netherlands in the 1720s. The process at work was not copy-cat perversion: on the contrary, a trial at assizes, if reported, provoked the vigilance of policemen or prurient freelances who previously may have been scarcely aware of the offence (it was a Devon magistrate acting on his own initiative, and apparently inspired by trials elsewhere, who collected evidence which forced Lord Courtenay, weeping like a child, to flee abroad in 1811). It was the authorities whose minds were affected by discussion of such trials, not the lifelong practitioners of the acts under discussion. But to admit this would have thrown the law into doubt.[64]

Historians too have tended towards a suppression based either on horror or *naïveté*. They have not had the same urge to sustain stereotypical labelling, but have often been the dupes of it. 'There is one class of case of which I shall not be expected to speak at all,' wrote the great historian of naval courts martial. 'To ignore the fact that it is there would be dishonest. To dwell on it would be an outrage.' An otherwise astute biographer of King James I dismisses the possibility that the handsome young Earl of Montgomery was his catamite – 'Montgomery was far too tough, smelt too much of the stables, and was too single-mindedly preoccupied with hounds . . . to fill the part' – as if older men are only attracted to perfumed youths with artistic pretensions and always recoil from the company of a strapping young extrovert.[65]

There were other suppressions of discourse. For example a boy drummer executed for a 'detestable' crime in 1811 'made a most ample confession in writing, immediately previous to his execution . . . but it is impossible to give it literally, for the person who took it, in the presence of a magistrate, said the recital made him so sick he could not proceed.' Holloway similarly protested his regret that he 'sullied the idea of manhood with this history of human depravity' and boasted that he withheld the worst details about 'the gully-hole of breathing-infamy in Vere Street' because the circumstances 'afflict me with the same sensation that a crimping knife on my side would create'.[66]

Syphilis, as we learnt in chapter 2, drew from Smollett images of the dunghill: sodomy, for Holloway, excited thoughts of a gully-hole. Both had in common the association of danger with dirt.

CHAPTER FOUR

―――⊶∘⊷―――

Dance as They Desire:
The Construction and Criminalization
of Homosexuality

The laws of God, the laws of man,
He may keep that will and can;
Not I: let God and man decree
Laws for themselves and not for me;
And if my ways are not as theirs
Let them mind their own affairs.
Their deeds I judge and much condemn,
Yet when did I make laws for them?
Please yourselves, say I, and they
Need only look the other way.
But no, they will not; they must still
Wrest their neighbour to their will,
And make me dance as they desire
With jail and gallows and hell-fire.
And how am I to face the odds
Of man's bedevilment and God's?
I, a stranger and afraid
In a world I never made.
They will be master, right or wrong;
Though both are foolish, both are
                                    strong.
And since, my soul, we cannot fly
To Saturn nor to Mercury,
Keep we must, if keep we can,
These foreign laws of God and man.
                              A. E. HOUSMAN

We distrust whatever is vague, formless or anomalous, and try always to confine ourselves within limits. In nineteenth- and twentieth-century Britain our detestation of anomalies has resulted in constant attempts to impose rules upon the conduct of relations between men. Some men are ravenous for other men's bodies, feeling an insatiable need to possess or be consumed; some men feel sexual curiosity about other men's bodies; some men take from other men an occasional casual pleasure that is almost autoerotic; some men admire the grace or power of the male form without erotic stirrings; some men only feel secure when immersed in male camaraderie; circumstances may force some men to live or work or die surrounded exclusively by other men; some men like one another. Most men misunderstand womankind in general, and hate or fear a particular woman at a particular time. Men and women may desire one another's bodies, may fall in love with each other, may achieve orgasms in heterosexual intercourse, may feel glowing unity in such intercourse, but men and women understand themselves and hence their own kind best. All this confusion engenders fear, which in turn drives many people to seek sanctuary in factitious rules or desperate denials.

The preceding chapter described how, after 1700, the confluence of a variety of circumstances resulted in a robust labelling process. This chapter will trace how the social changes that occurred after 1850 duly changed these labels, with the result that a new network of rules and denials evolved, achieving a particular force and form in the 1890s when the convergence of long-term trends and specific incidents constructed a new perception of the homosexual as criminal. The search for self-knowledge and for creeds to live by, which accompanied increasing literacy, provides the context for these developments. I suggested in chapter three that the increasing popularity of personal or confessional diaries in the late seventeenth century showed that people were increasingly aware of being separate individuals, and presaged new anxieties about individual sexuality. In Victorian Britain, as Gladstone and thousands of other diarists showed, this tendency to agonized but incomplete self-appraisal reached a new, higher pitch. People tried to understand themselves, sought self-discipline and self-improvement, set themselves rules of life and inevitably deceived themselves too. Many of them strove for enlightenment and self-control particularly in matters sexual, and felt confused or irritable when confronted by their own failures, or by the contrary behaviour practised by those around them.

This muddle was worst where men's feelings for one another were involved. As this chapter recounts, in the late nineteenth century large areas of male emotions and experience were foreclosed. Fears of interdicted sexual desires and fears of punishment for those desires came to inhibit men from showing emotions that were thought feminine, or sissy, or queer: gentleness and sensitivity and kindness and creativity all became suspect to some eyes. Not only were homosexual tendencies sublimated, consciously disciplined, unrecognized or furiously denied, but inhibitions were imposed on male affections and mentorship. By the early twentieth century youths were only granted adult status after assenting to arbitrary and contradictory definitions of who they were, what they wanted and what they might do: otherwise magistrates called them delinquent or psychiatrists stigmatized them as victims of arrested development. As I demonstrate, there was an obligatory repudiation of the basic affections, attractions and physical inquisitiveness that men share. This repudiation was sometimes taken to desperate extremes, as by the physician who wrote in 1906 that 'normally, the adult man produces on another man an absolutely repulsive effect from the sexual point of view'.[1] In a culture where people's attempts at self-awareness were so often shaped by the books and articles they read, where introspection so often followed literary models or was expressed in written form, the printed word had immense power. Partly as a result, so the evidence of this chapter suggests, the tense, angry, hate-filled words which had almost invariably characterized public discussions of homosexuality were far more audible and powerful than any calm acceptance of homosexual acts, uttered in private.

Victorian guides for visitors to London 'knocking shops' gave early demonstrations of the processes of repudiation and vilification that this chapter describes. *The Yokel's Preceptor, or More Sprees in London* (1855) recorded the increase of 'monsters in the shape of men, commonly designated *Margeries, Pooffs*', and after calling for the death penalty as the only hope of 'crushing the bestiality', went on to specify which streets were 'thronged with them'. The publisher realized that some men who bought his book, whatever their domestic disposition, hoped to take the opportunity while visiting the capital to have sexual relations with

other men, perhaps anonymously and without the cloying atten-
tiveness that was often demanded within marriage. The idea was
ritually anathematized to the reader, who was then advised how to
experience it. 'Will the reader credit it, but such is nevertheless the
fact, that these monsters actually walk the streets, the same as the
whores, looking out for a chance!' exclaimed the *Yokel's
Preceptor*. Around Charing Cross visitors would find 'posted bills
in the windows of several respectable [bars] cautioning the public
to "Beware of Sods"!' – a convenient signpost for anyone who
wanted to find a sod, whether to beat up or fuck. 'They generally
congregate around the picture shops, and are to be known by their
effeminate air, their fashionable dress &c. When they see what
they imagine to be a chance, they place their fingers in a peculiar
manner underneath the tails of their coat, and wag them about –
their method of giving the office.' Such books colluded in their
reader's self-deception and created a potential for violence. As a
Brazilian who became a millionaire by working as a male
tranvestite prostitute said, 'the people who point at me in the street
during the day, sleep in my bed at night.'[2]

The new rules and sharper definitions were based on falsehood,
but were despotic in their power. Thus the mid-Victorian Admiralty blamed women prostitutes for venereal infections in the Navy
in order to divert attention from sodomy among sailors. The
'familiar scene' of a warship docking at an English naval harbour
with seventy sailors 'affected by recent venereal sores of a bad
kind, not one of them having seen the face of a woman for more
than a year' was depicted by Josephine Butler, the campaigner
against the Contagious Diseases Act. 'To such dissolute sailors the
cowardly official says, "Inform, inform us of the *woman* who has
infected you." The men ashamed to confess that they had infected
each other point to any woman.' It became almost an assumption
of national culture that homosexuality was what was practised by
other people, living altogether elsewhere, in recognizably distinct
communities. When an MP representing a deprived urban constituency declared in Parliament in 1890 that agricultural labourers
and 'poor people' as well as the rich were 'frequently' charged at
Assizes with homosexual practices, a sporting squire from Shrop-
shire protested at this calumny on farmworkers, 'who at all events
in my particular county do not bear that character'. A regime of
deception and denial was enforced: the possibility of sexual

Gold-miners dancing together in the Transvaal in the late nineteenth century. There were no European women in the little town of Barberton, hence this cheerful scene. If it had happened in central London all the dancers would have been suspected of 'unnatural vice', and would have been arrested in a police raid. But like Australian station hands or American cowboys, South African miners were untainted with suspicion. Some of the men in this picture doubtless wanted nothing more than a hearty, carefree evening. Others with some drink inside them will have been glad of some sex later. The varieties of motive were lost in the crude stereotypes that developed from the 1890s.

intercourse between any but abnormal men was dismissed as a diseased fantasy. As part of this process, it was insisted that homosexuals were effeminate in manner or feeble in physique. 'Sexual continence before marriage is perfectly consistent with normal health,' opined a venereologist in 1920 in a typical exercise of denial. 'Otherwise,' he said incredulously, 'we must assume that sailors, explorers, Australian station hands, American cowboys, religious celibates and the like tend to be unhealthy, or to practise "unnatural vice".' Likewise a correspondent of the *British Journal of Venereal Diseases*, reporting in 1929 on a case where eleven

boys at a boarding school were found to have infected one another
with gonorrhoea, noted with surprise that they were not all runts:
'the boys who have fallen to these depths of degradation were not
those in whom the stigma of physical and mental degeneration
were apparent, but rather those boys who were physically and
mentally the *élite* of the school – at least in so far as they included
in their numbers the head prefect and athletes of no mean
distinction.'[3]

Truth had increasingly to be denied, or personal experiences
treated as if they had never happened, as preconditions of
acceptance as a male adult. The kinship between boys, and the
reality of eroticism between adolescent men, was ignored or made
terrifying by promulgation of superstitious untruths. Persistently
and reiteratively men in authority, whether legislators, lawyers or
physicians, spoke and behaved as if they had never been adolescents.
Harry Daley, the son of a Lowestoft fisherman, recalled his
early sexual initiation before the First World War. Another boy

> took out his large cock, the first I'd seen with hair round
> it, spat in his hand, and started to masturbate in the
> proper manner. After a minute or two he said he was
> tired and asked me to do it for him, which I did with
> pleasure.
>
> Thus began one of the happiest periods of my life; the
> real beginning of my happy life; the first awakening to
> knowledge of the pleasure and warmth in other people's
> bodies and affection; the realization that physical
> contact consolidates and increases the pleasure and
> happiness to be got from mutual affection . . . It was all
> open and uncomplicated. We were not shy amongst
> ourselves. Whenever in our wanderings we came to a
> secret place, a wood, a shed or a deserted building, we
> would merrily wank away. Some boys were independent;
> others gave, or expected to receive, mild affection.
>
> Nowadays, for some reason or other, this traditional
> experience is thought to be undesirable . . . We continued
> happily and unworried for a long time, until the sort
> of people one finds on the fringes of church life, noticing
> the dark rings under our eyes, warned us that boys who
> played with themselves went mad and had to be locked

away. This was a typical mean, dirty-minded trick, for they had been boys themselves and knew it was not true. In any case it didn't stop us. Henceforth we wanked and worried, whereas formerly we had experienced nothing but satisfaction and contentment.[4]

There is no intrinsic superiority in an orgasm reached in private, and nothing alien about mutual masturbation between young men, but it became a condition of adulthood for Daley's contemporaries to negate their own experience by pretending that there was.

There was particular distortion and amnesia among the ruling class with boarding school experience. 'Every boy of good looks had a female name, and was recognized either as a public prostitute or as some bigger fellow's "bitch",' John Addington Symonds wrote of the 'dung-hill' that was Harrow School in the 1850s. 'The talk in the dormitories and the studies was incredibly obscene . . . one could not avoid seeing acts of onanism, mutual masturbation, the sport of naked boys in bed together.' Harrow's pupils were 'drawn from the lower aristocracy and the moneyed classes for the most part; idleness, plethoric wealth, hereditary stupidity and parvenu grossness combining to form a singularly corrupt amalgam', Symonds recalled. Norman Cookson, 'a red-faced strumpet, with flabby cheeks and sensual mouth', who became a manufacturer of lead and an internationally renowned connoisseur of orchids, was 'the most infamous trench of our house'. As Symonds recounted shortly before his death, he had 'seen nothing more repulsive in my life – except once at the Alhambra in Leicester Square, when I saw a jealous man tear the ear-rings out of the ruptured lobes of a prostitute's ears, and all the men in the saloon rose raging at him for his brutality – I have seen nothing more disgusting in my life . . . than the inhuman manner in which this poor creature Cookson came afterwards to be treated by his former lovers.' After his fellow Harrovians 'had rolled upon the floor with him and had exposed his person in public – they took to trampling upon him. Whenever he appeared in that mean dining room, about those dirty passages, upon the sordid court . . . [William] Currey [later Fellow at Trinity College, Cambridge and a School Inspector], and [Richard] Clayton [later a banker] and [Henry] Barker [later a soldier] and the rest of the brood squirted saliva and what they called their gobs upon their bitch, cuffed and kicked him at their mercy, shied books at him, and drove him with obscene curses whimpering to his den.'[5]

Such recollections were erased, at least publicly, by other contemporaries, perhaps because they were too painful. Often schoolboy love was a substitute for family affection. Adolescent amities were for some the safest and most comforting experience of life. For Byron 'boyhood was the age of kindness and affection, unspoiled by selfish interests'. Feelings between teachers and pupils were sometimes intense and enduring and, as late as 1888, there was still enough innocence for an elderly schoolmaster, writing to his former pupil, Dufferin, by then the Indian Viceroy, to describe himself as 'your old tutor and lover'. The ultimate idealization of this experience was left to a bogus nineteenth-century outsider. 'At school, friendship is a passion,' Disraeli romanced in 1844. 'It entrances the being; it tears the soul. All loves of after life can never bring its rapture, or its wretchedness; no bliss so absorbing, no pangs of jealousy or despair so crushing and so keen! What tenderness and what devotion; what illimitable confidence; what infinite revelations of inmost thoughts; what ecstatic present and romantic future; what bitter estrangements and melting reconciliations; what scenes of wild recrimination, agitating explanations, passionate correspondence; what insane sensitiveness, and what frantic sensibility; what earthquakes of the heart, and whirlwinds of the soul, are confined in that simple phrase of schoolboy's friendship!' Few public men felt safe to acknowledge such experience. It was possibly unprecedented in the early 1950s when a former Ambassador and Cabinet Minister, Duff Cooper, paying tribute in his memoirs to a younger schoolfellow killed in the First World War, commented: 'Normal young men with broad interests and healthy appetites can afford to gild their masculine friendships with a little of the gold they will lavish on their first love affairs, and there is nothing in my life upon which I look back with less remorse than the almost passionate affection I felt for my greatest friend.'[6]

Other politicians understood themselves less well. In the 1870s an Eton master, Oscar Browning, had been accused by the headmaster of paying 'irrepressible attentions' to a pupil, George Curzon: the ensuing rumpus resonated throughout the public school world, although for half a century Browning and Curzon remained in affectionate correspondence. As an adult Curzon was 'epicene', to quote his official biographer, 'where his personal friends were concerned', but in the presence of strangers he was terrified of revealing his tender or feminine side. It was not that he was aware of sexual desire for men, but he was susceptible to all forms of beauty, including male beauty. He craved understanding from other men, and he was often overwhelmed by emotions which, according to the stereotypes of his world, were effeminate. Partly in consequence Curzon, as Viceroy of India, was swift to punish the sexual transgressions of those in his power, whether natives or Europeans: in terror at being overcome by his own femininity, he was harsh and furious at the sexual ambivalence of others. He had 'so little sympathy with the form of vice under discussion', he wrote when Sir Hector MacDonald, the general commanding the Ceylonese troops, was revealed as a homosexual in 1903, that he did 'not waste one drop of regret' upon the man's suicide. 'Such a brute is best kept out of the way.' He was vigilant for signs of 'abominable practices' by adolescent Maharajas: young Bhurtpore was 'a confirmed sodomite', Holkar 'notoriously guilty', Ulwar and Jodhpur 'infected with the same virus', he reported to the Secretary of State for India, Lord George Hamilton, with a mixture of effulgent disgust and prurient relish. Ulwar, despite being 'an active youth and a splendid polo player', enjoyed 'unnatural vice' and therefore as both punishment and cure, was temporarily deprived of power in his state 'and placed in the hands of a British officer under a strict system of discipline and control'. That 'young ruffian' Jodhpur was 'saturated with syphilis', contracted sodomitically according to Curzon, and 'totally unfitted' to govern his state. Curzon ordered him into the Cadets Corps 'for another two years of discipline', but instead the youth left Delhi 'and lived for some days in the house of the chief agent in his abominable lusts'. Ignoring his wife's affair with a young sirdar, 'he indulged in constant dissolute orgies in the palace' until Curzon decreed that he 'be treated like a confirmed drunkard or a madman is, that is, kept under medical restraint'. He added, 'Far the best thing would be that the boy should die.' Hamilton, who recently had described Jodhpur 'as sincere' and likeable, although 'unprepossessing' physically 'and a sad contrast to the handsome young Rajputs who were in attendance upon him', quickly emphasized that despite meeting the young man 'only . . . once', he recalled his 'evil countenance' and was 'not in the least surprised that he has lapsed back into . . . the special Oriental vice'. In this interchange there was a complicated mixture of sincere indignation at indecent acts, anxiety about sexual indiscipline among the leaders of a subject people which might lead to the fall of the Raj, a good deal of perfectly human self-deception and on Curzon's side, at least, a taste for punishing or humiliating those in his power. There were no open or honest memories of Eton; no realization that what he feared most were the feminine traits in himself.[7]

Interestingly and conversely, the suppressed homoeroticism which pervaded the Oxford and Anglo-Catholic movements was recognized. The institutions and religious practices of Anglo-Catholicism attracted gay men partly because it enabled them to 'express their sense of difference in an oblique and symbolical way', and also because of the prevalence of intense, demonstrative friendships among its early followers. Youths troubled by sexual impulses which they could not acknowledge were consoled by the prospect of devoting themselves to a celibate existence among other men. Anglo-Catholic churches with their 'dim Gothic glooms, the sombre hues of stained glass, the incense-wreathed acolytes, the muttering priests, the bedizened banners and altars and images' (to quote Compton Mackenzie) provided a voluptuous oblivion for shop assistants and office clerks who dreaded the ugliness of life and the dreariness of forbidden desire. Despite their doctrinal and liturgical particularities, Anglo-Catholics remained within the established Church and deprecated Roman Catholicism: their ritualism might seem rebellious, but they could at least feel superior to worshippers who gave allegiance to Rome.[8]

Overall, however, the code of conformity was powerful, narrow and intimidating. 'Have you noticed how all these blackguards were musical?' an MP asked after the denunciation of a homosexual coterie in 1883. In the Edwardian period Tom Driberg's elder brothers 'on discovering that (like many homosexuals) I could not whistle . . . persisted in trying to make me master this primitive form of music', and reproved him 'for striking a match, on the edge of the box, *away* from me: that was the woman's way, they said, men always struck matches *towards* them'. 'He brushes his hair for twenty minutes at a time – you're not going to tell me that's normal,' exclaimed a policeman accusing a colleague of homosexuality twenty years later. These stereotypes led some homosexuals into frantic lifelong compensatory behaviour, even into travesties of masculine roughness. 'All my life', wrote Lord Alfred Douglas, 'I have angrily and violently resented the suggestion that I ever had anything feminine about me.' As a schoolboy 'I was so determined to be "manly" that I deliberately went about insufficiently clothed in winter . . . Although by nature rather nervous and apprehensive, I cultivated insensibility to pain, and whenever any danger appeared I trained myself to rush out to meet it.' Although many influences were at work, this compensatory cult of virile aggression extended to choice of sexual partner: men were able to escape the implications of the labelling process by acting as aggressive men, having sex with aggressive men, and despising other tastes as weak. Thus in the 1940s Driberg picked up a young soldier: 'he had had no sex for some time, and offered just the right combination of lust and affection . . . when our passions were partially assuaged, he leaned back on the pillow and said in his Scottish accent, gnomically: "Only sissies like women . . . Real men prefairr male flesh."'⁹

Questions of maleness and feminity, or of aggression and passivity, whether explicitly erotic or not, were liable to as many different answers as there were individuals. Yet in nineteenth-century Britain there was a craving for the certitude of universal rules and axioms. 'Real belief in any religious doctrine is feeble and precarious,' wrote John Stuart Mill in mid century, 'but the opinion of its necessity for moral and social purposes [is] almost universal.' Surrounded by religious perplexities, by fears of social dissolution, and by the sense of personal isolation which became so characteristic of western Europeans in the nineteenth century, people wanted rules which were strict and certain. Anomalies of gender and desire, individual feelings which went so deep and could be so different, were frightening in their implications for conscientious souls trying to live a straightforward moral life according to eternal precepts – dismaying, too, for those who were feeling the essential isolation of modern life. The biographer of the Victorian publisher Alexander Macmillan wrote of his subject, 'To him the family was a God-given institution to relieve the isolation of the individual – the feeling expressed in Matthew Arnold's line "we mortal millions live alone."' In this feeling Macmillan typified the middle class of his era, who turned to an idyll of the family in self-defence and then defended their precarious idyll by attacking those outside it. Gradually, almost imperceptibly, the vocabulary of Continental researchers, who sought to decide whether sexual deviants could be identified by criminologists or held legally responsible for their acts, began to infiltrate British thought, offering a rigid impersonal structure on which to impale what was so often vague, incidental and individual.[10]

Until 1869, when Karoly Benkert coined the word '*Homosexualität*' while arguing against extending Prussian laws against sodomy to the newly unified Germany, there were literally no 'homosexuals', although a multitude of encounters occurred which would later be described as homosexual. Some years later Leopold Casper, a German urologist who had settled in New York, divided homosexual desire into two categories: 'innate', stemming from tainted heredity, or 'acquired', originating from a vicious environment. All this classification had momentous results. To define any action alters the perception of it: beliefs, imposed and distorted by language, reinforce social pressure. The newly created homosexual was told that his sexual acts determined his identity, and was absolved from the dilemma of self-assessment. His existence was dogmatized as being the product of either constitutional flaws or psychological aberration: a mysterious twist of physiology or early family discordance were to blame. Men were categorized according to partial, selectively chosen aspects of their character and behaviour: their social and legal status was defined by this classification, and the inadequacy of these concepts, the fact that some realities eluded them, was ignored. In a period in which most western people moved from a natural to a mechanical environment, the concept of sexual 'normality' emerged, as if human beings were identical to other animals, with no taste for variety and no possibility of choice. In a denial of the essence of humanity, human sexual desire was equated with farmyard tumescence or the instincts of jungle creatures. The precise quasi-clinical language used to describe such theories reinforced belief in their objective reality or verifiable existence: it also supported tyrannous or contemptuous attitudes of medical scientists.[11]

Nevertheless until the 1880s British medical scrutiny of homosexuality was neither extensive nor systematic. English medicine was slow to follow the French and Germans. In 1884, the neurologist Sir George Savage, successively of Bethlem Hospital and Earlswood Idiot Asylum, contributed a case history to the Medico-Psychological Association's *Journal of Mental Science* which shows that the construction of homosexuality had yet little grip even on medical specialists.

Savage's patient was a travelling salesman aged 28, 'of middle height, anaemic and emotional', whose loneliness had led him to hate himself and his desires. The patient 'felt he must kill himself' because although 'he did not feel any real mental depression . . . he felt so ashamed of his unnatural state that he wished he were dead, to prevent scandal to his family.' Savage characterized his patient as 'industrious and hard-working', 'a professing Christian' who 'had never indulged in worldly amusements', and had even renounced his one pleasure of music,

> as it took him into society, where he met other men. At eleven he learnt to masturbate, and had continued the habit ever since [but] never indulged in sexual congress. He says he has no desire or lust after women, and . . . thinks he never did have any lust for women.
>
> He told his employer of his feeling, and said that he felt that he must embrace him. This the master resented, and said if he 'came any more of that stuff' he should discharge him.
>
> He says in America he was fairly comfortable, because the men were only of moderate size and height; but that in England, where there are so many men over six feet, he is perfectly miserable. He says the sight of a fine man causes him to have an erection, and if he is forced to be in society he has an emission.
>
> He has no loss of memory, no tremulousness; his senses appear to be normal in every respect, and his reasoning powers in no way affected.
>
> I recommended him to follow his occupation with energy, to seek mixed society, to go to places of amusement in cities, and to pursue his musical tastes . . . I have met with only one another man, who was in a general hospital, who had similar symptoms, but he had a malformation of his genitalia, and his sex was at least doubtful.
>
> In one female patient, in Bethlem [asylum], there

was powerful lust towards those of her own sex. She died, and an infantile uterus was discovered. One wonders if this perversion is as rare as it appears, when we meet with trials such as have been held in Ireland.[12]

This case history, particularly if it is coupled with a famous trial of 1871 of two transvestites, Ernest ('Stella') Boulton and Fred ('Fanny') Park, has several points of significance. The reference to the Irish trials – in which the sexual escapades of a senior police detective and some Dublin officials were turned into 'a vile weapon in the hands of unscrupulous politicians to attack the Government in office' – shows the importance of occasional prosecutions in creating a public image of a separate, quasi-criminal caste, and in providing the only context for reference even among medical specialists like Savage. These rare interventions by the Law made a disproportionately large contribution to the definition of homosexuals as a special and hateful minority (even though several of the men in the Dublin episode were married). Boulton and Park's case, in which the youths were acquitted of conspiracy to commit a felony by cross-dressing, also shows lawyers and doctors floundering for a conceptual frame for the evidence. One barrister attacked 'the newfound treasures of French literature upon the subject – which thank God is still foreign to the libraries of British surgeons'. Savage's account also shows that regardless of this low level of awareness, and despite comparative social tolerance (a salesman who made sexual overtures to his employer would doubtless have been summarily dismissed at the end of the century), the patient felt shame and guilt. Noticeably, too, Savage and those concerned with the Boulton and Park case explored the possibility of hermaphroditism as a behavioural explanation[13]

Yet within a few years of Savage penning his case history, a clearer sickness model for homosexuality was evident, accentuating homosexuals' feelings of guilt, emotional stuntedness and self-loathing. The main influences for this medical assertiveness came from Paris and Turin. The social and political context for these Continental writings considerably diverged from conditions in late Victorian Britain, but their irrelevance to what was happening across the North Sea if anything enhanced their utility. European medico-forensic theories were adopted in their entirety in Britain not because they fitted precisely or were apt, but because they covered so generally and comprehensively matters which were essentially amorphous.

The decline of Roman Catholic power in France, the development of a secular state, and national defeat by Germany in the war of 1870 created a crisis of confidence and direction, in which the French appealed to the authority of physicians for certitude and discipline. In the three decades after 1870 about one-third of those elected to the French Chamber of Deputies were medical practitioners, and by the early 1880s they were pathologizing social ills in order to justify a medically-influenced policy of intervention: 'the population of large towns', as a Paris physician wrote in 1893, should be treated like that of 'the hospital'. Many subscribed to a new notion of degeneracy, introduced by Benedict-Augustin Morel, who saw the insane as 'throwbacks' and criminals as primitive retrogressives: his theories were expressed in their highest artistic form in Emile Zola's *Rougon-Macquart* sequence of novels (1871–93) which examines the effects of heredity and criminal degeneracy across several generations of one French family.[14]

The professor of psychiatry at Turin, Cesare Lombroso, who popularized Morel's theories, coupled homosexual desire with criminality as elements detrimental to the progress of civilization: born criminals and born perverts needed asylum treatment rather than penal servitude. 'Homosexual offenders whose crime has been occasioned by residence in barracks, or colleges, or by a forced celibacy, plainly will not relapse when the cause has been removed,' he wrote. 'It will be sufficient in their case to impose a conditional punishment, for they are not to be confused with the homosexual offenders who are born such, and who manifest their evil propensities from childhood without being determined by special causes. These should be confined from their youth, as they are a source of contagion.'

According to Lombroso, 'modern civilization', particularly mass education, irritated 'the nervous system, which, in its turn, demands stimulations and pleasure that must always be new and more and more keen . . . hence the great numbers of educated offenders'. From such arguments British physicians derived a view of homosexuality as the product of over-refinement. 'The intellectual development of man has destroyed the pristine balance between the various functions of the body, and civilization, with its artificial conditions of existence, has [stimulated] the growth of perverted tendencies,' declared the *British Medical Journal* after Wilde's conviction.[15] Oscar Wilde succumbed to this view after his imprisonment. 'The terrible offences of which he was rightly found guilty', so he petitioned the Home Secretary from Reading Gaol in 1896, 'are forms of sexual madness': he begged 'that he may be taken abroad by his friends and may put himself under medical care so that the sexual insanity from which he suffers may be cured'. He wrote of his 'monstrous sexual perversion', 'loathsome modes of erotomania' and 'insanity of perverted sensual instinct'.

Such views were broadcast and magnified by Max Nordau, a Hungarian physician and admirer of Lombroso, who settled in Paris in 1880, became President of the Zionist Congress and called for the development of 'muscle Jews' (to replace weakling 'coffee house Jews') who could seize a national homeland. His book *Entartung*, published in London under the title *Degeneration* in 1895, carried considerable influence. 'The disposition of the time is curiously confused, a compound of feverish restlessness and blunted discouragement, of fearful presage ... of imminent perdition and extinction,' wailed Nordau. Stability and social custom 'totter and plunge, and they are suffered to reel and fall, because man is weary, and there is no faith that is worth an effort to uphold them.' The world was disintegrating. Believing that 'only a chaste leadership can survive challenge from the lower infidel classes' and that 'morality' was 'an organized instinct', he saw 'perversion' as a threat not only to the social hierarchy but to national power. The greatest enemy of society was the egotist (perverts were always egotists) who 'turns in wrathful discontent against Nature, society and public institutions, irritated and offended by them, because he does not know how to accommodate himself to them'. Nordau attacked effeminate foppery – 'the predilection for strange costume is a pathological aberration of a racial instinct' – and denounced sexually ambiguous 'Egomaniacs, Decadents and Aesthetes' as belonging 'to the elements of the race which are most inimical to society ... They fritter away their life in solitary, unprofitable, aesthetic debauch, and all that their organs, which are in full regression, are still good for is enervating enjoyment.' Nordau's programme of national revitalization called for 'characterization of the leading degenerates as mentally diseased; unmasking and stigmatizing of their imitators as enemies to society; cautioning the public against the lies of these parasites'.[16]

These Continental theories were swiftly absorbed by the British. The volume on *Degeneracy* in the Contemporary Science series edited by the sexual liberationist Havelock Ellis and published in 1898 spoke of 'sexual perverts' as 'belonging to a still blacker phase of biology' than prostitutes: they were 'moral imbeciles', or 'degenerate lunatics', to whom 'the whole moral and governmental order appears as a mere hindrance to egotistic ambition'. 'Without interest for aught good or beautiful, albeit capable of a sentimentality which is shallow cant', such people were 'repellent by their lack of love for children or relatives, and of all social inclinations, and by cold hearted indifference to the weal or woe of those nearest to them'. They were insensible 'to either the respect or the scorn of others, without control of conscience and without sense or remorse of evil. Morality they do not understand. Law is nothing more than police regulation. The greatest crimes are regarded as mere transgressions of some arbitrary order . . . These ethically defective persons, when incapable of holding a place in society, are often converted into candidates for the workhouse or the insane hospital, one or the other of which places they reach after they have been, as children, the terror of parents and teachers, through their untruthfulness, laziness and general meanness, and in youth the shame of the family and the torment of the community.'[17]

This pseudo-scientific denigration – with its implication that these men were passive and pettish – convinced even the men that it traduced. Self-oppression by homosexual men became commonplace, and often reflected the language of degenerationist psychiatry. 'The usual traits of the genuine invert character' were listed in 1930 by Kenneth Ingram, the homosexual editor of the *Police Journal*. 'He is often markedly youthful in physical appearance, and he is always curiously immature in certain sides of mental development . . . His incurable romanticism, the mysterious importance which he loves to give to his cult, his comparative effeminacy, his extreme sensitiveness, the inconsistency of his attachments, his indifference or in some cases his sexual antipathy to women, his inclination to regard life frivolously, or else by psychological reaction to be abnormally pessimistic, and his curious tendency to see or to pretend to see evidence of homosexuality in other people where they do not in the least exist, are due not simply to the sense of social ostracism: these are the characteristics of the nursery, fairy-story, phantasy ego.' Somerset Maugham (of whom one biographer concludes, 'homosexuality, and his need to pretend ignorance of it, had contributed to the death of his heart'), ascribed the 'tortured fantasy and sinister strangeness' of El Greco's art to 'sexual abnormality'. Maugham, who had trained at a London medical school in the 1890s, analysed the 'innate frivolity' of homosexuals in terms inspired by the degenerationist theories he encountered in his youth.[18]

There was a wider context to British anxieties about homosexuality, namely the flight to domesticity which characterized the behaviour of late nineteenth-century middle-class Englishmen and women. The outburst of hostility against sodomites in the 1720s had occurred when the new ideal of the companionate marriage had rendered people's emotions raw; in the next century the people who marshalled themselves against homosexuality were those who wanted to fortify themselves against the ominous new forces of nineteenth-century life by retreating into an inviolate idyll of the safe, unselfish family unthreatened by hidden desires. In 1854 the Roman Catholic tradition of the immaculate conception of Jesus was raised to the level of dogma by Pope Pius IX: by papal definition, the Blessed Virgin Mother was freed from original sin in a supreme historical example of denial – in this case the child's wish to deny that parents have sex, or that the family may be a nest of carnality. The denial was not exclusive to Roman Catholics. 'The purpose is to guard and defend the household,' declared Frederick Temple, later Archbishop of Canterbury, in 1883: 'to consecrate a circle within which there shall be the warmest, strongest, deepest affection without the slight touch of . . . passion.' Of course this dream was unreal, and domesticity can seethe with lust and hate; but Egotists who sought to determine their own reality threatened this safe reverie, and had to be punished.[19]

The Victorians lived in 'an age in which great promises turned into great threats; in which changes, even changes for the better, aroused anxiety as they implied that concealed and dangerous desires might become reality', as Peter Gay describes in his study of

The Bourgeois Experience. Family life was conceptualized anew as the only safe haven in a hostile world, and children were invested with an unprecedented significance in the scheme of things; indeed, our notions about childhood are mere adaptions of those conceived during the Victorian era. Childhood was at once idealized and feared: its representation was split into the antithetical extremes of innocent felicity within the family and of lawless vice elsewhere. 'Everywhere childhood is regarded as a privileged period, of which happiness should be the indefeasible possession,' declared that wise, generous and romantic diplomat, the Marquess of Dufferin and Ava, in 1867. 'For that short time which is so aptly called the age of innocence the inexorable pressure of our moral responsibilities is suspended . . . Free and careless we wander up and down a transient Eden, while the glad voice of nature without bids us rejoice, and within the sanction of an untroubled conscience re-echoes the loving invitation.' At their best, children were as pure and sexless as Adam before the Fall, in Dufferin's idyll. At worst childhood was a pandemonium of evil and corruption:

> at the very centre and core of European civilization premature decrepitude and precocious depravity too often poison the very springs of existence. Bad food, bad air, bad companionship, the want of proper nursing, the total absence of proper education, render hundreds of thousands of miserable young creatures ignorant of what it is to be well and of what it is to be innocent. To such happiness is a term as incomprehensible as virtue; industry, and I might add honesty, is almost a physical impossibility; while the irritation and mental depravity which are too often developed by disease only invest with a still more sinister character the unbridled passions and the wayward instincts of youth.

The evils of a slum childhood were true to Dufferin's description, but it was partly because good men like him invoked childhood as Eden or hoped that children who were sexually ignorant were devoid of sexual feelings, that childish eroticism was so threatening to the idealization of childhood. It aggravated adult anxieties about masturbation, and occasioned frantic efforts to identify the influences which corrupted the perfect innocence of childhood.

The influences, it was insisted, must be external, not internal: they derived not from members of the family but from Others, elsewhere. One headmaster, the Revd Edward Lyttelton, writing in 1887, typically believed that 'solitary vice' was 'dangerous and deplorable' because it was 'learnt', not instinctual. Boys were 'innocent' of masturbation until inspired to 'foul practices' by other boys who spread 'corruption' through the school. In these efforts to characterize the family as a sexless sanctuary, and children as creatures without desires, the homosexual (perceived as an outsider from family life) increasingly became suspected of corrupting children. Precisely because they were so irrelevant to the causes of children's eroticism they became irresistible for use as scapegoats.[20]

Dufferin and his wife created for their children a delightful domestic felicity, as many charming family letters testify; yet the realities of Victorian family life often fell far short of his ideal. Domesticity failed as a sanctuary from ugliness and cruelty. By mid-century English middle- and upper-class households were 'conspicuous for the barrier of cold, harsh and emphatically inhuman reserve which cuts off anything like that friendly, considerate, sympathetic intercourse which ought to mark every family relation', John Morley wrote in 1870. Home was often where life became miserable, where people became estranged from their feelings and from the rest of humankind. 'A habit of reserve in all things was instilled into the minds of the young as an almost religious doctrine,' wrote Lady Cowper of the same period. 'We were taught, both by example and precept, that our thoughts and feelings were not intended to be dissected for the benefit of others, and indeed were hardly allowed to be admitted to examination by ourselves.' She was horrified in the 1890s that 'the custom of analysing things and people' had 'grown into such stupendous proportions': after years of repression, she felt 'overwhelmed with an avalanche of the scraps and shreds into which have been torn the feelings and the desires, the speculations and calculations, the beliefs and doubts . . . of each and every one'. Her language shows how dangerous and bewildering it could be to face one's Self or express one's needs: 'if we wantonly destroy this great and splendid gift' of emotional isolation, 'we shall find ourselves ere long in the quicksands of licence which we mistook in our waywardness for the rocks of freedom.' The collective life of many families could only survive if the individual Selves that comprised it were ignored.[21]

It was in the circle of the family that life began to go wrong; so it was to an ideal of the family that people turned to get things right. Those who took another course, such as male homosexuals, did something inexcusable. Their rejection of domesticity touched other people's sorest feelings and most bitter disappointments. Moreover they seemed to defy Christian theology. That unforgiving bachelor bishop, Cosmo Lang, writing in 1906, stressed as absolute Truths fundamental to Christianity that 'a personal sense of sin' was the foundation of character and that the 'deepest and most important' human relationship was that of a person with God. 'He is the unity of all the rest; and therefore the very basis of our life . . . To be wrong there, is to be utterly wrong.' The British conscience, 'trained by the long centuries of God's discipline of this race', knew 'that our relationship with Him is meant to be that of sons living in free dependence upon a Father, finding more and more in obedience to Him their perfect freedom . . . That filial union is the true meaning of our life.' If anything disturbed this unity, 'it is the force we call sin', essentially 'self-will, self-satisfaction, the assertion of independence of God'. Cosmo Lang emphasized 'the great truth of the Fatherhood of God', whom he called 'The Moral Governor of the World'. All originated in the identification of fathers with goodness, of fathers as 'Almighty Governors', and hence of authority with goodness. For Christians there were only two states of life: 'one centred in God . . . obedient to the leading of God . . . the other, centred in self . . . moving in thought, desire and will away from God. Between these two states most men hover to and fro, but gradually the main motive of the will – God or self – carries them, to the one or the other.' As people hovered between God and Self, so they hovered between heterosexuality and homosexuality. If God triumphed, people attained 'the home-life for which we are made, and in which alone we can find joy and rest'. Homosexuals, as we have seen, were defined as Egotists – as those centred in Self – who seemed to reject the patriarchy of Christianity as they rejected the patriarchy of the family. And yet, it was not their experience that fathers were good, or families safe. 'A man's worst enemies are his parents,' the bisexual novelist Norman Douglas decided. As an Edwardian child, Tom Driberg found the idea of domestic intimacy 'detestable in its suffocating cosiness'. He considered the family to be 'an institution destructive of true affection, a nexus of possessiveness, vindictiveness and jealousy' and found solace in other boys and men because 'the people of my grandparents' and parents' generations were great haters, and the hatred was concentrated most intensely within the family'.[22]

There were additional reasons why the British proved responsive to the views of Lombroso and Nordau. Nations are most apprehensive of ruin at the height of their power, and dread prostration when at their zenith. Increasing industrial competition from Germany and the United States, large territorial additions to the Empire in Africa and Asia, challenges to traditional naval invincibility, the splendid Jubilees but also the mortality of Queen Victoria, left the British aware not only of their triumphs but of their vulnerability. Joseph Chamberlain likened Britain to a 'weary Titan, staggering under the too-vast orb of his fate', and Nordau's book was published at a time when many people sensed that British glory was at its apotheosis: henceforth there could only be decline. Just at this moment when the British were fretting that they were an enervate race, Nordau and Lombroso issued their dire remonstrance against over-civilized egotists and epicene aesthetes. The conjunction was fatal. Doctors, journalists, politicians and laity were convinced alike. 'The burden is heavy; the world is a weary Titan; our creeds are outworn; we are very old, and our dolls are stuffed with sawdust; the century is waning, and big causes and enduring pleasures are not worthwhile; our lean bodies and jaded passions need stimulants and enticements,' wrote a physician, Sir Clifford Allbutt, in 1895, when offering sombre counsel against 'the encroachment of peoples of lower standards and lower ethical capacities upon the seats of nations'.[23]

But it was the vitiation of male might at this critically insecure moment in the history of the empire that counted most. Homosexuals were a threat to imperial aggression and their proliferation was an augury of collapse: they were the rubble before the avalanche. Just as Nordau and Krafft-Ebing foresaw homosexuals being 'numerous enough to elect a majority of deputies having the same tendency', so the paintings of Aubrey Beardsley were denounced by the demotic critic Harry Quilter as 'perverted' for depicting 'manhood and womanhood . . . mingled together . . . in a monstrous sexless amalgam, miserable, morbid, dreary and unnatural'. The *Yellow Book*, a progressive Victorian periodical, was according to Quilter 'corrupt to the last degree, enfeebling and enervating'. It conjured up for him the horror of men who were not aggressively male.

> Just fancy a nation of Beardsleys! Conceive politics, commerce, law and religion approached from this standpoint, applied in this manner . . . Art is, we are told with sickening reiteration, but a reflection of life; why should we not have a Beardsley bishop addressing a Beardsley congregation, or, say, Mr Gully [Speaker in Parliament], *à la* Beardsley, reproving an emasculated House of Commons.

Such references persisted. 'Egotistical decadents' and 'neurotic curiosities' existed 'to the injury of national truth and wholesome strength', declared a Kensington clergyman in 1916. 'We have no use for them. They render nothing to Caesar. And we do not think they render anything to God.'[24]

It was not coincidental that the poetry of Walt Whitman had lately inspired English homosexuals like Edward Carpenter to consider the prospect of an idyll of socialist brotherhood in which sexual equality obliterated class distinctions. Late nineteenth-and early twentieth-century public apologists for homosexuality often bedecked sexual acts with sentimental and factitious socialism. This proved as much a disservice to their aim of decriminalization as it was counterproductive in eradicating fright and vicious exhortation as instruments of public policy. 'If there is one set of human beings I detest, it is the English upper middle class,' Symonds wrote in 1891. 'The smallness and selfishness – the miserably mean scale of life and conception – of the upper English bourgeoisie' were loathsome 'because they are so infernally stupid and hedged in (like their own petty fields and petty parks) with palings of conventionalities, and stuffed with the artificial manures of comfort like their own fat flowerless meadows'. He railed against the habit of his own class 'of hiding their real selves under shells of convention'. He boasted 'a very miscellaneous set of friends, including all classes of society from a hairdresser to a Duke', which diversity pleasantly 'complicates social relations & taxes the range of sympathy'. He deluded himself that 'the blending of Social Strata in masculine love', to quote a letter of

1893, 'abolishes class distinctions, & opens by a single operation the cataract-blinded eye to the futilities . . . If it could be acknowledged & extended, it would do very much to further the advent of the right kind of socialism.'[25]

In later life Symonds enjoyed an affair with a muscular young Swiss sledge-driver. There seems to have been affection on both sides: Symonds was accepted by his lover's family, financed their hotel business, encouraged his lover to marry, and in turn experienced a happiness and satisfaction which, amongst other effects, improved his writing. 'There will be nothing surprising in this to those who have seen the humorous generosity, the unquestioning ease with which the unsophisticated young male in any country can respond to the aching introspective need of the intellectual,' as Rupert Croft-Cooke, another writer experienced in these matters, has explained. 'Never wavering in his ultimate desire for women, with nothing in the least extraneous in his nature, unspoilt by doubt, having no need to rationalize or probe into motive, or to look for explanation or defence, he can give himself with grace and cheerfulness, even with enthusiasm, and this is enchanting to a more tried and experienced partner. He finds no mystique in this and has no wordy hesitations or self-conscious constraints. There may be an element of sexuality in what he does, or one of gainfulness, but generally it is a boundless careless instinct which often leads to happy and enduring relationships.'[26] Seventy years later the relations between another poet, W. H. Auden, and a younger married Alpine man were similar. The affections of Symonds and his fellow propagandist Edward Carpenter were a private concern, seemingly delightful; but the priggish, self-deceiving miasma of political reform with which they enveloped their affairs can only have provoked antagonism in a non-socialist country, and have added to the labelling process a new detail as ridiculous and inaccurate as any other.

There was enough anxiety already. Public references to homosexuals increased in the final years of the nineteenth century. 'There is no doubt that of late years a certain offence – I will not give it a name – has become more rife than it ever was before,' the House of Commons was warned in 1890. More enthusiastically, in 1891, Symonds saw 'signs' throughout Europe 'of an awakening of enthusiastic relations between men' of 'a passionate character'.[27] This was reflected in the publication of novels such as

Monsieur Venus (1889) by Marguerite Vallette, *Footsteps of Fate* by Louis Couperus (translated into English in 1891), Oscar Wilde's *Picture of Dorian Gray* (1891), and *Un Rate* by Countess de Martel de Janville who used the pseudonym Gyp, which became more widely available in 1891. But then came the catastrophe of Oscar Wilde's arrest.

The preliminaries to this detonation were haphazard. The House of Commons resolved to suspend restrictions on women suspected of transmitting venereal disease in 1883, although it was not until January 1886 that the repeal of the laws came into effect. As a replacement the social purity movement drew up a Criminal Law Amendment Bill intended to launch a new campaign of moral coercion. A newspaper exposé in 1885 of the 'inveigling and capture and horrible treatment of young girls who are quite innocent and know nothing of what is going to be done to them' entitled "The Maiden Tribute to Modern Babylon" 'created huge excitement' by its 'plain speaking and hideous details'. Its author W. T. Stead depicted the sale for £5 of girl virgins to elderly aristocratic rakes and threatened to confront 'princes, peers and MPs with the victims of their sins'. This stunt was welcomed by agitators for social purity who loathed the sexual precocity of working-class girls, whom they regarded as passive victims of male sexual abuse. 'On the whole, the good outweighs the evil,' wrote the Revd Randall Davidson of Stead's sensational journalism. 'The wave of moral wrath and indignation which has been evoked will sweep things before it.' The Bill, hitherto 'supposed to be hopelessly doomed', was carried in the House of Commons without a division because no MP dared to be seen in the aftermath of Stead's articles to vote against it.[28]

One of the main parliamentary opponents of the Bill was George Cavendish-Bentinck, 'the typical high Tory' who believed that 'everything' in Britain was 'going to the devil'. If national policy had been left to him 'we should still be confronted with . . . press-gangs, slave-trades, total absence of educational provision, wholesale pauperism, abuses of labour in factories, in short . . . retrogression of civilization', according to his prospective son-in-law, Sir Edward Walter Hamilton, in 1886. 'A little, mean drunken aristocrat, without the slightest capacity for business,' according to another contemporary, 'he is notorious in the House of Commons for his muddled speeches, and unsteady gait after

A characteristically jaunty sketch of Henry Labouchere, whose facetious amendment to the Criminal Law Amendment Bill caused so much trouble and misery.

dinner.' In opposing the new legislation Cavendish-Bentinck joined Henry Labouchere, a Radical politician of equally cynical mind, who shared his interest in actresses. 'The mobility, springiness and delicacy of his figure might have suggested the graces of a dancing master,' wrote his friend William O'Brien, the Irish politician who took a conspicuous part in denouncing the Dublin homosexual coterie during 1884. 'His grimace . . . needed but a daub of red paint on the cheek, and a pair of baggy white breeches, with his hands in the pockets, to equip him to set a circus in a roar.' Whether dancing-master or clown, Labouchere was an unscrupulous mischief-maker with a passion for provocative conduct.[29]

Cavendish-Bentinck and Labouchere introduced an amendment fixing the female age of consent at 21, arguing that it was 'absurd' in a bill intended 'to protect young girls . . . to say that they would punish any person who procured or endeavoured to procure a woman of 30, 40 or 50 or goodness knew what age to become . . . a common prostitute'. When this was defeated, Labouchere introduced a further unsuccessful amendment, setting the age of consent at 18: a fellow MP, who shared the doubts of Cavendish-Bentinck and Labouchere, suggested that these amendments were a ploy to show 'the absurdity of the whole of the Bill'. Even on the day that he moved his amendment on homosexuality, Labouchere attacked the Criminal Law Amendment Bill as 'very badly drawn up' and full of muddled amendments: 'in matters such as these the greatest care ought to be taken not to confound immorality with crime, not to over-run in well-meaning enthusiasm . . . and not to play into the hands of blackmailers.'[30]

It is against this background that one should scrutinize the eleventh clause of the Criminal Law Amendment Act, which has become known as Labouchere's Amendment, and was passed by the House of Commons late at night on 6 August 1885. It provided that 'any male person who, in public or private, commits, or is a party to the commission of, or procures or attempts to procure the commission by any male person of any act of gross indecency with another male person, shall be guilty of a misdemeanour, and being convicted thereof shall be liable at the discretion of the court to be imprisoned for any term not exceeding two years, with or without hard labour.' Labouchere's Amendment was 'a disgrace to legislation', according to Symonds, 'by its vagueness of diction and the obvious incitement to false accusation', but this may have been its purpose. The clause was so vague, and despite Labouchere's declared anxiety about blackmailers, so obviously a blackmailers' charter with its reference to acts in private, that like his earlier amendments on the age of consent it seems an extravagant whimsy intended to spoil the Bill and force it to be referred to committee. Labouchere, according to O'Brien, had 'an incurable addiction to persiflage' and was an 'exquisitely malicious scoffer'; 'inflamed', as Frank Harris suggested, 'with a desire to make the law ridiculous', it was in character for him to propose 'that the section be extended so as to apply to people of the same sex who indulged in familiarities . . . The puritan faction had no logical objection to the extension, and it became the law of the land.' It was a piece of obstructive banter akin to the proposal in 1965 by Field Marshal Montgomery, during parliamentary debate on the decriminalization of homosexuality, that the age of consent should be eighty, not twenty-one, for men.[31]

As soon as Labouchere's clause was put before the House of Commons, a lawyer MP queried whether it 'was within the scope of the Bill' as it 'dealt with a totally different class of offence to that against which the Bill was directed', but the Speaker, Arthur Peel, ruled that 'anything' might 'be introduced' to amend the Bill. In different circumstances the amendment might have been ruled out of order, but Peel was keen to clear the legislative arrears so that the caretaker Salisbury Government which had been in power since June could prorogue Parliament and call a general election. It was late at night, few MPs were present, and no one challenged his ruling. Only one MP spoke against the amendment, and he limited himself to one cautious sentence.[32]

Britain in consequence was saddled with 'Labby's inexpansible legislation', as Symonds described it. The amendment criminalized all homosexual acts, not simply sodomy, and left Britain as the only European country in which mutual masturbation by men was interdicted. Most legal constraints had been removed in France under the Napoleonic Code. Although Germany and the Austro-Hungarian empire had laws against homosexuality, these were inconsistently applied, and some toleration was shown to the invert. Italy decriminalized sex between men in 1889, so long as public decency or minors were not violated.[33] Labouchere's clause ignored the Offences Against the Person Act of 1861 which rendered those convicted of buggery liable to punishments derived from Henry VIII's legislation. This 1861 Act had been seldom invoked, and successful prosecutions were rare; but it appears from a Home Office review of 1910 that although the penalties under Labouchere's amendment were lenient in comparison, the effect of the 1885 clause was to increase hostility to homosexual acts, as was manifested by more prosecutions under the 1861 law. Labouchere's amendment, with its weak provisions about evidence, and its consequent exposure of 'consent' and 'procuring' to expansive judicial interpretation, became a terrible instrument for inflicting misery.

Before Labouchere's amendment the law was 'insufficient', or so he claimed in 1890, because sodomy 'had to be proved by an accessory', while other sexual activities like mutual masturbation between men 'were not regarded as crimes at all'. He claimed in 1890 that after receiving a report from Stead on the prevalence of homosexuality, he consulted the Attorney-General, Sir Henry James, and the Home Secretary, Cross, before adapting a clause from the French penal code which he then introduced as an amendment to the Bill before Parliament. In fact France had decriminalized homosexuality between consenting adults during the Revolution almost a century earlier, and only retained legislation against the corruption of youths (although there was hostility against sexual relations between men). Similarly his claim to have worked with Stead's co-operation is dubious. The two men detested one another: Labouchere derided Stead's involvement with the Purity Leaguers, opposed the provisions of the Criminal Law Amendment Bill regarding the age of consent, exulted when Stead was imprisoned for indiscretions during his campaign, and never mentioned Stead's supposed report at the time when his amendment was debated. Stead and the Purity Leaguers in turn ignored Labouchere's amendment: it was scarcely mentioned in Stead's newspaper, Labouchere was ostracized by Christian moralists as a rake, and when in 1895 he tried to take some credit for facilitating the prosecution of 'Pretty Fanny authors' like Wilde 'whose minds are essentially diseased', Stead sprang to the playwright's public defence. There was a 'ridiculous disparity' between those who seduced youths and those who seduced girls, Stead wrote in a gibe at libertines like Labouchere and Cavendish-Bentinck. 'If Oscar Wilde, instead of indulging in dirty tricks of indecent familiarity with boys and men, had ruined the lives of half a dozen innocent simpletons of girls, or had broken up the home of his friend by corrupting his friend's wife, no one could have laid a finger upon him,' Stead raged in an attempt to prevent Labouchere joining Wilde's prosecutors as the heroes of the hour. 'The male is sacrosanct: the female is fair game. To have burdened society with a dozen bastards, to have destroyed a happy home with his lawless lust – of these the criminal law takes no account. But let him act indecently to a young rascal who is well able to take care of himself, and who can by no possibility bring a child into the world as a result of his corruption, then judges can hardly contain themselves.'[34]

The outlawing of homosexuality separated affection from sexuality, and increased the isolation and stylization of many men. Young Harry Daley found himself being called 'dirty little bugger' by hostile groups in the street after he began an open affair with a sailor during the First World War: 'I couldn't believe that love and affection – which had brought me such happiness – were things to be ashamed of, and was incredulous when told I could be sent to prison and, nastily, "That's probably where you'll end up."' (In fact he became a policeman.) Daley soon came to feel that he 'was living on the edge of a precipice' and 'should not have done too badly if I reached twenty-five without being flung into prison'. Those who practise clandestine activities try to reduce risk and optimize effectiveness. In the case of homosexuals, this often prompted a search for anonymity, with minute ritual before the sexual act and immediate separation afterwards. The tendency was to minimize emotional involvement while maximizing orgasmic yield. 'Hellenic love may be a splendid ideal for the homosexual but under modern conditions, with a police force trained to spot it, even provoke manifestations of it and prosecute it, it soon lost its glamour and refinement and, driven underground, it becomes mere promiscuity,' according to Rupert Croft-Cooke, who was gaoled after questionable police proceedings under Labouchere's amendment. 'Most of the ruttish inverts of today, following an obsessed existence in queer meeting-places all over the world, started with the hope of some ethical purpose in their lives, dreamed of male relationships as honourable as marriage, tried to create something from their friendships to compensate for the sterility of them, but with time and persecution fell into facile lechery.'[35]

Yet at first little changed: the authorities were reluctant to apply Labouchere's amendment. Lord Hannen, the senior judge of the Divorce Court, admitted privately in 1890 'some very remarkable things about the way in which a judge evades the law, while charging Grand Juries' in such cases. The reason for these evasions was betrayed by Lord Chancellor Halsbury who urged caution when the prosecution of Lord Arthur Somerset's circle was contemplated in 1889. 'If', wrote Halsbury, 'the social position of some of the parties will make a great sensation this will give very wide publicity, and consequently will spread very extensively matter of the most revolting and mischievous kind, the spread of which I am satisfied will produce enormous evil.' This was part of a longstanding tradition. Sir Thomas Henry, who was chief magistrate at Bow Street in the 1870s, 'thought the policy of prosecution in these cases was very doubtful, as the publicity attaching to them aroused morbid curiosity, and undoubtedly induced imitation'. Sir Howard Vincent, who was first Director of Criminal Investigations at Scotland Yard in 1878–84, wanted all such cases to be heard *in camera* as he deplored the way in which 'every item nauseous and sensational is detailed and magnified for the benefit of young boys and girls, especially in the Sunday and halfpenny press.' Reflecting this tradition, the judiciary was more concerned to repress public discourse on the subject of homosexuality than to apply Labouchere's amendment. These priorities emphasized the constant fear that 'male solicitation by males' was, in Vincent's phrase, an 'increasing scourge'.[36]

Labouchere's amendment, if it was intended to stop homosexual acts, was counter-productive, particularly as it was only under his clause that Oscar Wilde could have been prosecuted in 1895: Wilde's public ruin resulted in a higher number of individuals labelling themselves as exclusively homosexual then ever before. 'Always, so long as it stays remembered, the name of Oscar Wilde is likely to carry with it a shadowy implication of that strange pathological trouble which caused his downfall,' Laurence Housman wrote a quarter of a century later: 'his downfall did at least this great service to humanity, that – by the sheer force of notoriety – it made the "unmentionable" mentionable.' Wilde's entrapment and imprisonment were proof of the danger attending deviance. His trials resulted in highly explicit labelling which imposed and emphasized new antitheses in acceptable and abhorrent conduct. His ruin was a triumph of extremism, which left a heritage of extremism. Henceforth to achieve self-recognition as a homosexual, despite the risks and interdictions, required such heavy commitment that few people, having struggled to achieve it, were willing to relinquish one iota of their achievement. If a man made the dangerous and forbidding journey into the ostracized subculture there were no rewards in questioning its pretence to homosexual exclusivity, although every member of the subculture knew that it included husbands and womanizers too.[37]

Wilde's libel action of March 1895 against the Marquess of Queensberry, the father of his lover Lord Alfred Douglas, caused convulsive change. Occurring at the moment of maximum impact in Britain of degenerationist psychiatry, which had sponsored painful doubts about the virility of the race, its effects were cataclysmic. But even the evidence disclosed in the libel action might not have made Wilde's criminal prosecution inevitable under Labouchere's amendment in April and May 1895 had it not

A contemporary sketch of one of the youths who worked at the male brothel in Cleveland Street which was the centre of the scandal in 1890 which drove Lord Arthur Somerset into exile. He was a telegraph messenger boy with the delightful name of Charles Thickbroom: one of the other youths who worked at Cleveland Street was a clerk called Newlove.

been for other circumstances which gave the affair political implications. Labouchere had alleged during the scandal involving Lord Arthur Somerset and his telegraph messenger boys in 1890 that the Prime Minister, Salisbury, had joined in a cover-up. In 1895 there was added anxiety to avoid the semblance of sheltering privileged malefactors because the current Prime Minister, Lord Rosebery, was implicated in the Wilde fiasco. In 1893 Queensberry's eldest son, Lord Drumlanrig, had been created Baron Kelhead in the United Kingdom peerage (all the Queensberry titles being Scottish), at the instigation of Rosebery, who was susceptible to the company of handsome young men. This barony which Rosebery obtained for Drumlanrig excited Queensberry to insensate rage: he sent a preposterous jeremiad to Queen Victoria, inflicted a jealous tirade on Prime Minister Gladstone and followed Rosebery to Germany, intending to horsewhip him publicly for his influence on Drumlanrig, from which course he was dissuaded by the Prince of Wales, who happened to be staying nearby. Drumlanrig died of a gunshot wound shortly before his wedding in 1894, and was believed to have committed suicide either to escape scandal or in despair at his impending marriage: it therefore seemed ominous when Queensberry began calling Wilde 'a damned cur and coward of the Rosebery type'.[38]

Rosebery's friend Sir Edward Walter Hamilton heard of Queensberry's 'insulting card' accusing Wilde of 'posing as a sodomite' on 10 March, and even in his private diary could only bear to record that the card bore 'some opprobrious epithet which can be more easily grasped than written'. A month later he recorded: 'The Oscar Wilde [libel] case is proceeding; and some horrible disclosures are being made. It seems impossible that a British Jury can do otherwise than acquit Queensberry of defaming O. Wilde's character by imputing to him the character of "posing as" an unmentionable creature. The net seems to be closing round the brute.' Later, during the last of the criminal trials against Wilde in May, Hamilton noted, 'A verdict of guilty would remove what appears to be a wide-felt impression that the Judge & Jury were on the last occasion *got at*, in order to shield others of a higher status in life' – a reference to Labouchere's allegation against Salisbury during Somerset's scandal. When four days later Wilde was sentenced to two years hard labour, Hamilton was 'more glad than I can say about the verdict; for I never had a shadow of doubt about the guilt of the two beasts, and there was . . . a very prevalent suspicion abroad that the Government were trying to hush up the case in order to screen certain people of higher rank in life.' The authorities were obliged to prosecute Wilde to avoid imputations of partiality rather than act with the discretion which the Government's law officers preferred in such matters. During March Rosebery went to his Newmarket house where acute insomnia brought him to the verge of collapse: as Lord Esher recorded at the time, 'the Newmarket [horse-racing] scum say that . . . his insomnia was caused by terror of being in the

Wilde scandal.' (Rosebery retired from public office months later, and his later swings between elation and melancholy led some to suspect that he sought solace in cocaine.) If it had not been for these fatal convergences a great deal of misery might have been averted.[39]

Wilde's case was more than a sordid prosecution under a foolish law. It led immediately to an attempt to suppress all public mention of homosexuality, and compromised artistic individualism for a generation. During Wilde's trial, Sir Sidney Low, the editor of a London evening newspaper, the *St James's Gazette*, which appealed to a 'high-class public', found the evidence so 'repulsive' that he decided that his newspaper 'should have no part in this public scandal' and announced that it would print 'nothing but the brief statement that the trial was proceeding'. Low felt his 'action was generally approved', 'several advertisers showing their approval of our conduct by giving us new or enlarged orders'; but although no circulation was lost by this decision, Low's proprietor, Waldorf Astor, 'pointed out to me that such credit as I myself and my associates derived from our reticence was gained at his expense', because evening newspapers which reported Wilde's trial 'in excessive detail . . . very nearly doubled their circulation'. During the sensation, Halsbury, the former Lord Chancellor (described by a fellow judge, Sumner, as 'the quintessence of noxious geniality'), consulted Low about the best method to prevent such 'scandals' in future. After the collapse of Rosebery's Government, and his reappointment to the Woolsack, Halsbury introduced the Publication of Indecent Evidence Bill in 1896. He claimed that 'fathers of families' recognized that reports of prosecutions under Labouchere's amendment did 'infinite mischief' and should be prohibited by law. 'The evil only existed in *causes célèbres*, and the difficulty, danger and mischief arose when those cases were being heard, as the most minute and most disgusting details of every part of the evidence were brought forward.' Halsbury was supported by the Conservative Prime Minister, Salisbury. After all that had been said, written and done about homoeroticism in the previous decade, Salisbury felt it was suitable for him to become the first British party leader to pronounce on the causes and effects of homosexuality. 'It is a well-ascertained effect that the publication of details in cases of that kind has a horrible though undoubtedly direct action in producing an imitation of the crime,' Salisbury told the House of Lords. He had been assured by 'a very distinguished doctor . . . that after one of these cases appeared in the newspapers he heard of numbers of cases of crime of the same kind which were not brought forward. There appeared to be a kind of epidemic in consequence of the case published.' Halsbury's proposal was opposed by the Lord Chief Justice and the Master of the Rolls: after pressure from newspaper proprietors, it was abandoned, but it was the most explicit example of a far wider inhibition on the written word.[40]

'It is especially important', *Lancet* averred, 'that such matters should not be discussed by the man in the street, not to mention the boy and girl in the street.' They were not even to be contemplated by the scholar in his library. Havelock Ellis's austere study of *Sexual Inversion* (1897) was rejected by several publishers ('one or two adding that they would have [published] with pleasure had it not been their privilege to live in England'), declared obscene, and made the subject of a court order for the destruction of all copies. The British Museum Library, despite possessing a copy, hid its existence from readers by excluding it from the catalogue. Desart, Director of Public Prosecutions during Wilde's trials, noted that for about eighteen months afterwards, chief constables reported 'a perfect outburst of that offence all through the country'. He used this data to oppose legislation which would have criminalized lesbian acts. 'How many people does one suppose really are so vile, so unbalanced, so neurotic, so decadent to do this?' Desart asked in 1921. He answered 'an extremely small minority', and thought it would be 'a very great mischief' to create a new legal offence of female homosexuality, 'to bring it to the notice of women who have never heard of it, never thought of it, never dreamed of it'.[41]

Wilde's downfall stimulated the Pharisees. 'All those creeping things that riot in the decay of nobler natures hastened to their repast,' as Macaulay wrote of the fall of Byron. 'It is not every day that the savage envy of aspiring dunces is gratified by the agonies of such a spirit, and the degradation of such a name.' Harry Quilter, writing as he prided himself 'in the plainest words', celebrated that 'the fall of the great high-priest of aestheticism' had ensured that 'the newest developments of blasphemy, indecency and disease receive only half-hearted and timid approval'. Quilter (see plate) decried 'the morbid extravagances of hysterically neurotic and erotic imagination', and insisted that there were many 'subjects in themselves so repellent, so enervating and so unprofitable' that they should be 'excluded' from literary or artistic representation. He inveighed against books 'induced by morbid conditions of the brain' whose 'power for evil' was 'the transformation of [sexual] instinct . . . quivering with nervousness'. Such writing was 'as repugnant to healthy men as . . . to pure-minded women': its authors and their friends 'must be detected, exposed and destroyed'.[42]

Philistinism was given a fillip. 'Books are a mere form of self-indulgence, and in no way better than any other form of self-indulgence,' wrote the backwoodsman Lord Harberton in an article inveighing against 'The Arrogance of Culture' in 1915. 'The kind of people who derive the greatest pleasure from art and literature are neurotics, decadents and sexual psychopaths.' But no less than on barbarian frontiers, metropolitan literary life was conquered by a fetish for healthiness. In 1895 the publication of *Jude the Obscure* was greeted with such obtuse malignancy that Thomas Hardy abandoned writing novels altogether. The literary taste of his countrymen veered towards adventure stories like those of Sir Rider Haggard and Sir Anthony Hope Hawkins. As a reaction against Wilde's epicene aristocrats, readers turned to lower middle-class men like the characters created by H. G. Wells, Kipps and Mr Polly. It was not until 1928, when Evelyn Waugh published *Decline and Fall*, that the aristocracy were restored to English literature (as opposed to popular romantic fiction).

Similarly, sportsplaying became a qualification of healthy manhood less, as was claimed, because games encouraged team-work, than because they developed male competitiveness and aggression in a way that accorded with a sub-Darwinian view of Natural Order as an endless struggle for each individual and each nation to prove that they were mightiest. 'Undersized men [were] sexually vicious' because they played 'no healthy games', Dr G. E. Morrison, a physician and *The Times* correspondent in Peking, wrote in 1910. 'Nature is the art of God, and the spirit of sport pervades it, for Nature is healthy and joyful,' declared an author praising 'British Games as Preparatory Exercises for the Greater Game of War' in 1916. Wilde's antonyms 'beautiful' and 'ugly' were replaced by 'healthy' and 'unhealthy' which connoted anything but physical salubrity. 'Wilde, together with all he stood for, was "unhealthy",' as one novelist wrote. 'Low Church was healthy, High Church with all that lace and bowing and scraping was unhealthy while Popery positively festered.' Bohemianism was healthy only if manifest in 'wide-brimmed black hats, huge pipes, beefy appetites for food and chorus girls, but nothing aesthetic or precious'. Outsiders were as suspect as individualists. 'All foreign-ness was unhealthy – the only healthy place to visit outside England were the colonies in which to carry the white man's burden through malarial swamps. Plain dirty stories were healthy enough, subtle ones were an expression of degeneracy. It was all right to like to see a woman well turned out – to know anything about her clothes was poisonous. In art galleries you might "know what you liked" but any other knowledge of art was suspect. A man could smoke a pipe, large and heavy if possible, but cigarettes were for boys and effeminates. Perhaps the unhealthiest thing of all was to know anything about decor in the home – a healthy man left that sort of fal-lal to the wife.'[43]

One example of this commitment to healthiness was given by the critic T. W. H. Crosland. In the words of Crosland's biographer in 1928, Wilde was 'a despicable fiend . . . whose name stands today for the vilest, most influential and most insidious cult in this country'. Crosland himself wrote in 1912 of Wilde's 'crowning devilry', *De Profundis*: 'a blacker, fiercer, falser, craftier, more grovelling or more abominable piece of writing never fell from mortal pen . . . his genius belonged essentially to the stews.' Crosland went to the trouble of collecting evidence from rent boys against literary men who praised Wilde's work ('one dirty Sodomite bestowing lavish whitewash upon another'), and explained during a lawsuit of 1915 'that he objected to the spreading of Wilde's doctrines among the "cheap" public' such as 'office boys': although educated men from 'the thinking public would take care of themselves', the publication of Wilde's books in cheap editions 'was a danger to the public morals'.[44]

The violence which Wilde provoked was shown during the First World War when Beverley Nichols was discovered as a teenager by his father reading *The Picture of Dorian Gray*:

> he seemed to choke. The purple deepened on his fat cheeks. He turned to me with an expression of such murderous hate that I stepped towards the wall.

'You filthy little bastard!' he screamed . . . 'Don't you dare speak to me . . . you . . . you scum!' He hurled the book at my head . . . he struck me across the mouth.

'Now . . . you pretty little bastard . . . you *pretty* little boy' (and as he said the word 'pretty' he sent his voice high and shrill, in a parody of the typical homosexual intonation) 'watch me!' . . . My father opened the book, very slowly, cleared his throat, and spat on the title page. Having spat once, he spat again; the action appeared to stimulate him. Soon his chin was covered with saliva. Then, with a swift animal gesture, he lifted the book to his mouth, closed his teeth over some of the pages, and began tearing them to shreds . . . I could conceive no crime that could possibly cause any man's name to be so hated [and asked] 'What did Wilde do?'

'What did he *do*?' He shook his head; the crime was too terrible to pass his lips. 'Oh, my son . . . my son!' he groaned. And sinking on to the bed, he burst into tears.

At dawn the next morning the father returned to his son's bedroom to explain the crime of Oscar Wilde. 'It's unfit for a decent man to say,' he said, before writing some words on a scrap of paper and issuing a final threat: 'If ever I catch you reading a book by that man again, or if ever I so much as hear you mention his name . . . I'll cut your liver out.' After his departure the son read the paper he had left. 'This was what he had written: ILLUM CRIMEN HORRIBILE QUOD NON NOMINANDUM EST.'[45]

Legislation against homosexual solicitation followed Wilde's ruin. A section of the Vagrancy Law Amendment Act of 1898 was framed 'to lay hold of a certain kind of blackguard who is unmentionable in decent society'. The Royal Commission on the Police reported in 1908 that the London police 'rarely' intervened in cases of male solicitation and were satisfied that the legislation was not used to abuse 'the disreputable class of men who solicit other men', but a deputy chairman of London Sessions appointed in 1911 was so struck by 'the large increase' in cases of 'unnatural crime' that he 'decided to try the effect of birching' as a deterrent. There were 23 sentences of 15 strokes in London during the twelve months to October 1912. Two men so condemned applied to the Court of Criminal Appeal, where they received no sympathy from the Lord Chief Justice, Alverstone. 'If ever there was a case for corporal punishment it is for that particular class of offence,' he said in judgment, hinting that the sentence would be increased if it was allowed to go to appeal. 'Flogging is right,' agreed the Liberal Home Secretary, McKenna. 'The evil has been steadily growing of late years, during a period when flogging was not administered': the birch was 'a deterrent and tending towards the absolute suppression of this particular class of unnatural vice in our midst'. McKenna was supported by Conservative backbenchers like Colonel Amelius Lockwood: 'people who have lost all sense . . . and all ideas of anything which makes a man a man' deserved 'one remedy only, a short, sharp appeal to their feelings.' Predictably one MP offered himself as flogger. How many more would today?[46]

In the Edwardian period there were calls to introduce flogging as a penalty for the 'defilement' of minors, with Sir Edward Troup of the Home Office betraying the class assumptions of the agitation when he minuted in 1905 that 'the British workman has a wholesome dislike to the idea of being flogged.' Only the poor were child molesters: certainly the rich could never be flogged. In fact there were only 29 prosecutions of men for sexually assaulting males under 16 in 1910, and 49 such cases in 1912: the idea of flogging for those convicted was rejected as likely to cause parliamentary ferment, especially as the Home Office foresaw embarrassing regional discrepancies between the number of flogging sentences, with judges in some courts getting overexcited by the opportunities given them to birch.[47]

Prison-sentencing policy for homosexuals was reviewed in 1910 by Winston Churchill, who was then Home Secretary. 'Only circumstances of rare and peculiar aggravation should', he concluded, 'be sufficient to justify a sentence of over ten years' penal servitude for a single offence unaccompanied by danger to life. Where wealth is deliberately employed to the systematic corruption of minors; where force is used with such brutality as to produce permanent injury; where there is vile treachery, as in the case of a schoolmaster, or where there is evidence of habitual concentration of a man's main activities upon criminal intercourse of this character, then that limit may be exceeded.' Prosecutions were brought under the Offences Against the Person Act of 1861 (which provided for a minimum sentence of ten years and a maximum of life imprisonment), rather than Labouchere's amendment (with its maximum sentence of two years), and Churchill considered seven years' penal servitude as an appropriate 'standard'. He decided not to remit some sentences exceeding ten years. Of a schoolmaster who 'repeatedly committed the full offence with several of his pupils during at least four years before his conviction', he felt a ten-year sentence passed in 1903 was appropriate: 'when there is moral corruption, the consequences to the victim are much worse than when there is merely a violent assault.' But he felt another sentence of 1903 of ten years 'excessive' in the case of a man convicted of sodomy in a common lodging house. 'The prisoner has already two frightful sentences of seven years' penal servitude, one for stealing lime juice and one for stealing apples,' Churchill commented. 'It is not impossible that he contracted his unnatural habits in prison.' There was also the case of a cattleman aged 23 sentenced in 1903 for an act of forcible sodomy in which the passive partner was injured. The prisoner seems to have been so disturbed that he made a bogus confession of murder and Churchill ruled that he should be released after ten years. He admonished his officials for the slackly prejudicial report on the case which they prepared for him. 'There is not much use in stating "The Captain of the boat on which he worked called him the greatest blackguard he knew." Such gossip may figure in the Police reports; it ought not to be quoted in a case of fourteen years' penal servitude.'[48]

It seems from the cases brought before Churchill that the 1861 law was invoked against unsavoury men whom the police wanted to put away for other reasons. The Home Office record of E. J. Bennett (sentenced to ten years in 1902) read: 'More than one offence was proved against him, and he was probably a systematic corruptor of boys. He tried to blackmail one of his victims, who was respectably employed.' There was clearly insufficient evidence about boys to include in any criminal charge, and this may have been innuendo: the transgression which brought such condign punishment seems to have been the embarrassment with which he threatened a consenting partner who was his social superior. Similarly the Home Office wrote of Thomas Shannon that he 'enticed' his sixteen-year-old stepson 'into bed with him and at once committed the full offence. The boy said, "I screamed out; it hurt me." He at once complained to the police; he was bleeding and in pain for several days. The crime was probably deliberate; a pot of vaseline partly used was found in the room.' The changes and evidence were so framed that Shannon was sentenced to fifteen years in 1905. But again it seems relevant that the police reported of Shannon 'that he never did any work and lived off the proceeds of crime'. Churchill consulted the lawyer and future Lord Chancellor, F. E. Smith, 'who as a prominent Conservative' regarded 'the treatment of crime and criminals from a different standpoint', but, on the evidence, they agreed that Shannon 'should be released as soon as may be'. The police had wanted to nail a man with eleven previous criminal convictions, and prompted by Labouchere and Wilde, used the 1861 act to put him out of circulation. Churchill's minutes as Home Secretary suggest that he thought that the law was being exercised unevenly and sometimes too severely; but his greatest concern focused on the nature of the evidence submitted to him, the methods by which the police in some cases collected it and the motives which sometimes lay behind a police decision to bring charges. These were concerns which were to exercise many people as they had Churchill after 1910.[49]

The hunting of homosexuals became a sport for some policemen, an almost recreational duty distinct from the difficult or dangerous task of catching thieves or preventing violence. Whenever, in the period between the wars, the London police arrested 'a Nancy-Boy', he was 'treated as an inanimate object without feeling', as one constable recorded. 'They rubbed his face with toilet paper to procure evidence of make-up, joked and laughed about him as if he were not present, and always found the same sized tin of vaseline in his pocket.' At his police station, Hammersmith, there was a small group which 'specialised in catching homosexuals. They hardly talked of anything else, working themselves into a non-stop giggling fit when they had an appreciative audience, sprinkling their anecdotes with "dirty bastards" lest anyone should think they found pleasure in what they talked about so much. They were often struck off uniform duty and, slightly disguised, concealed themselves in the bushes and urinals on Putney towpath, bringing in triumphantly about once a fortnight a couple of lonely old gentlemen caught wanking one another off, and for the next month tittering and sniggering with their friends over the details.'[50]

Public lavatories and parks were the locations for clandestine and anonymous homosexual encounters. This is a difficult area for the historian to chronicle, but these cruising grounds were clearly not just the result of legal persecution or the suppression of the subculture. At the time of the raids on molly clubs in the 1720s when public acts of sexual intercourse were more common, places like Moorfields attracted cruisers. A Conservative MP called William Bankes was accused of indecency with a soldier in a public lavatory at Westminster in 1833: although acquitted with the help of character witnesses on that occasion, he fled abroad when charged with a similar offence in a London park in 1841. Jack Saul, the rent boy narrator of *The Cities of the Plain* (1881), was picked up in a cruising area of Soho. Before 1914 Hampstead Heath and other large parks around London were nocturnal gathering places for men seeking quick sex with other men free from emotional exchanges – and were also a magnet for blackmailers, who (as *The Cities of the Plain* and other sources confirm) found younger and more inexperienced men susceptible to extortion. The best-known place for importuning in London was under the County Fire Office arches at Piccadilly Circus, which kept this character until the 1980s. Men were taunted, 'Been up the Dilly lately, dear?' even by village bumpkins. Other favourite spots were the urinals at Victoria and South Kensington stations. Small dark side-streets like Brydges Place, Dove Mews, Dudmaston Mews or Falconberg Mews were favoured by men wanting quick sex on the spot, while busier, better-lit places like Clareville Street, Leicester Square or Grosvenor Hill were cruising grounds for men who wanted to pick up someone and take him to a room. (Kenneth Ingram claimed that 'all exhibitionist obscene public writing in public places was heterosexual' before the First World War, but that by 1930 it was 'almost invariably homosexual'.)[51]

The armed services were increasingly anxious about homosexual desire: sex between men, particularly between men of different ranks, threatened hierarchical order. In fact the Guards were famed for their sexual availability to other men. 'Oh! the gallant Blues! oh, my beautiful Boy! oh, my brave Screw! What recollections!' wrote a middle-aged homosexual in 1850 after the death of a young Guardsman who had been his lover. 'When a young fellow joins, someone of us breaks him in and teaches him the trick; but there is little need of that, for it seems to come naturally to almost every young man, so few have escaped the demoralization of schools or crowded homes. We then have no difficulty in passing him on to some gentleman,' a Guardsman was reported saying thirty years later. 'Although of course we all do it for money, we also do it because we really like it, and if gentlemen gave us no money, we should do it all the same. Many of us were married, but that makes no difference [except that] we . . . do . . . not let the gentlemen know it, because married men are not in request.' There was a half-formed assumption among military authorities that homosexual acts were inevitable when men 'were corked up like soldiers in a camp' but that such acts were 'incredible' when men had access to women, to quote St John Brodrick of the War Office, writing in 1889.[52]

It was only from the 1890s on that the authorities became at all preoccupied with the subject, trying to hunt out contagion or showing signs of panic about what they thought was happening. The Indian Army's commanders protested in 1894 that if 'disorderly houses' were suppressed 'even more deplorable evils' than venereal diseases would occur ('there is already an increase in unnatural crimes'). During the First World War, the authorities tolerated prostitution, with its high risk of venereal transmission, to curtail the increased tendency to homosexual acts which they decried. 'If prostitution in a reasonable manner is rendered impossible we are likely to see an increase in worse forms of vice,' wrote an Under-Secretary at the Home Office during this time, specifying 'young officers' committing 'acts of indecency with young males'. By 1915 'the condition of things in certain busy parts of the West End of London was a scandal to civilization,' according to Sir Archibald Bodkin, soon to become Director of Public Prosecutions. The Recorder of London agreed in 1918 that 'such conduct was rife in London': it was 'appalling' that 'in many cases the persons involved were educated men'. There was said to be an increase of 119% in Home Office figures for prosecutions for 'unnatural offences' between 1915 and 1923 (compared with a 46% increase for procuring abortions and 200% for bigamy). In the period 1920–4 there was in England and Wales an annual average of 62 prosecutions for 'unnatural offences', 215 for attempted sodomy or indecent assault and 176 for indecency. Homosexuality 'spread with the rapidity of an uncontrolled epidemic', wrote Fischer and Dubois in their *History of Sexual*

Life During the World War. 'In some prison camps homosexuality claimed practically all the inmates. One by one the soldiers fell victims to the attractions of unnatural love. Even those who were by temperament the most hostile to the practice were gradually won over by the supplication of their homosexual comrades, although they themselves, in civil life, may not have even known what homosexuality was . . . The men who, after years of such practices, either came to like them, or were completely demoralized by them, could not return to normal existence. A great many of them lived like outcasts, while others, unable to bear their degradation, sought the only way out in suicide.' The survival after the Armistice in 1918 of 'many prisoners of war thus mutilated in spirit has been more tragic than that of the combatant mutilated in body'.[53]

The dangers of wartime produced in many people a rigid mental outlook and a need for strong regulatory institutions, as exemplified in the unprecented government controls over social and economic life which were introduced in the period from 1915. Nationally and privately there was vigilance for signs of disorder – political, economic or emotional – and many people willingly surrendered themselves to the grip of steel-hard conventions of thought. It is of little surprise, then, that there was a new sensitivity, and heightened fears, about sexual acts which made a nonsense of stereotypes of male aggression and social order.

Moreover, as homosexuals were perceived, to quote one psychiatrist, as 'a secret brotherhood, a kind of freemasonry that is recognized by signs', the spy manias, social tension and national insecurity of wartime provoked fears that male homosexuality was an instrument of German espionage. 'One revolting phase of German life is the aberrations of an ever-increasing rout of erotomaniacs' exercising 'great influence on German society, politics and public opinion', warned a right-wing journalist, Arnold White, in 1916. 'Some of the best intelligence officers in the world have been engaged since the war began in handling the difficult problem of the infection of Londoners, especially including soldiers, by the doctrine of the German urnings,' he explained, borrowing Ulrichs' Teuton-sounding word for homosexuals. The legalization of homosexuality was one 'of the broadstones of the German Empire': Germany wanted 'to abolish civilization as we know it, to substitute Sodom or Gomorrah for the New Jerusalem, and to infect clean nations with Hunnish erotomania'. Men only volunteered as British soldiers to defend their hearths and homes, 'but if the conception of home life is replaced by the *Kultur* of urnings, the spirit of the Anglo-Saxon world . . . perishes.' The authorities 'charged with the difficult and painful duty of controlling the depraved missionaries of German urnings' were handicapped by English common law. 'Espionage is punished by death at the Tower of London, but there is a form of invasion which is as deadly as espionage: the systematic seduction of young British soldiers by the German urnings and their agents.' White invoked the spirits of Stead and Labouchere to obtain new criminal sanctions against homosexuals. 'Under the present law the maximum penalty is two years in prison. The German urnings and their agents deserve shooting . . . Failure to intern all Germans is due to the invisible hand that protects urnings of enemy race . . . When the blonde beast is an urning he commands the urnings in other lands. They are moles. They burrow. They plot. They are hardest at work when they are most silent.'[54]

The nature of this panic emerges in the official reaction to Fred Barnes (see plate), a music hall singer who was arrested with a sailor in Hyde Park between the wars. In consequence he was officially banned from attending the Royal Tournament, the annual naval, military and aviation tattoo then held annually at Olympia, in case he corrupted the men. This humiliation seemed so provocative and petty that every year he tried to evade the cordon. A hullabaloo erupted with men rushing hither and thither each time Barnes was spotted inside Olympia. The Military Police felt 'personally insulted' and hunted him down fast and furiously. Against these forces of self-righteous authority 'scores of young sailors' meanwhile sprang to action and ran 'to find him first, to warn him of danger and hide him', as Harry Daley, who was often on duty, described. 'Surely the laughing young sailors also had sympathy for a hunted thing; and perhaps amused admiration for one who confronted with this frightening restriction imposed by the combined authority of the War Office, Air Ministry and Admiralty, should remain undaunted.' Perhaps too there was indignation that an amiably silly crooner should be thought such a dangerous pollutant that he had to be hunted down and expelled from the Royal Tournament.[55]

SOME SEAFARING GENTLEMEN MAY BE PARTICULAR

The stereotype of homosexuals as effeminate and pettish was reinforced by popular humour. This cartoon from a down-market British Sunday newspaper of 1929 is an example.

Women took an unprecedented part in the administrative expansion and industrial production required by the First World War, and as a reward, the Representation of the Peoples Act of 1918, which among other provisions disenfranchized conscientious objectors for five years, allowed women to vote for the first time. Women however were given a more demanding residential qualification for the vote, and had to be aged 30 (rather than 21), as it was feared that without this inequality, women would outnumber men in the electorate. It was a similar fear of female encroachment upon the male domain, a desire to preserve feminine submission and phallocentric power, that prompted an attempt in 1921 to amend the Criminal Law Amendment Bill to extend the penalties attaching to male homosexuality to lesbian acts. This amendment was sponsored by three Conservative MPs, Frederick MacQuisten, a Scottish lawyer, Sir Ernest Wild, who later became a judge and Recorder of London, and the vain, bumptious 'bounder' Howard Gritten. None of these MPs commanded respect in the House of Commons. MacQuisten was 'one of its distinctive personalities', because of his pungent humour and 'intense dislike of what appeared to him to be needless interference in the liberty of the subject' which led him to become 'the champion of the "small man", shopkeeper, stall-keeper, Scottish crofter or whoever'. Yet though MacQuisten, with his instinctive attachment to old ways and his humourous sallies delivered in a querulous high-set voice, was popular in the bars and smoking rooms of Parliament, in its debating chamber he was a maverick who was often quoted but whose views seldom carried any weight. Similarly it was said of Wild's membership of the Commons, 'though his voice was often heard, it cannot be said that he made any mark in the House': as a judge 'his sentences marked a healthy reaction from the sentimentality which, in its sympathy for the prisoner, forgets the wrongs of the victim.'[56]

When 'these moral weaknesses ... become prevalent ... in any country, it is the beginning of the nation's downfall', MacQuisten asserted to the Commons when introducing his proposal 'to stamp out an evil which is capable of sapping the highest and the best in civilization'. 'One cannot in a public assembly go into the details; it is more a matter for medical science and for neurologists; but all lawyers who have had criminal or divorce practice know that there is in modern social life an undercurrent of dreadful degradation' which it would be largely possible 'to eradicate' if punished by law. MacQuisten associated lesbianism with the depravity of rich users of narcotics: 'Neurologists will tell you how largely the spread of the use of cocaine and other drugs is due to the dreadful nerve deterioration which besets many of the idle part of our population.' Finally he frightened fellow MPs with the humiliating thought that they might be scorned by their wives and cuckolded by another woman: 'only tonight' he had spoken to a man whose 'home had been ruined by the wiles of one abandoned female, who had pursued his wife, and later some other conduct happened with a male person which enabled him to get a divorce'.[57]

Sir Ernest Wild's support of MacQuisten was consonant with his views on feminity. A vigorous opponent of the suffragettes, he believed that life 'was essentially a dogfight' which 'was much more pleasant when man was the top dog and woman was made . . . to do what he wished'. His idealization of womanhood moved him to poetry of an excruciating but revealing character:

> Let her be fair,
>   With silken hair,
> Rippling in waves of gold,
>   Child of the Snow-king,
> Rapture invoking,
> Seventeen winters old:
>   Eyes azure-tinted,
> Rosebuds imprinted
> On lips and dimpled cheek,
>   Form supple, slender,
> Needing defender,
> Womanly, wayward, weak.

Women who were not wayward and weak, or did not want men on top, gave Wild apprehension. Although his disgust at the physical acts of lesbianism was sincere, the threat to the traditional male role of dominance (not only in sexual acts but in social structures) caused him as much anxiety as anything else. Beyond that, he feared women as daughters of Eve, eternal temptresses working for men's ruin. 'When a woman is bad she is bad, and when she is bad she would drag you down to hell,' he declared. As to discussing lesbianism with fellow MPs, Wild hated 'to pollute the House with details of these abominations', but offered the assurance of 'nerve specialists' that 'the asylums are largely peopled by nymphomaniacs and people who indulge in this vice.' Wild identified lesbianism with national decline. It 'saps the fundamental institutions of society', he warned 'because it is a well-known fact that any woman who indulges in this vice will have nothing whatever to do with the other sex. It debauches young girls, and it produces . . . insanity.' Everyone who believed in 'the punishment of vice' would desire laws which suppressed 'a vice that must tend to cause our race to decline'.[58]

'I do not suppose that there are any members of the Labour party who know in the least what is intended by the Clause,' declared Colonel Josiah Wedgwood, a Liberal MP who opposed MacQuisten's amendment on the principle that to involve lawyers in suppressing 'vice' only spread knowledge of it. Lesbianism 'was legislated against by the Roman emperors in the past, and the Roman emperors were a very good example of the sort of people who legislated against vice. They practised every vice on earth in their youth, and when they got old they passed laws against it.' The only other MP to contradict MacQuisten was Colonel J. T. C. Moore-Brabazon, who forty years later as Lord Brabazon of Tara helped to decriminalize male homosexuality. In 1921 Moore-Brabazon felt obliged to disguise his sympathy with homosexuals. He argued that fear of punishment had never succeeded in suppressing homosexuality. 'Perverts' could be dealt with in three ways. They could be executed which, 'though drastic' at least 'stamp[ed] them out'. The second alternative was to treat them as 'lunatics, and lock them up for the rest of their lives'. But 'the best method' was to 'leave them entirely alone'. MacQuisten's proposal would only succeed in 'introducing into the minds of perfectly innocent people the most revolting thoughts'. The amendment was passed by 148 votes against 53, but was rejected in the House of Lords after being denounced by the Lord Chancellor, Birkenhead, and more tellingly, by the former Director of Public Prosecutions, Desart. (An increase in the penalties attaching to male homosexuality was considered by some MPs in 1931, but lapsed when a general election was called.)[59]

The emergence of the identity of the modern homosexual is as contradictory a story as might be expected from its component parts. On the surface Labouchere's facetious amendment, the baleful fears implicit in degenerationist psychiatry, the insecurity of the British Empire at its apogee, the crisis of the Wilde trials all combined to produce an outburst of projective hatred. Subsuming all these events were trends and attitudes which had been simmering long before the crisis of the 1890s which culminated in the Wilde trials. Labelling had begun a century earlier. Men's feelings about one another had been causing them increasing tension. Men had consequently developed elaborate rules and rituals to cope with the expectations of maleness: lies and brutality were indispensable to their enforcement.

With such complex causes, some of them so wilfully misunderstood, it is not surprising that there was confusion in the identification. On the one hand, by 1918, homosexuals were said by a senior judge, Sumner, to bear 'the hallmark of a specialized and extraordinary class as much as if they had carried on their bodies some physical peculiarities': and yet at the same time the existence of homosexuality within one's own social circle or geographical locality was often denied despite all evidence. Just as seventeenth-century English people hesitated to connect violent legal or ecclesiastical condemnations with familiar sexual acts, so 'an unspeakable of the Oscar Wilde sort' (to quote a character in E. M. Forster's novel *Maurice*) was loaded with so much revulsion that people had difficulty in relating these dismal connotations to men whom they knew. Beverley Nichols has described one early twentieth-century homosexual, Egerton Edwards, in terms which show the inability of many people, even after the Wilde trials, to recognize the possibility of homosexuality being practised by their acquaintances. 'He was to suffer the tortures of the damned, to attempt suicide, to be shut in a mental home, and to escape from it – to sink into a gutter of sensuality and to die a strange and lonely death before he had reached middle age . . . But when I first saw him, he seemed enchanting . . . He was about thirty, dark, pale, with a romantic cast of features . . . He was remarkably elegant; he wore brown suede shoes with his white flannel trousers, and there was an orchid in the button-hole of his double-breasted jacket. A solitaire emerald glittered on the little finger of his left hand, and he smoked Turkish cigarettes through a long black holder . . . Towards the end, when his looks were fading, his face was heavily rouged, and the mascara on his eye lashes was so thick that after a game of tennis, in which he performed with an erratic faun-like brilliance, his cheeks were streaked with dark rivulets. His clothes, his walk, the books he read, the company he kept . . . blazoned [homosexuality] all over him, [but] my parents had no suspicion of it; if they had guessed, they would never have allowed him in the house.'

Nichols' parents were revealingly obtuse about Egie's eccentricities. 'Did he paint his face? How amusing! Was he seen in strange company, late at night, in the local inns? He was a "Bohemian"! Did he openly proclaim his aversion to young women? He was a "dark horse" and probably kept a mistress on the sly! And did he, from the outset, show an extraordinary interest in myself, asking me to dine, to go to concerts, giving me expensive presents? It was just his "kindness"; he was eminently a "nice" friend. His grandfather was a baronet, and his people moved in very respectable circles.' How could such a person be an outcast?[60]

Although the late nineteenth-century definition of the homosexual inhibited male friendships and encouraged ostracism, the stereotype that was established was so inaccurate and yet so powerful that many men were able to perform repeated homosexual acts without being labelled homosexual. Sailors, explorers, Australian station-hands, cowboys, athletes, head prefects of schools, policemen who importuned other men in urinals and who talked compulsively of homosexuals when off duty, soldiers who went to homosexual pubs for repeated bouts of sex with other men: all of these, as we have seen, engaged in the activity, but were excluded from the identity. The force of stereotyping depended on what type of sexual partner was pursued or preferred, and when they were pursued; upon which sexual roles were assumed, and when. Labelling required self-deception, deliberate ignorance and strict inhibitions on the way in which sexuality was discussed. Everything about the process was unreal except the sorrows, wasted opportunities and denials of life which it created.[61]

CHAPTER FIVE

―――∞○∞―――

Venus Decomposing:
Sex, Disease and Punishment in the Nineteenth and Early Twentieth Centuries

> It's so unspeakably loathsome. O, if only it had been an ordinary illness.
>
> HENRIK IBSEN, *Ghosts*

> People here are crazy upon this horrid subject.
>
> LORD CROSS to LORD DUFFERIN,
> 17 May 1888

> The shadow of another cleaves to me,
> And makes me one pollution.
>
> LORD TENNYSON, 'Guinevere'

Responses to venereal diseases were redelineated in the nineteenth century as threats to Christian faith and social order took a new and more menacing form. As ideologies strengthened to the detriment of traditional worship, as social values changed or resisted change, sexual control and habits generally, and sexual diseases specifically, were invested with additional anxieties. At the same time there were convulsive demographic changes. Britain's population increased by ten millions between 1801 and 1851, with most of this increase accommodated by industrialized cities. By 1851 more than half of London's population aged twenty or more had not been born there: when country labourers became town labourers, far from the reproaches of squire, parson and neighbours, they abandoned church attendance, or any religious observance. Nearly 80% of the population lived in conurbations by the end of the century. This rejection of obedience to God was shocking not only to the clergy but to all Christian consciences; and coupled with the filth and degradation of slum life, it seemed to portend the decay of towns and cities into lawless badlands where the old etiquette and deference were lost. 'Men's instincts are utterly corrupt, and . . . everywhere, except under the influence of religion and tradition, they resort to practices ruinous to their race, and lower than any that are practised by the beast,' warned the Duke of Argyll in 1896.[1]

The moral defilement of the poor would, it was feared, lead to social disorder. A typical expression of those fears came from Mrs Edith Lyttelton Gell, wife of the first chairman of the Toynbee Hall settlement in east London and a society matron imbued with the Christian work ethic ('Whoever fears God, fears to sit at ease'). She denounced 'the smart world in all its paltriness, its futility and its vice' for setting a bad example in the 1890s. 'Evil is very infectious, and the sins of the highest (like the cut of their sleeves and the set of their skirts) have a tendency to filter down through all the grades and shades of society.' To maintain 'social order', and to resist 'the paid agitator with whose mischievous nonsense the rural districts are infested', it was essential for 'superiors' to set an example of disdain for 'pleasurable life'. Some Christians in authority were content if their dependants buckled under to show the semblance rather than genuine faith. It was conformity to authority – Obedience – that was prized. Sheffield Police Court's missionary (the Edwardian equivalent of a probation officer) averred in 1910 that 90% of the poor made no pretence of faith, but had the 'fear of God in their hearts', and were therefore willing to 'bear a good deal'. Those 'with no fear of God' were 'a law to themselves': their sexual relations were 'incredibly evil'. The whole nation was weakened by the 'horrible' sexuality 'in the squalid parts of our large towns': rather than poor diet or bad accommodation, the immorality and disobedience of the lower orders was 'breeding a puny and all but imbecile race'. The middle and upper classes in nineteenth- and early twentieth-century Britain believed in God, or in the social expedience of professing Christian obedience, and disbelieved in an open democracy based on universal suffrage. The poor however desired universal male suffrage and abandoned Christian practices. By 1895 Winnington-Ingram, then Rector of Bethnal Green and afterwards Bishop of London, estimated that only 1 per cent of men in his slum parish regularly attended church or chapel. The context for changing attitudes to sex, disease and punishment was provided by this struggle of classes and faiths. The presumed connections between sexual self-control and social restraint, or between obedient love of God and respect for secular authorities, led to a complex interplay. By the 1920s the urban poor, even if they did not feel victorious, had fulfilled the fears of Mrs Lyttelton Gell and those who thought like her. Britain in the 1920s was not only committed to universal adult suffrage, but to the distress of many was a secularized society and becoming increasingly pronounced in that tendency.[2]

In this battle for control 'medical and moral science' were 'allied', or so the physician Forbes Winslow wrote in 1840: their allegiance set the context for attitudes to venereal diseases from this period onwards. The Christian mentality and medical practice were inextricably intertwined: even when the Christian faith was explicitly denied. Many people hankering after certainty have wanted to believe that the objective truths of science empowered moral goodness. Others have identified uncertainty with illness, Matthew Arnold for example in the 1850s writing of

> this strange disease of modern life,
> With its sick hurry, its divided aims.

Diseases were weapons in the battle to enforce social order; medical ideas were never sacrosanct questions of scientific interpretation, but were given shape and meaning by the social context in which they were conceived. Syphilis was never a matter of pure diagnosis and cure: nor were other diseases such as tuberculosis, cholera, chlorosis or cancer. Early nineteenth-century cholera epidemics were seen by medical men as the scourge of sinners: the predisposing causes of infection were identified as drunkenness, dirtiness or any sort of imprudent or impulsive conduct. Those who fell ill were culpable; in a time of fear and anxiety, partly as a result of residual superstition, every type of lively or conspicuous behaviour was censured. While it is absurd to historicize all disease, and untenable to argue that all illness is socially constituted, some diseases *are* defined by both biological and cultural influences which affect epidemiological perceptions: only by understanding the way in which a disease is influenced by class, race, ethnicity, gender or other arcane forces can its natural basis be understood. It is important to add that the mediation of medicine exerts such powerful social pressure precisely because it seems to transcend social factors, and to lie in some natural or purely scientific realm.[3]

Medicine, in trying to relieve the burden of disease, relied upon the exercise of authority (derived from science) and reflected the power structures within which it existed. Its practitioners were in intimate contact with patients during crises of birth and death. They interpreted personal experiences in scientific language and met patients in circumstances which enforced their authority. People who are in pain or in fear of death yearn for reassurance, grasp at any hope or power, and will gladly surrender their private judgment for the chance of relief. In the nineteenth century they often welcomed imperious behaviour from physicians who were accorded the status of Almighty Fathers intervening between the forces of life and death (and often savagely scorned and repelled as fallen, broken deities when their interventions failed). Particularly in nineteenth-century Britain, when religious certitudes were crumbling, professional authority was a godsend in defining human needs or explaining actions and events. The more that science discredited received opinion, or undermined individual experience, the greater grew the power of those claiming special authority and objectivity. This power was reflected even in the language of those like Cosmo Lang who rejoiced in the 'stern, searching and severe' message of the New Testament, but used medical analogies in his theology. Writing in 1906, he compared 'the working of a germ of disease in the human body' (an unspecified disease, whose progress however resembles that of syphilis) to the stealthy festering of sin which results in the death of a soul as surely as the germ results in the death of the body. 'Sin is within us as a disease which is gradually and most certainly alienating us from the life of God and bringing us towards death. We are all infected by it.' Confession and penitence were 'the first essential of health'.[4]

The ways in which medical authority was exercised were inseparable from the social position of physicians. They were marginal members of the bourgeoisie, neither capitalists nor workers, surviving with ambiguous and precarious status. Some doctors were great powers in the land, like Trollope's Sir Omricon

Pie, to whom prime ministers and dukes came as suppliants, or the Royal Physician, Lord Dawson of Penn, who hastened the death of George V because he did not think a king's death should be announced first in the evening newspapers. Other medical practitioners were seedy and degraded sawbones, guzzling gin in a tenement, or like the half-qualified Lambeth abortionist Neil Cream, deadening himself with opiates. A doctor's status depended upon his patients as much as his property, family connections, educational background or hospital appointments. All of these in turn could influence his diagnosis and treatment. As the social position of physicians was unusually exposed, their aspirations were correspondingly pronounced. Because of their social marginality, physicians tended to stress middle-class values expressed in scientific phraseology: they stereotyped the poor as undisciplined, improvident and immoral, and the aristocracy as sybarites, indicting both classes for deviating from middle-class normality.[5]

The career of the venereologist Sir Alfred Cooper demonstrates the workings of the patron-patient system and the role of social ambition in medicine. Cooper had a hard start to life because of his father's early death, and had little success with his practice until he was consulted by a rich man who lived by chance in the vicinity of his waiting room. 'The patient was so satisfied with young Cooper's appearance, manner and treatment, that he gave him the benefit of his patronage,' to quote the *British Medical Journal* in 1908: 'Cooper soon afterwards began to prosper, his geniality and tact being powerful factors in his favour.' He established himself as honorary surgeon to fashionable regiments with nicknames like the Devil's Own, and became popular in St James's clubs and as a Freemason. His manner was perfectly judged for the rich young blades who came to him with venereal infections. The status of his clientele was further elevated when he took as his patient the wild young Duke of Hamilton and Brandon: 'unweighted by any sense of responsibility and beset by all the deadly sins in a far greater degree than perhaps any other young nobleman', as one obituarist described, Hamilton 'seemed strong enough to fell an ox with his fist', but had desperate need of a venereologist. In gratitude he not only gave Cooper a holiday house in Scotland, but 'introduced [him] into high society, for which he was by nature fitted'. Cooper became 'a fine judge of claret', physician to royal princes, married the Duke of Fife's sister, was knighted, and as another doctor wrote in awe, 'was more than once selected to shoot with Lord Ashburnham and Prince Duleep Singh, famed as the pick of good shots'. He was a dependant of the rich, but lived gloriously: and left sufficient substance for his son to marry a duke's daughter and become a Cabinet minister.[6]

Language has been a powerful force in sexual expression, and in the oppression of those who have not accepted coercive discipline. Those who had the misfortune to contract syphilis were often labelled as rebels or deviants, or depicted as culprits. Increasingly their course of life was vilified, and their personal experiences falsified to serve social policy. Their example was used to frighten and to discipline. 'To be good, according to the vulgar standard of goodness,' wrote Oscar Wilde, 'merely requires a certain amount of sordid terror, a certain lack of imaginative thought, and a certain low passion for middle-class respectability.' Syphilis, as if it was not nasty enough, was appropriated to inspire sordid terror, to stunt imaginative development and to deny human diversity. The physical reality of syphilis was distorted not only to degrade those with the disease, but to frighten people away, to quote an Anglican clergyman of 1889, from the 'dangerously narrow borderland between fastness and positive vice'.[7] Dread of venereal disease was stimulated as a matter of public policy: the sexual act was forced to connote danger.

Given the restrictions on sexual discourse that existed in Britain, and which will be examined in more detail later, 'French novels' were directly or indirectly, the source of many Englishmen's ideas of eroticism. One of the best known was Zola's *Nana* (1880), in which representations of the perils of sexual exuberance reached their apotheosis in the death of the vivacious and beautiful prostitute heroine. The final paragraph reads:

> What lay on the pillow was a charnel-house, a heap of pus and blood, a shovelful of putrid flesh. The pustules had invaded the whole face, so that one pock touched the next. Withered and sunken, they had taken on the greyish colour of mud, and on that shapeless pulp, in which the features had ceased to be discernible, they already looked like mould from the grave. One eye, the left eye, had completely foundered in the bubbling purulence, and the other, which remained half open,

looked like a dark, decaying hole. The nose was still suppurating. A large reddish crust starting on one of the cheeks was invading the mouth, twisting it into a horrible grin. And around this grotesque and horrible mask of death, the hair, the beautiful hair, still blazed like sunlight and flowed in a stream of gold. Venus was decomposing.

Nana did not die of syphilis in Zola's account, but her death was hastened by her eroticism: the penalty of carnality was decomposition. Zola's unforgettable language was that of a great novelist, but those who professed to examine syphilis clinically were scarcely less lurid. The language in which 'this mournful subject' was discussed endlessly reiterated the 'horrible realities' of syphilis, its 'terrible doom' and 'extremely loathsome' forms, to quote an article of 1869.[8]

According to a doctor testifying to a Government committee of 1904, syphilis was 'a foul and loathsome disease' implying 'a breach of the moral laws'. Public knowledge of such a disease not only caused 'shame and reproach' but, if known to the diseased's employers, would 'probably' result in dismissal. Syphilis was seen in 1913 as 'a truly horrible and dangerous disease . . . because of the hideous potentialities, its insidious latency, its terrible, and often fatal, later effects'. It represented, according to the oculist Sir James Barrett, 'the pathological and seamy side of society'. Syphilis not only disgraced individuals, but was thought to jeopardize the nation's existence. Another physician, Sir Victor Horsley, lamented in 1904 that, owing to improved treatment, many syphilitics survived to 'produce stunted and diseased offspring': he stopped short of advocating that they be forcibly sterilized, 'though I think they deserve to be'. Venereal disease was a 'problem of enormous but unknown dimensions', declared the President of the Eugenics Education Society, Leonard Darwin, in 1917, on behalf of those who feared that syphilis would lead to 'general racial degeneracy, or to an *indefinable* deterioration in the nation in the future'.[9]

Nor was syphilis simply corrupt and morbid in every sense: it was an invisible and ubiquitous contagion that could attack anyone in almost any form. 'This most destructive enemy', wrote a mid-Victorian, is not only 'ceaseless . . . in the midst of us' but 'pervades every rank of society; its traces may be discovered in almost every family; its Protean and ever-changing forms are too numerous to be computed, and often elude detection even by the most experienced eyes; it attacks by preference the young and vigorous.' In his excitement the writer even seemed to declare that chastity or monogamy were futile against syphilis even if they were widely possible: 'it respects neither virtue, nor purity, nor innocence, which are alike defenceless against its indiscriminating and corrupting influence.' An Edwardian commentator described those with syphilis or gonorrhoea as a 'poisoned army' which 'moves about in slum and drawing-room, unsuspected and unspotted', and Lord Ranksborough in 1919 called syphilis an 'invisible demon'.[10]

Syphilis was the target of every hostile feeling. The aggression and anxiety which so many people inwardly harboured found a focus in venereal disease. 'It is the greatest enemy we have in our midst,' according to Lord Downham, who was President of the Local Government Board, the forerunner of the Ministry of Health. 'It is the enemy of man, the enemy of woman, the enemy of the child, the enemy of the home, the enemy of the nation, and the enemy of the Empire.' It was the universal enemy. 'This secret scourge', according to his successor, Lord Rhondda, 'is an Imperial question, I might call it a worldwide question.'[11]

The medical impact of these infections was never understated. Whatever the prognosis given in private by physicians to patients (and these were sometimes too optimistic), public statements from the medical profession were almost invariably dire. Pathologically it was 'the fourth of the killing diseases and – worse still – the first of the misery producing diseases', one authority wrote. Venereal diseases, declared Sir Archdall Reid in 1920, 'constitute a principal, if not quite the principal, cause of poverty, insanity, paralysis, blindness, heart disease, disfigurement, sterility, disablement and the life of pain to which many women are condemned'.[12]

The corollary of making nineteenth-century laws 'a school of public discipline' or repository of 'public conscience', as described in the preceding chapter, was that the threat of social disgrace and rejection coerced people into abstaining from illicit pleasures. People were only frightened of what the neighbours would say if neighbours were predictably censorious, or if transgressors were fixed for life with the stigma of badness. 'The conviction that moral character is unalterable, [that] a single bad action implies that future actions of the same kind will, under similar circumstances, also be bad' was, according to Schopenhauer, writing in mid-century, 'well expressed by the English use of the word *character* as meaning credit, reputation, honour.' One lapse into illicit conduct had irreversible effects. A good character, once lost, could not be recovered: otherwise the system of coercion and ostracism would disintegrate. Thus any unmarried woman who gave herself to a man was judged to have betrayed 'the whole female race, because its welfare would be destroyed if every woman were to do likewise; so she is cast out with shame as one who has lost her honour,' Schopenhauer observed. She was defiled and contagious: 'no woman will have anything more to do with her: she is avoided like the plague.' Meddling rudeness and fears of contamination were justified almost as Christ's work. Such developments spawned a divisive, suspicious unkindness between women. 'English ladies are conspicuous over all the world for the sour, merciless and undiscriminating austerity with which they repulse the efforts of a woman who has gone wrong to set herself socially right again,' John Morley confirmed in 1870. Quite apart from the inherent perniciousness of harsh and meddlesome moralizing, such attitudes could engender a world in which petty malice was habitual and in which aspersions blackened the most ordinary social interchanges. People were nasty because they had forgotten how to be otherwise. A young woman shortly to marry Lord Dufferin and Clandeboye visited his neighbours Lord and Lady de Ros in 1861. 'I do hate that sort of *crushing* ill nature which quietly ascribes to *bad motives* innocent actions, and that biting sneering sarcasm (in which the de Ros's excel) which seems like some burning wind to scorch and dry up every particle of good out of the character over which it passes,' she reported later to her fiancé. 'I got so tired of hearing characters killed, morning, noon and night.'[13]

Venereal diseases provided useful ammunition for this glum, fearful and often cruel mentality. Over and over again a distinction was drawn between 'guilty' and 'innocent' patients. Lord Gainford, sometime President of the Board of Education, spoke in 1917 of 'poor suffering children in the slum areas . . . innocent in themselves, but unfortunately . . . called upon to bear the sins of their fathers'. Lord Burnham, a newspaper owner who tried to take a generous attitude towards those with venereal disease, still spoke in 1919 of men suffering 'the effects of their own misconduct'.[14]

This compulsion to label the majority of those with the disease as culprits encouraged the myth that infection was a just affliction for wrongdoing. One Conservative politician, Joseph Henley ('the shrewdness of his homely sayings gained him the esteem of all parties'), opposed legislative measures against venereal disease in 1866 because they would 'remove all the penalties which a higher Power had imposed upon sin, and to give the opportunity of sin without the punishment'. 'In his wisdom and mercy towards fallen men, God has been pleased', declared the Roman Catholic Bishop of Victoria, Charles Richard Alford, to establish 'as a natural result' of fornication 'shame, disease, pain and even death. There are many who would be guilty of the sin, could they with certainty escape the threatened penalty. They would crowd the harlots' houses could they hope to escape the lurking pestilence.' Of course people gripped by such cruel superstitions were liable to confuse themselves and fall into contradiction. Although Randall Davidson, Archbishop of Canterbury, told the House of Lords in 1919 that the argument that venereal diseases were 'a Divine . . . mode of punishing wrongdoing' was 'undesirable and ineffective', only a year earlier his chaplain had summoned a doctor to discuss a standard lecture being given to soldiers on safer sex techniques, had 'said that the Archbishop considered it had immoral tendencies' and had attributed to Davidson the belief 'that in a lecture on such a subject, it ought, at least, to be plainly stated that venereal disease is God's punishment for sin'. Most probably, Davidson wavered in his notions. Ratepayers in places like Plymouth opposed local measures to reduce venereal disease lest this increase municipal expenditure: they demanded, 'why should we tax ourselves for the purpose of putting down a disease which some people say is a just punishment for particular offences.' It was rare for such bigotry to win medical concurrence. 'Far from considering syphilis an evil', a London surgeon called Samuel Solly declared in 1860 that 'he regarded it, on the contrary, as a blessing, and believed that it was inflicted by the Almighty to act as a restraint upon the indulgence of evil passions. Could the disease be exterminated, which he hoped it could not, fornication would ride rampant through the land.' This view was so unwelcome to his colleagues that it cost Solly the Presidency of the Royal College of Surgeons, which was his by reversion, in 1870.[15]

The idea of guilt became inseparable from venereal infections: it perplexed the morbidly disturbed and haunted the furtively guilty. Thus the Brides in the Bath murderer, George Joseph Smith, who married and drowned a succession of women whose lives he had insured, falsely accused the first of his victims of having infected him. 'You have blighted all my bright hopes of a happy future,' he wrote to her in 1910. 'I have caught from you a disease which is called the bad disorder. For you to be in such a state proves you could not have kept yourself morally clean.' Smith himself was a bigamist and professional seducer, with a string of criminal convictions, whose life had been anything but 'clean'; but he projected the dirt onto his victim, a bank manager's lonely daughter who was vulnerable to him precisely because of her purity. 'For the sake of my health and honour', he told her, 'I must go to London and act entirely under doctor's advice.' With his guilty past and guilty intentions, it was not by chance that in his projective paroxysm Smith accused the woman whom he was shortly to murder of having a guilty disease. Some criminologists have suggested that the murders in 1888–9 of Whitechapel prostitutes by Jack the Ripper were committed in vengeance by a man who had contracted a venereal infection from a whore, but this is unproven. It is true that, apart from Smith, other men who took their hatred of women to the extreme of multiple murder were obsessed with syphilis. Frederick Deeming, who killed several women and cemented their bodies under kitchen or scullery floors, 'said that he had murdered these women because they spread a vile infection' before he was hanged in 1892. A similar suggestion was made about Neil Cream, who poisoned several Lambeth prostitutes – with strychnine, to inflict the utmost pain – in the same year.[16]

Much of the official response to venereal diseases was dictated by their impact on the armed forces. Indeed the role of journeying soldiers in transmitting infection had been notorious since the siege of Naples and its sequel in the 1490s. The bounds of controversy were set by naval and military statistics of infection, the accuracy of which mattered less then the uses to which they were put. During the Crimean War venereal diseases vitiated troop strength almost as seriously as malnutrition, tuberculosis and dysentery. Florence Nightingale and her allies wrestled to solve the problem in the late 1850s, but without avail. By 1860 one-quarter of the Foot Guards in London had syphilis. One-third of all sick cases among soldiers were venereal in origin by 1864, and hospital admissions for gonorrhoea or syphilis accounted for 30% of troop strength. In the Navy venereal patients accounted for 12.5% of sailors admitted in 1862. Troops returning from service in India were a grave source of infection: it was estimated that two-thirds of military hospital patients at Baroda as early as 1824 were venereal, and that 31% of the army strength in Bengal was so infected in 1828. Lock hospitals were first established in the subcontinent in 1805, but were often shut to save money, sometimes under the pretext that levels of infection had abated. The rate of venereal infection in the Army rose steeply in 1862, following the return to Britain of troops from India where disease was rife, and this increase so shocked the Secretary for War, Lord de Grey (later Ripon), that he introduced several members of the medical profession to his Cabinet colleague, the Duke of Somerset, who was First Lord of the Admiralty.[17]

De Grey was an evangelical friend of Christians like F. D. Maurice, Charles Kingsley and Thomas Hughes. A 'hard-working, conscientious, kindly' man with faith in Victorian progress and Christian redemption, he 'only saw the real lions in the path, and them he would, without hesitation, attack with any available weapon', to quote a friend. In contrast Somerset 'was a typical Whig aristocrat: haughty and sarcastic in manner, able as an administrator, unusually well read, with some scientific knowledge, a free-thinker in religion, as to which he cared neither to conceal nor to propagate his opinions'. After discussions between de Grey and Somerset, the Christian meliorist and the agnostic pessimist, and other consultations by them, a parliamentary committee was appointed under the chairmanship of Admiral Lord Clarence Paget, MP, the Secretary of the Admiralty. This committee's proposals were presented by Paget to the House of Commons in 1864, at dinner time when only about fifty MPs were present, and were passed without debate as the first Contagious Diseases Act. The phrase 'Contagious Diseases' was taken from the Contagious Diseases (Animals) Act, appropriately enough because official policy towards venereal disease in prostitutes

Earl de Grey (afterwards Marquess of Ripon), the Christian
meliorist who described himself as one of the chief authors of the
Contagious Diseases Acts.

resembled their strategy against cattle plague and scab, and
several MPs confused Paget's proposals with existing animal
legislation.[18]

The new law empowered the compulsory hospitalization of any
woman who, on the sworn evidence of one policeman in closed
court, before a magistrate, was 'suspected' of being 'a prostitute'
in 'protected districts' surrounding major Army camps and naval
bases, such as Aldershot, Shorncliffe, Salisbury and Rochester in
England, Cork, The Curragh and Dublin in Ireland, and after
1869, Canterbury, Devonport and Winchester. The Act defined

neither prostitution nor soliciting. The magistrate could, if he judged the case proven, commit the woman for examination by an Army surgeon, with detention and treatment in a special hospital for up to three months if she was found to be diseased. (Three months was far too short a time for an effective cure.) These arrangements were initially seen as humane and progressive efforts in confronting an undeniable evil.[19]

The Contagious Diseases Acts were enforced from 1864 until 1883 against a scapegoated minority, women. The men who framed this legislation believed that exact scientific laws of social improvement could be identified and enforced. They saw the laws as part of the mid nineteenth-century scheme of urban sanitary reform, compulsory vaccination against smallpox and factory acts; a scheme which it was easier to develop if women were treated as particularly responsible for spreading venereal infections. Periodical examinations of soldiers for syphilis had been abandoned in 1859 as 'repugnant to the feelings of the men', except in the Coldstream Guards where they continued at intervals of ten days for every man up to the rank of corporal who was a bachelor (officers were not subjected to such indignity). But whores had no legal rights, and were so degraded that further indignities seemed not to matter. The prostitute could be treated, in Dr William Acton's phrase, as an 'emissary of death'. This feeling reflected men's fear of powerful and mysterious temptresses or betrayed male fantasies about women's bodies as devouring holes or pits of muck. Even Tennyson in 1858 had likened the wiles of the adulterous Queen Guinevere to the surreptitious, lethal spread of syphilis among unprotected lovers:

> taken everywhere for pure,
> She like a new disease, unknown to men,
> Creeps, no precaution used, among the crowd,
> Makes wicked lightnings of her eyes, and saps
> The fealty of our friends, and stirs the pulse
> With devil's leaps, and poisons half the young.

It was women, with their devilish flirting or witch-like ways, who were threatening the fraternity of men and spreading poison through the crowd.[20]

The lack of discourse which characterized the parliamentary passage of the Contagious Diseases Act was seen as crucial to its progress. A War Office spokesman attributed its successful operation 'without scandal, or any local public discussion' to the fact that its costs were centrally funded, and that the law was applied by the police with 'very great tact'; secrecy was maintained so far as possible. As de Grey said, the War Office always intended 'to work the Act as quietly as possible', and his officials agreed that in this respect, 'it has been worked remarkably well by the police.' 'It would never do', testified a Liverpool medical man, for anyone dealing with prostitution to 'be opening to the daylight what they went there for'.[21]

As Lord Palmerston's Government failed to fund the special hospitals stipulated under Paget's original Act of 1864, the law's futility was soon unmistakable, and it was revised in 1866. A new Act introduced by Paget provided for compulsory three-monthly examinations of prostitutes, again on the sworn evidence of one policeman, in closed court, before a single magistrate, and introduced compulsory regular examination of suspected women within a radius of ten miles of a protected area. A further clause, notoriously ill-drafted, made a brothel-keeper harbouring diseased prostitutes liable to two years' imprisonment with hard labour. This Act of 1866 was again passed virtually without debate, at 2 a.m., with most MPs ignorant of its purpose and provisions: it was a fine illustration of the evils which result from legislation passed late at night. Gladstone, who had been rescuing prostitutes since his youth and was a member of the Cabinet, still thought that the 1866 Act applied to animals.[22]

Like its predecessor, the Act was anomalous. Some prostitutes lived outside the radius of ten miles around a protected area, and went by train to pick up men; others lived near the camps under the protection of officers, certain that local police would not dare to accuse them. Women brought before a magistrate could forestall an examination order by asserting that they were menstruating: a claim which often so revolted the (male) magistrate that he dismissed the case immediately. As a result of these continuing deficiencies, the 1866 Act was amended in 1869: the protected area was given a radius of 15 miles with the hope that the higher cost of travel would deter prostitutes from commuting to their customers at military bases; a new clause provided for five days' compulsory incarceration of women before examination without commital procedure or trial, with no provision for release by habeas corpus, so as to prevent women escaping examination by claiming that they were menstruating.

Prostitutes detained under the Acts were given few chances to change their lives, and were confined in huts or barracks primitively adapted into hospitals. The women were examined in washrooms supplied only with cold water; the process was hurried and brutal; speculum examinations were painful, especially when performed by hearty physicians contemptuous of their patients. Examinations were often conducted at a known time each week in a room which could be seen by loiterers outside: at Devonport, for example, they occurred fortnightly on Thursday at the dockyard, whose workers cheered the women when they arrived, and jostled at the windows to watch the speculum examinations. Within the dockyard this event was known as Fuck Fair, and local children refined a new game of 'doctors, prostitutes and examinations'. As a result women detained at Aldershot were kept behind blinds drawn to prevent passing soldiers from seeing the inmates, and were thus condemned to exist in perpetual murkiness. Each hospital had solitary confinement cells for refractory patients, and the matrons reported that many women arrived in such a state of fury or excitement that they needed 'taming' in their cells. In chapel, as befitted 'fallen women', they were kept in silence behind screens, like convicts.[23]

Nevertheless Francis Mallalieu, a superintendent of the Contagious Diseases Police, believed that he was exercising 'a law of kindness to the women': while Lord Lilford found it a source of national pride that Britain had 'a voluntary system of protection', characterized by 'kindness and good treatment', in contrast to 'the continental system of coercion'. The actual implementation of these laws involved coercive exploitation, possibly of an extensive sort. A study of Victorian prostitution in York has shown that about one-sixth of men using local whores were police officers, and policemen must have been tempted to demand sex with women as the price of excluding them from Contagious Diseases examinations. Given the pleasure that many men receive from the sexual humiliation of women, and the contempt in which whores were held, it must have been irresistible for some policemen to exert duress or extort intercourse, and then to denounce the women they had used. This double use of male power would have been an ultimate gratification to some. The reality of 'voluntary submission', as it was described by Berkeley Hill of the London Lock Hospital, was coercive discipline: there was little resistance to the Acts or misconduct, an Admiralty official reported with satisfaction in 1868, because inmates were 'punished by a fortnight or a month's imprisonment for breaking some article in the room, or some trifling thing of that kind'. In contrast to these official pretences, as Sir Harcourt Johnstone said in 1875, moralizing 'advice' had 'little' effect precisely because it was 'compulsory'; 'in fact these women know just as well as we do that they are not imprisoned from motives of kindness, but to give security to men' even if the policy was covered 'with the cloak of a spurious morality or with a coating of State varnish'.[24]

It was possible to brutalize women, and yet to maintain they were being humanised, partly by a failure of imagination, and partly because the victims of the Acts already seemed so debased. 'These Acts affect the very dregs of the population – the lowest kind of prostitute on the one hand, and on the other the most vicious of the common soldiers,' claimed the Liberal politician John Morley a year later. There were 'masses of men and women who are virtually in the condition of barbarians, and whose practices can only be repressed by the same wisely coercive methods which have always been essential to raise a barbarous community into a civilized state'. The fate of camp followers, or army prostitutes, was indeed miserable: they became prostitutes at puberty and survived on their meagre earnings, rotten with venereal scabs, until wrecked by beatings, hunger and delirium tremens. One venereologist described the prostitutes known as Bushrangers who lived in sand caves outside Aldershot military camp, half-naked and semi-insensate with adulterated liquor: 'The women were very dirty – in fact filthy, covered with vermin, like idiots in their manner, very badly diseased; they almost burrowed in the ground like rabbits, digging holes for themselves in the sandbanks' (their counterparts at The Curragh at Dublin sheltered in hedges and were hence known as the Curragh wrens). Supporters of the Acts claimed that the legislation was 'marvellous' for such creatures, to quote Sir Claud Alexander of the Grenadier Guards: the loss of personal liberty was nothing compared to serving God. The prostitute was redeemed and uplifted by the Acts. 'Think of her as she once crouched and burrowed in the ground at Aldershot, calling out in her agony –

THE GREAT SOCIAL EVIL.

TIME:—Midnight. A Sketch not a Hundred Miles from the Haymarket.

Bella. "AH! FANNY! HOW LONG HAVE YOU BEEN *GAY?*"

"Do not touch me or I shall fall to pieces", and of her as she now is in hospital, attended, sympathized with and cared for. Think of her as she once crouched naked behind the bushes of the Curragh, and of her now clothed and in her right mind . . . Violate, if you please, the principles of Magna Charta, but do not violate the commands' of the Almighty.[25]

The Acts yielded some benefits. Both juvenile prostitution and the incidence of venereal disease were slightly reduced within areas covered by the legislation, although it is likely that infected prostitutes moved elsewhere (particularly to London) to pursue their livelihoods. Lord Lilford's committee which reported in 1868 found it 'frightful' that an infected prostitute 'must still ply her trade or starve', and therefore moved to London or another town where the Acts did not apply. 'To deaden her feelings she lives in a whirl of drunkenness and debauchery, delaying her cure and spreading the disease to the utmost of her power.'[26]

The secrecy surrounding the Acts of 1864–6, and the inhibitions on public discourse, meant that opposition to the legislation was slow to muster. A formidable agitation ignited after 1870, led by a redoubtable campaigner, Josephine Butler. 'Men steeped in sin . . . have hypocritically cloaked their own sensuality in the outward garb of punishing the being whom they alone have brought to shame,' the abolitionists felt. Such men made prostitutes 'the scapegoat of their brutishness – of their animal passions unhallowed by affection, and have paraded their own self-righteousness by driving her into the wilderness of social outlawry, moral degradation, and physical disease'. Josephine Butler in turn was attacked as '. . . frenzied, unsexed, and utterly without shame'. There was also a more subtle or patronizing devaluation of the efforts of her supporters. 'Declamatory *a priori* methods are the incurable vice of women when they come to political subjects,' explained John Morley in 1870 on behalf of those who 'believe in the progress of the human race . . . but only on condition of enlightened and strenuous effort on the part of persons of superior character and opportunity', such as himself. His first priority was to save 'an unborn generation from a deadly disease' which would leave it 'tormented and enfeebled by the vices of its ancestors', and thus he deplored the tendency of Josephine Butler's group 'to sacrifice the health and vigour of unborn creatures to the "rights" of harlotry to spread disease without interference'.[27]

It was not until 1883 that a motion against compulsory examination was carried in the House of Commons. This success was less a consequence of long agitation than the fact that some repealers persuaded the National Liberal Federation to declare its opposition to the Acts. Gladstone's Government needed the Federation's cooperation, and the Contagious Diseases Acts were a useful issue in political bargaining: although his Cabinet was divided on the issue, they agreed to allow Liberal MPs to vote howsoever they wished. In the event the House of Commons divided to vote earlier than Tory whips had expected, and they failed to collect their usual supporters in time. The Acts were suspended until financial grants for Contagious Diseases Police and lock hospitals in protected areas were abolished in 1885–6.[28]

The workings of the Contagious Diseases Acts in Britain are usually considered in isolation, but they were in reality inseparable from the policies followed in the Indian Empire, which had for so long been a source of infection whenever British troops returned from service there. A system of lock hospitals, combined with legally enforcible examination of whores ('Queen's ladies') living in 'regimental bazaars', was inaugurated there in 1864 to inconsistent effect; and policies were thrown into further disarray by the appointment of the Marquess of Ripon as Viceroy in 1880. In his own words he had been (as Lord de Grey), twenty years earlier, 'one of the authors' of the first Contagious Diseases Act in Britain, but he had since converted to Roman Catholicism, and judged that the Indian legislation went 'far beyond the English laws' by imposing 'a system of registration, not only of prostitutes, but of brothel-keepers, which the framers of the English law thought extremely objectionable'. Informed by his officials that registration was indispensable under Indian conditions, he hoped to dismantle the system.[29]

As a consequence of Ripon's susceptibilities, combined with other agitation, the Indian Contagious Diseases Acts were gradually suspended after 1881, and by 1888 were operating only in Bombay, Madras and Bassein, Lower Burma. The political pressures which necessitated this were almost universally deplored by British officials in India. 'For a young man who cannot marry and who cannot attain to the high moral standard required for the repression of physiological natural instincts, there are only two ways of satisfaction, *viz.* masturbation and mercenary love,' wrote the Surgeon General of India in 1886. 'The former . . . leads to disorder both of body and mind; the latter, to the fearful dangers of venereal.' He denied that compulsory examination 'exerts a deteriorating moral influence on the women' because 'for the confirmed prostitute no further degeneration is possible'. Prostitution differed entirely between Britain and India, wrote the senior civilian responsible for the Indian Army, Sir George Chesney, in 1888. Any whore operating 'west of Buda Pesth' he characterized as 'a fallen woman who, having been seduced from virtue in the first instance, is compelled by want and disgrace to pursue . . . a loathsome calling hateful to herself, and who, having once become a social outcast, can hardly ever . . . escape from the . . . degradation into which she has fallen'. But it was different for Orientals. 'India abounds in castes or sects of prostitutes with whom the calling is hereditary, who are born in and bred to that profession, and who in their turn bring up children to be the same.' Indians lost no self-respect by prostituting themselves: Indian whoredom was 'not attended with the misery and degradation which are its companions in the west'. Chesney took an over-idealized view of Indian conditions since even the Calcutta Public Health Committee, which supported state regulation of prostitution, reported 'horrible foams of suffering' among the 'pitiable and revolting' women 'who crawl to the Lock Hospitals, to die in torture'.[30]

The attitudes of men like Chesney led newspapers like *The Christian* to produce headlines such as BRITISH INDIAN GOVERNMENT IN AGREEMENT WITH HELL: INFIDEL GOVERNMENT IN INDIA. The proposal by a senior medical officer of the Indian Army that medical officers should instruct soldiers with 'practical hygienic knowledge' to avoid 'the consequences of the risks' (washing immediately after intercourse, or using condoms where available) was denounced as 'a hideous, filthy and infidel suggestion' by Alfred Dyer, editor of the influential Indian weekly *Sentinel*. 'No wonder that under . . . officials who countenance and allow their unholy expedients, the British Army in India is rotting away, and that the British soldier is being made into a half-brute and a half-devil,' Dyer exclaimed in 1888. 'Because God is true to His Word, and to the law of cause and effect which He has set in the human body, such remedies must necessarily be as futile as they are filthy.' Bowing to the

This woodcut (ascribed to Albrecht Dürer) was the first visual representation of a syphilitic, dated 1496. With his long hair, plumed hat, voluminous cloak and slashed shoes, the syphilitic is depicted as a fop, and perhaps also would have been identifiable to the German readers of this broadside as a foreigner, specifically a Frenchman. The zodiacal signs above the syphilitic's head attribute the origin of the disease to the conjunction in 1484 of five planets in the sign of the Scorpion, the zodiacal sign ruling genitalia.

Hogarth's famous picture of venereal patients consulting a quack is discussed in the text *(page 49)*.

The earliest identified male transvestite. Edward Hyde, Lord Cornbury, afterwards Earl of Clarendon, dressed to resemble his cousin Queen Anne while serving as Governor of New York.

Lord George Germain (Viscount Sackville) and Sir Benjamin Thomson
(Count von Rumford) whose affair in the 1770s and 1780s was well-known.

A broadsheet of 1816 depicting Sir Eyre Coote ('the curious beast') enjoying his sado-masochistic romps with the schoolboys of Christ's Hospital.

This broadsheet of 1822 depicts the arrest in a Haymarket tavern of the Bishop of Clogher and Guardsman Moverley. The arresting officer makes two punning allusions: to Sodom (from which Lot fled) and to sodomy ('come to the back hole'). While some bystanders want to send the miscreants to the pillory or hang them in chains, others think they belong in China or Turkey, countries where the English imagined sodomy was prevalent.

The Bishop of SODOM and his Fancy GOMORRAH.

As 'this monster' the Bishop of Clogher is taken away, a bystander explains that he has been 'making a mistake in the fundamental laws of the kingdom'. Guardsman Moverley is admonished, 'step on don't be ashamed to follow your deary'. Other bystanders comment on the prevalence of sodomy among parsons and the peerage, while others gibe at Lord Courtenay, William Beckford and Sir Eyre Coote. A street girl says vindictively, 'give it him well, it's such monsters as these will be the ruin of us poor girls'.

The Victorian Lord Chancellor, the Earl of Halsbury, contributed powerfully to the new social construction of homosexuality in the 1880s and 1890s, and was an important influence on the increased intervention of police and lawyers in matters of personal sexuality.

Harry Quilter, fist suitably covered in leather, was a journalist who excelled himself in attacking Oscar Wilde after his downfall, and the doyen of the new wave of critics who extolled philistinism and brutality after 1895.

pressure of Christian moralists, many cantonment lock hospitals were experimentally closed during Ripon's viceroyalty. In a typical case, at Rawalpindi, where the hospital shut in 1884, it was reported by the commanding officer that the percentage of venereal cases doubled in a year. Forty-four per cent of the garrison had in twelve months been 'poisoned by this disease', which was gaining in virulence. 'The blood of the greater part of the Army is being rapidly polluted, and it is clear that the health and constitution of a vast proportion of the whole British nation is being rapidly, gratuitously and needlessly destroyed.'[31]

Ripon's successor as Viceroy, Dufferin, wanted to 'take whatever precautions are possible to prevent diseased women contaminating our soldiers, without offering the latter ostentatious facilities for getting at healthy ones': which meant abandoning the Contagious Diseases Acts, but strengthening the lock hospital system and retaining cantonments. 'The young and inexperienced soldiers who are annually brought to India' ran higher risks than 'older and more experienced men', he wrote. Dyer was 'a fanatical cad' and 'the shrieking sisterhood ... who have constituted themselves the champions of military chastity' would 'allow death and disease to be propagated wholesale throughout the British Army'. Chesney was equally scornful of 'preachers' who demanded of other people 'a life of absolute chastity' outside marriage. Such preachers were mostly married, 'and the standard of morality which denounces fornication, and assumes that all sexual intercourse is innocent if covered by the sanction of marriage is to say the least a lamentably low one.' Fornication caused much of the world's misery, but an equal measure of misery was 'due to improvident and reckless marriages, to bringing children into the world without the means of supporting them, to the ruin of woman's health for the gratification of the man's passion. That the one state of things is wholly bad and the other wholly good and pure, is an absolutely false presentment.'[32]

As a result of the moralists' persistence, and various indiscretions or silly, wanton falsehoods by the military authorities, the lock hospital system and cantonment rules were abolished in principle in 1888, and in actuality in 1894. This led to counter-agitation. 'We have only to thank the absurd prudery and noisy shouting of ... narrow-minded fanatics' for the ill-health of the British Army: 'not only our young soldiers, but young England is being demoralized,' complained a soldier, Lord Malmesbury, in *The Times* in 1895. He felt that the nation was weakened and national traditions were corrupted by syphilis. 'Bring in again the Contagious Diseases Act and help the struggling humanity of the rising generation to be able to defend our shores and keep Englishmen as they were in the olden days.' By 1896 the annual rate of VD admissions among British troops in India had reached 52%, and a governmental committee of enquiry was appointed under Lord Onslow, then Under-Secretary of State at the India Office.[33]

Onslow's committee reported that 26,247 men in 1894, representing only 37%, of British troops in India, had never contracted venereal disease, whether in India or at home; and that annually some 13,000 soldiers left India, most of them for civilian life in Britain, of whom only 4% were already married. If 96% of the men returning to settle in Britain were bachelors, and if over 60% of them had contracted a venereal infection at some time, the level of disease potentially introduced from India was considerable. To emphasize its warnings, Onslow's report described the syphilis wards – known as the Inferno – at the Army hospital at Netley in Hampshire. On the occasion of Onslow's visit, 74% of the 263 patients at Netley had a history of syphilis: the average age of the 263 men was under twenty-five years. All the Inferno patients had 'a most shocking appearance; some lay there having obviously but a short time to live; others were unrecognizable from disfigurement by reason of the destruction of their features, or had lost their palates, their eyesight, or their sense of hearing; others again were in a state of extreme emaciation, their joints distorted and diseased.' The term of military service had expired for several patients, but they could not be discharged, 'incapacitated as they are to earn their livelihood, or in a condition so repulsive that they could not mix with their fellow men'. Family and friends 'refuse to receive them, and it is inexpedient to discharge them only to seek the asylum of the poorhouse; so they remain at Netley in increasing numbers'.[34]

A system of periodic examination of prostitutes under new cantonment rules was reintroduced in India in 1897 as a result of Onslow's report. Hospital admissions of British soldiers in India for VD fell from 48.6% in 1897 to 36.3% in 1898 and 29.9% in 1900. The rate of venereal infection fell among soldiers generally from 27.5% in 1885 to 5.1% in 1913 and among British sailors from an annual level of 17.1% in 1889 to 7.3% in 1914. Soldiers were not provided with prophylaxis throughout this period, and sailors only for a few years. This fall was due to many influences, including more out-patient treatment, longer and more effective treatment which cured the infection rather than just symptoms, and the provision of lotions with which men could cleanse themselves immediately after exposure to risk. The reimposition of medical examination of whores in Indian military cantonments does seem to have alleviated infection rates, but most improvement was due to better treatment and more information about hygiene, and to safer forms of sex. Without these advances more and more strapping young men would have been doomed to the Inferno.[35]

Even in the armed forces, where officers regarded morale as contingent on the men getting hearty sexual relief, there were those who wanted to identify, humiliate and punish sexual culprits. Lord Kitchener, when Commander-in-Chief of the Indian Army, 1902–9, 'made a great appeal everywhere on moral grounds' and ordered that any soldier under his command who contracted venereal disease was prohibited for three months after leaving hospital from using the regimental swimming-bath. A public notice was displayed announcing: 'Private ——, having been in hospital with venereal disease, is not allowed to use this bath, in order to prevent his contaminating his comrades.' This regulation was medical nonsense, as no soldier was released from hospital in a condition which could lead to infections through swimming-bath water, and was intended to humiliate and isolate. Under Kitchener's command, men were 'inspected continually' for venereal disease and 'punished' if infected, partly by deductions from pay. Army chaplains might laud this 'use of the moral methods', but Kitchener's emphasis on carnal guilt and his impulse to public excoriation of sexuality derived from his own private difficulties. He was a misogynist who surrounded himself with handsome young officers whom he described as his 'happy family of boys'. He was devoted to his aide-de-camp, Oswald FitzGerald, who 'established himself so securely in the affections of his chief that Kitchener never looked elsewhere', according to the Field Marshal's decorous biographer. 'FitzGerald, like Kitchener, was a bachelor and a natural celibate; he devoted . . . his life exclusively to Kitchener, and . . . never quitted Kitchener's side until they met death together' in 1916. Yet when, in 1903, a fellow general, Sir Hector Macdonald, was found 'to have had a perfect lust' for Ceylonese youths, Kitchener demanded that 'the brute' be court-martialled and then 'be shot' (instead 'the poor wretch', so Curzon the Viceroy reported, 'shot himself at some hotel in Europe'). Upon those who were not happily celibate, who behaved in a way that he dared not admit to himself that he wished to emulate, Kitchener inflicted those baleful tendencies listed by Edmund White as 'fostering guilt, intimidation, suppressed desire and worship of might'.[36]

The punishment of people with venereal disease harmed national health. The great venereologist Colonel Lawrence Harrison contrasted attitudes which prevailed until the First World War in the London police force – where it was 'a very severe crime to contract venereal disease' – with the Brigade of Guards, where 'it was considered a crime to conceal it, otherwise there was no penalty.' As a result Guardsmen attended Harrison's clinic at Rochester Row at the earliest moment of primary infection, usually made quick recoveries, and were less prone to disseminate disease: whereas policemen concealed their infection unless 'some complication compelled them to seek medical treatment', with calamitous effects on their own health and that of others. Until 1917 both the Government's health insurance scheme and approved private insurance schemes refused to pay benefit to those stricken with syphilis and gonorrhoea as they were 'misconduct diseases', which led both to concealment and to the diseased eschewing treatment.[37]

Most officers believed it was unreasonable 'to expect the youngsters to keep the trenches for England intact, and their chastity inviolable at one and the same time', to quote General F. P. Crozier. 'The abnormal life, the shattered nerves, the longing to forget, if even for one brief moment, the absence from home and the inculcation of barbaric habits in our manhood, tempered by the most beautiful acts of heroism . . . even unto death, lead directly and inevitably to . . . free love on a large, elaborate and ever-expanding scale.' Nevertheless soldiers in the First World War who contracted venereal infection were relegated to the bottom of the list for leave and had their pay docked. There were always officers so tense about their own images of masculine mastery that they attacked prophylaxis as liable to 'unman a man' by making 'him think that there is no need to exercise self-control'. Equally frustrated and vindictive clergy seethed with bitterness, like the chaplains attached to New Zealand regiments in 1917 who, furious at the failure of their appeals against fornication, proposed a poster threatening venereal cases with loss of all pay, publishing of names at home and other civil disabilities for five years.[38]

The identification and punishment of transgressors was integral to some personal versions of Christianity. The twisted progression from religious idealism to the salacity and cruelty of the British gutter press which is so obtrusive in the history of English divorce laws shows the wider context for the mistreatment of venereal patients. 'Place the adulterer in the criminal's dock; let him stand in the face of the Court by the side of the forger and the burglar, who are not more guilty then he,' urged the Bishop of Lincoln when the law establishing the first divorce court was being enacted in 1857. Samuel Wilberforce, then Bishop of Oxford, agreed: 'the proper course would be to render adultery a disgraceful crime, and to punish it as such.' These punitive and criminal traditions dominated the practice of divorce law. *The Times* marked the divorce (with damages of £10,000) obtained by Charles Cavendish in 1866 after his wife eloped with Lord Cecil Gordon-Moore with an editorial which dwelt on 'the extraordinary perversity which seems to rush into crime from some abnormal satisfaction in the crime itself'. Gordon-Moore was 'criminal' and Lady Elinor Cavendish had 'a sheer propensity to guilt'.[39]

For a long time publicity was seen as crucial to the moral workings of divorce law. Although Queen Victoria thought that the public reporting of divorce court proceedings were more 'pernicious to the public morals' than French novels, many others, such as Sir Robert Peacock, Chief Constable of Manchester from 1898 until 1926 and President of the Chief Constables Association, wanted to ensure that publicity of divorce proceedings was sufficiently unpleasant to deter potential adulterers. Journalists, too, were sure of their public – even divine – duty in the matter. W. T. Stead ('a puritan, and proud to bear the name,' as he said) asserted the privileges of his profession in 1910: 'The simple faith of our forefathers in the All-Seeing Eye of God has departed from the Man in the street. Our only modern substitute for Him is the press. Gag the press under whatever pretexts of prudish propriety you please, and you destroy the last remaining pillory by which it is possible to impose some restraint upon the lawless lust of man . . . The Divorce Court is the modern substitute for the Day of Judgment, not because of the decrees which it pronounces, but because of the publicity which it secures.' A greater editor than Stead, C. P. Scott of the *Manchester Guardian*, agreed. The report of the divorce in 1909 of Sir Walter George Stirling was 'a moral document of extraordinary interest – the spectacle of these people who had every luxury that wealth could produce and never did a day's work for themselves or anybody . . . is an appalling thing . . . that concerns the nation,' he moralized. It was not until 1926, after Lord Ampthill's son had been accused of 'hunnish practices' in the Russell divorce case of 1922–4, that the Government restricted reporting of divorce cases to the identity of partners, a concise statement of charges and counter-charges, points of law submitted and the judge's summing-up. The intention of divorce law was to deter adultery by punishing its practitioners with opprobrium: but in consequence, appearances overshadowed substance. The sin became not adultery itself, but its exposure.[40]

It was against this background of codified hypocrisy that the question was raised of compulsory notification by doctors, or even physical isolation, of venereal cases. The Notification of Diseases Act of 1889 succeeded in reducing some contagious diseases by involving local authorities in enforcing restrictions on infectious people. It was repeatedly but unsuccessfully urged that venereal diseases should be brought under this law. Syphilis was 'such a fearful disease that I would do anything in the world to stop it', to quote Sir Alfred Cooper. He wanted above all the reassurance that action was being taken, and the act for action's sake which seemed simplest and most immediate was notification. Another sentiment hard to condemn was horror that 'it is open to any diseased drab to tempt and poison with venereal disease any inexperienced boy, or to any diseased scoundrel to poison, perhaps his own wife and children, perhaps even to death, and the law lifts not a finger in protest, providing the poisoning is done for private profit or pleasure, and in the most cruel and treacherous way conceivable.' Notification under the 1889 law, and registration of the identities of syphilitics, or their banishment to institutions where they could not have intercourse with the clean world, seemed likely to prevent the possibility of transmission. But for others the attraction of notification was its persecution of transgressors, intimidation of voluptuous instincts and symbolic violence against one's own threatening lust. 'I was three years at Cambridge, and I have spent my life among soldiers, and my experience is that the chief agent for keeping a man clean has been the fear of consequences,' declared a cavalry major-general, Lord Ranksborough, in 1919. 'It has been the athlete's and the sportsman's fear of the consequences that has been the chief motive. We should not diminish that fear . . . [but] make it into a terror . . . by publicity' in the form of notification. 'I am aware of the arguments against it—the stigma, and the difficulty with the doctors, and the danger of driving it underground. But it has been underground ever since I can remember, and the question is—Do we intend to kill this invisible demon? If we do we shall not succeed by stroking its back in the dark . . . if we are going to tackle this scourge and destroy it we can only do it by the daylight of notification.' Ranksborough's brutal vehemence, with its fearful *double entendre*, represented the true intentions of many of those who wanted compulsory notification. Medical justifications might be invoked, but the real reasons were more primitive.[41]

The medical members of the Vigilance Association for the Defence of Personal Rights put the case against compulsory notification in 1882. 'We consider that a Physician's first duty is to his patients; that all other considerations are subordinate; and that the secrets revealed to us at the bedside, or those discovered by us in our intercourse with those who honour us with their confidence, ought to be as sacred as those of the confessional . . . we should be false to our trust and dishonour the profession were we to accept the post of informers in any sense hostile to the interests of those who employ us.' Notification was self-defeating, 'since it will lead to evasion, wilful errors of diagnosis, falsehood, concealment and consequent spread of disease'. People would resort, often with medical connivance, to any device to escape the apparatus of notification. The proposal was 'vicious' because 'compulsory notification will, as surely as night succeeds day, lead to compulsory isolation'.[42]

Opponents of notification of venereal diseases argued that if the medical profession bore the onus of furnishing information, patients would either decide against seeking treatment, choose doctors not for their reputation as healers but for their willingness to disregard the law, or approach shady amateurs, such as abortionists. This warning was certainly vindicated by the examples furnished by another stigmatized disease, tuberculosis, whose victims were also liable to social ostracism, dismissal from jobs, or eviction from homes: after it was made a notifiable disease in 1912, tubercular patients avoided doctors who were notorious as keen notifiers, and consulted practitioners who were sufficiently compassionate or complaisant not to notify the authorities, or to delay notification until the disease was terminal. Even before this experience with turberculosis, the neurologist Sir Frederick Mott warned that compulsory notification 'might lead to disease not being divulged, and not being treated'. Other doctors predicted that compulsory notification would create new opportunities for blackmail: as it was often unclear which sexual partner had infected the other, an extortionist who had the original infection could threaten to accuse the real victim, knowing that publicity or the rigmarole of notification would enhance the suffering of the victim. This opinion (that notification would be useless without the State maintaining intimate knowledge of the conduct of millions of citizens) prevailed among most venereologists: it was not seriously questioned by anyone with administrative or medical experiences in the area after the 1920s. Notification was reduced to being the pet obsession of a few anti-libertarian politicians, or a bludgeon for those who liked to displace their own tensions onto strangers.[43]

Evasion, wilful error, falsehood and concealment, to paraphrase the medical petition of 1882, were practised by doctors in certification of causes of death. Because of the stigma attached to tuberculosis, families and doctors often substituted 'bronchitis' as the cause of tubercular deaths until at least the 1930s, if not far longer. Sir Victor Horsley lamented in 1904 that death certificates were regarded as family documents rather than the scientific basis of national statistics, and that it was therefore impossible to assess the incidence and effects of venereal disease. He urged that death certificates should be regarded as scientific documents, issued in confidence by physicians to the Government's Registrar-General, for divulgence only at the latter's discretion to the friends or family of the deceased. Horsley's recommendation was endorsed by Sir Almeric FitzRoy's Committee on Physical Deterioration, but no government action was taken to implement this recommendation.

Just as Sir William Petty and John Graunt had complained that seventeenth-century Bills of Mortality understated the fatal incidence of syphilis in London to preserve the reputation of the dead, or the feelings of surviving family, so many medical practitioners certified deaths without specifying their venereal cause. Indeed, if they did, relations sometimes contested the certification. In 1930 a financier, Andrew Wilson Tait, died at his house near Holland Park aged 54. His last years had been marred by illness and by a serious business malpractice which in retrospect was attributable to his confused mental state. The cause of death was initially registered by his doctor as 'General Paralysis of Insanity' – that is, tertiary syphilis – but his widow was sufficiently rich and distressed to obtain from Lord Horder, the King's doctor, a statutory declaration that cause of death was chronic meningo-encephalitis. This declaration was endorsed on his death certificate by the Registrar of Births and Deaths in 1931, although the earlier attributed cause of death could not be erased.[44]

The transmission of venereal diseases was admitted as an element in the practice of late nineteenth-century divorce law in England, over three centuries later than in Scotland. The wife of Lord Borthwick had lodged a judicial complaint of marital cruelty the year before he died at Edinburgh in 1582 'of the French disease': in England wilfully communicated venereal disease was accepted as evidence of adultery to substantiate a claim for judicial separation, but was not in itself grounds for divorce. This interpretation of the law seems to have altered after Lord Hannen succeeded Lord Penzance as the judge presiding over the English divorce courts in 1872. The position had certainly changed by 1890 when Lord Connemara ('a real Irishman – good natured, careless and muddle-headed . . . popular, genial and plausible') was divorced by his wife on the grounds of his adultery with her lady's maid and his cruelty 'in communicating to her a certain complaint caught in loose company, a good many years ago'. Three physicians testified on her behalf, including the venereologist Berkeley Hill. Connemara, who had to resign as Governor of Madras before the case was heard, protested that his wife's accusation of syphilis was 'a morbid delusion' against which he prepared no defence as 'up to the last, I did not think the monstrous charges wd be pressed.' He made an unsuccessful counter-suit alleging her adultery with one of her medical advisers, whom she later married. (*The Times*, which reported most divorce proceedings in detail, announced of this case, 'the details of the cruelty charge . . . are unfit for publication.') Connemara was extremely upset at the judgment, and some sympathizers thought her accusation was a vindictive fantasy. Lady Connemara was certainly either emotionally disturbed or in an early stage of general paralysis: Lord Dufferin in the late 1880s found her 'very odd and fanciful', Queen Victoria judged her irrational and by 1893 she was denying to Lord Derby that she was mad, but claiming that her food was poisoned. The Connemara divorce caused a considerable stir: the fact that it was such a dirty business, the vehemence of accusation and denial, the obfuscation of the evidence, the anxious intervention of third parties, were all reminders of the stigmata which remained inseparable from syphilis.[45]

So far little has been said in this chapter about the treatment of sexual diseases, particularly amongst the civilian population. Despite the importance of providing medical facilities to restrain levels of infection, there was persistent neglect. Until the institution of the National Health Service in 1948, hospitals were managed by committees of physicians and philanthropists, and were financed by charitable appeals and subscriptions from members of the public. At many hospitals, public subscribers pressed the management committee to exclude venereal patients from general wards. 'There was a great agitation, ladies complained of their maids, suffering from some slight malady, being put next to prostitutes in beds, and the result of it was that eventually almost all the prostitutes gravitated to the Female Lock Hospital,' one venereologist recalled in 1910.[46]

Medical staff colluded with those members of the public who opposed taking venereal cases as in-patients. During the early 1870s London hospitals such as St George's, St Mary's or University College did not admit venereal patients, while the London Hospital, located at Whitechapel 'in a poor and teeming neighbourhood much infected with venereal disease', reluctantly lifted its prohibition on such patients to provide fifteen beds for women. For a time the Royal Free Hospital had twenty-six beds for female cases, but in the 1860s these were abandoned 'owing to loss of funds occasioned by the outcry raised against this hospital in one of the medical journals'. There was minimal venereal care in workhouse infirmaries, and most dispensaries refused to treat venereal cases of any kind so as to keep themselves undefiled by any taint which might come from prostitution. Similarly Liverpool's three general hospitals, the Hull General Infirmary and many other provincial hospitals were 'governed by the same purist spirit' which excluded venereal cases. Despite evidence at Winchester of 'immense benefit' from the introduction of a ward for venereal patients, 'that same spirit fought long and resolutely for their exclusion, and at length prevailed': the governors of Colchester Hospital not only excluded venereal patients, but rejected a government offer to pay for building a ward.[47]

At leading teaching hospitals, venereal beds were seldom provided, which deprived students of opportunities to learn about diagnosis and treatment. A government inspector was told by several hospitals as late as 1913 that it would be contrary to their statutes to receive venereal cases. 'In others I heard that it was unreasonable to expect subscribers to spend their money on rescuing persons from the consequences of their own sins, and in one hospital at least it was hinted that the whole subject was unsavoury, and that they did not wish to be connected with it even as regards outpatients,' he reported. All these hospitals admitted advanced cases of syphilis and late complications of gonorrhoea, and he was exasperated that many hospital beds occupied by tertiary cases would be free if there was more efficient treatment at primary stage. No beds or wards were reserved for infective venereal cases in thirty general hospitals visited by him in London and the provinces, and although most accepted out-patients for treatment, there was no provision of out-patient departments open at hours which suited the working class. In one London general hospital a rule precluded the treatment of unmarried women with venereal disease, although no such rule existed for bachelors, and in the same hospital maternity cases amongst the unmarried were turned away. This policy of exclusion harmed the health of the nation.[48]

Forty-six per cent of surgical cases at the Royal Free Hospital in 1853 were venereal. Bart's Hospital estimated in 1868 that about half of the 6,000 registered out-patients seen annually were venereal, as were about one-half of patients in their casualty department. University College Hospital, London, estimated at the same date that the out-patients department saw about 25,800 cases of venereal disease annually, or about 43 per cent of total patients. A surgeon at St George's Hospital in London, who saw on average 240 patients weekly in the mid nineteenth century, estimated that one-quarter of them had syphilitic symptoms. Fifteen per cent of patients at the Hospital for Diseases of the Throat were syphilitic by the late 1860s. The Royal Free Hospital treated a daily average of 117 venereal patients in the same decade, and 20 per cent of patients at Moorfields Opthalmic Hospital had advanced syphilis. The Resident Surgeon at the Queen's Hospital in Birmingham computed in the 1860s that 'one out of every two and a half of the out-patients was directly or indirectly affected by venereal.' Even if these levels of infection were higher than in country districts or provincial towns, a tragically large proportion of those infected with venereal disease were living and dying untreated. Many hospitals outside the metropolis had few if any venereal patients: for example Nottingham General Hospital, serving a populous industrial area, treated a 'very small' number of secondary syphilitics, but 'seldom' saw primary infections as 'quacks get hold of them' first.[49]

London, with a population of over two and a half million, including perhaps 18,000 prostitutes, had only 184 hospital beds for women with venereal disease in 1868. The London Lock Hospital treated only 754 patients, of whom 681 were discharged as cured and 8 discharged when they were found to be pregnant; this hospital received an annual government subsidy of about £25 per bed, with the additional annual cost of about £10 per bed met from charitable endowments. Other lock hospitals had been opened at Glasgow (1805), Newcastle (1813), Manchester (1819), Liverpool (1834), Leeds (1842), Bristol (1870) and Birmingham (1881). These institutions initially admitted only women, especially prostitutes, but later opened male lock wards and out-patient clinics. In common with all hospitals reliant on private donations, lock hospitals did more than provide medical relief for the poor. They enabled rich patrons who subscribed to the hospital to prove their charity by distributing tickets of admission to the dependent poor, and instilled the working-class women confined in them with the deference that was thought to be indispensable to social discipline. Lock hospitals were the Cinderellas of the voluntary hospital system – badly funded, with staff who lacked professional status. A *Lancet* obituary in 1926 of one

London Lock Hospital surgeon typically 'regretted that a man with such a gift for surgery should have early specialized in venereal disease'. Hospital committees felt unable to raise money by advertisement, gala concerts or bazaars; and because of the low status attached to venereology as a medical specialization doctors had difficulty in attracting benefactors. Lock hospital trustees in their annual reports depicted their patients as reprehensible, excused public indifference to the charity and were apologetic about the medical services which they provided.[50]

It seems that specialist institutions for venereal cases, which had to emphasize their efforts at moral reclamation in order to raise funds, subjected inmates to a particularly sententious regime, full of interfering religiosity, treating patients more as culprits than staff would in a general hospital. 'English prostitutes sink rapidly from one grade of their wretched life to a lower and lower one, until they reach the lowest depths of misery and infamy,' wrote a commentator of progressive sympathies in 1869: 'only in . . . exceptional cases do they ever escape from their degraded position.' Since this view of lock hospital patients as infamous and irredeemable was almost universal, they were not surprisingly regarded as undeserving of kindness or sympathy.[51]

Patients at the London Lock Hospital, which had about 30,000 entrants annually before 1914, but 100,000 by 1920, were treated by surgeons like James Lane (1825–91), Matthew Berkeley Hill (1833–92) and John Astley Bloxam (1843–1926). Lane himself contracted syphilis, probably from a patient: 'In the prime of his life, and when a career of prosperity appeared to be within his grasp', he was stricken with locomotor ataxy, which, though slow in its progress, was attended by almost unendurable agonies which forced him to retire in the 1880s. He had been a strong believer in the compulsory regulation of those with venereal disease, particularly working-class women. Berkeley Hill studied venereal diseases under the great authority Ricord in Paris, and with Alfred Cooper published two important textbooks on the subject. Hill believed that many women patients had 'very little self-control' and only responded to 'fear of . . . punishment': holding these views he was as active as Lane in defending the Contagious Diseases Acts, advocating their extension nationally, and equally he deplored their repeal. Their colleague Bloxam 'regarded himself as a disciplinarian', and was 'a surgeon of the old school' who 'created a sensation' by pioneering the transplant of part of a finger to form the base of a new nose after tertiary syphilis had rotted it away: 'his methods, so far as antiseptic or aseptic technique were concerned, might be conservative, but his results were remarkably good.' The ethos of coercive discipline created by men like Lane, Hill and Bloxam is ugly to imagine.[52]

This subjugation of the patient was not exclusively the fate of the poor. 'I am undergoing the extremely unpleasant operation known as the "cold water cure",' wrote the syphilitic Lord Binning from an 'obscure village' near Frankfurt in the late 1880s. 'I am wrapped in wet sheets, douched, fed on nothing but gruel and otherwise ill treated . . . I have been nothing bettered by this horrible place, but rather the worse, and grow yellower and more miserable every day, and the doctor notwithstanding wants me to stay on.' Binning was 'a very nice-looking and pleasant and cheery young gentleman', so Lord Dufferin wrote; but the cold-water cure was calculated to crush cheeriness. The punitive element in expensive private treatment, and the disciplining of patients who had previously 'lived loosely', was commonplace.[53]

Patients were vulnerable in the aftermath of diagnosis, or in the early stages of treatment, and whether they persisted in the course prescribed by their medical adviser often depended on the sympathy or bullying which they encountered. Oscar Wilde's discovery in 1878 that he had caught syphilis from an Oxford prostitute shattered even his insouciance and pitched him into a crisis of penitence in which he nearly embraced Roman Catholicism. The novelist Violet Hunt caught syphilis in the late 1890s, although she did not discover that she was infected until 1906, when one of her suitors 'with tears in his eyes told me to my face I had a disgraceful illness . . . only he did not name it or do more than hint.' She was warned by another admirer who saw 'my spots on my forehead and said, "You ought not to go out."' She consulted Middlesex Hospital's aural surgeon, Dr Stephen Paget, who 'looked at me and spoke to me as to something unclean . . . it was most inglorious moment of my life.' Paget's disapproval may have been imagined by her in a state of hyper-sensivity and guilt: but whatever the truth of his conduct, she left his consultation knowing 'what fallen women feel'. Like many other syphilitics, she did not attend her doctor again, preferring continued infection to the disdain of Paget.[54]

In a different context, but with similar assumptions, a medical practitioner describing his treatment of merchant seamen for venereal diseases at Liverpool between the world wars, after painting a lurid picture of bars with 'bright lights, fiery liquids and . . . the female vampires of dockland', described his patients as 'bone lazy': the only sailors who tried to 'retain their self-respect' were those who served in luxury liners or Royal Navy Reservists in whom 'the discipline inculcated at our naval barracks bears perennial fruit'. He was keen to assert medical authority – his patients were 'given plainly to understand' that 'rules of diet and conduct' must be obeyed – and contemptuous of ignorance or fear. He characterized his patients as 'too lazy to follow out instructions given verbally, too lazy to read the short notes on treatment printed on every patient's identity card, and too fond of mine host's nut-brown ale'. As to non-whites,

> Natives of British India are notoriously bad attenders. They make their first appearance either alone or destitute of English, or surrounded by a host of mess-mates who quickly fill the waiting room with their persons and their gibberish . . . After some parley one of the gang . . . acts as interpreter for the unfortunate afflicted, and thereafter matters proceed smoothly until one proceeds to do a vein puncture or to incise a suppurating bubo. Then one finds the use of a needle is a sore point with the Hindu.

The Liverpudlian doctor concluded with contempt, 'a second attendance is rare': but this may have had less to do with Hindus' supposed fear of needles than with his own punitive and offensive attitude, or by the way he wielded his needle on those whom he considered lesser races.[55]

Scientific advances in venereology had been continuous. Benjamin Bell had proved in 1793 that syphilis and gonorrhoea were separate illnesses, and later William Wallace inoculated healthy Dubliners to demonstrate that the syphilitic rash, like the initial genital ulcer, was contagious. Wallace in 1834 also announced potassium iodide as a cure for secondary infections. His claims for this technique were modest, but after his death in 1838 other writers pitched exaggerated claims for potassium iodide as a panacea which could be substituted for mercury. As the smell of salivated patients was so obnoxious, and mercurial treatment resulted in a loss or (as in Oscar Wilde's case) a blackening of the teeth, there was an exaggerated reaction towards using potassium iodide instead. The best results from iodide seemed to occur when it was used in conjunction with mercury in tertiary syphilis involving nervous or vascular decay; but like mercury, it did not cure the disease, although it was reputed to do so.

Philippe Ricord finally discredited Hunter by redemonstrating the distinctions between syphilis and gonorrhoea in 1837. He also divided the course of the disease into three stages – primary, secondary and tertiary – which made it easier to understand the symptoms which syphilis presented. By popularizing the use of the vaginal speculum, Ricord made advances in comprehending vaginal and uterine syphilitic lesions. Nevertheless he made some blunders. He regarded silver nitrate as a panacea for syphilis, using it in fearsomely strong solutions in the urethra and vagina. He did not consider gonorrhoea to be a specific disease, and discounted the possibility of secondary and tertiary syphilitic lesions being contagious.[56]

After 1850 it was increasingly recognized that patients died of other diseases, such as bronchitis or inflammation of the bowels or infantile cholera, to which they would not have succumbed if they had not been constitutionally syphilitic. Once morbid anatomy became subject to scientific enquiry, other confirmations were made. Sir Samuel Wilks held the first recorded examination of the corpse of a man who had died of syphilis: 'this necropsy was a revelation to him, as it showed that the internal organs could be affected in the same way as the exterior of the body.' After an interval, 'this great fact was accepted by the profession at large', and by the 1870s syphilis was recognized to cause inflammation of lymphatic and other glands, rheumatic inflammation of joints such as knees and ankles, or of the eyes; inflammation and suppuration of the eye's mucous membranes leading to blindness; inflammation of the bladder or kidneys; or urethral obstructions; and sundry other types of ulceration. Leg paralysis (tabes dorsalis) was also finally accepted as a tertiary manifestation of syphilis.[57]

For the first time in four centuries the medical status of venereal diseases changed substantially. In 1879 a German, Niesser, isolated the causative microbe of gonorrhoea: over twenty years later, Ilya Metchnikoff and Pierre Roux experimented with the syphilitic virus on apes, finding that the more the animal experimented upon resembled man, the closer the disease was in character and virulence to human syphilis. In 1905 Fritz Schaudinn and Erich Hoffman identified the specific organism of syphilis, the *spirochaeta* or *treponema pallidum*. In 1906 the German bacteriologist August von Wasserman announced his discovery of serodiagnosis in syphilis, known as the Wasserman test or Wasserman reaction. This blood test was highly specific and sensitive, although external factors sometimes caused a false positive reaction, and in its early days misinterpretations through technical error occurred. Soon afterwards, further work by Metchnikoff and Roux proved that inoculation with the syphilitic virus could be rendered completely inactive in humans by applying subchloride of mercury (or calomel) in ointment form within a few hours of infection. Once Metchnikoff had demonstrated that this prevented syphilis by destroying the poisonous microbe, his method was adopted on the European continent. It was tried by the German Navy in the year that his final paper was published (1905), an Army Order governing prophylaxis which was issued in Austria in 1907 reduced infection by 62% in some regiments, while in the same year a similar military decree was published in France. Even before Metchnikoff's discovery German sailors and soldiers were given antiseptic ointment and an injection of protdeargol before 'going on the loose', and had access on board ship to automatic dispensing machines providing these. But in Britain there was little ventilation of Metchnikoff's technique of self-disinfection, although as one contemporary wrote in 1918, 'his calomel ointment, if applied as and when directed, *does* confer absolute safety.'[58]

Venereal disease is usually contracted at a definite time, and those exposed to infection know the exact moment of risk: with the identification of efficient methods of self-disinfection, few other diseases offered such opportunities for prevention. The micro-organisms causing infection were frail, and could be destroyed by antiseptic reaching them; but once they penetrated the surface of the skin, beyond the reach of antiseptics, they multiplied rapidly, and long treatment was required to destroy every single microbe. When the antiseptic was of prescribed strength, used within the prescribed limits of time and properly applied at the point of infection, it was infallible; but if through drunkenness, carelessness or misfortune, the antiseptic was wrongly compounded, or the time-limit was exceeded, or some point of infection was missed, failures occurred. As a result of these possible sources of failure, it could only be claimed that, whereas an individual could secure absolute and unconditional immunity, in the general population only relative immunity was obtainable.

There were other obstacles to the use of Metchnikoff's ointment. General Sir Alexander Godley provided prophylactic facilities for his troops in Egypt in 1914–16 – 'privately and without putting anything on paper' to forestall objections from his political masters – but found that 'from sentimental reasons' the ointment was seldom used: 'on being assured by the woman that she is clean' men felt that 'to use the ointment was an insult to her'. Prostitutes refused to let men use the ointment as it caused blistering, especially where women accommodated twenty or thirty men nightly. Some men collected tins of Metchnikoff's concoctions to barter for women or beer, and clandestine demand developed when Egyptians started using the ointment to cure lice in their hair.[59]

Other forms of prophylaxis became more widely available. Condoms were a limited and expensive commodity made of sheep gut until the 1850s, when it was realized that the recent development of Charles Goodyear's vulcanization process meant that they could be mass-produced in rubber form. The size of families as measured by marriage cohorts began to decline in the 1860s, and the annual birthrate, after reaching a peak of 36.3 births per thousand of the population in 1876, fell by 33% in the period to 1914. The firm of E. Lambert and Sons of Dalston, which became the leading provisioner of condoms, was founded in 1877, in which year the world's first birth control organization, the Malthusian League, was founded. Its leaders were secularists who preferred the insertion of contraceptive sponges in women to the use of condoms by men; but the unquestionable popularization of sheathes after 1870 played a part in making sex safer from venereal infections.[60]

Beyond the refinement of preventive techniques, a new era in therapy was inaugurated, with repercussions not only for venereal diseases, but eventually for a wider range of illness, by the announcement in 1910 by the German scientist Paul Ehrlich that he had discovered a powerful specific for curing syphilis: known as Salvarsan, this wonder-drug was shortly followed by a refinement, Neo-Salvarsan. These discoveries caused an international furore. He received the Nobel Prize for medicine jointly with Metchnik-off, but was besieged by detractors, including doctors who resented Salvarsan depriving them of lifelong patients, and moralists who attacked him for removing the punitive element from fornication. Within a few years he died, exhausted by 'interruption, traduction, foolish malice and senseless hatred in which he was forced to continue his laboriously conscientious work'.[61]

Many objected to Salvarsan. In its early days, it was adminis-tered by intramuscular injection which led to some deaths when practised by inexperienced or careless doctors: these difficulties diminished when Ehrlich devised a method of injection into the vein. Nevertheless a decade later Dr Mary Scharlieb, a member of the Royal Commission on Venereal Diseases, was still insisting on Salvarsan's imperfections. The technique of administration 'was extremely cumbrous and the whole proceeding needed much meticulous care and skill that it was practically beyond the power of the ordinary practitioner to adminster the drug'. She still felt in 1924 that Salvarsan was 'the treasure of the few, but not the possession of mankind'. This was because, in her heart, she did not want a mass cure for syphilis: without the fear which the disease excited, she believed people would explore desires which were otherwise fugitive. Quacks were equally hostile to Salvarsan. It gave patients faith in modern therapeutics, and diminished the numbers who turned in despair to quacks when orthodox medicine gave no relief. Clever German commercial propaganda, according to one unregistered practitioner, created 'grandiose notions' about Salvarsan. He found it bizarre that 'reputable newspapers, which had never been known to allude, however distantly, to syphilis, began to discuss its new treatment', and implied that German agents had bribed newspaper editors. Whatever the cause of this journalistic candour, open discourse was fatal to the ignorance and shame on which quacks preyed.[62]

These advances in preventive medicine and therapeutic cures seemed to undermine the basis of moral persuasion as practised since the lapse of the Contagious Diseases Acts. Sir Alfred Pearce Gould, surgeon at Middlesex Hospital and President of the Boys

Brigade, agreed with Gibbs of the London Lock Hospital that young men had traditionally been 'prevented from having intercourse' by 'fear of pregnancy and fear of venereal disease'. A shrewder observer, Sir Archdall Reid, had the more subtle insight that 'fear drives men, not from sexual intercourse, but from the prostitute to hunt after the amateur'. Sir John Robertson, who was Birmingham's Medical Officer of Health until the 1920s, similarly insisted that 'supplying prophylactic outfits will more surely destroy the family life of this nation than any other method you could advocate. To destroy the family is to destroy the nation. It was to similar methods that the glory of ancient Rome owed its eclipse.' His opinion (in effect that Birmingham marriages were only held together by fear of venereal disease) was widely quoted (indeed by Davidson, Archbishop of Canterbury, in the House of Lords). He dismissed his opponents 'as persons desiring to salve their consciences because they themselves have been incontinent, or as persons who pander to something which may be popular'. Considering whether doctors had 'any moral right to withhold knowledge because of an ulterior consequence', Robertson insisted that no one could ignore 'the amount of damage the knowledge is going to do' to national morality: he therefore deprecated publicizing medical methods of preventing venereal infection. 'The sale of packets by chemists, or any general education among the youth of the country concerning the use of these packets would lead to a lowering of the moral standard,' agreed a physician specializing in children's medicine in 1920. 'That class of the population which is kept straight' by 'fear of disease would slide in the wrong direction': 'it would be easy enough to teach prophylaxis; it would be a very difficult matter to unteach it.' He was a compassionate altruist, but the prisoner of a mentality which believed that sensualists could only be controlled by fear, whether of losing their lives or their souls, a mentality fearful of the independence of mind and action that would ensue if knowledge was uncontrolled, if the power that derives from information was diffused outside the ranks of the privileged.[63]

Lady Barrett, an obstetrician at the Royal Free Hospital in London, opposed the use of condoms as likely to prevent conception: 'it is better for the nation to have the children, and less immoral, than to interfere with the natural consequences of an act,' she adjured, adding that 'a greater evil' than illegitimacy was 'for young people to indulge in promiscuous intercourse and use unnatural means to avoid the consequences'. She equated 'promiscuity in sexual intercourse' with 'excess', and representing the Federation of Medical Women denounced a pamphlet on self-disinfection issued by the Society for Preventing Venereal Disease as 'disgusting'. She wanted 'a campaign to teach people continence' because any publicity for prophylactic methods would end by 'polluting the minds of all young people'. Early medical women felt vulnerable when discussing sexual conduct, and until the Second World War struck reactionary poses, repudiating female sexual appetite in a way which was contradicted by a survey conducted in the 1890s by an American woman physician, Clelia Mosher. Middle-class women were prepared to acknowledge their desire for orgasm, or their sexual experiences of other pleasures, in a confidential questionnaire; but in other circumstances such candour was unsafe. When Lady Barrett died in 1945, her obituary in the *Lancet* praised her as 'the perfect hostess' whose 'home life with her husband . . . was of the happiest': 'charmingly feminine in appearance and dress, she gained many adherents to the cause of medical education for women, and her dignified example was much help in practice to others.' Women pioneers in medicine were exposed to exceptional scrutiny from male colleagues and only seemed innocuous if they remained 'charmingly feminine': they coped with the social and sexual insecurities of medical men, and controlled their own unease, by declaring themselves as enemies of eroticism, as living proof that women's desires were not insatiable and that the prerogatives of masculinity were unchallenged. Typically a manifesto issued in 1920 by the Federation of Medical Women, while 'not advocating the retention of disease in order that the fear of infection may deter from promiscuous indulgence', warned that if condoms were freely available, 'promiscuous intercourse would be looked upon as free from the risk of infection, and to a great extent free from the risk of conception . . . a phase of society would be produced as vicious and degenerate as any of which history has record . . . moral degeneration and sex excesses would rot the very foundation of society.'[64]

Against all these opinions from physicians worried by the threat of an increasingly secularized and urban nation, there were others who welcomed the new power of science to weaken religious dogma or to dispel old fears. Stern talk about immorality was no longer enough, wrote an observer in 1913 who wanted campaigns against venereal disease to be based on recent scientific advances. 'Youth is human, and humanity is frail. No code of ethics will ever help here.' Sexuality, as the strongest force in human nature, was entitled to expression and protection. Fear of venereal disease was 'only a slight deterrent of immorality', according to a lay writer with considerable experience, Ettie Rout, in 1920. Opposition to publicizing methods of prophylaxis, she believed, sprang less 'from the desire to prevent sin, as from the desire to secure the poisoning of the sinner; packets are objectionable to such prejudiced minds because they enable men to be immoral without suffering for it.' Others defended male (if not female) lust. 'Let us face the facts,' urged a Harley Street venereologist. 'More than half of our young manhood, and the better rather than the worse half, are occasionally carried away by the sexual urge': the most valuable qualities of citizenship were 'associated with virility'. This particular physician was an atheist who looked forward to the full secularization of Britain and was heavily influenced by Darwinian thought: he was also profoundly phallocentric in his assumptions, rather in the manner of the Contagious Diseases Acts sixty years earlier with their explicit contempt for women.[65]

In discussing whether sexual continence was compatible with good health, a distinction was drawn between men and women. Dr William Acton, influential in his time although now regarded as a mountebank, called the attribution of erotic passion to women 'a vile aspersion'. Women, according to Charles Gibbs, were natural 'abstainers' from intercourse. Other medical specialists could be found offering vague impressions that 'passion' was not 'as strong in women as in men'. Medical explanations for this perceived difference were never based on male inability to bring their women partners to orgasm: indeed an undercurrent of fear or suspicion of female orgasm survived from the seventeenth-century hypothesis that women scattered venereal infections when stirred to pleasure. One doctor in 1864, advising the Admiralty on syphilis, described how 'when a young and vigorous man has sexual intercourse with a female having a spasm in the vagina, he too often . . . injures himself. The next day . . . he rushes to his medical adviser, who, if he is a prudent man, will have the female examined before he gives an opinion.' In 90% of cases the woman will be found to have had an orgasm, 'but to be perfectly healthy otherwise': 'wounds' sustained by a man from an orgasmic woman could 'be cured by rest and ablution'.[66]

This attitude resulted in a dual standard of treatment for venereal infections. The deathrate from cardiac aneurysm in women (which was caused in a proportion of cases by venereal infection) rose from 11 per million in 1922 to 26 per million in 1938 because 'of the very great increase in syphilis amongst women' during the First World War and 'of the very low proportion who received any treatment', according to a Ministry of Health official: the deathrate for men rose from 45 to 52 per million in the same period, which smaller rate of increase reflected the superior medical treatment which men received in the armed forces.[67]

The reluctance to publicize scientific advances in confronting venereal diseases, or to popularize safer sexual practices, has been shown; but the censorship exercised on the subject was even more sweeping. The final section of this chapter explores the controls on discourse about sexual diseases, the consequences of these restrictions, and the meaning of the narrow discussion and stylized images that were permissible. Partly from well-judged distrust of advertising quacks, partly because it is harder to keep people frightened if they are in command of the facts of a subject, and partly from a genuine sense of what Sir James Barrett called 'the inherent nastiness of the subject', discussion of venereal diseases was repressed: for a long time the only acceptable discourse was couched in stylized middle-class colloquialisms, which meant nothing to the poor, and seemed risible to young people who fancied themselves to be sophisticated. The Indecent Advertisements Act of 1889 was directed 'against persons who advertise their specifics against a certain class of diseases of a nameless character': although one target were quack handbills offering cures for masturbation or syphilis handed out on the streets of cities, the law's proponent, the Earl of Meath, opposed the 'filthy' advertisement of condoms, whether as preventives of venereal disease or pregnancy, as 'inducements to promiscuous sexual intercourse'. Meath was a Christian philanthropist of great energy, who deplored the tragedy of Victorian urban deprivation, with the physiques of the young ruined by bad housing, bad air and sleazy recreation; he sought to mitigate these evils by founding organizations to improve the health of young city-dwellers such as the Lads Drill Association, the British Institute for Social Service and the Duty and Discipline Movement. London owes many of its parks and playgrounds to Meath's efforts, and after a long and unselfish campaign by him, the great reform of compulsory physical exercise in British elementary schools was introduced in 1902. When he denounced postal circulars 'by which thousands of young men have their prospects of life destroyed' he was admirable in his wish to stop the exploitation of masturbatory anxieties, just as he was sincere in his horror at 'this stream of pollution, which is contaminating the minds of the young'; but as a contingency of his fine intentions, knowledge of preventives of what Lord Chancellor Halsbury in 1889 still called the 'secret disease' was restricted, and discussion of the subject over the next two decades became perhaps more inhibited than at any time before or since.[68]

Secrecy and squeamishness enveloped the subject: the rich and poor alike were left bewildered and ashamed. The impulse to censor, of which Meath's Act was evidence, left people of all ages and classes in a state of sad and dangerous ignorance. Queen Victoria's second son, Prince Alfred, Duke of Edinburgh, had a 'mysterious malady' which meant that his life was 'not one that would be accepted by an Insurance office' and died aged 55: his son, young Prince Alfred, was diagnosed to have syphilis and was discharged from his regiment, whereupon his mother, 'disgusted and embarrassed by his disease', exiled him to Romania. There his condition deteriorated rapidly – 'He hardly recognizes anyone and often does not know what he says, poor boy' – and he died, attended only by his tutor and one servant, in 1899, aged 24. Queen Victoria's best-known recent biographer states that he died of tuberculosis, *The Times* reported that he 'had been suffering from chronic cerebral affection' and 'depression', but the *Complete Peerage* attests that he shot himself: it is certain that he died forsaken by his family, who then began 'to lament and weep at his having died quite alone'. The Royal Family's confusion – their incomprehension that such an infection could strike at them, their denial that he needed comfort – was encapsulated by the princeling's aunt: 'It is true that he was giddy & wild, as many young men alas are, & that he contracted an illness, of which I know next to nothing, as I have never heard or asked anything

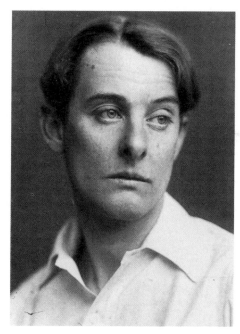

Lord Alfred Douglas

Oscar Wilde

Fred Barnes, the music hall entertainer, who was annually expelled from the Royal Tournament because the naval and military authorities thought him such a threat. Official horror at Barnes' innocuous presence epitomized prevailing notions about the danger of corruption by homosexuals at their most extreme and absurd.

This sequence of pictures dating from 1871 was entitled 'Up in the World – Down on her Luck'. It confirmed the view that however gaily a woman began a life of prostitution, however rich her protectors, she always ended her days in the gutter, cold, wet, miserable and ruined.

Even one lapse from the straight and narrow was often thought unforgive-able. Transgressors were ostracized or expelled from the family circle. This typical Victorian image of an unmarried mother with her child was entitled 'Erring Daughter Cast Out Into Snow'.

about it, one dislikes thinking about it, & still more speaking or writing about it.' A few years later, at a family tea party of Lowestoft peasants and fisherfolk, a scene occurred which superficially had nothing in common with the ostracism and death of the grandson of a Russian Czar and of Queen Victoria: but the circumstances were miserably similar. There was the same fear of defilement and the same cruel ignorance.

> Suddenly Uncle Willie said, 'The police met our boat when we came in and took one of our poor young chaps away.'
>
> 'Oh!' said Aunt Milly, 'What had *he* been up to?'
>
> 'He got a nasty disease about him and put it up his young brother,' replied Uncle Willie with great simplicity.
>
> Dead silence, of course, and red faces ... They all enjoyed a rude joke if it was open and straightforwardly told on a subject within their experience. But this was different. Uncle Willie apparently took the silence as a token of sympathy, for at last he said sadly, 'Poor young chap'. He had probably been thinking 'How sad to be young – at sea with a feared, painful and shameful disease – nobody to help, advise or console – then to hurt someone you love and fall into the hands of the police' ... The reports on the case later showed the fisherman and his brother to have been victims of superstition and ignorance. Many people in those days believed, perhaps not until desperate circumstances forced them to do so, that venereal disease would vanish if passed on to a completely innocent person. The local magistrates who condemned the fisherman from the bench were the very people, with their combined influence and narrow-mindedness, who prevented more enlightened people from bringing these subjects into the open.

The illness and emotional pain of Prince Alfred and the young fisherman were alike aggravated by the cult of reticence which reached its apogee in the quarter-century after the suspension of the Contagious Diseases Acts.[69]

It was to redress such dismal isolation and fear that in 1909

Henry Robson, a Bournemouth general practitioner interested in eugenics, published a book entitled *Sexual Disease and its Medical Prevention* which gave a clear and succinct account of the prevalence, symptoms, pathology and prevention of venereal diseases, including a description of Metchnikoff's prophylactic methods. Robson was the first doctor on the British Medical Register to write a book advocating the scientific prevention of venereal disease, and was indeed threatened before doing so that he might be prosecuted or struck off the Register (as had happened to a Leeds dermatologist, Dr Henry Allbutt, author of a popular guide to contraception, *The Wife's Handbook*, which sold over 250,000 copies from its publication in 1886 to the turn of the century). Although his book was written for the public rather than doctors, newspapers refused to review it, circulating libraries and booksellers would not handle it and the medical press barely mentioned it. This boycott was only lifted after the outbreak of war in 1914.[70]

There was other censorship. Eugene Brieux's celebrated play about syphilis, *Les Avaries*, known in England as *Damaged Goods*, was translated from the French by Sir John Pollock, and together with two other plays by Brieux and a preface by George Bernard Shaw, was offered to several publishers. Each declined to take the risk of publishing *Damaged Goods*, at least one firm replying that their other authors would sever all connections if a play about syphilis was issued under their imprint: it was not until 1911, when Brieux was elected to the French Academy, that publication became feasible. The office of Lord Sandhurst, who as Lord Chamberlain controlled theatrical censorship, banned the play, which only appeared on the British stage in a series of private performances in 1914. Several newspapers refused to send their drama critics to the production: 'others were extremely abusive in their notices, [but] the tone of the press as a whole was markedly respectful, even friendly, to the undertaking.' This production of 1914 was seen by only a few subscribers to the Authors Producing Society, specially formed to produce plays banned by the Lord Chamberlain's censors; but the topicality of venereal disease during the World War led to a revolution in the moral conscience of Sandhurst's staff, who raised the interdiction on *Damaged Goods* in 1917. Their decision enabled the play to be performed nightly for months at St Martin's Theatre, and to be revived as part of a public health campaign during the next syphilitic epidemic in 1943. It was also adapted into an American film, *Marriage Forbidden*, distributed in Britain in 1939.[71]

Discourse was censored in other ways. There were commercial restrictions on making discussions of syphilis available to the masses. In 1913 the multiple newsagents W. H. Smith refused to stock in its bookstalls a pamphlet entitled 'The Doctors and Venereal Disease' reprinted from the *English Review*: 'Admirable as the article is in many ways, we hardly think it is suitable for display in so public a place as a Railway Bookstall, and besides this, most of our Railway Contracts specially disbar us from selling books &c. dealing with this subject,' Smiths explained. It suggests an extraordinary set of preoccupations that railway managers planning to rent bookshops on their station platforms should include provisions in the leases preventing the sale of pamphlets on syphilis.[72]

The writings of Brieux and Robson were the most admirable examples of the more liberated discourse which began just before the First World War, but there were many more vulgar and influential ebullitions. A typical journalistic account of the fearful perils of sex was given by W. N. Willis, co-author of *The White Slaves of London*. Ostensibly devoted to attacking fornication, miscegenation and the keeping of Asian common-law wives by Europeans working in the Orient, his book *Western Men with Eastern Morals* (1913) is prurient and titillating, providing mildly pornographic stories under the guise of disapprobation, always with death awaiting those who yield to their sexual natures, with emphasis on the racial superiority of Anglo-Saxons. 'I am afraid that the contents of this chapter will come as a shock to a good many of my readers,' he announces at one stage. 'All I can say is that I regret the necessity; but, after all, it is surely in the interests of both the white rulers and of the coloured dependent races that the truth should be told.'

Willis describes visiting a Singapore brothel with 'a rollicking lot of young men of the bulldog breed', of whom one in particular 'was a splendid sample of healthy British manhood' with a good job and family: 'His mother, sister, and two brothers were highly thought of in the village in which the family had lived for a couple of hundred years.' Willis describes the whores' antics in lingering detail: 'One big-nosed, dark-eyed, hatchet-faced sample of the

Hebrew breed, who could only speak Russian, stood on her head in the room, whilst a sea-captain, for diversion, poured champagne over her. It was a sickening, lewd sight.' Gradually the young men disappear behind curtains with the whores ('just imported from Russia . . . speaking Yiddish') while Willis is ejected from the brothel for quarrelling with the Madame's native protector ('He glanced at me, and showed his knowledge of the Western vernacular by asking "Who the —— I was". I replied coolly, "I am an Englishman"'). Within days 'the splendid sample of healthy British manhood' is stricken with syphilis, and Willis adopts the role of officious friend visiting the sickbed.

> The hospital is full of young and old, withering steadily, but too surely, away to their last resting place. It supplies pictures of disease which cannot, for sheer decency, be described. I can only say that the sight I saw was so sickening and repulsively horrible that I was ill for days.

Willis lingers on the remorse of the syphilitic. 'He had lost heart, the blow was so sudden, so terrible to his young, once healthy and vigorous body, that he almost abandoned hope while he lay, hour and hour, in that half-way house to death, silently weeping when the memory of his mother conjured up the days of innocent love, of goodness and of happiness, in the old home where he was born . . . Too late he realized that this was the natural result of a minute or two of supposed pleasure – an embrace and a kiss of death, from a strumpet bred in Odessa.' Willis' preoccupation with Russian Jewesses had factual justification: from the 1880s until the 1920s a combination of factors – Russian pogroms forcing rural Jews into overcrowded urban ghettos, poverty undermining family solidarity and authority, more accessible intercontinental travel – resulted in the conspicuous and unprecedented involvement of Yiddish-speaking Jews both in brothel-owning and in trafficking in young Jewesses for the purposes of prostitution, particularly in South America, Asia and the northern and southernmost parts of Africa. The uses made of this by anti-Semites were vile.[73]

Syphilis became so frightful – the object of so much hostile projection, associated with so many bad feelings, the focus of so much fear and guilt – that an extraordinary cycle of deprivation and discipline began. Misinformation about the subject was informally imparted or ignorance assiduously imposed, the better to foster the anxiety and fear that was thought to keep people conscious of danger and sin. Children were deprived of emotional or physical satisfaction: every minute of their waking day was controlled.

Willis emphasized racial integrity, and other writers on venereal diseases were preoccupied with preserving the integrity of class distinctions. Lord Malmesbury was quoted earlier regretting that syphilis was attacking the etiquette and traditions of 'olden days', the family of the 'bulldog breed' youth idealized by Willis had been settled in the same pure, contented village for centuries, and other writers on the subject equally yearned for a dreamland, where all the rules were kept, and nothing decomposed or disintegrated. Thus Major Arthur Corbett-Smith, editor of the *Journal of State Medicine* and lecturer at the Royal Institute of Public Health, in 1919 published a letter to a godson aged 18 warning about the risks of venereal infection. He recalled the letter which he had sent the boy on the day of his baptism.

> 'Tell your father', I said, 'to teach you how to play with a straight bat and to stand up to the fastest bowling; how to ride clean across country and not to funk the fences; how to bring down a pheasant coming fast over the tree tops in a high wind. And tell your Mother to teach you, for her sake, to be gentle and courteous in reverence to all women.'

This strain of idealized reverence continued: 'a pretty English girl is one of the loveliest things God ever made, and if they are not to be admired and made a fuss over (within reason) I don't quite see why they were ever created.' (He excepted working-class girls from this encomium, recalling that he himself had severed one youthful flirtation when he found the girl's parents kept a stationers' shop). In order to mitigate 'sex-hunger', he urged his godson to continue 'hard physical exercise' for 'as long as you can after you leave school'. An active social life among the refined and well-connected would help to banish lust. 'Go and visit, too, at a few good houses and meet nice people. Cultivate the acquaintance of a few charming women, pay little attentions, and so on, and you will probably find as much female companionship as you want.' Keeping caste was essential to avoid venereal disease.

> If a young fellow has been brought up with a love of the open air – and it is this love which has made the Britisher what he is – I can see no danger in his comradeship with a nice girl . . . He will never be really content in carrying on a flirtation with a golden-haired maiden in a photographer's shop, or with a waitress in his favourite tea shop. It really isn't worth it.

Corbett-Smith tried to be practical about the difficulties of celibacy for a youth. To prevent 'overmuch accumulation of semen', Nature had provided 'a safety-valve', in the form of wet dreams, or what Corbett-Smith's contemporaries called 'nocturnal pollution'. He consoled his godson that the 'temporary discomfort', as he described a wet dream, was 'a very trifling affair besides that which a woman experiences every month', and advised against masturbation. 'I do beg you, old man, not to imagine that you ought to seek relief in, shall we say, an irregular way . . . I am well backed by medical opinion that there is absolutely no necessity.' His language at this junction becomes tense with double-meanings. 'The remedy lies in your own hands,' he declared. 'If you fight it down once or twice, throw yourself into some extra hard work, get a long day on the golf links, or a good tramp across Surrey commons, you will find that things come to adjust themselves.'[74]

It was better if young men hoarded their semen inside themselves, and were given no guidance to think of women as anything but receptacles in which to deposit semen. Since the clergy, headmasters and pensioned officers who pontificated were largely dead to women's feelings, they discouraged curiosity about female desire or responses. Albert David, headmaster of Rugby and later Bishop of Liverpool, recommended a sex education manual to the Royal Commission on Venereal Diseases precisely because 'it dealt very reverently and frankly (without mentioning the female side at all) with the boy's own difficulties'.[75]

Corbett-Smith's avuncular homily ('"look to the end", as old Aristotle said,' it concludes, 'Here is a little cheque to help you through the Summer Half') is typical of its genre. Its explicitly middle-class approach with references to 'nice people' living near

Surrey commons, its adulation of a social style in which one's godsons shoot pheasant rather than flirt with waitresses, its mimicry of a tone of voice which is bluff but worldly, its soldierly tributes to the virility of the golf links, its patronizing but protective attitude to middle-class English girls and its contempt for young women who earn their own livings or have sexual imaginations of their own, the phallocentric nature of its perception of human sexuality: all are characteristic of the period. The only British adolescents worth discussing were those with a hope of attending universities. The British undergraduate above all things, Corbett-Smith believed, wanted to be ' a good sportsman; and you cannot ride straight to hounds, or row in the Eights, or make a century at cricket, if you spend your evenings in a café or a girl's bedroom.' As he explained,

> Your French, German or Russian student sees things
> differently . . . So long as our young men maintain the
> fine ideal of being 'sportsmen' and of playing the game
> for their side, not looking on while others do the work,
> so long will they be the envy of their contemporaries
> across the water in their freedom from sexual disease.

Corbett-Smith offered as an example 'of the young Britisher's attitude towards women', his knowledge of Shanghai's brothels, where 'over and over again I have known instances of our fellow country-men resorting to these houses solely for the sake of the girls' society, a couple of dances, a drink, perhaps not so much as a kiss . . . east of Suez, where the sexual impulse is enormously strengthened, it seems almost incredible.' This national pride persisted to the last moments of Corbett-Smith's life in 1945 when, after sending a letter to the local police headed 'Corbett-Smith on his self-despatch', he swathed his head in a Union Jack flag and shot himself on Margate Promenade.[76]

'The vilest abortionist is he who attempts to mould a child's character,' wrote George Bernard Shaw: but the views of school-masters were powerful in forming experience and constructing images of sexual infections. 'Groping about, as we all are, for the best way of helping boys,' the Revd Albert David of Rugby School told the Royal Commission on Venereal Disease of 1914, he had decided that 'to speak at all effectively' to boys about sex, he needed to do so with 'aversion, so that one's tongue almost stumbles over the words'. He believed that sex education should work up a 'boy's own natural shame', without making him 'curious': otherwise there would be the catastrophe that 'you let him loose with additional opportunity of exercising his imagination.' Human imagination became a source of disease: private fantasies or personal exploration were presented as something like a national menace. The recognition that individuals had private needs was denied. 'It is selfishness which is at the bottom of all vice,' according to the Revd Edward Lyttelton, successively headmaster of Haileybury and Eton, so boys' wishes had to be hidden from them: they had to think of anything but their own selfish urges. Children and adults alike had to be separated from feelings.[77]

J. L. A. Paton, High Master of Manchester Grammar School, advised the Royal Commission on Venereal Diseases in 1914 on 'training' young men to avoid risk of exposure to syphilis. 'The mother or nurse must begin to train' each boy as a toddler: 'inhibitions must be imposed, and the child must be taught there are certain parts of its own body it must not touch.' He judged 'self-control' and 'regularity' in bowel movements – 'what the mother calls the little duties of life' – to be important in avoiding sensual or affectionate children: a full bladder or bowels would increase the child's awareness of its own body, and regularity in the timing of lavatory visits would imbue discipline and physical self-control. 'It is a mistake to be too much given to caresses, to fondle the child too much,' Paton continued. 'The erotic instinct is already there, and it is one which we want to repress.' He praised the traditional Scottish mother who 'never used to kiss her boy' as likely to produce an emotionally reserved and unerotic man less likely to contract venereal infection. At school Paton inculcated 'the duty of chastity' together with 'school patriotism and civic feeling': 'any sort of indulgence in dirty talk, or dirty writing, means instant expulsion.' Contaminating influences must be isolated. Paton did everything possible 'to encourage hardiness and a love of fresh air and cold water' in a boy: 'it preoccupies his mind with manly things, and it postpones the sexual impulse.' Speaking 'as a man of sense', he blamed 'high feeding', that is good food and tasteful cooking, as the cause 'of our having so many young people who are just like pistols at full cock, strongly oversexed'.[78]

Venus Decomposing

With their terror of full cocks, with a moral heaviness that squashed spontaneity and personal pleasures, men like David, Lyttelton and Paton created a spectre of misery which has yet to be exorcized. They only partly succeeded in stopping people thinking for themselves about themselves: they failed to reverse the secularizing tendency which was turning notions of sin and penitence into notions of delinquency and correction, or of deviance and cure. Yet the underlying compulsion to punish remained. In other respects too, though the influence of headmasterly dreads and threats went underground, it persists in a fetid nether-region of the subconscious, contaminating the lives and imaginations of people who consider themselves untouched by the fears and ferocity of long-dead pedagogues. Venus in decomposing made a great deal more than sexual intercourse seem rotten.

CHAPTER SIX

Packets and Fanatics

I have never come across anyone in whom the moral sense was dominant who was not heartless, cruel, vindictive, log-stupid and entirely lacking in the smallest sense of humanity. Moral people, as they are termed, are simple beasts.   OSCAR WILDE

The terrible nature of this scourge comes home when one sees it, so to speak, wholesale. Passing through lines of tents in an outlying portion of a camp, impressed by the silence and loneliness, I asked, 'Where are the soldiers?' At command a bugle sounded, and out of the tents came between 500 and 600 victims of the disease, stricken in one of our pest-haunted sea-ports. It was a tragic sight, the sorrow of which was heightened by the knowledge that the offender's cross is not borne by the sinner alone. The gonococcus is a germ of terrible social malignancy, while the spirochete of syphilis, transcending the imagination of Ezekiel, visits upon the innocent mother and children the iniquity of the father, perhaps after long years of bitter repentance for 'his trespass that he hath trespassed and for the sin that he hath sinned'.

SIR WILLIAM OSLER, 1915

Thousands go to their doom from want of self-control; in vain did the great venereal camps, at which 90,000 men were treated in this country alone, point to GOD's judgment on an immoral life; in vain do the ruined health

of wives and children and the distorted and
disfigured limbs of children warn, like some
hideous spectre, the foolish youth of today
from the way of death.
BISHOP WINNINGTON-INGRAM, 1920

In 1913 there was appointed a Royal Commission on Venereal
Diseases, the report of which was decisive in directing preventive
health campaigns against sexually transmitted diseases in Britain:
indeed its influence continues today. The Commissioners' report
and its implementation were controversial. The protagonists in
this controversy were people of pronounced types, and their
personalities as much as the arguments they deployed were given
form by prevailing mentalities. In this chapter I devote some detail
to the characters, private motives and public conduct of those
involved because I believe it is the best way to recover and
understand the dominant and conflicting mentalities which have
fashioned policies towards venereal diseases in Britain for most of
the twentieth century. The conflict between professing Christians
and avowed agnostics, between those who insisted on the
Christian basis of society and those who demanded its complete
secularization, had as one of its battlefields the prevention and
cure of venereal diseases. The Christian forces, as we shall see,
won the battle, but found it was a pyrrhic victory.

International conferences on venereal diseases which were held
at Brussels in 1899 and 1902 stimulated interest across Europe in
social policy and medical research. Discussions on both occasions
were almost unanimous that state regulation of prostitution had
not reduced rates of infection, and led the College of Surgeons and
the British Medical Association to ask the Prime Minister,
Salisbury, for a Royal Commission to investigate the subject; but
Whitehall's horror of public sensitivities on the subject was
invincible, and in 1899 it was 'decided that public opinion was not
yet sufficiently enlightened to make a Government enquiry useful'.
The Reports presented in 1905 by the Royal Commission on the
Poor Laws deplored the 'terrible havoc' wrought by venereal
disease, particularly through infant mortality and childhood
illness, and were used by Colonel C. W. Long MP in his unsuccessful attempt to provoke a new government enquiry; in the

following few years the Advisory Board of Army Medical Services, and Royal Commissions on Feeble-Mindedness and on Divorce all gave attention to the subject. A petition was presented in 1911 asking that workhouse authorities should have power to detain venereally diseased paupers, but this too was rejected by the Government. Most officials and politicans wanted to avoid a subject which excited such contention, many regarded the remonstrances of moralists like the committee of the National Vigilance Association as vulgar and meddlesome impertinence and some at least had an inchoate reluctance to interfere in what they suspected was the proper punishment for sin. Even when, just before the First World War, the House of Commons voted that £50,000 be spent on laboratories to diagnose and treat venereal diseases, the Treasury intervened to stop this sum being spent, and a figure of £25,000 was substituted.[1]

Scientific advances, particularly Wasserman's test and Salvarsan, increased medical and lay interest in venereal diseases, and added to the pressure on the Government. In 1912 the Royal Society of Medicine and the Eugenics Education Society appointed a joint committee to study venereal diseases; in August of the following year special sessions were devoted to the subject at an international medical congress in London. Some weeks earlier a venereologist, Sir Malcolm Morris, urged in the *Lancet* the appointment of a Royal Commission, stressing the need for notification and for extended use of modern treatment. This call from Morris was echoed in a letter signed by several leading physicians which was published in the *Morning Post*. Other support came from the *Daily Telegraph*, whose proprietor Lord Burnham was sympathetic to medical reform on this subject, and the *Pall Mall Gazette*.

Morris lamented that the sexual reticence which had characterized the British 'since the Puritan era' prevented any attempt at legislative control of syphilis, which he dubbed 'dire' and 'a racial poison'. The case for legislation on notification and treatment seemed to him 'incomparably stronger' because syphilis was transmitted from parent to child, 'so that the offspring of a syphilitic may be born not with a mere predisposition to the disease, as in tuberculosis, but with the virus actually in its tissues, to cause, it may be, hideous deformity or blindness, or deafness, or epilepsy, or idiocy, ending often in premature though not untimely death.' Morris based part of his appeal for government intervention on the claim that venereal diseases jeopardized national security at a time when both Anglo-German relations and Balkan diplomacy were unsettled. 'In these days of a falling birthrate and of an international rivalry in which the weight of numbers are factors of national success or failure, a disease which is so frequent a cause of abortion, which at the best diminishes efficiency and at its worst consigns its victims to our asylums and infirmaries and workhouses and prisons, or to an early grave, cannot continue to be a matter of indifference to the State.'[2]

Such arguments were made irresistible by the discreet exertions in government circles of a few well-placed allies of Morris, notably Sir Almeric FitzRoy, Clerk of the Privy Council. A highly-strung man, hypersensitive and overweeningly snobbish, FitzRoy looked more like a buck of the Regency period than a civil servant, and indeed his caustic cynicism made him widely disliked in Whitehall. Intolerant, narcissistic, posturing and soured by life, he prided himself on being 'a man of the world'. His own sexuality was confused. His diaries are full of romantic ebullitions about strapping young peers and tall peeresses, indicative of repressed craving: he was eventually obliged to resign in 1923 as Clerk of the Privy Council after being charged with pestering girls in Hyde Park.[3]

In 1903–4, following the war in South Africa, FitzRoy obtained the appointment (with himself as Chairman) of a government Committee on Physical Deterioration, ostensibly in response to the War Office's shock at the feebleness of the soldiers which it recruited to fight in the Transvaal in 1899–1902. The Commiteee owed its appointment to the Duke of Devonshire, FitzRoy's mentor, and included such officials as the Board of Education's Inspector of Physical Training and the Inspector of Marine Recruiting: although there is no doubt that there was concern in Whitehall at the poor physique of working-class servicemen, FitzRoy's obsession with bodily perfection was significant to the formation and workings of the committee. Just as FitzRoy's influence with Devonshire was crucial to the appointment of the Committee on Physical Deterioration, so his intimacy with the veteran politician John Morley (by now Lord President of the Council as Lord Morley of Blackburn) was decisive in promoting a new Royal Commission on Venereal Diseases. In a speech inaugurating the International Medical Congress of 1913 Morley denounced the 'sheer moral cowardice in shrinking from a large and serious enquiry into the extent, causes and palliatives of this hideous scourge'; and two days after the Congress had called for confidential notification, and for enlarged facilities for treatment, Morley announced the appointment of a government enquiry.

The appointment of the Royal Commission prompted an incident of little intrinsic importance, which was nonetheless typical of the reckless opportunism which has characterized journalistic treatment of sexually transmitted diseases. Morley, as the minister responsible for appointing the Commission, received a letter from *The Times* alleging that its rival the *Morning Post* had supported medical pressure for an enquiry into venereal diseases 'solely [with] the view to increasing its circulation among the doctors', attributing sordid motives to the paper's editor and attaching 'ignominious and contemptible' responsibility for the campaign to the President of the Royal College of Physicians, Sir Thomas Barlow. FitzRoy dismissed the letter from *The Times* as 'journalistic jealousy', and it is clear that its staff wanted to discourage the appointment of an official enquiry into the disease, not from any sincere medical conviction, but so as to rob their competitor of the credit of a successful campaign. *The Times* remained ambivalent about publicizing the campaign against venereal disease. Although it covered wartime developments on the subject without inhibition, it became reluctant to publish correspondence from medical experts about prophylaxis, possibly because its proprietor Lord Northcliffe was believed to have been stricken with tertiary syphilis by 1915, and reputedly died of general paralysis in 1922.[4] Medical examination of prostitutes, or any reversion to the methods of the Contagious Diseases Acts, were excluded from the remit of the Royal Commission, as the Liberal Government was anxious to avoid confrontation with the suffragette successors of Josephine Butler: a desire which was a constant theme of official policy towards venereal disease for at least half a century after 1885. Various possible chairmen of the Royal Commission were mooted including the divorce judge Lord Mersey, other lawyers like Lord Desart, or Morley, who 'deemed the task too incongruous as the closing effort of his literary life'. After several refusals, the Government was 'compelled' to appoint Lord Sydenham, 'in spite of the fact that an ex-soldier was a somewhat queer substitute for a lawyer.'[5]

Long before his appointment to this post, Sydenham was notorious for 'egregious vanity'. Originally a professional soldier, he had been until 1907 Secretary of the Committee of Imperial Defence, a strategic co-ordinating body in Whitehall, and also served as a colonial governor in Australia and India. On his retirement from government service in 1913 he had received a peerage and become director of an armaments company. Restless, meddlesome, ambitious and masterful, he was adept in the surreptitious manipulation of journalists, possessed 'remarkable powers of self-deception', and was 'insensitive, clumsy, uncouth, and infinitely boring'. He was an inveterate and unscrupulous intriguer, who festered with grievances, and became 'the most uncompromising exponent of the most extreme Conservative views'. This fierce and gloomy old man hated modern social trends, and was a die-hard opponent of Irish independence, Indian self-government and Jews. His wife meanwhile led the British Women's Patriotic League, a body opposed to 'the presence of aliens and naturalized aliens' in Britain as 'exercising an evil influence upon family life and public morals' tantamount to 'a moral epidemic'. Together the Sydenhams shared a muddled congeries of pseudo-scientific or demi-eugenist beliefs about the need for 'a moral code' to maintain imperial power and keep undiluted 'the blood of our Nordic race'.[6]

The other members of the Royal Commission included FitzRoy and another Whitehall mandarin, Sir Kenelm Digby, a former Oxford law don and judge, who had been Permanent Under-Secretary at the Home Office until 1903. The medical profession was represented by Sir Malcolm Morris, the venereologist whose article in *Lancet* had stimulated the appointment of the enquiry; Sir Arthur Newsholme, Principal Medical Officer of the Local Government Board; the neurologist Sir Frederick Mott; Dame Mary Scharlieb, a gynaecologist and obstetrician; Mrs E. M. Burgwin, Inspector of the Feeble-Minded and a pioneer in educating mental defectives; J. E. Lane of the London Lock Hospital; and Sir John Collie, then Medical Examiner for London County Council. The political world was represented by the Labour MP, Philip Snowden, and a Liberal backbencher, Sir David Brynmor Jones, who was later, in a fit of 'Celtic irascibility', to storm out of the Commission 'to the scarcely concealed relief of his colleagues' after a disagreement with Sydenham in November

1913, and thereafter took little part in its deliberations.[7] Christianity was represented by Louise Creighton, an Anglican bishop's widow; by Canon J. W. Horsley, a former mayer of the slum district of Southwark known for his interest in temperance; and the Revd J. Scott Lidgett, a Wesleyan minister who was editor of the *Methodist Times* and for fifty-eight years Warden of the Bermondsey Settlement in an adjacent slum district.

Many of the Commissioners approached the subject with apprehension or bias. Several later published memoirs in which they expressed repugnance for their work. 'This was the very last task I should have chosen,' wrote Sydenham, 'I found my duties difficult and often unpleasant.' Snowden, Lidgett and Scharlieb found the subject 'very unpleasant', 'distressing' and 'repulsive' respectively. Three members of the Royal Commission – Newsholme, Morris and Scharlieb – also sat on a private committee under Bishop Boyd-Carpenter appointed in 1913 by the elaborately named National Council of Public Morals for the Promotion of Race Regeneration, Spiritual, Moral and Physical to investigate contraception and the birthrate. As its title indicates, Boyd-Carpenter's committee was committed to a vision of Christian morality allied to selfless duty to the Empire. Other Commissioners such as Mrs Burgwin publicly sympathized with the aims of this Council of Public Morals, while Lidgett and Mrs Creighton were both members of the National Vigilance Association. Scharlieb and Lidgett were Vice-Presidents of the London Public Morality Council.[8]

Sir Malcolm Morris, who was with FitzRoy one of the chief begetters of the enquiry, had been associated with public health campaigns against tuberculosis before diverting his attention to venereal diseases. From the early 1880s he was medical editor for the publishers Cassell, and edited the *Practitioner* in 1895–1902: through commissioning articles and books he was intimate with most medical specialists of his era, and rose to a position of influence in the medical world. His temperament was important to the methods of the Royal Commission and to the direction taken by its successor, the National Council for Combating Venereal Disease. 'In spite of Morris's virility and decisiveness, there was something feminine in his character which was both amusing, annoying and attractive,' according to one friend. 'To merely rational acquaintances it made him appear superficial, with more of the mentality of the advocate than the scientist; to the judicial he might seem one-sided; while to his friends this very same feminine trait showed up only as sensitiveness and affection.' He revelled in committee work, where he was subtle and resourceful: his tendency to intrigue, and his zest for backstair approaches, made him resemble Sydenham.[9]

The most distinguished medical member of the Commission was Sir Frederick Mott, who devoted his life to research on the central nervous system. As pathologist to London County Council asylums from 1895 until 1923, based first at Claybury Asylum and later at the Maudsley Hospital, he superintended a vast amount of research and published many important articles. He believed that mental disorders were correlated with bodily changes or grounded in physiology, and was hostile to Freudian doctrines of psycho-analysis. His greatest achievement was to prove (what had been earlier hypothesized) that general paralysis of insanity was due to tertiary syphilis, and had nothing to do with nervous inheritance or with the stresses of modern life. This proof had given double relief: it encouraged the work of those trying to prevent the disease, and reduced the fear of descendants of general paralytics that they would be afflicted with the condition. Mott also studied asylum dysentery, which had been ascribed to nervous afflictions of the intestine, but which he proved to be caused by poor hygiene. Mott was an early authority on shellshock – which he largely attributed to physical damage of the central nervous system caused by the noise of exploding shells, rather than to psychical disorder – and studied the importance of the degeneration of the thyroid and other endocrine and sexual organs in cases of insanity. He was also interested in eugenics and in reducing 'feeble-minded stocks' of the population. He was single-minded in his search for scientific truth, and for a medical scientist was unusually free from vanity or envy.[10]

In addition to his work for London County Council, Sir John Collie was Physician at the Hospital for Epilepsy and Paralysis in Maida Vale, President of the Special Medical Board for Neurasthenia and Functional Nervous Diseases, and medical adviser to several insurance companies. Author of treatises entitled *Malingering and Feigned Sickness* (1917) and *Fraud in Medico-Legal Practice* (1932), Collie spent much of his professional life helping businesses to resist compensation claims from injured employees.

He took pride in outwitting half-educated claimants and sarcastically dedicated both textbooks 'to my friend the British Workman to whom I owe so much'. His attitude may be judged from *Malingering*: 'most sick and injured workmen belong to a class whose education is incomplete [so] they are peculiarly unfit to take a detached view of themselves, especially when ill. Many working men of fair education, who in ordinary matters can act quite logically, and whose mental equilibrium is properly balanced, seem to be congenitally incapable of appreciating ordinary moral obligations when it rests with them to decide whether they shall or shall not return to work . . . Such people are victimized by their unstable nervous systems. Too often they make no stand against morbid introspection [and become] self-centred.' Collie's professional work was devoted to extirpating 'moral malingering' and driving his patients into 'self-control, self-respect and a return to work'. For 'fraud and hysteria' alike he recommended 'firmness', claiming (inaccurately) that 'nervous weakness' was unknown in Asia and in Africa, where 'the absence of sick pay aborts any growth of perverted sensations'. He also took the pose of a world-weary cynic: 'no-one who has any experience of human nature credits anything said by anyone about sexual affairs.'[11]

Among the Commissioners who were clergy, the Wesleyan Methodist, Lidgett, had a longstanding interest in venereal diseases: he was the favourite nephew of the redoubtable Lady Bunting, Josephine Butler's ally in agitating for repeal of the Contagious Diseases Acts. Lady Bunting devoted herself 'to the self-sacrificing service of moral causes, especially to the rescue and uplifting of imperilled and unfortunate women', according to Lidgett, and was an influence that 'inspired' his 'lifework'. He was 'an austere and exacting man with few intimate friends', who believed that 'religious convictions made [for] respectability'.[12]

Horsley had been a prison chaplain for ten years, during which time he had taken particular interest in the suicidal gestures of 'drunken women and silly girls'. A historian of Victorian suicide describes Horsley as a smug dogmatist with generous instincts, who believed that 'suicide, like every other kind of sin, crime and misery, was caused by intemperance, impurity, laziness and bad temper, and nothing else'. His copious writings on the subject can be summarized as preaching that suicide attempts could be reduced if magistrates gave a few exemplary sentences, if newspapers stopped reporting cases sympathetically or in detail, if inebriates were sent to reformatories, if workhouses stopped producing sulky, silly girls, and if all children were taught the duty of self-control. He brought the same brisk views to syphilitics and suicides alike. Much of his busybodying seems to have been a defence against any sort of introspection: irritated by the 'chronic levity' of young women, he was sustained in his work by bustle: 'one has not the time to be depressed, nor the desire to moan over failures,' he wrote. According to FitzRoy, Horsley's examination of witnesses before the enquiry was 'marked by puerile vanity and inconsequent fumblings', but the clergyman's sentimental radicalism was ill-matched to the frozen aristocratic hauteur affected by FitzRoy: Horsley's autobiography was subtitled *Memories of a 'Sky Pilot' in the Prison and the Slum*, a phrase calculated to revolt FitzRoy. 'Mrs Creighton and Canon Horsley, in the true spirit of clerical dogmatism, cannot detach themselves from the special prepossessions in which training and, in the lady's case, a certain bias have soaked them,' FitzRoy complained in 1915. 'Canon Horsley, it is true, claims to represent nothing but his own bald inspirations, which he deems authoritative, if not divine; but Mrs Creighton cannot think except in the terms of woman, jaundiced and embittered by the exaggerations of amour propre.'[13]

Certainly Louise Creighton believed her fellow women were 'bound' to fight for 'social purity'; she professed to oppose 'antagonism against men, whose weakness and wrongdoing is so clearly the cause of the degradation of numberless women, and of the suffering and disease which follows'; but in practice her indignation at 'the double standard of morals' expected of men and women made her a tactless and ineffective member of the Commission. 'Her whole mind was set on righteousness,' according to one admirer. 'Downright in manner and speech, with small regard for the graces and little diplomacies of life, she appeared at times uncompromising and even formidable.' FitzRoy loathed the company of she-dragons; 'Canon Horsley and Mrs Creighton were perhaps the least useful members; the interventions of the former were as frequent as ineffective, and the asperities of the lady's mind were in constant collision with sound policy,' FitzRoy noted. 'Even when she was in the right, her accents were provocative, and on certain points she was the dupe of tyrannical prepossession.'[14]

A strong Christian commitment was shared by other colleagues. Mary Scharlieb was a redoubtable woman who had been so shocked by the suffering of Hindu and Muhammadan women in the Orient that, despite opposition, she qualified at Madras Medical School in the 1870s: although she never had an operating knife in her hand until she was forty, she became one of the greatest abdominal surgeons of her era. From 1887 she was active in temperance work and the reclamation of English prostitutes: a woman of deep religious conviction, her faith dominated her life, including her approach to sexuality and prophylaxis. Compassionate and humorous, with high motives and wide experience, her attitude to sexual pathology was narrow and tendentious: she wrote, 'the horror of the subject consists not in the prevention and treatment of venereal diseases, but in the selfishness and moral slackness to which they are due.' She opposed the attempts of Marie Stopes to propagate birth control among the working classes: forty years' medical experience had convinced her that 'artificial limitation of the family causes damage to a woman's nervous system' and particularly created permanent psychological obstacles to conception tantamount to sterility. Contraception, she wrote in 1921, was 'not in the real interests of the wife, since by removing all fear of consequences from the mind of the husband it removes the only potent check on his desires, and thus . . . removes the wife's best protection against the slavery of too frequent intercourse.' Apart from this assumption of the beastliness of male sexual voracity, she viewed publicity for contraceptive methods in the same light as publicity for venereal prophylaxis: it was 'a moral wrong' to spread such knowledge as it would reach those 'outside conscience'. Emphasizing her professional background against the 'non-medical' training of Stopes, she wrote,

> Mankind is already over-sexed: the absence of all restraints, such as times and seasons impose on other animals, is probably the result of the over-exercise of this gracious gift, and anything which tends still further to increase the already super-abundant sexuality of man is an injury and not an advantage, both physically and morally . . . nations which practise artificial prevention of conception, and who therefore have no restraint on

their sexual passions, are likely to become effeminate and degenerate. The removal of the sanction of matrimony, and the unhindered and unbalanced sexual indulgence that would follow, would war against self-control, chivalry and self-respect.

These opinions, represented as pathological facts, were controverted by other physicians. Few other medical practitioners believed that the mother of a small family was more prone to nervous disorder at menopause, but rather that the unwilling celibate, or the exhausted woman, who had borne child after child beyond her strength, fell victim to their nerves. There was no evidence, as Scharlieb implied, that the father of a large family was more sexually abstemious than a father who used contraception: indeed, on the contrary, the fitting by a man of a condom on himself usually required a measure of that self-control which Scharlieb insisted was so important. Her objection that contraception for unmarried women was immoral overlooked that it was preferable for a woman who fornicated to remain childless, rather than for her to burden the State with the duty of support, or to be compelled to use abortionists.[15]

Scharlieb's colleague on the Royal Commission, Mrs Burgwin, similarly testified, in 1914 to Bishop Boyd-Carpenter's Council on Public Morals, that women who 'thwarted Nature' by using the 'terrible crime' of contraception became 'physical wrecks', that children from large families 'have frequently better physique' and that married couples who practised contraception 'necessarily lower [their] moral tone' and lack any 'conception of right or wrong, and of what human duty is, if they use this means'. Her testimony was intolerant, censorious, dogmatic and impossibly exacting in its standards. She felt women with small families were more inclined to waste money, and asserted righteously, 'either people should abstain from marriage or they should accept the full responsibilities of it.' The poor, she affirmed, ought to be 'segregated' to prevent marriage or intercourse, rather than given contraceptives, and she opposed the use of condoms as a prophylactic against venereal infection, believing 'chastity is the only correct remedy.'[16]

From the outset in 1913, FitzRoy, Morley, Morris and Sydenham had intended that the Commissioners should return an unanimous Report which it was thought would therefore carry more authority, and the efforts taken in 1915–16 to ensure this were ruthless.[17] The Report itself reflected the group mentality which has been shown in my description of the Commissioners, and which was so representative of the industrious and high-minded professional and administrative classes of the era. The Commissioners recognized the harm to national health, and the depths of personal misery, caused by venereal diseases: they were humane, conscientious people who wanted to take the most bold and constructive steps to cure these diseases that scientific knowledge and administrative efficiency would allow. But at the same time they were Christians horrified by the consequences for eternity of trifling with moral laws; they believed that sensualists were unceasingly enticed yet tormented by sin, that Hell could be defined as slavery to insatiable sin. They could not bring themselves to relieve the punishment of sin or mitigate the fears of sinners; but unlike the Victorian framers of the Contagious Diseases Acts they accepted no distinction between male and female sinners. As a result their recommendations were generous, but lethally incomplete. Only two of their main recommendations were not adopted by the Government: confidential registration of causes of death, and a uniform national system of medical records. But recommendations for better facilities for laboratory diagnosis, using the Wasserman test, the organization of treatment centres by county and borough councils, and the provision of Salvarsan or its substitutes without charge were adopted. It was also agreed to permit patients to attend treatment centres distant from their homes, so as not to be recognized.

Sydenham's report was presented to the Local Government Board. Its President at the time, Walter Long, was 'emphatically a "safe" man', but 'quite obviously a very stupid man' in the view of contemporaries. 'He always wanted to do the right thing and always (equally) in the wrong way.' Long took the opinion of his department's Principal Medical Officer, Newsholme, who was one of the Commissioners, and within a few days local authorities were directed to provide clinics and out-patient facilities, with Salvarsan prescribed as medication, together with health education on venereal diseases. Central government provided 75% of the cost of these services, as the Commissioners advised. The Local Government Board also urged local authorities to establish treatment centres in each town with a population exceeding 20,000, and to appoint full-time venereal disease officers (68 clinics were open by June 1917). Long's civil servants were so overburdened by the organizational problems of establishing new venereal disease centres to co-exist with existing treatment centres that they delegated all educational and propaganda work – much of it politically contentious and therefore unwelcome – to an independent body, the National Council for Combating Venereal Disease, which had been formed in 1914, but which only launched into active life after the presentation of Sydenham's Report. It was evidence of the intense national concern that had been aroused that a public appeal in 1916 for funds for the NCCVD raised £18,000 in a few weeks.[18]

This was an impressive but partial effort. Buried inside their long Report, the Commissioners put two sentences which conceded that mercury could 'destroy or arrest the multiplication of the spirochaetes', and that Metchnikoff had shown that calomel cream applied to the site of a syphilitic inoculation in apes prevented infection. Without other inferences or comment, the Report added, 'This procedure has been shown to be also protective to man.' Many doctors found it inexcusable that the Commissioners chose to expurgate an important item of sanitary information, and to imply to the Government and to the public that Metchnikoff had done no more than produce syphilis in a few monkeys. The Commissioners' silence was purposive, and attributable either to their fear of the presumed hostility of public opinion, or to their disapproval of the spread of any knowledge concerning the prevention of venereal infections by medical means.[19]

At least one member of the Commission, Mott, had previously written that 'it would be well' if Metchnikoff's prophylactic methods 'were widely known and practised in the civil population', and he publicly emphasized this opinion on several occasions. As Mott later confirmed, he and at least one other Commissioner wished to mention the efficacy of Metchnikoff's formula of calomel and carbolic acid or Condy's fluid of potassium permanganate in their Report, but 'were deterred from doing so' in the interest of unanimity: 'they did not want to smash the whole Commission up.' He felt that Metchnikoff's ointment had been vindicated in treating the armed forces and should be extended to civilians. 'I have all along taken that view,' declared Mott, and had pressed it on Sydenham and Morris, 'but I was told that it was impossible': to other members, notably the clergy and Mrs Creighton, the thought was too terrible, and so a discovery with which the medical world was ringing, and which was then being used to protect 20 million belligerents, was passed almost in silence. Mott relinquished the point in the hope of securing an effective and unanimous report in other respects.[20]

Commissioners like Mrs Creighton were worried by the 'dangers' which accompanied 'the indiscriminate distribution of knowledge'. Writing in 1914, before the Commission reported, she affirmed that knowledge of social evils was 'of the utmost value' when there was a certainty that 'sane and wise thinking [would] influence conduct and public opinion'; but she had a horror of unrestricted knowledge among those with different ethical standards or social background who might reach conclusions or urge solutions, 'rash and ill-considered' as she called them, different from her own. Her fellow Commissioner, Newsholme, a humane man who was perhaps the leading authority on public health in Britain, similarly believed that 'non-personal and indiscriminate instruction' in prophylaxis would 'increase the amount of promiscuity, which is the real enemy to be fought'. He wanted moral training from early childhood. 'Knowledge is necessary, but in practical life it is attitude more than knowledge that counts. The real failure in life consists in the shirking of . . . self-control.' This attitude permeated the Commission and shaped its strategy of suppression.[21]

The Commissioners were prisoners of a mentality which believed that knowledge was the preserve of the few: a source of political power and private corruption which it would be dangerous for the newly literate masses to enjoy. Thus the intention of Lord Meath's Indecent Advertisements Act of 1889 was to protect people who had received a smattering of 'education in our Board Schools', workers 'in factories and workshops' for whom 'in the evening the only resort is the streets' from handbills about venereal diseases: their corruptibility was sharply distinguished at the time by Lord Kimberley (Foreign Secretary in Rosebery's Government) from the incorruptibility of educated gentlemen who wished 'to introduce a copy of Aristophanes or Boccaccio into a house'. This outlook prevailed until modern times. Counsel prosecuting a bookseller who stocked sex education textbooks by reputable sexologists opened his (successful) case in 1950 by emphasizing the need to keep such books away from the less educated: books which were not obscene if sold in a shop in a rich thoroughfare like Kensington High Street nevertheless were obscene if sold in a shop in unfashionable Blackpool, he argued. Similarly a seizure order by Glasgow magistrates placed on Flaubert's *Madame Bovary* was justified at the Home Office in 1954 with the comment: 'what can be studied by an undergraduate is not necessarily fit reading for the entire population.' Under the Obscene Publications Act of 1959, the price of a book was one of the 'relevant circumstances' for the courts to consider when deciding who was likely to read the book and consequently whether it would 'deprave and corrupt'.[22]

When the paperback publishers of D. H. Lawrence's novel *Lady Chatterley's Lover* were charged with obscenity in 1960, the prosecuting barrister showed this traditional anxiety about the dissolution of working-class discipline under the influence of eroticism in his famous question to the jury: 'Is this a book that you would even wish your wife or your servants to read?' His objection was not only that the novel 'sets out to commend sensuality almost as a virtue', but that it was being sold at a price of 3½ shillings which would put the book within the grasp of the masses. Similarly the Conservative lawyer, Hailsham, would 'have preferred to see it between boards and priced at 30 shillings', as he told the House of Lords (the Labour party's deputy leader, Hattersley, took a similar stance in 1989 when opposing a paperback edition of Salman Rushdie's *Satanic Verses*). Cleland's novel *Fanny Hill*, first published in 1748–9 under the title *Memoirs of a Woman of Pleasure*, was not prosecuted under the 1959 act when available in an edition costing two guineas, but was successfully prosecuted when issued as a cheap paperback in 1963. When Hitler's *Mein Kampf* was republished in English after many years in 1969 the publishers were at pains to emphasize that 'the selling price was set intentionally high so as to avoid any imputation of catering to a mass audience': there was indignation when a paperback version (again priced over the average) was finally issued in 1972. It requires a curious reading of German history in the 1930s to believe that the rich alone were immune from infection by Hitler's doctrines, or contributed nothing to the destruction of Weimar democracy. This patronizing censorship based on class discrimination remains at the heart of British public life.[23]

This hostility to working-class eroticism – this refusal to trust the less educated with the facts and images of sexuality – was ubiquitous. It even affected senior military officers, who as a caste regarded army morale as contingent on sexual activity and were hostile both to civilian pressure to shut brothels and to moralizing about continence. 'A good judge of war' declared in 1918 that 'a man – or a boy . . . could not fight well unless he could love well'; but when 'habits acquired in the billets of France or Flanders', to quote the libidinous General F. P. Crozier, 'spread rapidly to Mayfair and Whitechapel, and all the places in between', officers became uneasy. Nevertheless when Sir Thomas Barlow, President of the Royal College of Physicians, suggested to the Government in November 1914 that the police be empowered to exclude prostitues from military areas, the Home and War Offices were aghast at the prospect of reviving the controversies which surrounded the Contagious Diseases Acts. A policy of prevarication was adopted, with lectures, improved recreational facilities and support for volunteer female patrols intended to shame prostitutes. For a year and a half the two ministries tried to shuffle responsibility for dealing with prostitution onto each other, with the War Office insisting to the public for a long time that the military rate of venereal infection of 4.8% was lower than in peacetime. Politicians and civil servants alike were paralysed by their desire not to provoke the suffragettes, and by memories of Josephine Butler's campaigns. This response was the antithesis of that of the Americans, for whom the elimination of venereal diseases among its combatants seemed sufficiently important to justify coercion and intimidation. Conversely the British were wary of parliamentary or popular opposition if they infringed civil liberties.[24]

There was a class element to this *laissez-faire*. 'The officers are better off,' Crozier wrote. 'Comparative luxury, knowledge [of prophylaxis], and armour [condoms] stand them in good stead.' But while officers had the freedom to sleep 'the night in Lina's arms, after a not too good dinner and minding one's p's and q's', the ranks had to make 'the best of it in a thorny ditch' with whomever they could pick up: without condoms, or knowledge of their efficacy, they ended up 'standing in a queue later at the Red

Lamp clinic' seeking disinfection. 'As there are in the ranks of the British Army some of the finest middle- and lower middle-class stock in the Kingdom, it is not surprising that young men find themselves in this strange queue, who would, in times of peace, have hesitated to line up outside a music hall.'[25]

Eventually, in 1916, an Army Order was issued directing that soldiers who had exposed themselves to the risk of venereal disease should attend treatment within 24 hours of *infection*, but did not specify if this meant *exposure to infection* or the time when the soldier first noticed the disease. The order was prefaced with the sentence: 'Suggestions with regard to prevention which would imply the adoption of any system of prophylaxis which might be said to afford opportunities for unrestrained vice could not be accepted by the Army Council.' This was a sop to those, like Scharlieb or Mrs Creighton, who wanted to maintain the pretence that ablution rooms were not for prevention of infection, but for early post-coital treatment.

There was bitter contention over statistics. In Portsmouth, for example, with good facilities for disinfection of troops, Lord Sandhurst, representing the Government in a parliamentary debate in 1919, stated that the infection rate was two and a half times that of the United Kingdom average. These figures were stigmatized by Sir Archdall Reid as 'enormously inaccurate', and were contradicted by the major-general formerly in command at Portsmouth, who stated that in the first nine months of 1917, approximately 3,750 men served under him, of whom five contracted venereal disease. After some obfuscation, the Government conceded that Sandhurst's figures were 'very much too high': but this incident excited suspicion of the Government's good faith.[26]

Of Allied troops who visited Paris on leave, but without prophylaxis, in the summer of 1917, 20 per cent contracted venereal disease; but in the five months from November 1917, when prophylactic kits were provided, this figure fell to 3 per cent. Venereal disease was sometimes deliberately contracted, and at one stage during the war, infected prostitutes in London and Paris earned more money than healthy ones, as soldiers wanted to be invalided and escape fighting. Elsewhere 'men, driven insane by the ordeal of battle, bought and sold tubercle sputum and gonorrhoeal discharge, and deliberately infected themselves for the purpose of securing evacuation from the firing line to the Base

Hospitals.' Some soldiers sold their discharges to fellow combatants, who would infect their genitals with it, or most tragically of all, smeared their eyes 'and came in blind'. All these cases were cited as evidence of the failure of prophylaxis.[27]

Infection rates for troops from Australia, Canada and New Zealand were higher, because their soldiers were on average younger, seldom married and had no homes to visit when on leave. After providing prophylaxis the Canadians cut their infection rate from 22% in 1915 to 8% in 1918, and the Australians from 16.7% in September 1917 to 13.2% a year later. Pressure steadily mounted for action against venereal disease from representatives of the colonial administrations. Sir Robert Borden, the Canadian Prime Minister, spoke in 1917 of venereal disease being 'carried to every dominion of the Empire, and the future of our race damaged beyond any comprehension'. In the same year a clause was added to the Criminal Law Amendment Bill then before Parliament making it a criminal offence for a person with 'venereal disease in a communicable form' to 'have sexual intercourse', a clause which was intended, in the words of a former Home Secretary, 'to make the provisions of our Statute law fit the moral sense of the whole community'. When, after delays, the Bill was enacted in peacetime, this clause was omitted; but the Government's concession of this principle made an interim order to protect soldiers irresistible: in March 1918 clause 40D was added to the Defence of the Realm Act making it an offence for any woman with communicable venereal disease to have 'sexual intercourse with any member of the armed forces or any of His Majesty's allies, or solicit or invite any member to have sexual intercourse with her'. Women charged under this regulation could be remanded for medical examination for not less than a week – a provision which would have been less objectionable if it had been applied to men too.[28]

The War Office, which was responsible for implementing this law, preferred to ignore it, so that by July 1918 there had been under one hundred convictions, although the Government misled colonial leaders into believing that prosecutions had been far more widespread. Later in the summer politicians felt that the continuance of clause 40D would be unpopular among women voters, who would be enfranchised for the first time at the general election, and moved towards abrogating the clause. So as not to enrage colonial leaders, this decision, born of political expediency, was masked by the appointment in October 1918 of a government committee under a judge, Lord Moulton, with Sir Malcolm Morris as one of the members, to consider amending 40D. In the event, following the Armistice in November, Moulton's committee, together with clause 40D, was quietly abandoned. The War Office declined a request by Sydenham to circulate to demobilized soldiers a memorandum on venereal diseases which he had prepared.

The Army's success with prophylaxis vitiated the Commissioner's attempt to expurgate Metchnikoff's discoveries, but there is another aspect of Sydenham's Report which deserves scrutiny. After hearing specialist medical opinion, it recommended legislation (which was enacted in 1917) imposing a penalty of up to two years' imprisonment on anyone who treated or publicly offered to treat or advised on treatment of venereal disease, or prescribed remedies. This interdiction was intended to stop advertising by quacks, some of whom were unscrupulous in their charges and methods, and others of whom blackmailed clients with threats to denounce their infection; but until 1925 it also prevented pharmacists from recommending such self-disinfectants as Condy's fluid or Metchnikoff's formula to customers who asked them for advice. Witnesses representing the General Medical Council who testified before the Commission were emphatic that 'quack' and 'free practitioner' were synonymous, and treated quackery as heresy was under the Inquisition. Indeed, when a hapless spokesman for herbalists and unqualified practitioners appeared before the Commission, FitzRoy assumed the role of Torquemada, and subjected his victim to a cascade of mockery and denigration, with Sydenham and his medical colleagues scarcely less hostile. (The persistent hatred of unqualified practitioners was demonstrated in the American film *No Greater Sin* distributed in Britain in 1942, featuring the trial and vindication of a young man who when he realized that his wife and their foetus were venereally infected killed the quack who had told him before his marriage that he was cured.)[29]

One anomaly of this legislation was that it became a criminal offence for a pharmacist to answer a customer's enquiry about what chemical preparation might be taken to avoid venereal disease, although no offence was committed by either party if the customer knew what to ask for and the pharmacist sold it. This penalized the ignorant, and, as the sexologist Norman Haire wrote, was 'based on the theory that people can be made moral by fear of consequences'. The Act made no distinction between preparations and medicines for external or internal use, nor did it consider whether they were intended for prevention, cure or relief. The Minister of Health, Neville Chamberlain, confessed to a delegation of 1923, which urged him to revise this Act, that even lawyers had difficulty in interpreting it, but later that year the Law Officers of the Crown gave the Ministry of Health a new legal interpretation, to the effect that chemists could verbally recommend preparations to customers, so long as they did not offer any written or printed advice. (One of the law officers, Sir Thomas Inskip, later protested that the 'gratification of sexual appetite' was 'an unsavoury subject' in itself.) The Director of Public Prosecutions, Sir Archibald Bodkin, deprecated the law which he had to apply: 'Section 2 somewhat remarkably forbids public advertisement of any preparations, even if they would be suitable and intended solely for prevention, although prevention would appear', Bodkin advised, 'desirable to emphasize and make known'.[30]

Bodkin claimed in 1925 that cases against pharmacists were hard to prove or prosecute under the Act, and there were occasional cases of pharmacists who were deservedly prosecuted for giving bad advice or useless medicines (a Dudley pharmacist was fined £20 in 1934 for recommending and selling a futile concoction to a young gonorrhoeic); but on other occasions the law was quickly and easily applied for purposes far from those for which it was framed. In 1930 a pharmacist who published a booklet on contraception was prosecuted, because it contained information on treating infections, although the avowed intention of the authorities at Reading was to suppress the booklet before it could provide teenagers with information on contraception. Another case at Manchester caused disquiet. A man was sentenced in 1927 to six weeks' imprisonment by a magistrate connected with the NCCVD for selling a leaflet on prophylaxis which was scarcely distinguishable from literature distributed by some local authorities. Although the man was eccentric, he had been encouraged in his work by various medical officers of health and by military camp commanders: his conviction created a 'contradictory and deplorable legal position', and was inevitable given the vindictive handling of his trial by the NCCVD magistrate, who was strongly committed to preventing free dissemination of knowledge. This law still applied over fifty years after its enactment. In 1970 a youth called Richard Branson (afterwards head of Virgin Records and manufacturer of Mates condoms), who had founded the Student Advisory Centre in Piccadilly, offering advice on sexual and drug problems to young people, was convicted under the 1917 law. There is little doubt that the police used the old Act to harry Branson, whose iconoclastic views they found objectionable; he was charged after another young man accused of possessing drugs was acquitted at trial with the help of Branson's testimony.[31]

Sydenham himself was President of the NCCVD in 1915–20, and his coadjutors from the Commission such as Morris and Scharlieb were active in its work. Its aims were to provide information on the prevalence of venereal diseases and the necessity for early treatment; to promote the provision of greater facilities for treatment; to increase the opportunities for medical study of these diseases; 'to encourage and assist the dissemination of a sound knowledge of the physiological laws of life, in order to raise the standard both of health and conduct'; and to organize lectures and literature about its aims. The NCCVD received a government grant of £16,250 in 1916, and during 1918–29 annually received between £10,000 and £15,000 from central government, the first time that the Treasury made a grant for propaganda to a private body.[32]

Sir Charters Symonds, a surgeon at Guy's Hospital who was Vice-President of the NCCVD, recalled that in the foundation phase of the Council, 'care was taken to avoid suggesting that means should be taken to prevent infection', for which 'reason the term "prevention" first employed [in the Council's title] was changed to Combating'. The reasons for this were explicit. 'I strongly feel that there is a distinct moral difference between telling people to go about with disinfecting packets in their pockets, and urging them if they fall into temptation to take the earliest possible treatment,' Sydenham declared in the House of Lords in 1919. 'My Council gave earnest consideration to the point, and decided to have nothing to do with the former policy' because 'indiscriminate distribution' of these packets would 'arouse ... curiosity and ... lead into vice men who would otherwise recoil from it'.[33]

'All reference to disinfection was taboo,' according to a venereologist who offered help to the NCCVD at the end of the war: 'employment as a lecturer was conditional on agreement not to mention or recommend personal disinfection as a method of combating venereal disease.' Indeed this attitude was taken to such an extreme that the early publications of the NCCVD 'permitted the recommendation of a very mild and, therefore, often ineffectual disinfectant (sodium stearate [soap] and water) after sexual risk, but forbade the recommendation of an effective disinfectant (such as potassium permanganate and water)'.[34]

After his Report had been presented, 'Sydenham laid on his Commissioners the duty to do all the propaganda work of which they were capable', and several did so with great energy. Morris in 1917 published a book about venereal disease whose supposedly distasteful subject was obscured under the title of *The Nation's Health*. Schoolteachers, the clergy, scoutmasters and social workers, who needed information to instruct others, were sent lecturers by the NCCVD, as were meetings of the general public organized by friendly societies, mothers' unions, girls' clubs, munitions workers, and so forth. 'It was a very difficult duty at first,' recalled Scharlieb, who lectured all over England. 'The situation was novel, it was necessary to speak on a subject that was unknown to audiences that were at heart unwilling to be taught. The very name of the venereal diseases was repulsive to the public, and not infrequently those who invited me to lecture did their best to disguise it under a more attractive title ... nothing but a realization of national danger and an appreciation of individual duty could have made it possible to tell the whole truth ... so as to help and not disgust the audience.' The reaction to such lectures is conveyed by the response to an address to the Richmond branch of the Women's Co-operative Guild in 1917. 'A speaker from the Civil Liberty Council lectured us upon Venereal Diseases, and moral risks for our sons,' wrote Virginia Woolf who was present. 'I felt the audience was queer, and as no one spoke, I got up and thanked her, whereupon two women left the room, and I saw that another gigantic fat one was in tears.' One woman 'told the lecturer it was a most cruel speech, and only a childless woman could have made it "for we mothers try to forget what our sons have to go through". Then she began to cry. Did you ever hear such – nonsense it seems to me. The poor speaker said she was used to it.' Woolf's servants told her afterwards that 'indignation was expressed by most of the women' at public mention of VD. Her cook 'after being a little shocked . . . agreed that it was most important that women should have knowledge in such matters – and then she told me stories of friends and relations, and how they'd suffered.' Virginia Woolf herself was not without prejudice on the subject, as she believed that venereal infections were the fate of social classes other than her own: she found it bizarre that the poor did not 'discuss these questions openly, considering how much more they are affected by them than we are'.[35]

Throughout the period 1914–42 the Secretary of the NCCVD was Sybil Neville-Rolfe, the wife of a naval commander and the daughter of an admiral. Widowed at the age of twenty in 1906, she consoled herself with reforming prostitutes and studying eugenics for some years, and became General Secretary of the NCCVD on its foundation. Forceful in 'persuading influential (and possibly only half-convinced) people to help in her good causes', according to an admirer, 'her tactics were irritating; but they were so patently employed only to further the welfare work to which she was devoted . . . that irritation soon gave way at least to amused tolerance.'[36]

The NCCVD rapidly drew criticism as a 'little knot of intensely prejudiced and incapable private people, to which is now opposed a mass of scientific and instructed opinion immensely more weighty than its own', to quote Sir Archdall Reid. He despised the 'tortuous' reasoning whereby the NCCVD employed lecturers to 'expound the horrors of these maladies' who were 'forbidden to explain how they may be prevented'. The trouble, he felt, was that the NCCVD was 'under ecclesiastical control', a mere 'appanage' of Randall Davidson, Archbishop of Canterbury. It is true that the Archbishop was active in pressing his belief that 'medical science [must] take a wider view than the purely physical one', and that there was 'peril' that if methods of prophylaxis were publicized, Britain would forsake 'sound principles of moral conduct . . . upon which the well being of English homes depended'. Nevertheless neither the NCCVD nor its successor body, the British Social Hygiene Council, ever enjoyed enthusiastic support from the Churches. They had the support of individual Christians among both clergy and laity but, as an Oxford college chaplain wrote in 1933, 'the bishops themselves tend to be influenced by rather than to influence trends of thought' and avoided questions of 'social hygiene'.[37]

Mary Scharlieb, with her Christian bias, urged on behalf of the NCCVD that packets 'had been only partly successful' even when used by soldiers and sailors well instructed on how to use them. She inferred that packets would provide little protection to civilians, 'since they were to be used by men undisciplined and untaught ... probably suffering from emotional disturbance at the time when the appliances should be used.' To Scharlieb 'the offer to make unchastity safe was a blow at the nation's morals', and as a gynaecologist she warned 'that the method was practically inapplicable to women and that therefore a potent source of infection was left untouched'. The Victorian dual standard of sexuality, or the phallocentric policies made notorious by the Contagious Diseases Acts, were (so she suspected) being surreptitiously perpetuated.[38]

The NCCVD supported early treatment of persons infected, or supposed to be infected, with appropriate facilities in hospitals or elsewhere, but opposed provision of facilities for immediate self-disinfection. Yet the success of preventive treatment depended on the shortness of time between exposure to infection and the use of a disinfectant: in most cases, unless a disinfectant had been provided before the risk was run, the earliest possible moment for successful disinfection would be missed. The NCCVD's scheme for local treatment centres where antisepsis could be provided on application inevitably entailed delay: and the moral difference between possessing a disinfectant before copulation and seeking disinfection afterwards seemed factitious to the Council's few early critics.

One luminary of the NCCVD was Dr Edward Turner who in addition to several hospital appointments in London was a member of the Social Hygiene Advisory Committee of the Colonial Office, an executive member of the London Public Morality Council and an Inspector in the Special Constabulary. Turner was the British Medical Association's representative on the NCCVD from 1915 (chairing its medical committee in 1919–22), and Vice-President of the NCCVD between 1921 and 1931, responsible after Morris's death in 1924 for its liaison with the Ministry of Health. During and after the war he addressed some 2,000 public meetings on venereal disease, and his resonant voice reached perhaps a million men. 'Not for him any fine chopping of logic, but a forthright slashing frontal attack that was almost overwhelming in its force and weight,' wrote Dr Bishop Harman, an ophthalmic colleague. Turner 'detested venereal disease with his whole soul, and he spent himself journeying from place to place lecturing to crowded audiences of men . . . [with] his bluff, hearty speech, [and] manner of taking his audience into his confidence.' 'I treat sick persons, I do not tell them how they can deliberately run into danger and attempt to avoid results,' Turner declared to justify his opposition to 'the issue of packets and preaching of self-disinfection'. He practised in one of the richest parts of London, but treated few cases of venereal disease, doubtless because his indiscreet and censorious reputation preceded him: as he admitted, 'any boy whom I might know who had this disease would go to any doctor but myself to be treated.' Thirteen young officers came to him during the war with gonorrhoea or syphilis, and with his gullible puritanism, he believed nine of them who offered 'their word of honour that under no circumstances would they have gone wrong unless they had been taught and instructed in the use of packets'. One can imagine the circumstances in which miserable youths produced this excuse to deflect Turner's remorseless disapprobation. Like Scharlieb he equated venereal prophylaxis with contraception. The advertisement and supply of 'packets' would ruin morals and complete the evil work begun by 'Malthusian propaganda'.[39]

Another founder of the NCCVD was the obstetrician Sir Francis Champneys, known for his high principles and austere faith: he was a devotee of sacred music, contributed to the Anglican hymnal and had a church organ built in his drawing room (see plate). A vice-president of the London Public Morality Council, his language and belief typified the NCCVD's leadership in the 1920s. Champneys believed that fornication and adultery were the worst of mortal sins, 'which, without repentance and amendment, destroy the soul', and that it was 'apostasy' to condone them in any way. 'Inasmuch as the soul is immortal while the body is mortal, a mortal disease of the soul is far more important than a disease of the body, however physically dangerous,' he asserted: 'a person dying of syphilis innocently acquired is far better off than a person who commits either of these mortal sins with complete physical safety and does not repent . . . the complete abolition of venereal disease without corresponding abolition of unchastity would only leave the modern world where the ancient world was when it drew down the unmeasured denunciation of the Apostles.' Champneys preferred 'that venereal diseases should be imperfectly combated than that, in an attempt to prevent them, men should be enticed into mortal sin'; to accept 'that in the public interest it is better that some young men should fall, rather than that venereal disease should fail to be prevented in some cases of incontinence, would be to repudiate Christianity.'[40]

There was vigorous opposition to the views of Champneys, Turner and their colleagues. Lay people were alarmed when a doctor announced that, though able to prevent disease, he would refrain from doing so out of conscientious scruples which the laity did not share. Doctors forfeited public confidence when they suggested that prevention of disease was a matter for their personal discretion according to their individual theories of social science. Champneys' appeal to avoid fornication lest disease be contracted evoked 'about as contemptible a motive as can well be imagined', to quote Hugh Elliot, who questioned 'whether the Creator is likely to show favour to a person who refrains from fornication, not because it is opposed to the Word of God, but for fear he should acquire venereal disease'. Elliot had recently published a major study of the Victorian philosopher Herbert Spencer, whose arguments for the pre-eminence of the individual over society and of science over religion were congenial to him. He represented the most powerful intellectual tradition of nineteenth-century secularism. Elliot asked 'those better acquainted with the motives of the Creator, whether a man whose spirit is moved towards fornication, but who desists lest he contract disease, is more likely to achieve salvation than another man of the same moral tone but less worldly prudence'. The religiosity of Champneys seemed medieval to Elliot. 'A true religion would restrain a man from fornication, for the simple reason that it was against the word of God; a true morality would restrain him because fornication would offend all his natural sentiments; but the religion of medievalism would propose to restrain him by the fear of the disease.' This appeal to craven instincts and low self-interest insulted those at whom it was directed. It accorded 'with the old idea of Hell, as a place where sinners are everlastingly submitted to the pains of burning': Champneys wanted 'the retention of a minor hell as a means of deterrence', whereas Elliot believed that 'the abolition of horrifying penalties does not ... promote wickedness, but leads to more gentleness and charity, in which a true morality flourishes.' To Elliot it seemed that the NCCVD 'never learnt anything by experience, but always guided their activities by their prepossessions and obsessions of the moment ... worked up in the guise of ingenious schemes for social regeneration ... Their shifting and uneasy minds still clung to the gospel of suffering and pain.'[41]

The NCCVD for a short period enjoyed universal support for its work, but several of its supporters objected that its promotion of 'moral hygiene' entailed a resolve to discredit and suppress physical hygiene. Their discontent was further aggravated by government intervention. In January 1919 the Minister of Health, Dr Christopher Addison, appointed a committee on the dangers of infectious epidemics during the process of naval and military demobilization. Its Chairman was Waldorf Astor, Parliamentary Secretary to the Ministry of Health, a modest, conscientious and unselfish ascetic, who was converted to Christian Science in 1924. Venereal infections were considered by this committee, and after taking evidence from medical, service and other opinion, they reported in August 1919 'their unanimous view that the true safeguard against these diseases is individual continence and a high standard of moral life' with 'sound public opinion and a healthy national tone'. Astor reported that prophylactic packets gave 'a false sense of security', especially as the Army's carefully organized packet system 'would be unattainable in the civil community', where the sexually active were not susceptible to control. 'Energy should not be dissipated on measures of doubtful value, but concentrated rather on wise propaganda and the provision of early, prompt and skilled treatment, in order to diminish the prevalence of these diseases.' The premise of Astor's Report that without 100 per cent success in preventive medical techniques, 'a false sense of security' was given, and that therefore propaganda about prophylaxis should be eschewed, was without parallel in other branches of medicine. If this requirement of total success had been widely applied, diphtheria or tetanus anti-toxin, quinine, the use of antisepsis or asepsis in surgery and all preventive surgery would have been abandoned.[42]

The Astor Report so irritated the secularists of the NCCVD that several of them resigned in 1919 to set up the Society for the Prevention of Venereal Disease. The first President of the SPVD was Lord Willoughby de Broke, leader of the die-hard group in the House of Lords dubbed by Lord Dufferin and Ava as 'the Slashem and Bashem Party'. A picturesque, bluff-spoken fox-hunting squire (see plate), he combined romantic ideals about the duties of a landed gentleman with radical views on social policy. A fervent believer in military conscription, and hence in working-class soldiery with strong physiques, he hankered after a Britain ruled by hereditary leaders enjoying the chivalrous dues of an idealized feudal order. Together with this quixotic blimp, the Vice-Presidents of the new society included Rudyard Kipling, H. G. Wells, Fellows of the Royal Society such as Sir Leonard Hill and Sir Ray Lankester, Lt General Sir Francis Lloyd, and the armaments manufacturer Vincent Vickers. The van of the SPVD consisted of four 'sturdy and uncompromising fighters – Lord Willoughby de Broke, Sir Archdall Reid, Sir Bryan Donkin and Sir Frederick Mott, who were all die-hards of the bulldog breed and would never countenance compromise or expediency if such entailed the very slightest surrender of principle'. The SPVD's Secretary, Bayly, later successfully sued Astor for likening 'the packet people' to supporters of licensed brothels in their belief 'that man is frankly an immoral animal, and that it is the duty of the State to make the indulgence of his animal passions as safe as possible'. (Astor had denounced the SPVD for proposing to educate adolescents in the use of packets: 'I cannot imagine anything more revolting to fathers and mothers that their sons and daughters should be taught how to indulge in promiscuous sexual intercourse with impunity . . . a combination of Hun material efficiency and Latin unchastity totally alien to Anglo-Saxon tradition and conscience.')[43]

Mott was muted in public, inhibited by his fatal decision in 1916 to succumb to the blandishments of Sir Malcolm Morris and the pressure of Lord Sydenham to suppress mention of prophylaxis. The SPVD's most vociferous medical leaders were Sir Bryan Donkin and Sir Archdall Reid. Donkin made his early mark as physician at the East London Hospital for Children, later developing interests in neurology and criminology. He wrote prolifically on such subjects as the influence of heredity in mental disease, the role of venereal contamination in mental pathology, and the connections between disease and crime, between fraud and spiritualism, and between faith and credulity. He was a humanist who deployed 'close and often destructive logic' against religious mysticism and loathed psychoanalysis. Decisive in his views, 'to hear him conversing with women, which he was very fond of doing, even on difficult subjects, was a lesson in good breeding,' according to a medical friend, Sir Seymour Sharkey. 'He spoke with as much care and consideration as he showed to men, but treated them with infinite gentleness, and so gained many a devoted friend.' Reid had travelled the world as a game-hunter and mineral prospector before settling as a general practitioner at Southsea in 1887. He published in 1896 an ambitious and vigorously argued monograph on evolution, in which his knowledge of primitive life and tropical pathology was reinforced by acute and ruthless study of literature on the subject. His *Principles of Heredity* (1905) offered a complete scheme of biological evolution under which humankind's mental and physical character was acquired, not innate. He looked forward to a national eugenics policy whereby the weaker members of the race would die out while the others gradually developed racial immunity to disease.[44]

The Secretary of the SPVD in 1919–28 was Dr Hugh Wansy Bayly, a man as energetic and formidable as both Donkin and Reid. A venereologist of volatile political enthusiasms, he was in 1920–2 simultaneously associated with the Nationalist party of Horatio Bottomley (a demagogue later imprisoned for embezzlement), a member of the Labour party, a shortlisted parliamentary candidate for Lord Rothermere's Anti-Waste League and an unsuccessful Imperial Conservative and anti-prohibitionist candidate in the general election of 1922. Later in 1923–4 he founded the Ex-Service Men's National Movement and the Workers' Liberty and Employment League, both naive bodies of fascist tendencies, and he was the self-styled expert on Nordic racial biology advising a campaign led by Lord Queensborough and Lady Sydenham against alien immigrants. Like Reid he was interested in genetic evolution, but he bastardized Darwinian theory by arguing that 'the logic of biology' insisted that there was 'no equal moral standard' between male and female sexuality. He epitomized the dogmatist who peddled personal nostrums under the guise of objective scientific facts. 'A small coterie of faddists, knowing naught of and caring less for biology, have made equality of the sexes in everything a foolish and ephemeral slogan,' he fulminated in 1930. 'It is incredible and absurd to suppose that Woman, through countless ages, should have concentrated her energies on her mother role and left physical and intellectual strife to Man, if such specialization . . . had been prejudicial to race advancement.' From these 'logical and reasoned theories' and 'proved scientific facts' he proceeded to deny 'that women shine in politics, in business, in learned professions, or even in art', and to denigrate women compulsively and comprehensively. If Mary Scharlieb and Louise Creighton at the NCCVD represented the heirs of Josephine Butler and other radical women, Bayly with his commitment to prophylaxis was the standard-bearer within the SPVD of Victorian medical practitioners' defence of the dual standard of sexuality and the supreme prerogative of phallic desire. Bayly, like Donkin and Reid, prided himself on his rationalism (while in reality, like the others, he was a highly emotional man): each of the trio was a deliberate and embittered enemy of Christianity generally, and the Christians of the NCCVD specifically. Bayly wrote in the 1930s that there was 'no human being more intellectually immoral, more unscrupulous in withholding, twisting or exaggerating evidence, more imbued with the savage doctrine that the end justifies the means, than . . . an official of an emotional cult obsessed with the delusion that they have ethical and religious sanction for their cause'.[45]

The SPVD in many ways resembled the Malthusian League, founded in 1877 as the world's first birth control society. It was fiercely secularist, smaller in membership than the NCCVD, attractive to people of eccentric or even disreputably reactionary political views. It was combative, intolerant and marginalized; yet its aims might be thought progressive or enlightened, and were so noisily propounded as to carry themselves far and wide. Its representatives urged the provision by public authorities of washing places, attached to lavatories in streets, stations and hotels, with good lighting, warm water and scrupulous cleanliness, open at all hours of day and night. They suggested that each would have an attendant responsible for their cleanliness and for keeping the apparatus and medicaments in good order; the latter would have been a weak solution of permanganate of potash and a supply of calomel ointment, for which a charge of threepence would have covered the cost. They derided the hopes which the NCCVD attached to Early Treatment Centres: 'treatment centres cannot compass any material degree of success unless they are widely advertised; and wide advertisement will make people ashamed to go to them.' Whereas the NCCVD assumed that most 'irregular intercourse' occurred with prostitutes in brothels, the SPVD recognized that 'the immense mass of immorality is not with prostitutes' but occurred in 'parks and fields, in lanes and passages, in brothels, hotels and private houses'. (Sir Edward Henry, the Commissioner of Police for London, stated in 1906 that in the previous year, there had been over 1,000 prosecutions in the metropolitan area for copulating in public places such as streets, alleys and parks; 63% of soldiers who had contracted a venereal infection while in England in one survey of the First World War had done so in the open air; and a quarter of a century later a public health inspector found 23 used condoms in a Birmingham road which was frequented by young people who had nowhere else to fornicate at night – one of the facts which made Winnington-Ingram, Bishop of London, exclaim of condoms in 1934, 'I would like to make a bonfire of them and dance round it.')[46]

Despite the way in which the SPVD was marginalized as a small group of rancorous eccentrics, it shook the NCCVD and gradually undermined the prevailing Christian denial of prophylaxis. It increased the secularization of medical and official thought concerning the reduction of venereal infections. The belligerence of Bayly, Donkin, Reid and Willoughby de Broke caused offence, as was intended. In the early 1920s there were several attempts to conciliate the warring factions. Sydenham wearied of the controversy, and retired as President of the NCCVD in 1920; his successor, a young Conservative politician called Lord Gorell, argued unsuccessfully in 1921 for the appointment of a new Royal Commission, chaired by the Imperial Proconsul Lord Milner, to arbitrate in the row and to consider the desirability of compulsory notification, which had been excluded from Sydenham's terms of reference in deference to suffragette feeling.

The attitude of the newly formed Ministry of Health was decisive. Sir Arthur Robinson, the most senior civil servant at the Ministry, held 'very strong views' about self-disinfection. 'Even if the practicability of effective self-disinfection were established, the moral and social objections to it are so weighty as to outweigh the medical arguments for it,' Robinson wrote in 1921. 'But the practicability of effective self-disinfection is not established in the least – the moral and social objections remain in full force and I am clear the Ministry should give no countenance to it.' Addison's successor as Minister of Health, Sir Alfred Mond, regarded compulsory notification, which had not been recommended by the Royal Commission but which was urged by Gorell, as a policy which the House of Commons would never approve because it infringed personal liberty. Mond suspected that notification would deter 'people suffering from the disease from seeking medical aid and so do more harm than good' and was 'apprehensive' that the activities of the NCCVD 'would lead to a perverted view being taken of . . . the relation of the sexes with possibly calamitous results socially and racially'; he had 'secret sympathy with the scientific basis of the prevention doctrine' advanced by Bayly, Donkin and Reid, but said he could not politically survive 'the opposition that would be aroused if he adopted it officially'.[47]

It was to resolve this impasse, in 1921–2, that the Royal Physician, Lord Dawson of Penn, persuaded the Ministry of Health that it was desirable for another committee to evaluate the case for self-disinfection and pacify the SPVD and NCCVD. The Ministry welcomed his idea, but were keen to avoid direct responsibility: membership of the new Committee was not decided by civil servants, but delegated to an advisory selection committee chaired by Dawson, which included six medical knights. The Chairman of the new Committee was Lord Trevethin, 'peppery and a bad organizer', who had recently retired as Lord Chief Justice, and the Vice-Chairman was another judge, Tomlin. Trevethin was recommended as 'a man of the world' free of prejudice or eccentricity: Lord Tomlin was Counsel to the Royal College of Physicians, and a man of some scientific attainments. Their selection was intended to ensure that a tone of judicious impartiality would pervade the Report, which Dawson wanted to be acknowledged as conclusive. Other members of Trevethin's Committee included physicians representing the Eugenist Society, the Admiralty, the Air Force, the Home Office, the House of Commons, the London County Council, Oxford University and several venereologists. Their remit was to report upon 'the best medical measures for preventing venereal disease in the civil community, having regard to administrative practicability, including costs'. After twenty-eight meetings, they reported that 'the success of any general public facilities for self-disinfection is likely in the civil community to be very small', and that money would be best spent on public health education and treatment facilities rather than facilities for self-disinfection, although ablution centres in areas like docks were desirable. Sexual continence, rather than medical meaures, was identified as the only absolute preventive of infection, though Trevethin's Report accepted that sheathes provided 'a measure of protection'. It urged that the Venereal Diseases Act of 1917 should be interpreted to allow qualified pharmacists to sell disinfectants with printed instructions approved by competent authorities. Compulsory notification was dismissed as likely to cause concealment, and useless until the Government took powers to detain patients.[48]

Trevethin replaced Gorell as President of the NCCVD in 1923, and was on the brink of reaching agreement for the unification of his organization with the SPVD when Willoughby de Broke died suddenly in December 1923. This interrupted negotiations, but it seemed possible that an accommodation might be reached when Sir Auckland Geddes (a physician who had recently been a Cabinet minister) succeeeded Trevethin as President of the NCCVD and Willoughby de Broke as President of the SPVD. Geddes however was an autocrat who soon irritated Bayly, and the two societies were never reconciled.[49] In 1925 the NCCVD's name was altered to the British Social Hygiene Council as a reflection of reduced public interest in venereal diseases, as well as to stress their intimacy with the newly formed American Social Hygiene Council and to signal their interest in improving 'Social and Racial Health' by 'promoting all those factors essential to the good life which depend on the inherent quality and personal behaviour of the individual in his capacity as a social unit of the community'.[50] During the ensuing decade the SPVD declined into desuetude. The sequel to these events will be recounted in the next chapter; it is enough to conclude that in the 1920s the SPVD leadership was justified in feeling savage at the Royal Commission for its suppressions, and at the NCCVD for its complicity. 'The chicanery and the humbug, the uncourageous fanaticism, the treachery to the Army and the nation, the flood of useless misery and disease, the slaughter of the innocents – these', as Archdall Reid wrote, 'will not be forgotten, but will stink in the nostrils of the nation for ever more.'[51]

CHAPTER SEVEN

─◦◦◦─

The Eaten Heart:
Syphilis since the 1920s

Blind,
Deaf,
Stunted,
Scarred,
With teeth fast set on edge;
What soul is there
Within that carrion's case
Riddled with the workings of the pallid
    spirochaete.
What soul?

Blind,
Hot,
Drunken
Lust.
The father ate of sour grapes,
And in a moment soured
The very source of life.
The fouled beginning
Breeds a foul descent
And Death.

DR N. BISHOP HARMAN,
'The Wages of Sin', 1928

What's syph? Syph is something that only boys
get. Boys like you. Boys who tell lies. Boys who
do not do as they're told. Boys who try to
dodge their work instead of facing it like men.

JAMES HANLEY, *Boy* (1931)

We were right, yes, we were right
To smash the false idealities of the last age,
The humbug, the soft cruelty, the
   mawkishness,
The heavy tyrannical sentimentality,
The inability to face facts;
All of which linger on so damnably among us.
   RICHARD ALDINGTON, 'The Eaten Heart'

This chapter chronicles venereal diseases in Britain over the last sixty years, a period in which the medical character of syphilis and gonorrhoea were transformed by antibiotics, but in which the stigma attached to the disease was only nominally adjusted. There remained a high level of public ignorance about symptoms and cures, and a punitive attitude to patients persisted, although it sometimes was more subtle in its expression. There was slow and often reluctant recognition that venereal infection could no longer be described simply as 'the handmaid of prostitution'. Catchwords changed – 'sinner' was replaced by 'delinquent' – but moralists well beyond the age of highest sexual activity continued to preach and nag, and were usually faithful to the first precept of all moralists since St Paul: be unkind in order to make people good. Syphilis could justly be depicted by an expert in 1924 as 'a greater menace' to national health than cancer or tuberculosis: as 'a peculiarly disabling and killing disease which is gnawing deeply into the vitals of the race' (in 1924 out of a total mortality of 473,235, syphilis killed 60,335, cancer accounted for 50,389 and tuberculosis slew 41,103). But as mortality rates fell in the following quarter century, the fear, dread and secrecy surrounding the disease proved less eradicable than the microbes.[1]

There has been a repeated conflict since the 1920s between those venereologists who sought to treat patients on the basis of a straightforward scientific approach to therapy unencumbered with moral judgments, and those who reflected other public and medical sentiment which prefers the social uses of disease to dominate therapeutics. The latter school emphasizes individual responsibility for infection: with different degrees of explicitness, it sees venereal diseases as blameworthy, as a punishment for those who transgress moral codes or for those whose dirty behaviour threatens to soil everyone. VD, in the Central Office of Information's phrase of the late 1940s (see illustration on page 275), was the punishment of unclean people capable of vile crimes: 'a great evil and a grave menace to the whole nation and to the future of our race'.[2]

Public attention to venereal disease diminished in the 1920s: a declining preoccupation with racial purity, boredom with furious medical controversies, wider access to apparatus for washing or self-disinfection after intercourse, the opening of rehabilitation hostels for young women who had been infected, and therapies like bismuth or Salvarsan combined to reduce the problem. Above all there was an increase in the number of clinics and an improvement in the scientific services available to treat new cases: by 1938 there were 188 venereal disease treatment centres in England and Wales supported by 99 pathological laboratories, including a central laboratory set up in 1924. Infant deaths certified as attributable to syphilis fell from 2.03 per 1,000 registered births in 1917 to 0.2 per 1,000 in 1938. The incidence of new syphilitic infection fell by almost 50 per cent in the fifteen years after 1917, with most of this improvement occurring by 1924 as the result of the educational breakthrough in methods of prophylaxis and cure which followed the public discourse and controversy of 1917–21. There were 6,421 cases of new syphilitic infection in men and 2,683 cases in women during 1931, but the overall rate of new infections fell by over 45% in the period to 1939, in which year there were 3,574 male and 1,412 female cases reported respectively. The war caused a resurgence of new infections, which peaked in 1946 at 10,705 for men and 6,970 for women: but by 1950 new infections were down to 2,678 and 1,465 for the two sexes. The total recorded cases of gonorrhoea fell from 35,693 in 1938 to 26,369 in 1942, although there was subsequently a further rise. These improvements were not attributable to an outburst of sexual continence or an increased number of hymens unbreached until the marriage night: 27,753 children were born to unwed mothers in 1938, representing 4.2% of the total annual birthrate. In that year 42% of women aged under 20 who married were pregnant at the time; 31% of women who married at the age of 20 were pregnant, falling to 10% of women marrying at the age of 25. Half of a survey of men aged between 16 and 45 conducted in 1941 believed in the acceptability of premarital sexual intercourse 'if you are in love with your girl', compared with only 2% who believed in sex with either 'any casual girl acquaintance' or a prostitute.[3]

Apart from the provision of better facilities for treatment, there was more careful behaviour by people at higher risk of catching disease. 'The White seafarer is becoming less thoughtless and indifferent on the matter of his own responsibility for the spread of V.D.,' wrote the Medical Superintendent of the Seaman's Hospital in 1929, reporting that increasingly sailors remained under treatment until their primary or secondary syphilis had healed and they were safe from relapse. Fatalism nonetheless persisted in some quarters. James Hanley, who was a merchant seaman in 1914–24, published an autobiographical novel on maritime life in 1931 in which the fate of a boy who contracts syphilis in Alexandria is regarded as hopeless by his shipmates: 'When it's dark just take a header overboard and that's the end of it,' advises the steward, shortly before the captain suffocates the youth with his greatcoat and throws the corpse into the sea.[4A]

Controversy about sheathes as a preventive of venereal disease during the war of 1914–18 publicized their contraceptive value (so that the birthrate among the unskilled and semi-skilled fell by 14.4 per cent between 1923 and 1933). Their imminent arrival as a subject of less restricted discourse was signalled by the publication in 1917 of Norman Douglas' elegant novel *South Wind*. One of its characters, an American called van Koppen, pondering as a teenager 'certain coarse organic impulses', 'had both the wit to realize the hygienic importance of a certain type of goods and the pertinacity to insist on cheapening their price, in the interests of public health'. By a national advertising campaign with the catchphrase that condoms should be 'within reach of the humblest home', van Koppen succeeded in 'shattering the Paris monopoly' of such products and was soon able to retire 'on a relatively modest competence of fifteen million dollars a year'. Two years earlier it would have been unthinkable for a novel to make ironic fun of condom manufacturers, but *South Wind* was deservedly a best-seller. Moreover, as Norman Douglas teasingly predicted, sales of sheathes increased enormously: one British manufacturer alone was producing 8.5 million condoms yearly by 1934. Although many were used as marital contraceptives, others were bought by young fornicators who were exposed to infection. Free samples were sent to couples who announced their engagement in newspapers, automatic vending machines were left on the pavement outside chemists' shops at night or installed in public houses

1. The Earl of Meath, the Christian philanthropist responsible for the Indecent Advertisements Act which temporarily suppressed discourse on venereal diseases.

2. Randall Davidson, Archbishop of Canterbury 1903-28, whose contradictory interventions in questions of sexual morality reflected Christian anguish at the creeping secularization of the age.

3. Cosmo Lang, the proud prelate who succeeded Davidson as Archbishop of Canterbury. After many years spent ruthlessly trying to impose his views on sexual morality, he finally conceded in 1937 that Britain had 'a largely non-Christian population'.

4. Arthur Winnington-Ingram, Bishop of London from 1901 until 1939, who was prominent in public morality councils and wanted to make a bonfire of all the condoms in the country and dance round it. He detested the dirt and corruption of city life, and is appropriately depicted here in a quasi-rural idyll at Fulham Palace.

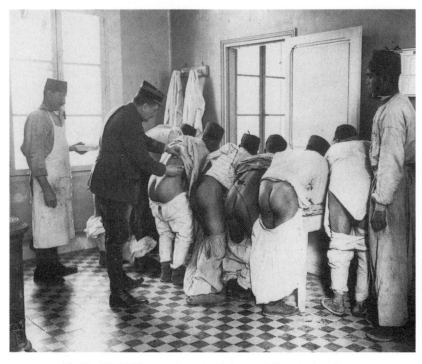

The First World War not only resulted in increased dissemination of venereal infections, but also in much greater public discussion of methods of
prevention and cure. Surprisingly little illustrative material survives. This
photograph of Algerian riflemen in the French army receiving treatment for
syphilis in 1916 is an exception. It is significant that the troops selected to be
photographed in this somewhat undignified posture were not European.
There was still a tendency to present syphilis as the affliction of Others who
were both dirty and foreign.

Two members of the Royal Commission on Venereal Diseases: Philip Snowden *(right)*, the Labour minister, in Downing Street – Snowden was likened by one contemporary to Robespierre, the sea-green incorruptible. Reverend John Scott Lidgett *(below front)*, at a gathering of Wesleyan ministers – Lidgett was one of the most austere leaders of the Nonconformist community in Britain.

Lord Willoughby de Broke, the President of the Society for Preventing Venereal Disease which wanted full publicity and free availability of prophylactics.

Sir Francis Champneys, the obstetrician and vice-president of the National Council for Combating Venereal Diseases. He believed that if a country adopted widespread prophylaxis, its citizens would lose their souls to Hell.

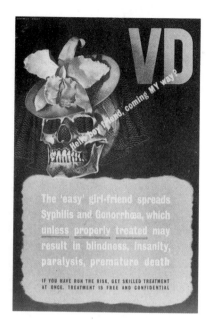

Ministry of Health posters counselling the public
on venereal diseases from the late 1940s and
early 1950s.

1. Sir Alfred Mond (Lord Melchett), who as Minister of Health in the 1920s privately sympathised with those who wished to make methods of prophylaxis against venereal disease freely available, but dared not do so on political grounds. Lord Winterton used to interrupt his parliamentary speeches with cries of 'Silence in the Ghetto'.

2. Earl Winterton, possibly the most voluble homophobe in Parliament in the 1950s.

3. Sir David Maxwell Fyfe, Home Secretary during the increased persecution of gay men in the early 1950s, and furious in his later denunciations of homosexuality.

4. Rupert Croft-Cooke, the author who was imprisoned for homosexuality in 1953 and suffered police harassment after his release.

EVERY TIME
YOU SLEEP WITH A GIRL,
YOU SLEEP WITH ALL
HER OLD BOYFRIENDS.

These days you can't be too careful.

You see, sexually transmitted diseases aren't that fussy ...ey don't care whether you're male or female, straight or ...ly, promiscuous or choosy.

On average, you're likely to have six sexual relationships in ...ur life. So, if you sleep with six other average people you are ...tually part of a chain of contacts that totals a staggering ..,656 people No wonder AIDS is spreading.

Already a person dies of the disease every day, and the ...tish Medical Association figures suggest that by 1991, some ...,000 people in Britain will be affected.

And, with the virus itself changing five times faster than other viruses, hope of a cure seems distant. It's terrifying news. But there is something you can do to protect yourself. Use a condom.

Because it's been shown that condoms help prevent the transfer of the virus (they'll also reduce the risk of VD, cervical cancer and unwanted pregnancy).

Mates condoms are just as reliable and just as sensitive as other brands. The range includes Ribbed Mates, Natural Mates and Coloured Mates – all of which carry the BSI Kite-mark

They're widely available in pubs, newsagents, clubs, record stores, garages, chemists and supermarkets.

They're made by one of the world's largest manufacturers. Yet they cost less than other condoms.

And all profits from Mates Healthcare Ltd are going to help fight AIDS. We'll be producing leaflets, videos and information packs to educate people in 'Safer Sex' techniques.

Because prevention is better than cure

We also plan to give money to hospices and counselling services for those dying of the disease

So, when you use a Mates condom, you won't have to worry about the present and you'll also be helping to safeguard everyone's future.

MATES. YOU MAKE LOVE. THEY MAKE SENSE.

THESE DAYS, WOMEN ARE ONLY
INTERESTED IN MEN
WHO ARE WELL EQUIPPED.

"THEY'RE AWFULLY FIDDLY TO PUT ON.
ISN'T THAT HALF THE FUN?"

(which had the 'indefensible' effect according to Lord Darcy de Knath of 'converting the poor man's club into premises for retailing the accessories of the brothel'). As Cosmo Lang complained when Archbishop of Canterbury, garages sold sheathes to people who hired 'a motor car for a joy ride' – the joy in question being a fuck on the back seat or in a field beyond the reach of parents or landladies. The suggestion of the divorce judge, Merrivale, that it was criminal to supply unmarried people with condoms ('the facilities which render prostitution comparatively safe') was not pursued, although the House of Lords in 1934 tried to restrict the public sale and display of 'these filthy things' despite their contribution to reducing the level of disease.[4B]

The treatment centres which proliferated between the wars were not wholly effective. The ideal VD Officer imbued with 'the public health ideal', according to Harrison, 'sees in his patient someone who is a potential danger to the community, not merely a person whose sufferings are to be alleviated, and he regards default from treatment not merely as a sin, the consequences of which will fall on the patient's own head, but as a hindrance to the attainment of the great object of the V.D. scheme, since the default may lead to the spread of disease.' To forestall patients defaulting from a complete course of treatment, the personality of staff at a treatment centre was more important than its accessibility or the anonymity of its surroundings. As one patient wrote in 1935, 'I was reading something about Patients going to the "Free Centre" and not taking it Serious Enough, well you can take it from me that all the patients I have met were serious enough, and a smile and a joke inside is like the Sun shining, and makes you think that you are not so bad after all, and if you keep plodding ahead everything will be alright.' The public regarded venereal patients as 'outcasts, although actually such patients are not different from anybody else', wrote the physician in charge of the Rochester and Gravesend treatment centres in 1930. 'There is no more disgrace in having V.D. than in having influenza; the disgrace, if there is any, is in the immorality which goes before. But as the majority of people are more or less immoral at one time or another, why should the lucky ones, who have escaped disease, hold up the finger of scorn at those who have not escaped? . . . This hypocrisy does exist, and is a great deterrent to many going to the V.D. Clinics, especially women; they do not want to go because they think they will be labelled as venereal and disgraced.' Harrison's prototype clinic at St Thomas's Hospital was known as the Lydia Department to reduce the embarrassment felt by those attending for the first time when asking for directions to the VD clinic: and the stigma of infection caused other complications. Many women infected by their husbands felt 'shame so profound' that they loathed attending VD clinics because they had a 'deep-rooted, elemental feeling' that they would be 'further degraded by having to sit with such women as are sure to come there', and often ceased treatment when the symptoms had been relieved, rather than when the infection had been eliminated. There was a high default rate among women attending VD clinics. 'Women patients are very shy of new nurses, and a rather censorious, slightly rough nurse can empty a clinic in a very short time,' Harrison wrote. There was 'constant searing fear', another venereologist reported of young women with VD, that friends or employers might discover that they had a venereal infection and that they would then be ostracized or lose their job 'as utterly outcast and degraded'.[5]

Some patients found the attitude of clinic staff hostile or humiliating, and ceased to attend as soon as their immediate symptoms had been cured. This antagonism was doubtless imagined in certain cases by patients agitated about their attendance, but in other instances their feeling that treatment was accompanied by a punitive manner was justified. Jobs at such clinics carried low prestige for physicians or nurses: 'I could not ask my nice nurses to do such work; you would have to have special staff, and they would have to be housed by themselves,' said the matron of a provincial hospital in 1935 when threatened with the possibility of a new treatment centre at her hospital. Only a minority worked there by first choice: in the late 1930s the Ministry of Health found that of 357 medical officers in their 188 centres, only 63 were venereal disease specialists, of whom just 44 were in charge. The remainder professed other branches of medicine. A significant number were bitter at finding themselves in jobs which they had not wanted at the beginning of their careers, and vented their frustration on patients. ('Two of the greatest evils in British social life are venereal disease and the Press,' wrote Sir Robert Bruce Lockhart in 1937: 'they cannot command the services of first-class men. No young medical student who has any hopes of success dreams of taking up venereal disease because there is a social stigma on "pox-doctors". For the same reason no decent man goes into journalism.')[6]

In contrast to the efficacy of treatment centres, and the competence and compassion with which some were administered, the management of lock hospitals remained unsatisfactory. The lock wards of Edinburgh Royal Infirmary were described by one doctor who worked in them as 'awful': he saw up to 150 out-patients in each evening session, and only had help from the hospital gate-keeper in preparing the patient's arm with a tourniquet and iodine for injections of Neo-Salvarsan. Female patients were treated mainly by 'a devoted and capable sister, whose good moral influence on the girls was considerable and probably of more value than her medicines', but until 1919 the wardmaster for male patients was an old soldier chosen for his ability to impose order rather than for his nursing knowledge or desire to help patients. He exploited everyone within his power, exacting payment for services from patients, and battening onto them once they had left hospital. With barred windows, locked doors and the prohibition of visitors, male patients were isolated within the institution: after a daily parade, they were marched to the basement to earn their keep by chopping firewood for the rest of the hospital. In the early 1920s both men and women were treated in small theatres adjoining the two lock wards, where overcrowding prevented privacy, asepsis and detailed examination. Out-patients were seen in a temporary wooden hut which was dingy and whose facilities were inadequate. These conditions continued until 1934, when a new building was erected, with two floors allocated to venereal patients. This department was considered as late as 1960 'among the best designed and equipped in Britain' by one of its doctors who, in a phrase which shows the priorities which can develop within institutional hierarchies, lamented that 'alas the venereologists by their attention to preventive medicine have so reduced their work that they agreed in 1958 to give up one floor to satisfy the constantly growing demand for dermatological treatment.'[7]

The oldest specialist institution for venereal cases, the London Lock Hospital, perturbed the Ministry of Health throughout the 1920s. It was headed by Charles Gibbs (1868–1943), who had been elected Assistant Surgeon there in 1897, and was Senior Surgeon from 1907 until his death. He was also in charge for many years of the venereal department at Charing Cross Hospital, and served as a medical officer during two wars. Gibbs conformed to a familiar but egregious type within teaching hospitals. 'He was a ruthless leg-puller' who 'taught vividly and with tremendous gusto', according to one student. He was 'either very much liked or disliked; and he also either liked students (and staff) or actively disliked them.' He had a caustic tongue which he never scrupled to use, although in fairness it was generally to emphasize some telling teaching point. Gibbs' approach to his patients was heavy with judgment. 'During the war . . . the morality of the women of this country deteriorated horribly,' he declared in 1920. 'I mean the bare-faced manner in which young girls of sixteen or seventeen would come into one's consulting room and say, "My boy has given me the clap"!' He preferred those patients who were submissive and remorseful.[8]

His conduct of the men's lock hospital at Dean Street in Soho and the women's lock hospital at Harrow Road was all that could be expected from this description. Colonel Lawrence Harrison, Director of the Lydia Department at St Thomas's Hospital which was the model for other venereal treatment centres, inspected all the lock facilities in 1920 and again in 1922, in his role as the Ministry of Health's adviser on venereal disease. Harrison found Gibbs stubborn and inefficient, and judged that it would be 'impossible' to improve conditions while Gibbs remained Senior Surgeon. Gibbs' approach was disliked by colleagues within the hospital, but this did not result in constructive reforms. Although 'good individual work' was done by some senior members of the staff, Harrison judged that 'it cannot make for good instruction of younger men that they should learn in a school where such diametrically opposed opinions prevail.' Until 1923 the Hospital produced 'grossly inadequate' returns on their patients, and Gibbs had a subjective and unsubstantiated view of the categories of admission. Harrison deprecated 'these hospitals from the public health point of view', but concluded, 'we cannot hope to change them.'[9]

New complaints reached the Ministry of Health in 1925 from Lord FitzAlan of Derwent, who was leader of the Roman Catholic laity in Britain. He complained that although one Roman Catholic woman was allowed to visit women and children at the Harrow Road building, priests were prevented from seeing patients. Investigation of FitzAlan's complaint disclosed that the managers of the lock charity discouraged any visitors who might criticize conditions. As a result, in 1926, Harrison returned with Dame

Janet Campbell, the Ministry of Health's medical adviser on women and children, to inspect facilities and treatment. They found patients were deplorably fed and subjected to deliberate discomfort; children born to unwedded women in the lock hospital had been refused baptism because they were 'born in sin', and patients were forbidden to visit the hospital chapel unaccompanied. They expressed concern at the case of a woman patient who had been sent to the hospital with a misdiagnosed ophthalmic condition, who was found to be uninfected, but who nevertheless contracted gonorrhoea which blinded her as the result of bad hygiene during her medical examination. Both Campbell and Harrison were doctors as well as civil servants, and identified two cases in which women patients had died in childbirth at the lock hospital after poor treatment. 'Any social work done appears to depend on the goodwill of the Matron and the more or less haphazard activities of certain voluntary workers,' they reported. Although the hospital Secretary, H. J. Eason, deflected these criticisms before the hospital's governing body of clergy, doctors and philanthropists, in 1927 the Women's Committee of the hospital, a group of professional and upper-class women charged with fund-raising and other supervisory benevolence, resigned in protest at his methods. The London County Council also withdrew its annual grant of over £10,000 to the hospital. 'This *mis*management is gross, the most glaring example of mismanagement I remember,' wrote Britain's Chief Medical Officer, Sir George Newman, in a private memorandum. 'It is a scandal that such conduct of a hospital should be allowed.' Later in 1927 Davidson, the Archbishop of Canterbury, gave an ultimatum to Newman that he and Sir Thomas Barlow, a Royal Physician, would resign from the hospital Committee unless there was an enquiry into its management. The Archbishop was 'much disturbed', condemning both the chaplain and the 'misdeeds' of Eason, whom he called 'dishonest'. These criticisms were echoed by Sir Arthur Robinson, the senior civil servant at the Ministry of Health, a man famously reserved and cautious, who called Eason 'nasty'.[10]

This threat from Davidson and Barlow forced the Ministry to appoint a Committee of Enquiry chaired by Sir John Eldon Bankes, a Lord Justice of Appeal. After interviewing many of those involved, and after inspecting facilities, Bankes and his colleagues confirmed that patients were treated as 'moral outcasts', and were 'constantly' made to feel 'the subjects of moral disapproval'. In other respects, too, Eason's regime was condemned by their Report, which, despite political pressure and a parliamentary debate in 1929, Neville Chamberlain, the Minister of Health, refused to publish. When, soon afterwards, the Conservatives were defeated at a general election, Chamberlain's Labour successor made Eldon Bankes' Report available to the public.[11]

Despite this indictment, the governors of the hospital refused to replace Eason, although other outside personnel were introduced. New women members such as the Countess of Leitrim were recruited; the management board was strengthened by two bankers, J. F. W. Deacon and Lord Kinnaird, and two politicians, Sir Samuel Strang Steel and Alderman Leonard Snell of Paddington (described by Harrison as 'a broad minded gentleman quite out of sympathy with any repressive, condemnatory attitude towards the patients'). Even so, reforms were slow. As Harrison noted in 1931, 'the same Secretary [Eason], the same Senior Surgeon [Gibbs], the same Chaplain [Revd G. C. Rubie], hold office as before the Inquiry'; the new matron and new social service worker had been promoted from amongst existing staff. 'There has been no new blood in the higher offices.' There was 'a great improvement in the cleanliness and orderliness' of the men's hospital at Dean Street, where however some facilities remained 'disgusting'. The children's ward at Harrow Road had also been 'cleaned and painted' to look 'brighter', but to Harrison's eye 'the construction of the Harrow Road hospital with its windows with small panes set high up on thick walls still gives it very much the appearance of a work-house.' Gibbs opposed unified medical control, and the surgical staff were so ill-coordinated that the Matron and Charge Sister at Dean Street both resigned in 1930 in frustration, as did another governor in 1931. Under the regime of the early 1930s, class differentiation and coercion continued: patients were 'classified into (1) Victims, (2) Better-class patients, such as shop-assistants, typists, etc., and (3) Union, Prison and incorrigible patients, the different classes being accommodated on different floors'. Adults were given four hours' moral or religious instruction daily, together with a religious service at which attendance was voluntary.[12]

Elsewhere the operation of clinics seemed threatened by a legal decision which jeopardized the confidential basis of their opera-tions. In 1920 Sir Stanford Cade of Westminster Hospital was pressed against his wishes by Mr Justice McCardie to testify that a woman had syphilis in a divorce case in which she alleged the cruelty of her husband in transmitting the disease to her. This incursion on confidentiality was regretted by almost all venereologists, whose concern was increased seven years later when the Director of the Venereal Department of Birmingham General Hospital, Dr Eric Assinder, was ordered in court to testify against a husband being sued for divorce whom he had treated for venereal disease in 1924. This case attracted national attention, partly because it was again tried by Sir Henry McCardie, a judge who enjoyed sermonizing on social issues. McCardie's treatment of Assinder, and other remarks during the case, drew publicity. Officials at the Ministry of Health regretted McCardie's ruling: 'medical secrecy', wrote one, was essential for 'the success and efficiency of the V.D. clinics'. Venereologists were equally adamant: 'in the case of venereal disease fear of disclosure and of consequent discredit in the eyes of society operates more powerfully than in any other class of disease in deterring the patient from confiding the knowledge of his trouble to another person.' In the event McCardie's unpopularity in political and judicial circles led him to depression and suicide in 1933, and other judges were not so rebarbative in their rulings. Ultimately the main achievement of these incidents was to unite venereologists in their commitment to confidentiality, and to enhance public awareness of that resolve.[13]

Disapproval of venereal patients and particularly of sexually independent women persisted. In 1927 Dr Tytler Burke, the Venereal Diseases Officer of Salford, wrote a study to emphasize that in venereal disease policy, 'the accommodating young woman or the enthusiastic amateur must, for all practical purposes, be classed as a prostitute although she may not come within the police definition.' At least half of those who attended his clinic were middle-or upper-middle-class women, with husbands in their thirties who became infected adulterously while their wives were pregnant constituting 'the majority of cases', but beyond counselling that male continence was not unhealthy, he had more to say about the 'psycho-pathological phenomenon' of any woman who fornicated:

> Unlike her regular and professional sister, she is, as a rule, definitely and deliberately immoral. She experiences a

thrill of satisfaction from nibbling at forbidden fruit . . .
Deliberate wrongdoing gives her immense enjoyment.
She is a sexual kleptomaniac. Her conduct is an expression of vicarious criminality. She is a degenerate, an
abnormality, the female equivalent of the hooligan and
apache. She is equally to be found in the palace and the
hovel. She is amenable to little except incarceration in an
asylum, and yet but rarely is she a lunatic. She is often
extremely difficult to detect although she exists in such
large numbers. Such women are . . . very heavily infected, especially with gonorrhoea, and exceedingly few of
them ever . . . request treatment. This type of woman
reaches her zenith in the nymphomaniac; but every
variety is found, from the Madonna-faced maiden who
indulges in *flirtage* between dances to Messalina. Her
ranks were strongly reinforced during the war, and
immediately post-war, period.[14]

For Burke, then, it was not just women who did not keep their
virginity inviolable who were criminals and degenerates and
dirtbags of disease — women almost impossible to identify, yet
everywhere—but even maidens flirting with youths at dances. There
was something about women, clearly, which upset Burke: yet he
was not a crank but universally respected as an authority on his
subject.

A few years later, in 1935, he submitted a report to the Lancashire
authorities highlighting the men 'in charge of trams, motor lorries,
charabancs, taxis, railway engines and railway signal cabins who
have been suffering from serious syphilitic involvement of the brain
and spinal cord'. Of the men who attended Salford's Municipal
Clinic with venereal infections between 1928 and 1934, 748 (or
over 12 per cent) were road transport drivers. As syphilis ultimately
lowered visual, auditory and mental perceptions such patients were
potentially 'a serious menace to life, limb and property', just as a
motorist with general paralysis of insanity 'was very much more
dangerous than a drunk man in the same position'. Burke blamed
this high level of infection on 'the lorry-girl' whose 'nefarious
activities require the urgent attention of the police and of the
Ministry of Transport'. He described how young women travelled
the country with lorry drivers, offering sexual intercourse for a

hitched lift, or accommodating as many as six men a night for a shilling upwards each.[15]

Burke not only forwarded his report to the Ministry of Health, but also made it available to journalists: a story headlined 'Vampires of the Shadows' appeared in the *News of the World*. This in turn drew him into correspondence with a Fulham lorry driver, Frank Bricknell, whose letters were copied to the Ministry. One at least deserves to be quoted for its insights into the mind of a working-class layman with a morbid interest in venereal disease and a prurient hostility to female sexuality. 'It pleases me to know that you are a man who can see plain facts,' Bricknell wrote to Burke:

> You ask if I can give you more information on the subject, well Doctor, I believe I can set my knowledge of this into book form. This is no idle boast. I have always had a passion for studying human nature and its peculiar characteristics. This is why I have learned so much of this loathesome business.
>
> I have purposely picked this type of prostitute up on my travels, and have been amazed at the different stages of life these women have emerged from . . . May I Sir, to try and express myself more clearly, place the prostitutes of this country into their respective category . . . No 1, the Society Prostitute who can boast an up-to-date flat right in the heart of society. Their fee would keep me for a month. This type . . . does not concern any V.D. specialist. They pay for experience and are, of course, as we may put it 'safe'. No 2, 'The Prowler'. This type have worked their profession to a fine art. When coming towards you they suddenly twist their ankle, ask you the way to the nearest Tube or ask you if you have any change as they badly want to phone but have not the requisite coppers. All these methods bring about the desired 'stop' without exciting the attention of any 'busy' [policeman], to use their phrase . . . type no 3 . . . you can hardly call them women has fallen far below the cannibal. They portray degradation itself. They are 'Lorry Girls', degenerates from the streets who . . . to be quite frank with you, Sir, 'loans' her body

to you for a mere pittance – a cup of tea and a roll and a
few coppers.

Frank Bricknell took the view that the problem should be delegated
by the police to vigilantes who could waylay prostitutes and carry
them away forcibly for inspection at venereal disease clinics:

> I have decided to 'take the bull by the horns' and become
> a speak-easy. I state quite definitely that it is impossible
> for a policeman . . . to disguise himself sufficiently to
> enable him to 'hang around' and witness this sort of
> thing . . . Now a suggestion in confidence. Any person
> who is well versed in this matter, with a small car and a
> 'friend' armed with the necessary documents to pick up a
> 'lorry girl' suspect and proceed with her to the nearest
> town's V.D. clinic would in a short time convince a dozen
> 'Ministrys' that this is something not to be scoffed at . . .
>
> I have a personal hatred for publicity in any form, but if
> my humble name is going to help you any, well go ahead,
> use my name and address and good luck to your
> efforts . . . If I can rest assured that I have helped you in
> your clean-up and thereby made all my pals' jobs much
> safer on the road, I shall be content.[16]

Not all correspondents were so keen to abuse women verbally and
physically under the mask of public morality, and some sent cries of
misery or desperation. One result of this stress on the evils of lorry
girl 'vampires', or the insistence that fornicating women were no
better than prostitutes, was that some women who knew perfectly
well that they were not whores just because they took sexual
pleasure believed that they therefore could not contract syphilis or
gonorrhoea. 'Many a girl imagines that she may indulge in promiscuity' without risk of venereal disease because 'that only happens to
bad women who are on the streets', quoted Burke, without realizing
his own contribution to this fallacy.[17]

There was still heavy emphasis on personal decorum ('the use of
bad language broke down barriers of self-control and brought
people over the edge,' warned a naval Surgeon in 1926), but among
more professional writers the futility or delinquency of venereal
patients was increasingly stressed instead of their selfish sinfulness.
A social worker in London County Council's Public Health

Department, arguing in the 1940s that the worst residue of infection was among women who depended upon prostitution for survival, complained that it was 'almost impossible' to keep prostitutes in attendance for more than two visits to a VD clinic. They were 'extremely irresponsible people', often 'on the borderline of mental deficiency', 'mostly very young', 'not disagreeable' but 'utterly feckless and unreliable'. This was the judgment of an experienced and well-intentioned woman which carries authority: but such judgments tended to be self-reinforcing and to reflect the assumptions with which the women were approached. A study of the Tyneside area in 1943–4 tried to define the characteristics of 'promiscuous women' according to a set of values that were clear, but not universal, and which on the study's own evidence were irrelevant to the women's experiences. 'Some are from homes which are adequately furnished, well kept, and in which the mother especially cares for the difficult daughter.' Other girls were from 'unhappy and broken homes' or 'of poor mentality and easily led, whilst a few are high spirited and adventurous'. The homes of adulterous married women were often 'dirty and ill-kempt', but 'a few are surprisingly clean': 'perhaps the most common characteristics are a lack of self-discipline and an absence of any consciously held standard of life.' The authors blamed 'vast sums of money' which were spent on 'advertisements for cosmetics, clothing and alcohol as well as on cinema productions, displaying an artificial standard of luxury and spurious sentiment' for encouraging sensuality. 'By contrast with this colourful existence the child from the poor home is with rare exceptions compelled to earn a living in monotonous or uncongenial work, to dwell in a drab house often in a district of unrelieved ugliness.' The Tyneside researchers convinced themselves that but for advertising and films showing luxuriant pleasure, young women would be less tempted into fornication or prostitution – a view which was often propounded during the following thirty years but which is controverted by the ubiquity of fornication and prostitution long before Hollywood or advertising agencies existed. People had always fornicated for pleasure, or prostituted themselves because they needed money. These were not new habits, nor just the fault of Mae West and Errol Flynn.[18]

Increasingly after the 1920s psychological techniques were applied to control and classify venereal patients. Articles by Sir Cyril Burt, the London County Council's psychologist, published in 1926, on the 'sex delinquency of girls' gave valuable insights into such subjects as prostitution and venereal disease, but also gave a false new scientific patina to older prejudices about female sexuality. In 1948 E. D. Wittkower, psychiatrist to the Dermatological Department at St Bartholomew's Hospital attached to the Tavistock Psychoanalytical Clinic, who had investigated venereal soldiers under the auspices of the War Office, published a paper which tried to define the personality of the archetypal venereal disease patient. He found that they 'frequently come from . . . homes in which parents were separated, divorced or dead'; 'that delinquency and criminality are common in venereal disease patients before, and unrelated to, their illness'; that they were 'heavy drinkers' and often 'emotionally, sexually and socially immature' – evidence of 'emotional immaturity' being taken equally as either 'unaggressive' or 'over-aggressive' behaviour, definitions which could be used to include almost everyone. Wittkower's implication that venereal disease patients were 'delinquents' was repudiated by other physicians. Surgeon-Commander Coulter speaking in 1948 'was convinced that the average sailor who contracted venereal disease was a magnificent specimen' and was 'horrified to think that the virility which existed in his service from Nelson downwards should be in any way associated with delinquency'. Another physician, talking of 'fighting soldiers of the finest type', thought they were 'subjected to more temptations than the ordinary soldier' precisely because they were such 'fine physical specimens'.[19]

Against this background of treatment centres and adapting social attitudes, the position of the BSHC grew vulnerable during the 1930s. It received grants from the Government of £8,998 in the financial year 1926–7, £6,990 in 1927–8, £6,000 in 1928–9 and £12,000 in 1929–30, which sums were augmented by about £2,000 from local authorities. Nevertheless by 1930, 60 out of 146 British local authorities had undertaken no preventive health education campaigns against venereal disease for at least five years, while others had spent only nominal amounts. Whereas the London County Council spent £1,334 on publicity and education about venereal disease in 1929–30, the great city of Birmingham spent only £7, and the populous industrial town of Barnsley just £1. Devonshire spent £259; but another county, Essex, only £13. This niggardly approach became an acute problem for the BSHC after the passage of Neville Chamberlain's Local Government Act of

1929. Under the Venereal Diseases Scheme of 1916, counties and county boroughs had been responsible for running their own venereal diseases health service, supported by a central government grant of 75 per cent of the cost of approved schemes. However, the Act of 1929 consolidated this specific grant into the block grant paid by the central government to local authorities for other grant-aided services such as maternity and child welfare, tuberculosis treatment and the welfare of the blind. It also devolved the central government's responsibility for funding the BSHC to local authorities, setting contributions at the rate of either 3 shillings or 5 shillings per thousand of the population. Of the 146 local authorities, 32 declined to contribute in 1930, and as the economic situation deteriorated after 1931, this problem increased.[20]

When Sir Basil Blackett, President of the BSHC 1929–35, remonstrated about the response of local authorities, Ministry of Health officials were unsympathetic. 'The BSHC are far outstepping their province, which is propaganda, and are arrogating to themselves the direction and criticisms of the V.D. work of local authorities,' complained Sir Arthur MacNalty, their senior medical officer, in 1931. He and his colleagues resented Blackett's implication that they were 'supine' in their relations with recalcitrant local authorities, and would not tolerate an outside organization 'criticizing the Ministry's considered views'. He conceded that some provincial medical officers 'are not proficient and do not trouble to make themselves proficient in modern methods' of diagnosis and treatment, and accepted other criticisms from Blackett, but felt that the 'misdirected activity' and 'castigatory' tone of the BSHC were equally culpable.[21]

Whitehall was not uniformly hostile to the organization: the Colonial Office appreciated the BSHC's campaigns against commercialized vice in Cyprus, India, Jamaica and Malaysia (some of which outposts of empire were visited by Mrs Neville-Rolfe or her coadjutors), and made a regular financial grant to the Council in the 1930s. The Marquess of Dufferin and Ava, as Under-Secretary of State for the Colonies, opened an Imperial Social Hygiene Congress organized by the BSHC in 1937, and Leo Amery, a former Colonial Secretary, was President during 1936–9. It is noticeable that Ministers of Health were far less involved: their officials at the Ministry gradually lost confidence in the BSHC. As early as 1931 Harrison thought the BSHC 'defective' because it lacked a medically-qualified secretary. 'The activities of Mrs Rolfe have always been marked by zeal without discretion & Sir B. Blackett seems unable or unwilling to restrain her,' argued Sir Arthur Robinson. Medical officers in the provinces were irritated by her termagant ways and by the hectoring propaganda of her workers. A conference of East Anglian venereal disease officers shortly before the Second World War dismissed BSHC literature as 'mostly wastepaper', and felt their films (with titles like *Waste*, *The Flaw* and *Whatsoever a Man Soweth*) and lectures 'attracted the wrong type of audience'. According to Harrison, 'it did not seem that the BSHC had any friend in the room.' At a meeting attended by venereal disease officers and medical officers of health from the Midlands there was near unanimity 'that the only effect of these dramatic films seemed to be some increase in neurasthenia'; after they were shown in an area, people morbidly obsessed with sex, but with no symptoms of venereal infection, pestered treatment centres for unnecessary examinations. 'The British Social Hygiene lectures were out of touch with their audience,' one doctor declared with general approval: 'he did not see how an exposition of the "development of a daisy" was going to teach rough miners how to avoid V.D.' According to a Leicestershire doctor, the BSHC's 'freely advertised public lectures attracted a varied crowd comprising middle-aged persons, a few past and present patients, a few neurasthenics and the morbidly curious'. Young people at risk seldom attended, unless the lectures were delivered at factories, with compulsory attendance for employees; 'a young audience, receptive for knowledge and keen for guidance ... created a different atmosphere in which discussions were intelligent and valuable.' This was seldom the case with the effusions of the BSHC's volunteers. The Medical Office of Health for the Isle of Wight typically urged that leaders like Sybil Neville-Rolfe of 'voluntary societies ought to be strangled'.[22]

Similar criticisms spread, particularly among women, after the outbreak of the Second World War. 'This hush-hush attitude is all wrong and the ignorance of the disease is appalling,' declared a middle-class middle-aged woman who was interviewed at random in 1943. 'My own mother had never even heard of it. Myself – doing [hospital] voluntary work and very curious why one ward was definitely "no admittance" – got no explanations. I went to Uncle and asked if I could borrow his books on the subject. Uncle said

"No", didn't think it was necessary for me to know. Tried my cousin – he said, "You don't want to read that stuff." I got him to do some explaining – not very much, because the whole subject just seemed closed to anyone outside the medical profession.' But there is evidence that from the late 1930s women were less willing to tolerate euphemisms and expurgations.[23]

The work of the BSHC received other assessment, when in 1942–3 Mass Observation surveyed civilian opinion on venereal disease. Less than a quarter of those interviewed showed embarrassment at being questioned on such a topic: male investigators interviewed men, and women interviewed women, but twice as many men as women showed embarrassment. About seven times as many men as women objected to venereal disease being discussed in newspapers or on the radio, only 2% of women opposing public discussion. 'Women, whose knowledge of VD is in any case much slighter than men's, were much more appreciative of this publicity than men, who at present possess a much wider general sex knowledge'; indeed a few women (but no men) claimed never to have heard of venereal diseases until the current public health campaign. Several men 'disliked the removal of the taboo', particularly if meant their wives and daughters learnt about venereal disease. 'The less educated were ready to talk freely more often than the middle class, and in general the studies . . . suggest that middle-class people as a whole are less informed of the elementary facts, more scared of the subject.' Mass Observation found 'a welter of half knowledge and superstition . . . far worse and more damaging to the community than complete ignorance'. Few respondents knew how to recognize early symptoms of infection, but 'most people' had 'some idea of the final stages of syphilis, at times distorted into deep-seated personal fears'. Among the small minority of respondents who knew anything of prophylaxis there was 'muddle and confusion'. A plethora of superstitions survived about transmission: respondents mentioned that infection was possible through pores of the skin, or by sharing lavatories, touching banisters, using other people's towels, pipes or hairbrushes, wearing their clothes, kissing infected people, using public or swimming baths, intercourse with menstruating women, stroking infected dogs, or falling astride a ladder. It was still widely believed that intercourse with a virgin would effect a cure by passing the disease to the other person; and the belief that venereal disease was only transmissible from women to men was still current in rural districts. Drinking huge quantities of beer was believed to wash gonorrhoea away. Younger people wanted to regard venereal diseases in the same way as tuberculosis or chickenpox, but found 'themselves in a quandary because of deep-seated distaste for the whole question of VD'. One young electrician was quoted as a typical example: 'I have profound feelings of horror and disgust connected with anything to do with VD . . . I would kill myself if I contracted it *from whatever cause.*' A physician later reported that 'many people with venereal disease felt that [it] was something which had polluted them more or less permanently.'[24]

In the late 1930s the increasing likelihood of war revived memories of the problems met during 1914–18. The BSHC's President, Amery, wanted his organization to be given a leading role in a Social Hygiene Board to be set up by Whitehall to represent civil and military interests. Judging from the earlier experience of world war, he expected 'a rapid influx into camp neighbourhoods of girls rendered promiscuous in sex habits through mass hysteria as well as of women of the professional prostitute type'. Sir Francis Fremantle, another Conservative politician associated with the BSHC, similarly forewarned the Minister of Health, Walter Elliott, of 'powder magazines in the form of the blue-eyed village maid' that would be lying around after the outbreak of war. In the event, following the outbreak of war, voluntary donations to the BSHC shrivelled up; given the inadequacy of its local government funding, the organization had to survive for a time on a bank overdraft, while trying without avail to find a sympathetic philanthropist. The Ministry of Health hardened its heart, and with effect from 1942 centralized all health education in the Central Council for Health Education, which enjoyed a direct government subsidy. To the distress of Mrs Neville-Rolfe and her followers, the BSHC had to agree that in return for the Ministry paying its debts, it would transfer all its responsibilities on venereal disease propaganda, together with films and other equipment, to the Central Council, which took on some BSHC members as advisers for three years.[25]

Wartime conditions, with the constant imminence of separation and death, the concentration of fear, desperation and loneliness, and the sexual allure of the blackout, led to less restrained carnality. 'A great danger is like wine, it makes men affectionate,' as de Tocqueville wrote. In many quarters there was reluctance to relinquish the image of the prostitute as the predominant source of contagion. An analysis of new venereal cases in the industrial town of Salford during 1941 found that half of the patients were prostitutes, 20 per cent of infections were conjugally transmitted, and that the remaining 30 per cent were 'amateurs': a pejorative term which showed that the Salford authorities judged that unmarried women who chose to enjoy sexual intercourse were amateur prostitutes, or deserved to be treated as such, and were the antithesis of decent womanhood. This perception progressively weakened as the war wore on. 'The vast majority of the sexual exposures were wholly uncommercial and on a friendly basis,' a US Army report on venereal disease in Britain concluded a few years later. The view of the fornicating woman as demi-whore, 'no better than she is', was shaken over the period 1942–5.[26]

British servicemen outside Britain were equally impulsive in their search for pleasure. There is a huge literature on sex and the Second World War: one account of conditions and disease in the east Mediterranean should suffice. The Berka was a slum in Cairo a few hundred yards from Shepheard's Hotel, which housed 90 per cent of Cairo's licensed brothels and contained up to 600 licensed prostitutes. The local Provost Marshal estimated that 90,000 men visited the Berka for sexual intercourse each month. Those women who were licensed were inspected by Egyptian doctors twice weekly, but knew the exact time of their examination in advance, and prepared themselves by using powerful antiseptics and astringents. 'The medical inspection averaged thirty seconds per woman – the dexterity of the examiners was incredible.' Most of the women had positive reactions to the Wasserman test, but were allowed to ply their trade if they had taken a course of neoarsphenamine and bismuth. 'In the Canal Area, where Suez, Ismalia and Port Said were hotbeds of vice, the brothels were situated in filthy slums in the native districts, in which plague and other contagious diseases were prevalent.' Once the British commander placed these districts out of bounds, there was a fall in venereal infection rates; in August 1942 Cairo brothels were also put out of bounds, although 'Alexandria was excepted at the urgent request of the non-medical representatives of the Royal Navy.' Within six months the incidence of infection at Cairo was almost halved. It proved impossible to enforce the order in Palestine: troops flocked to the brothels of Haifa and Tel Aviv. 'In Cyprus there was a minimal attempt to adhere to the policy; but what could be expected in a land where half-a-crown bought a bottle of brandy, a woman and gonorrhoea?'[27]

It was only after the arrival of US troops in Britain in 1942, which prompted a steep rise in venereal infection, that the British Government became energetic. US Army medical officers were astonished at the near-invisibility of public health campaigns and at the legal constraints on contact-tracing. The Japanese invasion of Malaya caused a shortage of rubber, with which the British Government coped by giving condoms a lower production priority than teats for infant feeding. British condoms were considered uncomfortable, and the only half-jocular belief that they were 'too small' for GI's penises made men reluctant to wear them in case they were suspected of underendowment. Moreover few American soldiers attended prophylactic stations because most of their sexual intercourse was with women friends rather than prostitutes: 'under these circumstances', to quote a US Army report, soldiers 'were much less impressed with the desirability or necessity of prophylaxis'.[28]

From 1939 the Ministry of Health sought co-operation from the British Broadcasting Corporation and newspapers in a public education campaign, but it was not until after the Americans arrived in 1942 that officials persuaded the media to experiment in frankness. Journalists and broadcasters, according to Sir Weldon Dalrymple-Champneys of the Ministry of Health, 'had considerable misgivings which proved quite groundless for public opinion had advanced much further than they suspected between the wars'. Certainly the number of people who consulted treatment centres but proved not to be infected rose from 39,008 in 1939 to 72,689 in 1944, which was partly attributable to increased public awareness and partly to the 'increased nervousness' of those who were morbidly 'apprehensive and suggestible' about syphilis.[29]

Journalistic prudery remained an obstacle to effective public health campaigns of any sort. In 1942 a national effort to convince people to wash their hands after defecating was abandoned because newspapers could not bring themselves to print the word 'water-closet': in 1943 advertisements describing the incidence of syphilis and gonorrhoea, the dangers of transmission to a new generation and the benefits of early treatment were altered to satisfy the delicacy of newspaper editors who insisted that a parenthesis identifying syphilis and gonorrhoea with pox and clap should be expunged. They also refused to print the sentence 'Professional prostitutes are not the only source of infection' as admitting a fact which they preferred to deny. Their bowdlerization of another sentence – 'The first sign of syphilis is a small ulcer on or near the sex organs' – by deleting any reference to sex organs caused grotesque misery as people all over Britain with ulcers on other parts of their body feared they had VD and appealed to doctors or the Ministry of Health for advice. These bowdlerizing editors were hard-bitten types who had worked for such men as the first Lord Rothermere, proprietor of the *Daily Mail*, with his senile concupiscence for young and inexperienced 'yum yums', or the *Daily Express*'s Lord Beaverbrook whom G. M. Young said had the manner of a backstreet abortionist and who for many years lived in a menage with Lord and Lady Grantley: but lip-smacking morality was what sold their papers. As *Lancet* commented, the expurgated VD advertisement of 1943 was 'designed to reach the simplest people' for whom a barricade of unfamiliar terms was almost as impenetrable 'as a barricade of silence'. In medical experience the patient who denied having gonorrhoea, but said he was 'a fair martyr' to clap, was not exceptional.[30]

War conditions revived calls to make syphilis and gonorrhoea notifiable diseases. A movement in this direction had existed even in peacetime. During 1928 the municipal authority of Edinburgh included in a bill which they sponsored in the House of Commons a clause for compulsory notification of venereal infections, and although this clause was withdrawn, BSHC members from the industrial provinces (like the Cardiff Public Health Committee) continued to press in the 1930s for a system of compulsory notification. A fascinating survey in 1935 of 434 patients at Burke's Salford clinic found that all 134 women and all but 5 of 300 men favoured the compulsory (but free and confidential) treatment of people with VD. The Ministry of Health discouraged such moves: 'the chief disadvantages of compulsory notification are the tendency to promote concealment or delay in seeking treatment,' it told one correspondent, adding that notification would only complicate matters with 'the risk of false certification . . . and the labour of tracing people who reported with false names and addresses'. Predictably agitation for compulsory notification revived during the war: Dr Edith Summerskill, a Labour MP, advocated compulsory notification of venereal disease and obligatory blood tests for all pregnant women.[31]

In November 1942, after consultations which had lasted since October 1940 but had been transformed by American intervention, Defence Regulation 33B was enacted: this stipulated that anyone who had been reported by a venereal diseases specialist as being suspected of having infected two or more of their patients might be compelled to undergo medical examination and to remain under treatment until pronounced free of the disease 'in a communicable form'. Two or more accusations were required before legal action was taken so as to forestall blackmailers (who might threaten to denounce persons as their source of infection) or to guard against genuine mistakes by patients reporting the source of their infection. Nevertheless it was curious that the individual informed against could be detained under Regulation 33B, but not the two informants involved, although they might be equally capable of transmitting an infection. In practice such compulsion was only applied to a small number of sources. In 1944, for example, out of 8,339 contacts (of whom 246 were men) reported under Regulation 33B, only 3,696 (including 109 men) were traced, of whom 2,858 (including 84 men) agreed to be examined. The number of contacts reported in 1944 by more than one other person totalled 827 (including only 4 men): 235 agreed to be examined, 417 were ordered to attend examination, and the rest proved untraceable. There were only 82 prosecutions under Regulation 33B in 1944, either for not attending compulsory examination, or discontinuing treatment before being pronounced free from communicable disease. The regulation expired in December 1947, although a Labour MP, Richard Marsh, tried to restore it in 1962–3.[32]

William Temple, Archbishop of Canterbury, who was President of the Central Council of Health Education, threatened to resign over the issue of Regulation 33B, which he alleged treated 'a moral problem as if it were primarily a medical problem': it seemed to him 'evil' that the Government's chief 'concern over infectious contacts is to make fornication medically safe'. But there was a decline in ecclesiastical influence over venereal disease policy which reflected a decline in the power of Christianity in general. Temple's predecessor as archbishop, Cosmo Lang, had acknowledged during the enactment of the divorce reforms of 1937 that Britain had 'a largely non-Christian population': Sir Francis Fremantle noted in 1942 that a recent opinion poll had shown 'that only about 20 per cent of the population owe any allegiance to the Church'. Intellectual giants of Victorian Britain like Cardinal Newman had devoted their lives to fighting the collapse of faith, and by the 1890s slum clergy like Winnington-Ingram estimated that only 1% of their parishioners practised Christian belief. By the 1930s the atheism of the poor had spread to other classes: true Christian faith was rarer, but belief in traditional Christian precepts of obedience, and in the social and political dangers that ensued if people did not submit to authority, was as strong as in Newman's day. Although ecclesiastical influence had declined, officialdom was empowered by Christian teaching on obedience and conformity to authority, and was disposed to perpetuate the vestiges of its influence. From the 1930s to the present day politicians and administrators confronted by issues of sexuality have invoked Christian values while not themselves professing Christianity: in some cases this inconsistency has been rooted in crude opportunism and hypocrisy, in other cases it expresses the bafflement of decent people trying to do their best with complexities not of their making.[33]

Amongst the laity there was the usual outburst of confused but primitive suggestions all aimed at combating the wartime increase in venereal infection. One correspondent of the Ministry of Health advocated that the identity cards of people with venereal disease should be indelibly stamped 'V.D.' on the assumption that the nation would start demanding to see other people's identity cards before having sex with them. Another correspondent believed 'these diseases are mostly voluntary': that because they arose from an act of intercourse decided on by deployment of an individual's own free will, the infection was self-inflicted. On this basis that the patient was culpable, he urged the Ministry to make syphilis '*an illegal disease*' and to impose 'stern government measures to check it'. Such people found it impossible to be specific about suitable 'stern measures' or the benefits for disease control in criminalizing infections, but felt better after venting their rage on strangers.[34]

In 1943 a Joint Committee on Venereal Disease was established by the Government, partly as a result of American concern at the health of their soldiers stationed in Britain. Comprising representatives of the Admiralty, War Office, Air Ministry, Home Office and the police, 'it met in an atmosphere charged with emotion, by reason of highly coloured press reports,' according to its chairman, Dalrymple-Champneys, who found himself 'confronted with an extremely difficult situation having international complications'. Amongst other recommendations, Dalrymple-Champneys' Committee urged the routine blood-testing of every pregnant woman for syphilis, and proposed measures to compel the parents of congenitally syphilitic children to take treatment together with their offspring; but a related committee of 1944 advised against any system of compulsory notification as unworkable. A German law of 1927, 'which provided confidential notification and compulsory treatment of defaulters, serves as a typical example of a failure', as the Venereal Diseases Officer for Lancashire wrote. 'The causes of failure were lack of co-operation by the medical profession, the local authorities and the public, together with lack of money to provide the necessary staff for the complicated administration and lack of facilities for compulsory treatment.' Medical people were conscious of the correlation between a nation's form of government and its legislation on sexual hygiene: the fact that fascist Italy in 1931 and Nazi Germany after 1933 had reintroduced state regulation discredited medical *dirigisme* in British judgment in the 1940s. (Hitler's view that curing syphilis was '*the only decisive factor in the nation's existence*', that incurable syphilitics must be segregated and that 'modern life must be freed from the suffocating miasma of our modern eroticism' was disavowed by the BSHC as early as 1934.)[35]

The BSHC became increasingly isolated. A spokesman of the British Medical Association's Committee on Industrial Health felt by 1943 that 'the preach and treat' school had failed, 'and he favoured the school which said "educate and disinfect".' The BSHC's position was summarized by its early wartime Medical Secretary, Dr Otto May. 'Either promiscuity was desirable, or not desirable. If desirable, all that was necessary was instruction in prophylaxis. If not desirable, then the basis of education in social hygiene must be . . . healthy family life.' May had previously been medical adviser to a life insurance company, and had absorbed many of the assumptions of his employer about the family as an economic and social unit. He wanted venereal disease propaganda 'which would harness the sex urge to a constructive use in the social fabric, and not a destructive use'. In his view 'the strength of the primitive sex urge' had been exaggerated: the use of prophylactics should not be aired publicly, 'but [was] a matter for personal discussion between doctor and patient'. Twenty years earlier May advocated the teaching of personal prophylaxis in his monograph on *The Prevention of Venereal Diseases*, but as he said in 1943, 'he was older now and had come to the conclusion that the advocacy of prophylaxis implied a sanction for misconduct which would be much more powerful than its deterrent effect.'[36]

The Society for the Prevention of Venereal Disease continued to propagandize. Its wartime chairman was Dr Robert Lyster, who inveighed against the 'prudery, hypocrisy and cant' of those 'opponents of prophylaxis [who] do not wish to destroy these diseases'. Lyster was in the tradition of SPVD mavericks: energetic, domineering and intolerant, he was venereal diseases officer for the camps and barracks around Winchester in the First World War, edited *Public Health* from 1918 until 1925, lectured for thirty years in public health and forensic medicine at St Bart's Hospital, was Medical Officer of Hampshire, three times a Labour parliamentary candidate and a lonely socialist member of Bournemouth town council. Of the NCCVD, he complained, 'They talk glibly about "the education of the people" but they fight grimly to prevent the public knowing the very simple facts about prevention.'[37]

Venereal diseases continued to attract busybodies and bores. Alderman Mrs Bonham Pigg conjures up an appalling prospect of wartime *ennui* in St Pancras, where she operated, by urging 'that everyone could and should help to dispel ignorance' by constantly talking about the subject: 'those engaged in Air Raid Precaution circles, firewatching and other civic duties could do good conversational work on the subject.' The doom of spending a night firewatching on a St Pancras rooftop with someone who reiteratively and unrelentingly talked with self-conscious frankness about the perils of syphilis must have been one of the worst horrors of the Blitz.[38]

Until penicillin became widely available after the war, syphilis was treated according to the recommendations of an expert committee of the League of Nations convened in 1928. Its report of 1935 recommended that adults with primary infections should receive a minimum of four courses each consisting of eight injections of neoarsphenamine concurrently with the same number of bismuth, with the addition of two further bismuth injections. Sulphapyridine when first marketed in 1938 seemed to achieve brilliant success in treating gonorrhoea, although during the war it was largely superceded by sulphathiazole.

Even before the efficacy of penicillin was established, pillars of the BSHC such as Sir Drummond Shiels were optimistic that 'the taboo concerning venereal diseases' would 'disappear within a generation'. Lord Winster in 1943 hoped 'that one good effect' of the war would be 'to dispel the unhealthy atmosphere of fear, mystery and hypocrisy which has cloaked the venereal diseases for so long'. The *British Journal of Venereal Diseases* reported in 1948, 'easier and quicker methods of treatment for venereal disease had led to increased promiscuity, as the fear and dread of these infections which formerly had acted as a partial deterrent was now practically removed.' The chairman of a regional hospital board in the 1950s rejected an appeal for reconstruction work on a venereal clinic with the remark 'We don't want to spend money on these dying diseases.' An article published in 1959 by the pharmaceutical company Glaxo Laboratories (which had pioneered deep fermentation production of penicillin in Britain) affirmed, 'The chance of contracting syphilis in most of Britain is today almost nil, and the implications of this disease, as naturally also of gonorrhoea, to the patient are negligible.' Such optimism lasted for less than twenty years, and the Chief Medical Officer's report for 1965 identified venereal disease as a 'large and intractable' problem despite modern treatment: 'many' doctors and nurses, he judged, viewed the subject with 'distaste . . . and in some quarters there is still a conspiracy of silence.'[39]

With the rise of this new biomedical optimism there was less stress on fresh air and manly exercise as preventives of venereal infection. The traditional view of games-playing as a way to stop the 'bad' behaviour that led to fornication was often articulated before the Second World War. But from the 1940s such opinions receded, and were increasingly thought both self-deluding and blimpish.[40]

In other respects the nature of venereal disease control changed as the result of penicillin. By 1950 when the number of new infections was the lowest recorded, a venereologist at St Mary's Hospital in

Paddington predicted that 'with continued peacetime conditions and vigilance at our ports (our links with the vast reservoir of infection overseas), the outlook for the future should be good.' In the event 2,570 British soldiers in Korea were treated for venereal disease between November 1950 and September 1951: and there was a marked increase in gonorrhoea infections after 1955, until the annual number of new cases approached 35,000 by 1959. This was attributed to increased sexual activity generally and to the 'reservoir' of undiscovered gonoccocal infection among prostitutes and other women: homosexuals were also identified as 'an important factor', together with male immigrants from the Caribbean who (when separated from their families) were reported as using prostitutes. Fifty per cent of new male cases of gonorrhoea in 1960 occurred in immigrants, half of whom came from the West Indies.[41]

The wider availability of penicillin did not seem an unqualified boon to health propagandists or to moralists. In 1947 the US Army (see illustration overleaf) redirected their educational efforts from publicizing prophylaxis to 'appeals to self-control and sublimation': they stressed that 'sometimes Penicillin doesn't work', and found these failures all too gratifying for their higher purpose. British officials felt 'that the moral approach does not come happily from a Government Department' and could seldom 'be effectively adopted on a poster': instead their approach was to offer sound medical advice, presented in a darkly ominous way that kept alive some of the shame and apprehension surrounding venereal diseases. Government posters issued in the late 1940s and 1950s (see plate) still referred to 'a grave menace' threatening not only 'the whole nation', but 'the future of our race'. People with venereal diseases were filthy pollutants ('clean living is the only safeguard') who had shown criminal irresponsibility: long after penicillin had become available it was insisted that to transmit syphilis was 'a vile crime'. The chief aim of the British educational campaign launched in 1948 was to encourage people to seek immediate and effective treatment from qualified practitioners, but this sensible message was sometimes inaudible amidst all the ominous phrases about 'evil'. Many posters – 'A Shadow on His Future' and 'Here Comes the Bride' are representative – used the image of darkening shadows to create morbid anxieties. The frightfulness of women – the fear of what is inside a cunt which makes some men regard the opposite sex as both objects of desire and as eerie, incomprehensible and hostile creatures – seems exemplified in one lurid black and mauve design for the Central Office of Information (see back cover).[42]

There was regret in government departments at science's triumph over the spirochaete and a hankering for the old regime for fear. These feelings were often muddled up with an anxiety that the power of modern science would lead to social disintegration or the ruin of Divine Mysteries. 'The worst passage in the book', wrote a member of the Home Office in 1953 when it was contemplating prosecuting Kinsey's *Sexual Behaviour in the Human Female* for obscenity, 'is the statement on page 327 that present methods of simple and rapid cures for the two principal venereal diseases make their spread through premarital coitus a relatively unimportant matter. Fear of disease is perhaps the most potent factor in restraining many young people from promiscuous immorality . . . and to remove that deterrent gratuitously . . . [is] monstrously irresponsible.' The loss of belief in God, it was minuted by another Home Office man in 1955, 'accelerated by the rapid sweep and magnitude of scientific discoveries and the omnipotence and the omniscience of man', coupled with 'whipped up publicity that draws a false and seductive glamour over the

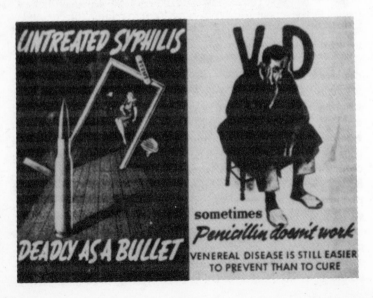

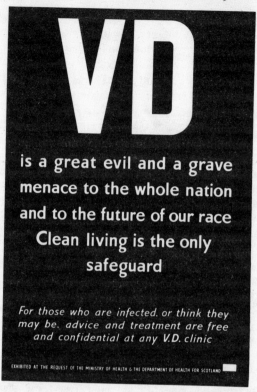

VD

is a great evil and a grave
menace to the whole nation
and to the future of our race
Clean living is the only
safeguard

*For those who are infected. or think they
may be. advice and treatment are free
and confidential at any V.D. clinic*

EXHIBITED AT THE REQUEST OF THE MINISTRY OF HEALTH & THE DEPARTMENT OF HEALTH FOR SCOTLAND

"love lives" of film stars' was warping teenage morals. He deplored that 'increasing emphasis' was being 'laid on the pleasure aspect of sex', and was hostile to sexually independent women. 'Is the woman who repeatedly remarries and regularly gets a divorce with substantial alimony less of a prostitute than the street walker because she sells her favours under the respectable camouflage of a civil wedding?' he demanded. Before antibiotics, 'the fear of contracting venereal diseases acted strongly as a deterrent to sexual promiscuity' because infection entailed 'a long drawn out penance' and was 'disabling and disfiguring'. The end of such suffering did not seem to him an unmixed advantage.[43]

That women might be autonomous sexual beings was as frightening a notion as ever to some people, and girls reared in the 1950s and 1960s were still taught about their sexual identity in misogynist language in the tradition of Dr Tytler Burke. 'The desire to get

V.D.

CAN BE CURED
—if treated early

. . . so skilled advice should be sought IMMEDIATELY if there is cause for suspicion. A specialist's advice and treatment (if necessary) are FREE at all V.D. clinics, where penicillin is now extensively used.

What are the venereal diseases? In this country Syphilis and Gonorrhoea. If not skilfully treated in its early stages, *Syphilis* is often a killing disease. Untreated *Gonorrhoea* is also serious, and may cause chronic ill-health or inability to have children.

How are they caught? Almost always through sexual intercourse with an infected person, who may have no obvious signs of disease. Accidental infection from cups, 'seats', towels, etc. is extremely rare.

What are the signs? The smallest sore place appearing on or near the sex organs up to 90 days after infection, or the slightest discharge from them, may be the only signs of infection.

Can an unborn child be infected? Yes. If a woman has Syphilis her baby may be born dead, or diseased, but skilled treatment before or during pregnancy will almost always ensure a healthy baby.

How can these diseases be avoided? By not running the risk. Clean living is a real safeguard. Contraceptives cannot rule out the risk of infection.

TREATMENT

A specialist's advice and treatment can be obtained *free* at the local clinic. The addresses of the treatment centres, and times of sessions, are given on local posters; or may be obtained from the offices of the Medical Officer of Health. In case of difficulty apply for further information to the Medical Adviser, Scottish Council for Health Education, 3, Castle Street, Edinburgh, 2.

If you write, mark your envelope **'CONFIDENTIAL'**

ISSUED BY THE DEPARTMENT OF HEALTH FOR SCOTLAND
AND THE SCOTTISH COUNCIL FOR HEALTH EDUCATION

married is a healthy, normal instinct because it leads to wifehood and motherhood without which no woman's life can be complete,' declared Veronica Dengel in a book published by the progressive firm of Faber. 'Almost every woman wants marriage. It is a normal impulse inspired by nature for the purpose of continuing the race. An honest woman admits it; the wise woman has a PLAN. Be clever, of course; don't reveal your plan.' Veronica Dengel advised a woman in search of a husband to get an office job (avoiding 'insurance offices, banks, public utilities, department stores' where women employees outnumber the men: 'too much competition there') in the type of business or factory which 'attract more men than women'. Indifference should be feigned initially to tantalize the man: 'don't let him kiss you goodnight', let him 'observe your abilities as a hostess', remember 'the way to a man's heart is still through his stomach!' In conversation 'men like you to understand and share their interest in their job, their hobbies, their ambitions . . . Ask him his opinion about politics, current events, the news': but 'if you are a business woman, don't talk about your own job' because 'it would strike a false note.' As the courtship proceeds, 'don't be persuaded to public displays of affection . . . Not only does it cheapen the couple – but it is most embarrassing for others around, especially children.' As to sexual play, 'petting is unwholesome and indecent – an unwarranted, unlicensed exploring . . . physical harm will come because, sooner or later, the casual petter will complete the sexual act; and after the initial experience can be led into promiscuity . . . Very, very few girls admit any enjoyment of the sexual relationship.' Premarital intercourse was 'wrong': psychiatrists had 'proved' the 'mental imbalance' of fornicators. 'The girl who enters marriage clean and sweet and completely chaste is very precious to her husband . . . He wants the security of positive knowledge that she belongs to him alone. It builds his faith, confidence and fidelity; it bolsters his uncertain moments.' As Dengel summarized, echoing Sir Ernest Wild who had wanted to criminalize lesbianism in the 1920s, 'The best man is never as good as the best woman; but the worst man can never be as bad as the worst woman.'[44]

These attitudes were undermined by the advent in the 1960s of the contraceptive pill, which enabled women to take more responsibility for contraception and which led to a much wider acknowledgment of female desires. The efficacy of the pill, the publicity which it brought to other contraceptives such as intra- uterine devices, the free availability of contraceptives under Britain's National Health Service which was enacted against government wishes after a campaign in 1972–3 by peeresses in the House of Lords: all these things changed sexual practices and some sexual attitudes. Not the least benefit of the pill was to discredit the plenitude of ineffective or ruinous contraceptives that had hitherto been sold. In the early 1960s there were over one hundred chemical contraceptives sold in Britain (including creams, jellies, pastes, suppositories, foaming tablets and aerosol foam), of which almost half failed all tests as spermicidal agents. Only 37 declared their contents on the container (as contraceptives were excluded from the Pharmacy and Medicines Act of 1941 as the result of ill-considered moralist fretting) and some seem to have been positively injurious to health. The advent of the contraceptive pill dealt a death-blow to these quack products, and so alarmed the London Rubber Company, which had a near-monopoly of British condom sales, that in 1965 it funded the Genetic Studies Unit, which disseminated such misleading and alarming information about contraceptive pills that the Institute of Public Relations invoked its disciplinary procedure. Beyond this marketing convulsion, the popularization of the contraceptive pill in the mid 1960s is said to have revolutionized attitudes and created the Permissive Society. It did nothing of the sort. It changed sexual practices, but it scarcely altered the accretion of guilt that surrounds sex.[45]

The Permissive Society is a phrase which has different meanings for different people. In its most positive but most rarely used sense, it indicates a cluster of attitudes intended to acknowledge the sexual prerogatives and desires of women as equal to those of men, and intended to shed the idea of punishment and shame which have traditionally smothered sexuality. In its most positive idealization, the Permissive Society was intended to de-eroticize guilt and to discard the false mystification, sentimentality and manipulative obscurity which ecclesiastics as well as writers like Corbett-Smith or Veronica Dengel had propagated about sex; it was intended to establish sexual intercourse as a recreational pleasure rather than a procreative duty, as a series of imaginative acts to satisfy physical and emotional curiosity, rather than as the chief distinction in an adult life between a chaste and a monogamous existence. Of course, this was an ideal that was always under attack, both from disturbed people and sincere Christians. In the latter category in this period stood Dr. Ernest Claxton, Assistant Secretary of the British Medical Association, who denounced, 'extra- and pre-marital intercourse' as 'medically dangerous, morally degrading and nationally destructive'. As late as 1977 Claxton warned that 'sex indulgence is like a drug of addiction', that young women tempted by petting should 'keep away from the edge of the precipice' and that there was 'a conspiracy' of 'people who want to destroy our way of life' by encouraging 'sex indulgence' identical to that which destroyed the Roman Empire. (Masturbation, he counselled in a sex education manual for adolescents in 1977, was physically harmful if 'indulged in frequently', 'sheer self-indulgence for self-gratification'; people who excused masturbation 'only say this because they like doing it themselves'.) Even if Claxton's views were not representative of the medical profession collectively, they were amplified by journalists, and influenced the BMA's public pronouncements, notably their deplorably misleading report on *Venereal Disease and Young People* (1964). Meanwhile, clergymen as well as physicians continued to fulminate against non-procreative sex. 'To accept the pleasures of sexual attitudes and practices without relating them to the purposes for which these pleasures were intended is a form of perversion and must be condemned as delinquent,' wrote the Methodist preacher, Lord Soper, expressing the crux of Christian objections to unbridled sexuality's denial of consequences. But (as so often) this plea for individuals to respect their sexual partners, and not to objectify them, slid quickly into rancorous and crankish spluttering. 'A boy who takes sex because he wants it will tend to take somebody else's goods for precisely the same reason,' Soper pronounced. 'The girl who is encouraged to see nothing wrong in pleasing herself with somebody else's body will be unlikely to see any objection in pleasing herself with someone else's money.'[46]

But the Permissive Society as an idealized place in which the individual sexual wishes of both men and women are tolerated and satisfied in conditions of mutual respect has a debased counterpart, constructed from false images which draw on men's wish to revenge themselves on women or degrade the objects of their desire. This Permissive Society is presented as the social expression of sexual freedom, but it is a parody of true freedom. The preconditions of freedom are justice and equality, yet there has been precious little of either in all the sexual coupling and sexual discourse of the last quarter century. This Permissive Society is largely perceived as it is depicted in the gutter press, which with its page-three pin-ups is overwhelmingly concerned with maintaining men's subordination of women, by sexualizing women's inferior status, by objectifying their bodies. Its images present women as whores: they take the same phallocentric view as Dr Tytler Burke, Salford's Venereal Diseases Officer, or Frank Bricknell, the lorry driver, both quoted earlier. One of the ultimate icons of this Permissive Society is Mary Millington, who until her suicide was the tabloids' favourite pornographic star. My most vivid memory of her is her posing naked in a photograph pinned to the wall of a London office: several of the male employees had each stuck a matchstick into her cunt. Women, however, are forbidden by employers to display at work photographs of naked men however anodyne, and have been known to be threatened with dismissal if they protest. Where is the sexual justice or equality in this? The Permissive Society is a horrible journalistic vulgarization, intended to reinforce male supremacy: hence the homophobia of tabloid journalists, who despise men who are sexual with other men because they suspect them of taking the passive role of women, and who hate lesbians for defying the primacy of the penis. The Permissive Society is a debased stunt intended to verify and vindicate all the emptiest and most brutal clichés of male sexual identity. If true sexual freedom is ever obtained, it will involve something more than taking sexual partners without noticing that they are individuals too. The pre-conditions of sexual freedom are that people should not be punished or demeaned for the individuality of their sexuality: that they should not be threatened with fear, guilt or shame. As the rest of this book will show, we have never been near a state of sexual freedom, still less of sexual justice.[47]

For example, despite antibiotics, venereal diseases retain their power to excite shame and anxiety. When Richard Marsh tried to legislate for the compulsory treatment of the diseases in the 1960s, he 'was bombarded with an enormous volume of correspondence', some 'from cranks of one type and another, but a great deal from ordinary people equally disturbed'. Yet neither ordinary people, nor disturbed people, have ever bombarded their MPs with letters about tuberculosis, or rheumatism, or the common cold. The author of an article entitled 'VD and the Young' published in a weekly magazine in 1976 'received many letters from readers asking why we should waste time on this nasty subject, often quoting Romans 6.23: "Sin pays its wages"'. More recently, in 1988, an account of Barbara Binding, the proprietor of a private venereal disease clinic, describes her as making

> her living from the people who do not have sexually transmitted diseases. The overwhelming majority of those paying the £35 consultation fee are what she calls the Worried Well. 'There is almost nothing wrong with my patients. Sometimes we go for weeks without finding anything.'
>
> To many, she says, taking a VD test is like exorcizing a ghost. They feel guilt about some sexual encounter and convince themselves they have caught something. When they are told they have not, their conscience is somehow eased. And there are the obsessives, who take test after test even though they have no grounds for fear.[48]

A survey by the National Secular Society published in 1970 showed that of 42 books on sex education, most did not mention venereal diseases at all, or else mentioned them as a threat in pre-marital sex without giving information about symptoms. Another survey in that decade on suitable methods to prevent the spread of venereal disease found that 34 per cent of respondents recommended more publicity and more public education; but other comments included:

> 'Brand everyone who has got it. Tattoo them on the backside.'
> 'You can catch it from a toilet seat, and you can't stop that, can you?'
> 'Everyone I go with is spotless. I always make enquiries first.'
> 'It's up to the schools to teach girls to keep themselves clean, as men pick it up from them.'
> 'Make everyone bath in the morning and at night.'[49]

These replies demonstrate the primitive urge to identify and punish transgressors no less than the persistence of the myth that nice clean girls don't get VD.

Patients were still traduced. When a disc jockey, John Peel, admitted on radio that he had venereal disease, there was public protest, and when he subsequently appeared as a witness for the defence in the trial for obscenity of the Schoolkids issue of *Oz* magazine in 1971 his infection was raised in court by prosecuting counsel to impugn his probity. In the same year, too, one of the complaints of the prosecution in the trial for obscenity of the *Little Red Schoolbook* (which, based on Mao Tse-tung's handbook, advised children on their rights on everything from homework to oral sex) was that it 'treats VD more or less as the common cold', describing symptoms and cure, without any terrifying or punitive overtones. The bacteriologist Lord Stamp wanted VD to be portrayed to the young as an especially 'rotten disease . . . colour films on the subject might be the answer': a Tory MP, Peter Bruinvels, speaking in 1986, was outraged that in sex education classes at school, 'VD comes across as something that can be treated as simply as a case of measles.' A correspondent of this author in the same year, whose 'fear of VD' had inhibited his sexual experience, remonstrated with my belief that 'moralistic hectoring' about the retribution of syphilis did no good. 'You might as well say that punishing robbers does not stop robberies,' he wrote: 'However, disband the police force for 6 months and see if the robbery rate remains constant.' Such people found it intolerably threatening that modern medicine was trying to regard VD as no more rotten than any other serious infection: anxious to sustain a regime of retributive fear, they furiously denied the fact that syphilis *can* be treated as simply as measles, and fought to keep the disease as a deterrent, like prison for thieves or the rope for murderers.[50]

In 1971 there were 1,606 cases (1,270 men and 336 women) notified of early infectious syphilis (compared with 8,432 in 1951), and 55,914 (37,929 men and 17,985 women) of gonorrhoea. The age group at highest risk continued to be between 18 and 24. Fifteen per cent of new cases of syphilis, and 3.4 per cent of new cases of gonorrhoea, were contracted abroad. One-third of men who caught gonorrhoea did so from their regular sexual partners, emphasizing the oversimplification of the equation with promiscuity: one does not catch VD from having sex with a lot of people, but by having one partner who is infected. The risk clearly increases with the number of sexual partners, but it is ultimately a question of care and experience rather than of numbers. One half of people who caught a venereal infection when young had married within a few years and had remained faithful to their partner, however many partners they may have had when younger. Those who were sexually active as teenagers, research showed, betrayed no distinctive signs of moral turpitude or emotional disturbance, and had often settled down and married by the age of 25. Some public health campaigns did not reflect the great decline in syphilis, but gave undue emphasis to morbid and repugnant photographs of untreated or advanced cases. Moralists in the 1960s and 1970s often referred to a rise in gonorrhoeal infections which they attributed to 'promiscuity' despite the fact that the number of new cases of syphilis had fallen. It would have been as sensible to cite the decrease in syphilis to argue that there was decreased 'promiscuity'. (The incidence of syphilis fell by 64% in the ten years to 1988, with only 1,463 new cases seen at National Health Service genito-urinary clinics in 1988; the incidence of gonorrhoea fell by 57%, to 22,884 new cases over the same period.)[51]

A handbook on *Alternative London* published in the 1970s warned of VD clinics, 'some just add a touch of punishment as part of their free service.' One such experience was described by a woman in 1973:

> While I was in the undignified and vulnerable position immediately prior to examination, the doctor asked me what I thought was wrong. I replied that as far as I knew nothing: but my boyfriend had suspicious symptoms so I thought I'd better come along just in case. At this, the doctor remarked in a loud whisper to the nurse, 'Hum, lot of guilty consciences today'. Moral indignity was added to physical, and the humiliation was complete.

'It is still true that visiting some of the older VD clinics can make a person feel like a social outcast,' a medical researcher noted in 1976. 'There is room for improvement in the physical surroundings and in the attitude of staff.' Certain doctors desired this forbidding environment as a moral deterrent. 'A visit to a VD clinic can have a valuable effect,' Dr Dalzell-Ward of the Health Education Council believed. 'It can be a warning and a preventative agent.' It is hard to think of another disease which a physician would welcome young people contracting as a warning and a preventative: it would be thought disgraceful to welcome cancer in a cigarette smoker or a coronary for an overeater as having 'a valuable effect'. The Dalzell-Ward theory of prevention was in any case flawed: research in the 1960s among young people who had visited a VD clinic at least once found that only 32 per cent were afraid of venereal disease.[52]

As shown by the conviction in 1970 of Richard Branson under the Venereal Diseases Act of 1918, VD clinics could not advertise in public: posters were only permitted in public lavatories, which aggravated the furtive and dirty reputation surrounding the diseases. There were occasional recrudescences of police stupidity: Newcastle-upon-Tyne police on one occasion confiscated Health Education Council posters from a community advice centre on the pretext of indecency. Few of the 190 clinics listed their addresses or telephone numbers in directories. It was only a decade and a half after Branson's victimization that a former ward sister, Barbara Binding, obtained special dispensation from the Department of Health and Society Security to advertise treatment for VD, and was thus able to open the country's first private clinic for sexually transmitted diseases, the Regents Park Clinic, in 1985. Even so she had difficulty in advertising. The *Yellow Pages* telephone directories only agreed to include her advertisement after hesitation, and magazines such as *Punch* and *What's On* refused it. The Metropolitan Police ruled that the clinic could only advertise in London taxis if the phrase 'sexually transmitted diseases' was replaced with the euphemism 'personally transmitted diseases' ('"Not nice for families," they said').[53]

Research funded by the Nuffield Foundation in association with the Health Education Council in the 1970s found that 'people in authority, including teachers, seem reluctant to admit that VD can be cured fairly easily.' Partly as a result 42 per cent of men and 59 per cent of women did not mention VD clinics as a way of getting cured: and 9 per cent were frightened of clinics, partly because of the myth that the disease was cured not by penicillin but by vigorous surgical manipulation inside the penis ('they scrape the penis to get the scabs out'). This myth was sufficiently prevalent to reach Charles Highway, the blasé eighteen-year-old sophisticate in Martin Amis's novel *The Rachel Papers* (1973). He finds that he has been infected with clap by a girl studying at an Oxford secretarial college. 'All weekend I cried, beat my head against the bathroom door, thought of ways of committing suicide, ran off into the woods and screamed as loud as I could, considered lopping off my rig with a razor blade, slept in a nettle-bed of nerves. I half-wanted to tell my father; I knew he wouldn't mind, but it would have disgusted me to have his efficient sympathy.' Instead, 'after six hours of incognito leprosy at school', Highway consults a school friend whose father is a doctor. 'Via girls, Durex, promiscuity, I brought the subject up – quite hypothetically of course.' His friend's reply is 'vehement':

> 'It's hell, apparently. They stuff stuff up your arse to sort of . . . bring it out. Then they bung this needle-thin umbrella down your cock and press a button that fans it out. Then, *then*, yank it out, really hard'. He made a tugging gesture with his spoon.
>
> 'What, they give you an anaesthetic first?'
>
> 'No. No point. It's too sensitive . . . Anyway you've got to be able to get a rise first before they can get in. Obviously. Then they *wrench* it out, and all the scabs and crabs come with it'. He sipped his coffee. 'You usually faint'.[54]

When the bibulous and libidinous Soho journalist Jeffrey Bernard was having a smear taken from his penis at a VD clinic in 1985, he noticed that the hands of the smear-taking nurse had 'love' and 'hate' tattooed on their fingers. It is an arresting and apt image: a rake's penis in the impersonal grip of hands indelibly marked with those two words so tightly bound to venereal diseases, 'love' and 'hate'. It is not just that they evoke the antithesis between Eros and death; but also that the two alternate approaches to treating venereal diseases are born of either love or hate. Publicly, venereal patients have too often been perceived as bad characters: an official of the International Hospitals Association described them as 'a menace to society' and even Colonel Harrison, the father of compassionate venereology, described them as a 'danger to the community'.[55] The unreliable motives of the culpability school of sexual hygiene, the success of good scientific therapy, the value of calm advice on prophylaxis, the unpredictable behaviour of people who have been frightened rather than convinced: these are the facts of venereal disease in Britain in the twentieth century. Superstitious savagery, dread of human reality, pontifical regulations born of fear all ought to be suspect. Kindness is the sanest of powers, particularly the kindness of strangers.

CHAPTER EIGHT

⟡

Nights of Insult:
Male Homosexuality since the 1940s

Every society has the tendency to degrade and,
as it were, to starve out its adversaries – at least
in its perception.
>   FRIEDRICH NIETZSCHE

        under every no
Lay a passion for yes that had never been
broken.
>   WALLACE STEVENS, 'Esthétique du Mal'

Nights of Insult let you pass
Watched by every human love
>   W. H. AUDEN, 'Lullaby'

This chapter scrutinizes attitudes to male homosexuality since the
Second World War, with Lord Wolfenden's Committee of
1954–7 on the reform of laws relating to homosexuality as its
focal point. The irony of the campaign for decriminalization was
that it aggravated social labelling; the campaign for repeal excited
repressive attitudes or habits of verbal abuse which in some people
had previously been dormant. The controversies which surrounded Wolfenden's deliberations were made more strident by the
over-reaction of certain politicians, lawyers and journalists
against components in their own psychological make-up: their
desperate repudiation of their own instincts was more harmful
than the behaviour of conscious, practising homosexuals whose
existence they earned notoriety by denouncing. This torrent of
disturbed opinion used distinctive terminology. An atmosphere of

threatening conspiracies was maintained by words like 'insidious', 'corruption', 'perverted' or 'indulgence'. Social labelling was sustained by inhibiting discourse to an idiom of 'unnatural vices', the 'abominable crime' and 'unmentionable' practices. These inflammatory catchphrases enabled people to speak and write without thinking too hard what they meant. This vocabulary of fear and hate spread assumptions which were more pervasive after legal reform than they had been before.[1]

The 'social distinctness' of male homosexuals was described by one psychiatrist in 1947. English family life promoted 'a solidarity in which the homosexual has little or no part; and this makes him painfully aware that the real social unit is the group and not the individual.' He could move freely in society only so long as his homosexuality was undisclosed. 'The feeling of difference, the social stigma, the legal penalties – all these close off the domain of inversion.' In many circles it was impermissible for men who did not practise homosexuality to show indifference to the defilers – let alone sympathy. Thus those who by error entered a homosexual bar 'leave as soon as possible', a physician wrote in 1952. 'If they make any comment, it will be some harsh invective as if the mere sight has sullied them.' A committee of Anglican clergy and physicians reported three years later 'that as long as the present law exists many a normal man who would like to offer the invert the ordinary friendship he craves . . . dare not take the risk' of abuse or gossip. These prohibitions instilled fear and panic which in turn created defensive behaviour. One defence was not to admit one's homosexuality to family and friends, or even to oneself. Of 127 homosexuals interviewed in the late 1950s, 31% thought their homosexuality was 'very secret', 32% judged it was known only to other homosexuals, 21% reported that close friends knew but not casual acquaintances, and 13% considered themselves recognizably homosexual. 'The whole thing is so often bedevilled with nervousness and also by the dreadful business of lies, wangles, subterfuges and time-table manipulations,' a man who kept his homosexuality secret from family and friends explained at the time of the Wolfenden enquiry. 'The double life aspect of the thing is a constant irritant. Whether this is the same thing as guilt, the psychiatrist could tell. But the result is the same . . . nagging pain and ceaseless awareness.' Other men escaped from isolation, sadness and indignation by denying their distinctness, as by insisting 'I'm not queer, I'm just playing the queers.' This was a dreary and confusing option whose frustrations often enraged its exponents into bursts of violence against their sexual partners.[2]

All this stereotyping and ostracism were counterproductive. They assuaged some superficial fears of contagion, satisfied the fretful piety of pleasure-haters and provided targets for bullies; but they did not stop homosexuality. A mire was dug of tension and confusion, of distrust and false loyalty, without benefit to national purity. 'We have compelled them to think of themselves as outlaws, as members of a great secret society, of a superior persecuted minority, and therefore they do what most of us would do in the same circumstances – they help one another,' J. B. Priestley wrote in 1957. 'All those gobbling red-faced types, who make such a fuss of their hatred of homosexuality that they tend to arouse suspicion, who are so outraged by any suggestion that our laws on this subject are barbarous and stupid ... [en]sure that the homosexual influence in our cultural life will at least be as strong as ever.'[3]

The labelling that relied on polarities of sexual preference was harsh on those who belied the process. According to one observer of gay clubs in London during the 1950s, bisexuals were 'considered immoral' and as 'only concerned with sensuality, the sex of the love object being immaterial'. This intolerance was necessary to validate the self-deception that everyone was either homosexual or not. Similarly medical opinion distinguished between the 'inborn homosexual', for whom attempts at medical treatment or the imposition of penal servitude were 'a moral outrage', and 'acquired, functional or psychological homosexuality [which] falls within an entirely different category from that of true homosexuality'. As a physician claimed in 1947 in condemnation of 'bisexuality or pseudo-homosexuality', most 'wrong-doers' indicted for 'homosexual offences are not natural inverts in the medical sense of the term, but merely immature heterosexuals or bisexuals; as a result, the reasonable claim of *bona fide* inverts to a just recognition of their rights as a social minority is gravely prejudiced by the actions of others who in no way can join in this claim, but who by popular misconception and in the eyes of the law are grouped indiscriminately with true homosexuals as criminally-minded perverts.' The self-indulgence of bisexuals was delaying 'the true homosexual being rescued from the clutches of a law which sometimes operates with medieval barbarity'.[4]

Among moralists, similar disapproval was expressed. A report circulated in 1955 by the Church of England Moral Welfare Council contrasted 'the genuine invert' (who suffered from 'a condition') with 'the pervert'. Perverts were those creatures whose behaviour undermined rigid categorization and who were there-fore objects of hostility. Denigrated as heterosexuals who engaged in homosexuality rather than acknowledged as people who felt labels were irrelevant to their own feelings and experience, they were consigned to two categories, one more contemptible than the other. There was 'the casual (to be distinguished from the bisexual) . . . who, from motives of curiosity, or in exceptional circumstances – life in the services, or in prison, or in a situation of particular temptation or emotion – may engage in one or more homosexual acts, but who easily and rapidly assumes again a heterosexual orientation'; but lower still, the 'habitual pervert' engaged in regular homosexual acts, either as a prostitute, 'or for the purposes of blackmail, or in search of new sensual satisfactions, or simply because to do evil for evil's sake has a fascination of its own'. The implication of this view was that young working-class men were 'habitual perverts'. At a level whose expression was inchoate there was a refusal to believe that a vigorous young work-ing-class man would desire sex with other men for its intrinsic pleas-ure or because it satisfied his wider sense of his identity and needs. Since such young men were so far from stereotyped expectations, they were perceived as twisted by some extra mercenary kink.[5]

As the *Medical Press* noted in 1947, homosexuality conjured popular 'images of the jaded roué . . . who, having run the gamut of normal experience, now turns to new sources of gratification in much the same way as the Roman gourmands, tired of honest mutton, turned to peacocks' brains'. Sir Norwood East, a former prison doctor attached to the Maudsley psychiatric hospital, believed that 'some people turn to homosexuality when satiated with pleasures obtained from women', rather than realizing that some men rejected women, and sought other men, because they found heterosexual relations unfulfilling. There was an imaginative failure to realize that some people could find, after experimenta-tion, their own gender sexually or emotionally more satisfying. Such a choice, it was judged, must be the perversity of a self-indulgent lecher.[6]

Laura Hutton of the Tavistock Clinic in London, writing in

1949, defined the man who was 'born' homosexual because of an endocrinic imbalance as a '"sissy" or "pansy", who suffers the greater scorn and contumely of his fellow-men, solely because of a bodily abnormality for which he is no more responsible than he would be for a congenital club foot'. This type were 'often rather poor specimens, both from the point of view of physique and of character' but 'endowed with peculiar sensitiveness to beauty and with creative ability'. They needed different treatment from men ('ordinarily fine specimens of manhood') whose 'early psychological difficulties have led to an abnormal choice of love object' but who responded to psychotherapy. Hutton's patronizing language, with its comparison of homosexual desire to a club foot, had many counterparts among contemporaries striving for tolerance towards gay men: the progressive *Encyclopaedia of Sexual Knowledge*, in its edition of 1957, with the kindest of intentions, compared the homosexual to 'a hunchback' and Lord Arran, who led the parliamentary campaign to decriminalize homosexuality, described homosexuals in 1965 as 'the odd men out: the ones with the limp'.[7]

Male homosexuality was fixed with such opprobrium that many youths felt bewilderment or despair once they recognized the nature of their desires. Among a sample interviewed in the 1950s, 40% had been too frightened to seek advice, and the experiences of those who did tell others were sometimes bizarre, or evidenced the suppressed desires of those in authority. Confidences were distorted, abused or rejected by their recipients. The following six experiences seem representative.

> I told our family doctor I was homosexual. He seemed to get rather excited about it. He questioned me about the kind of man that attracted me and then asked if I was attracted to a man like him. He was a mousey little man with thick glasses and in the brashness of youth I said, 'Good heavens no, doctor!' I didn't think much more about it at the time; not until many years later when I heard he'd committed suicide.

> The doctor told me to lie on the couch and loosen my clothing. Then he passed his hands over me, telling me to think beautiful thoughts and forget my evil actions.

> He told me to pull up my socks, find a nice girl and get married.

I told my doctor I wanted to see a psychiatrist. He said I was a namby-pamby. He told me to get a piece of paper and draw pictures of nude women. I think he was off his rocker.

I told my brother who told my sister and together we decided to go to see my uncle who is a specialist. He told me I needed more exercise. He reduced me to tears.

[A Roman Catholic priest] said, 'You can't be homosexual if you're a civil engineer. Only artists and actors and people like that are homosexual.'

I told my mother and father that I was homosexual. They simply would not believe me.[8]

Many isolated young homosexuals thought the only way to meet other men was by visiting public places like lavatories. As they became more experienced, learnt how to recognize other homosexuals and were shown other rendezvous, they often ceased to visit public places in search of partners. This meant that it was seldom the habituated homosexual, but often young, isolated or inexperienced men who were arrested by the police for importuning. (The other types of men apprehended were those so ashamed of their homosexuality that they sought quick and anonymous encounters in public places from which they would flee as soon as they had attained orgasm; or those whose pleasure was heightened by a sense of danger.) In London in the 1950s few men sought partners in homosexual clubs (which like the eighteenth-century molly clubs were more social oases than pick-up joints), although certain bars, like the Piccadilly, the Standard, the White Bear and Murphy's Irish House, streets, and cinemas like the Biograph in Victoria were important. Gay bars were less discreet than the clubs. With the exception of a few pubs which had a private arrangement with the police, these pubs were regularly raided. This police assiduity was ostensibly intended to disperse 'homosexual coteries', but had the opposite effect. 'The entire clientèle would transfer its custom, by some mysterious means of mutual agreement, to another pub, which for several months would be crowded night after night, until it was raided in its turn,' as one habitué described. The official version was different. 'These pests descend like locusts on some licensed premises, drive out the respectable clientèle and literally take over the custom of the house,' so Sir Laurence Dunne, the Chief Metropolitan Magistrate, described. Before the publican 'realises it, the damage is done; his respectable customers have deserted him, and he has either to accept the custom of the perverts or put up his shutters. The perverts in mass are even more noisome than singly. They often wear articles of feminine clothing, answer to feminine names and use the filthiest of language and innuendo.'[9]

There was medical, religious and lay pressure towards chastity as the price of toleration for the homosexual temperament. Homosexuality did not create 'outcasts or pariahs' if 'the actual sex expression is diverted elsewhere', wrote a former editor of the *Police Gazette*, Kenneth Ingram. The invert should abandon 'the atmosphere of curious cults and immoral intrigues' for 'a fuller mission' in life. 'He will be neither an absurdity, nor a scourge, nor one whose sense of affectional values is vitiated by the phantastic imagination that he belongs to a more aesthetic and higher aristocratic order. By becoming more than an invert, he will not lose the gifts which he intuitively realizes to be his peculiar possession. He must be changed only by being developed. He is abnormal only because he is undeveloped.' It is easy to preach chastity if you are not obliged to practise it yourself. Ingram was a homosexual who, sadly, found it possible from middle age to practise what he preached: but other advocates of sublimation lacked that excuse. Homosexuality 'can develop on the highest plane', Sir Norwood East urged in 1947. 'The life of the chaste homosexual may be more complicated, sublimated and specialized than that of the chaste heterosexual [but] may be encouraged by the knowledge that continence is consistent with full health and efficiency.' If homosexuals could not channel their sexual drives into religious or artistic inspiration, they were counselled to emulate the worthy lives of spinsters engaged in charitable deeds and voluntary work. Inverts could 'expect nothing but a prospect of transitory attachments, disillusionments and loneliness in old age', reported a committee of Anglican clergy and physicians in 1955. 'But this is the expectation of many normal women who long for marriage and emotional security yet who accept their condition, and by seeking to sublimate their sexual lives in various socially useful ways achieve personal fulfilment. Along the same lines lies a partial solution, at least, for the homosexual.'[10]

The view that prison incarceration was indispensable to produce a state of mind responsive to psychotherapy was sometimes propounded, but this ignored the fact that the supposed cure required the stigma of imprisonment and destroyed the patient's civil life. In any event, out of 1,065 men imprisoned for homosexual offences in 1955, only 158 were judged suitable for psychotherapy, and only 65 were so treated. The value of such treatment was doubtful. It was often inexpedient or embarrassing for the patient to tell the physician that his treatment was ineffective, while other men remanded for reports pretended to have been 'cured' in order to avoid gaol. Apart from psychotherapy, other treatment was tried. In the 1940s there were experiments to direct men's sexual desires by injections of male hormones (androgens) and female hormones (oestrogens). Scientists and moralists hoped 'that the eternal verities of "masculine" and "feminine" might, indeed, be embodied in a simple chemical form'. Physical castration had been shown not to inhibit male homosexual activity, except by preventing active anal intercourse: castrati could still fellate or masturbate other men, or take the passive role. But chemical castration was thought more effective in reducing libido, and in cases of 'gross indecency' in the 1950s there was a vogue for imposing compulsory hormone treatment as an alternative to prison even though such treatment could result in the growth of breasts. It seems to have had little long-term effect except to confuse and humiliate its recipients. (The Home Office forbade prison medical officers to give hormonal treatment to homosexual inmates lest it cause infertility, and thus condemn ex-prisoners to the sin of non-procreative copulation if, once 'cured', they practised heterosexuality.)[11]

Views of punishment and therapy varied. A 22-year-old farm labourer called Ron was debauched at an early age by a gardener, and together they were later sentenced in the early 1950s to five and seven years' imprisonment respectively. Both were kept at Wormwood Scrubs, where they saw one another almost daily. As a fellow prisoner described:

> Neither of them had been offered any help during that time by psychiatrist or doctor. One day, an Assistant Governor, a man who professed to be a Christian, visited Ron in his cell.
>
> 'Well', he asked, 'have you made up your mind to change your habits when you get outside?'

'How can I?' said Ron. 'Every day I see the man who started it all. I keep on remembering. Sir, can't I be put somewhere else, so that I can get away from him?'

The Assistant Governor smiled. 'That's all part of the punishment,' he said.[12]

Gay men were characterized in terms of anal acts: 'buggers are two men who work themselves up into such a state of mutual admiration that one puts his piss-pipe up the other's arse,' to quote the definition given to Sir John Betjeman in boyhood by his father. The reality was different. The psychotherapist attached to Wormwood Scrubs prison in London during the 1940s reported that the majority of those imprisoned for homosexual acts had practised mutual masturbation, 'what, among schoolboys, would be termed "smutty or sexual fun and games"': the sexual conduct of most of those imprisoned 'could scarcely be called abnormal in the early teens'. Michael Schofield, whose medical researches were perhaps the most valuable of the period, reported that 'pseudo-homosexuals' restricted their acts with men to sodomy because it most closely resembled the heterosexual act, and that mutual masturbation and slicklegging were more common acts between 'genuine inverts'. Given the obsession with buggery, it is worth giving in detail the figures of Schofield. Among the 127 men interviewed by him in the late 1950s, mutual masturbation was the technique used at first homosexual experience for 61%, of which 77% had experienced this before they were seventeen. Beginning with slicklegging, other techniques were gradually learnt and became more frequent as men grew older. Among the sample, mutual masturbation was the usual technique in 17% but the preferred technique for only 5% – figures which probably reflected the number of isolated and guilty men whose sexual encounters were limited to a quick unbuttoning and fumble in a park or lavatory. Slicklegging was the usual technique of 35% and the preferred technique of 37%. Fellatio was the most usual technique for 7% and the preferred technique for 9%. Twenty-two per cent of the sample had never experienced passive anal intercourse and 28% had never experienced active anal intercourse. About half of those who undertook anal intercourse were willing to be either active or passive. Passive anal intercourse was the most usual technique for 22%, but active anal intercourse for only 10%: in other words less than one-third regularly had anal intercourse. (Of the sample, 10% had had no homosexual experiences in the last year, 23% one partner only, 41% from 2 to 11 partners, 16% from 12 to 24 partners, and 13% over 24 partners, 42% of the group had experienced heterosexual intercourse, but only 18% of these had had such experiences for any length of time.)[13]

'In practice the homosexual who observes a reasonable discretion in his affairs is in no danger from the police,' the psychiatrist David Stafford-Clark of Maudsley hospital judged in 1947. 'Reasonable discretion implies not only avoidance of public or commercial exploitation of his inversion, but also the good fortune to steer clear of the bisexual psychopath who may masquerade as a true invert in order to gain opportunities for subsequent blackmail, a practice which involves little risk for the blackmailer who can usually support his claim to be an innocent victim of indecent and entirely unwelcome overtures, by producing a temporarily infatuated girl-friend as evidence of his own normality.' The velleities of Stafford-Clark were unreal, and became much more demonstrably so within the next few years. Professional men might pontificate in this way, and assuage doubts about the justice or sense of the law, but others knew to their cost that conditions were not as safe and comfortable as Stafford-Clark wished to imagine. 'The law is very much alive, and heavy penalties are incurred by anyone who breaks it,' wrote Peter Wildeblood after a gaol sentence for homosexuality in the 1950s. 'A homosexual who gives way to his impulses, even if he is doing no conceivable harm to anyone, therefore runs appalling risks.'[14]

A trial at Abergavenny in 1942 (reported among national newspapers only in the *News of the World*) illustrated the dangers which were faced by those who practised a criminal sexuality. Twenty-four men were charged after an investigation provoked by a youth complaining of overtures from a cinema manager. A boy of nineteen threw himself under a train before coming to trial, while at least two other defendants tried to hang or poison themselves, of whom one, a chef, was sentenced to three months' imprisonment for attempted suicide as well as ten years' penal servitude. Although the *News of the World* spoke of 'an orgy of perversion' at Abergavenny, the judge, Sir John Singleton (a bachelor with a 'detached' mind who 'could generally get from a jury the verdict he thought would meet the justice of the case', in whose court 'the slightest departure from the correct standards of decorum were apt to recoil unpleasantly on the head of the delinquent') emphasized in his summing up 'that Abergavenny is not a happy hunting ground for such people'. Singleton ordered women to leave the court before evidence was heard. Of the defendants, eighteen received gaol sentences of from ten months to twelve years, with thirteen of them receiving a total of 57 years; the younger men who received lighter sentences seem to have collaborated with the police, one of whose officers stated that with four exceptions, 'who were normal, all the accused were of a certain type'. His definition of normality, which doubtless rested on accepting the quartet's assurance that they were 'not queer but playing the queers', was not examined. There was the usual association of homosexuality with effete upper-class men, so that an 18-year-old factory worker from Barking recounted to police 'his association with men in luxury flats in the West End', for which he got 15 months. The defendants were described in contemptuous language. A young café assistant from Chelsea 'was said to be a conscientious objector and a member of the Peace Pledge Union', both of which acts were brave in the wartime atmosphere of 1942 but could be represented to popular opinion as cowardly; he was also described as 'a timid, undersized, pathetic person'. A young actor/playwright from Hammersmith 'was described by an Army doctor as a psychopathic personality with suicidal tendencies'. The first of the defendants to be sentenced was mocked for fainting – although his sentence of ten years perhaps justified such a reaction. A middle-aged window-dresser, whom Singleton also gave a condign sentence, 'was stated by the police' to be 'detested by all decent minded men who worked on the premises with him', and was derided for keeping powderpuffs and cosmetics in his bedroom; in fact he sounds a charming queen, who was nicknamed 'The Marquis', and wrote unpublished novels under the pseudonym of Miss Amanda Flame.[15]

'There is something mean and stuffy about a courtroom which seems to bring to a common level of bathos all the high drama, the scorching cruelty, the treachery, the cupidity and bloodthirstiness, the failure, distraction and whining fear which are associated with the penal code,' Rupert Croft-Cooke reflected during his trial in 1953 (see plate). 'I felt this meanness and stuffiness as I looked at the plump, self-satisfied faces before me, I felt it rising from the very varnish of the places . . . something not exactly evil, but smugly malicious and pawky.' Just as Singleton at the Abergavenny trial of 1942 banished all women from his courtroom, so a decade later the judge who tried Croft-Cooke announced at the start of the hearing 'that the case about to be heard was a very unpleasant one' – an exaggeration for a case alleging gross indecency with a sailor at the defendant's house, and moreover an exaggeration bound to prejudice a jury. Croft- Cooke's judge suggested that all women present in court should leave which they did: one doughty woman blushed scarlet but remained until she noticed that she was alone of her sex. Wild, the Recorder of London a decade earlier, was emphatic that women should not sit as jurors in cases involving homosexuality, as if the physiology of anal intercourse was more shocking than childbirth. In the 1950s women were still some-times excluded from the jury list on days that such cases came to trial.[16]

In 1938 there were 134 prosecutions in England for sodomy and bestiality, 822 for attempted sodomy and indecent assaults and 320 for gross indecency. Fifteen years later, in 1952, these figures had risen to 670, to 3,087 and to 1,686 respectively. In the period between 1930 and 1955 homosexual offences known to the police increased by 850 per cent compared with 223 per cent for all indictable offences. Partly the level of prosecutions in the earlier period reflected the difficulties of securing a conviction. The Departmental Committee on Sexual Offences against Young Persons reported in 1926 that 'sometimes juries are loth to convict, even when the evidence is clear', either 'because they find it hard to accept as true the shocking facts submitted for their verdict, or it may be due to an insufficient appreciation of the gravity of the offence'. Between the wars George Melly's father sat on a jury which acquitted a man accused of sodomy. Asked later if the defendant was guilty, he replied, 'O yes, but half the jury didn't think it was possible and the rest of us didn't think it mattered.'[17]

Despite the lower level of arrests in the inter-war period, blackmail supposedly abounded. The former Lord Chancellor, Jowitt, claimed in 1954 that at least 95 per cent of the blackmail cases of which he had been apprised when Attorney-General in 1929–32 had been founded on allegations of homosexuality – a memory which if accurate suggests extraordinary fears and tensions. Seventy-one cases of blackmail were reported to the police in England and Wales between 1950 and 1953, of which 32 involved homosexuality; of a total of 125 blackmail cases known to the Scottish police in the decade from January 1946, only one involved homosexuality. Policemen working in pairs were however known to blackmail homosexuals (two officers were convicted of attempted blackmail in 1955), and there were deterrents to reporting blackmail. When a bus driver complained to the police in the early 1950s that he had been blackmailed by a male shop assistant with whom he had previously been sexually involved for seven years, the Director of Public Prosecutions advised that no action should be taken for demanding money with menaces: but both men were charged with buggery, and were each sentenced to nine months' imprisonment. As with police arrests, there is evidence that the young, inexperienced and isolated were the preferred prey of blackmailers; but of its essence, the extent and pattern of blackmail is unascertainable.[18]

The focusing of hostile anxiety on a hateful minority of homosexuals, first remarked during the Napoleonic Wars, and revived during 1915–18, was a feature of the Second World War. Lord Chorley, who was a senior official at the Ministry of Home Security in 1941–2, recalled in 1965 'that if there was any question of making an Order [of detainment without trial] against a man under the Defence Regulations, it was indeed a strong element in the case against him that he was known to be a homosexual. Many men spent time during the war shut up for very little other reason.' The wartime blackout facilitated sex between strangers, and long absences from home, living in proximity to other men, with the fear of imminent death, led to relief of sexual tension by men who seldom conformed to stereotype. The wartime Home Secretary, Herbert Morrison, has been described by his biographers as 'prudish and puritanical', with 'tough and punitive' personal instincts. His wife had refused to copulate with him for twenty years: as a result he was notorious for his roaming hands at parties and as Home Secretary expressed his wish to see a woman hanged. Homosexuality left him tense and embarrassed, but he supported Sir Theobald Mathew, a devout Roman Catholic who was appointed Director of Public Prosecutions in 1944, who believed that homosexuality was increasing and should be combated. Mathew felt that the lives of male adolescents had undergone 'complete change' as the result of the extended duration of education and National Service, creating an unprecedented atmosphere in which homosexuality 'can be easily acquired and become ingrained'. He thought very few men were '"genuine" homosexuals'. Most of those who came before the courts were men who 'through curiosity, hero worship or cupidity, allowed themselves to be initiated into these practices, and have persisted in them, until their capacity to control or limit their homosexual desires has ceased to exist.' He believed that by the time most men became entangled in the criminal laws surrounding homosexuality, they were 'past reformation', which makes his policy of prosecution seem more like persecution. The only real solutions that he could list were to ensure '(a) that boys and young men should be taught that these habits are dirty, degrading and harmful, and the negation of decent manhood, and (b) that every practicable precaution should be taken to ensure that those in charge of boys and young men are themselves free from this taint'.[19]

Hostility to homosexuality fed on accounts of trials in newspapers like the *News of the World*. The men running the lurid press were 'a cold-eyed bunch of businessmen who peddled tragedy, sensation and heartbreak as casually as though they were cartloads of cabbages', in the words of a journalist who worked for the presslord Rothermere. 'The false, overcoloured and sentimental view of life reflected in these newspapers was due to the cynical belief of these men that this was what the public wanted.' For many people crime reporters were the only source of information about homosexuality, and they concluded that all homosexuals were chorister-molesting vicars or men who groped other men in subterranean lavatories in a fetid atmosphere of urine.[20]

Anxieties were increased by the publication of Alfred Kinsey's report on *Sexual Behaviour in the Human Male* (1948). Interest in this research was so great that a diplomat, Guy Burgess, who owned one of the first copies in England, was so frightened of it being stolen that he hid it in a place where he thought no one would look – the Foreign Secretary's In-Tray – and its findings were so objectionable to some people that the Home Office contemplated its prosecution for obscenity. After interviewing a large sample of North Americans, Kinsey reported that 37% of the total male population had homosexual experience to the point of orgasm between adolescence and old age, and that another 13% reacted erotically to other men without having overt homosexual contacts after adolescence. Equally significantly, he found that of men who had left school aged about 14 or 15, 6.9% used homosexual outlets before they were 20, compared with 10.8% of those with education at high school level aged about 17, and 2.4% of college graduates: yet it was the high school category which deplored and mocked homosexuality most. Kinsey's implication that homosexuality was present in every corner and class of Britain, and was not the deviance of a small, excoriated and identifiable minority, terrified some people.[21]

Other events in 1951 added to the insecurities created by Kinsey. Britain lost its political control over Iran and Egypt, leading to a crisis of imperial self-confidence comparable with that of the 1890s when the degenerationist theories of Lombroso and Nordau had caused such anti-homosexual excitement in Britain. In the ensuing decade, as the British Empire disintegrated in Malaysia, Africa, and Cyprus, fears about military loss of control were over and over again identified with sexual lack of control: the disintegration of heterosexuality, it was reiterated, had been a feature of the disintegration of the Roman Empire, as it would be for the British Empire. 'One wonders at the type of mind that even considers the legalization of what the law of Moses condemned to instant death,' wrote a correspondent in the *News Chronicle* a year after the British fiasco at Suez. 'God has been good to Britain. Let us beware lest we tempt Him to wrath.' An older man with past homosexual experiences suggested that such acts were 'harmful' because they rendered men 'weak in initiative, invention and purposefulness', and 'spread like wildfire'. This fear of an exhausted nation, coupled with anxiety about loss of control, was widespread. Thus Tudor Rees quoted the dictum of a fellow judge, Avory, that 'an irresistible impulse is an impulse that must be resisted' and wrote in 1955 of homosexuals as men dominated by 'an unconquerable demon'. It was his view that people 'find themselves so out of control of their own emotions that they commit vicious offences just because they, being free to fall, succumb through an utter failure to resist'.[22]

Fears were stimulated by the disclosure in 1951 that two British diplomats, Guy Burgess and Donald Maclean, who had fled to Russia, had been Soviet spies for years. Burgess was homosexual and Maclean was bisexual. By then Morrison was Foreign Secretary with responsibility for the absconding diplomats, and under pressure from the Americans a campaign began against homosexuals in government service, which was given extra edge as the scions of British espionage convinced themselves that they would never unravel the deceptions until they had mastered the world of 'crypto-homosexuals'. The United States Government, beset by Senator Joseph McCarthy's paranoia about communist Enemies Within, pressed the British to identify homosexuals as security risks. Quite apart from the risks of blackmail, 'indulgence in acts of sex perversion weakens the moral fibre of an individual to a degree that he is not suitable for a position of responsibility,' to quote a Senate sub-committee report. 'Most perverts tend to congregate at the same restaurants, night clubs and bars' and had an over-riding loyalty to one another. Predictably McCarthy's chief coadjutor, Roy Cohn, who brought furious zeal to the accusation and persecution of homosexuality, was a homosexual himself, livid in his public denial of his tastes (he tried to silence critics by remarking that one young man of whom he was fond later married Miss Universe and fathered seven children). 'Positive vetting' of civil servants holding responsible jobs, to seek 'serious character weaknesses', was introduced by the British in 1952. During the following year Commander E. A. Cole of Scotland Yard spent three months in America consulting Federal Bureau of Investigation experts about the strategy and methods of a homosexual purge. Some members of Britain's security forces became obsessed with homosexuality, incessantly and repetitively enquiring into supposed sexual irregularities. When in the mid 1970s a paranoid cadre of MI5 officers, convinced that Britain was disintegrating, launched Operation Clockwork Orange to smear and undermine Labour party leaders and progressive Conservatives, accusations of homosexuality were a favoured technique. As late as 1985 a Cabinet minister who had drawn the resentment of a group of British security officers was beset by lies planted among journalists, and fed to fellow politicians, that he had made sexual overtures to schoolboys. The campaign of innuendo undermined his political standing and served to deter other ministers disposed to monitor the practice of espionage. It was also a reminder of how often paranoiacs resort to accusations of homosexuality against their supposed enemies. Doubtless some of the MI5 smearers were engaging in a self-repudiation as desperate, contemptible and transparent as Roy Cohn's.[23]

As part of these fears, the Admiralty in 1954 issued new Fleet

Orders stressing 'the horrible character of unnatural vice' and instructing naval officers 'to stamp out the evil'. In grotesquely specific language and detail, the Admiralty described how officers were to inspect sailor's underwear for seminal or faecal stains, or jars of vaseline or hair gel for pubic hairs, and set regulations for the scrutiny of men's bodies for signs of homosexual use. Conscious that this obsessive need to investigate and control sex would be seen by many men on board ships as hypocritical dirty-minded meddling, the Admiralty ordered its officers to enlist 'the help of the steadier and more reliable men on the Lower Deck' to resist the deplorably common tendency 'to treat these matters with levity'. The response they feared almost as much as homosexuality was having their horrors laughed at. Around the same time the War Office, frightened of the 'essentially secret nature' of homosexuality and apprehensive of 'contamination by civilian sources', introduced new regulations against it. When soldiers were 'all boxed up with their own kind', Lieutenant-General Sir Kenneth McLean (on special duty at the War Office) told a House of Commons committee, 'we must stamp on this the moment it is found.' If a sergeant put his hand on a soldier, even without gross indecency, 'we want to jump on that at once,' a legal expert from the War Office confirmed. The Air Ministry were less keen than the other service departments to 'pounce' or 'stamp out'. Homosexuality was 'almost entirely confined to ground trades', they told the Wolfenden Committee. Air-crews were immune to its 'corrupting influence' because they were 'all selected individuals with a paramount interest in flying'. Aviators were heroes, not deviants: hurtling about the heavens in aircraft was so thrilling that men hardly needed the extra thrill of sex, or so the Air Ministry seemed to believe. One military anxiety was however much diminished by the 1950s. 'The old unholy traffic between soldiers of the Guards and Household Cavalry and perverts in the Royal Parks is now a thing of the past,' Sir Laurence Dunne reported after two decades as a London magistrate. 'Education and a higher moral sense has [sic] played its part, but *I fear* that the abolition of the old tight overalls worn by other ranks walking out is a strong contributory factor; battle dress or khaki serge lacks the aphrodisiac appeal of the old walking out dress.'[24]

The chief result of this anxiety about national security was the prosecution of Peter Wildeblood, diplomatic correspondent of the

Daily Mail, who was tried together with Lord Montagu of Beaulieu and Michael Pitt-Rivers in 1954. The background to the case was complicated. In 1953 Montagu and another man were accused of committing an unnatural offence and an indecent assault on two boy scouts. The circumstances of the allegation were implausible, and it was proved to the judge's satisfaction that the police had tampered with one important piece of evidence. Montagu was acquitted on the graver charge, but the jury disagreed about the indecent assault, at which point Mathew's Directorate of Public Prosecutions decided that Montagu should be retried at the next sessions. Three weeks later Montagu's cousin, Michael Pitt-Rivers, together with their friend Wildeblood, were arrested on several charges of indecency with two RAF men in 1952 and were also accused with Montagu of conspiring to commit them. (Wildeblood the diplomatic correspondent was arrested by a superintendent from Special Branch, a feature which betrayed the British wish to assure the US Government that they were purging sensitively placed or socially prominent homosexuals.) At Winchester Assizes in March 1954 the scouts charge was dropped from the indictment, but the publicity it had already attracted was prejudicial. The principal prosecution witnesses were the airmen, Edward McNally and John Reynolds, one of whom had been badgered almost to tears until he made a statement. They were 'perverts, men of the lowest possible character . . . who apparently cheerfully accepted corruption', in the words of prosecuting counsel. They committed 'unnatural offences . . . under the seductive influence of lavish hospitality' from Montagu, Wildeblood and Pitt-Rivers, 'who were so infinitely their social superiors'. (Prosecuting counsel 'was an impressive man, with purple jowls hanging down over his collar', Wildeblood recalled: 'His voice was fruity and passionate; it shook with horror as he described the scandalous liaison between witnesses and the accused.') Sir Theobald Mathew took an unusual interest in the case, not only promising McNally and Reynolds immunity from prosecution, however many offences they admitted, but taking the trouble to be in court when sentences were passed (18 months for Pitt-Rivers and Wildeblood; 12 months for Montagu). No attempt was made to pursue other men incriminated by McNally and Reynolds, but Mathew betrayed a passion to ruin Montagu. As to McNally, 'when questioned about details he became vague and evasive, twisting, turning, contradicting his previous evidence and saying he didn't remember'; but on the main point he had been well enough schooled, 'repeating over and over again in the same incongruous words: "Mr Wildeblood committed an offence against me."'[25]

Fears of class betrayal or of disintegrating social boundaries were fundamental to this affair. Mathew always believed that his department should intervene in cases of 'special gravity' where men 'in authority' (like peers) had 'used their position to make victims or accomplices of those . . . under their influence'. (Homosexual acts, a metropolitan magistrate told the Wolfenden Committee, were 'morally wrong, physically dirty and progressively degrading', but became 'even more anti-social where the participants are not of equal status', as for example with 'the artistic genius' or 'the man of wealth or title and the friend from a simpler walk of life'.) It was not just the prosecutor's ludicrous emphasis that Montagu and Wildeblood had plied McNally and Reynolds with a bottle of champagne in a luxurious Kensington flat when in fact a bottle of champagne cider was shared in a tiny bedsitter. But Wildeblood and Montagu, like Croft-Cooke, had been open in disregarding the rigidity of the English class system. 'I instinctively rebelled against a system by which a man, whatever his personal qualities might be, was indelibly labelled "Top Drawer", "Middle Drawer" or "Bottom Drawer", merely by the manner in which he spoke,' Wildeblood later wrote. For four years he had served next to working men in the RAF. 'Now that the war for freedom was over, I was no longer supposed to speak to them, because they were not "my class". The social rules seemed to me as ridiculous as those imitation traditions which I had had to learn at school. The homosexual world knows no such boundaries – which is precisely why it is so much hated and feared by many of our political diehards.' Montagu's offence was that he befriended men who, to paraphrase prosecuting counsel, were 'infinitely his social inferior'.[26]

The personal factor was important in this campaign of prosecution. The Home Secretary from 1951 until 1954 was Sir David Maxwell Fyfe, a notorious homophobe. The Metropolitan Police Commissioner appointed in 1953, Sir John Nott-Bower, was a bigot: convictions for male soliciting or importuning rose to an average of about 40 per month in the West End of London in the years after his appointment. As one MP who monitored these developments wrote, 'Promotion in the junior ranks of the force had always depended to a considerable extent upon the number of convictions a particular officer has been able to secure, and when the news filters down to the lower ranks that the authorities are interested in a particular type of offender the inference is obvious, especially as in this instance it was easier and incidentally safer and less troublesome for a police officer to catch a homosexual than a burglar.' The Chief Metropolitan Magistrate appointed in 1948, Sir Laurence Dunne, was as hostile as Fyfe or Nott-Bower to homosexuals, whom he called 'male harpies' or 'the lowest of the low', and blamed them for turning 'the West End street urinals [into] plague spots after dark'. For offences other than public indecency, he wanted sentences to be 'uniform and severe' and he opposed any relaxation in the laws or in their enforcement (such as imitating Dutch tolerance, or adopting the Code Napoléon):

> I decline to be impressed by the view taken in other countries. They have their problems: we have ours . . . this aberration is on the increase, and I believe it would weaken the hand of the law in dealing with what is admitted by all, save addicts, to be an evil. To countenance homosexual practices in private is playing with fire. Appetites are progressive, and a homosexual sated with practices with adults, without hindrance, will be far more likely to tempt a jaded appetite with youth. A great deal of encouragement is already given by unthinking people who affect to find something funny and not reprehensible in their conduct . . . it would be disastrous to give further tacit encouragement by altering the law.

With this lurid language – invoking flames, addiction and national disaster but deprecating cheery tolerance – the fears of men like Dunne, Fyfe, Mathew and Nott-Bower all fed on one another. As a result many men found themselves suddenly ensnared 'in the cruel machinery of accusation, defence, punishment – the whole rigmarole invented by society to quell those insufficiently inconspicuous'.[27]

There were increasing numbers of mass prosecutions in which one man was promised immunity from prosecution if he testified against others, or was prosecuted on a less serious charge of indecency in return for denouncing other men of his sexual acquaintance. In the absence of other admissible proof, the police resorted to intensive interrogation of chains of men in order to extract admissions of guilt. In the three years to March 1956, 94% of the 480 men convicted of homosexual acts in England and Wales signed written statements admitting their guilt. Homosexuals are not exceptionally prone to self-incrimination; but they were subjected to exceptional pressure when detained for questioning. In many cases police searched the rooms of suspected men, taking letters, photographs, books or other possessions as evidence that the man had homosexual tastes. During trials, judges often admitted such evidence despite the usual judicial rule that evidence was inadmissible merely to prove that the accused had a propensity to commit a crime similar to that with which he was charged. As a man sentenced to seven months' imprisonment later recalled,

> At the police station I was shown letters I had written to this man. They were quite harmless, although a few phrases could be interpreted to mean that we'd had sex. The policeman told me that they did not want me and that it was in my interest to tell them about the other man. They would move heaven and earth to see I didn't get into trouble. So after a lot of persuasion and some strong arm methods, I signed a statement admitting sex three times.

The suddenness and ferocity of the police onslaught stunned many of their victims. Knowing that a policeman wanted to interview him, another young man called at his local police station:

> I never had any fears. I suppose everyone thinks it can't happen to me. He was an awful detective – threats, swear words – 'I'll fucking well bash you; you're bloody clever; I can always go to your family'. Yet the funny thing was . . . I didn't want to be late for work. So I told them to write down what they liked and I'd sign it.

Police officers relied on the surprise and inexperience of many of those charged:

> At the police station they were very nice, gave me cigarettes and called me by my Christian name. I was persuaded to rely on their sympathy. I was so green I didn't even realize I had been charged. This was on a Friday, and they said to come back on Monday and they thought everything would be cleared up by then. On

> Monday, before I knew what was happening, I was
> whipped into Court and given three months . . . I had
> no solicitor and I said nothing in Court.

Because publicity could lead to loss of home, jobs, friends and
family, and because so many of the men were isolated and naive,
police were free to intimidate, as three other men recorded.

> Some people are so incensed by the idea of homosexu-
> ality that police methods that wouldn't be tolerated for
> a moment in other crimes are allowed when they're after
> queers . . . The worst thing is this threat of exposure or
> violence which the police use to persuade people to tell
> tales about others.

> I was taken to the police station where I was given quite
> a grilling. They threatened to get my landlord into
> trouble. They also threatened to arrest Jack unless I
> admitted it and they used my job as a lever to persuade
> me to make a statement.

> My friend was visited by the police. They were having
> one of those round-ups in another part of the country
> and on one of these blokes they found my friend's name
> and address. Nothing else, just the name and address.
> But that did not stop the police coming round three
> times, once at the place where he worked. They didn't
> find nothing but my friend had so much explaining to
> do, we felt we'd better leave the house and live
> somewhere else.

Often police made an unnecessary visit to the accused's workplace
so that his employer or colleagues realized that he was in trouble
for homosexuality.[28]

One example of these techniques began in 1954 when an
eighteen-year-old public school boy propositioned a fellow pas-
senger on the train from Exeter to Taunton. The other man proved
to be a railway policeman who initiated an investigation which
resulted in 17 men being prosecuted. Informal promises made to
some of the youth's contacts were reflected in the sentences given
by Sir Roland Oliver at Taunton Assizes. Soldiers aged 18 and 19,
and two aircraftmen aged 20, were all bound over for two years,
and two labourers aged 22 were put on probation for three years.

But older men, from a higher social class, had more damaging evidence put against them, depicting them as corrupters of younger inferiors, and received gaol sentences. One of these men, a businessman of 37 with a brave war record, who was married with a child, died in his cell immediately after being sentenced to imprisonment of one year. The tricks of such cases having been learnt by the Somerset police, another 13 men were prosecuted at Taunton in 1955. 'The pogroms', wrote a Somerset resident in 1958, 'continue, one in this neighbourhood having started with long and weary police-court proceedings on the eve of Christmas, so that the festival may presumably be spent in contemplation of the Spring Assize.' There was an identical pattern on each occasion. 'The police go round from house to house, bringing ruin in their train, always attacking the youngest men first, extracting information with lengthy questioning and specious promises of light sentences as they proceed from clue to clue, i.e. from home to home, often up to twenty.' In Somerset there were still 'moralists in high places who imagine that they do good by this cruelty'. Throughout Britain so-called 'stale' cases were dredged up by the police on the basis of informants' accusations – in a typical case of 1954 a man was charged with an offence committed ten years earlier – for which the chief evidence was statements, extracted under duress, by men implicating one another in a chain.[29]

These mass arrests excited fears among some judges about the proliferation of 'coteries of buggers', in Lord Chief Justice Goddard's phrase, where 'the most horrible things go on'. This view of sinister cells of deviants was popularized in lurid newspapers like the *Sunday Pictorial* whose pioneering series on homosexuality in 1952 declared that the practice was 'most prevalent among the Intellectuals'. Even a Home Office minister affirmed in 1954 that the increase in prosecutions 'must reflect a very considerable increase in the numbers of offences actually committed'.[30]

The publicity surrounding these trials upset lawyers and spread anxiety. 'The population of Taunton was [not] more debased than other groups of the community, but once vice got established it spread like a pestilence, and unless held in check spread indefinitely,' Sir Roland Oliver judged at the Somerset pogrom of 1954. 'It is my duty for the sake of mankind,' said Sir Geoffrey Streatfield a month later when sentencing to ten years' imprisonment a young man who had recently been certified as schizophrenic. 'It is a shocking thing,' apostrophized a Marylebone magistrate in the same week, fining a blind man £5 for indecency with another man, 'because he is employed as a physiotherapist and no one can contemplate the mischief that might be caused by such a man.' Perhaps he imagined that the blind man was going to masturbate physiotherapy patients against their wishes or without their realizing that this was not conventional treatment: it is difficult to guess what other 'mischief' he had in mind. 'Wherever I go I find the same ugly story,' Sir Wintringham Stable observed from the bench at Buckinghamshire Assizes in 1955. 'I don't know what is happening to this nation. The percentage of cases of this class which we have today is absolutely terrifying. If this evil is allowed to spread, it will corrupt the men of the nation.' Sir Donald Finnemore, sentencing a man at Devon Assizes, called for 'one prison [to be] especially set aside for these cases'. Finnemore was a bachelor, devoted to the Baptist faith and the Boys Brigade, who was no stranger to sublimation and wanted an isolation prison 'where men of this kind who cannot control themselves' could do 'useful work'. Segregation would stop what another judge, Tudor Rees, described in 1955 as 'the guilty planting corruption in the innocent'; but Rees feared that the atmosphere would be so 'congenial to their temperaments' that 'the element of punishment or of reform would be entirely absent.' A senior police officer concerned with investigating London vice similarly dismissed Finnemore's proposal. 'I have known men so dominated with these homosexual impulses that they would, I am quite sure, commit an offence for the express purpose of being sent to such a place,' he warned. 'A life sentence to be served there would to them be a paradise.'[31]

Aspersions were cast on the judiciary if they were lenient. When one magistrate remanded a man for treatment, a policeman sneered that the offender had escaped a prison sentence because the magistrate was 'an old queer himself'. Some lawyers responsible for a man's defence were so ambivalent about homosexuality that they put up a carelessly prepared or weak defence in court. One barrister who regarded 'all homosexual behaviour – not merely buggery – with absolute disgust' was known to the Howard League for Penal Reform, which commented that fortunately he was 'conscious of his attitude; the danger lies more in those who are not conscious of it, and such prejudice doubtless plays a part in the widely divergent sentences inflicted.'[32]

Police prurience and silliness were often evident. Croft-Cooke, who found during his prosecution in 1953 that 'human society has a filthy mind in which evil is believed more readily even than the neutral', has described how the police illegally searched his house after his arrest, and 'gleefully confiscated' two bamboo canes used for training morning-glory from two flowerpots. 'Have you ever seen Mr Croft-Cooke with a cane in his hand?' they demanded of his acquaintances, doubtless as 'the result of some ghastly indoctrination they had undergone under a lecturing expert on sexual offenders'.[33]

Croft-Cooke's case provided another example of 'the bedlam of noxious prejudices' which Fyfe encouraged. Three days after his release from Wormwood Scrubs in 1954, he was visited by a man who would not give his name but seemed to be a plain-clothes policeman. The visitor had heard that Croft-Cooke was writing a memoir of his experiences with police and prison officers, including the dubious methods by which corroborative evidence had been secured to ensure his conviction. The policeman in mufti warned Croft-Cooke that he might suffer 'irreparable harm' if he published details of how his conviction was obtained: 'If mistakes were made by anyone, if anyone went too far, I mean, it's best forgotten now.' When Croft-Cooke demurred, and added that Fyfe's 'filthy witch-hunt' was continuing apace, his visitor smiled in agreement. 'It is,' he said, 'and, you know a second conviction is very much more easily obtained than a first, especially when the first has been well publicized. It needs only the word of one person, a policeman perhaps or someone who has been given an interest in the matter. If you weren't believed before, you are scarcely likely to be believed again, are you? Write about prison by all means but the other things: well, you wouldn't like another term, would you? I mean it would be Wandsworth this time. Not nearly so comfortable as the Scrubs. You think it over.'[34]

Conviction made a man vulnerable to continued police attention. The playwright who was sentenced at Abergavenny by Singleton in 1942 was dogged by his criminal record. Twelve years later, when police across Britain were looking to improve their rate of convictions by locating easy prosecutions for homosexuality, he found himself charged by Welsh police with attempting to procure another man. By then he had some reputation as a BBC dramatist so his arrest was reported in the *News of the World*; yet his ardent self-defence, and the flimsy suppositions on which the police case was based, resulted not only in his acquittal but in sympathetic comments from the judge after the verdict. He was not the only victim accused on the police assumption that the knowledge in a small community of a previous conviction was the best evidence for securing a new conviction.[35]

The underworld created by this harassment was dreary, distrustful, dangerous and self-hating. The nervous irritation caused by the precautions and constraints of a secret life poisoned relationships. Schofield in 1952 described a man of 42 working as a buyer in a department store:

> He spends a lot of his off-duty hours prowling around . . . with the idea of meeting other men. He is somewhat cynical . . . and is convinced that people who hang around these meeting places are 'no good and not to be trusted, and that includes me'. He refuses to go to the rooms of other men and as he lives with his married sister, it is impossible to take his partner back to his home . . . When he meets a willing partner, no names or addresses are exchanged and his sexual activities are either performed in the park or in some back alley or, very occasionally, in a hotel room . . . He cuts down the preliminaries as much as possible because 'a queer's conversation is strictly limited'. He is a confirmed 'oncer' and has a strong guilt about orgasm. He says that after he has had sexual experience with someone, he has a feeling of revulsion towards him . . . the whole experience is over in about thirty minutes . . . he hurries away from his partner as soon after the climax as possible.

Three other men whom he interviewed made similar points. The effects of stereotyping and of immersion in an introverted community, at once embattled and self-hating, were destructive. One respondent described having a partner who accepted sex only on terms of complete emotional severance.

> When I was 17 I fell violently in love with a man about twenty years older. One day there was a whole crowd of us at a party and I kissed the back of his neck while he

was playing the piano. He turned round and hit me in the face and there was the hell of an uproar. All the same he asked me to go camping with him a few weeks later and we had sex together. We used to have sex together quite a lot after that, but he used to get angry if I showed any affection or tried to make love.

The bitchiness and competitiveness of other homosexuals trapped in a precarious criminal world made men slide into a permanent state of doubt, insecurity and guilt.

I've fallen badly for a few people but it has never lasted. Perhaps that's my fault. I don't know. Sometimes it's been broken up by gossip.

A third man had grown a carapace against hurt:

The chances of meeting someone now are nil. I move in a circle where affairs are ridiculed and I'm known as a hard cynical bitch . . . I've carefully protected myself against the chance of falling for someone and the protection is now complete and I couldn't break out of it even if I wanted to.[36]

As a result of the furore that surrounded police techniques, Fyfe in 1954 proposed appointing a Royal Commission on Sexual Offences. His main concern was prostitution. Conditions in Mayfair and Soho streets were 'deplorable', he told the Cabinet, 'probably without parallel in the capital cities of other civilized countries'. He wanted legal reforms to be recommended by a Royal Commission to prevent streetwalking. 'A "call girl" system has at least this advantage,' he wrote, 'it removed a public scandal from the streets and at the same time exposes young men to less easy and obvious temptation.' Although Fyfe opposed relaxing laws against homosexuality, he feared that if prostitution was the subject of enquiry it would be impossible to exclude other sexual offences. 'The most profitable line of development is to improve, so far as finances permit, the facilities for the treatment of homosexuals sentenced by the courts.' At a Cabinet meeting on 24 February to consider Fyfe's proposal, 'special doubt was expressed about the expediency of attempting to amend the criminal laws relating to homosexuality', and a decision was deferred. In the next discussion, on 17 March, the Prime Minister, Churchill, suggested that 'the prudent course would be to take no action' except to encourage a backbench MP to introduce a bill to restrict press reports of trials for homosexuality. This resurrection of the idea of Halsbury's Publication of Indecent Evidence Bill of 1896 had support from other Cabinet ministers, who liked to think that male desire for other men would not exist without publicity. It was not until mid April that Fyfe extracted reluctant Cabinet agreement to appoint a departmental committee (not a Royal Commission) on sexual offences. Around this time Fyfe asked for a report on 96 cases of men who were in prison for homosexual offences. He interpreted the report as meaning that only 15 of them were 'genuine inverts': the other 81 'were simply not standing up to wickedness' and had practised homosexuality for 'reasons such as boredom with women, desire for sensation and money'.[37]

While the Cabinet was agonizing over the issue, an elderly peer, Winterton, initiated a debate in the House of Lords in May 1954 on Homosexual Crime. It had been 'constantly impressed' on Winterton in childhood 'that the punishment for wickedness was eternal immurement after death in Hell; I used sometimes to go to bed in terror that I might die in my sleep and find myself in a dreadful furnace surrounded by burning coals to which I had been condemned by the Almighty for having been naughty during the day.' From these horrors he grew up into an 'absurd dissenting nanny goat', often choleric when speaking in Parliament, jerking his body with tension and rubbing his hands together so violently that on one occasion he dislocated a thumb. With his 'good looks and perpetual youthfulness', Winterton had a 'devastating' streak of devilry: in Parliament when Sir Alfred Mond, a Jewish MP, 'was obstructive or obtrusive, Winterton would murmur audibly "Silence in the Ghetto"', which according to one admirer 'produced the desired effect'. Hating 'the filthy, disgusting and unnatural vice of homosexuality', he believed it was an 'obsessive, uncontrollable mania' which if tolerated would 'weaken the moral fibre and injure the physique' of the British: 'we should go the way of other countries in the past, who were once great but became decadent through corrosive and corrupting immorality.' He brimmed with misinformation, citing 'an eminent legal authority' to confirm that 'adult homosexualists ... attack children.'

Wilde's trial had 'acted as a moral purge' by stopping the 'horrible series of attacks' among Oxford undergraduates and rendering homosexuality 'taboo' in the university, he alleged, and had driven abroad 'undesirable men about town ... belonging to well-known families' whose corruption of Guardsmen had been 'a bane to commanding officers, employers and parents'. Referring to the ovation received by Sir John Gielgud on returning to the theatre after a conviction (an indication that London theatrical audiences resented the new persecutory regime that was disfiguring the country), he thought this inconceivable in the heyday of actors like Sir Herbert Beerbohm Tree, Sir John Hare and Cyril Maude. 'We were members of the same club,' Winterton attested: 'It is inconceivable that they would have been guilty of the disgusting offence of male importuning.' Perverts as ever were the hated Others: not the men one knew.[38]

Press reaction to the Winterton debate was suggestive. The *Daily Mail*, under the headline SEX VICE: VETERAN PEER SPEAKS OUT, reported Winterton's speech in full, but curtailed all the other speeches, so that his neurotic and untruthful ebullition was invested with authority. As so often the most rabid and distorted comment proved the most memorable. The editor of the *Sunday Express* complained that 'an emotional crusade' was 'developing to legalize perversion, and even to sanctify perverts ... STUFF AND NONSENSE. Perversion is very largely a practice of the too idle and the too rich. It does not flourish in lands where men work hard and brows sweat with honest labour. It is a wicked mischief, destructive not only of men but of nations.'[39]

A former public school headmaster, Wolfenden, was appointed to chair the Committee enquiring into sexual offences which Churchill's Cabinet had reluctantly agreed to appoint in 1954. Its other members included parliamentarians, lawyers, physicians, clergy and provincial worthies. For some time Wolfenden and his contacts at the Home Office felt so self-conscious about the subject, or worried about offending their women typists, that they substituted for the Committee's title 'Homosexuality and Prostitution' the brand name of a biscuit, 'Huntley and Palmers'. One Home Office man, for example, discussing whether homosexuals should testify to Wolfenden, wrote that it might be helpful to 'let the Committee see what a few Huntleys look and behave like'. Wolfenden was sufficiently aware of his personal vulnerability to decide that it would be prudent to avoid public lavatories in London while he chaired the Committee.⁴⁰

The appointment of Wolfenden changed policing and sentencing immediately. There was reduced police intervention and a relaxation of judicial anxieties. The criminal statistics for 1956 showed that the police reported 17% fewer homosexual offences than in 1955, prosecutions fell by 12%, convictions by 11% and the numbers imprisoned by 28%. Continued controversy over the inconsistency of police attitudes in different areas forced Attorneys-General in the mid 1960s to request all chief constables that no prosecutions should be brought without the approval of the Director of Public Prosecutions in cases where blackmail was involved, or involving acts in private between consenting adults, or in 'stale' cases where the acts had happened more than twelve months earlier. In the nine months to the end of April 1965, 76 such cases were reported to the DPP, on which it was decided to take action on 55 per cent. Sentencing policy had changed already, and the number of custodial sentences for homosexual offences fell from 781 in 1954 to 370 in 1963.⁴¹

Wolfenden's Committee began by interviewing the Lord Chief Justice, Goddard, to seek his opinion on the relation between morality and law. Goddard was a judge who felt 'physically sick' when trying 'buggers', yet he had a crucial role in setting the bearings of the subsequent enquiry. By nature he was imperceptive and illiberal, frightened of women (as his daughter believed) but perhaps frightened more of himself. In the judgment of one contemporary, 'Goddard's influence on the cause of penal reform was almost unrelievedly malign; with a coarse callousness (his fondness for dirty jokes can hardly have been entirely coincidental) there went not only a desperate ignorance of the springs of human behaviour (including, of course, his own) but what seemed like a positive pride in his ignorance.' Goddard did not believe that private acts other than buggery between adult males should be the concern of criminal law: such acts 'have none of the attributes generally considered to be the constituents of a crime except that they excite disgust and repulsion'. Many 'moral offences' such as 'the seduction and desertion of a young girl, or adultery which breaks up a home when there are children' were 'far more anti-social' yet not criminal. In trials of gross indecency, he thought that generally one of the defendants 'is an addict' to homosexuality, but 'not by any means both'. It was common to find that one of the pair had 'an irreproachable character and one just cannot understand how he came to be acting thus'. Goddard's explanation was that in gross indecency cases 'a man slightly under the influence of drink . . . hardly realizes what the other is up to.' But in buggery 'if the parties are adults they are I believe both invariably addicts', and he felt 'strongly that buggery ought always to be treated as a crime . . . It is such a horrible and revolting thing and a practitioner is such a depraved creature that he ought in my opinion to be put out of circulation.' Goddard saw 'a wide difference between the decadent young man who finds or thinks he finds satisfaction in good-looking youths to the extent of masturbation and the bugger who is nearly always a habitual'. He regretted that 'as a recent notorious case showed men who have good war records and can properly be classed as brave may be addicted to this vice but, if they are, they are in my opinion such public dangers that they ought to be segregated.' He wanted penalties for male importuning to be 'drastically increased' and thought for rent boys 'a whipping would probably be the best thing' (a sentiment shared by some of their clients including the occasional Tory MP).[42]

Apart from oral and written evidence tendered to the Wolfenden Committee, a plethora of books and articles were published for general readership. Thus Sir Compton Mackenzie's novel *Thin Ice* (1956), inspired by the lives of two politicians, Sir Harold Nicolson and Tom Driberg, has been praised as 'a first-person narrative in the voice of a blackmailed homosexual . . . which openly attacked the injustices of the existing laws'. In fact the narrator is a heterosexual widower who never ceases to emphasize his loathing and ignorance of the homosexual world. In order to make his case for repeal of Labouchere's Amendment palatable to 'normal' readers, Mackenzie presents a bleak image of the homosexual 'temperament' or 'horrible mania' as his characters call it. 'No homosexual in pursuit of passion can be loyal to a friend': 'extravagant promiscuousness' was too compelling. One character is 'a plump round-faced man with finikin gestures' gossiping with a male hairdresser who 'sibilated' his replies. The blackmailer is a 'slim young man', 'sinister' and 'detestable', talking in 'the pettish accents of wounded vanity', from whose 'narrowed eyes' the narrator feels 'repulsion such as some people get from a snake'. When in 1941 the narrator visits a gay club in Soho to recover his friend's compromising letter he feels 'nausea' at the scene: 'a young man walked with mincing steps to a piano in the inner room and after smoothing back his hair with an arm arched like a swan's neck began to play one of those lugubrious tunes imported from America which now stir the emotions of the British young. Two other young men tripped across to lean over the pianist at each end of the piano and gaze at the player with calves' eyes that were apparently intended to express intense admiration of his performance. I asked myself furiously why the devil none of these idle young epicenes had been called up. . . . Two more young men started dancing together . . . if sidling about can be given the name of dancing. At other tables elderly men watched the dancers with apparent pleasure.' The only honest or affectionate homosexual in the book is a youth whom the narrator sends back in tears to his parents in Bromley with £50 and a homily ('I hope this beastly business has taught you a lesson, Weeks. The kind of life you've been leading can only end in misery and disgrace'); he expiates his shame by getting killed in the war, provoking the final judgment that 'he has died for his country which is something to be proud of.'[43]

Other arguments for reform were equally pragmatic. One of the charges against homosexuals was that they were 'an exclusive and cohesive freemasonry'. This was not surprising as both laws and social labelling presumed their exclusion from the rest of the community; but it aggravated fears of national security and imperial disintegration. Among inverts there was 'often a *camaraderie* of a remarkable kind', one group warned: 'If in any department of life persons feel that they are being treated unjustly and there is no redress, *moral deterioration* sets in.' The intervention of the law was creating 'an aggrieved and self-conscious minority which becomes the *centre for dissatisfaction and ferment*'.[44]

A Home Office official minuted in 1955 that the implication of criminal laws was 'that enjoyment of homosexual intercourse is so exotic and intense as insidiously to draw those who practise it away from normal sexual intercourse and its natural results: so insidious that society must protect itself by penalizing the act'. This presumption of the supreme and incomparable ecstasy of homosexuality worked, he feared, as one of 'the strongest arguments in the seducer's favour'. A man engaged in tempting another man, so he seemed to think, would suggest that homosexual acts were more delicious than any other: why else were laws needed against them? He believed that 'many homosexuals, far from thinking themselves a persecuted minority, take pride in their different taste and regard themselves as having been clever enough to by-pass nature and enjoy gratifying their sexual desires without the possible consequence of normal intercourse.' They regarded themselves as 'superior to the ordinary run of people' precisely because they were singled out by law. 'If the fruit were not so severely forbidden many fewer would be tempted to indulge in what for most people would be otherwise just an unspeakably dirty act, and further, the intense publicity that attends trials at present would not then act, as it does now, as a stimulus to experiments of a homosexual character.' He accepted however that if the law was changed, 'it would be necessary to safeguard the young with greater stringency even than at present with penalties for contamination heavier and more deterring than they are now.'[45]

Police and legal witnesses who testified to Wolfenden believed that seduction in youth was decisive in producing homosexuality, and as the Committee reported, this notion alarmed parents. When it was discovered that a son had homosexual experience, parental reaction was often to repudiate their own responsibility, and heap blame on someone else. They would insist that their boy had been seduced, that he was the victim of an evil trick, that his defiler should be exposed and shamed before the community. In other cases men in trouble with the authorities tried to exonerate themselves by blaming their homosexuality on seduction when younger. But as one man recounted in the 1950s,

> The probation officer said to me, 'And what evil person perverted you?' I told him this was a lot of nonsense and if people had told him about being perverted in childhood, he was having the wool pulled over his eyes and he ought to be bright enough to see they were just seeking sympathy by shifting the blame onto someone else.

In many instances, moreover, the supposed young victim was in truth the seducer, who had exerted guile and tenacity to catch an older boy or man. The fantasy that boys were usually used as passive partners in anal sex was equally untrue. Most boys permitted only mutual masturbation, and Schofield's research suggested that homosexuals rejected sex with younger teenagers precisely because boys' sexual repertoire was limited and their sexual technique less gratifying.[46]

Medical witnesses before Wolfenden were unanimous that seductions had little effect in inducing a settled pattern of homosexual behaviour. Seduction only had lasting effects if its direction corresponded with inherent tendencies in the subject. With one exception (a Scottish lawyer called Gilbert Adair), all members of the Wolfenden Committee rejected the seduction theory – although twenty years later, perhaps having forgotten the evidence, one member, the Marquess of Lothian, had 'little doubt that homosexuality is on the increase' and opposed reducing the age of male homosexual consent to 18 because 'homosexual floodgates might be opened', especially as by the 1970s there was 'much greater awareness about homosexuality'.[47]

Legal witnesses provided varied evidence. Several pressure groups for legal reform supported the decriminalization of homosexuality on the grounds that current laws were inexpedient, inequitably administered or an obsolete infringement of individual choice – but never from a position of open sympathy with homosexuality. Other organizations, such as the Law Society, representing British solicitors, opposed any change. 'Both buggery and gross indecency should remain criminal offences when committed in private between consenting adults of full age,' they submitted. 'The offences are productive of great evils inasmuch as they (i) tend to reduce the inclination to marry; (ii) militate against the procreation of children; (iii) are calculated to result in damage to the State if they get too strong a hold; (iv) are likely (if legalized in private between genuine homosexuals) to contaminate others (and particularly the young); (v) may, if allowed to go unchecked, result in male brothels; and (vi) probably tend to spread venereal disease.'[48]

The predatoriness of homosexuals became axiomatic. One London railway station was 'a hunting ground for the homos', according to a police officer, stalked by men 'with an uncanny sense or instinct in their quest'. The Church of England Social and Moral Welfare Council favoured defining the age of consent at 21, to protect young conscripts to the armed forces 'compelled to live for two years in a predominantly male community' and facing 'special risks of mixing with homosexuals'. Tudor Rees thought this impracticable:

> How is the man who sets out on his filthy errand to be satisfied that the other person has, in fact, reached the prescribed age? Would he, to be on the safe side, get the other's birth certificate? Homosexuals are not made that way, and would not engage in such practices if they were endowed with such prudence.

At Chatham during the war, 'men came down in great numbers to sleuth young naval ratings,' the Bishop of Rochester lamented in 1957: 'men were sucked in and held on to, as it were, by an octopus of corruption.' Homosexuality was so like 'drug addiction' that there was need for the law 'to protect men from being made into homosexual addicts and then let loose on the world with their predatory corruption'.[49]

The British Medical Association's evidence to Wolfenden was tendered by a committee; but as Alex Comfort noted, the document was written in 'its rhetorical passages by a single person of definitive and restrictive opinions' (possibly its Assistant Secretary, Dr Ernest Claxton). So far as copulation was concerned, the word 'indulgence' was always used in preference to the word 'enjoyment'. One passage lamented how 'doctors observe their patients in an environment favourable to sexual indulgence, and surrounded by irresponsibility, selfishness and a preoccupation with immediate materialistic satisfaction'; another pronounced that 'personal discipline and unselfishness have little place' in homosexual thought. The written evidence emphasized religious conversion as a 'cure' for homosexuality, and included two appendices on the value of evangelism. Despite consulting many physicians, the only one quoted at length was the psychiatrist at Liverpool Prison who stated, *inter alia*, 'in cases of homosexuality of no matter what grade or type, cure "is a goal only reached after striving and fighting oneself, with victory probably the greatest satisfaction one can experience", as one of my patients put it, but it is a fight which one cannot undertake alone, and if there is any other solution than belief in Christian doctrine and principles and faith then I do not know it.' In another appendix, Claxton urged the formation of a treatment centre where inverts would receive

Christian inspiration mixed with farmwork, forestry and market gardening: anything that was the antithesis of the bright lights of Piccadilly. 'Sorrow, remorse and loathing of the habit and a willingness to accept forgiveness' would be developed in each inmate, Claxton proposed; 'his mind, motives and will then become reinforced by a Superior Will and he acquires faith to believe that he can be different.' Apart from hypothesizing that self-loathing and fighting oneself were sound medical courses, the BMA encouraged the conspiracy theory of homosexuality. Its evidence noted that male homosexuals aroused public hostility by placing 'their loyalty to one another above their loyalty to the institution or government they serve'. Such supreme personal loyalty was 'a special problem' where homosexuals worked in churches, Parliament, the civil service, armed forces, journalism or the theatre.[50]

What this religious approach (endorsed by the BMA evidence) meant was shown by another contemporary report on homosexuality by Anglican doctors and clergy. Unrepentant sinners were doomed to eternal damnation, they judged. 'When conscience and the faculty of self-criticism have been finally killed by long continued habit of rationalization or determined continuance in what was once known to be sin, then there can be no shame leading to repentance, and where there is no repentance there can be no divine forgiveness. The Hell to which a man thus *brings himself* is no arbitrary fiat of a vengeful God. It is the fact which gives to morality its ultimate meaning.' A male homosexual who continued 'doing what he knows is wrong, living with a perpetually uneasy conscience' would find that the conflict might drive him to neurosis or suicide. 'So close is the association of mind with body that an actual physical disease may develop, the origin of which is this spiritual conflict of conscience against will.' The best course was for the 'sodomite' to face his 'sin' without 'self-excuse'. A wonderful transformation would ensue. He would recognize that however great his sins against other males, 'he has fundamentally been in rebellion against God.' He would feel his 'weakness' and desire 'cleansing . . . When pride has been humbled, God can act in forgiving love. What for the sodomite . . . is felt as the bitterness of self-reproach, the pain of a guilty conscience and the tragedy of a life that is morally soiled, is taken up into the sufferings of Christ.'[51]

One member of the Wolfenden Committee, the Scottish lawyer Gilbert Adair, submitted a minority report which, in Lord Longford's words, suggested that 'homosexualism between consenting adults cannot be regarded as their affair alone; they are not just corrupting each other, but are liable to spread the infection far and wide.' In Adair's own phrase, 'the presence in a district of . . . adult male lovers living openly and notoriously under the approval of the law is bound to have a regrettable and pernicious effect on the young people of the community.' But otherwise the majority proposed changes both in the law and its enforcement, the chief of these being the decriminalization of homosexual acts in private by men aged 21 or more.[52]

The Times, Manchester Guardian, Observer and *News Chronicle* welcomed the Report with few reservations. The *Daily Mirror* trumpeted that no newspaper would hesitate to publish its opinion of the Report, but omitted the main proposals about homosexuality. The *Daily Telegraph* feared that homosexuality, if legalized, might spread like an infection. The *Sunday Times*, though not entirely hostile, warned that the 'basic national moral standard' was being 'undermined by libertarian cults and the steady sapping of welfare Socialism'. The *Evening Standard* judged Wolfenden's proposals on homosexuality to be 'bad, retrograde and utterly to be condemned'. The *Daily Mail* judged that Wolfenden's 'proposals to legalize degradation in our midst' would result in the fall of the Empire; the *Sunday Graphic* found that the Report extended a smiling benediction to the Sins of Sodom. *The British Journal of Venereal Diseases* welcomed Wolfenden's Report as 'enlightened and realistic' in its proposed measures to eliminate streetwalking prostitutes; but limited itself to commenting that Wolfenden's recommendations on homosexuality 'are unacceptable to many'.[53]

Fyfe's successor as Home Secretary, Butler, initially favoured implementing Wolfenden's recommendations on both prostitution and homosexuality, but abandoned this plan after his Junior Minister, Renton, refused to support the proposals affecting homosexuals. A Street Offences Act was passed to eliminate streetwalking by women prostitutes, and negotiations with the Government for the introduction of a Homosexual Reform Bill by a backbench MP were sympathetically received by Sir Charles Fletcher-Cooke, who replaced Renton in 1961. Progress was then blocked by the Lord Chancellor, Kilmuir, who (as Sir David Maxwell Fyfe) had taken such an ignominious role in persecuting homosexuals. He refused to sit at Cabinet meetings where the 'filthy subject' was discussed: 'such is the disgust and horror', as one MP commented, 'which some men need to express as their defence against admitting the existence of their own homosexual feelings.' After being dismissed from the Cabinet in 1962, and suffering from increasing mental depression, he emerged as a strong opponent of decriminalization, attacking 'the proselytization which goes out from sodomitic societies and buggery clubs' as tending to encourage 'lying and cruelty and indecency', and insisting that it would be 'a great pity' to accept reform and thus admit 'that the law on this point has been wrong in England for nearly 500 years'.[54]

'Some blood-chilling conjectures are now appearing in quarters where it is customary to think with the bowels,' one journalist reported in the weeks after the publication of Wolfenden when many minds indeed were morbidly dwelling in the bowels. The Report conceded that there was 'some case' for retaining anal intercourse as an offence, and Fisher, Archbishop of Canterbury, speaking in 1957, believed that if this could be done, 'it would relieve the anxieties, fears and indignation of a great many people.' Even many homosexuals, he suggested, 'feel that in that extreme offence there is a degree of depravity to which they are thankful not to have fallen or in which they are especially reluctant to be partners'. During subsequent reform of the laws, a former Lord Chancellor, Dilhorne, introduced an amendment which kept sodomy and attempted sodomy as criminal offences, while decriminalizing other homosexual acts. Under the influence of legal precedents stretching back to the woman impregnated by a baboon described by Dilhorne's seventeenth-century ancestor Coke, he saw no 'valid distinction' between 'sodomy with a male person' and 'sodomy with an animal'. The sexual use of the anus, usually filled with rotting exeretory matter, evoked for men like Fyfe 'the iridescence of decay'; but in the 1930s Dr Eustace Chesser found that 30 per cent of wives whom he surveyed in Manchester had experienced anal intercourse, 19 per cent of French men and 15 per cent of French women frequently indulged in the practice in the early 1970s, and 15 per cent of women attending the genito-urinary clinic of a London hospital reported doing so in 1987. Yet during the 1970s a university lecturer whose home was raided by police unsuccessfully searching for drugs was sentenced to imprisonment after photographs were found of him buggering his girlfriend, and another man was gaoled for 18 months after a woman complained to police that he had stolen her watch and photographs showing their consensual sodomy were found during a police search (he was acquitted of stealing the watch and the woman was not prosecuted for participating in sodomy). In 1988 a widow who regularly had sexual intercourse with a younger handyman on the drawing room floor of her home, but who became distressed when he took her into the bedroom and the noise of their fucking prompted a neighbour to bang on the wall in protest, reported to the police that he had attempted buggery, for which attempt he was sentenced to one year's imprisonment. The Court of Appeal in the 1970s held that although husbands who returned home drunk might sodomize their wives by mistake, deliberate acts (by implication non-marital acts) should be discouraged. A judge in 1974, charging the jury in a blue-film trial, invoked Jehovah's visitation on Sodom and stressed that under British law, as 'in every civilized country', 'the unnatural and horrible offence of sodomy' was considered 'as serious as committing manslaughter'.[55]

Initially MPs were disturbed by Wolfenden's recommendations on homosexuality and strikingly un-selfaware about the ways in which they expressed that disturbance. 'You've no idea how many there are about,' a 'violently anti-queer' MP told a homosexual at a dinner party. 'I've got the knack of recognizing them and if you'd seen as many as I have, you'd be horrified by it.' MPs interpreted freedom for homosexuality as a personal threat: 'unknowingly they equated relaxations of the law with the relaxation of the control which they were anxious at all costs to preserve over their own repudiated feelings,' according to the intuition of Leo Abse, who successfully guided decriminalizing legislation through the House of Commons in 1967. 'It was fitting that repeatedly my opponents should have taken as their rallying cry the assertion that "the floodgates would open" if the law were to be changed: for the flood they feared was the flood of their own desires, and the gates for whose security they were so concerned were really those of their own repressions.' Abse could only allay parliamentary anxieties by 'insisting that compassion was needed for a totally separate group, quite unlike the absolutely normal male males of the Commons', as he recounted. 'To hint that the homosexual component in a man's nature plays a large part in helping him to understand and thus form a deep relationship with a woman, would have aroused discomfort: and to point out that the conduct of some of the philanderers in the House, compulsively chasing women, was determined by a ceaseless flight from their feelings for men, would have been disastrous.' During parliamentary debates there was reiterated insistence by speakers that they were innocent of the subject on which they were speaking. Like Wolfenden and his Home Office liaison writing of Huntley and Palmers, Lord Mathers in 1957 stressed that Wolfenden dealt with 'matters entirely outwith my knowledge' before urging homosexuals to use Christian prayer to 'rid themselves of the bonds that have hitherto held them in thrall'. Others who seemed sympathetic to reform, and supported the

'What I particularly admired about the debate was the way that every speaker managed to give the impression that he personally had never met a homosexual in his life.'

1.vii.60

325

Wolfenden proposals, only felt able to do so by talking, as Lord Molson did in 1965, 'of deplorable public activities' which should be decriminalized in order to be rid of evils like blackmail; or protesting 'very real revulsion' about the acts which were to be removed from police investigation. Such were the compulsory acts of denial forced upon men. Arran even protected his supporters with the disclaimer that homosexuality 'had been universally condemned from start to finish . . . by every single Member of this House'. These devices provoked Lord Snow to remark on 'the curious unworldliness' of debate: parliamentarians all spoke as if they had 'never met a homosexual, as though these were something strange like the white rhinoceros'.[56]

A cartoon by Osbert Lancaster published in the *Daily Express* in 1960 is pertinent (see illustration on page 325). The proponents of reform repudiated not only homosexuality, but homosexuals. They argued that the existing law degraded or corrupted the police charged with enforcing it, that it facilitated blackmail, that it was ineffective, that its severity compared with equivalent laws on the European mainland reflected poorly on Britain's reputation for tolerance or justice. Almost no one spoke positively of homosexuality. The liberalization of the law in 1967 marked less a triumph for national toleration than the acme of the Victorian middle-class taste for privacy. For more than a century, to recall Peter Gay's argument from chapter four, the middle classes had placed a higher and higher value on domestic privacy: on the notion that an Englishman's home was his castle, that the affections exchanged there were privileged and to be excluded from state interference, it was a lair where people could recuperate from life in their own way and in safety from intruders. The Wolfenden Report, and its aftermath, endlessly echoed with phrases about 'acts between consenting male adults, *in private*'. There was no attempt to emancipate male homosexuals and little sense of striking a blow against bigotry. Instead the notion of privacy received its ultimate tribute: sexual outlaws were given tolerance within the law conditional on their acceptance of privacy. When the reform was being passed in 1967 Arran warned gay men that 'any form of public flaunting' would make the sponsors of the reform law 'regret . . . what they have done', and Abse has repeatedly lamented since that gay men have not been private enough in their practices, as he expected. In other words, the liberalization of

1967 was not a victory of toleration over bigotry, or of the much vaunted 'permissive' forces of the 1960s over traditional values. Reform was achieved because of the inexpediency of the old law, and the abuses in its enforcement that stood revealed; concessions to homosexuality were extended as one side of a bargain, with the acceptance by gay men of notions of privacy, or social invisibility, as the pay-off. In the process there had been a national debate lasting almost a decade in which the voices of the sexually relaxed had been less audible than those of the fearfully strident. There had not been so effective a labelling process since the trials of Oscar Wilde.[57]

It is claimed that the 1967 reform led to a revolution in attitudes: that decriminalization emancipated men from guilt about homosexual acts or that the stigma was erased. The idea that the influence of centuries of verbal violence, legal harassment and social ostracism could be removed in a couple of decades does not bear a moment's scrutiny. Men in their twenties in 1967 had been at the age of sexual awakening during the worst excesses of Fyfe and Mathew. The claim that the trauma of those ugly times no longer had any effect can only be advanced by people who deliberately repress their imagination or etiolate their memory. Some gay men pitched themselves with abandon into fucking, making 'an ecstatic break with years of glances and guises, the furtive past we left behind'. People's essential bisexuality was denied as furiously as ever: male homosexuals remained a favourite object of projective fear. The most that can be claimed is that Wolfenden's Report was the finest flower of Victorian notions of privacy, and the Arran—Abse Act marked their apogee. Ever since, respect for domestic privacy had been declining in Britain, particularly since 1979. The private doings of individuals have come under increased scrutiny from officialdom and journalists: catchwords about the private sanctity of an English home have become hollow. The Arran—Abse law did not change national attitudes to sexual polluters, nor could any act of parliament be expected to do so: it merely changed the framework within which the law operated. Convictions of men for homosexual acts increased after 1967, and the authoritative survey of *British Social Attitudes* published in 1983 (well before HIV had received publicity in the country) found that about 65 per cent of respondents believed that homosexual relationships were 'always' or 'mostly' wrong. Homosexuals, having 'broken' an 'unwritten' agreement that they would be tolerated if family values (such as privacy about feelings) were affirmed, 'got the backlash they asked for', to quote Digby Anderson of the Social Policy Unit in 1986.[58]

It is true that the implementation of Wolfenden's recommendations on homosexuality extended legal sanction to individual tolerance, giving official support to the instinct and sympathies which had led a theatrical audience to rise in ovation of Sir John Gielgud when he resumed acting after his conviction in 1954. For many people the reform of laws on homosexuality seemed an essential primary change in creating a more tolerant and pluralistic society, or in shedding the mentality which insisted on punishing social non-conformity or ostracizing transgressors. The social obligation to revile gay men, like the pressure to avoid associating with them in case one was suspected of sharing their vice, was reduced. It became easier to profess casual acceptance of other people's homosexual acts. But the Sexual Offences Act of 1967 did nothing to eliminate the hard core of bigotry and hatred: nor could this be expected without a much wider social recognition of the need for sexual justice, not only for relations between the same sexes, but for everyone.

All this was clear in 1977 when Arran unsuccessfully introduced legislation to reduce the age of male homosexual consent from 21 to 18. (68 boys between the ages of 14 and 17 were prosecuted in England for buggery in 1975, 51 for attempting to commit buggery and 6 for indecency between males: of that number 56 were found guilty.) Calm voices were drowned in a frenzy of opposition to Arran's proposal which was led by Lord Halsbury, grandson of the Lord Chancellor who had such influence on the nineteenth-century social construction of homosexuality. Halsbury stigmatized male homosexuality as 'a syndrome whose symptoms were exhibitionism, promiscuity, proselytism, and a vainglorious boastfulness about the merits of being homosexual', but felt less threatened by women homosexuals – 'the sick are conspicuously absent' and that is why lesbianism is not a social problem.' The Bishop of Birmingham pronounced homosexual acts as a 'deviation from the natural order and . . . contrary to the divine intention': Christianity was again supported by science, with the bacteriologist Lord Stamp insisting that 'the breakdown of the procreative function of man can only be regarded as unnatural.' Lothian was afraid that 'homosexual bullies' would exploit 'a submissive society' in order 'to intimidate the weak' into corrupt ways. Lord Macleod of Fuinary (believing against all evidence that adolescent sexual experimentation fixed lifelong orientation, and believing even more extraordinarily that the law was a proven deterrent against teenage homosexuality) warned that 'young men will be led up the garden path who might otherwise shortly be married and be happy.' He expostulated, 'If we do not want to topple, as the Roman Empire toppled, let us defy all legislation that attempts to unseat the moral law.' ('The most obvious of all ways in which to write off a country', the backwoodsman Lord Clifford of Chudleigh had told Parliament in the previous year, 'is to persuade children to become homosexual.') Almost every speaker denied, or more often ignored, the evidence accepted by Wolfenden that teenage seduction was a negligible factor. Such remarks legitimized hostility to male homosexuals by their parliamentary utterance.[59]

As usual the House of Lords enabled obscure but well-intentioned people to voice the fear and anger of the muddled and the inarticulate. Whatever the phrase 'permissive society' was supposed to mean, the reality was that under the surface neither private troubles nor public dangers had changed much. 'Women's right to speak in defence of the innocent is greater than that of any man,' declared the Countess of Loudoun during the Arran debate of 1977. 'Are we to encourage the infectious growth of this filthy disease by giving the authority of Parliament to the spreading of corruption and perversion among a new generation of young men?' Arran's Bill was intended 'to extend the tentacles of evil, to withhold the protection of the law from the innocent, the gullible, from the simple youth who has just arrived in the big city and the boy who is charmed and overcome by cheap flattery and easy money. In whose favour is it? No one's but the pervert and the money grubbers, waiting to pounce.' Homosexual acts were 'a crime against society' she insisted. Homosexuality defiled: 'you cannot be a homosexual alone, which inevitably leads to the corruption and perversion of others, which is a symptom of the disease.' Just like 'an attack of cholera, such an outbreak must be contained and isolated'.[60]

But something worse than cholera was germinating.

—❦—

CHAPTER NINE

Hating Others: AIDS

We hate others because we hate ourselves.

CESARE PAVESE

It is evil which generally has the upper hand,
and folly makes the most noise. Fate is cruel,
and mankind pitiable.

ARTHUR SCHOPENHAUER

Their ramparts guard a wilderness;
And hate, arousing out of shame,
Flares up into a wondrous flame:
They curse; they strike; they break the wall
Which buries them beneath its fall.

WILLIAM SOUTAR

AIDS is a cruel and silly neologism, as Bruce Chatwin wrote. 'Aid' connotes succour and comfort: yet the word becomes a horror once a hissing sibilant is added to it (rather as the serpentine sibilance of the word 'syphilis' has seemed so apt through the ages). HIV are far preferable initials: AIDS excites panic and despair, emotions which can only facilitate the spread of disease. HIV will kill millions of people, but fear of its contagion is spoiling the lives of millions more. In reality it is infectious but not contagious; but whether transmitted accidentally or deliberately, intimately or indirectly, its micro-organisms are fearful because like the spirochaete of syphilis they seem invincible, invisible, and ubiquitous. The virus has been depicted (particularly by commentators who equate hedonism with national weakness) not only as attacking the body of individuals, but as an invasion of society itself. HIV, which cannot be transmitted by casual contact and need not be transmitted by sexual contact, has provoked a contagion panic disproportionate to the risk of contraction. It has excited the destructive terror that festers when our troubles are attributable to infection spread by other people: the rank belief that patients must be punished or eradicated has erupted in consequence.[1]

The first person known to have died as a result of AIDS in Britain was Terrence Higgins, in July 1982, and for perhaps a year after that it was possible to deny that anything significant was occurring, as people tend to do in the first stage of an epidemic. But once the existence of a medical crisis was recognized, as with cholera in the 1840s or tuberculosis in the early twentieth century, groups or individuals were identified as blameworthy, traduced as dirty or contagious, and punished as miscreants. In Britain, as a consequence, HIV has been perceived less as a virus that must be conquered than as an affliction of the undisciplined. Blame, in all its forms, has only negative results: it spreads confusion and victimizes the weak. Blame helps no one and nothing except the spread of the virus.

It is in the nature of broadcast or published comment on AIDS that it is usually the most punitive remarks that give discussion force or form, or remain most memorable. The Social Services Committee of the House of Commons investigated AIDS in 1987, collecting and analysing expert opinion in a constructive and humane way, yet reading its verbatim minutes, one is left with the disproportionate memory of one MP, Nicholas Winterton, who believed that 'sitting in judgment' on patients was essential to cope with 'a killer disease', that public health education should be framed to 'frighten' people from 'an unnatural sexual habit' and whose general view was summarized by a sympathizer a few months later as 'that all AIDS victims should be completely cut off from society to protect the majority'. Stories of theatre cleaners who, for example, boycotted gay actors, or of schools which boycotted public swimming pools where gay men swam, all because they were frightened of the AIDS contagion, are usually published with denials that HIV can be transmitted by casual contact, but their focus nevertheless engenders rather than allays fear, stimulating anxiety rather than alleviating it.[2]

This chapter examines this impulse to blame, and some of its negative consequences. It does not describe the work of those medical scientists investigating the structure and action of HIV, whose research has been treated abundantly elsewhere; nor does it emphasize the few positive results of HIV, such as the changes in medical attitudes on the specialist wards of some London hospitals, where nurses and physicians have spurned the tradition that emotionally involved health care is bad health care, and do not try to divorce their actions from their feelings. I assume also – perhaps too easily – that my readers can imagine the sheer sadness of AIDS: the exhausting rage against the meaningless of the syndrome, its swathe of destruction and the cruelty that it has provoked. 'A tragedy', wrote Thomas Hardy, 'exhibits a state of things in the life of an individual which unavoidably causes some natural aim or desire of his to end in catastrophe when carried out.' AIDS is a tragedy.

Instead I show how in Britain contagion fears have been politicized in order to attempt to frighten people into accepting a regime in which sexual appetite is regulated, eroticism is repressed, social conformity equated with health and conspicuous people of all sorts are treated as undesirable. All those individuals for whom social controls are not just a necessary evil to keep society intact, but a bulwark against personal disintegration, or a pleasure when exercized aggressively against the weak, have been aroused to a fervent pitch. Chiliasts who relish crises and drastic restrictions have been granted their heart's desire as we career towards the end of another millenium. 'If the world is to survive this plague we must be prepared to pay as a nation, whatever price is demanded, whatever the sacrifice, whatever the curtailment of the present freedoms,' wrote a Notting Hill man in 1986. 'If it is shown that homosexuals in this country spawned it, nurtured it, propagated it, then released it into the wider community and then remain the largest single source of it, then I want that source controlled. Naturally I want all other sources controlled, blocked, contained; drug users, blood transfusions, multiple heterosexual activity [but] it seems sensible to start with what is the largest single source.' In fact it seems less sensible than emotionally gratifying.[3]

There has been an attack on pleasure for its own sake, a vindictive sanctimony about other people's ills has flourished, with a chorus of triumphant censure unknown in this country since the swansong of the pleasure-haters around the time of the First World War. 'The Church should condemn both those who catch this fatal disease and those who transmit it to others,' wrote a Kensington man in 1987: 'Christianity without morality is nothing.' People with AIDS are condemned, and told to go away and die without expending anyone else's time or money. 'I am fed up being continually bombarded with the AIDS problem,' as a correspondent of the *Daily Express* declared in 1988. 'The majority of victims have only themselves to blame because of their sexual activities and needle sharing. I abhor the amount of money being spent on them and feel no sympathy for them whatsoever.'[4]

The excessive attention given to the curious notion of 'revenge sex' has been characteristic. A few Soho rent-boys have been induced to tell journalists that they are trying to transmit HIV to their male contacts as 'revenge' for themselves being infected, although there seems to be a muddle about modes of transmission in some of these rumours. Fantasies about revenge sex have a long pedigree: in literature they occur in such stories as (syphilitic) Guy de Maupassant's *Bed 29*, and similar notions were aired in the sixteenth century to explain the dissemination of syphilis at the siege of Naples. Although I have heard people say that the best way to ensure good treatment (medically and otherwise) for people with AIDS would be for the Prime Minister's son, Mark Thatcher, or her most responsive Cabinet colleague, Cecil Parkinson, to fall ill, no one schemes to infect them. But the threat of revenge plots has caused persistent excitement. 'The AIDS scare could start a backlash of violence against gays, Government ministers believe,' the *Sun* newspaper reported in 1986. 'They fear a wave of "queer-bashing" may lead to bisexuals passing the disease on to women in revenge.' The Chief Rabbi, Lord Jakobovits, has predicted that compulsory testing for HIV will have to be introduced to defend the nation against people who are HIV+ and deliberately seek to spread the virus so as to outnumber the rest of the population. 'Pressure will grow to identify carriers of the disease; and my concern is the moral issue as to whether we are entitled to expose innocent citizens to the danger of infection. If it indeed transpires that there are considerable numbers of carriers, this minority may seek security by deliberately spreading the contagion to escape what they experience as discrimination.'[5]

The context for these ideas, and for this outburst of human unkindness, has been set by journalists. As few people in Britain have experience of AIDS, perceptions have been nurtured by press

200 witch docs on alert

- TWO hundred witch doctors are being called to a crisis conference to fight the AIDS menace.

- Worried health chiefs in South Africa fear the killer disease could spread rapidly among the country's blacks, who prefer witch doctors to ordinary doctors.

- They estimate 80 per cent of blacks go for treatment with herbal roots and magic rituals.

- "We have to convince the witch doctors that AIDS is spread by personal contact," said AIDS expert Dr Reuben Sher.

SCOURGE OF THE EIGHTIES

For a long time the slogan 'Scourge of the Eighties', together with a macabre picture intimating mortality by showing the skull beneath the skin, accompanied every news report about AIDS in the *Sun*. This grisly and degrading logo enabled readers immediately to identify an AIDS story. This example was printed in December 1986.

coverage which offers inflammatory phrases like 'Gay Plague', 'Gay Menace' and 'Gay Killer Bug', even though the transmission of HIV both from male to female and female to male has been demonstrated since 1983. (In one recent study of European patients, the rate of male to female transmission among 155 couples where the man was HIV+ or had AIDS was 27%, with the duration of sexual relationships and the frequency of sexual contact proving irrelevant to whether the virus was transmitted: the use of condoms was the most significant preventive.) One explanation for this insistent depiction, against the evidence, of gay men as killers, the only possible cause and source of HIV, may be a displaced desire to kill them. The people whom one accuses of wanting to destroy oneself are the people one wishes to destroy. In any case the characterization of homosexuality as a lethal contagion has ancient antecedents, and was popularized during the controversies that surrounded the Wolfenden Committee's deliberations. As this book has repeatedly shown, early misfortunes and later sexual disappointments have always turned a portion of humankind into bullies: sexual diseases have always excited brutish responses.[6]

Moralists have seized HIV as a tailor-made pretext for touting the ideological or social segregation of people whom they judge to be deviant, delinquent or just different. For people who contracted HIV 'through blood transfusions, or accidentally, there can be nothing but deep sympathy', wrote the conservative commentator George Gale in 1985. 'But what of those who contract it as a direct consequence of their behaviour?' he asked. 'Homosexuals who are not promiscuous are no more at risk than the rest of us,' he asserted inaccurately – a man with only one male partner can still get AIDS if that partner is HIV+. 'Those who choose promiscuity and unnatural methods of sexual gratification choose thereby to put themselves at risk.' Under this view people who had contracted the virus before its existence was known could not plead ignorance to mitigate their misconduct: ignorance, too, was a condition which deserved to be despised and punished. Sympathetic reports about Rock Hudson and Lord Avon, who had both been stricken by AIDS, were 'intended to make the disease respectable', Gale wrote. 'I trust they fail.' Rather than concede the diversity of human sexual desire, Gale insisted that AIDS was a penalty for transgression, 'a disease avoidable by decent living', and that 'this being so', the privacy of those with the disease should be stripped bare, so that discriminatory action could be taken against them and their past conduct judged. It was 'outrageous' to keep 'information about those suffering from the disease' as 'confidential'. People with AIDS were too contagious to be trusted. 'It is more important to protect the lives of those who might innocently or accidentally catch the disease than to protect the reputation of those who have caught the disease through their own self-indulgence.'[7]

Both the penis and the rectum are sexual as well as excretory organs. Practices which some cultures regard as normal may impress members of other cultures as vile or perverse. Thus when a woman complained to a Zambian court that her husband was a sexual pervert whose deviance might be a means to cast a spell on her, the court upheld her complaint and ordered the police to mount guard against her husband's unnatural pleasure – which consisted in his trying to kiss and suck her breasts during foreplay.

Fellatio and cunnilingus have been practised through the centuries, with what incidence no one knows. Many people still find oral sex repellent, although it seems that its pleasures have been more freely enjoyed in western industrialized countries since the 1950s. Rectal intercourse has similarly pleasured some men and women through the millenia, although others have found it uncomfortable or boring, and others have been revolted by the suggestion. The idea that it is natural to use the penis for sex, even though one excretes through it, but that it is somehow unnatural to use the rectum, although the same conditions obtain, is inconsistent. It has been rightly stressed that HIV is transmissible during buggery from the semen of the active partner into the bloodstream of the passive partner, the interior of whose rectum may be torn by the pushing of the penis. The phrase 'rectal trauma' has been seized on by moralists who assert that this proves the unnaturalness or deviance of using the rectum for a purpose which they are inspired to say was not divinely intended. Homosexual men have HIV, they pronounce, as a punishment for abusing their arses. The inconvenient fact that heterosexually transmitted HIV is rife in sub-Saharan Africa has been explained by the racist hypothesis that black people are so primitive that they have a greater predilection for brutal acts of buggery on their women, or else thrust into vaginas with such animal violence as to rip them. The hypothesis that vaginas also sustain microscopic tears when penetrated by penises, and can hence be infected by HIV, or that vaginal juices can transmit HIV into blood-swollen penises, has not provoked a comparable outcry about 'vaginal traumas' or 'penile traumas'; still less the triumphant judgment that this proves that penetrative heterosexual copulation is unnatural or against Divine purpose, and that the deviants who indulge in it deserve what they get. Objectively the discrimination between penises and rectums is nonsense; given the greater horror that shit commands over urine in our culture, the distinction is understandable; but nonsense is still nonsense, whether acculturated, atavistic or adopted as an excuse for journalistic bullying.[8]

British newspapers in the 1980s were replete with journalists who were in a rage to displace their aggression onto other people. One such opinion-maker was the *Star*'s columnist Ray Mills, who in 1986 described his 'political philosophy' as 'encompassed by the four point plan: Hang 'em, flog 'em, castrate 'em and send 'em home.' His enmities included almost all teachers and their cretinous students/pupils. Spongers and skivers. Vandals and litter louts . . . Hippies, peace people, drop outs . . . Wooftahs, poof-tahs, nancy boys, queers, lezzies – the perverts whose mortal sin is to so abuse the delightful word 'gay' as to render it unfit for human consumption . . . the strident, shrieking, hairy-nippled harridans whose claim to be feminists is a revolting contradiction in terms.[9]

Mills' views of homosexuality would have been unpublishable in a British national newspaper before HIV. He recalled that when he 'was just a lad, it was rumoured among the smokers behind the school cycle shed that there existed men who were not as other men, and quite unlike our dads'. Fortunately they were easily identifiable and easy to exclude: their 'limp wrists and mincing gait . . . were an infallible guide to their proclivities'. Nowadays all was horribly 'changed'. The world was 'packed with homosex-uals' as the result of 'a sinister move . . . to make homo-sexuality . . . damned near compulsory'.

Insidiously, almost imperceptibly, the perverts have got the heterosexual majority with their backs against the wall (the safest place actually . . .) . . . The freaks pro-claim their twisted morality nightly on TV . . . Where it may end of course is by natural causes. The woofters have had a dreadful plague visited upon them, which we call AIDS . . . Since the perverts offend the laws of God and nature, is it fanciful to suggest that one or both is striking back? . . . Little queers or big queers, Mills has had enough of them all – the Lesbians, the bisexuals and transsexuals, the hermaphrodites, catamites and gender benders who brazenly flaunt their sexual failings to the disgust . . . of the silent majority.
A blight on them all.[10]

This sort of rage against life was ignited in many people by AIDS. A 'red hot *Sun* exclusive' of 1985 reported that the Revd Robert Simpson 'vowed yesterday that he would take his teenage son to a mountain and shoot him if the boy had the deadly disease AIDS'. In this debased version of the biblical story of Abraham and Isaac, Simpson 'would pull the trigger on [the] rest of his family' too. 'The fighting vicar says he has nothing against gays,' reported the *Sun*, 'it is not their fault if they were born with more female hormones than male.' Nevertheless he deplored 'unnatural acts', beseeching 'the Government to repeal the law on homosexuality between consenting adults and prostitution – and to punish promiscuity'. AIDS was 'like the Black Plague' in this Christian's view. 'It could wipe out Britain. Family will be against family.' The Simpson family would in fact be turned against itself, if its *paterfamilias* started shooting it, but such are the terrors and furies that contagion and adolescent randiness evoke in some people that the *Sun* carried a photograph of the priest holding his rifle at point-blank range at a youth. Its journalists gave no hint that it was unreasonable for a father to commit murder rather than accept that his son was gay and ill, although it was perhaps revelatory when it quoted the son as commenting of his father, 'sometimes I think he would like to shoot me whether I had AIDS or not.'[11]

HIV was over and over again stressed as a threat to families and was therefore used to attack all those outside domestic monogamy. Welcoming the Cabinet committee 'HA' on AIDS formed in November 1986 (disbanded by Margaret Thatcher in September 1989), the *Spectator* advised that in addition to a 'fierce' health education campaign, 'the Government's policy should be to create a climate in which to be tested for AIDS is the price of social acceptance, and where monogamy and chastity are encouraged.' At one moment the British Medical Association advised all those who had more than one sexual partner in the previous year not to donate blood: non-monogamous people were stigmatized as viciously as blacks or junkies or queers have been. 'If you are promiscuous you will probably die,' one citizen wrote to a local newspaper, 'and if you are prepared to put other people's lives at risk in your own selfish quest for a few minutes' pleasure, then the world is better off without you.'[12]

The virus was depicted as nemesis. Thus in 1985 the *News of the World* reported the death of a man with AIDS. 'Eddie Cairns had the world at his feet . . . handsome, talented and on his way to the top. But he was also a fast living homosexual. Eddie, 34, died alone in a miserable council flat on the edge of an industrial estate.' Suppressing the fact that as well as being gay, Cairns was a haemophiliac who may have contracted the virus through infected blood plasma, the newspaper asserted 'he was promiscuous and went full tilt at life and used to go to a lot of wild parties and gay discos': this *joie de vivre* led to his 'downfall'.[13]

Broadcasters and journalists could seldom accept men who had contracted HIV through sexual contacts as anything other than guilty victims. Television viewers were 'offered the whispered voices of broken men, disclosed in lonely bedsits and lonely isolation wards, hoarsely and desperately repeating the "need" for monogamy, in tones of deep regret and not infrequently of self-recrimination and blame'. A woman journalist interviewed a friend of mine who died as a result of AIDS in 1987. When a photograph of him was being taken, she snapped: 'this is a serious subject: *stop* looking so happy.' When he told her that the two years since his diagnosis had been the richest and most meaningful of his life, she said, 'You've been brainwashed, I don't believe you, and our readers don't want to read this.' The proposed feature on him was never published: if people with AIDS did not conform to the desideratum of guilty victim, journalists did not want to know about them. Other images that did not fit stereotype were excluded. When the singer Sir Peter Pears died in 1986 no mention was made in his obituary in *The Times* of his lifelong homosexual partnership with the composer Lord Britten; but when the choreographer Sir Robert Helpmann died shortly afterwards, his obituarist stressed his 'strange, haunting and rather frightening' appearance: 'A homosexual of the proselytizing kind, he could turn young men on the borderline his way.' It was worth publicizing when a homosexual was 'dangerous' company, but not otherwise.[14]

HIV is depicted as one of the few calamities that can unseat privilege or unsettle the fortunes of the powerful – whether of nations or of individuals. There is repellent glee from outsiders when the young and rich found that their privileges were no defence against HIV – a discovery which must have been particularly crushing for those concerned. In 1988 the *Daily Express* reported the *Sun*'s revelation that Henry Tennant, son of Lord Glenconner, 'had caught the killer virus through liaisons with homosexuals'. Married with one son, Tennant was described as a 'society misfit who became weird because of an obsession with transcendental meditation'. A family friend was quoted as saying, 'Lord Glenconner could have cut him out of his will. His anger would have been understandable.' It was not explained what is comprehensible about disinheriting a gentle young man as punishment for contracting a life-threatening virus. A few months later the *News of the World* reported that Henry Tennant's brother Charlie, 'a hopeless heroin addict', had 'contracted AIDS'. Its journalists (who like most British reporters seemed unable to distinguish the condition of carrying HIV from the full onset of AIDS, or the intermediate AIDS-Related Complex, known as ARC) moralized that 'the fabulously rich' Tennant family 'despite their wealth' could not 'fend off the stream of heartbreaking dramas'. Readers were incited to feel satisfaction at this death-blow to hubris.[15]

The old fantasies that homosexuality was a particular vice of the rich were revived. One of the greatest objections by the Moral Right to greater public discourse about sex – which enabled more young working-class men to be open about homosexuality rather than pose as 'not queer but playing the queers' – was the damage that it inflicted on the delusion that homosexuality was a vice containable in the privileged classes. 'Russell Harty could not have paid a higher price for using rent boys,' wrote a woman journalist after the broadcaster's death in 1988 from hepatitis B. *Sun* readers were told:

> If you have a teenage child, you can't stop him or her running away if they are determined to do so, You CAN hope the law will protect them.
>   Only these days it doesn't. It protects the rich and famous instead.

The suspicion that sinister influence was being exerted to protect the perversions of the privileged had long antecedents. The wish of some journalists that the police should launch prosecutions on the slightest hint of sexual transgression by celebrities, with the sequel of a sensational trial in which the evidence is hotly contested, is self-serving. As Winthrop Mackworth Praed wrote as long ago as 1823,

> And guilt hath wed legality;
>   And useful through the nation
> Is prurience to publicity
>   And sin to circulation.

Tabloid journalists cannot be accused of protecting the prominent, although they do facilitate the business of blackmailers. In 1988, for example, the *Sun* published letters written by a judge, Martin Bowley, to his male lover, which had been stolen by another man who wanted to blackmail the lover into sleeping with him and who sent them to the *Sun* when he refused. The Lord Chancellor, Mackay of Clashfern, accepted Bowley's resignation as a judge, a senior official of his department telling journalists that homosexuality was still regarded as 'very risky' for judges and that he would be 'surprised' if there were more than a few homosexual judges.[16]

Newspapers were zealous in identifying those who had contracted HIV, or were dying as a result of AIDS. There is no point in having transgressors, as ninteenth-century moralists knew, unless they can be exposed to the scorn and fear of their neighbours, or marked as irretrievable outcasts. Stephen Barry, former valet of the Prince of Wales, was gloatingly described as trembling with distress as he protested that he only had a persistent throat infection to journalists who called at his home in the months before his death as a result of AIDS in 1986. Another newspaper published the death certificates of three British Airways stewards who died as a result of AIDS, together with the names and addresses of their next of kin. One of the Sunday prurients paid a bribe of £100 in 1987 to obtain confidential hospital records which identified two physicians, and was fined £10,000 for contempt of court by publishing an article headlined SCANDAL OF THE DOCS WITH AIDS in defiance of a court order banning it from publishing details of the cases.[17]

A *News of the World* story in 1987 headlined SCANDAL OF THE AIDS COLONY said that

> Britain's first leper colony for AIDS victims had been set up in a council tower block housing hundreds of healthy families. Over 200 sufferers of the deadly disease are waiting to die in the sordid ghetto aptly named World's End. Another 400 in the block off the King's Road in Chelsea are AIDS carriers . . .
>
> Local residents – paying £87 a week for nightmare surroundings – are happy to move somewhere cheaper and better.

> Other victims use an underground gay contact net-
> work to move in with friends and sufferers already
> living there.
>
> An innocent mother of three children in World's End
> revealed last night: 'I've found dirty hypodermic needles
> on the stairs. And one prostitute who knows she has
> AIDS regularly uses her flat as a meeting place for gays.
> I'm terrified for my children'.

The *Daily Express* picked up the story, suggesting more cautiously that there was a 'fear' that as many as 600 residents were 'contaminated'. Local councillors denounced these reports as 'lies', a view which was upheld by the Press Council after a complaint from the Royal Borough of Kensington and Chelsea. The treatment of this contagion stunt typified the need to present AIDS as an attack on that fantasy of neo-conservative moralists, the stability and sanctity of family life, in which children are always happy, healthy and safe if left with the love of their good parents. People with AIDS were projected as living at the opposite extreme to this illusory idyll. Sadly it needs no ingenuity to connect such beliefs with the remarks of Dame Cicely Saunders who tried to justify the reluctance of hospices to admit people with AIDS. 'As we welcome whole families for our unlimited visiting hours, any change of policy would mean a considerable programme of local education,' she wrote in 1986. Families can't be let near people with AIDS: homosexuals and drug users by implication do not have families.[18]

The perceived threat to family life was manifest in other ways. The Rating Guidelines in *AIDS Bulletin No. 4* issued in 1987 by Mercantile and General Reinsurance recommended that any life insurance proposal from a bisexual male should be 'usually declined'. Whereas the response to a proposal from a male homosexual depended upon investigation of his sexual or medical history, sexual practices or HIV antibody status, no such allow-ance was made for bisexuals, even if they tested negative for HIV. This is unwarranted by the facts: an important survey of 1984–7 at the West London Hospital found that practising bisexual men had a much lower prevalence of HIV infection (5%) than exclusively homosexual men (30%), possibly because the bisex-uals had tended to non-penetrative sex with other men. In practice people of all sexual preferences who admitted to having had negative tests for HIV were refused life assurance, despite companies claiming that no one would be debarred from cover merely because they had been tested. Yet the discrimination against bisexuals was particularly flagitious and revealing: the world of house mortgages and life insurance is based on assumptions about the immutability of family life, about the strict division of gender and about the reliability of public roles and private conduct. The existence of bisexual desire is far more threatening to this carefully constructed and precisely delineated world than anything that homosexuals may say or do. They are perceived as subverting the whole system, which is why they alone have been excluded from it as rigorously as people with fully developed AIDS. Not the least mournful falsification surrounding the HIV panic has been the antithesizing of homosexual and heterosexual acts: the diversity of sexual desire has been depicted as a danger to the whole human race, and the tendency is even discernible to discourage men from recognizing supposedly 'feminine' feelings in themselves. The decision by men who are in touch with their bisexuality that they must sever their feelings for other men, that they must act as if sexual or emotional intimacies are only permissible or safe with women is an impoverishment; like all falsifications, it is only storing disruption for the future.[19]

HIV was dragged into every sensational story where death was involved, as in the Hungerford massacre of 1987 when 'gunman Michael Ryan went on a killing spree because he was scared he had AIDS,' to quote the *Sun*. 'Detectives think the gay killer who shot dead 16 people was driven berserk by his terror.' His crime seemed so unreasonable that he was portrayed as a man whose sexual appetites were equally against reason or nature. Repudiated by women, he threatened them directly with guns and indirectly with his polluting penis. 'Ryan believed women were beyond his grasp, so he turned to men', including a 'bisexual ex-soldier' whose wife 'must be tested for the killer virus AIDS,' *Sun* readers learned. The wife was quoted as saying, 'It's horrible. I never really thought it would happen to me.' Violence was conjured up in other ways. 'Grim-faced ministers emerged from a Cabinet meeting yesterday fearful that the killer plague AIDS will spark violence on the streets of Britain,' the *Sun* reported in 1986 at a time when contagion was 'spreading like wildfire' in its judgment. 'The prospect of bloodshed as terrified citizens make "reprisal" attacks on homosexuals and drug addicts is now seen as a real threat.' In fact citizens were too fearful to go near enough to attack people with AIDS, but instead, in Hammersmith, they burned down their homes.[20]

The impulse to blame and reject sick people has led to the supposedly 'guilty' individuals who are HIV+ being depicted not only as a threat to the innocent majority, but as wholly culpable for their own condition. 'AIDS is a totally self-inflicted illness', except in those 'much more morally reprehensible cases' where people were 'inflicting AIDS on their unborn children', a government spokesman said in the House of Commons in 1986. Robert Maxwell, the millionaire appointed by the Government to head its AIDS charity, was similarly wont to speak of 'guilty' and 'innocent' people with AIDS, although he was later persuaded to modify his distinction to 'careless' and 'innocent'. Princess Anne in a speech to the World AIDS Summit held in London in 1988 declared that 'the real tragedy is the innocent victims – the people who have been infected unknowingly, perhaps as the result of a blood transfusion, and the few who have been infected knowingly, by sufferers seeking revenge.' AIDS, she said, was 'self-inflicted'. Yet no disease is a 'classic own goal, scored by the human race on itself', to quote another phrase used by the Princess Royal: AIDS results from a virus, and is no one's fault. No individual or group deserves the syndrome or is guilty of getting it, and it serves no purpose except the propagation of the virus to talk in these terms. Her remarks prompted further punitive and discriminatory ebullitions. While the medical correspondent of the *Daily Express* responded that 'in medical terms, there are no innocents and no guilty patients – just victims', three columns away on the same page the editorial writer took a more brutal approach. 'BRAVO, Princess Anne!' he proclaimed, congratulating her for 'straight-talking'. Only 'a small proportion' of people with AIDS, such as haemophiliacs, were 'victims'; but 'the main carriers', homosexuals, were culprits 'suffering the consequences of their own voluntary acts'. It was 'absurd' to pretend they were not ill through their own 'fault'. A few days later the *Daily Express* reported that 20% of a survey of 1,000 women thought AIDS 'a just punishment for promiscuity'.[21]

AIDS has been stressed as a syndrome hitting 'other people', the doom of strangers or foreigners. For a brief period in its early days some associates of the Terrence Higgins Trust counselled people seeking safe sex to confine their intercourse to people whom they knew and trusted: catastrophic advice based on the all too human hope that the people one knew would never carry the virus and that it was only unknown people who were endangered. 'AIDS is a foreign thing,' according to a Chinese official responsible for testing the blood of foreign residents for HIV. 'There's no AIDS in Tewkesbury,' declared the local Environmental Health Officer in 1986 on the basis of inchoate assumptions about the universal heterosexuality of a Gloucestershire market town. 'There will be no AIDS in Israel,' I was told two months later by a Zionist peer of considerable influence in Britain. 'People from Spelthorne won't get AIDS,' a councillor said when first told that London boroughs were each to appoint AIDS officers. When this denial that HIV would invade one's experience became untenable, there was incredulous regret that 'AIDS is no longer the disease of a homosexual ghetto,' to recall a lament of the *Spectator* in November 1986. Rupert Murdoch's journalists were equally appalled when (to abbreviate a headline of 1987) MIDDLE-CLASS GIRLS GET WARNING OF AIDS RISK.[22]

The results of this conceptualization were unmitigatedly harmful. Newspapers repeatedly confused seropositivity with having AIDS. In 1986 a man and woman, both described as aged 21 and 'with AIDS', appeared in a London magistrates court charged with shoplifting. The authorities were thrown into a panic about contagion, apparently fearing that HIV could be transmitted by breathing or from saliva through the skin. Originally the police did not want to transfer the couple from the cells to the court, and throughout the hearing they and the ushers wore protective gloves. Eight shop employees were reported as having AIDS tests (although, assuming that they had contracted HIV from the shoplifters' blood, this would not show on a test until many months later) and the chairman of the magistrates' bench said, 'I would ask everyone to leave this court unless they don't mind the risk of catching AIDS.'[23]

Asked to repair a telephone at a tiny gay club for men and women at Taunton, British Telecom in December 1986 sent three engineers, a supervisor and a manager, all wearing protective gloves. The engineers had originally demanded masks as well and also that they be met by someone from the club with a medical certificate attesting that he or she did not have AIDS. (During a period of three months in 1987, the London Lesbian and Gay Switchboard reported over 100 serious faults with its telephones; but their complaints were ignored, or repair work was not undertaken properly: a British Telecom official admitted that their engineers 'might take a less sympathetic view of complaints from gays than from other customers'.) The following month, when magistrates granted a registration certificate when the club moved premises, the Taunton Deane Licensed Victuallers Association protested. 'We don't like homosexuals on our doorsteps,' other publicans stated, threatening that there would be a 'bloodbath' within a year as their customers 'seeing a homosexual will want to cause trouble'. Elsewhere, just before Christmas 1986, the leader of South Staffordshire District Council, Bill Brownhill, announced his solution to AIDS would be to 'gas 90 per cent of queers'. Twelve lesbian women and gay men who went to his garden at Wombourne to protest were arrested by the police for breach of the peace, fingerprinted by an officer wearing protective gloves, asked by police to take a HIV test, handcuffed when they appeared in court and remanded in custody over Christmas on prosecution allegations, refuted by the defence, that none had been confirmed as having provided truthful names and addresses. All charges were subsequently dropped, although a lesbian who was said to have spat at a police officer was threatened with a charge of attempted murder. Protective rubber gloves are not recommended as necessary in police guidelines except for officers conducting body searches where an exposed needle may be found; but the fear of contagion, and the almost wilful misunderstanding of the transmission of HIV, overbore every other consideration.[24]

The panic resulted in prejudice by employers. During an investigation into sex discrimination by an airline, which for thirty years refused to interview men for jobs as aircraft cabin staff, the company told the Equal Opportunities Commission that HIV mainly affected homosexuals, that 30% of men applying for cabin jobs were homosexual, that cabin staff were promiscuous and AIDS might be transmitted by blood or saliva from male cabin attendants to passengers. The wife of a HIV+ haemophiliac was dismissed from her job as a cleaner in a bakery after fellow staff complained. 'We have food around,' said the owner, 'it would have been a real hazard.' But HIV cannot be breathed onto food, and it would have been no hazard. One of the projectionists at a cinema in Letchworth began disinfecting door handles because he was afraid that he would catch AIDS from a fellow projectionist who was homosexual, Michael Buck. Although it is impossible to catch HIV in such a way, after 17 years working in the cinema, Buck was sacked in 1986. At the age of 45, he was unable to find another job; and only received £2,000 damages in settlement in 1988. The Government resisted Labour party attempts to amend the Employment Act of 1989 so as to illegalize discrimination against employees on the grounds that the latter are HIV + or are believed to be at risk of contracting the virus. The Government's claim that such provisions were unnecessary was untenable given the avowed policy of employers like Texaco Oil to require a negative HIV test as a prerequisite of employment, or the monstrous action in July 1989 of Torbay Health Authority, which dismissed a woman nurse whose husband had died a few days earlier as a result of AIDS with the mealy-mouthed protest that it did so only for her own good. The truth is that the Government opposed any measure which increased the rights of an employee against an employer, and still more any measure that might by implication benefit any of the minorities stigmatized by HIV. Their attitude was purblind and unjust.[25]

It is unreasonable to expect physicians to be immune from the fears and anxieties that beset the laity. Many respond to HIV with visceral instincts of punishment and control. One in six general practitioners in east Berkshire surveyed in 1988 believed that the best way to control HIV would be to recriminalize homosexuality. The mother of a brilliant young scholar who died as a result of AIDS in 1984 has recorded the 'moral righteousness and insensitivity of the consultant'. Her son was put in an isolation ward and his visitors had to wear masks. After asking to see the consultant physician, she had to wait eight hours for an interview of three minutes, at which she was told for the first time that he had AIDS, which 'should come as no surprise given his lifestyle'. She was eventually granted another and even briefer interview.

> I was worried that my other son who shared a bathroom with Richard might get AIDS. The consultant just

giggled and said: 'Not unless he has been up to the same shenanigans and mixing with the same company'. That was the level of his counselling.

Mike Gill, who lived in the small Cornish town of Penryn, found himself ostracized after he was diagnosed HIV+ following the death in the mid 1980s of his lover as a result of AIDS. He was banned from his local pub, received hate mail, had dog shit shoved through his letter box and was shunned by friends. His parents received abusive telephone calls and were snubbed by acquaintances. He was refused treatment by four different dentists and forbidden to take communion wine from the chalice. When admitted to hospital in Truro in 1986, suffering from incontinence and severe weight loss, nurses used full barrier procedures with him, wearing disposable caps, gloves and masks. His food was served on paper dishes. Staff were reluctant to empty his bed pans, and an auxiliary suggested that he should urinate in a sink. 'I had the image of a hospital being caring,' he recalled in 1988, 'but it was like twisting the knife in.'[26]

There are shining exceptions to this medical insensitivity, expitomized by the approach at the London Lighthouse at Notting Hill, where it is never forgotten that body and mind can never be separated, that mental well-being helps physical well-being, and that patients should have control of their own health so far as possible. The principles of the Lighthouse and other specialist wards in major London hospitals that actions should seldom be dissociated from feelings are little publicized, but remain unforgettable to those who have been exposed to them. Richard Wells, the Royal College of Nursing's adviser on AIDS, spoke in 1987 of the particular problems of 'looking after a group of people who for five years have been told by the media that they are not worthy of care, and that they are going to die. Death for most people is extremely difficult; for the young it is even more difficult.' Yet as Jacqui Elliott, who leads the AIDS nurses at Middlesex Hospital, has insisted, it is possible to change patients' 'hopelessness into hopefulness by the care we can give'.[27]

The Royal College of Nursing reported in 1986 that some AIDS patients were unnecessarily isolated by hospitals 'which had over-reacted and had unfair attitudes towards the original population of patients at risk – male homosexuals and drug addicts'. In 1987 the *British Medical Journal* received several reports of physicians who refused to see or treat HIV+ patients and heard of a general practitioner who had removed a seropositive patient from his list. Although a great deal improved, more than a year later a HIV+ woman who gave birth to a daughter at Hillingdon Hospital felt that she and her children were treated 'like lepers'. They were subjected to 'barrier nursing', and isolated in a room converted from an office. 'I was told to stay in there,' she said. 'It was as if they were scared they'd catch AIDS if I opened the door . . . they kept missing me out when they brought the meals round.' One surgeon wrote in the *BMJ* that he 'reserve[d] the right to decline to operate on those in whom recent or continuing infection with HIV is likely, other than in life threatening circumstances'. He implied that risks to other patients, medical staff and their families, coupled with the 'voluntary sexual perversion or mainline drug abuse' of most HIV+ patients justified withdrawal of medical care. The voluntary cigarette-smoking which leads to lung cancer, or the voluntary overeating which results in obesity and heart disease, are never adduced by physicians, it hardly needs to be added, as reasons which justify withdrawal of medical care: only sexually transmitted diseases provoke this sort of anxious hostility.[28]

The blaming of drug users or gay men, epitomized by the stance of this surgeon, inevitably fuels hostility to other people with HIV. A boy who at the age of 8 developed AIDS from infected blood plasma was excluded from his school, shunned by family friends and after he died aged 10, only hospital staff attended his funeral. His parents received 'only malice and hate from most if not all their neighbours, including churchgoers', as David Watters, Secretary of the Haemophiliac Society, recounted. Such people 'deserve much more than tawdry and cowardly moralizing'. A Scottish woman who was the first to adopt a HIV+ child has been distracted by the attempts of a newspaper to trace and identify her – presumably so that she and her child can be subjected to the same ostracism. Watters arrives at his office on most mornings to find vile messages on his telephone answering machine. Two weeks before the death as the result of AIDS of one young haemophiliac man, 'BEWARE AIDS IN HERE' was daubed in two-foot high letters on the wall outside his Hartlepool home. Other members of his family were persecuted, including his brother's divorced wife,

who was driven to a mental breakdown, with six weeks' hospitalization, by a 'campaign of hate' which left her 'the innocent victim of
AIDS thugs'. Her son aged three 'was shunned by his playmates
who wrongly feared he could pass on the disease'. Their house
'was pelted with eggs and late at night the thugs would stand
outside shouting "AIDS". Strangers knocked on her front door to
ask if she or her son had AIDS. When she travelled by bus, or
visited a pub, people announced, "Don't sit next to her, you might
catch AIDS"'. Beyond making other people's lives miserable, the
only achievement of such mindless persecution is to impede
control of the pandemic. A wish to avoid the misery of neighbourhood malignants is one reason why a survey of 1987 in north-west
England showed that only five out of a sample of 15 haemophiliac
boys had been told by their parents that they were HIV+. Doctors
had agreed before testing them not to tell those who were
seropositive until they were 18, although some will probably have
started fucking before then, and the virus will have a better chance
of propagation.[29]

Tory MP Vivian Bendall may attack as a 'pretty poor show' the
practice of putting haemophiliacs with AIDS in hospital beds next
to patients who had contacted the virus by injecting drugs, but in
reality all these distinctions are spurious. Gay men or drug users
who decide not to take an antibody test, because they recognize
that it may jeopardize their job or home, or because they feel that
there is no longer any consensus of decency to protect them from
politically motivated harassment, are like the parents of the
haemophiliacs in north-west England: they prefer that the truth
should not be known because the truth has become so
dangerous.[30]

At the same time the official response has not been repressive.
Calls for mass compulsory testing for HIV were rejected: although
the Government took powers for the compulsory detention in
hospital of a person with AIDS, the law has been invoked in only
one case. Whereas the Federal Government in the USA has felt
that it would be compromised by co-operation with gay activists,
the AIDS activists of the Terrence Higgins Trust have been used as
advisers on official responses to the epidemic. Tony Whitehead,
the first chair of THT, and a former drug user and male prostitute,
was co-opted onto the educational and social advisory group
formed by Sir Donald Acheson, Chief Medical Officer to the

Department of Health and Social Security, for example, and helped to direct government policy in a direction which was neither personally restrictive nor punitive. Despite the brutal and widespread stigmatization of gays that has occurred as a result of AIDS, the health crisis has occasioned the first official recognition of groups of gay men as potentially valuable contributors to the policy-making process. However, since 1988 the AIDS policy community has been more formally institutionalized, drawing increasingly on the traditional hierarchies and established professional structures for advice, to the detriment of THT's influence. In the period from 1983 until 1988, AIDS policy-making in Britain was essentially open and pluralistic; by late 1989 it was closed and consensual. The introduction of needle exchange schemes, despite the opposition of some Tory politicians, will probably be seen by posterity as the last flower of the AIDS policy community's finest period.[31]

Admittedly it was only after eighteen months of anxious procrastination, in January 1986, when the British Government was aroused to the fear of HIV 'leaking' into the white heterosexual community, that the need for concerted action was accepted. (By then the greatest changes by men in abandoning high risk activities like anoreceptive intercourse with casual partners had already occurred.) The public health advertising campaign launched later in 1986 was budgeted at £20 million, compared with £30 million spent advertising the privatized issue of shares in the nationalized gas supply company, British Gas, but the content of the Government's advice was equitable and resisted prejudice against any of the minorities identified with HIV. It proclaimed:

> Anyone can get it, gay or straight, male or female, already 30,000 people are infected. At the moment the infection is mainly confined to relatively small groups of people in this country. But it is spreading.

A leaflet sent out in 1986 to every household in the country indicated the usual means of HIV transmission and enjoined fidelity ('It is safest to stick to one sexual partner'): a government circular issued to employers on employment issues relating to HIV was equally laudable in confronting 'unnecessary fears and worry' and effective in giving temperate advice. Later, in 1988, the Health

Education Authority produced its AIDS Charter, advertised in national newspapers, which called for people with HIV and AIDS to be 'treated with care, sympathy and dignity':

> those with AIDS, particularly homosexual men, have been stigmatized, and AIDS has been associated with 'undesirable minorities'.
>
> The reality is that AIDS is everyone's business. Men, women and children. In a few years time most people will know of somebody infected with HIV, and realize the tragic consequences of a disease for which there is no cure and no vaccine in sight.

This approach has been courageous, and unwelcome to some government supporters.[32]

The latter often insist that HIV will not infiltrate the 'ordinary' population and denounce the attention given to the virus as pandering to perverts. In 1988 the *Sunday Telegraph* published an article headlined IS THERE A HOMOSEXUAL CONSPIRACY? based on interviews with 'opinion-formers, many of whom dared not give their names, in the Church, in government, in medicine and in television'. An anonymous policy-maker was quoted as saying of the genesis of the public health campaigns in 1986: 'What neither ministers nor senior officials knew at the time was how entrenched homosexuals were in the upper reaches of the medical establishment dealing with venereology, and that they and their sympathizers were a substantial element in the Chief Medical Officer's advisory committee on AIDS.' He alleged that the 'main purpose' of safer sex pamphlets produced by voluntary organizations like the Terrence Higgins Trust 'was to promote a homosexual lifestyle'. The government campaign, with its slogan 'Don't Die of Ignorance', might 'foster an attitude where young men felt they'd missed out if they hadn't done it . . . of course, homosexuals wanted that, because they need a steady supply of young men with whom to engage in their activities.' Britain's public health campaign has hence been used to stress the untrustworthiness of homosexuals, their conspiratorial nature and their exploitation of illicit loyalties in the cause of sexual subversion. The Government had 'not reckoned with the entrenched power of the homosexual community in medicine and the civil service', agreed a journalist in the *Daily Express* in the same week of 1988. 'It is high time it grasped the real nettle.' It was this sort of propaganda which hastened the marginalization of people from the Terrence Higgins Trust in the official AIDS policy community during 1988–9, with consequences that are already proving harmful not only to people with HIV but to national health.[33]

Government advertising warnings of HIV transmission by drug users sharing needles have been less effective. The most desirable message to convey to intravenous drug users is that their 'works' can be easily disinfected each time after use by a couple of infusions of household bleach; but this simple lesson in life-saving has been deemed politically inconceivable because it gives tacit countenance to drug-taking. Instead a fortune has been spent on an advertising campaign which will only impress or frighten middle-aged people with no exposure to drugs. The Government's intention has been to deter people starting on drugs (to some of our political masters and mistresses existent drug-takers are not worth saving), and they have failed ignominiously. The gaunt, sallow youth on the Heroin Screws You Up poster has been adopted as a pin-up on the bedroom walls of young women, his moody self-destructiveness being sexually attractive to many people. The images of the Shooting Up Once Can Screw You Up Forever campaign were equally enticing: people drawn to this sort of life will be pleasurably excited by elegantly photographed pictures of sleaze and the debris of drug-taking (bloodied needles to some people are no less alluring than images of the blades with which heroin is cut into lines for snorting, or the tinfoil on which heroin can be heated and inhaled by users Chasing the Dragon). The advertisements focused on heroin only served to make self-defined 'family' men and women feel better, assuring them that the threat of HIV was located elsewhere with forces inimical to domesticity. One government poster of 1987–8 identified each needle mark on a user's body as financed by a different theft from his family: the fact that his mother's wedding ring was one of these 'hits' – that he robbed her of the symbol of married life – epitomized the way in which HIV was seen as the affliction of those who would break family values asunder.

Among people who believe that they don't know anyone with HIV or AIDS, the publicity that has had most effect has been not the circulars and leaflets issued by the government, but television advertisements and journalistic glosses on the official propaganda. The young in particular have been left untouched by the scrupulous advice in the leaflets. In Britain children have been so scared by other negative messages about HIV that they believe adult loving relationships will be impossible for them. There has been a tendency for moralists to present the equation 'sex = death' in order to frighten adolescents into celibacy. The British Government's television advertisements, with their imagery of icebergs, tombstones and funeral wreathes, have been unrelentingly negative; as have counterparts like the Australian Government's television advertisement suggesting a family being mown down at a bowling alley by a thunderous and inexorable ten-pin ball of AIDS, or the French poster of a huge and ominous black mass like an alien spaceship overshadowing the country, with slogans that translate as 'It depends on each of us to erase that shadow' and 'France doesn't want to die of AIDS.' This approach is less likely to influence people at risk than to increase the numbers of 'the worried well', healthy people long documented as consulting clinical advice on sexually transmitted diseases, for whom anxiety about syphilis and now HIV acts as a way of expressing their sexual guilt or anxiety, or their general vulnerability and depression. 'We are producing a generation of cripples who are scared of sex,' to quote officers of the International Association for Planned Parenthood in 1988. The Government's fearful advertising campaign has already 'had a terrible effect on children. Primary school children are now anxious about AIDS. Parents and teachers won't talk to them about it . . . The skull and crossbones approach is especially frightening for children because they do not have access to other information.' Not only is a generation growing up for whom carnal pleasure will be associated with terror; but adolescents are not offered any safe way to express their sexuality, which, after all, is omnipresent, and will not be dissipated either by will-power or by the nagging of elders. This is reckless, because the easiest reaction to a crude bombardment of fear is denial, the insistence that HIV is the affliction of other people. The mean age of British people known to be HIV+ in 1988 was twenty-five years old. Young people need to understand that they may be at risk of infection themselves, yet most AIDS education aimed at the young uses fear as the main motive for changing behaviour. The positive and even pleasurable aspects of safer sexual behaviour have been ignored: feeling part of a group, emulating an admired role model, or being lovingly protective are all powerful reasons for some forms of conduct, yet there is little hint of these approaches in official propaganda. Instead the young are offered a crude appeal to contagion fears.[34]

Richard Branson's initiative in launching Mates condoms led to a lot of personalized jibes and generalized cavilling from right-wing columnists in the better quality British newspapers. The *News of the World* in 1987 published a lurid and tendentious account of activities at his Heaven nightclub. Its report seemed intended to discredit 'father-of-two Branson' as a hypocrite catering for those who sought 'the ultimate in depravity'.

A more constructive approach, which is likely to prove more effective, can be seen in the advertising for Mates, the brand of condoms launched in 1987 as a non-profit-making, half-price alternative to Durex. Mates were the conception of the millionaire Richard Branson (one of the last people to be prosecuted under the Venereal Diseases Act of 1917, as described previously). Branson wished to encourage the use of condoms by the young, to reduce embarrassment in the buying and selling of condoms, and to make them available in shops, garages, bars and fast-food restaurants. The profits were donated to an AIDS-related charity: heavily subsidized Mates were sold to family planning clinics, with two million other condoms donated to organizations connected with HIV. The annual value of British condom sales is estimated at between £25 and £30 million; within a year Mates had won a market share of at least 20 per cent. They estimated that half of their customers were new users (young people concerned about HIV) with the rest representing brand-switching from Durex. This success was little due to their undercutting of Durex: research showed that many people thought that Mates's low price meant that they were inferior, and when their price was raised to 10% below that of Durex, sales rose. The real success of Mates was effected by their advertising which, though exiguously funded, has (together with the Terrence Higgins Trust's advertisements in gay newspapers) been the main spur to encouraging people to practise 'safer sex' to reduce risk of HIV infection. Thus a survey published late in 1988 of 400 people in the Bristol area aged 16 to 21 showed that 40% were sexually active before the age of 16, 6% had four or more partners in the previous year and 92% felt that they were at no risk of HIV infection: results which hardly suggest that the Government's scary propaganda has convinced the people to whom it should matter most. Campaigns would probably be more effective if they were nationally oriented, but locally based, and targeted at specific forms of risky behaviour. It is facile to expect the Government to achieve much: the response of any self-respecting rebellious teenager, admonished to a life of celibacy by a middle-aged politician, will be to rush out in search of as much sex as possible with as many people as are available. Officials and politicians have been expected to make an abrupt and imaginative change of outlook for which nothing in their training has prepared them. For example one of Mates' earliest advertisements (see plate) used an idea which had previously been conceived for the government health campaign, but which the senior hierarchy of the Department of Health and Social Security had rejected as too upsetting. Effective contraception since the 1960s made possible the gorgeous luxury of cheerful casual sex without consequences. It made a reality of the fantasy that for one night, with one person, one could step out of time into sensual oblivion, and pick up the rest of one's life the next day as if little had happened: a widely desired fantasy whose reality had been confined before the 1960s mainly to the more expensive brothels. This has now been ruined, as fantasies always are. With the advent of HIV, there is always the possibility that there *will* be consequences, that somewhere in the chain of previous fucks will reside someone carrying HIV. The loss of this idyll – it lasted less than twenty years – is a sadness, to be mourned. The message in Mates' advertisement 'Every time you sleep with a girl' (there was an equivalent for sleeping with a boy) is all too true; and it says much for the vulnerability of the DHSS's officials that they could not bear to accept it.[35]

Other Mates advertising has wittily celebrated eroticism and done much to promote safer sex. It has been deftly targeted at special groups. Whereas other condoms manufacturers have tended to ignore gay users (with particularly unpleasant overtones in the USA), Mates have advertised in gay newspapers urging readers to 'be a carrier' – not of HIV but of condoms. Mates have broken a previously impenetrable barrier of sales resistance: getting women to buy condoms. Mates' sales in a cosmetic retail chain like Bodyshop quickly outpaced their sales at the great retail chemists, Boots, just as Mates' dispensing machines in women's lavatories have more users than those in men's lavatories. The cheerful advertisement 'Women are only interested in men who are well equipped' (see plate), placed in women's magazines, takes joy in the male body: it charms rather than grates on the reader, and has had more constructive influence on sexually active young women than the millions of pounds spent by the Government. This approach shines in contrast to that of the popular British newspapers, which only celebrate images of the male body in their de-eroticized pictures of sportsmen, which present women merely as equipment for men's fantasies or as aids to orgasm, and which have propagated so much confused or wicked nonsense about HIV. The task of putting on a condom is thought a passion-killer: rather than nagging about its advisability, though, Mates' advertisement 'They're awfully fiddly to put on' eroticizes the experience, turns it from a dreary, sordid necessity of hygiene into a new refinement of foreplay. Condoms suffer from a traditionally shameful association: Mates, shrewdly, offer the image of fun. Instead of badgering people into chastity, or frightening people into the sort of panic in which bad, impulsive decisions get taken, Mates have encouraged the taking of individual decisions in a relaxed atmosphere. What could connote less panic than the image of the couple in their advertisement 'We'd like everyone to make love with their eyes open'?

The confusion which surrounds HIV is exemplified by the medley of nonsense spluttered about condoms. As against syphilis or gonorrhoea, they are if properly used a reliable, but not infallible, barrier against HIV infection. Until the launch of Mates condoms, however, the London International Group (formerly known as the London Rubber Company) which had a near-monopoly of the British condom market were chary of their image, especially as they were trying to diversify their interests into non-sexual rubber products. As a result the conglomerate, which manufactured over 90% of the condoms sold in Britain, 'refrained from aiming at the British homosexual market', so *The Times* reported in 1986, 'perhaps for fear of tarnishing its image'. If this is true, it raises interesting questions about the contribution of commercial criteria to the epidemiology of HIV. Research by the Central Birmingham Health Authority published in 1988 showed that between 10 and 15 per cent of men in the city aged between 16 and 75 – up to 30,000 men – visited prostitutes in the city, with women seeing an average of 18 clients weekly. Ninety per cent of the Birmingham women required condoms to be worn (although many agreed to unprotected sex for more money), in contrast to Hamburg, where 90 per cent of men visiting brothels refused to wear condoms. Elsewhere in Britain, however, prostitutes were discouraged from carrying condoms because police used possession of condoms as evidence for obtaining convictions. Women who carry condoms are automatically suspect to some men. A woman lawyer who was stopped by a customs officer at Heathrow Airport in 1987 was strip-searched, arrested and cautioned after an unused packet of condoms was found in her luggage. This was at a time when the Government was urging foreign travellers to take prophylactics with them; but Customs and Excise treat condoms as a prima-facie indication of drug smuggling.[36]

This was not the only fatuity perpetrated by Customs and Excise. Until 1986, when they abandoned obscenity charges against Gay's the Word bookshop in Bloomsbury (one of the most pleasant and commodious bookshops in London, but often depicted by journalists as a pornographic gully-hole), none of the American or European gay newspapers containing the best current information about AIDS was allowed into Britain. Sir Donald Acheson, the Government's Chief Medical Officer of Health, could only obtain magazines like the *New York Native* or the *Advocate*, which he needed to design the official preventive health programme but which were seized by customs officers, by having them smuggled in diplomatic bags.[37]

There was a recrudescence of fears about homosexuality vitiating the armed forces. At present masculinity is imagined as completely closed off. A man, under the dominant myth, must be masculine all the way through: femininity appears alien, and the threat of its infiltration is savagely suppressed. Fighting men – combatants in armies and navies – are for many people the apotheosis of masculinity and, although men's temperaments have both masculine and feminine components, it is insisted that they surrender their passivity and compete as aggressive all-male men. This cult of masculinity, with its repudiation of passivity, anxiety about external threats and preoccupation with militarism, is exemplified in an anonymous letter sent in 1982 to Peter Tatchell, who was reviled by his opponents in the Bermondsey parliamentary by-election as a gay man. 'When I lived in Bermondsey, until my family were bombed out while I was fighting to protect this country from outside evils,' wrote his correspondent, 'Bermondsey was a place where men were men, and women counted as "manholes"; and members of the "Middlesex Regiment" would not be tolerated.' Like most myths, that of masculinity is precarious, and the higher level of contagion fears in the country led to increased sensitivity about emotional and erotic ambivalence, or latent and active homosexuality among troops.[38]

In 1987 a Tory MP, Teddy Taylor, denounced 'an active minority of armed forces personnel [who] are bringing their services into disrepute' after cases in which a soldier in the Royal Horse Artillery complained of being sexually assaulted with a vacuum cleaner and in which two Scottish soldiers were imprisoned for ordering recruits to have sex with each other. The 'tradition' in another Scottish regiment where recruits endured an initiation ceremony in which they were forced to mark time with a piece of string connecting their scrotum to their ankles also ended in a court martial. A sixteen-stone fishmonger who buggered two army privates, and fellated other troops who reportedly thought he was a woman, was gaoled a few weeks later amidst much publicity. This concentrated on the brilliant impersonation that had apparently duped so many virile youths. There was no imaginative effort to understand how a young man, after an evening's drinking, feels randy, wants to come, but doesn't feel able to do so in a blatantly homosexual act; and who therefore needs little convincing that the sixteen-stone fishmonger who wants to fellate him is really a woman. When, after a barbecue, an Army sergeant aged 34 kissed a fusilier aged 19, the latter 'was so terrified he ran back to his camp, and hid, shaking and sobbing, under an Army truck', a later court martial in 1988 was told. 'He was distraught and frothing at the mouth,' according to a witness. The sergeant was acquitted of 'indecency and embracing a fellow soldier contrary to good order and military discipline' after claiming that the young soldier, who 'was upset and wanted to leave the Army', gave him 'a kiss or a slobber' on the cheek while being comforted, but then 'seemed to go a bit funny . . . screamed and ran off'. The belief implicit in these reports that it is natural to shake, sob or froth at the mouth because one has been kissed by another man, or that embraces between men subvert 'good order' were not questioned: these absurdities demonstrate the ruthlessness with which male affections and mentorship are proscribed, or curiosity about other male bodies is denied, except in brutal and impersonal rituals.[39]

The police, predictably, were prone to extreme anxieties about HIV. After allegations in 1988 of homosexuality at Hendon Police College, a policeman was quoted as saying,

> This was not a case of coppers dropping their trousers and mooning. We are talking about sexual acts taking place between men in the bar. This is very serious. People like that are not fit to become police officers.

The pretence that displays of male bottoms are a safe, unerotic and manly ritual but that homosexual acts were incompatible with police work is an example of the most primitive form of splitting. Elsewhere the identification of HIV with homosexuality resulted in displays of crude police contagion panics. During 1988 a car stolen in Edinburgh was crashed into a lorry at Hawick. Blood from the injured driver was splattered over the front of the car and when police ordered a test, he was found to be HIV+. 'Rather than risk further infection, police had the car burned and compressed.' The metalwork of a car splashed with HIV+ blood can be disinfected easily, but cars are highly sexual objects to some men, and this one had to be set alight and crunched up before policemen felt safe.[40]

Prisons have been a focus of panic. One prisoner had his head shaved, with the consent of the medical officer, 'because you've got HIV bugs and they jump around.' At Leeds and Wandsworth Prisons, new inmates who are recognized as gay or as intravenous drug users are confined to a special unit until they agree to be tested for HIV. A drug user at one London prison was stripped and kept in a lighted cell for 48 hours until he agreed to be tested. Testing is not accompanied by effective counselling, and the results are not confidential. After a positive test, prisoners are almost invariably segregated, and (although the director of the Prison Medical Service has stated that this is unnecessary) are often prevented from associating with other prisoners by being excluded from work, attending classes or playing sports. In the prison hospital at Brixton prisoners who are HIV+ are forced to eat off different coloured plates from other patients – a stupidity without medical justification. One does not catch the virus from ceramics. Despite the recommendation of its own Advisory Council on the Misuse of Drugs, endorsed by the World Health Organization, the Home Office resisted providing condoms to prisoners lest this be seen to condone 'homosexual rape' inside gaols – as if most homosexuality among incarcerated men is not consensual. In an act of casuistry, the Home Office argued that issuing condoms to prisoners would implicate it in illegality: because every part of a prison is under surveillance, no part of it can legally be described as private, but under the Arran—Abse Act of 1967, a homosexual act between two consenting adults is only legal if conducted in private. The Prison Reform Trust estimated in 1988 that up to 30 per cent of men in prison engage in homosexual acts; but no one knows what proportion of these acts comprise mutual masturbation or slicklegging, with little if any risk of HIV transmission, any more than they know how many prisoners share needles when injecting drugs. A research project proposed by the chair of the Prison Department's AIDS Advisory Committee to establish the facts on drug use and sexual intercourse in gaols was vetoed by the Home Office, with the backing of the Home Secretary, Douglas Hurd; ministry representatives will only admit 'off-the-record' that homosexual acts occur in prison. For political convenience, they prefer to suppress facts, although acknowledging the reality of homosexual acts and intravenous drug use in prison no more 'condones immorality' than the Home Office's annual publication of criminal statistics condones burglary. The only immorality is to facilitate the spread of HIV by denial or suppression of the truth. Of course the truth might be alarming, and excite agitation for compulsory HIV testing of prisoners, or the segregation of seropositive prisoners. 'Prisons are filling up with anonymous AIDS carriers ideally placed to spread the virus to all and sundry,' wrote a HIV+ inmate of Dartmoor Prison in 1988. 'This poses a direct threat to staff and prisoners that cannot be countered or neutralized in any way other than to separate carriers and screen all incoming prisoners. The Home Office wants AIDS carriers located in main wings, mixing freely with other men and women, and I thank God the prison officers have resisted this folly. If it had been carried out prisoners would have mutinied and carriers would have been murdered by panic-stricken mobs.' Prison officers protested that they were at risk from the blood of prisoners in concerted and universal denial that any of them could ever have sexual contacts with other men. The reaction of the Prison Officers' Association to the first case of an infected officer is to be dreaded: in their fury to deny the possibility of a sexual transfer they will insist that he was infected by blood, saliva, breath or judging by Brixton's arrangements a meal plate, and will insist on segregating HIV+ prisoners. Overall the slovenliness and suppressions which characterize the Home Office's response justify the speculation that Margaret Thatcher's Government is largely indifferent whether or not prisoners become infected with a life-threatening virus. 'Victorian values', which she espouses, included little concern with the physical health of prisoners, as Wilde discovered in Reading Gaol: and *The Times* in 1988 revealingly reported 'a senior Conservative MP' as declaring that 'Prisoners should be given condoms to control the spread of AIDS among the *general* population.' The spread of HIV among prisoners is by implication discounted: criminals don't matter.[41A]

The Government's dislike of independent research producing possibly uncongenial results can be traced to the top. A long-awaited government-funded survey of sexual practices, designed to measure the possible spread of HIV, was delayed and in September 1989 vetoed by the Prime Minister, Margaret Thatcher.

She felt squeamish about the reporting of its results, judged that the survey's value did not 'justify asking people intimate questions about their personal lives', and suspected that the public would be too shy or offended to participate. In fact the survey had already been test-piloted on 1,000 people, with the usual rate of response for social surveys – 70 per cent. The test offered some interesting indicators. Sixty-four per cent said that foreigners carrying the virus should be banned from entering Britain, and one in six believed that employers should have the right to dismiss infected employees. The majority wanted HIV + people to carry identity cards, and supported universal testing. Nearly half of respondents agreed that people with AIDS had only themselves to blame. Eighty per cent of people knew that condoms reduced the risk of HIV infection, but 59% of male respondents said they never used them. The average number of times that respondents copulated was 1.51 times weekly, although the frequency of partners and age of earliest sexual activity was subject to wide variations. The meaning of these results, and their implications for policy-making, were obscured by Thatcher's hostility to social research, which so often comes to refute her prejudices. While happy to have adulterers in her Cabinet, her party base is strongest among the kind of Tories who prefer to deny the realities of AIDS. Many of her supporters believe that people with HIV are culpable. For people of such a disposition a sex survey seemed a waste of money, spent on undeserving people. 'The Prime Minister's decision means that more people will die of AIDS,' the *Sunday Correspondent* concluded in an editorial. 'They will pay a high price for the prejudices of some elements in the Conservative Party – and of the Prime Minister.'[41B]

The Advisory Council on the Misuse of Drugs (mentioned previously) also recommended measures (such as needle exchange schemes) to forestall intravenous drug users from becoming conduits of disease into the general population. Their suggestions received little support and no funding from the Government. Fifty per cent of intravenous drug users in Edinburgh in 1988 were HIV+, a proportion as high as that in New York. A responsible estimate suggested that 1% of all men in Edinburgh aged between 15 and 44 were HIV+. The city had twice the infection rate of London: elsewhere in Scotland, Dundee had an equal prevalence of HIV to parts of London, and in Glasgow it was higher. Edinburgh's high incidence occurred because a police crack-down in 1983–4 on drug-taking coincided with the initial spread of HIV and resulted in an acute shortage of syringes, which was perpetuated by physicians and pharmacists who feared prosecution under Scottish common law for 'reckless conduct' if they supplied users with new ones. Facilities for addicts were pitiful and the official attitude to addicts was rigidly punitive. Clean syringes were hard to obtain, psychiatric help almost non-existent and there was hostility to prescribing controlled amounts of drugs to addicts as a means of gradually helping them to achieve abstinence. In Glasgow an experimental needle exchange clinic which was opened in 1987 proved a failure after local residents set up a picket and threatened to photograph visitors, thus frightening addicts away. Yet government ministers were loath to provide free syringes, free condoms or controlled drug supplies lest such pragmatism provoked its backbenchers to attack them as 'soft'. The Health Secretary John Moore lacked the courage to withstand backbench grumbling in order to confront the problem imaginatively, with results which are beginning to prove disastrous.[42]

Apart from this orchestrated rejection of drug users, there was also a wider backlash against homosexuals. In 1987, 24% of 'young readers' of the *Sunday Mirror* agreed with the newspaper's proposition that 'gays deserve AIDS', and a *News of the World* survey suggested that 56% out of 12,000 respondents believed that 'AIDS carriers should be sterilized and given treatment to curb their sexual appetite', with 51% in favour of recriminalization of homosexuality. Amongst respondents, 70.9% wanted people with AIDS to be isolated in hospital, 24.5% wanted them isolated in camps and 4.6% on islands. According to a Gallup Poll for the *Sunday Telegraph* published in 1988, 62 per cent of people said that homosexual acts were 'wrong', 15 per cent felt that they were 'right' and 17 per cent volunteered that 'it depends.' Men were more hostile than women. A poll conducted for London Weekend Television in January 1988 showed that only 48% of those questioned thought that consenting homosexual acts should be legal, compared with 61% recorded by a poll in March 1985. Forty-three per cent in 1988 thought such relations should be illegal, as against 27% in 1985. Sixty-eight per cent believed that homosexuals should not display affection in public.[43]

Gay men were implicated in every sort of sexual deviance. Peregrine Worsthorne, editorializing in the *Sunday Telegraph* in 1988 about child incest in Cleveland, seemed to believe that the problem had been inspired by 'hedonistic' homosexuals:

> A few years ago homosexuality was regarded with scarcely less disgust than is child abuse today. Respectable people recoiled with horror at the thought of men doing what they do to each other. How can sentient beings do such things? Only to be told by the progressives to stop being narrow-minded prudes.
>
> Now that society has stopped being narrow-minded, pretty well anything goes in the homosexual world – some of it so disgusting as to be quite indescribable. Is it any wonder that those tempted to sexual abuse of children have begun to feel that if there really is to be a free-for-all, they, too, should be part of the all?

Worsthorne was wrestling with a paradox whose importance he misunderstood. In the years immediately before the outburst of publicity about the sexual abuse of children in Cleveland, it had been stressed that HIV was easily transmissible in acts of buggery: insistently and repetitively, buggery had been depicted as the dangerous and specialized vice of an exclusive type, the male homosexual. Yet the revelations from Cleveland in 1987–8 made it all too clear that heterosexual males practise buggery, and that the younger the child, the less its gender matters to the abuser. In other words, the stereotyping so sedulously fostered around HIV had once again proved inaccurate: buggery was not a separate and extreme act which was the preserve of male homosexuals, but part of a continuous strand of fantasy and desire (in which the sex of the person fucked was often a matter of indifference) encompassing the conventionally benign figures of Father, Uncle and Grandfather, the heterosexual villains of Cleveland. The overturning of the buggery stereotype left people feeling threatened and helpless: the predictable response was to try to reinstate the myth, to insist more than ever on the culpability of gay men, whose attractiveness as scapegoats was enhanced precisely because they were so irrelevant to what happened in Cleveland.[44]

The dual standards of the legal system meanwhile became more obtrusive. A woman social worker gave a Christmas party in 1985 at which she enjoyed sexual acts ('gross indecency') with two youths aged 15 and 16 in her care, for which she was tried at a magistrates court and given a suspended sentence of six months. After her arrest she 'sang very loudly to the police' about a male social worker who had also attended the party. He was sentenced at Mold Crown Court by Sir William Mars-Jones to a prison sentence of three years and three months for 'gross indecency' at the party with a consenting sixteen-year-old man. The courts began to use binding-over orders to punish homosexuals who had not been found guilty of any criminal offence. In one case two men were charged with insulting behaviour after publicly kissing. Despite being acquitted of the criminal charge, they were bound over by the court to keep the peace for eighteen months. One can only conclude that although found not guilty of crime, they were found guilty of being gay. It was increasingly reported that police were charging men suspected of gross indecency or soliciting under local by-laws or under the Public Order Act of 1986 rather than under the appropriate sections of the Sexual Offences Act. This prevented the possibility of a jury trial.[45]

Whereas in some cultures a cuckolded husband is assured of judicial sympathy if he kills his wife's lover in a rage, amongst the British it is a man who has been homosexually propositioned who expects leniency when he is tried for murder. A young Englishman accused of having beaten a Spanish taxi driver to death in 1987 explained, 'the bloke touched me up and I must have gone spare' – an explanation which *News of the World* readers were expected to find comprehensive. When Neil Anderson made a pass at his former employee Roger Pellicci, the latter responded by hitting his head with a telephone answering machine, then he beat the 'body repeatedly with a stick and poured inflammable liquid over it to make it look like a homosexual killing' – howsoever that can be identified. Sentencing Pellicci in 1986 to five years' imprisonment, the judge accepted the defence plea that he had 'long suffered from homosexual panic' rendering him 'grossly over-reactive to any form of homosexual approach'. One wonders what sympathy a judge would feel for a gay man or woman who entered a defence of 'heterosexual panic' at a murder trial. Given such attitudes it is not surprising that a Coventry youth, who decided that he had caught AIDS after drinking from the same bottle as a gay man, whom he then punched to death, was sentenced to an imprison-ment of only three months.[46]

Class prejudice has permeated the British reaction to HIV. Characteristically when Mombasa and Malindi were put out of bounds to British soldiers in Kenya lest they consort with HIV+ prostitutes, the official interdiction was not extended to officers. The restrictions which are deemed acceptable as regards the working class are not applied to the upper middle class. AIDS has enabled Conservatives such as the *Sunday Telegraph*'s editor, Worsthorne, to voice the attitudes of the Victorian pleasure-haters who were fearful of working-class sexuality. Like a vigilante for those nineteenth-century societies for suppressing the vices of persons with low incomes mocked by the Revd Sydney Smith, Worsthorne has railed against the poor enjoying the same pleasures as the rich. 'We are living today with the trickle-down consequences of the permissive society,' he warned in 1988.

> Originally only the better-off and better-educated sections of society were affected . . . Twenty years later, however, *Joy of Sex* goings-on have gone down-market to the yobbo elements of society whose whole approach is a great deal more orgiastic . . . sexual licence has been democratized, and what was possibly just tolerable . . . when confined to a small, sophisticated clique of well-heeled liberated progressives becomes a national scan-dal when adopted by the poor and ignorant.

> The rot set in at the top and can only be eradicated by changed attitudes at the top . . . sexual drives need to be repressed in the interest of civilization . . . What is needed is a general convention of restraint, supported by social sanctions more than by law, with which adulterers, say, as well as child abusers, are required to conform.[47]

Lord Halsbury, who led opposition to the Arran Bill of 1977 to reduce the age of male homosexual consent to 18, was equally prominent in the 1980s. A few Labour-controlled municipal authorities inaugurated the provision of services specifically for gay men and women, or instituted policies to provide accurate information about homosexuality for schoolchildren. One or two of their publications were crass, but some of the books said to be available from the London boroughs of Lambeth and Hackney were figments of the imagination of journalists or local politicians, and the contents of other publications were misrepresented by equally inventive outsiders. One particular book – *Jenny lives with Eric and Martin*, which told the story of a child living with her father and his male lover – was made the focus of particular obloquy although it was never put before a pupil or used in a London schoolroom. Its offence was to publicize a reality which many people have an urgent need to deny: that sexual desire is not a matter of antitheses but of a wide and continuous spectrum of heterosexual and homosexual wishes, that children unexceptionally, as a matter of fact, have parents who are bisexual by instinct if not always in acts. Huge sums were said to have been squandered on perverts. In fact two of the most criticized boroughs, Camden and Haringey, had total annual budgets in 1987–8 of £138 million and £204 million respectively, of which the lesbian/gay budgets accounted for 0.096 per cent and 0.06 per cent, that is £133,000 and £127,000. This expenditure on cultural and counselling services, and discouragement of school bigotry, seemed preferable to Councillor Brownhill of Staffordshire's suggestion (mentioned previously) to 'gas queers'. The campaign in Haringey was led by a Conservative councillor and parliamentary candidate, Peter Murphy, who believed that all homosexual acts, including those between women, involved sodomy. When challenged on his statement that Judaism took its teaching on homosexuality from the Catholic Church, he replied, 'I'm not an intellectual', and when asked by a journalist to explain how a natural, God-given urge to heterosexuality could be corrupted by schoolteachers saying that homosexuality was acceptable, he responded, 'I suggest you write an article portraying me as a right-wing fascist.'[48]

Halsbury introduced a bill in December 1986 to prevent local authorities from giving financial or other assistance to anyone for the purpose of publishing or promoting 'homosexuality as a pretended family relationship' or for the purpose of teaching such acceptability in a maintained school. Under the original proposals even the provision of local authority buildings for a guest speaker was forbidden. It was an extraordinary measure since its supporters only attacked publications recommended by the Inner London Education Authority; there were no complaints about local authorities in Wales or Scotland, and almost none outside

London. Originally the Government recognized the absurdity of allowing metropolitan habits to determine legislation for the whole nation and rejected Halsbury's Bill as 'unnecessary'; but later, after an abrupt reversal, its germ was incorporated into the Local Government Act of 1988 (in a clause whose number changed so often that for convenience it will be called the Halsbury Clause in this book). As amended by the Government in the final enactment, Halsbury's Clause stated that a local authority shall not '(a) intentionally promote homosexuality or publish material with the intention of promoting homosexuality, (b) promote the teaching in any maintained school of the acceptability of homosexuality as a pretended family relationship'. An amendment stating that the Clause should not 'prohibit the doing of anything for the purpose of discouraging discrimination against any homosexual person, and designed to protect the civil rights of any such person' was defeated, as was a similar amendment on the provision of counselling, both at the instigation of a government whip. The American equivalent of this proposal was Senator Jesse Helms' Amendment to a Labor, Health and Human Services and Education Bill of 1987 prohibiting the use of US government funds 'to provide AIDS education, information or prevention materials and activities that promote, encourage or condone homosexual sexual activities or the intravenous use of illegal drugs'.[49]

During adolescence Halsbury himself had been lectured by parents and schoolmasters on the dangers of 'pubertal curiosity' and homosexuality. 'As an older boy,' he recalled in 1977, 'I was expected to collaborate with my headmaster and housemaster in discouraging it wherever I could.' He had been 'always warned against it . . . because a habit once started may become a permanency and can only lead to unhappiness.' The subject remained a preoccupation, and Halsbury had collected 'files and files of it' by 1986, in which year he became President of the National Council for Christian Standards in Society. Lesbians were far less of a problem than male homosexuals, in his opinion:

> They do not molest little girls. They do not indulge in disgusting and unnatural practices like buggery. They are not wildly promiscuous and do not spread venereal

disease. It is part of the softening-up propaganda that lesbians and gays are nearly always referred to in that order. The relatively harmless lesbian leads on to the vicious gay . . . They will push us off the pavement if we give them a chance.

His preferred type of homosexual was segregated and self-hating. The 'best' letter which he received during the controversy over his Bill was from a man declaring 'how fed up I am with my fellow homosexuals', so Halsbury quoted. 'They have brought it upon themselves, their unpopularity . . . I cannot stand the sight of them. I wish they would keep themselves to themselves.'[50]

What sort of textbook might Halsbury and his supporters have found unobjectionable? Dr Jonathan Rodney's *Handbook of Sex Knowledge*, used in schools in the 1960s, declared that it was 'obvious that sexual love among persons of the same sex is a perversion because . . . such a practice cannot result in procreation'. Rodney implied that the social ostracism of homosexuals was necessary for public safety; unrestricted mixing would lead to self-discovery and the revelation of people's inherent bisexuality. 'The greatest *danger* in homosexuality lies in the introduction of normal people to it,' he fretted. 'An act which will produce nothing but disgust in a normal individual may quite easily become more acceptable, until the time arrives when the normal person by full acceptance of the abnormal act becomes a pervert too.' Few children will have noticed the grotesque inconsistency in Rodney's concept of normality, but most will have absorbed his message of repudiation and fear: don't try to understand yourself and keep away from queers.[51]

Halsbury's Bill was drafted by a Conservative lawyer, Lord Campbell of Alloway, who feared that 'positive images' of homosexuality 'involve a direct attack on heterosexual family life' by undermining 'paternalistic disciplines' and teaching children that heterosexual reproduction was 'a positive social mischief in an overpopulated world'. Books with 'contact addresses' for the young who wished to contact advisory organizations like the London Lesbian and Gay Switchboard were 'a lure to pervert the young', so Campbell approvingly quoted a police officer as saying. In fact these Switchboards, which young people can telephone for counselling, are not proselytizing organizations, but have given comfort and advice to the confused and isolated. The need they meet was indicated by a survey in 1983 of 400 homosexuals aged between 15 and 21, of whom 25% felt isolated, 21% had met verbal abuse, 20% had been beaten up, and 10% had been thrown out of their homes: yet the only example of 'promotion' which one indignant MP, Greenway, could provide, when challenged, from his own constituency was the homosexual 'incitement to children' of displaying the telephone number of the Lesbian and Gay Switchboard on notice-boards. Halsbury, Campbell and their supporters used fears of contagion as a way to put their assertions beyond dispute. Corruption fantasies about homosexuality described in previous chapters were transformed into contagion theories of AIDS. To attribute danger to an act is the quickest way to stop people thinking clearly. Halsbury began by talking of male homosexuality 'corrupting' children and 'ultimately ... our society itself'. 'Lesbians are no danger,' said his supporter Longford, but male homosexuals were. Lord Fitt had 'absolutely no doubt that a significant number of present AIDS carriers ... were given positive education in homosexuality when they were at school'. AIDS indeed, as the government spokesman Skelmersdale said, was 'Banquo's ghost haunting this debate', and while not blaming his political opponents for disseminating AIDS, he urged them 'to distance themselves in the public mind from charges of encouraging the spread of the disease'. So far as the Government was concerned, 'insiduous propaganda for homosexuality' was entirely 'dangerous'.[52]

The recrudescence of such vicious nonsense would have been impossible without HIV. Inside and outside Parliament HIV was the pretext for the Halsbury campaign. Under the headline LABOUR'S CASH AIDS THE NEW BLACK DEATH, Lord Wyatt of Weeford asserted with almost total inaccuracy in the *News of the World*,

> The start of AIDS was homosexual love-making.
> Promiscuous women are vulnerable, making love to promiscuous bisexuals.
> Then they pass AIDS on to normal men.
> Yet some Labour councils encourage AIDS with grants to homosexual centres ... They also encourage children to experiment with sex.

This is murder.

This identification of the AIDS contagion with the contagion of homosexuality was made repeatedly and aggressively. 'It is not the gay way of life that bothers reasonable people,' wrote Professor John Vincent, 'it is the gay way of death.' Some Conservative politicians revelled in this apprehension. 'The desperate disease of AIDS starts with and comes mainly from homosexuals,' declared Dame Jill Knight when introducing the Halsbury Bill against 'iniquitous corruption of children' to the House of Commons in 1987, 'yet some of that which is being taught to children in our schools would undoubtedly lead to a great spread of AIDS.' She assented to the view that 'homosexuality means AIDS and that AIDS means homosexuality'. Other MPs agreed. 'Eighty-nine per cent of the people who have *promoted* the disease of AIDS have been homosexual,' wrote a government minister, Angela Rumbold, who believed that one of the principal ways of transmitting HIV was via saliva. 'I have recently been told that a London borough has decreed that each of its schools must have at least one homosexual teacher,' reported a retired microbiologist who still believed in 1988 that HIV was transmissible by non-sexual and non-blood methods. 'If this is true, it means that a most interesting epidemiological experiment is already under way.'[53]

Even cursory thought will show that the effect, if any, of the Halsbury Clause will be further to facilitate the spread of HIV. The burden of the Clause – especially as its supporters rejected amendments which were intended to discourage discrimination against homosexuals and to facilitate counselling at school age – was to leave teenage lesbians and gay youths more isolated, anxious and exposed. It sent the message that their sexuality was deprecated and that violence against their persons was socially legitimized. With the spread of HIV every young person beginning an active sexual life (whether with the same or the opposite sex) needs to do so carefully and soberly, measuring risks and avoiding unsafe practices; but a homoerotically inclined young man who has seen little but physical and verbal violence against homosexuality, who has been reared in an environment where positive images of it are prohibited by the Government, will be in the worst possible state to avoid HIV. His sexual feelings for other men will have been bottled up for years, he will be tense and confused, isolated and inexperienced, and when he finally picks up another man, he will be probably in a drunken whirl, angry and reckless, certainly in the worst possible state to remember safe sex or to avoid HIV infection.

Homosexuality means having a propensity for sexual relations with people of one's own sex. One cannot 'promote' (to use Halsbury's word) a propensity. The concept of promotion, if it had any meaning, meant persuading people to become homosexuals. 'It is an absurd idea that one can go into a classroom, to a meeting, or on a holiday course,' as Lord Falkland said in debate in 1988, 'and that someone can make attractive the idea that one can change the drift of one's own sexuality.' Resolutely ignoring Wolfenden's conclusion that teenage seduction was a negligible factor in producing homosexuality, Halsbury's supporters, like Lord Ingleby ('Homosexuality clearly is not what God intended for human beings'), deplored 'public money' being 'used to indoctrinate children'. Indeed many of Halsbury's followers seemed sympathetic to his grandfather's wish that mention of homosexuality should be stopped. Although male consensual homosexuality had been decriminalized, 'that does not mean', as the government minister Skelmersdale said, 'that it should be publicized'.[54]

Supporters of the Halsbury Clause claimed that homosexual tastes were acquired by seduction in youth. If this was believed, why was the law not applied to private schools and why do Conservatives confine their sons in boarding schools where 'pubertal curiosity' shows so many of them the pleasures of youthful homosexuality? Halsbury had already sent his son Tiverton to board at Stowe, founded by an inspirational but homosexual headmaster, J. F. Roxburgh. Why did so many of the peers who voted for the Clause risk sending their sons to boarding-schools like Eton? Because they regarded adolescent homosexuality as 'only a phase', which is discarded by upper middle-class young men when they attain public responsibilities. Networks of male loyalty and affection are reproduced in confined all-male institutions like the Church, Army and clubs, but open discussion of homosexuality in state schools is construed as threatening because it makes all sexual behaviour more open and more democratic. Throughout the Halsbury debates it was *male* homosexuality which excited fears: the fear that heterosexuality has such a frail hold that a teacher, stumbling through a sex education class, might unseat it altogether; the fear that the family is so fragile that it will be destroyed by homosexuals who refuse to live in it or bisexuals who 'pretend' to live in it; the fear that without laws forbidding public expression of homosexuality, humanity will be seduced into racial suicide. Among supporters of the Amendment, there was another influence at work. Many of the male journalists or politicians who were keenest on persecution were misogynists, whose contempt for women was all too well attested to by their private dealings. Their hostility to everything 'passive' or female was displaced onto those men who could be caricatured as passive or feminine.[55]

The deluge of misinformation surrounding the Halsbury Clause transformed anxieties about HIV into anti-gay violence. Sham concern about what Lord Hailsham once called 'a proselytizing religion' aggravated and disguised vicious acts perpetrated by those who hated homosexuality. In the months to May 1988 when the Clause came into effect, 'queer-bashers' terrorized customers at the Vauxhall Tavern, a gay man was stabbed as he waited for a bus at King's Cross, shots were fired into the crowded London Apprentice pub, there was an attempt to bomb a lesbian and gay discothèque at Leeds and a hall at Milton Keynes was set ablaze by arsonists shortly before a meeting to oppose the Clause was to take place. In December 1987 an arson attack on the offices of the newspaper *Capital Gay* caused damage worth £20,000. Its editor telephoned Dame Jill Knight inviting her to visit the office and see the damage. Before hanging up she said, 'I am not doing any damage whatsoever. Children need protecting. I will not have the perversion of children.' When this arson attack was raised in the House of Commons in a debate on the Halsbury Clause, a Tory MP was understood to shout 'quite right': Dame Elaine Kellett-Bowman affirmed that 'intolerance of evil should grow.' In the same week a poisonous gas canister was thrown into a gay bar at Chatham resulting in the hospitalization of forty people. Reading Matters bookshop in Haringey (which was the subject of several inaccurate or untruthful newspaper reports) received threats that it would be bombed or burned, or its staff killed: when Haringey Tory councillors tabled a motion for the council to suspend its grant to the 'homosexual' shop, there were chants of 'burn it down' from the gallery. The home of a drag performer, Terry

Latour, was firebombed after he had received anonymous telephone abuse as a 'queer bastard'. Strathclyde Regional Council threatened to withdraw grants to students unions unless they undertook to disband lesbian/gay societies and stop campaigning for homosexual equality. East Sussex Education Authority banned a Home Office-funded information pack about voluntary organizations because the London Lesbian and Gay Centre was among the 100 organizations listed. Manchester University Press withdrew from its agreement to publish a collection of essays entitled *Positively Gay*, edited by two academics, because the university wanted to avoid offering 'a hostage to fortune' to the 'Far Right'. The Opera House at Glyndebourne was asked in 1989 to withdraw Britten's *Death in Venice* from school peformances because it might contravene the clause.[56]

Media coverage of this controversy was skewed. It concentrated on 'respectable' issues such as whether Shakespeare's sonnets or the novellas of Ronald Firbank would be excluded from public libraries under the legislation, but never questioned the assumptions about corruption and public safety which characterized the supporters of Halsbury and Knight. With the exception of actors and Arts Council peers fretting about Shakespeare and Firbank, opponents of the new law were represented as wild and outrageous, as people dwelling far beyond the margins of respectability. Thus one should compare the descriptions of four gay actors who interrupted a House of Commons debate on the Halsbury Clause in 1987 ('These homosexuals should take their handbags and lipstick elsewhere,' said a Tory MP, Terry Dicks, 'God help any of them who taught such filth to my grandchild') with the sympathetic reporting of the cheers and claps with which in the same week residents of Swanage greeted the defeat in the House of Lords of a bill permitting the development of a marina on its seafront. Though there was no intrinsic difference between the interruptions, the actors were vilified as effeminate deviants and the Swanage ratepayers admired as pillars of conformity.[57]

Aside from the evidence of the Halsbury controversy, the identification or marginalization of homosexuality has become an increasingly prominent theme in British political life since the identification of HIV. It has been used to stigmatize and isolate opponents of government policy, especially after a Cabinet committee decided that, as counter-propaganda against the women's peace camp at Greenham protesting against the siting in Britain of US Cruise missiles, the dissidents should be depicted in off-the-record government press briefings as dangerously contagious: dirty, smelly lesbians, who were dangerous because their unhygienic living conditions threatened public health, their sexuality threatened national morality and their pacifism threatened national security. From the moment of its election in 1979 the Conservative Government emphasized the limits of the powers of government and proclaimed individual freedom. Margaret Thatcher spoke of a 'disease' of crime: 'we must strengthen the family,' she told a Conservative Women's Conference, or else Britain would face 'social problems which no government could possibly cure – or perhaps even cope with.' But her Government faced a dilemma: it could not easily indict a society which had been in its charge for years without discrediting its own policies. Threats to social order therefore had to be displaced outside its control, and responsibility for disintegration had to be projected onto other individuals and institutions. In this case, the Church of England was selected for blame. The Conservative party launched a 'whispering campaign' against the Archbishop of Canterbury founded on two grievances: his comments at the remembrance service for the dead of the Falklands War in 1982, which were insufficiently jubilant, and the Church of England's report on urban deprivation, *Faith in the City*, which was deemed hostile to government policies. The Chief Rabbi, Sir Immanuel Jakobovits, was given a barony in 1988 because 'his uncompromising God-helps-those-who-help-themselves approach to Jewish religion greatly impresses Mrs Thatcher, who finds it a refreshing change from . . . the often wimpish Anglican approach of the Archbishop of Canterbury.' Jakobovits wrote a free-market counterblast to *Faith in the City* entitled *From Doom to Hope* which was regarded in Downing Street as 'a symphony of commonsense'. On the subject of coition, the rabbi believed that until the public health campaign of 1986–7 there were 'homes in which the concept of pre-marital sex was unknown' and he also opined that homosexuality should be brought back into the penal code 'as blasphemy still is'. Homosexuality resembled kleptomania, a disease whose consequences were not more tolerable because of their aetiology. 'To argue from natural predisposition is a slippery slope which would lead to the collapse of the entire moral order, which is founded on the recognition of the freedom to choose good or evil.'⁵⁸

Douglas Hurd, the Home Secretary, wanted both to deter the clergy from criticizing government policies and to enlist them in creating a 'social cohesion' to remedy the social divisiveness of some government policies. Secular Anglicanism was objectionable if it fretted about love and justice instead of belauding patriotism, discipline and family order. Some politicians posed as the guardians of national morals in order to give a moral base to expedient self-interest. It was against this background that the issue of homosexual clergy became a weapon in a battle for political control in which the real targets were not gay vicars but the bench of bishops. In February 1988, for example, Hurd went into 'the lion's den', as the *Daily Express* described the General Synod of the Church of England, and 'left the clerics in no doubt that he feels they are failing Britain'. In Hurd's own words, there were 'limits to the extent in which the Church should become immersed in a political agenda'. What was needed was for 'Church and State to rebuild the moral standards and values' which would ensure 'a cohesive and united nation', he told the Synod. 'What society most desperately needs from the Churches today is a clear, definite and repeated statement on personal morality.' Yet government ministers often fornicate or exchange old marriage partners for new. Hurd, who divorced his first wife and married his secretary in 1982, was perhaps not thinking of God's commandment against adultery, nor of the vows of lifelong fidelity made before God, when he railed against a nation oblivious to biblical teaching on personal morality, just as the MPs who inveighed most shrilly against public obscenity in a debate of 1986 were invariably men who within the previous few years had attracted celebrity as adulterers.⁵⁹

It was against this background that in November 1987 an Essex clergyman, A. R. Higton, proposed a motion to the General Synod declaring that fornication, adultery and homosexual practices were sinful in all circumstances and that Christian leaders should be exemplary in their behaviour as a condition of being appointed to or remaining in office. Tolerance of homosexual acts he believed 'undermined the central message of the Christian faith . . . that sin is sin'. It was no defence that some 'homosexuals are nice people . . since when was being nicely perverted better than being simply perverted?' Homosexuality was physically and

PULPIT POOFS CAN STAY

Runcie . . . defended gays

Church votes not to kick them out

GAYS PEDDLE KINKY BOOKS IN A CHURCH!

By ANNETTE WITHERIDGE

A SICKENING trade in gay sex and child porn books has been uncovered . . .in a church!

These headlines in the *Sun* and the *News of the World* which appeared during the furore about homosexuality and Anglicanism in 1987 were scarcely more sensational than those in the supposedly better quality newspapers.

psychologically 'disturbing', as AIDS showed. The Synod tried to evade the controversy raised by Higton (which included an outburst of tabloid newspaper revelations about gay vicars, or 'pulpit poofs' as the *Sun* called them – see left) by passing a compromise resolution which declared that homosexuality 'falls short' of the 'Christian ideal', but which did not declare it evil or sinful.[60]

Many bishops in their public statements began rejecting what they did or said in private. Bishops who had acted with charity to homosexual clergy proclaimed their disinclination to appoint homosexuals in their dioceses. The Bishop of Ripon led the way in declaring that he would not ordain practising homosexuals, thereby causing much quiet sadness among many Yorkshire Christians, and a swell of triumph among vindictive and selective moralists. Thus the lay organizer at a Sowerby church scapegoated gay clergy as one of the abrogations of traditional practice which have occasioned low attendance at church:

> homosexual clergy spells the sordid cliché of queer curates and choirboys. Homosexuality is abhorred by scripture and disowned by zoology, says George. 'It doesn't exist in any other animal'. (He has clearly never passed a field of bullocks). What does he feel about a non-practising gay? 'Non-practising?' he bellows: 'What does that mean?' And his wife interjects: 'It's always there underneath and you never know what might happen'. George says he would also 'hound' gays out of the teaching profession.[61]

Following the Higton debate, the hierarchy of the Church of England decided to persecute homosexual clergymen. 'For so long the Church has been accused of liberal temporizing on moral issues, but now, at last, it is to take a stand – or rather take a stick to beat those who are most vulnerable,' wrote the Revd Peter Mullen of Yorkshire. 'I know five priests who are practising homosexuals. It is no coincidence that they are the tenderest, most compassionately effective priests I have ever met. None of them is a pederast, seducer or child-abuser . . . they feel despised and rejected by the Church which they have served sacrificially for (in some cases) thirty years and more.' The fuss about gay vicars within the Anglican Church gave the impression that sexual misdemeanour was the only sin.

What of covetousness, meanness of spirit, jealousy or pride? When did the Archbishop of Canterbury last discipline a cleric for covetousness, or when was a member last expelled from the Mother's Union for jealousy or backbiting, or a bishop unfrocked for pride? 'Do not judge a fornicator if you are chaste,' as a medieval abbot advised, 'for if you do, you too are violating the law as much as he is. For He who said thou shalt not fornicate also said thou shalt not judge.' Anglican luminaries pretended to distinguish between possession of a homosexual temperament and homosexual acts. This odd distinction supposes that God created people whose lives were to require perpetual involuntary sacrifice and whose sexual inclinations were to remain forever unfulfilled. In every other aspect of modern theology, churchmen insist that it is a grave error to separate orientation from practice. Just as Christianity has abandoned dietary laws, it should shed its adhesion to exclusive views of human sexuality, views which originated in societies where the frail existence of semi-nomadic people required that sexual energy should not be dissipated in acts that did not potentially add to the population.[62]

HIV also had its malign influence on broadcasting. The regular depiction of adultery or fornication on television was denounced by one advertising executive advising on a health education campaign about AIDS. 'Counselling sexual restraint in these circumstances is like trying to extol celibacy in a whorehouse.' Television 'must stop selling "real life"' and 'start portraying life the way it should be'.[63] In other words, reality must be repudiated, under the pretext of AIDS, so that a false idealization of existence can be pretended and enforced. Instead of carnality, the suggestion is that people should be encouraged to put their energy and imagination into work, into the accumulation of money and possessions, into safe objects rather than into desires and affections which complicate, endanger and enrich human existence.

Censorship has tightened. In 1985 Gay's the Word bookshop in Bloomsbury was prosecuted under Customs and Excise legislation dating from 1876, covering not only medical books on HIV and mild erotica, but also books by Jean Genet, Kate Millett, Jean-Paul Sartre, Edmund White, Tennessee Williams and Oscar Wilde. The charges were only abandoned in 1986 after a pertinacious defence campaign which stressed that the prosecution contravened European Economic Community statutes. The only common factor to the books which were seized was their reference to homosexuality. Customs officers regarded the subject as intrinsically indecent and depiction of male nudity as inherently offensive. While there has been little official sympathy for the attempts since 1986 by Clare Short, MP (dubbed 'Crazy Clare' by the *Sun* newspaper) to introduce a bill 'to make illegal the display of pictures of naked or partially naked women in sexually provocative poses in newspapers', there has been an eruption in favour of Winston Churchill's attempt in the same year to impose new obscenity laws on television after the broadcasting of Derek Jarman's film *Sebastiane*, an exasperatingly slow reverie which attempted to demystify the male body by its repetitive photography of penises. Controls on male sexual imagery and texts have increased. There was obsessive concern among Churchill's supporters about the anus, although the Bill was packaged as above all concerned with protecting children from corruption. A play televized at 11.30 p.m. entitled *Two of Us*, depicting the homosexual affinity between two teenage boys, was only broadcast after the excision of a scene in which they kissed (not very erotically), and led a Tory MP, Harry Greenway, to protest that the BBC was 'implanting ideas into the minds of the young and vulnerable with the possibility of interesting them in a perverted lifestyle'. (As a matter of fact although perhaps 10% of the population is lesbian or gay, a survey of 1986 showed that 1.85% of television time and 0.9% of wireless broadcasting depicted gay or lesbian people.)[64]

New legislation on private videos, or the proposed fiscal controls over satellite television, provide other examples of an impetus to codify and regulate the distribution of all sexual images. The notion accepted by Wolfenden, and enjoyed by the British in the 1960s, that what one thought and did in one's own home was not a matter for state intervention, it being eroded. Privacy is being abandoned. Just as the private doings of vicars are suddenly to be scrutinized and judged, so are those of all other citizens seemingly. Britain is experiencing a revival of the subsuming principle of Lord Campbell's Obscenity Act of 1857: the restriction of erotic images and discouragement of private fantasies will tend to develop public homogenity (a formula which Hurd calls 'social adhesion'). These restrictions rely on contagion fears. Erotic images are equated with 'sick' pornography, or are said to be a danger as they incite people to sex which is no longer 'safe'.

The Conservative party's election manifesto of 1987 declared that there was 'deep public concern over the display of sex and violence on television', and promised 'stronger and more effective arrangements to reflect that concern'. Hurd, as Home Secretary, 'summoned' the heads of British television to a meeting in September at which they agreed to restrict the import of 'sexually explicit' US programmes. Yet the annual Independent Broadcasting Association survey on *Attitudes to Broadcasting* published in the same year found that under 20% of viewers spontaneously mentioned violence as a recent source of offence to them on television, and those complaining that there was 'too much sex' were about as numerous as those grousing that there were 'too many old films'. Nevertheless in 1988 the Government appointed a new Broadcasting Standards Council chaired by Lord Rees-Mogg, who had recently distinguished himself as a critic of the conditional morality of 'the condoms campaign' about AIDS. Public broadcasting in Britain is set to become a bromide.[65]

What are the meanings and lessons of all this? This book has examined human unkindness and fears of contagion across five centuries. It has shown the ways that people behave when they are worried that their world is going to disintegrate. It has offered a historical exploration of the primitive impulses to blame, attack and exclude others which relentlessly recur. It has recalled some of the ways in which our culture has persistently treated sex as dangerous and dirty. I have discussed fear: not only fear of sex, but fear of arcane loyalties and of subversive desires which will destroy society; of national disintegration as well as of personal disintegration. Ostracism and bullying have been two themes. The survival of the nation and of family life have sometimes only seemed guaranteed by the brutalizing of scapegoats.

What else have preceding chapters suggested? That it is common to want to punish the ill; that the Church of England is becoming paralysingly fretful about what Robert Graves called strife below the hipbone; that revulsions about the anus have less to do with the pleasure or pain of buggery than with the fears of decay and mortality which it evokes. Since the stereotyping of the molly began in the eighteenth century, there has been an extraordinary regime of self-deception and denial among men. Enclosed groups like the Army or police force have had to maintain ridiculous pretences about the nature of male mentorship and gender. Throughout British society there have been pressures never to recognize or admit one's own feelings, to separate one's actions from one's emotions, to repudiate one's desires and to punish other people who seem to practise their own freely. Homosexuality has to be rendered recognizably extraordinary – invested with terrifying 'Otherness' – so as to help people forget or ignore the potential for it in themselves. 'Without gays, straights are not "straight",' as Simon Watney writes, which is why homosexuality is so emphatically depicted 'as either an *absence* or *excess* of manliness'.[66] It needs to be feared as a spreading scourge – a myth sustained by the pretence that the habit is the result of contamination during teenage seduction. People whose behaviour threatens to explode all these fantasies and self-inflicted untruths – bisexuals for example – seem particularly dangerous and have become special targets of abuse.

AIDS is not merely a vile syndrome which has occasioned physical and verbal attacks on scapegoats; it also provides a pretext to undermine personal privacy and to regulate an individual's imagination. Under the dizzying rush of contagion fears, people are discouraged from thinking for themselves, or from fulfilling their own wishes: such conduct is dubbed 'selfish', and perceived as a national peril. AIDS has created a retinue of fears. It has created counsels of expedient self-deception: thus fidelity enforced by the threat of illness poses as proof of true emotional commitment; desires are not only to remain unconsummated, but the reality of their existence is to be denied. In the cause of saving lives endangered by AIDS both the essence and variety of human life can be tragically denied. To fear sex is to fear our shared humanity.

> Some say the world will end in fire,
> Some say in ice.
> From what I've tasted of desire
> I hold with those who favour fire.
> But if it had to perish twice,
> I think I know enough of hate
> To say that for destruction ice
> Is also great
> And would suffice.

> ROBERT FROST

Select Bibliography

Select Bibliography

UNPUBLISHED

Bodleian Library, Oxford: papers of 2nd Baron Monk Bretton, J. S. Sandars.

British Library: Harleian manuscripts, and papers of Sir Henry Campbell-Bannerman, William Cole, 1st Viscount Cross, Sir Almeric FitzRoy, W. E. Gladstone, Sir Edward Walter Hamilton, Sir Robert Peel, 1st Marquess of Ripon, John Wilkes.

Churchill College, Cambridge: papers of 2nd Viscount Esher.

India Office Library: papers of 1st Viscount Cross, 1st Marquess Curzon of Kedleston, 1st Marquess of Dufferin and Ava, 9th Earl of Elgin and 13th Earl of Kincardine.

Mitchell Library, Sydney, New South Wales: papers of Dr G. E. Morrison.

Northern Ireland Record Office, Belfast: papers of 1st Marquess of Dufferin and Ava.

Public Record Office: papers of Cabinet Office, Directorate of Public Prosecutions, Home Office, Ministry of Health, Ministry of Information, War Office.

PUBLISHED (place of publication London unless otherwise stated)

This is neither a comprehensive list of relevant books and articles, nor even a list of those studies whereby knowledge upon the subject has lately been increased, but a selective guide to the main sources of this book and to the most suggestive further reading.

Acton, William, *Prostitution Considered in its Moral, Social and Sanitary Aspects in London and Other Large Cities: with Proposals for Mitigation and Prevention of its Attendant Evil.* 1857.

Altman, Dennis, *AIDS and the New Puritanism.* 1986.

Ballhatchet, Kenneth, *Race, Sex and Class under the Raj: Imperial Attitudes and Policies and their Critics 1793–1905*. 1980.

Boucé, P. G., *Sexuality in Eighteenth Century Britain*. Manchester, 1982.

Brandt, Allan M., *No Magic Bullet: a Social History of Venereal Disease in the United States since 1880*. New York and Oxford, 1985.

Bray, Alan, *Homosexuality in Renaissance England*. 1982.

Bristow, Edward, *Vice and Vigilance: Purity Movements in Britain since 1700*. Dublin, 1977.

Bristow, Edward, *Prostitution and Prejudice: The Jewish Fight against White Slavery 1870–1939*. Oxford, 1982.

Brown, Peter, *The Body and Society: Men, Women and Sexual Renunciation in Early Christianity*. 1989.

Cam, Joseph, *A Short Account of the Venereal Diseases*. 1719.

Carter, Erica & Watney, Simon, eds., *Taking Liberties: AIDS and Cultural Politics*. 1989.

Chamberlen, Paul, *The Second Part of the Practical Scheme Containing Directions for the Use of the Anodyne Necklace*. 1728.

Cleugh, James, *Secret Enemy*. 1954.

Clowes, William, *A Briefe and Neccessarie Treatise. Touching the Cure of Disease called Morbus Gallicus*. 1585.

Comfort, Alex, *The Anxiety Makers: Some Curious Preoccupations of the Medical Profession*. 1967.

Crimp, George, ed., *AIDS: Cultural Analysis and Cultural Activism*. Cambridge, Mass., 1988.

Croft-Cooke, Rupert, *Feasting with Panthers: a new consideration of some late Victorian writers*. 1967.

Croft-Cooke, Rupert, *The Verdict of You All*. 1955.

Crompton, Louis, *Byron and Greek Love: Homophobia in 19th-century England*. 1985.

Daley, Harry, *This Small Cloud*. 1987.

Dodd, William, *Rise, Progress and Present State of the Magdalen Hospital for the Reception of Penitent Prostitutes*. 1770.

Douglas, Mary, *Purity and Danger*. 1966.

Dreuilhe, Emmanuel, *Mortal Embrace: Living with AIDS*. 1989.

Fee, Elizabeth and Fox, Daniel, eds., *AIDS: the Burdens of History*. Berkeley, Calif., 1988.

Finnegan, Frances, *Poverty and Prostitution: a study of Victorian prostitutes in York*. Cambridge, 1979.

Gay, Peter, *The Bourgeois Experience: Victoria to Freud*:

vol. 1, *Education of the Senses*. Oxford and New York, 1984.

vol. 2 *The Tender Passion*. Oxford and New York, 1986.

Goodich, Michael, *The Unmentionable Vice: Homosexuality in the Later Medieval Period*. 1979.

Harrison, Brian, 'Underneath the Victorians', *Victorian Studies*, 10 (1966–7).

Harrison, Fraser, *The Dark Angel: Aspects of Victorian Sexuality*. 1977.

Harvey, Gideon, *Great Venus Unmasked, or a More Exact Discovery of the Venereal Evil or French Disease*. 1672.

Holloway, Robert, *Phoenix of Sodom, or the Vere Street Coterie . . . 1813*.

Hyde, Harford Montgomery, *The Other Love: An Historical and Contemporary Survey of Homosexuality in Britain*. 1970.

Johnson, Wendell Stacy, *Living in Sin: the Victorian Sexual Revolution*. Chicago, 1979.

Maccubin, Robert P., ed., *Unauthorised Sexual Behaviour during the Enlightenment*. 1985.

McHugh, Paul, *Prostitution and Victorian Social Reform*. 1980.

Mars-Jones, Adam, and White, Edmund, *The Darker Proof: Stories from a Crisis*. 1987.

Marten, John, *A Treatise of all the Degrees and Symptoms of the Venereal Disease in Both Sexes*. 1708.

Monette, Paul, *Borrowed Time*. 1988.

Morgan, Fidelis, *A Misogynists' Sourcebook*. 1989.

Mort, Frank, *Dangerous Sexualities: Medico-Moral Politics in England since 1830*. 1987.

Nicols, Beverley, *Father Figure*. 1972.

Pearsall, Ronald, *The Worm in the Bud: The World of Victorian Sexuality*. 1969.

Pearson, Michael, *The Age of Consent: Victorian Prostitution and its Enemies*. Newton Abbot, 1972.

'Pickles', *Queens*. 1984.

Power, Sir D'Arcy and Murray, K., eds., *A System of Syphilis*. 6 vols., Oxford, 1908–10.

Rees, Tudor and Usill, Harley V., eds., *They Stand Apart: a critical survey of homosexuality*. 1955.

Rosebury, Theodore, *Microbes and Morals*. New York, 1971.

Rossiaud, Jacques, *Medieval Prostitution*. Oxford, 1988.

Scott, Benjamin, *A State Iniquity; Its Rise; Extension and Overthrow*. 1890 (repr. New York, 1968).

Shilts, Randy, *And the Band Played On*. 1988.

Sigsworth, E. M. and Wyke, T. J., 'A Study of Victorian Prostitution and Venereal Disease', in Martha Vicinius, ed., *Suffer and Be Still: Women in the Victorian Age.* 1972.

Smith, F. B., 'Ethics and disease in the late nineteenth century: the Contagious Diseases Acts', *Historical Studies* [Australia], 15 (1971).

Smith, F. B., 'Labouchere's Amendment to the Criminal Law Amendment Bill', *Historical Studies* [Australia], 17 (1976).

Smith, Joan, *Misogynies.* 1989.

Soloway, Richard A., *Birth Control and the Population Question in England 1877–1930.* 1982.

Spinke, John, *Quackery Unmasked.* 1709.

Stone, Lawrence, *The Family, Sex and Marriage in England 1500–1800.* 1977.

Vass, Antony A., *AIDS – A Plague in Us.* St Ives, 1986.

Wagner, Peter, *Eros Revived: Erotica of the Enlightenment in England and America.* 1988.

Walkowitz, Judith, *Prostitution and Victorian Society.* Cambridge, 1980.

Watney, Simon, *Policing Desire: Pornography, AIDS and the Media.* 1987.

Weeks, Jeffrey, *Coming Out: Homosexual Politics in Britain, from the Nineteenth Century to the Present.* 1977.

Weeks, Jeffrey, *Sex, Politics and Society: the regulation of sexuality since 1800.* 1981.

Weeks, Jeffrey, *Sexuality and its Discontents: Meanings, Myths and Sexualities.* 1985.

Wildeblood, Peter, *Against the Law.* 1955.

Wynne-Finch, Heneage, *Fracastor: Syphilis or the French Disease.* 1935.

Young, Wayland, *Eros Denied: Studies in Exclusion.* 1964.

Notes

Notes

The notes first provide the sources of quotations used in the text in order of their use, followed by the citation of other sources for the paragraph, and sometimes concluding with the citation of yet other sources relevant to the substance of the paragraph.

Place of publication of books is London unless otherwise specified.

CHAPTER ONE

1 Panos Institute, *AIDS and the Third World* (1986); Thomas C. Quinn, Jonathan Mann *et al.*, 'AIDS in Africa: An Epidemiological Paradigm', *Science*, 234, 21 Nov. 1986, pp. 955–63; 'Joh's Condomania: "Condom vending machines could stop Australia being a great nation"', *New Australian Express* (London), 10 Sept. 1987; World Health Organization figures, quoted *Independent*, 7 June 1988.

2 For a suggestive book on drug users, see Marek Kohn, *Narcomania: on Heroin (1987)*. Another useful source on HIV is Dennis Altman, *AIDS and the New Puritanism* (1986).

3 Simon Watney, *Policing Desire: Pornography, AIDS and the Media* (1987), p. 3; Lord Dacre of Glanton in Hugh Lloyd-Jones, Valerie Pearl and Blair Worden eds., *History and Imagination* (1981), p. 12; the epigraph for this chapter is from ibid., pp. 358–9.

4 Sander L. Gilman, *Difference and Pathology: Stereotypes of Sexuality, Race and Madness* (1985), pp. 1–2, 18; Mary Douglas, *Purity and Danger* (1966), pp. 36–7; Percy Bysshe Shelley, 'The Revolt of Islam', VIII, iv, 2.

5 Logan Pearsall Smith, *Little Essays drawn from the writings of Santayana* (1920), p. 52; P. G. Boucé, 'Some sexual beliefs and myths in eighteenth-century Britain', in

P. G. Boucé ed., *Sexuality in Eighteenth Century Britain* (Manchester, 1982), p. 30; Lawrence Stone, *The Family, Sex and Marriage in England 1500–1800* (1977), p. 495; Peter Brown, *The Body and Society: Men, Women and Sexual Renunciation in Early Christianity* (1989), pp. 20–1; Mary Whitehouse, *Whatever happened to sex?* (1977), pp. 67–8.

6 Douglas, *Purity*, pp. 2–5, 113, 133.

7 Lord Sidney Godolphin Osborne, 'Immortal Sewerage', in Viscount Ingestre ed., *Meliora, or Better Times to Come* (1853), pp. 9, 11, 16–17. See also Arnold White ed., *The Letters of Sidney Godolphin Osborne* (1890), pp. ix–xxiv and *passim*.

8 Peter Gay, *Education of the Senses* (New York and Oxford, 1984), captions between pp. 182–3; Theodor Rosebury, *Microbes and Morals* (New York, 1971), pp. 168–9.

9 Harleian Ms. 7312, British Library, folios 143–4; Sir Malcolm Morris in *Lancet*, 28 June 1913; Sir Austen Chamberlain, quoted P. S. O'Connor, 'Venus and the Lonely Kiwi', *New Zealand Journal of History*, 1 (1967), p. 27; Lynda Lee-Potter in *Daily Mail*, 3 Dec. 1986.

10 Hugh Elliott, 'Venereal Prophylaxis', *Nineteenth Century*, 84 (1918), p. 175; 'Brave Angel Beverley Killed By Aids', *News of the World*, 6 Sept. 1987.

11 Christopher Chavasse, Bishop of Rochester, House of Lords debates,

4 Dec. 1957, 206, col. 797.

12 Douglas, *Purity*, pp. 35–40.

13 Edward Gibbon, *Decline and Fall of the Roman Empire*, 4, ch. 44; Howard Becker, *Outsiders* (Glencoe, Ill, 1964), p. 14.

14 Russell Barry, Bishop of Southwell, House of Lords debates, 19 May 1954, 187, cols. 751, 753; Eric Fuchs, *Desire and Love* (Cambridge, 1986), p. 203 (originally published at Geneva in 1979 as *Le Désir et la Tendresse*), quoted Roger Scruton, *Sexual Desire: a Philosphical Investigation*, (1986), p. 309; Brown, *Body and Society*, pp. 9–11.

15 Antony Vass, *AIDS: A Plague in Us* (St Ives, 1986), pp. 20, 29; William Nayler, 'Walking Time Bombs', *Medicine in Society*, 11/3 (1985), p. 9; *The Times*, 17 Jan. 1987.

16 House of Lords debates, 16 June 1966, 275, col. 158; Robert Rhodes James ed., *Chips, the Diaries of Sir Henry Channon* (1967), p. 23.

17 João Trevisan, *Perverts in Paradise* (1986), p. 9; Jeffrey Weeks, *Coming Out* (1977), p. 3; Michael Goodich, *The Unmentionable Vice: Homosexuality in the Later Medieval Period* (Santa Barbara, 1979); Louis Crompton, *Byron and Greek Love: Homophobia in 19th-Century England* (1985), p. 13; L. W. M. Kettle, *Salome's Last Veil* (1977), pp. 191–2.

18 Arthur N. Gilbert, 'Buggery and the British Navy 1700–1861', *Journal of Social Studies*, 10 (1976), p. 88, and 'Sexual Deviance and Disaster During the Napoleonic Wars', *Albion*, 9 (1977), p. 99; George Bataille, *Death and Sensuality: A Study of Eroticism and Taboo* (New York, 1962), p. 11; Robert Holloway, *Phoenix of Sodom* (1813), pp. 15–16; W. Sorley Brown, *The Genius of T. W. H. Crosland* (1928), pp. 286, 295; Arnold White, 'Efficiency and Vice', *English Review*, 22 (1916), p. 452.

19 Goodich, *Unmentionable Vice*, p. 82; Charles Churchill, 'The Times' (1764), lines 419, 555, in James Laver ed., *Works of Charles Churchill*, 2 (1933), pp. 419, 421;

Holloway, *Phoenix*, pp. 17, 29, 30, 42; T. P. O'Connor, House of Commons debates, 28 Feb. 1890, 341, cols 1588, 1593; Frederick MacQuisten, House of Commons debates, 4 Aug. 1921, 145, col. 1800.

20 William Acton, *Prostitution* (1968 edn), p. 64; Elaine Showalter, 'Syphilis, Sexuality and the Fiction of the Fin de Siècle', in Ruth Bernard Yeazell ed., *Sex, Politics and Science in the Nineteenth-Century Novel* (1986), p. 93; *Westminster Review*, 36 (1869), pp. 179–81, 186, 198, 201–2.

21 Showalter, 'Syphilis, Sexuality', pp. 90–1, 103.

22 *Lancet*, 6 Sept. 1930, p. 545; Osborne Morgan, House of Commons debates, 20 April 1883, 278, col. 784; St John Brodrick to George Curzon, 7 May 1883, Mss Eur F 111/9A; William Temple, Archbishop of Canterbury, quoted *British Journal of Venereal Diseases* (hereafter *BJVD*), 18 (1942), p. 86.

23 Beverley Nichols, *Father Figure* (1972), pp. 74–5.

CHAPTER TWO

1 James H. Jones, *Bad Blood: the Tuskegee Syphilis Experiment* (1981), p. 3.

2 R. R. Wilcox, 'Venereal Disease in the Bible', *BJVD*, 25 (1949), pp. 28–33.

3 E. W. Hirsch, 'A Historical Survey of Gonorrhoea', *Annals of Medical History* (hereafter *AMH*), 2 (1930), p. 416.

4 R. S. Morton, *Venereal Diseases* (1966), pp. 19–20; H. L. Wehrbein, 'Therapy in Gonorrhoea', *AMH*, 7 (1935), pp. 492–3.

5 J. Johnston Abraham in Heneage Wynne-Finch ed., *Fracastor: Syphilis or the French Disease* (1935), p. 8.

6 J. L. Miller, 'History of Syphilis', *AMH*, 2 (1930), p. 396; Iwan Bloch's history of syphilis in Sir D'Arcy Power and J. Keogh Murray eds., *A System of Syphilis*, 1 (1908), pp. 6–20 & *passim*; Owsei Temkin, 'Therapeutic Trends and the Treat-

ment of Syphilis before 1900', *Bulletin of the History of Medicine*, 29 (1955), pp. 309–16; J. Johnston Abraham, 'Some Account of the History of the Treatment of Syphilis', *BJVD*, 24 (1948), pp. 153–61; J. D. Rolleston, 'The Folklore of Venereal Disease', *BJVD*, 18 (1942), pp. 1–13.

7 Charles Henderson Melville, 'The History and Epidemiology of Syphilis in the More Important Armies', in Power and Murray, *Syphilis*, 6 (1910), pp. 8–9; R. R. Riaz de Isla, *Tractado contra el mal serpinto* (Seville, 1539); Bloch, op. cit.

8 Fracastor, book 1, lines 322–73; D. W. Montgomery, 'Hieronymus Fracastorius, the author of the poem called Syphilis', *AMH*, 2 (1930), p. 410.

9 Miller, 'Syphilis', p. 395; Wynne-Finch, *Fracastor*, p. 21; Bloch, op. cit.

10 M. A. Waugh, 'Venereal Diseases in Sixteenth-Century England', *Medical History*, 17 (1973), p. 192; Morton, *Venereal Diseases*, p. 23; Miller, 'Syphilis', p. 397.

11 Richard Wiseman, *Severall Chirurgicall Treatises* (1676), book 8, p. 66; Gideon Harvey, *Great Venus Unmasked, or a more Exact Discovery of the Venereal Evil or French Disease* (1672), p. 23; John Cam, *A Short Account of the Venereal Diseases* (1719), p. ii.

12 Ralph Johnstone, *Report on Venereal Diseases*, Cd. 7029 of 1913, p. 3; cf. Leon Elaut, 'John Andree's Essay on Gonorrhoea', *Medical History*, 14 (1975), pp. 87–90.

13 Wynne-Finch, *Fracastor*, pp. 10–11; Joseph Grunpeck, *Tractatus de pestilentiali score* (Augsburg, 1494); William Pusey, *The History and Epidemiology of Syphilis* (Springfield, Ill, 1933), p. 10).

14 Charles Creighton, *History of the Epidemics in Britain* (Cambridge, 1891), pp. 417–9; Miller, 'Syphilis', pp. 397–8; syphilis was called 'grandgore' in this document, a name which persisted in Scotland for over a century.

15 Waugh, 'Venereal Diseases', pp. 193–4; Sir Arthur MacNalty, *Henry VIII – A Difficult Patient*

(1952), p. 161; Creighton, *Epidemics*, pp. 414–5, 420, 422.

16 Stanislav Andreski, 'The Syphilitic Shock: Puritanism, Capitalism and a Medical Factor', *Encounter*, 55 (Oct. 1980), p. 78; Anthony Wood, *History and Antiquities of the University of Oxford*, 1 (1792), p. 514; Margaret Pelling, 'Appearances and Reality: barber-surgeons, the body and disease', in W. L. Beier and R. Finlay eds., *London 1500–1700: the Making of the Metropolis* (1986), pp. 89, 99.

17 William Clowes, *A Briefe and Necessarie Treatise, Touching the Cure of the Disease called Morbus Gallicus* (1585), pp. iii, iv, 2, 44–5. This was the first major account of syphilis written in English, but Andrew Boord's *Breviary of Health* (1547), the first printed medical text by a physician written in English, includes a section on venereal diseases. See Waugh, 'Venereal Diseases', pp. 194–5; Margaret Pelling, 'Appearances and Reality', pp. 98–100 & *passim*; Joanna Innes, 'Prisons for the poor: English bridewells 1555–1800', in Francis Snyder and Douglas Hay eds., *Labour, Law and Crime* (1987), pp. 46–7, 55 & *passim*.

18 Clowes, *Treatise*, p. 3.

19 W. E. H. Lecky, *History of European Morals* (1869), p. 123; Blair Worden, 'Oliver Cromwell and the Sin of Achan', in Derek Beales and Geoffrey Best eds., *History, Society and the Churches* (1985), p. 128; cf. Blair Worden, 'Providence and Politics in Cromwellian England', *Past & Present*, 109 (1985), pp. 55–99.

20 Pelling, 'Appearances and Reality', p. 99; Harry Porter ed., *Puritanism in Tudor England* (1970), pp. 7, 217–8.

21 Roy Porter, 'Mixed Feelings: the Enlightenment and Sexuality', in Boucé, *Sexuality in Eighteenth-Century England*, p. 3; David M. Vieth ed., *The Collected Poems of John Wilmot, Earl of Rochester* (1968), pp. 38–9, 95; Robert Latham and William Matthews eds., *Diaries of Samuel Pepys*, 5 (1971), pp. 17, 224, & vol. 8 (1974), p. 588; Harold Brooks ed.,

The Poems of John Oldham (Oxford, 1987), p. xliii.

22 Edward Walford, *Old and New London*, 5 (1877), pp. 215, 528.

23 *Life and Times of Selina, Countess of Huntingdon*, 1 (1839), p. 165; Revd Edward Betham to Revd William Cole, 14 Aug. 1764, Add. Ms. 5832; Martin Madan, *An Account of the Triumphant Death of F.S., A Converted Prostitute* (1763), pp. 4, 8; Sir Walter Besant, *London North of the Thames* (1911), p. 183; Martin Madan, *Thelyphthora* (1780).

24 William Dodd, *The Rise, Progress and Present State of the Magdalen Hospital for the Reception of Penitent Prostitutes* (1770 edn), pp. i, 1, 4, 6, 7, 10, 44, 226–7; Sir Victor Pritchett, *The Living Novel* (1946), p. 109.

25 Thomas Scott, *The Force of Truth* (1779), and T. Scott, *Four Sermons on Repentance* (1802); British Museum Print Room, 'View of the Lock Chapel near Hyde Park Corner, where a Gospel Ministry', 134166.

26 James Cleugh, *Secret Enemy* (1954), pp. 102–3; Morton, *Venereal Disease*, p. 21.

27 Paul Chamberlen, *The Second Part of the Practical Scheme Containing Directions for the Use of the Anodyne Necklace* (1728 edn), p. 12; Joseph Cam, *A Short Account of the Venereal Disease* (1719), pp. 50, 60; John Marten, *A Treatise of all the Degrees and Symptoms of the Venereal Disease in Both Sexes* (1708), pp. x, xix-xx, 43.

28 Wiseman, *Treatises*, p. 5; Marten, *Treatise*, pp. 41, 43.

29 J. D. Rolleston, 'Venereal Disease in Pepys' Diary', *BJVD*, 18 (1942), pp. 169–73; Mynors Bright, Lord Braybrooke and H. B. Wheatley eds., *The Diary of Samuel Pepys*, 6 (1923), pp. 151, 155–7, 163–4, 174; compare Margaret Pelling, 'Healing the Sick Poor: Social Policy and Disability in Norwich 1550–1640', *Medical History*, 29 (1985), p. 80; W. J. Bynum, 'Treating the Wages of Sin: Venereal Disease and Specialism in Eighteenth-Century Britain', in W. J. Bynum and R. Porter

eds., *Medical Fringe and Medical Orthodoxy 1750–1850* (1986), p.9.

30 Ulrich von Hutten, *Von Der wunderlichen Arzeni, des Harzes Guaiacum gennant, und wieman die Franzosen beilen soll* (Strasburg, 1519); cf. line 56 in Oldham's Satyr IV, 'I sweat like Clapt Debauch in Hot House shit': Brooks, *Oldham*, p. 52.

31 Wiseman, *Treatises*, pp. 6, 15; Harvey, *Great Venus*, pp. 83–4.

32 Marten, *Treatise*, p. xxiii.

33 Shakespeare, *Timon of Athens*, IV, 3, 150–65; Samuel Butler, *Hudibras*, 1, 64; Roger Thompson, *Unfit for Modest Ears* (London, 1979), p. 113; *Tatler*, 7 December 1710; L. W. Harrison, 'An Elegant Early 18th-Century Piece of V.D. Propaganda: An Essay on Noses by Joseph Addison', *BJVD*, 19 (1943), p. 79–81; Sir D'Arcy Power, 'Clap and the Pox in English Literature', *BJVD*, 14 (1938), pp. 105–117.

34 John Martin and Geoffrey Parker, *The Spanish Armada* (1988), p. 261; Arthur Schopenhauer, 'What a Man represents', *Parerga and Paralipomena* (1851), trans. by E. F. J. Payne (Oxford, 1974).

35 Harvey, *Great Venus*, pp. 4, 36, 98.

36 Harvey, *Great Venus*, pp. 4, 37.

37 W. E. H. Lecky, *History of European Morals*, 2 (1877), p. 283; Vieth, *Rochester*, p. 183; Keith Thomas, 'The Double Standard', *Journal of History of Ideas*, 20 (1959), pp. 197, 207.

38 Harvey, *Great Venus*, pp. 28, 62.

39 Marten, *Treatise*, p. 67.

40 Harvey, *Great Venus*, p. 63.

41 Harvey, *Great Venus*, p. 64.

42 Chamberlen, *Scheme*, pp. 7, 11, 13, 15.

43 *Select Trials of the Old Bailey*, 2 (1742), p. 371; Bynum, 'Wages of Sin', p. 5.

44 Robert L. S. Cowley, *Marriage à la Mode: a re-view of Hogarth's narrative art* (Manchester, 1983), pp. 84–92. For an account of the power of one venereologist, Baron von Struensee, see W. J. Reddaway, 'King Christian VII', *English Historical Review*, 31 (1916), pp. 59–84; P. Nors, *The Court of Christian VII of Denmark* (1928), pp. 97–

101; James Cleugh, *Secret Enemy* (1954), p. 130–1.

45 A. E. W. McLachlan, 'Chatterton's Syphilis', *BJVD*, 18 (1942), p. 84.

46 Marten, *Treatise*, pp. ix, xxxiii, xxxvi; Cam, *Short Account* pp. iii–iv, 25; John Spinke, *Quackery Unmask'd* (1709), pp. 5, 8–9; A. Fessler, 'Leaflets on the Treatment of Venereal Diseases', *BJVD*, 22 (1946), pp. 85–9, and Fessler, 'Advertisements on the Treatment of Venereal Diseases', *BJVD*, 25 (1949), pp. 84–7.

47 Angus McLaren, *Birth Control in Nineteenth-Century England* (1978), p. 21–2; Marten, *Treatise*, p. 63, 54.

48 Simon Davis, 'A Night in Armour', *New Society*, 27 Feb. 1987, p. 15; *Complete Peerage*, 1 (1910), pp. 206–8, 2 (1912), p. 94.

49 E. J. Dingwall, 'Early Contraceptive Sheaths', *British Medical Journal*, hereafter *BMJ*, 3 Jan. 1953, pp. 40–1; Daniel Turner, *Syphilis: A Practical Dissertation on the Venereal Disease* (1717), p. 74, and F. A. Pottle, *Boswell's London Journal 1762–1763* (1966), p. 287, quoted McLaren, *Birth Control*, pp. 23–5.

50 Jean Astruc, *Treatise of the Venereal Disease* (1737), pp. 299–300, quoted McLaren, *Birth Control*, p. 23.

51 Cf. Robert Holloway, *The Rat-Trap* (1773), pp. 57–8: 'I have ever held the seduction of women a crime of the most atrocious nature; not only as it is a kind of political murder in itself, but the appendages to this vice augments its heinousness . . . What depredation, carnage and misery has this vice alone spread through the kingdom? It is really sickening to human nature to behold the innumerable wretches that fill the streets . . . doomed to perpetual penury, disease, barbarous insults, stinging indignities . . . How severe is fate, to seal a woman's transgression with an eternal stigma; if she errs but once, a life of contrition boots her nothing.'

CHAPTER THREE

1 Randolph Trumbach, 'Sodomitical Subcultures, Sodomitical Roles and the Gender Revolution of the Eighteenth Century', in Robert P. Maccubin ed., *Unauthorised Sexual Behaviour during the Enlightenment* (1985), pp. 109, 114; Mary McIntosh, 'The Homosexual Role', *Social Problems*, 16 (1968), pp. 183–5.

2 McIntosh, 'Homosexual Role', p. 185; Crompton, *Byron*, p. 262.

3 Alan Bray, *Homosexuality in Renaissance England* (1982), pp. 13–17; Harry Porter ed., *Puritanism in Tudor England* (1970), pp. 130–1; Brooks, *Oldham*, pp. 344–5; Sir Edward Coke, *Institutes of the Laws of England* (1644 edn), 3rd pt., ch. 10, p. 58.

4 Goodich, *Unmentionable Vice*, pp. ix, xv; D. A. Coward, 'Attitudes to Homosexuality in Eighteenth-Century France', *Journal of European Studies*, 10 (1980), p. 232; Coke, *Institutes*, pt. 3, ch. 10, p. 59.

5 Goodich, *Unmentionable Vice*, pp. 8–9; Coke, *Institutes*, pt. 3, p. 58; Bray, *Renaissance Homosexuality*, pp. 19–20; H. Montgomery Hyde, *The Other Love* (1970), p. 36.

6 Frankie Rubinstein, *A Dictionary of Shakespeare's Sexual Puns and their Significance* (1984), p. xiii; Bray, *Renaissance Homosexuality*, pp. 14, 16; Sir Francis Lockwood, counsel for Charles Tindal Gatty, reported *The Times*, 21 June 1893; on Dilhorne, see ch. 8, p. 323.

7 Bray, *Renaissance Homosexuality*, pp. 44–9, 70–1, 74–6; Stone, *Family Sex and Marriage*, p. 519; Coward, 'Attitudes', p. 234.

8 Bray, *Renaissance Homosexuality*, pp. 52–3; Stone, *Family Sex and Marriage*, pp. 516–7; A. L. Rowse, *Elizabethan Renaissance* (1971).

9 W. S. Lewis ed., *Horace Walpole's Correspondence*, 22 (1960), pp. 286–7; Vieth, *Rochester*, p. 51; Tobias

Smollett, *Roderick Random* (1748), ch. 51.

10 Caroline Bingham, 'Seventeenth-Century Attitudes Toward Deviant Sex', *Journal of Interdisciplinary History*, 1 (1970), pp. 447–72.

11 Bingham, 'Deviant Sex', pp. 455–6.

12 Bray, *Renaissance Homosexuality*, pp. 9, 69–70, 77–9; Eve Kosofsky Sedgwick, 'The Beast in the Closet', pp. 149–50; Robert H. McDonald, 'The Frightful Consequences of Onanism: Notes on the History of a Delusion', *Journal of the History of Ideas*, 28 (1967), p. 424; *Select Trials at the Old Bailey*, 3 (1742), p. 40.

13 G. S. Rousseau, 'The Pursuit of Homosexuality in the Eighteenth Century', in Maccubin, *Unauthorised Sexual Behaviour*, p. 137; Bingham, 'Deviant Sex', p. 467; Brooks, *Oldham*, p. 54.

14 Bingham, 'Deviant Sex', p. 467; Rey, 'Parisian Homosexuals Create a Lifestyle, 1700–1750: The Police Archives', in Maccubin, *Unauthorised Sexual Behaviour*, pp. 179, 189; Crompton, *Byron*, p. 223.

15 Arthur Ponsonby, *English Diaries* (1923), pp. 58–61, 66–70, 134–6; Richard Ollard, *Pepys* (1984), p. 327.

16 Stone, *Family, Sex and Marriage*, pp. 328, 396, 404.

17 Geoffrey Ashe, *Do what you will: a history of anti-morality* (1974), pp. 71–2; J. A. Noble, 'The Fiction of Sexuality', *Contemporary Review*, 67 (1895), p. 497; Francis Bickley ed., *The Diaries of Lord Glenbervie*, 2 (1928), p. 114.

18 Bickley, *Glenbervie*, 2, p. 114.

19 *Select Trials*, 3 (1742), p. 75; Roy Porter, *English Society in the Eighteenth Century* (1982), p. 160.

20 *Complete Peerage*, 3 (1913), pp. 14–15; 6 (1926), p. 47; Beilby Porteus, *Sermons on Several Subjects* (1803 edn), vol. 1, pp. 172–3.

20 Bickley, *Glenbervie*, 1, p. 249; Laver, *Churchill*, 2, p. 149; 'Humphrey Nettle' [William Jackson], *Sodom and Onan* (1776).

21 M. J. D. Roberts, 'The Society for the Suppression of Vice and its early critics 1802–1812', *Historical Journal*, 26 (1983), pp. 159–73; Joanna Innes, 'Politics and Morals: the reformation of manners movement in later eighteenth-century England', in E. Helmuth ed., *The Transformation of Political Culture in late 18th-Century England and Germany* (Oxford, 1990).

22 Stone, *Family, Sex and Marriage*, pp. 253–4; Arend Huussen, 'Sodomy in the Dutch Republic during the eighteenth century', in Maccubin, *Unauthorised Sexual Behaviour*, p. 176; Crompton, *Byron*, pp. 295–6; Dowager Marchioness of Dufferin and Ava, *My Russian and Turkish Journals*, (1916), p. 7.

23 Huussen, 'Sodomy in the Dutch Republic', pp. 169–78; Coward, 'Attitudes to Homosexuality', p. 237.

24 *Select Trials*, 2, p. 370; 3, p. 37; ch. entitled 'The Mollies Club' in Ned Ward, *A Compleat and Humorous Account of the Remarkable Club and Societies in the Cities of London and Westminster* [pp. 256–9 of 1756 edn]; Holloway, *Phoenix*, p. 28; Arnold Harvey, 'Prosecutions for Sodomy in England at the beginning of the nineteenth century', *Historical Journal*, 21 (1978), p. 944.

25 Bonamy Dobree ed., *Letters of Philip Dormer Stanhope, Fourth Earl of Chesterfield*, 6 (1932), pp. 2668, 2942.

26 *Complete Peerage*, 3, p. 267; Bickley, *Glenbervie*, 1, p. 77.

27 Gibbon, *Decline and Fall*, 4, ch. 44; Holloway, *Phoenix*, p. 13; Amphlett Micklewright, 'The Bishop of Clogher's Case', *Notes and Queries*, 214 (1969), p. 423. Lord Sefton seems to have been fascinated by the misfortunes of sodomites – he attended the execution of John Hepburn and Thomas White in 1810: *New Newgate Calendar*, 8 (1818), p. 280.

28 Holloway, *Phoenix*, pp. 11, 22.

29 W. Matthews ed., *Diary of Dudley Ryder 1715–16* (1939), p. 143; *Select Trials at the Old Bailey*, 1 (1742), p. 330; Mary Wollstonecraft, *A Vindication of the Rights of Women* (1792; 1970 edn), p. 182; Bickley, *Glenbervie*, 1, p. 89; cf.

Coward, 'Attitudes', pp. 235–6, on French attitudes to corruption of minors.

30 Holloway, *Phoenix*, p. 11; Crompton, *Byron*, p. 242; Coward, 'Attitudes', p. 233; Rey, 'Parisian Homosexuals', p. 185.

31 Churchill, 'The Times', lines 331–4; Bingham, 'Deviant Sex', p. 467.

32 W. H. Auden, *Forewords and Afterwords* (1973), p. 453.

33 Sir Kenneth Dover, *Greek Homosexuality* (1978); Ruggiero, *Boundaries*, pp. 114–17.

34 *Select Trials at the Old Bailey*, 1 (1742), pp. 106–7; Rey, 'Parisian Homosexuals', p. 184.

35 Barry Burg, *Sodomy and the Perception of Evil: English Sea Rovers in the Seventeenth-Century Caribbean* (1983), pp. 130–1.

36 Marten, *Treatise*, p. 68; Gilbert, 'Buggery and the British Navy', p. 78.

37 Alan Valentine, *Lord George Germain* (Oxford, 1962), pp. 456–7, 472–5; Piers Mackesy, *The Coward of Minden* (1979), pp. 34–5, 254–61. For other examples of sexual slander or calumny employed to ostracize political enemies, see Peter Wagner, *Eros Revived: Erotica of the Enlightenment in England and America* (1988), pp. 98, 344.

38 Andrew Baxter to John Wilkes, 23 June 1745, 3 Oct. 1745, 30 Dec. 1745, 10 May 1746, Add. Ms. 30867.

39 Bickley, *Glenbervie*, 1, p. 4.

40 Rochester, 'A Ramble in St James's Park', in Vieth, *Rochester*, p. 41; *Select Trials*, 3, p. 38; Holloway, *Phoenix*, pp. 8–9. By contrast 'the keeper of a house of ill-fame' for heterosexuals, David Robertson ('his aspect sallow and cadaverous, and his general appearance mean and despicable') was hanged for 'unnatural crime' in 1806: *New Newgate Calendar*, 7 (1818), p. 370.

41 Rey, 'Parisian Homosexuals', pp. 181, 188; Coward, 'Attitudes', p. 243; Lord Hawkesbury to Lord Sydney, 8 Nov. 1808, PRO HO 79/1/66; Bray, *Renaissance Homosexuality*, pp. 53–4; Harvey, 'Prosecu-

tions', p. 944.

42 Bray, *Renaissance Homosexuality*, pp. 92–3, 102, 108–9, 113; Crompton, *Byron*, pp. 161, 236–7.

43 Churchill, 'The Times', lines 285–96.

44 Smollett, *Random*, chs. 34–5.

45 Holloway, *Phoenix*, pp. 48, 50.

46 Smollett, *Random*, ch. 51; *Complete Peerage*, 3, p. 576; Hyde, *Other Love*, p. 79; Crompton, *Byron*, pp. 170–1. Another version of the verse quoted by Smollett is in *New Newgate Calendar*, 5 (1818), p. 104.

47 *Select Trials*, 1, pp. 281–2; 2, p. 271.

48 Holloway, *Phoenix*, pp. 17, 20, 34–43, 46, 51. For references to Holloway's other vituperations, such as his attack on the magistracy entitled *The Rat-Pack* (1774), I am indebted to Joanna Innes, of Somerville College, Oxford, whose comments have in other ways strengthened this chapter.

49 *Select Trials*, 2, pp. 362–4; for an account of moral policing and social order in eighteenth century London, see the account of the informing constable and carpenter, William Payne of Bell Yard, in Joanna Innes, *Inferior Politics: social problems and social policies in eighteenth-century Britain*, forthcoming.

50 *Select Trials*, 3, pp. 39–40; newspaper cutting of 4 Nov. 1810 in British Library cup 364 p 12.

51 Harvey, 'Prosecutions', pp. 939, 941 (with criminal statistics for trials, acquittals and executions for sodomy, 1749–1835, at pp. 947–8).

52 Rey, 'Parisians Homosexuals', pp. 182–3; Coward, 'Attitudes', pp. 235, 239.

53 Sir James Mackintosh, House of Commons debates, 21 May 1823, 9, col. 418; F. D. Maurice, quoted House of Lords debates, 24 June 1937, 105, col. 782; Sir Robert Anderson, 'Morality by Act of Parliament', *Contemporary Review*, 59 (1891), p. 78; Crompton, *Byron*, pp. 230–1.

54 Newspaper cuttings of 14 Oct. & 4 Nov. 1810 in British Library cup

364 p 12; Crompton, *Byron*, p. 21.

55 Sir Robert Peel to Sir James Graham, 17 Dec. 1842, Graham to Peel, 19 Dec. 1842, Add. Ms. 40448.

56 Harvey, 'Prosecutions', pp. 939–40; John D. Byrn, *Crime & Punishment in the Royal Navy: Discipline on the Leeward Islands Station 1784–1812* (Aldershot, 1989), pp. 77, 149–50; Nicholas Rodger, *The Wooden World: Anatomy of the Georgian Navy* (1986), pp. 80–1; Gilbert, 'Buggery', pp. 72–98.

57 *Gentleman's Magazine* (1762), p. 549; Frederick J. Stephens, *Catalogue of Political and Personal Satires in the Department of Prints and Drawings in the British Museum*, 4 (1883), p. 220; Gilbert, 'Sexual Deviance', pp. 106–7; Crompton, *Byron*, pp. 31–3, 164–71; British Library, newspaper cutting of 1810 in cup 364 p 12.

58 Gilbert, 'Sexual Deviance', p. 113; Holloway, *Phoenix*, p. 30.

59 Harvey, 'Prosecutions', p. 946.

60 Thomas Sherlock, *A Letter from the Lord Bishop of London to the Clergy and People of London and Westminster on the occasion of the late earthquakes* (1770 edn), pp. 3, 10; Sir Thomas Kendrick, *The Lisbon Earthquake* (1956), pp. 5, 10; Bray, *Renaissance Homosexuality*, pp. 29–30, 47; Ruggiero, *Boundaries of Eros*, pp. 109–10, 119, 121–2; Goodich, *Unmentionable Vice*, p. xiv.

61 Gilbert, 'Sexual Deviance', p. 108.

62 Harvey, 'Prosecutions', p. 942; Lord Hawkesbury to Lord Sydney, 8 Nov. 1808, PRO HO 79/1/66.

63 George Dawson to Archbishop Beresford of Armagh, quoted Micklewright, 'The Bishop of Clogher's Case', p. 425.

64 Earl of Desart, House of Lords debates, 15 Aug. 1921, 46, col. 572; Hyde, *Other Love*, p. 75.

65 Crompton, *Byron*, p. 25; David Hannay, *Naval Courts Martial* (Cambridge, 1914), p. ix; William McElwee, *Wisest Fool in Christendom* (1958), p. 176.

66 Holloway, *Phoenix*, pp. 14, 18, 24.

CHAPTER FOUR

1 Robert Rentoul, *Race Culture or Race Suicide? A Plan for the Unborn* (1906), p. 182; R. W. Connell, *Gender and Power: Society, the Person and Sexual Politics* (1987), pp. 147–8; Roger Scruton, *Sexual Desire*, pp. 284, 310; Guy Hocquenghem, *Homosexual Desire* (1978), pp. 10, 20–2, 25–6.

2 *Yokel's Preceptor* (1855), pp. 3, 5–7; Trevisan, *Perverts in Paradise*, p. 101.

3 Judith Walkowitz, *Prostitution & Victorian Society*, (Cambridge, 1980), p. 130; House of Commons debates, 28 Feb. 1890, col. 1585; Sir Archdall Reid, *Prevention of Venereal Disease* (1920), p. 129; H. L. Oldershaw, 'Outbreak of Gonorrhoea in a Residential Boy's School', *BJVD*, 5 (1929), p. 303.

4 Harry Daley, *This Small Cloud* (1986), pp. 22–3.

5 Phyllis Grosskurth ed., *The Memoirs of John Addington Symonds*, pp. 39, 94–5; D. J. Jeremy and C. Shaw eds., *Dictionary of Business Biography*, 1 (1985), pp. 772–3; for a contemporary account of homosexuality at Eton, see A. J. V. Cheetham and D. Parfit eds., *Eton Microcosm* (1964), pp. 92–4.

6 Sir Alfred Lyall, *The Life of the Marquis of Dufferin and Ava*, 1 (1905), p. 22; Crompton, *Byron*, pp. 75, 250; Eve Kosofsky Sedgwick, *Between Men* (New York, 1985), p. 176; Lord Norwich, *Old Men Forget* (1953), pp. 28–9. For other explorations of these themes see J. A. Mangan and James Walvin eds., *Manliness and Morality: Middle-Class Masculinity in Britain and America 1800–1940* (Manchester, 1987).

7 Lord Curzon of Kedleston to Lord George Hamilton, 16 July & 3 Dec. 1902, Hamilton to Curzon, 21 Mar. 1902, Mss Eur F 111/161; Curzon to Hamilton, 25 Mar., 13 Apr. & 28 May 1903, Hamilton to Curzon, 19 June 1903, Mss Eur F 111/162; Lord Ronaldshay, *The Life of Lord Curzon*, 1 (1928), p. 65; Kenneth

Rose, *Superior Person: a portrait of Curzon and his circle in late Victorian England* (1969), p. 31.

8 David Hilliard, 'UnEnglish and Unmanly: Anglo-Catholicism and Homosexuality', *Victorian Studies*, 25 (1982), pp. 184–5, 187–91, 203, 206, 209–10.

9 T. M. Healy, *Letters and Leaders of My Day* (1928), 1, p. 195; Daley, *Small Cloud*, p. 171; Lord Alfred Douglas, *Autobiography* (1929), p. 212; Tom Driberg, *Ruling Passions* (1977), pp. 30, 114.

10 John Stuart Mill, *Autobiography* (1873 edn), ch. 3, p. 70; Charles Graves, *Life and Letters of Alexander Macmillan* (1910), p. 388; Walter Houghton, *The Victorian Frame of Mind* (1957), pp. 62, 77, 100, 106.

11 Marjorie Rosenberg, 'Inventing the Homosexual', *Commentary*, 84 (Dec. 1987), p. 36; for an account of phrenologists' contribution to the emergence of the modern homosexual, see Michael Lynch, 'Here is Adhesiveness: From Friendship to Homosexuality', *Victorian Studies*, 29 (1985), pp. 68, 75, 88, 91.

12 George Savage, 'Case of Sexual Perversion in a Man', *Journal of Mental Science*, 30 (1884), pp. 390–1. For the Irish case, see William O'Brien, *Evening Memories* (1920), pp. 15–32.

13 Hyde, *Other Love*, pp. 94–8, 128; Jeffrey Weeks, 'Inverts, Perverts and Mary Annes: Male Prostitution and the Regulation of Homosexuality in England in the nineteenth and early twentieth centuries', *Journal of Homosexuality*, 6 (1980/1), pp. 116–7. For a bank employee dismissed under suspicion of an 'unnatural offence of a loathsome character', see Geoffrey Jones, *Banking and Empire in Iran* (1986), p. 142.

14 Jan Goldstein, *Console and Classify: the French Psychiatric Profession in the Nineteenth Century* (Cambridge, 1987), p. 265; Eugene Talbot, *Degeneracy, its Causes, Signs and Results* (1898), pp. 8–26; George Mosse, *Nationalism and Sexuality: Respectability and Abnormal Sexuality in Modern

Europe* (New York, 1985), pp. 34–7.

15 Cesare Lombroso, *Crime: its Causes and Remedies* (1911 edn), pp. 256–7, 260, 418; *BMJ*, 1 June 1895, p. 1226; Sir Rupert Hart-Davis, *The Letters of Oscar Wilde* (1962), pp. 401–4, 411.

16 Max Nordau, *Degeneration* (1895), pp. 2, 5–6, 259, 263, 318, 337, 540, 556, 560; Mosse, *Nationalism and Sexuality*, p. 42.

17 Talbot, *Degeneracy*, pp. 323–4.

18 Kenneth Ingram, *The Modern Attitude to the Sex Problem* (1930), p. 75; Ted Morgan, *Somerset Maugham* (1980), pp. 40, 591.

19 Gay, *Tender Passion*, p. 49; William Temple, quoted House of Lords debates, 20 Aug. 1907, 181, col. 387.

20 Gay, *Education of the Senses*, p. 422; Marquess of Dufferin and Ava, *Speeches and Addresses* (1882), pp. 75–6; Edward Lyttelton, *Causes and Prevention of Immorality in Schools* (1887), pp. 12–13.

21 John Morley, 'A Short Letter to Some Ladies', *Fortnightly Review*, 13 (1870), p. 375; Countess Cowper, 'The Decline of Reserve among Women', *Nineteenth Century*, 27 (1890), pp. 65–7, 71.

22 Lang, *Parables of Jesus*, pp. 241–3; Norman Douglas, *South Wind* (1917); Driberg, *Ruling Passions*, pp. 2, 29, 43.

23 Sir Clifford Allbutt, 'Nervous Diseases and Modern Life', *Contemporary Review*, 67 (1895), pp. 210, 221; J. A. Noble, 'The Fiction of Sexuality', *Contemporary Review*, 67 (1895), pp. 490, 497.

24 Harry Quilter, 'The Gospel of Intensity', *Contemporary Review*, 67 (1895), p. 778; Revd A. W. Gough, *The Times*, 8 April 1916.

25 Schueller and Peters, *Symonds Letters*, 3, pp. 592, 594, 723, 808.

26 Croft-Cooke, *Feasting with Panthers*, p. 125.

27 Labouchere, House of Commons debates, 28 Feb. 1890, col. 1534; Schueller and Peters, *Symonds Letters*, 3, pp. 553, 586–7.

28 G. K. A. Bell, *Randall Davidson*, 1

(1935), pp. 114–5; Lord Carnarvon to Sir Richard Cross, 12 July 1885, Add. Ms. 51268; Sir William Harcourt to Cross, 28 July 1885, Sir George Trevelyan to Cross, 1 Aug. 1885, Add. Ms. 51274; Earl of Lytton to Earl of Dufferin, Nov. 1885, Mss Eur F 130/21. Cf. Rennell Rodd to George Curzon, 10 May 1883, Mss Eur F 112/338 ('we have been abolishing the CD Acts here, a proceeding which I, radical of all that is most radical, must call damned folly and ignorant sentimentalism'), and Sir Arthur Blackwood to Lord Dufferin, 21 Feb. 1888, Mss Eur F 130/30 ('Thank God, the persistent, prayerful, self-sacrificing labours of many at home, among whom I am not worthy to be named, have succeeded after many years, in at last moving the conscience of the country, and in compelling the House of Commons to repeal the most degrading, iniquitous Acts that were ever passed [and] were only passed because the House was ignorant of what it was doing').

29 Diary of Sir Edward Walter Hamilton, 9 Nov. 1886, Add. Ms. 48645; ibid., 11 April 1891, Add. Ms. 48655; Paul McHugh, *Prostitution and Victorian Social Reform* (1980), p. 205; Sir John Colville, *Strange Inheritance* (Salisbury, 1983), pp. 102–3, 108, 151; O'Brien, *Evening Memories*, p. 6.

30 *Truth*, 6 Aug. 1885, quoted Smith, 'Labouchere's Amendment', pp. 169–70.

31 Symonds, quoted Croft-Cooke, *Feasting with Panthers*, p. 156; O'Brien, *Evening Memories*, pp. 6–7; Harris, quoted Smith, 'Labouchere's Amendment', pp. 166, 169; Viscount Montgomery of Alamein, House of Lords debates, 21 June 1965, 267, cols. 332, 342.

32 House of Commons debates, 6 Aug. 1885, 300, col. 1397.

33 Schueller and Peters, *Symonds Letters*, 3, p. 587.

34 House of Commons debates, 28 Feb. 1890, cols. 1534–5; *Review of Reviews*, 11 (1895), p. 492; Smith, 'Labouchere's Amendment',

pp. 172–3. For other examples of Labouchere retrospectively misrepresenting past events in his career, see Stephen Koss, *The Rise and Fall of the Political Press in Britain*, 1 (1981), pp. 193, 335.

35 Daley, *Small Cloud*, pp. 48, 74; Michael Pollak, 'Male Homosexuality', in P. Ariès and A. Bejin, *Western Sexuality*, p. 43; Croft-Cooke, *Feasting with Panthers*, p. 140.

36 Schueller and Peters, *Symonds Letters*, 3, p. 554; Smith, 'Labouchere's Amendment', p. 174; evidence of Sir Howard Vincent to Royal Commission on Police, 13 May 1907, Q. 45815/15, Cd. 4156 of 1908; cf. Lord Halsbury and Lord Davey, House of Lords debates, 16 June 1903, on 'cases which it is inadvisable to drag into the light of day' or 'to ventilate' (incest).

37 Laurence Housman, *Echo de Paris* (1923), p. 56; Sorley Brown, *Genius of Crosland*, p. 339; *Review of Reviews*, 11, p. 491; Weeks, *Coming Out*, pp. 21–2, 44.

38 Hyde, *Other Love*, pp. 116, 146; St John Brodrick to George Curzon, 8 Dec. 1889, Mss. Eur F 111/9B.

39 David Brooks ed., *The Destruction of Lord Rosebery: From the Diary of Sir Edward Walter Hamilton 1894–1895* (1986), pp. 225, 236, 250; James Lees-Milne, *Enigmatic Edwardian* (1986), pp. 97–9; on cocaine, see Lord George Hamilton to Lord Curzon of Kedleston, 5 March 1903, Mss Eur F 111/162: 'Rosebery made rather a curious speech the other day in the House of Lords. I am informed, by those who watch him, that the impression is he takes some drug before speaking, which makes him brilliant for the moment, but exceptionally flabby and invertebrate for the remainder of the day. He has got very big, and looks very much like the fat boy in Pickwick.' Compare the descriptions of Rosebery by a physician who met him: 'You are never sure of him. Is always playing a double part' (Diary of Dr G. E. Morrison, 25 Oct. 1899); 'a weak ill-formed mouth ... the same kind of mouth as Oscar Wilde ... name closely

associated with that of Oscar, Viscount Drumlanrig elder brother of Lord Alfred Douglas was his private secretary & committed suicide. He fainted when report bought him of punishment of Oscar' (ibid, 15 Nov. 1899), Morrison papers, State Library of New South Wales.

40 Croft-Cooke, *Feasting with Panthers*, pp. 9–10; Sidney Low, evidence to Royal Commission on Divorce, 21 Dec. 1910, QQ. 43346, 43348, 43354; Halsbury, House of Lords debates, 20 Mar. 1896, 38, cols. 1435–6; Lord Salisbury, ibid. col. 1445; Lord Sumner, quoted Mark de Wolfe Howe ed., *Holmes-Laski Letters*, (1953) I, p. 764; Gay, *Tender Passion*, pp. 203–4.

41 *Lancet*, 19 & 26 Nov. 1898, pp. 1344, 1431; Crompton, *Byron*, pp. 372–3; E. S. P. Haynes, 'The Taboos of the British Museum Library', *English Review*, 16 (1914), pp. 123–34; Houston Peterson, *Havelock Ellis, Philosopher of Love* (?1927), pp. 243–62; Earl of Desart, House of Lords debates, 15 Aug. 1921, 46, col. 573.

42 Quilter, 'Gospel of Intensity', pp. 761–82; cf. *National Review*, 26 (1895), p. 305.

43 Viscount Harberton, 'The Arrogance of Culture', *English Review*, 19 (1915), p. 146; Diary of G. E. Morrison, 19 Nov. 1910; John Astley Cooper, 'The British Imperial Spirit of Sport and the War', *United Empire*, 7 (1916), p. 581; Croft-Cooke, *Feasting with Panthers*, p. 287.

44 Brown, *Genius of Crosland*, pp. 222, 246–7, 258, 282, 284, 295, 309; *The Times*, 16 April 1915. For Crosland's blackmail of Lord Canterbury whom he alleged had had sex with a minor, see *The Times*, 20 Jan, 11, 12, 15 & 16 Feb. 1910; Douglas, *Autobiography*, pp. 232–3; H. Montgomery Hyde, *Lord Alfred Douglas* (1984), pp. 162–8. On Canterbury, see *The Times* 2 May 1916 & Charles à Court Repington, *The First World War* (1920), pp. 611–2.

45 Nichols, *Father Figure*, pp. 96–9. Lord Ritchie of Dundee (born 1919) similarly recalled that Wilde's name

was forbidden to be mentioned in the house when he was a child; perhaps significantly his eldest brother (born 1899; died 1927) was much beloved by the Bloomsbury set. House of Lords debates, 1 Feb. 1988, 492, col. 995; David Garnett ed., *Carrington: Letters and Extracts from her Diaries* (1970), pp. 265, 377. For the homophobic views of another brother (born 1902), see Lord Ritchie of Dundee to John Wolfenden, 21 July 1955, PRO HO 345/2.

46 Edward Bristow, *Vice and Vigilance* (Dublin, 1977), p. 171; Report of Royal Commission on Police, Cd. 4156 of 1908, p. 118; House of Commons debates, 12 Nov. 1912, 43, cols. 1855–61.

47 Sir Edward Troup, minute of 20 March 1905, and other papers in PRO HO 144/955.

48 Winston Churchill, minute of 29 August 1910, PRO HO 144/1098/197967.

49 Ibid.

50 Daley, *Small Cloud*, pp. 101, 213.

51 Hyde, *Other Love*, p. 94; Crompton, *Byron*, p. 358; Daley, *Small Cloud*, pp. 156–7; CHP/9, PRO HO 345/7; Ingram, *Sex Problem*, p. 68; cf. Paul Pry [Thomas Burke], *For Your Convenience* (1937).

52 John Sparrow, *Leaves from a Victorian Diary* (1985), p. 117; *Sins of the Cities of the Plain*, p. 64; St John Brodrick to George Curzon, 12 Nov. 1889, Mss Eur F 111/9B; J. R. Ackerley, *My Father and Myself* (1968), pp. 23–4 & *passim*.

53 Earl of Elgin and Kincardine to Henry Fowler, 22 May 1894, Mss Eur F 84/12; Sir Ernley Blackwell, quoted Suzann Buckley, 'The Failure to Resolve the Problem of Venereal Disease Among the Troops in Britain During World War I' in Brian Bond and Ian Roy eds., *War and Society*, 2 (1977), p. 67; *The Times* 11 Jan. 1918; Edith Tancred to Walter Elliott, 24 April 1940, PRO MH 55/1339; statistics in PRO HO 345/9; Fischer and Dubois, *Sexual Life*, pp. 416, 421–2.

54 Forel, *Sexual Life*, p. 243; Arnold White, 'Efficiency and Vice', *English Review*, 22 (1916), pp. 446–52.

For other propaganda hints about Hunnish vice, see Henry V. Fischer, *The Secret Memoirs of Bertha Krupp* (1916), pp. 5 & *passim*. Prussian homosexuality had received international publicity in the Eulenberg scandal of 1907, for a fascinating perspective on which see Norman Rich and M. H. Fisher eds., *The Holstein Papers*, 4 (Cambridge, 1963), pp. 447 & *passim*. Sir Valentine Chirol, head of the Foreign Department of *The Times*, considered that Berlin was 'the European capital where sodomy finds its chief home'. Diary of G. E. Morrison, 2 June 1909.

55 Daley, *Small Cloud*, pp. 98–9.

56 Sir Alexander Fuller-Acland-Hood to J. S. Sandars, 9 June 1910, Bodleian Library, Oxford, Eng Hist C/760; *The Times* 14 Sep. 1934 & 2 March 1940.

57 MacQuisten, House of Commons debates, 4 Aug. 1921, 145, cols. 1799–1800; cf. Virginia Berridge, 'The Origins of the English Drug Scene 1890–1930', *Medical History*, 32 (1988), pp. 51–64.

58 Robert Blackham, *Sir Ernest Wild* (1935), pp. 174, 177, 181; Wild, House of Commons debates, 4 Aug. 1921, 145, cols. 1803–4; cf. Craig, *Banned Books*, p. 89.

59 Colonel Josiah Wedgwood, House of Commons debates, 4 Aug. 1921, 145, cols. 1800–1; J. Moore-Brabazon, ibid., cols. 1804–6; Lord Desart, House of Lords debates, 15 Aug. 1921, 46, cols. 572–3; see also Iris Origo, *Images and Shadows* (1970), pp. 44–57, 62–3, 66–70, 134–5; *Spectator*, 4 Dec. 1942, p. 529. Further parliamentary discussion occurred during the reform of the divorce laws in 1937, when the Royal Physician, Lord Dawson of Penn, unsuccessfully proposed that spouses should have grounds for divorce 'if since the celebration of the marriage [either party has] been guilty of the practice of homosexuality'. A similar proposal had been put to the Royal Commission on Divorce by Desart in 1910. The views of Dawson and Desart were rejected by a law lord, Atkins, who considered homosexuality a 'permanent infirmity': Atkins judged it 'the result of wicked impulses which, like other wicked impulses, are capable of being controlled . . . by advice and by resolution': Lord Desart, evidence to Royal Commission on Divorce, 1 June 1910, Q. 15836; Lord Atkins, House of Lords debates, 7 July 1937, col. 145.

60 Weeks, *Coming Out*, p. 14, citing Sir Leon Radzinowitz, *A History of English Law, Grappling for Control* (1968), p. 432; Nichols, *Father Figure*, pp. 87–90. When a physician, Dr George Gray, met Sir Edmund Backhouse, the forger hermit of Peking, in 1911 he diagnosed 'pederastic tendencies' on the basis of Backhouse's 'soft flabby irresolute way, his feminine hands and feminine grip' – although sodomy had not occurred to another Peking physician, G. E. Morrison, when his friend Backhouse was 'in great pain with fissure of the anus' in 1904. Yet when Morrison met the Cambridge humanist Goldsworthy Lowes Dickinson in 1913, he did not hesitate to note: 'a man of vile aspect . . . [with] all the appearance of a pederast . . . He inspired me with a curious feeling of repugnance'. Diary of G. E. Morrison, 31 August 1904, 8 July 1911, 11 June 1913.

61 This paragraph follows the conclusions of George Chauncey, 'Christian Brotherhood or Sexual Perversion? Homosexual Identities and the Construction of Sexual Behaviour in the World War One Era', *Journal of Social History*, (1985), pp. 189–211. The idea and evidence in this article are superbly developed in Chauncey's *Gay New York*, forthcoming 1991.

CHAPTER FIVE

1 Duke of Argyll, House of Lords debates, 10 July 1896, 42, cols. 1196, 1199; W. Owen Chadwick, *The Victorian Church*, 1 (1966), pp. 325–6.

2 Edith Lyttelton Gell, 'Squandered Girlhood', *Nineteenth Century*, 32 (1892), pp. 936–7; Royal Commission on Divorce, 1910, QQ. 17997–

8, 18000–2; A. F. Winnington-Ingram, *Work in the Great Cities* (1895), p. 129;
F. M. L. Thompson, *The Rise of Respectable Society* (1988);
W. Owen Chadwick, *The Secularisation of the European Mind in the Nineteenth Century* (1976).

3 Forbes Winslow, *The Anatomy of Suicide*, (1840), p. 46; Charles Rosenberg, *The Cholera Years* (1962), p. 40; Karl Figlio, 'Chlorosis and chronic disease in nineteenth-century Britain: the social constitution of somatic illness in a capitalist society', *Social History*, 3 (1978), pp. 167–97; Richard Evans, *Death in Hamburg: society and politics in the cholera years 1830–1910* (Oxford, 1987).

4 Paul Starr, *The Social Transformation of American Medicine* (New York, 1982), pp. 1–3, 17, 19; Gay, *Education of Senses*, p. 313; Lang, *Parables of Jesus*, pp. 221, 227–8.

5 Figlio, 'Chlorosis', pp. 176–7; *The Times*, 8 & 10 March 1945.

6 Norwich, *Old Men Forget*, pp. 12–13, 17; *BMJ*, 14 March 1908, pp. 660–1; *Complete Peerage*, 6 (1926), pp. 275–6.

7 Oscar Wilde, 'The True Function and Value of Criticism: with some Remarks on the Importance of Doing Nothing', *Nineteenth Century*, 28 (1890), p. 458; Revd Henry Sidebotham, 'Monte Carlo', *Nineteenth Century*, 25 (1889), p. 554.

8 *Westminster Review*, 36 (1869), pp. 179–81, 186, 198, 201. For accounts of the deaths of two patients with tertiary syphilis, see Ackerley, *My Father and Myself*, pp. 85–91 & *passim*, and Randolph S. Churchill ed., *Winston S. Churchill, Companion Volume 1* (1967), pp. 499–547. For a rare account by a nineteenth-century woman with venereal disease, see Helena Whitbread ed., *I Know My Own Heart: the diaries of Anne Lister 1791–1840* (1988), pp. 149–50, 158–64.

9 Sir Almeric FitzRoy's Committee on Physical Deterioration (1904), QQ. 10532–3, 10891; Civis, 'Doctors and Venereal Disease', *English Review* (1913), 15, p. 253; Sir

James Barrett, *The Twin Ideals* (1918), pp. 465, 469; Leonard Darwin, 'The Dysgenic Effects of Venereal Diseases', *Eugenics Review*, 9 (1917), pp. 117–27.

10 *Westminster Review*, 36, p. 202; Civis, 'Doctors and Venereal Disease', p. 250; Lord Ranksborough, House of Lords debates, 10 Dec. 1919, 37, col. 880.

11 Lord Downham, House of Lords debates, 2 April 1919, 34, col. 85; Lord Rhondda to deputation on 24 Jan. 1917, PRO MH 55/530.

12 Hugh Elliott, 'Venereal Prophylaxis', *Nineteenth Century*, 84 (1918), p. 171; Sir Archdall Reid, *Prevention of Venereal Diseases* (1920), p. 25.

13 Arthur Schopenhauer, *The Wisdom of Life*, 1 (1890), pp. 75–81; John Morley, 'A Short Letter to Some Ladies', *Fortnightly Review*, 13 (1870), p. 375; Hariot Rowan-Hamilton to Earl of Dufferin, ? 18 Dec. 1861, Dufferin and Ava papers, MIC 22, Reel 6, vol xiv; for a more flattering account of Lord and Lady de Ros by Dufferin see Mrs J. R. Swinton, *A Sketch of the Life of Georgiana, Lady de Ros* (1893), pp. 113–16; C. E. D. Black, *The Marquess of Dufferin and Ava* (1903), p. 387; compare Sir Cyril Burt, 'The Contribution of Psychology to Social Hygiene', *Health and Empire*, 1 (1926), p. 33: 'The ostracism of the unchaste makes it harder for them to return to chastity'.

14 Lord Gainford, House of Lords debates, 8 March 1917, 24, col. 466; Lord Burnham, House of Lords debates, 2 April 1919, 34, col. 82.

15 Henley, House of Commons debates, 22 March 1866, 182, col. 815; Alford, quoted *Wesminster Review*, 37 (1870), p. 125; Edward H. Beardsley, 'Allied Against Sin: American and British Responses to Venereal Disease in World War One', *Medical History*, 20 (1976), p. 191; Reid, *Prevention*, p. 267; House of Lords debates, 2 April 1919, 34, col. 75; Select Committee on Contagious Diseases Acts (1868), QQ. 541, 961; *BMJ*,

30 Sept. 1871, p. 395; *Lancet*, 25 Feb. 1860, p. 198.

16 Eric Watson, *Trial of George Joseph Smith* (1922), pp. 87, 281; Edward Marjoribanks, *The Life of Sir Edward Marshall Hall* (1929), pp. 49–50; W. Teignmouth Shore, *Trial of Thomas Neil Cream* (1923), pp. 40, 170.

17 F. B. Smith, 'Ethics and disease in the late nineteenth century: the Contagious Diseases Acts', *Historical Studies* [Australia], 15 (1971), p. 131; House of Lords Select Committee (1868), Q. 1122.

18 Vincent, *Later Derby Diaries*, p. 108; Lord Buxton, quoted Lucien Wolf, *Lord Ripon*, 2 (1921), p. 322; White ed., *Osborne Letters*, I, p. xvi, II (1890), pp. 278–90; on Somerset, see also Duke of Argyll to Lord Dufferin, 25 July 1859, Dufferin and Ava papers, MIC 22, Reel 4, vol. X; Marquess of Dufferin and Ava to Lord Rosebery, 15 Oct. 1893, Dufferin and Ava papers D1071H/01/1.

19 Select Committee on Contagious Diseases Acts (1868), QQ. 500, 502.

20 Alfred Tennyson, 'Guinevere', lines 514–19; F. B. Smith, 'Ethics and Disease', pp. 118–19; Select Committee on Contagious Diseases Acts (1868), QQ. 711–16, 721–3, 945.

21 Select Committee on Contagious Diseases Acts (1868), QQ. 27, 102, 861.

22 Smith, 'Ethics and Disease', p. 120.

23 Smith, 'Ethics and Disease', p. 126.

24 Select Committee on Contagious Diseases Acts (1868), QQ. 206, 281, 461; Frances Finnegan, *Poverty and Prostitution: A Study of Victorian Prostitution in York* (1979), pp. 17, 63–5, 122, 147–9; Sir Harcourt Johnstone, House of Commons debates, 23 June 1875, 225, col. 366. On continental regulations see J. B. Post, 'A Foreign Office Survey of Venereal Disease and Prostitution Control Regulations 1869–70', *Medical History*, 22 (1978), pp. 327–34.

25 *Westminster Review*, 36 (1869), p. 188; Morley, 'Short Letter', p. 374; Smith, 'Ethics and Disease', pp. 126–7; Colonel Sir Claud

Alexander, House of Commons debates, 23 June 1875, 225, cols. 376, 381. For an appalling account of the destitution of diseased and drunken whores in York, see Finnegan, *Poverty and Prostitution*, pp. 136–42, 151–61.

26 Report of Select Committee on Contagious Diseases Acts (1868), p. 9.

27 Smith, 'Ethics and Disease', p. 133; *Westminster Review*, 37 (1870), pp. 143–4; Morley, 'Short Letter', pp. 372–3; Glen Petrie, *A Singular Iniquity: the campaigns of Josephine Butler* (1971); Kent, *Sex and Suffrage*, p. 10; for similar obloquy directed against women protestors against nuclear weaponry at Greenham Common, see Lady Caroline Blackwood, *On the Perimeter* (1986), p. 2 & *passim*.

28 James Stuart to W. E. Gladstone, 20 March 1884, Add. Ms. 44485, f. 306; Arnold Morley to Campbell-Bannerman, 12 March 1886, Campbell-Bannerman to Marquess of Ripon, Childers, Gladstone, 12 March 1886, Add. Ms. 41215, ff. 10–11; H. E. Garle, 'Abolition and After', *Health and Empire*, 10 (1935), pp. 14–26.

29 Kenneth Ballhatchett, *Race, Sex and Class under the Raj: Imperial Attitudes and Policies and their Critics 1793–1905* (1980), pp. 12–14, 17 & *passim*; Kerrie L. McPherson, *A Wilderness of Marshes: the origins of public health in Shanghai 1843–1893* (Oxford, 1987), pp. 213–57; Dufferin to Cross, 20 July 1888, F 130/11; Marquess of Ripon, minute of 21 Oct. 1880, Add. Ms. 43574; Ripon to Dufferin, 15 June 1888, Mss Eur F 130/30.

30 W. J. Moore, memorandum on CD Acts, Oct. 1886, & Calcutta Public Health Committee, Note on the question of state interference with Contagious Diseases in Calcutta, May 1887, both in Dufferin and Ava papers, D1071H/M10/2; Sir George Chesney, memorandum of 24 Sep. 1888, Dufferin and Ava papers D1071H/K2/4.

31 *The Christian*, 27 April 1888; Alfred S. Dyer, 'The Government

versus the Gospel in India', *Sentinel*, March 1888, Proceedings of India Council, May 1888, Nos. 1825 & 1829, Dufferin and Ava papers D1071H/M10/2.

32 Dufferin to Cross, 27 March 1888, D1071H/M10/2; Dufferin to Cross, 26 March & 29 June 1888, Mss Eur E243/24; Chesney, op. cit.

33 Dufferin to Duchess of Manchester, 6 June 1888, and Dufferin to Lord Arthur Russell, 29 June 1888, both in Mss Eur F130/29; Dufferin to Viscount Cross, 14 May, 8 & 29 June, 17 Aug. 1888, all in F130/11; Lord Malmesbury, 'The Health of the Army', *The Times*, 25 Sep. 1895; Sir George Arthur, *Some Letters from a Man of No Importance 1895–1914* (1928), p. 20.

34 Report of Departmental Committee on the Prevention of Venereal Disease among the British Troops in India, C. 8379, PP 1897, LXIII, paras. 13–15. For a later view see Karun Kumar Chatterji, *Syphilis in general practice, with special reference to the tropics* (1920).

35 Ballhatchett, *Race, Sex and Class*, pp. 94–5.

36 National Council of Public Morals, *Prevention of Venereal Disease*, (1920) pp. 32–3; Sir Philip Magnus, *Kitchener* (1958), p. 235; Lord Curzon of Kedleston to Lord George Hamilton, 25 March & 13 April 1903, Mss Eur F111/162, India Office Library; Arthur, *Some Letters*, p. 160; Sir George Arthur, *Further Letters from a Man of No Importance* (1932), pp. 114, 224; Edmund White, *States of Desire* (1986 edn), p. 55.

37 Col. Lawrence Harrison, 'Imperial Conference', *Health and Empire*, 1 (1926), p. 208; Sir Basil Blackett, 'Social Hygiene 1914–1935', *Health and Empire*, 10 (1935), p. 180.

38 F. P. Crozier, *A Brass Hat in No Man's Land* (1930), pp. 50–1, 127; Lord Derby, House of Lords debates, 11 April 1918, 29, col. 684; Public Morals, *Prevention of Venereal Disease*, pp. 156–7; O'Connor, 'Venus and the Lone Kiwi', p. 25.

39 House of Lords debates, 19 &

28 May, 9 June 1857, 145, cols. 537, 919, 1412; *The Times*, 3 March 1866.

40 A. C. Benson and Lord Esher, *The Letters of Queen Victoria 1837–1861*, 3, (1908), p. 378; W. T. Stead, evidence to Royal Commission on Divorce, 21 Dec. 1910, Q. 43403; C. P. Scott, ibid., QQ. 43527–8.

41 Sir Alfred Cooper, evidence to Fitz-Roy Committee on Physical Deterioration (1904), Q. 3871; Reid, *Prevention*, p. 17; Lord Ranksborough, House of Lords debates, 10 Dec. 1919, 37, col. 880.

42 *Protest of Medical Men against Compulsory Notification of Infectious Diseases* (1882), pp. 2, 5.

43 F. B. Smith, *The Retreat of Tuberculosis 1850–1950* (1988), pp. 68–70; Mott, evidence to FitzRoy Committee on Physical Deterioration, Q. 10469; Reid, *Prevention*, p. 18.

44 Lynda Bryder, *Below The Magic Mountain: A Social History of Tuberculosis in Twentieth-Century Britain* (Oxford, 1988), pp. 41–3, 73, 103–9, 260, 264–5; Stephen Paget, *Sir Victor Horsley* (1919), pp. 173–4, 209; D. J. Jeremy and C. Shaw eds., *Dictionary of Business Biography*, 5 (1986), p. 432.

45 *Complete Peerage* 2 (1912), p. 222; S. B. Atkinson, 'Some Medico-Legal Associations of Syphilis', in Sir D'Arcy Power and J. Keogh Murray eds., *A System of Syphilis*, 3 (1909), pp. 158–9; *The Times*, 28 Nov. 1890; John Vincent, *The Later Derby Diaries* (Bristol, 1981), p. 137; Lord Connemara to Lord Cross, 2 Dec. 1890 & 8 Feb. 1891, Mss Eur E243/45, India Office Library; Dufferin to Duchess of Manchester, 2 Jan. 1888, Mss Eur F130/29; Marquess of Dufferin and Ava to Queen Victoria, 3 Sep. 1889, Marquess of Dufferin and Ava to Sir Henry Ponsonby, 16 Sep. 1889, Dufferin and Ava to Connemara, 25 Sep. 1889 & 13 July 1890, Dufferin and Ava papers D1071H/N1/34.

46 Astley Bloxam, evidence to Royal Commission on Divorce, 7 Dec. 1910, Q. 40959; Ruth Hodgkinson, *Origins of the National Health Service* (1967), pp. 300–2.

47 *Westminster Review*, 37 (1870), pp.121–2; Select Committee on Contagious Diseases Acts (1868), Q. 348.

48 Ralph Johnston, *Report on Venereal Diseases*, Cd. 7029 of 1913, p. 20.

49 Select Committee on Contagious Diseases Acts (1868), QQ. 908–912, 1122; W. J. Moore, memorandum on Contagious Diseases Acts, Oct. 1886, Dufferin and Ava papers D1071H/M10/2.

50 Walkowitz, *Prostitution and Victorian Society*, pp. 59–61; *Lancet*, 30 Jan. 1926, p. 261.

51 Sir Alfred Cooper and Sir Victor Horsley, evidence to FitzRoy Committee on Physical Deterioration (1904), QQ. 3851, 3852, 10535; Gay, *Tender Passion*, pp. 374–8; *Westminster Review*, 36 (1869), p.187.

52 Public Morals, *Prevention of Venereal Disease*, p. 4; obituary of Lane, *BMJ*, 13 June 1891, p. 1312; obituary of Hill, *BMJ*, 16 Jan. 1892, p. 148; Select Committee on Contagious Diseases Acts (1868), Q. 295; obituary of Bloxam, *Lancet*, 30 Jan. 1926, p. 261. See Sir Edward F. Chapman to Surgeon-General of India, 30 June 1886: 'the study and practice of the treatment of venereal diseases by the medical profession has never yet led to distinction; yet there is no disease, in the present day, more injurious to mankind at large, and none calling more clearly for special professional skill': Dufferin and Ava papers D1071H/M10/2.

53 Lord Binning to Reginald Brett, c. 1887–8, papers of Viscount Esher 10/14, Churchill College, Cambridge; Lord Dufferin to Lord Terence Blackwood, 20 March 1888, India Office Library Mss Eur F130/29; compare Dufferin to Marquess of Lansdowne, 27 March 1888, and Dufferin to Earl of Haddington, 15 June 1888, ibid.

54 Ellman, *Wilde*, pp. 88–91; Morgan, *Somerset Maugham*, pp. 95–6; for Paget's obituary see *BMJ*, 22 May 1926, pp. 884–5; for some curious and untruthful comments by a lover of Violet Hunt on syphilis and the Imperial family of Hohenzollern, see Ford Madox Ford, *A History of Our Own Times* (Manchester, 1989), pp. 200–1; for the gonorrhoea of another woman novelist of this epoch, see Claire Tomalin, *Katherine Mansfield. A Secret Life* (1987), pp. 73–8.

55 A. O. Ross, 'The Problem of Treatment of Venereal Disease in the Mercantile Marine', *BJVD*, 5 (1929), pp. 210–11, 216, 219.

56 See generally W. A. Pusey, *The History and Epidemiology of Syphilis* (Springfield, Illinois, 1933).

57 Select Committee on Contagious Diseases Acts (1868), Q. 1075; *BMJ*, 18 Nov. 1911, p. 1385.

58 Sir Bryan Donkin, 'The Fight Against Venereal Infection', *Nineteenth Century*, 82 (1917), pp. 583–4; Hugh Elliott, 'Venereal Prophylaxis', *Nineteenth Century*, 84 (1918), p. 171; Sir Alfred Cooper, evidence to FitzRoy Committee on Physical Deterioration (1904), QQ. 3831–9.

59 P. S. O'Connor, 'Venus and the Lonely Kiwi', pp. 12–13.

60 Angus McLaren, *Birth Control in Nineteenth-Century England* (1978), pp. 120–1, 225; Richard Soloway, *Birth Control and the Population Question in England 1877-1930* (1982), pp. 3–4 & passim.

61 Cleugh, *Secret Enemy*, p. 185.

62 Dame Mary Scharlieb, *Reminiscences* (1924), p. 218; Maurice Ernest, *Beware of Harley Street* (1917), p. 8.

63 Public Morals, *Prevention of Venereal Disease*, pp. 3–4, 6–7; Reid, *Prevention*, p. 270; House of Lords debates, 2 April 1919, 34, col. 75; Public Morals, *Prevention of Venereal Disease*, pp. 4, 12, 20, 22–3, 170.

64 Public Morals, *Prevention of Venereal Diseases*, pp. 173–7, 234; Gay, *Education of Senses*, pp. 136–49; *Lancet*, 1 Sep. 1945, p. 290.

65 Civis, 'Venereal Disease', p. 252; Public Morals, *Prevention of*

Venereal Disease, p. 84; Wansy Bayly, *Triple Challenge* (1935), p. 376.

66 Quoted Porter, 'Mixed Feelings', p. 15; Public Morals, *Prevention of Venereal Disease*, pp. 2, 22; David McLoughlin, evidence 6 Dec. 1864 to Skey Committee on Pathology and Treatment of Venereal Disease, QQ. 64–5.

67 Harrison to Chief Medical Officer, 8 Nov. 1939, PRO MH 55/1333.

68 Barrett, *Twin Ideals*, p. 445; Earls of Meath and Halsbury, House of Lords debates, 8 April 1889, 334, cols. 1761–4; White, ed., *Osborne Letters*, II, pp. 286–7.

69 Countess of Longford, *Victoria RI* (1964), p. 551; *The Times*, 7 Feb. 1899; *Complete Peerage*, 5 (1926), p. 8; Helen Pukala, *The Last Romantic* (1985), p. 121; Daley, *Small Cloud*, p. 28.

70 Donkin, 'Fight against Venereal Infection', p. 588; Donkin, in Reid, *Prevention*, pp. 3–4; McLaren, *Birth Control*, pp. 112, 132–3.

71 Eugene Brieux, *Three Plays* (1917), forward and preface by Charlotte and George Bernard Shaw; 'Forbidden Marriage', *Health and Empire*, 14 (1939), p. 60. In the USA Brieux's sales were far larger than in Britain, and there were fewer obstacles to American productions of the play.

72 Charles Wilson, *First With The News* (1985), p. 379.

73 W. N. Willis, *Western Men with Eastern Morals* (1913), pp. 15–28, 110; Dufferin to Sir Arthur Godley, 8 June 1888, Mss Eur F 130/29; Edward J. Bristow, *Prostitution and Prejudice: the Jewish Fight against White Slavery 1870–1939* (Oxford, 1982); A. Bostock Hill, 'Notes of a Recent Visit to the Straits Settlements and the Federated Malay States', *Health and Empire*, 1 (1926), pp. 101–4.

74 Arthur Corbett-Smith, *The Problem of Sex Diseases* (1919), pp. 90–2, 94–5. For an earlier portrayal of a *declassé* syphilitic, see Samuel Warren, *Passages from the Diary of a Late Physician* (1854 edn), pp. 310–13, 317, 391–20.

75 Revd Albert David, evidence to

Royal Commission on Venereal Disease, 15 June 1914, Q. 16417; Harry Bisseker, *In Confidence: to boys* (1904). The latter book was published under the aegis of the Council of Medical Officers of Schools Association.

76 Corbett-Smith, *Problem*, pp. 79–80, 86, 102, 104; Arthur Engel, 'Immoral Intentions: the University of Oxford and the Problem of Prostitution 1827–1914', *Victorian Studies*, 23 (1979), pp. 79–107; Bristow, *Prostitution and Prejudice*, p. 24. Henri Champly in *The Road to Shanghai* (1934) exposed white slavery in China. Others followed Corbett-Smith in their desire to distinguish not only between men and women, but between the British and foreigners. Thus the headmaster Lyttelton declared in 1900 that 'the normal growth of animal desires [was] far stronger in the male than in the female, at least in England': Lyttelton, *Training of the Young*, p. 10.

77 David and Lyttelton, evidence to Royal Commission on Venereal Diseases, QQ. 16417, 16465, 16579.

78 J. L. A. Paton, evidence to Royal Commission on Venereal Diseases, 6 July 1914, QQ. 18849–50, 18854, 18877.

CHAPTER SIX

1 Douglas White, 'Eugenics and Venereal Disease', *Eugenics Review*, 5 (1914), p. 264; Leonard Darwin, 'The Eugenics Education Society and Venereal Disease', *Eugenics Review*, 8 (1917), pp. 213–7; evidence to Royal Commission on Divorce from Dr Astley Bloxam, Montagu Crackanthorpe, Sir Frederick Mott, J. E. Lane and others; PRO MH 55/531.

2 *Lancet*, 28 June 1913, pp. 1817–9. For further arguments that 'victory lies most nearly within the reach of that belligerent who possesses the greater reserve of healthy manhood', see E. T. Burke 'Venereal Diseases During the War', *Quarterly Review*, 233 (1920), pp. 304, 316.

3 *The Times*, 9 Oct. 1922, 11 Nov.

1922, 3 June 1935; another story persists of FitzRoy importuning men at South Kensington station: Hyde, *Other Love*, p. 201.

4 Diary of Sir Almeric FitzRoy, 11 August 1913, British Library Add. Ms. 48377; Donkin, 'The Fight Against Venereal Infection', p. 585; Harvey Cushing, *The Life of Sir William Osler*, 2 (1925), pp. 624, 631; Hamilton Fyfe, *Northcliffe, an Intimate Biography* (1930), pp. 314–28 & *passim*.

5 Diary of Sir Almeric FitzRoy, 8 & 12 Aug., 3 Oct. 1913, Add. Ms. 48377.

6 Diary of Sir Almeric FitzRoy, 1 Jan. 1913, Add. Ms. 48377; *The Times* 8 Feb. 1933; Peter Fraser, *Lord Esher* (1973), pp. 21, 106, 198; Lees-Milne, *Enigmatic Edwardian* (1986), p. 146; Bayly, *Triple Challenge*, pp. 313–4; Sydenham, House of Lords debates, 8 March 1917, 24, cols.465–6, and 2 April 1919, 34, col. 68; see also Diary of G. E. Morrison, 5 Nov. 1899, 29 Jan. 1903, 2 Oct. 1905, 21 Jan. 1906.

7 Diary of Sir Almeric FitzRoy, 24 Nov. 1913, Add. Ms. 48377.

8 Lord Sydenham, *My Working Life* (1927), p. 297; Lord Snowden, *Autobiography*, 1 (1934), p. 276; J. Scott Lidgett, *My Guided Life* (1936), p. 200; Scharlieb, *Reminiscences*, p. 212; National Council of Public Morals' National Birth Rate Commission, *The Declining Birth Rate* (1916) and *Problems of Population and Parenthood* (1920); Marquess of Aberdeen and Temair, *The Times*, 31 Oct. 1919; Monk Bretton papers, 107 (d).

9 See tributes by Sir St Clair Thomson and Sir Anderson Critchett in *BMJ*, 1 March 1924, pp. 407–9.

10 *BMJ*, 13 Nov. 1926, pp. 914–5; *Journal of Mental Science*, 72 (1926), pp. 317–20; Martin Stone, 'Shellshock and the Psychiatrists', in W. F. Bynum, Roy Porter and Michael Shepherd eds., *The Anatomy of Madness*, 2 (1985), pp. 251–2.

11 Sir John Collie, *Malingering* (1917), pp. 18, 20, 25, 32, 43; Collie, *Fraud in Medico-Legal Practice* (1932), pp. 1, 15. The other medical knight on the Commission was Sir Arthur Newsholme, who in a review of Bertrand Russell's *Marriage and Morals* wrote that it was 'pernicious, by instigating the substitute of a retrograde movement towards social and family anarchy and barbarism, in lieu of the slow but upward progress towards the ideal of monogamous married life for the majority of the people, and of chastity for those to whom this does not come': *Health and Empire*, 5 (1930), p. 67.

12 Lidgett, *My Guided Life*, p. 75; *Dictionary of National Biography*; *The Times* 18 June 1953; Royal Commission on Divorce, 29 Nov. 1910, Q. 39723. On the 'revolting' food at Lady Bunting's, see Diary of G. E. Morrison, 15 Jan. 1911.

13 Sir Almeric FitzRoy, *Memoirs*, 2 (1925), pp. 533, 582; Anderson, *Suicide*, pp. 319–20, 326–7; for Horsley as 'the terror of rack-renters', see Winnington-Ingram, *Work in Great Cities*, p. 130.

14 Louise Creighton, *The Social Disease* (1914), pp. 12, 14, 28–9; *The Times*, 16 April 1936; FitzRoy, *Memoirs*, 2, p. 614. Mrs Creighton's husband had been a great ecclesiastical historian who was successively Bishop of Peterborough and London, enjoying a high reputation for tolerance and humour. Yet 'O think, I beseech you, of the deep importance of every hour of your lives,' he preached; 'The days are evil, and in each succeeding generation there is war on earth . . . Oh fortify your hearts against all temptations to frivolity, to lounging, to trifling, to petty affectations which eat out the soul. Trust me, such things are unmanly and they are ungodly': Mandell Creighton, *The Claims of the Common Life* (1905), p. 36.

15 *Dictionary of National Biography*; Scharlieb, *Reminiscences*, pp. 213, 220; Lord Sydenham, 'Dame Mary

Scharlieb', *Health and Empire*, 5 (1930), pp. 262–4; *BMJ*, 16 July 1921, pp. 93–4.

16 Birth Rate Commission, *Declining Birth Rate*, pp. 217–9, 221–3, 226–7. On Mrs Burgwin, see Patricia Hollis, *Ladies Elect: Women in English Local Government 1865–1914* (Oxford, 1987).

17 FitzRoy, Diary of Sir Almeric, 6 Aug. 1913 & 20 Dec. 1915; Sydenham, *Working Life*, p. 297; Scharlieb, *Reminiscences*, p. 219.

18 *Morning Post*, 27 Sept. 1924; Howe, *Holmes-Laski Letters*, 1, p. 566; Sir Arthur Newsholme, *The Last Thirty Years in Public Health* (1936), p. 157.

19 Donkin, 'The Fight Against Venereal Infection', p. 585.

20 Public Morals, *Prevention of Venereal Disease*, p. 141.

21 Creighton, *Social Disease*, p. 14; Sir Arthur Newsholme, 'The Relative Roles of Compulsion and Education in Public Health Work', *Health Problems in Organised Society* (1927), ch. 9.

22 Earls of Aberdeen and Kimberley, House of Lords debates, 8 April 1889, 334, cols. 1764–6; Alec Craig, *The Banned Books of England* (1962), pp. 96, 108; J. H. Walker, memorandum of 15 August 1954, PRO HO 302/1.

23 Viscount Hailsham, House of Lords debates, 15 December 1960, 227, col. 572; John A. Sutherland, *Offensive Literature: Decensorship in Britain 1960–1982* (1982), pp. 27, 78.

24 Crozier, *Brass Hat*, pp. 57–8; Beardsley, 'Allied Against Sin, p. 202; Buckley, 'Failure to Resolve', p. 72; M. Cavaillon, 'France's Efforts against Venereal Disease', *Health and Empire*, 2 (1927), pp. 150–62; E. Jeanselme, 'On the Present Recrudescence of Syphilis in the Paris Districts', *Health and Empire*, 3 (1928), pp. 251–3.

25 Crozier, *Brass Hat*, pp. 127–8.

26 *The Times*, 16, 17 & 19 Dec. 1919, 3 Jan. 1920; Reid, *Prevention*, pp. 300–7; *BMJ*, 24 Jan. 1920.

27 Ettie Rout, quoted Public Morals, *Prevention of Venereal Disease*, p. 91, and Reid, *Prevention* (1920), p. 275; Fischer and Dubois, *Sexual Life*, pp. 381–2.

28 Buckley, 'Failure to Resolve', p. 72; Reid, *Prevention*, pp. 274–5; Herbert Samuel, House of Commons debates, 19 Feb. 1917, 90, col. 1105.

29 Ernest, *Beware of Harley Street*, p. 2; 'No Greater Sin' *Health and Empire*, 16 (1942), pp. 335–6; cf. E. M. Goodman, 'The Criminal Law Amendment Bill', *Review of Reviews*, 55 (1917), p. 369; Lords Rhondda, Sydenham and Gainsford, House of Lords debates, 8 March 1917, 24, cols. 456–66.

30 Ettie Rout to Sir Auckland Geddes, 28 Feb. 1925, Sir Archibald Bodkin to Ministry of Health, 26 Sept. 1925, PRO MH 55/182; Norman Haire, *Encyclopaedia of Sexual Knowledge* (1934; 1957 edn) p. 487; Craig, *Banned Books* (1962), p. 95; M. W. Schraenen, 'The Campaign against Medical Charlatanism – Comparison of Anti-Venereal Legislation', *Health and Empire*, 9 (1934), pp. 197–206.

31 E. J. Gordon Wallace, 'The Venereal Diseases Act, 1917', *Health and Empire*, 10 (1935), pp. 53–4; *Reading Standard*, 1 March 1930; *Berkshire Chronicle* 28 Feb. 1930; PRO MH 55/1322; Society for Prevention of Venereal Disease to Neville Chamberlain, 29 June 1927, PRO MH 55/192; *Morning Post*, 22 June 1927; Mick Brown, *Richard Branson* (1988), pp. 49–50.

32 Reid, *Prevention*, pp. 116–7.

33 *Lancet*, 6 Dec. 1919; House of Lords debates, 2 April 1919, 34, col. 67.

34 Bayly, *Triple Challenge*, pp. 331, 375.

35 Scharlieb, *Reminiscences*, pp. 212–3; Nigel Nicolson ed., *The Question of Things Happening: the Letters of Virginia Woolf*, 2 (1976), pp. 138–40.

36 Scharlieb, *Reminiscences*, p. 223; Leo Amery, *My Political Life*, 3 (1955), p. 208; *The Times*, 5 Aug. 1955; G. R. Searle, *Eugenics and*

Politics in Britain 1900–1914 (Leyden, 1976), pp. 10–17.

37 Reid, *Prevention*, p. 338; Archbishop of Canterbury, House of Lords debates, 2 April 1919, 34, cols. 70, 74–6; *Health and Empire*, 5 (1930), p. 162; T. W. Pym, 'Social Hygiene and Human Welfare: the task of the Religious Leader', *Health and Empire*, 8 (1933), p. 23.

38 Scharlieb, *Reminiscences*, p. 222. For the opposition of a leading suffragettist to prophylaxis as likely to encourage prostitution and to perpetuate dual standards of sexuality, see Mrs Henry Fawcett, *Review of Reviews*, 55 (1917), pp. 155–8.

39 *BMJ*, 11 July 1931, pp. 81–4; Monk Bretton papers, 107 (d); *Health and Empire*, 6 (1931), pp. 285–90; Boyd-Carpenter Committee, *Prevention of Venereal Disease* (1921), pp. 106–8.

40 *Lancet*, 9 August 1930, p. 325; information from Lady Dalrymple-Champneys, Nov. 1988; Monk Bretton papers, 107 (d); Sir Francis Champneys, 'The Fight Against Venereal Infection', *Nineteenth Century*, 82 (1917), p. 1051.

41 Elliott, 'Venereal Prophylaxis', pp. 172–9; Champneys, 'Prophylaxis', ibid., pp. 959–62.

42 Michael Astor, *Tribal Feeling* (1963), pp. 43, 47; Christopher Sykes, *Nancy* (1972), p. 146; Reid, *Prevention*, pp. 372–4; Bayly, *Triple Challenge*, pp. 203, 333–4; the members of Astor's Committee are listed in House of Lords debates, 10 Dec. 1919, 37, col. 876.

43 Marquess of Dufferin and Ava, House of Lords debates, 23 Nov. 1920, 42, col. 503; Bayly, *Triple Challenge*, p. 338; *Western Morning News*, 27 July 1922; for Willoughby de Broke's views, see House of Lords debates, 2 April 1919, 34, cols. 53–63, and 10 Dec. 1919, 37, cols. 840–53.

44 *Lancet*, 6 Aug. 1927 & 23 Nov. 1929.

45 Bayly, *Triple Challenge*, pp. 325–9, 374–5.

46 Reid, *Prevention*, p. 7; *Report on Prevention of Venereal Disease*, p. 130; Sir Edward Henry, evidence to Royal Commission on Police, 17 July 1906, Q. 67, Cd. 4156 of 1908; 'The Problem of Venereal Diseases in Wartime', *Health and Empire*, 14 (1939), pp. 153–4; Bishop of London, House of Lords debates, 13 Feb. 1934, 90, cols. 819–21.

47 Sir Arthur Robinson, minute of 9 March 1921, PRO MH 55/179; Sir Alfred Mond, minutes of Ministry of Health conference, 8 Dec. 1921, and minutes of meeting with Lord Dawson of Penn, 16 Dec. 1921, PRO MH 55/181.

48 Howe, *Holmes-Laski Letters*, 1, p. 330; *The Times*, 14 August 1935 & 4 August 1936. The six medical knights advising Lord Dawson were Sir Clifford Allbutt, Sir Anthony Bowlby, Sir Walter Fletcher, Sir Archibald Garrod, Sir Norman Moore and Sir John Thomson-Walker, together with Professor H. R. Kenwood. Trevethin's colleagues were Lord Tomlin, C. J. Bond of Leicester Royal Infirmary and the Eugenics Society, Surgeon Vice-Admiral Sir Reginald Bond, Professor Georges Dreyer of Oxford, Martin Flack of the RAF, Dr Dorothy Hare, Sir Francis Fremantle MP, a former county medical officer, Professor H. R. Kenwood of London University, Lt.-Gen. Sir William Leishman, Sir Frederick Menzies of the London County Council, Dr Morna Rawlins, an authority on venereal disease in women, Dr J. H. Sequeira and Sir Bernard Spilsbury the Home Office pathologist.

49 Geddes was succeeded as President of BSHC in 1925 by the Marquess of Willingdon, who was in turn succeeded in 1926 by the Marquess of Linlithgow. Later presidents were Sir Basil Blackett (1929), Leo Amery (1936) and Sir Walter Langdon-Brown (1939). Vice-presidents in the 1930s included physicians such as Professor Winifred Cullis or Sir Robert Philip, the educationalist Sir Cyril Norwood, the geologist Dame Maria Ogilvie Gordon, an imperial-minded politician Sir Edward Grigg (Lord Altrincham) and the Countess

of Shaftesbury. The rakish young
Lord Stanley of Alderley became
Chairman of its Appeal Committee
in 1934.

50 Sir Basil Blackett, 'Some Aspects of
Social Hygiene', *Health and
Empire*, 10 (1935), p. 4; Blackett,
'Progress in Social Hygiene 1914–
35', ibid., p. 171. The published
aims of BSHC were to 'strengthen
the family as the basic social unit',
'the development of control of the
racial instinct', 'to emphasize the
responsibility of the community and
the individual for preserving or
improving, by education and social
measures, the quality of future generations', 'to further social customs
which promote a high and equal
standard of sex conduct in men and
women', 'to promote the prevention
and treatment of venereal diseases
by appropriate educative, medical
and social measures', to resist 'commercialized vice' and to remove
'conditions conducive to promiscuity'. In Blackett's view, 'the great
enemy is IGNORANCE' (pp. 7,
11).

51 Reid, *Prevention*, p. 341.

CHAPTER SEVEN

1 E. T. Burke, 'The Toll of Secret
Disease', *Nineteenth Century*, 102
(1927), pp. 675–6, 682. This chap-
ter can be read in conjunction with
Allan Brandt, *No Magic Bullet*, op.
cit., and Elizabeth Fee, 'Sin versus
Science: Venereal Disease in
Twentieth-Century Baltimore', in
Elizabeth Fee and Daniel Fox eds.,
AIDS: the Burdens of History (Ber-
keley, Calif., and London, 1988),
pp. 121–46.

2 PRO Inf 13/198.

3 Memorandum on Venereal Disease
in Britain 1931, PRO MH 55/198;
PRO MH 55/1326; PRO MH 55/
1386; Albertine Winner, 'Venereal
Disease Hostels in London', *Health
and Empire*, 11 (1936), pp. 27-35;
G. Pugh Smith, 'Social Hygiene and
Audience', *Health and Empire*, 16
(1942), p. 294; *Lancet*, 6 March
1943, p. 314; Sir Weldon Dalrymple-Champneys, 'The Epidemiological Control of Venereal Dis-

ease', *BJVD*, 23 (1947), pp. 101–2;
L. W. Harrison, 'Venereal Dis-
eases', in Sir Arthur Salusbury Mac-
Nalty, *The Civilian Health and
Medical Services* (1953), pp. 116–7;
see generally Steven Humphries, *A
Secret World of Sex 1900–1950*
(1988).

4A 'Report of National Conference on
the Health and Welfare of the British Mercant Navy at Home and in
Ports Overseas', *Health and
Empire*, 4 (1929), pp. 93–168;
G. St. J. Orde Browne, 'Port Welfare in the Western Mediterranean',
ibid., 8 (1933), pp. 110–6; 'The
British Social Hygiene Council and
the Mercantile Marine', ibid., 10
(1935), pp. 27–42; 'The Welfare of
the Mercantile Marine', ibid., 10,
pp. 206–31; H. M. Hanschell, 'The
Problem of Venereal Disease in the
Mercantile Marine', *BJVD*, 5
(1929), p. 208; *BMJ*, 22 May 1943,
pp. 645–6 and Hanschell's letter,
idem, 26 June 1943, pp. 803–4;
James Hanley, *Boy* (1931), pp. 262,
269–71.

4B Douglas, *South Wind*, ch. 17; Lord
Dawson of Penn, House of Lords
debates, 13 Feb. 1934, 90,
cols. 806, 811; Bishop of London,
ibid., col. 819; Archbishop of Canterbury, ibid., col. 836; Lord Darcy
de Knath, House of Lords debates,
27 Feb. 1934, 90, col. 976; Francis
Watson, *Dawson of Penn* (1950),
pp. 245–8; David L. Lewis, 'Sex
and the Automobile: from Rumble
Seats to Rockin' Vans', essay in
David L. Lewis and Lawrence
Goldstein eds., *The Automobile
and American Culture* (Ann
Arbor, 1983); James J. Flink,
The Automobile Age (1988),
pp. 160–2.

5 L. W. Harrison, 'Tracing and Treat-
ing Contacts', *Health and Empire* 1
(1926), pp. 188–90; Harrison,
'How to Attract to Treatment and
Render Non-Infective the Largest
Proportion of the Infected Popula-
tion', ibid., 5 (1930), pp. 37, 39;
Hamish Nicol, 'Co-ordination of
Infant Welfare and Venereal Disease
Work', ibid., 5 (1930), 122–3; Mar-
garet Rorke, 'The Girl Mother in the
VD Clinic', ibid., 5 (1930), p. 225;

patient A2830 ('Happy Days') in
E. T. Burke, 'Are We To Have Compulsory Treatment of Venereal Disease?', ibid., 10 (1935), p. 122;
BMJ, 9 Jan. 1943, p. 53.

6 MacNalty, *Civilian Health*, p. 115; Blackett, 'Progress in Social Hygiene', p. 181; Kenneth Young ed., *The Diaries of Sir Robert Bruce Lockhart*, 1 (1973), pp. 381–2. For an account of treatment centres and 'definite wrong-doers', see Margaret Roeke, 'The Social Aspect of the Venereal Disease Treatment Centre', *Health and Empire*, 3 (1927), pp. 193–9; for a description of the VD clinic at Darlington, see T. Ferguson, 'A Survey of Some Findings in Clinic Administration', ibid., 5 (1930), pp. 105–8.

7 Robert Lees, 'The Lock Wards of Edinburgh Royal Infirmary', *BJVD*, 37 (1961), pp. 188–9; R. C. L. Batchelor, 'The Edinburgh Venereal Diseases Scheme', *Health and Empire*, 14 (1939), pp. 204–13; Margaret Thompson, 'The wages of sin: the problem of alcoholism and general paralysis in nineteenth-century Edinburgh', in W. F. Bynum, Roy Porter and Michael Shepherd eds., *The Anatomy of Madness*, 3 (1988), pp. 316–37; on later Edinburgh venereology, see obituaries of David Lees in *Health and Empire*, 9 (1934), pp. 4, 141–9.

8 *Lancet*, 16 Oct. 1943, p. 494; Public Morals, *Prevention of Venereal Disease*, p. 4.

9 Quoted in draft report of Sir John Eldon Bankes, PRO MH 55/201; on Harrison see *BMJ*, 23 May 1964, pp. 1386–7, and 27 June 1964, p. 1714.

10 Lord FitzAlan of Derwent to Neville Chamberlain, 8 May 1925, and Sir George Newman to Sir Arthur Robinson, 22 June 1927, PRO MH 55/200; Newman to Robinson, 14 Nov. 1927, and minute by Robinson, 10 Dec. 1927, PRO MH 55/201.

11 Cd. 3363 of 1929; *The Times*, 19 July 1929; Letitia Fairfield, 'In-Patient Provision for Venereal Diseases in L.C.C. Hospitals', *Health and Empire*, 7 (1932), pp. 16–21.

12 Harrison, memoranda on London Lock Hospital, 7 Feb. 1930 & 1931, and Annie Lord-Hoyle to Ministry of Health, 5 May 1930, PRO MH 55/202; *Daily Herald* 6 March 1931. For an account of some physicians working at the London Lock Hospital in the 1920s see obituary of Henry Corsi, *BMJ*, 14 Jan. 1950, pp. 130–1; obituary of J. Johnston Abraham, *BMJ*, 17 August 1963, p. 448; obituary of J. E. R. McDonagh, *BMJ*, 27 Feb. 1965, p. 594.

13 Garner v. Garner reported in *The Times* 14 Jan. 1920, pp. 5, 13, and in *The Times Law Reports*; PRO MH 55/184; George Pollock, *Mr Justice McCardie* (1934); C. J. MacAlister, 'Law and the Venereal Diseases', *Health and Empire* 7 (1932), pp. 38–54; *BMJ* 4 Jan. 1975, p. 43, for an obituary of Assinder (1889–1974).

14 Burke, 'Secret Disease', pp. 681–2; Burke, 'The Present Opportunity for a Review of the Venereal Diseases Scheme', *Health and Empire*, 6 (1931), p. 197; 'Modern Girls and Moral Values: Amateurs who Sin for Pleasure: What Knowledge Has Done', *Reynolds News*, 5 March 1922.

15 E. T. Burke, report of 18 April 1935 & memorandum of 29 August 1935, PRO MH 55/1371; on Burke, see *Health and Empire*, 9 (1934), p. 350; Burke, 'Congenital Syphilis', ibid., 11 (1936), pp. 92–100; review of his *Venereal Diseases* (1940) in *BMJ*, 4 Jan. 1941, p. 15, 7 June 1941, p. 871 for his forthright views, and 5 July 1941, p. 34, for obituary.

16 Frank S. Bricknell to E. T. Burke, 23 Aug. 1935, PRO MH 55/1371. See also 'Symposium: the transport worker and the lorry girl', *Health and Empire*, 11 (1936), pp. 5–14 (especially 'How A Lorry Driver Sees It, by A Man on the Road').

17 'Unhappy Wife' to Burke, 22 Aug. 1935, PRO MH 55/1371; Burke, 'Present Opportunity', p. 197; cf. Gladys Hall, *Prostitution: a survey and a challenge* (1933).

18 Fleet Surgeon W. E. Home, quoted G. D. Knox, 'Seamen and Venereal

Disease: Initiation of a Comprehensive Policy', *Health and Empire*, 1 (1926), p. 64; Margaret Wailes, 'The Social Aspect of the Venereal Diseases', *BJVD*, 21 (1945), p. 16; 'The Social Background of Venereal Disease', *BJVD*, 21 (1945), pp. 26–31; Barbara Meil Hobson, *Uneasy Virtue: the Politics of Prostitution and the American Reform Tradition* (New York, 1987), ch. 8 'The Unadjusted Girl', pp. 184–209; R. Marinkovitch, 'How to bring young infected women under treatment', *Health and Empire*, 14 (1939), pp. 75–9.

19 Cyril Burt, 'The Contribution of Psychology to Social Hygiene', *Health and Empire*, 1 (1926), pp. 13–37 (especially pp. 28–32); Burt, 'The Causes of Sex Delinquency in Girls', ibid., 251–71; Burt, 'Educational Psychology', *Health and Empire*, 6 (1931), pp. 200–10; E. D. Wittkower, 'The Psychological Aspects of Venereal Disease', *BJVD*, 24 (1948), pp. 59–60, 64.

20 'The Local Government Bill', *Health and Empire*, 4 (1929), pp. 30–46, 87–8; S. W. Hill, 'The Finance of Public Health Services: Revision of the Block Grants Scheme', ibid., 12 (1937), pp. 45–9.

21 Sir Arthur MacNalty, minute of 7 Jan. 1931, PRO MH 55/198; Sir Basil Blackett, 'Economic Aspects of Social Hygiene', *Health and Empire*, 4 (1929), pp. 301–12.

22 L. W. Harrison, minute of 3 Jan. 1931, Sir Arthur Robinson, minute of 14 Jan. 1931, PRO MH 55/198; L. Harrison, memoranda of 5 April 1939, 1 & 22 May 1939, PRO MH 55/1333; L. W. Harrison, 'Methods of Enlightenment of the General Public on Venereal Diseases', *BJVD*, 18 (1942), pp. 77–81; H. A. Hadfield, 'The Nature and Cause of Phobias, with Special Reference to Syphilophobia', *BJVD*, 14 (1938), p. 130; C. Hamilton Wilkie, quoted *BJVD*, 18 (1942), p. 88. For a description of Amery as 'a clever little cuss but a bit too cocksure', see Sir Walter Townley to G. E. Morrison, 12 May 1904, Morrison papers, vol. 48. For criticism of the

approach epitomized by Sybil Neville-Rolfe, or for examples of personal hostility to her, see also James McIntosh to Harrison, 8 Feb. 1939, PRO MH 55/1384; Walter Elliott to Sir Walter Langdon-Brown, 12 March 1940, PRO MH 55/1885; J. E. Pater, minutes of 30 March & 14 July 1939, Eric Macgregor, minute of 31 March 1939, and L. Harrison, minute of 5 Nov. 1940, PRO MH 55/1386.

23 *Lancet*, 6 March 1943, pp. 314–5.

24 *Lancet*, ibid.; *BJVD*, 24 (1948), p. 64; L. W. Harrison, 'Coordination of Maternity and Child Welfare Service with the Venereal Disease Service', *Health and Empire*, 1 (1926) pp. 169–72; Flora Lloyd, ibid., pp. 173–8.

25 Amery, memorandum of 26 Sep. 1938, and Sir Francis Fremantle to Walter Elliott, 21 August 1939, PRO MH 55/1384; John Costello, *Love, Sex and War: Changing Values 1939–45* (1985), p. 126. Cf. Fremantle, 'The Economics of Public Health', *Health and Empire*, 1 (1926), pp. 108–15; Otto May, 'Social Hygiene in Rearmament', ibid., 14 (1939), pp. 4–6; L. Crome, 'Some Medical Aspects of the Spanish War', ibid., 14 (1939), pp. 74–5; L.C.M.S. Amery, 'Progress in Social Hygiene', ibid., 14 (1939), pp. 141–50.

26 Alexis de Tocqueville, *Recollections* (1948 edn), p. 192; Salford Town Clerk to Ministry of Health, 26 Jan. 1942, PRO MH 55/1326; Costello, *Love*, p. 329.

27 Robert Forgan, 'Pox Britannica', *Health and Empire*, 15 (1941), pp. 108–17; 'The Treatment of Venereal Disease in the Army', ibid., 149–51; Robert Lees, 'Venereal Diseases in the Armed Forces Overseas', *BJVD*, 22 (1946), pp. 149–51; cf. H. E. Garle, 'The Struggle against Prostitution and Venereal Disease in Egypt', *Health and Empire*, 8 (1933), pp. 215–21 Miss L. D. Potter, 'Egypt and a changing outlook', ibid., pp. 105–9; F. Ray Bettley, 'The Medical Conduct of a Brothel', *BJVD*, 25 (1949), pp. 56–66.

28 Costello, *Love*, pp. 127, 328–9; for other American attitudes, see 'Drastic Venereal Diseases Legislation in the Argentine', *Health and Empire*, 12 (1937), pp. 50–2.

29 Dalrymple-Champneys, 'Venereal Diseases', p. 103. Radio Paris appointed a Social Hygiene Committee and broadcast lectures on venereal disease as early as 1930. *Lancet*, 6 Sep. 1930, p. 545. See also Norah Hill, 'What is Good Health Propaganda', *Health and Empire*, 14 (1939), pp. 12–19; for the description of a Ministry of Information film on venereal disease, see *Lancet*, 24 April 1943, p. 533.

30 Roger Wimbush, 'Broadcast Propaganda', *Health and Empire*, 15 (1940), pp. 14–16; 'At the Armstrongs', ibid., pp. 117–26, 152–62; 'The Council in the Country', ibid., pp. 130–3; *Lancet*, 27 Feb. 1943, p. 276; *Daily Mirror*, 19 Feb. 1943; Gordon Westwood (pseudonym of M. G. Schofield), *Society and the Homosexual* (1952), p. 22; *BJVD*, 5 (1929), p. 219; Stephen Koss, *The Rise and Fall of the Political Press in Britain*, 2 (1984), p. 477; J. A. Gere and J. H. A. Sparrow eds., *Geoffrey Madan's Notebooks* (Oxford, 1981), p. 76.

31 Burke, 'Compulsory Treatment of Venereal Diseases?', pp. 120–1; J. M. Mackintosh, 'Venereal Diseases', ibid., 16 (1941), pp. 258–64; Ministry of Health to S. Pickering, 29 April 1943; Ernest Brown (Minister of Health) to Thomas Hewlett, MP, 4 Jan. 1943, Brown to Alec Beechman MP, 4 March 1943, PRO MH 55/1326; *BMJ*, 2 Jan. 1943, p. 21.

32 W. K. Bernfeld, 'Medical Professional Secrecy with special reference to venereal diseases', *BJVD*, 43 (1967), p. 55; House of Commons debates, 3 July 1962, 662, cols. 291–4, 28 June 1963, 679, cols. 1920–5.

33 *BJVD*, 18 (1943), pp. 86, 91; *BMJ*, 6 March 1943, p. 290; F. A. Iremonger, *William Temple* (1948), pp. 448–50; J. G. Lockhart, *Cosmo*

Lang (1949), p. 235; *BJVD*, 17 (1942), p. 88).

34 Charles Taylor to Ernest Brown, 3 Aug. 1943, PRO MH 55/1326; Arthur Stringer to Brown, 29 March 1943, PRO MH 55/1326.

35 Dalrymple-Champneys, 'Venereal Diseases', pp. 101, 104; A. Fessler, 'Sociological and Psychological Factors in Venereal Disease', *BJVD*, 22 (1946), p. 25; 'Herr Hitler on Prostitution and Combating Venereal Disease', *Health and Empire*, 9 (1934), pp. 59–61; cf. Karl Marcus, 'How Swedish Combats Venereal Disease', *Health and Empire*, 1 (1926), pp. 125–30; Hans Haustien, 'The German Federal Law for Combating Venereal Diseases', ibid., 2 (1927), pp. 89–99; F. A. R. Sempkins, 'The Prostitute in Prussia', ibid., 2 (1927), pp. 252–5; H. Haustein, 'Recent Russian Literature on Venereal Diseases', ibid., 4 (1929), pp. 216–32; Edith Tancred, 'Social Aspects of Registration of Prostitutes in Budapest and Vienna', ibid., 5 (1930), pp. 227–30; Julio Bravo and Jose Fernandez de la Portilla, 'The Campaign against Venereal Disease in Spain', ibid., 9 (1934), pp. 229–35; Cavaillon, 'The European Economic Crisis and its Effects on the Venereal Disease Campaign', ibid., 10 (1935), pp. 266–81; E. H. Hermans, 'Anti-Venereal Campaign in Holland', ibid., 11 (1936), pp. 273–7; A. de Graaf, 'The Struggle against Prostitution in Holland', ibid., 278–83; Charles Csepai, 'Pre-Marriage Sexual Behaviour in Hungary', ibid., 12 (1937), pp. 35–41; Dr Gutt, 'Social Hygiene in Germany', ibid., 13 (1938), pp. 8–14; Dr Unger, 'Social Insurance in Germany', ibid., 37–44; R. R. Wilcox, 'Some American Ideas on Venereal Disease Control', *BMJ*, 30 Nov. 1946, pp. 825–7; Jones, *Bad Blood*.

36 *Lancet*, 6 March 1943, p. 314; cf. *Lancet*, 13 March 1943, pp. 350–1; *BJVD*, 18 (1943), pp. 81, 87; *BMJ*, 6 March 1943, p. 290; *BMJ* obituary of May, 31 August 1946,

p. 314; Lee K. Frankel, 'Life Insurance and Social Hygiene', *Health and Empire*, 1 (1926), pp. 116–20; O. May, 'Venereal Diseases in terms of Sickness Benefit', ibid., pp. 121–4.

37 *Lancet*, 10 April 1943 & 18 June 1955, p. 476, p. 1280. For the views of the President of the SPVD in the 1940s, see Lord Horder, 'Prevention of VD', *Observer*, 6 June 1948.

38 *BJVD*, 18 (1943), p. 91.

39 *BJVD*, 18 (1943), pp. 88–9; *BJVD*, 24 (1948), p. 66; PRO Inf 2/139 (for the Central Office of Information's anti-VD campaign of 1948); 'The Changing Pattern of Venereal Disease', *The Glaxo Volume*, 20 (1959), pp. 29, 32; Extract from Annual Report for 1965 of Chief Medical Officer, *BJVD*, 43 (1967), p. 65; cf. Thomas Eliot, 'Norway Conquers Venereal Diseases', *BJVD*, 31 (1955), pp. 1–8.

40 Leonard Bowden, quoted Gordon D. Knox, 'Seamen and Venereal Disease: Initiation of a Comprehensive Policy', *Health and Empire*, 1 (1926), pp. 63–4; papers by H. C. Squires and Sir Drummond Shiels on 'Social Hygiene and General Physical Fitness', ibid., 13 (1938), pp. 195–205; cf. J. A. Mangan, *The Games Ethic and Imperialism* (1986).

41 G. L. M. McElligott, 'Fatal Syphilis', *BJVD*, 29 (1953), p. 62; Anthony Head, House of Commons debates, 22 Nov. 1951, 494, p. 190; A. J. King and C. S. Nicol, 'The Problem of Gonorrhoea', *BJVD*, 37 (1961), pp. 91–3; cf. Axel Perdrup, 'Gonorrhoea in Denmark', *BJVD*, 37 (1961), pp. 115–9.

42 PRO Inf 2/139.

43 J. H. Walker to Sir Austin Strutt, 23 Sept. 1953, PRO HO 302/10; Hamilton Pearson, memorandum of 28 Nov. 1955, PRO HO 45/25306; cf. C. S. Nicol, 'Venereal Diseases: Moral Standards and Public Opinion', *BJVD*, 39 (1963), pp. 169–70, 172; for his obituary see *BMJ*, 5 May 1984, p. 1387.

44 Veronica Dengel, *All About You* (1954), pp. 224, 226, 230–2, 236, 238–41; cf. Eleanor French,

'Prostitution', *BJVD*, 31 (1955), p. 114.

45 Phyllis M. F. Fraser, 'Chemical Contraceptives', *BMJ*, 23 Nov. 1963, p. 1342; *BMJ*, 24 July & 7 Aug. 1965, pp. 244, 372.

46 Michael Schofield, *Promiscuity* (1976), pp. 17, 22, 40, 162; Pauline Perry, *Your Guide to the Opposite Sex* (1969); Lord Soper in C. H. Rolph ed., *Does Pornography Matter?* (1961), p. 49.

47 John Stoltenberg, *Refusing to be a man: essays on sex and justice*, (1990), pp. 118–26.

48 Richard Marsh, House of Commons debates, 28 June 1963, 679, col. 1920; Schofield, *Promiscuity*, p. 28; *New Society*, 18 Oct. 1973, pp. 135–7; *Independent*, 15 June 1988.

49 Schofield, *The Sexual Behaviour of Young Adults* (1973), pp. 80–2.

50 Andrew Lycett, 'The radio rebel comes of age', *The Times*, 11 Aug. 1987; Sutherland, *Offensive Literature*, p. 114; Tony Palmer, *The Trials of Oz* (1971); Jonathan Dimbleby, 'The Oz Trial', *New Statesman*, 30 July 1971; Lord Stamp, House of Lords debates, 12 Feb. 1973, 338, col. 1331; Peter Bruinvels, House of Commons debates, 21 Oct. 1986, 102, col. 1065; letter from L. A. Chambers, 27 Aug. 1986.

51 Schofield, *Promiscuity*, p. 29; *New Society*, 18 Oct. 1973; Lord Stamp, House of Lords debates, 12 Feb. 1973, 338, cols. 1327, 1330; Lord Somers, House of Lords debates, 14 Jan. 1976, 367, cols. 231–2; written answer to parliamentary question, House of Commons 23 June 1989.

52 Schofield, *Promiscuity*, pp. 31, 163; Schofield, *Young People*, p. 251; Jen Murray, 'VD and the young', *New Society*, 15 Nov. 1973, p. 422; Nicholas Saunders, *Alternative London*; Dalzell-Ward, quoted *Evening Standard*, 23 Oct. 1972. See also Germaine Greer's account in 1973 of having a check-up to verify that she was not infected. 'My NHS doctor in the Midlands fixed me with a terrible stare and asked

me what I expected, given the life I led': quoted Lord Stamp, House of Lords debates, 14 Jan. 1976, 367, col. 209.

53 Schofield, *Promiscuity*, p. 165; Schofield, *Young People*, 79; 'A Wealth of Worried Well', *Independent*, 15 June 1988.

54 Schofield, *Young People*, p. 78; Martin Amis, *The Rachel Papers* (1973), ch. 9 (p. 92 of 1984 edn); cf. Gavin Ewart, 'The Spirokeet', *Pleasures of the Flesh* (1966).

55 Jeffrey Bernard, 'Clinical', *Spectator*, 2 March 1985 (he was not diagnosed as having a venereal infection on this occasion); W. Alter, 'Venereal Diseases and the Hospital', *Health and Empire*, 9 (1934), p. 235.

CHAPTER EIGHT

1 Alex Comfort, 'A Matter of Science and Ethics: Reflections on the BMA Committee's Report on Homosexuality and Prostitution', *Lancet*, 21 Jan. 1956, pp. 147–9.

2 E. A. Bennett, 'The Social Aspects of Homosexuality', *Medical Press*, 3 Sept. 1947, pp. 207–10; Gordon Westwood (pseudonym of Michael Schofield), *Society and the Homosexual* (1952), p. 19; *A Minority* (1960), pp. 109, 179, 190; *Problem of Homosexuality*, pp. 22–3.

3 J. B. Priestley, *Reynolds News*, 10 Nov. 1957.

4 D. Stanley-Jones, 'Sexual Inversion', *Medical Press*, 3 Sept. 1947, pp. 213–4.

5 Church of England Moral Welfare Concil, *The Problem of Homosexuality* (1955), pp. 7–8.

6 *Medical Press*, 3 Sept. 1947, p. 216; cf. Albertine L. Winner, 'Homosexuality in Women', pp. 219–30.

7 Laura Hutton in Sybil Neville-Rolfe, pp. 418–9; Norman Haire *et al*, *Encylopaedia of Sexual Knowledge* (1957), p. 362; Earl of Arran, House of Lords debates, 12 May 1965, 266, col. 73.

8 Schofield, *Minority*, pp. 41–2.

9 Schofield, *Minority*, pp. 68–86; Peter Wildeblood, *Against the Law* (1955), p. 35; letters from E. Mor-

ris, Peter Denning and Bobbie Ashkettle (who ran several one-room clubs in Gerrard Street), *Capital Gay*, 21 Aug. 1987; Sir Laurence Dunn, CHP/5 of 1954, PRO HO 345/6; Simon Raven, 'Boys will be boys: the male prostitute in London', *Encounter*, 15 (1960), pp. 19–24.

10 Ingram, *Modern Attitudes*, p. 85; Sir Norwood East, 'Homosexuality', *Medical Press*, 3 Sept. 1947, p. 216; Moral Welfare Council, *Problem of Homosexuality*, p. 14 (italics in original).

11 Sir Hermann Mannheim, 'Some Criminological Aspects of Homosexuality', *Medical Press*, 3 Sept. 1947, p. 211; Andrew Hodges, *Alan Turing* (1983), p. 468; Arran, House of Lords debates, 12 May 1965, 266, col. 72; Schofield, *Minority*, pp. 42–50; Sir Frank Newsam to Sir John Wolfenden, 31 Jan. 1955, PRO HO 345/2.

12 Wildeblood, *Law*, p. 130.

13 *Medical Press*, 3 Sept. 1947, pp. 215, 218; Bevis Hillier, *Young Betjeman* (1988), p. 117; Schofield, *Society*, pp. 111–3; Schofield, *Minority*, pp. 92, 96, 125, 128–34, 158; Moral Welfare Council, *Problem of Homosexuality*, p. 16.

14 David Stafford-Clark, 'Medico-Legal Problem of Homosexuality', *Medical Press*, 3 Sept. 1947, p. 221 (& cf. *BMJ*, 30 Jan. 1943); Wildeblood, *Law*, p. 3.

15 *News of the World*, 23 Aug. & 8 Nov. 1942; *The Times* 7 Jan. 1957.

16 Rupert Croft-Cooke, *The Verdict of You All* (1955), pp. 33–4; Blackham, *Sir Ernest Wild*, p. 175; Wildeblood, *Law*, p. 66.

17 Departmental Committee on Sexual Offences against Young Persons (1926), para. 42; George Melly, *Rum, Bum and Concertina* (1977), p. 12.

18 Earl Jowitt, House of Lords debates, 19 May 1954, 187, col. 745; W. Conwy Roberts to Wolfenden, 22 April 1955, PRO HO 345/3; Anatole James to Wolfenden, 30 March 1955, PRO HO 345/2; *Manchester Guardian* (report of Crown v. Collister and

Warhurst), 29 March 1955; CHP/DR/25, PRO HO 345/11. For an account of homosexual blackmail see John Costello, *Mask of Treachery: Anthony Blunt, the Most Dangerous Spy in History* (1988).

19 Lord Chorley, House of Lords debates, 12 May 1965, 266, col. 149; Bernard Donoughue and G. W. Jones, *Herbert Morrison* (1973), pp. 174, 309; memorandum by Sir Theobald Mathew, CHP/7 of 1954, PRO HO 345/6.

20 Wildeblood, *Law*, p. 31.

21 Schofield, *Society*, pp. 29–30. See also J. H. Walker of the Home to Sir Austin Strutt, 23 Sep. 1953, on the 'disgraceful furore' surrounding publication of *Sexual Behaviour in the Human Female* which came 'fairly close to hinting that . . . the more a young girl allows herself to be lasciviously mauled, the better her chances of a happy marriage . . . this and similar passages will give great offence . . . and it is impossible to ensure that it will not encourage some youngsters to excess'. PRO HO 302/10. Kinsey's report had a forerunner more than 20 years earlier: the unjustly forgotten *Factors in the Sex Life of Twenty-Two Hundred Women*, by Katherine B. Davis, reviewed by Isabel Emslie Hulton, *Health and Empire*, 5 (1930), pp. 151–3.

22 *News Chronicle*, quoted *New Statesman*, 14 Sept. 1957, p. 307; Progressive League, p. 9; Tudor Rees & H. V. Usill, *They Stand Apart: a critical survey of the problem of homosexuality* (1955), pp. 17, 19–20; Hodges, *Turing*, pp. 459, 500–3; Earl of Kilmuir, House of Lords debates, 12 May 1965, 266, col. 76.

23A Barrie Penrose and Simon Freeman, *Conspiracy of Silence* (1986), pp. 363–4; Wildeblood, *Law*, pp. 45–7; Sidney Zion, *The Autobiography of Roy Zion* (Secaucus, New Jersey, 1988), p. 91.

23B Paul Foot, *Who framed Colin Wallace* (1989), pp. 28, *passim*.

24 Admiralty Fleet Orders, 29 Jan. 1954, PRO HO 345/7; memorandum by Air Ministry (with Annex B), CHP/46, and memorandum by War Office, CHP/47, PRO HO 345/8; Sir Laurence Dunne, CHP/5 of 1954, HO 345/6 (emphasis added).

25 Wildeblood, *Law*, p. 40; see also *News of the World*, 10, 24 & 31 Jan., 21 March 1954; Wildeblood's evidence to Wolfenden, CHP/51, PRO HO 345/8.

26 Wildeblood, *Law*, p. 26; Sir Theobald Mathew, CHP/7 of 1954, PRO HO 345/6; Harold F. R. Sturge, CHP/11, ibid.

27 Hyde, *Other Love*, p. 212; Croft-Cooke, *Verdict*, p. 10–11, 28; Schofield, *Society*, p. 120; Dunne, CHP/5, HO 345/6.

28 Schofield, *Minority*, pp. 137–9, 144, 146.

29 *News of the World*, 30 May, 6 June 1954, 30 Jan. 1955; R. D. Reid, *Spectator*, 3 Jan. 1958. It may have been significant to police conduct that Dr R. Sessions Hodge, of the Neuro-Psychiatric Department of Taunton's Musgrove Park Hospital, was a leading proponent of hormonal treatment for homosexuals, and testified on the subject to the Wolfenden committee. PRO HO 345/9. Sir Roland Oliver favoured decriminalizing homosexual acts between consenting males in private aged at least 18. CHP/13, HO 345/6.

30 Lord Goddard, House of Lords debates, 24 May 1965, 266, col. 665; Hodges, *Turing*, p. 502; Lord Lloyd, House of Lords debates, 19 May 1954, 187, col. 749.

31 *News of the World*, 30 May & 13 June 1954; Rees and Usill, *Apart*, pp. vii, 7–8.

32 Schofield, *Society*, p. 172; *Minority*, pp. 142–3.

33 Croft-Cooke, *Verdict*, p. 10.

34 Croft-Cooke, *Verdict*, pp. 251–2.

35 *News of the World*, 31 Jan. & 21 Feb. 1954.

36 Schofield, *Society*, pp. 121–3, 128, and *Minority*, p. 116.

37 Sir David Maxwell Fyfe, Cabinet memorandum C (54) 60 of 16 February 1954, PRO Cab 129/66; Cabinet meeting minutes, 24 Feb, 17 Mar. & 15 April 1954, PRO Cab 128/27/1; Kilmuir, House

of Lords debates, 12 May 1965, 266, col. 656.

38 Earl Winterton, *Fifty Tumultous Years* (1955), pp. 115–9; Rhodes James ed., *Chips: the Diaries of Sir Henry Channon*, p. 172; Arthur, *Further Letters*, pp. 117–8; *Times*, 28 Aug. 1962; Earl Winterton, House of Lords debates, 19 May 1954, 187, cols. 737–45; Alan Houghton Brodrick, *Near to Greatness: a life of Earl Winterton* (1965), pp. 252–5; cf. Desmond Donnelly and Sir Hugh Munro-Lucas-Tooth of Teananich, House of Commons debates, 28 April 1954, 526. For other comment at this time see *The Criminal Law and Sexual Offenders, a Report of the Joint Committee on Psychiatry and the Law appointed by the British Medical Association and the Magistrates' Association* (1954).

39 Wildeblood, *Law*, p. 128.

40 Lord Wolfenden, *Turning Points* (1976), pp. 132, 137; W. Conwy Roberts to Wolfenden, 28 June 1955, HO 345/2; Hyde, *Other Love*, pp. 260–1; *Lancet*, 14 Sept. 1957, p. 549.

41 Lord Stonham, House of Lords debates, 12 & 24 May 1965, 266, cols. 100, 643.

42 Wolfenden, *Turning Points*, p. 136; Lord Goddard, CHP/12 of Nov. 1954, PRO HO 345/6, and House of Lords debates, 12 May 1965, 266, col. 665; Bernard Levin, *The Times*, 8 June 1971.

43 Sir Compton Mackenzie, *Thin Ice* (1956), pp. 56, 81, 121, 170–1, 176, 192, 217, 220, 223; *Times Literary Supplement* 29 May 1987.

44 Progressive League, *Evidence submitted to the Home Office Committee on Homosexual Offences and Prostitution* (1955), pp. 3–4; Moral Welfare Council, *Problem of Homosexuality*, pp. 22–3.

45 Hamilton Pearson, memorandum of 28 November 1955, HO 45/25306.

46 Schofield, *Society*, pp. 161, 163–4.

47 Marquess of Lothian, House of Lords debates, 14 June 1977, 384, col. 36.

48 Memorandum of Council of Law Society, June 1955, CHP 61, PRO HO 345/8; on venereal disease see F. J. G. Jefferiss, 'Venereal Diseases and the Homosexual', *BJVD*, 32 (1956), pp. 17–20; Jefferies' evidence to Wolfenden committee, CHP/94, PRO HO 345/9; Henning Schmidt el al., 'Incidence of Homosexuals among Syphilitics', *BJVD*, 39 (1963), pp. 264–5; Robert Morton, *Venereal Diseases* (1966), pp. 128–30.

49 Rees and Usill, *Apart*, pp. 9, 15–16; Moral Welfare Council, *Problem of Homosexuality*, p. 16; Bishop of Rochester, House of Lords debates, 4 Dec. 1957, 206, cols. 797–8.

50 *BMJ*, 17 & 31 Dec. 1955; Alex Comfort, 'Science and Ethics', pp. 147–9; *Schofield, Minority*, pp. 50–1, 141; *Lancet*, 6 Aug. 1955, pp. 291–3, 13 Aug. 1955, pp. 346–7, 3 Sept. 1955, pp. 504–5. The BMA's attempt to arouse anxieties about arcane subversion led a mountebank MP to complain to the Speaker of the House of Commons that charging MPs with homosexuality was a breach of parliamentary privilege for which the BMA should be rebuked; but the Speaker evaded his stunt on a technicality. See *The People*, 18 Dec. 1955.

51 Moral Welfare Council, *Problem of Homosexuality*, p. 17. For evidence submitted to Wolfenden by a Roman Catholic committee selected by the Cardinal Archbishop of Westminster, see 'Homosexuality, Prostitution and the Law', *Dublin Review*, 230 (1956), pp. 57–65. For the evidence of the Church of England Moral Welfare Council to the same committee, see Derrick Sherwin Bailey, *Sexual Offenders and Social Punishment* (1956).

52 Lord Pakenham, House of Lords debates, 4 Dec. 1957, 206, col. 742.

53 Wolfenden, *Turning Points*, p. 141; *Lancet*, 14 Sept. 1957, p. 549; Lord Francis-Williams, 'Fleet Street Notebook'. *New Statesman*, 14 Sept. 1957, p. 310.

54 Cabinet meeting, 28 Nov. 1957 (which decided that it was impracticable to reform laws relating to

homosexuality), PRO Cab 128/31/2; Anthony Howard, *Rab Butler* (1987), pp. 264–5.

55 C. H. Rolph, 'Wolfenden Revisited', *New Statesman*, 28 Sept. 1957, p. 374; Archbishop of Canterbury, House of Lords debates, 4 Dec. 1957, 206, col. 757; Viscount Dilhorne, House of Lords debates, 21 June 1965, 267, col. 252; Earl of Kilmuir, House of Lords debates, 16 June 1966, 275, col. 156; Geoff Robertson, 'The Abominable Crime', *New Statesman*, 1 Nov. 1974, pp. 611–2; Oliver Gillie, 'Low AIDS Risk for Sexually Active Women', *Independent*, 12 Feb. 1988; 'Lover of "Lady Chatterley's Mother" jailed', *Daily Telegraph*, 6 Oct. 1988.

56 Schofield, *Minority*, p. 91; Leo Abse, *Private Member* (1973), pp. 146–9, 153; Earl of Kilmuir, House of Lords debates, 24 May 1965, 266, cols. 655, 659, and 21 June 1965, 267, col. 304; R. H. S. Crossman, *The Diaries of a Cabinet Minister*, 1 (1975), p. 561, 2 (1976), p. 97; Lord Mathers, House of Lords debates, 4 Dec. 1957, 206, cols. 821, 823; Lord Molson, House of Lords debates, 21 June 1965, 267, col. 308; Lord Byers, col. 310; Arran, House of Lords debates, 16 June 1966, 275, col. 160; Lord Snow, col. 167.

57 Arran, House of Lords debates, 21 July 1967, 285, col. 523; Leo Abse, 'Dying from feeling well', *Time and Tide* (winter 1986), pp. 48–9.

58 Richard Goldstein, quoted Altman, *AIDS and the New Puritanism*, p. 7; Digby Anderson on a television programme called *Weekend World*, quoted Sarah Benton, 'What are they afraid of?', *New Statesman*, 11 March 1988.

59 Earl of Halsbury, House of Lords debates, 14 June 1977, 384, cols. 14, 71: also Lord Campbell of Croy (col. 21), Bishop of Birmingham (col. 32), Lord Stamp (col. 52), Marquess of Lothian (cols. 36–7) and Lord Macleod of Fuinary (cols. 57–8); Lord Clifford of Chudleigh, House of Lords debates, 14 Jan. 1976, 367, col. 238.

60 Countess of Loudoun, House of Lords debates, 14 June 1977, 384, cols. 45–7.

CHAPTER NINE

1 Bruce Chatwin, 'AIDS panic', *London Review of Books*, 7 July 1988; Roy Porter, 'Ever since Eve: the fear of contagion', *Times Literary Supplement*, 27 May 1988; Renée Sabatier, *Blaming Others* (a report of the Panos Institute) (1988).

2 *New Statesman*, 13 March 1987; Chris Boffey, 'Campaign to ban AIDS docs', *Today*, 9 Nov. 1987; Watney, *Policing Desire*, p. 39; Nicholas Winterton, Social Services Committee minutes of evidence, QQ. 438–40, 472; cf. QQ. 14, 43–4, 58, 82, 281–3, 290–3, 306, 347, 715.

3 John Trustcombe, 'Homosexual Bomb Already Exploded', *Kensington News*, 27 Nov. 1986.

4 Letter of T. G. W. Potts, *Kensington and Chelsea Times*, 1 May 1987; letter of Mrs Celia Johnson, *Daily Express*, 16 March 1988.

5 *Sun*, 17 & 24 Nov. 1986 ('Scourge of the Eighties: 18 Vice Boys in AIDS Revenge: They want to spread plague'); Andrew Brown, 'An orthodox morality', *Independent*, 24 Nov. 1987; compare Jakobovits' views with those of one of Egypt's leading Islamic authorities: 'We should like all AIDS victims to stop them from harming the many members of society . . . We must purge society of the AIDS patient'. Sara el-Gammal, 'Kill all AIDS victims, Islamic scholar says' *Independent*, 4 July 1989.

6 European Study Group, 'Risk factors from male to female transmission of HIV', *BMJ*, 18 Feb. 1989, pp. 411–3.

7 George Gale, 'AIDS – And those who have a right to know', *Daily Express*, 30 August 1985.

8 James A. Brundage, *Law, Sex and Christian Society in Medieval Europe* (1988), pp. 7–8.

9 Ray Mills, 'The Angry Voice', *Star*, 2 Sep. 1986; on the word 'gay', cf. General Sir John Hackett, 'Connotations of gaiety', *Independent*,

11 Nov. 1987: 'I sat through a complete annual conference of the National Union of Students and went along in the course of it to a "gay evening". As I looked around the sad, raddled faces in the sparsely peopled room, I asked myself, in blunt, soldierly terms, whether I had ever seen a more miserable lot in my life! . . . [are] we now doomed to accept, in perpetuity, that "gaiety" has become no more than a synonym for sodomy.'

10 Ray Mills, 'The Angry Voice', *Star*, 9 Sep. 1986.

11 John Lisners, 'I'd Shoot My Son if he had AIDS, says Vicar', *Sun*, 14 Oct. 1985; Watney, *Desire*, pp. 94–5; Leo Bersani, 'Is the Rectum a Grave?' in Douglas Crimp ed., *AIDS, Cultural Analysis, Cultural Activism* (1988), pp. 199–200.

12 'How to stop a plague', *Spectator*, 8 November 1986; A. D. Carter, 'Deadly promiscuity', *Kensington News*, 27 Nov. 1986; D. MacIntyre and J. Laurence, 'Thatcher disbands Cabinet AIDS team', *Sunday Correspondent*, 17 Sept. 1989.

13 'Fast Eddie's Downfall', *News of the World*, 13 Jan. 1985.

14 Watney, *Desire*, p. 124; private information; for memories of Graham Gardner, see John Shine, 'Room with a View', *Leading Lights* (Dec. 1987); *The Times*, 4 April & 29 Sept. 1986.

15 *Sun*, 29 & 31 March 1988; Ashley Walton, 'Tennant family curse strikes again as heir catches AIDS: Parents' Love and Sympathy As They Tell Him See The World While You Still Have Time', *Daily Express*, 30 March 1988; James Weatherup and Phil Davies, 'Toff's Family Curse Strikes Junkie Charlie: Second Tennant Son Hit By AIDS', *News of the World*, 7 Aug. 1988.

16 Fiona McDonald Hull, 'Kids Deserve Protection', *Sun*, 29 July 1988; Sarah Helm, 'Mackay criticized over gay judge', *Independent*, 26 Jan. 1988.

17 Phil Reeves, 'Judge rules doctors with AIDS cannot be identified', and Ying Hui Tan, 'Identifying AIDS victims prohibited', *Independent*, 7 Nov. 1987; Oliver Gillie, 'Doctors with AIDS will not reveal disease to patients', *Independent*, 9 Nov. 1987; Nicholas Timmins, 'Doctors with AIDS can still practice', *Independent*, 16 Nov. 1987; Nick Constable and Carys Edwards, 'AIDS Doctor Who Died: We Heard Evil Rumours', editorial 'Make Every Doctor Take An AIDS Test' and Philip Johnston, 'Health Chiefs Shrug Off Danger', *Today*, 16 Nov. 1987.

18 Sandie Laming and Tim Spanton, 'Scandal of the AIDS Colony at World's End', *News of the World*, 13 Sept. 1987; Alastair Lawson-Tancred, 'Fury over "colony for AIDS"', *Kensington and Chelsea Times*, 18 Sept. 1987, and ibid., 27 Nov. 1987 & 27 Aug. 1988; Dame Cicely Saunders, 'Hospice service and AIDS victims', *Times*, 2 August 1986.

19 Mercantile and General Reinsurance, *AIDS Bulletin*, No. 4 (1987); 'AIDS tests bar to life insurance', *Independent*, 6 Feb. 1989; Brian Evans et al., 'Trends in sexual behaviour and risk factors for HIV infection among homosexual men 1984–7', *BMJ*, 28 Jan. 1989, p. 217; Rachel Johnson, *Oxford Myths* (1988), p. 159

20 Steven Warr, 'My AIDS fear, by wife of Ryan's gay pal', *Sun*, 28 August 1987; Alex Marunchak, 'AIDS Test on Maniac Rambo Killer', *News of the World*, 30 August 1988; *Sun*, 21 Nov. 1986.

21 John MacKay, House of Commons debates, 30 April 1986, 96, col. 918; Clare Dover, 'Anne in AIDS Row with Gays', 'Small Talk in the Shadow of Death' (with adjacent editorial), 'AIDS peril ignored', *Daily Express*, 27 & 28 Jan., 3 Feb. 1988.

22 Andrew Higgins, 'No AIDS please, we're Chinese', *Independent*, 17 Feb. 1988; Watney, *Desire*, p. 1; private information; Thomas Stuttaford, 'How AIDS threatens all of us', *Spectator*, 15 Nov. 1986; Thomson Prentice, 'Middle Class Girls Get Warning of AIDS Risk From First Sexual Act', *The Times*, 24 Aug. 1987. Terry McCarthy, 'Malaysians warn of Thai AIDS',

Independent, 14 Sept. 1989; cf. a statement from the director general of the Indian government's Council for Medical Research: 'This is a totally foreign disease, and the only way to stop its spread is to stop sexual contacts between Indians and foreigners': quoted Susan Sontag, *AIDS and its Metaphors* (New York, 1989).

23 Simon Watney, 'The Spectacle of AIDS', in Crimp, *AIDS*, p. 72; 'Court cleared for AIDS couple', *The Times* 21 March 1986.

24 Andrew Lumsden, 'The Moral Backlash: When grown men are babies', *New Statesman*, 21 Feb. 1987; Steve Platt, 'BT Bashing', *New Society*, 16 Oct. 1987.

25 Henry Elliott, 'Airline denies ban was due to AIDS', *Times*, 3 Feb. 1987; Thomas Prentice, 'Dismissal of carrier's wife criticized', *Times* 13 June 1987; Oliver Gillie, 'The law of intolerance', *Independent*, 3 March 1988; 'Gay worker wins legal fight', *Independent*, 16 Feb. 1988; Gavin Strang, 'The 1989 Employment Bill', Terrence Higgins *Trust Newsletter*, July 1989.

26 *BMJ* 20 Feb. 1988; Mrs Elizabeth Wilson, 'AIDS', *Spectator*, 8 Dec. 1984; Robin McKie, 'Doctors who do not care for the sick', *Observer*, 2 Dec. 1984.; Nicholas Schoon, 'Gay outcast fights back against fear of disease', *Independent*, 14 March 1988.

27 Lis Leigh, 'New approach to care for AIDS patients', *Sunday Times*, 22 Feb. 1987; Richard Wells and Jacqui Elliott, evidence to Social Services Select Committee of the House of Commons, 18 Feb. 1987, Q. 371.

28 Thomson Prentice, 'AIDS virus carriers in Britain could total up to 100,000', *Times* 3 Dec. 1986; Morven Kinlay, 'Nurses Shunned My AIDS Baby Cries Mum', *News of the World*, 31 Jan. 1988; P. J. Guy, 'AIDS: a doctor's duty', *BMJ*, 294 (1987), p. 445; Raanan Gillon, 'Refusal to treat AIDS and HIV positive patients', *BMJ*, 294 (1987), pp. 1332–3.

29 Neville Hodgkinson, 'Outcast boy dies of AIDS', *Sunday Times*,

6 March 1988; Emily Smyth, 'A love to be handled with plastic gloves', *Independent*, 9 Aug. 1988; Margaret Rooke, 'Family lives in fear of AIDS thugs', *News on Sunday*, 26 April 1987; Thomson Prentice, 'AIDS peril from boys who may have virus', *Times*, 5 Sept. 1987; Frances Peck, 'Blood brothers' fight against ignorance' *Independent*, 1 August 1989.

30 Clare Dover, 'Anger As Experts Say There's No Risk: Patients Face AIDS Victims in Next Bed', *Daily Express*, 31 March 1988; Martin Amis, 'Double Jeopardy: Making Sense of AIDS', in *The Moronic Inferno* (1986), pp. 187–8.

31 'Guy Brain talks to Tony Whitehead', *Terrence Higgins Trust Newsletter*, May 1989; Larry Kramer, *Reports from the Holocaust: the making of an AIDS activist* (New York, 1989).

32 Watney, *Desire*, p. 82; Kenneth Clarke's circular of 24 Nov. 1986, Department of Employment; 'AIDS Charter', *Independent*, 1 Dec. 1988; Brian Evans et al., 'Trends in Sexual Behaviour and risk factors for HIV infection among homosexual men 1984–7', *BMJ*, 28 Jan. 1989, p. 215.

33 Graham Turner, 'Is there a Homosexual Conspiracy?', *Sunday Telegraph*, 5 June 1988; James Davies, 'Back to the AIDS drawing board', *Daily Express*, 7 June 1988.

34 Oliver Gillie, 'Children scared by AIDS adverts', *Independent*, 5 Oct. 1988; Gill Gordon and Tony Klouda (of International Planned Parenthood Federation), *Preventing a crisis; AIDS and family planning work* (1988), pp. 155–6; Adam Lawrence, 'Anonymous AIDS Tests', *Independent*, 1 Dec. 1988; David Miller, Timothy Acton and Barbara Hedge, 'The worried well: their identification and management', *Journal of Royal College of Physicians*, 22 (July 1988), pp. 158–65; Celia Hall, 'Glossy health campaigns attacked for victim-blaming messages' *Independent*, 22 May 1989.

35 This section follows information and conversation with Richard

Watson, the effervescent Account Director handling Mates at the advertising agency Still Price Court Twivy D'Souza. The judgments in this section are however mine. On the Bristol survey see 'Fear of AIDS dismissed by the young', *Independent*, 15 Nov. 1988.

36 Robert Lander, 'Precautions boost for sales', *Times*, 15 Nov. 1986; John Craig, 'Condom arrest sparks protest', *Sunday Times*, 22 March 1987; *Independent*, 'AIDS unheeded', 31 March 1988, '30,000 men visit city's prostitutes', 19 May 1988; 'Free condoms on the rates urged to halt spread of AIDS', 9 August 1988; Christine Toomey, 'Turned off: AIDS dims the red lights over Hamburg', *Sunday Times*, 22 May 1988; Association of Metropolitan Authorities, *The Challenge to Local Authorities: HIV Infection and Drug Use* (1988); Pamela Nowicka, 'Conduct unbecoming in a lover', *Independent*, 14 Feb. 1989.

37 Laura Flanders, 'No Sex Please, We're British', *New York Native*, 18 May 1987; Watney, *Desire*, p. 13.

38 Anthony Easthope, *What A Man's Gotta Do: The Masculine Myth in Popular Culture* (1986), pp. 42–3; Peter Tatchell, *The Battle for Bermondsey* (1983), p. 72.

39 'Sex case soldiers', *Independent*, 22 Sept. 1987; Colin Bell, 'Atom Submarine Gay Sex Probe', *Daily Express*, 14 Dec. 1987; Mark Rosselli, 'Two soldiers jailed for assault', *Independent*, 7 Nov. 1987; Kieron Saunders, 'My Wrack and Ruin', *Sun*, 12 Jan. 1988; Bob McGowan, 'Sarge kissed me goodnight says the frightened Fusilier' & 'Secret shame of sarge cleared in kissing case', *Daily Express*, 20 & 21 April 1988. A naval chaplain, dying as a result of AIDS in 1987, told Navy staff of his condition and 'was allowed to stay on after an unblemished 12 year career, but was ordered never to speak publicly about catching AIDS': Andrew Alderson, 'AIDS kills chaplain', *Daily Express* 20 Dec. 1987.

40 *News of the World*, 7 Feb. 1988;

Kerry Gill, 'Stolen Car Infected with AIDS', *The Times*, 25 May 1988.

41A Jeremy Laurence, 'Condoms issue in jails to beat AIDS', *New Society*, 22 Jan. 1988; Sarah Helm, 'AIDS carrier warns of jail epidemic', *Independent*, 9 April 1988; 'BMA calls for condoms in gaols', *Guardian*, 7 July 1988; Robert Kilroy-Silk, 'When men are the victims', *The Times*, 21 Nov. 1987; Miranda Ingram, 'Victims of disbelief: the trauma of men who are raped', *Independent*, 29 June 1988; Kirsty Milne, 'Life Sentence: prisoners with AIDS', *New Statesman and Society*, 7 October 1988; Sarah Helm, 'Home Office vetoes research project into AIDS risk in jail', *Independent*, 2 Nov. 1988; Una Padel, 'AIDS research in prisons', *Independent*, 5 Nov. 1988; Anthony Storr, 'AIDS among prisoners', *Independent*, 9 Nov. 1988; 'Government has let people down on law and order', *The Times*, 12 Oct. 1988, (emphasis added).

41B John Jackson, 'How far would you go?' *Daily Mirror*, 18 Sept. 1989; *Sunday Correspondent* editorial, 17 Sept. 1989.

42 Thomson Prentice, 'AIDS peril from boys who carry virus', *The Times*, 5 Sept. 1987; 'Time for pragmatism over AIDS', *Independent*, 31 March 1988; 'The threat of AIDS', *New Society*, 1 April 1988; Geoff Rayner and Karen Gowler, 'The lessons of AIDS', *New Society*, 8 April 1988; Kate de Selincourt, 'Needle exchange schemes working', *New Statesman and Society*, 24 June 1988; Celia Hall, 'Doctors fear heterosexual AIDS epidemic in Scotland', *Independent*, 30 Jan. 1989.

43 Helena Kennedy, 'There is no case for the persecution of gays', *Listener*, 12 March 1987; Flanders, 'No Sex Please', op. cit.; Dalya Alberge, 'Arts figures fear gay censorship', *Independent*, 25 Jan. 1988; 'Two in three condemn homosexual acts and lifestyle', and Graham Turner, 'Is there a Homosexual Conspiracy?', *Sunday Telegraph*, 5 June 1988.

44 Peregrine Worsthorne, 'Cleveland: the high price for breaking taboos',

Sunday Telegraph, 10 July 1988; Beatrix Campbell, *Unofficial Secrets – Child Abuse: the Cleveland Case* (1988).

45 'Social worker's horrendous sentence', *Capital Gay*, 6 Feb. 1987; Gay London Policing Group, *Gay Men and Bind Overs* (1988); Philip Derbyshire, 'Charges against gay men', *New Statesman and Society*, 15 July 1988.

46 'Spanish Cabbie Touched Me Up', *News of the World*, 30 Aug. 1987; 'Gay panic led man to kill', *The Times*, 14 June 1986; Watney, *Desire*, p. 39.

47 'Test for diplomacy', *Times* editorial 14 Jan. 1987; John Lewis, 'Calls for tough AIDS action', *New Statesman and Society*, 10 June 1988; Worsthorne, 'Cleveland'.

48 Lord Willis, House of Lords debates, 1 Feb. 1988, 492, cols. 883–4; Christopher Smith, House of Commons debates, 15 Dec. 1987, 124, col. 1008; Sarah Benton, 'What are they afraid of?', *New Statesman*, 11 March 1988.

49 Lord Skelmersdale, House of Lords debates, 18 Dec. 1986, 483, col. 336; House of Lords debates, 1988, cols. 1030, 1034; on Helms see Douglas Crimp, 'How to have promiscuity in an epidemic', in Crimp, *AIDS*, pp. 259–65, 270.

50 Earl of Halsbury, House of Lords debates, 18 Dec. 1976, 483, cols. 310, 337; 1 Feb. 1988, col. 875.

51 Jonathan Rodney, *A Handbook of Sex Knowledge* (1961), p. 107, quoted Watney, *Desire*, p. 23 (emphasis added).

52 Lord Campbell of Alloway, 18 Dec. 1986, cols. 312–3; Halsbury, col. 311; Earl of Longford, col. 316; Lord Denning, col. 325; Lord Fitt, col. 330; Lord Skelmersdale, cols. 333–4; Ken Livingstone, House of Commons debates, 15 Dec. 1987, 124, cols. 1011–2, and Greenway, col. 1002.

53 Lord Wyatt of Weeford, *News of the World*, 9 November 1986; John Vincent, 'Labour in a Gay Fix', *Sun*, 3 Dec. 1986; Dame Jill Knight, House of Commons debates, 8 May 1987, 115, cols. 998–1000, 1011;

'Promoting AIDS', *New Society*, 27 Feb. 1988 (emphasis added); J. F. Watkins, 'Contagion and AIDS', *Times Literary Supplement*, 10 June 1988.

54 House of Lords debates: 18 Dec. 1986, Viscount Ingleby, col. 320, and Lord Skelmersdale, col. 333; 1 Feb. 1988: Lord McIntosh of Haringey, col. 887; Lord Hutchinson of Lullington, col. 896; Viscount Falkland, col. 868.

55 Benton, 'What are they afraid of?', op. cit.; Gavin Maxwell, *The House of Elrig* (1965), pp. 131–6; Lord Annan, *Roxburgh of Stowe* (1965).

56 Hailsham, 'Homosexuality and Society', in Rees and Usill, *They Stand Apart*, p. 22; Dame Elaine Kellett-Bowman, House of Commons debates, 15 Dec. 1987, 124, cols. 1009, 1024; 'Mystery Arson Attack', 'Arson is Right – MP' and 'CS Gas Attack on Kent Pub', *Capital Gay*, 18 Dec. 1987; *Independent* parliamentary report, 16 Dec. 1987; Jane Dibblin, 'Burn it down', *New Statesman*, 11 March 1988; Peter Tatchell, 'Results of Section 28', *Independent*, 24 May 1988; 'Arsonist attacks drag act's home', *Capital Gay*, 6 May 1988; Duncan Campbell and Nigel Townson, 'University press blocks gay book', *New Statesman and Society*, 12 August 1988; 'In brief', *Times Literary Supplement*, 16 Sept. 1988; 'Gay Bashing in the lanes of Brighton', *New Statesman and Society*, 29 Sept. 1988; Celia Dodd, 'The unwavering stand of an acceptable kind of rebel' *Independent*, 9 Aug. 1989.

57 Phil Dampier and David Kemp, 'Ragbag rap at gay demo in Commons', *Sun*, 17 Dec. 1987; John Pienaar, 'Cheers as marina bill is defeated', *Independent*, 16 December 1987.

58 John Pienaar, 'Thatcher warns of threat to family', *Independent*, 26 May 1988; Sarah Benton, 'Will God join the Tories?', *New Statesman*, 19 Feb. 1988; Andrew Brown, 'An orthodox morality', *Independent*, 24 Nov. 1987; Colin Hughes, unheadlined report, *Independent*, 11 Dec. 1987; Ross Benson, 'Good

59 House of Commons debates, 24 Jan. 1986 (vol. 90); Paul Wilenius and Norman Luck, 'Now Gummer Joins Morals Attack: War on Condom Culture Church', *Daily Express*, 9 Feb. 1988; Robert Gibson, 'Home Secretary Urges Churchmen to Launch a Moral Crusade', *Daily Express*, 11 Feb. 1988; 'Anger as Gummer calls gays disabled', *The Times*, 11 Feb. 1988.

60 Tony Higton, 'Time for the Church of England to re-affirm biblical morality', *Independent*, 11 Nov. 1987.

61 Adrianna Caudrey, 'The gay vicar and his flock', *New Society*, 15 Jan. 1988; Andrew Brown, 'Gay Christians lose church base', *Independent*, 17 May 1988.

62 Revd Peter Mullen, 'The persecution of homosexual clergy is cruel and unworthy', *Independent*, 23 Jan. 1988; Fr Philip Caraman, 'Noonday Devils kept at bay', *Literary Review*, Aug. 1988; Revd Edward Norman, 'A place for gay Christians?', *The Times*, 7 May 1988; compare Steve Doughty, 'Scandal of Gay Vicars', *Daily Mail*,

Lord, it's Rabbi Manny in the Peer show', *Daily Express*, 31 Dec. 1987.

12 Nov. 1987; Phil Dampier and Rob Skellon, 'Pulpit Poofs Can Stay', *Sun*, 12 Nov. 1987; Debbie Ambrose, 'Church: It's Still Godly to be Gay', *Today*, 12 Nov. 1987; Godfrey Barker, 'Epistle to Sodom and Gomorrah', *Daily Telegraph*, 12 Nov. 1987; Andrew Brown, 'Voices from the Wilderness', *Independent*, 22 Feb. 1988; A. Brown, 'Synod rallies round canon at centre of sex row' and 'Hypocrisy in high places', *Independent*, 8 & 10 July 1989.

63 Frank Lowe, 'If we want to stop AIDS we must stop selling real life', *London Standard*, 5 Nov. 1986.

64 'Anger over gay play', *Daily Express*, 22 March 1988; Jonathan Sanders, 'Breaking Taboos: Two of Us', *Gay Times*, May 1988; Watney, *Desire*, p. 98.

65 Richard Evans, 'TV to cut sex and violence from US', *The Times*, 30 Sep. 1987; Sir William Rees-Mogg, 'Why the only defence against AIDS is a change of sexual habits', *Independent*, 23 Feb. 1988; 'In the public service?', *New Society*, 20 May 1988.

66 Watney, *Desire*, p. 26.

Index

Index

Abingdon, 4th Earl of, 83
abortionists, 40, 160, 166, 184
Abse, Leo, 324–7, 361
Acheson, Sir Donald, 350, 358
Acton, Dr William, 169, 198
Adair, Gilbert, 319, 322
Addison, 1st Viscount, 237, 242
Addison, Joseph, 44
Admiralty, 108, 149, 198, 242, 270, 301–2
adultery, 4, 68–9
Advocate, 359
Africa, 2, 355
airmen, 302–3, 307
Air Ministry, 149, 242, 270, 302
Aldington, Richard, 246
Alexander, Sir Claud, 172
Alford, Charles, Bishop of Victoria, 165
Alfred, Prince, Duke of Edinburgh, 200–1
Allbut, Sir Clifford, 126
Allbutt, Dr Henry, 202
Alverstone, 1st Viscount, 143
Alzahavarius, 19
American Social Hygiene Council, 243
Amery, Leo, 261, 264
Amis, Martin, 284
Ampthill, 2nd Baron, 182
Anderson, Digby, 328
Anderson, Neil, 366
Anderton, James, 13
Anne, Queen of England, 74
Anne, Princess Royal, 344
Aretaeus the Cappadocian, 8–9, 18
Argyll, 2nd Duke of, 52
Argyll, 8th Duke of, 157
Aristophanes, 224
Arnold, Matthew, 115, 158
Arran, 8th Earl of, 290, 326–7, 328–9, 361
Ashburnham, 5th Earl of, 161
Assinder, Dr Eric, 255
Astor, 1st Viscount, 138
Astor, 2nd Viscount, 237–8
Atkins, Baron, 400
Auden, W. H., 78, 128, 286
Avicenna (Abu-Ali Al-Husain ibn Abdullah ibn Sina), 24
Avon, 2nd Earl of, 355

Avory, Sir Horace, 300

Backhouse, Sir Edmund, 400
Bamford, Thomas, 43
Bankes, Sir John Eldon, 253–4
Bankes, William, 146
Banner, Charles, 76
Barker, Henry, 111
Barlow, Sir Thomas, 214, 226, 253
Barnes, Fred, 149
Barrett, Lady, 196–7
Barrett, Sir James, 162, 199
Barry, Stephen, 341
Batten, Sir William, 55
Baxter, Andrew, 84–5
Bayly, Hugh Wansy, 239–41, 242, 243
Beardsley, Aubrey, 5, 126–7
Beaverbrook, 1st Baron, 267
Belhaven and Stenton, 2nd Baron, 52
Bell, Dr Benjamin, 191
Bendall, Vivian, 350
Benkert, Karoly, 116
Bennett, E. J., 144
Bentham, Jeremy, 57, 96
Bernard, Jeffrey, 285
Berridge, Revd John, 35, 37
bestiality, 59–60
Bethercourt, Jacques de, 16
Betjeman, Sir John, 294
Bhurtpore, Maharaja of, 113
bidets, 79
Binding, Barbara, 281, 284
Binning, Lord, 190
Birkenhead, 1st Earl of (F. E. Smith), 145, 153
Birmingham, Bishops of,
    William Boyd-Carpenter, 216, 221
    Laurence Brown, 328
Bismarck-Schönhausen, Prince Otto von, 72
Bjelke-Petersen, Sir Joh, 2
Blackett, Sir Basil, 261–2
blackmail, 90–1, 131, 297–8
Blantyre, 8th Baron, 84–5
Bloomfield, 1st Baron, 68
Bloxam, Dr John Astley, 189–90
Bodkin, Sir Archibald, 147, 230
Boleyn, Anne, Marchioness of Pembroke and Queen of England, 59

Booth, Sir Felix, 96–7
Borden, Sir Robert, 228
Borthwick, 6th Baron, 185
Boswell, James, 53
Bottomley, Horatio, 239
Bowley, Martin, 341
Boyd-Carpenter, William, 216, 221
Boys Brigade, 195–6, 309
Brabazon of Tara, 1st Baron, 153
Branson, Richard, 231, 284, 355
Brazil, 11, 108
Bricknell, Frank, 257–8, 280
Brieux, Eugène, 202–3
British Institute for Social Service, 200
British Journal of Venereal Diseases,
    109–10, 272, 322
British Medical Association, 211, 234,
    270, 279, 320–1, 338
British Social Hygiene Council, 243–4,
    260–4, 267, 270–1
British Telecom, 345–6
British Women's Patriotic League, 215
Britten, Benjamin, Baron, Lord, 339,
    375
Brodrick, St John, 1st Earl of Midleton,
    14, 147
brothels, 28, 107, 170, 249, 356
Brown, Laurence, 328
Browne, Sir Thomas, 16
Brownhill, Bill, 346, 368
Browning, Oscar, 112
Bruinvels, Peter, 282
Buckingham, 1st Duke of, 61
buggery, 58–61, 78–9, 294, 323–4, 365
Bunting, Lady, 218
Burdett, Sir Francis, 101
Burgess, Guy, 299, 300
Burgwin, Mrs E. M., 215, 216, 221
Burke, Edmund Tytler, 255–8, 267,
    275, 280
Burnham, 1st Baron, 212
Burnham, 1st Viscount, 165
Burt, Sir Cyril, 259–60
Butler, Josephine, 168, 174, 214, 218,
    226, 240
Butler, Samuel, 44
Butler of Saffron Walden, Baron, 322
Byron, 6th Baron, 66, 87, 112, 139

Cade, Sir Stanford, 255
Cairns, Eddie, 338–9
Cam, Joseph, 25, 51
Campbell, 1st Baron, 381
Campbell, Dame Janet, 252–3
Campbell of Alloway, Baron, 370–1

Canterbury, Archbishops of,
    Randall Davidson, 129, 165, 196,
        233, 253
    Geoffrey Fisher, 323
    Cosmo Lang, 125, 159, 249, 269
    Robert Runcie, 376, 380
    Frederick Temple, 122
    William Temple, 14, 268–9
Canterbury, 5th Viscount, 399
Carlisle, 5th Earl of, 69, 85
Carpenter, Edward, 127, 128
Casper, Leopold, 116
Castlehaven, 2nd Earl of, 63–4, 65, 93
Catherine, Princess of Aragon, 59
Cavendish, Charles, 181
Cavendish-Bentinck, George, 129–31,
    133
Central Office of Information, 246–7,
    274
Chamberlain, Sir Austen, 6
Chamberlain, Joseph, 126
Chamberlain, Neville, 230, 254, 260
Chamberlen, Paul, 39, 48
Champneys, Sir Francis, 235–6
Channon, Sir Henry ('Chips'), 10
Charles II, King of England, 33, 40, 57
Charles V, Holy Roman Emperor, 60
Charles VIII, King of France, 20, 21
Charles, Prince of Wales, 341
Charles Theodore, Elector of Bavaria,
    83
chasing the dragon, 353
chastity, 16, 31–2, 177, 180, 292
Chatterton, Thomas, 51
Chatwin, Bruce, 330
Chesney, Sir George, 176–7
Chesser, Dr Eustace, 323
Chesterfield, 4th Earl of, 74
China, 21, 345
Chorley, 1st Baron, 298
Christianity, 8–9, 31–8, 69–71, 181–2,
    376–80
    Anglo-Catholicism, 114
    Contagious Diseases Act, 167
    contraception, 220
    divine punishment, 6–7, 26–7, 101,
        165
    family sanctity, 122, 125
    India, 176–7
    legal sanctions, 58–9
    prophylaxis, 235–7, 240–41, 268–9
    social control, 156–9, 164, 172, 174
    Venereal Diseases Commission, 211
    Wolfenden Report, 319–21
Churchill, Charles, 13, 77, 88, 102

Churchill, Sir Winston Leonard Spencer, 143–5, 313
Churchill, Winston Spencer, 381
Church of England Social & Moral Welfare Council, 289, 319
cinema films, 5, 259, 275
Clap, Margaret, 86, 91
Clarendon, 3rd Earl of, 74
class distinction, 29–31, 205–7, 224–6, 304, 307–8, 367, 373–4
Claxton, Dr Ernest Edward, 279, 320–1
Clayton, Henry, 90
Clayton, Richard, 111
Cleland, John, 225
Cleveland, Duchess of (*formerly* Countess of Castlemaine), 40
Clifford of Chudleigh, 13th Baron, 329
Clogher, Bishop of (Percy Jocelyn), 103
Clowes, William, 30–1
clubs, 72–3, 85–6, 291–2, 317
Cobbett, William, 101
cocaine, 138, 152
Cockburn, William, 25
Coetlogon, Revd Charles de, 38
Cohn, Roy, 301
Coke, Sir Edward, 57–60, 323
Cole, Commander E. A., 301
Collie, Sir John, 215, 217–8
Colonial Office, 261, 324
Columbus, Christopher, 18–19
Comfort, Dr Alex, 320
companionate marriage, 67–8
condoms, 51–3, 79, 194, 266, 355–8
Coningsby, Sir Thomas, 66
Connemara, 1st Baron, 185–6
Contagious Diseases Acts, 108, 167–78, 214, 218, 226, 234
contraception, 220–1, 277–9
    see also condoms
Cook, James, 86, 91
Cookson, Norman, 111–2
Cooper, Sir Alfred, 160–1, 182, 189
Cooper, Duff, 1st Viscount Norwich, 112
Coote, Sir Eyre, 76, 94
Corbett-Smith, Arthur, 205–7, 278
Cornwallis, 1st Marquess, 83
Coulter, Jack Leonard Sagar, 260
Couperus, Louis, 129
Courtenay, 3rd Viscount (*later* 9th Earl of Devon), 103
Courtney, Ned, 90
Coventry of Aylesborough, 1st Baron, 63
Cowper, Countess, 124

Cream, Neil, 160, 166
Creighton, Louise, 216, 219, 224, 227, 240
Creighton, Mandell, Bishop of London, 216
Criminal Law Amendment bills, 129–35, 151–3, 228
Croft-Cooke, Rupert, 128, 134, 296–7, 304, 310
Crosland, T. W. H., 141
Cross, 1st Viscount, 133, 156
Crozier, General F. P., 180, 226–7
Cumberland, Prince Ernest, Duke of, 90
Cumberland, Prince Rupert, Duke of, 40
cunnilingus, 79
Currey, William, 111
Curzon of Kedleston, 1st Marquess, 14, 112–4, 180
Customs and Excise, Board of, 358, 380

Daily Express, 1, 267, 333, 339, 342, 344, 352–3, 377
Daily Mail, 267, 314, 322
Daily Mirror, 322
Daily Telegraph, 212, 322
Daley, Harry, 110–1, 134, 149, 201
Dalrymple-Champneys, Sir Weldon, 266, 270
Dalzell-Ward, Dr Arthur James, 283
Darcy de Knath, 17th Baron, 249
Darwin, Leonard, 162
David, Albert, Bishop of Liverpool, 206, 207, 209
Davidson, Randall, 1st Baron Davidson of Lambeth, Archbishop of Canterbury, 129, 165, 196, 233, 253
Dawson of Penn, 1st Viscount, 160, 242
Deacon, John Francis William, 254
Deeming, Frederick, 166
Defoe, Daniel, 77
De Grey, 2nd Earl, *later* 1st Marquess of Ripon, 167, 170, 175
Dengel, Veronica, 277, 278
Denis, Saint, 21
Derby, 15th Earl of, 186
De Ros, 23rd Baron, 164
Desart, 5th Earl of, 103, 139, 153, 214
Devonshire, 8th Duke of, 213
diaries, 66–7, 106
Diaz de Isla, Ruy, 21–2
Dicks, John, 93
Dicks, Terry, 375
Digby, Sir Kenelm, 215
Dilhorne, 1st Viscount, 60, 323

Index

Dingley, Charles, 36
Directorate of Public Prosecutions, 103, 298, 303, 315
Disraeli, Benjamin, 112
divine punishment, 6–7, 26–7, 101, 165
doctors, see physicians
Dodd, Revd William, 36–8
Donkin, Sir Bryan, 238–40, 241, 242
Donne, John, 60, 65
Dorchester, 2nd Earl of, 63
Dorset, 1st Duke of, 83
Dorset, 5th Duke of, 83
Douglas, Lord Alfred, 115, 136
Douglas, Norman, 125, 248
Douthwaite, Alan, 10
Downham, 1st Baron, 163
Downshire, Marchioness of, 68
Driberg, Tom (Lord Bradwell), 114–15, 125–6, 316
Drumlanrig, Viscount, 136–7
Dryden, John, 11, 42, 77
Dubois, E. X., 147–8
Dudley, 3rd Earl of, 10
Dufferin and Ava, 1st Marquess of (5th Baron Dufferin and Claneboye), 112, 123–4, 156, 164, 177, 186, 190
Dufferin and Ava, 3rd Marquess of, 238
Dufferin and Ava, 4th Marquess of, 261
Dufferin and Ava, Hariot, Marchioness of, 72, 124, 164
Dufferin and Claneboye, 5th Baron, see Dufferin and Ava, 1st Marquess of
Duffus, George, 79
Duleep Singh, Prince Frederick, 160
Dunne, Sir Laurence, 292, 302, 305
Durex condoms, 355–6
Duty and Discipline Movement, 200
Duvalier, Jean-Claude, 2
Dyer, Alfred, 176–7

Eames, Sir John, 95–6
Eason, H. J., 253, 254
East, Sir Norwood, 289, 292
Edward VII, King of England, 137
Edwards, Egerton, 154–5
Egremont, 3rd Earl of, 50
Egypt, 194, 265–6, 300
Ehrlich, Paul, 194–5
Elizabeth I, Queen of England, 30, 32, 57, 60
Elliott, Hugh, 236–7
Elliott, Jacqui, 348
Elliott, Walter, 264
Ellis, Havelock, 121, 139

'empires, fall of', 151, 196, 197, 300, 313, 314, 322, 329
Englefield, Sir Henry, 68
English Review, 203
Equal Opportunities Commission, 346
Esher, 2nd Viscount, 137
espionage, 148–9, 298–301
Ex-Servicemen's National Movement, 239
extortion, see blackmail
eugenics, 162, 212, 242
Evening Standard, 322

Falkland, 15th Viscount, 373
Fallopio, Gabriello, 52
family life, 67–8, 115–6, 122–3, 342
Fawkener, William, Clerk of the Council, 69
Federal Bureau of Investigation, 301
Federation of Medical Women, 197
fellatio, 77–80, 82, 282, 294
Ferdinand II, King of Naples, 20
Ferdinand V, King of Castile, 20
Ferdinand, Prince of Brunswick, 83
Fife, 1st Duke of, 160
Finnemore, Sir Donald, 309
Firbank, Ronald, 375
Fischer, H. C., 147–8
Fisher, Geoffrey, Baron Fisher of Lambeth, Archbishop of Canterbury, 323
Fitt, Baron, 371
FitzAlan of Derwent, 1st Viscount, 252
FitzGerald, Oswald, 179–80
FitzRoy, Sir Almeric, 184, 213, 216, 219, 221, 229
flagellation, 76, 94, 310
Flaubert, Gustave, 225
Fletcher-Cooke, Sir Charles, 322
flogging, 142–3, 316
Forster, E. M., 154
Fracastor, Hieronymus, 22–3, 31, 43
France, 14, 21, 28, 72, 86, 93, 96, 103, 119, 227, 323
Frazier, Sir Alexander, 40
Fremantle, Sir Francis, 264, 269
Friendship, John, 29
Frost, Robert, 383
Fyfe, see Kilmuir

Gainford, 1st Baron, 164
Gale, George, 335
Galen, 9, 23, 24
Gama, Vascò da, 21
Gascoigne, Sir Thomas, 63
Gay, John, 52

Gay, Peter, 122–3, 326
Gay's the Word Bookshop, 380
Geddes, 1st Baron, 243
Gell, Edith Lyttelton, 157–8
Genet, Jean, 380
George II, King of England, 51
George III, King of England, 83, 92
George V, King of England, 160
Germain, Lord George (1st Viscount Sackville), 83–4
Gibbon, Edward, 75, 102
Gibbs, Dr Charles, 196, 198, 251–2
Gielgud, Sir John, 314, 328
Gill, Mike, 348
Gladstone, William Ewart, 106, 137, 170, 175
Glaxo Laboratories, 272
Glenbervie, 1st Baron, 69, 83, 85
Glenconner, 3rd Baron, 339–40
Goddard, Lord, 308, 315–6
Godley, Sir Alexander, 194
gonorrhoea, 16–17, 24–5, 110, 283
Goodyear, Charles, 194
Gordon-Moore, Lord Cecil, 181
Gorell, 3rd Baron, 241, 242
Gould, Sir Alfred Pearce, 195–6
Grafton, 3rd Duke of, 70
Graham, Sir James, 97
Grantley, 6th Baron, 267
Graunt, John, 38, 185
Graves, Robert, 382
Gray, Dr George Douglas, 400
Greco, El (Domenikos Theotoko-poulos), 122
Greenway, Harry, 371, 381
Gritten, Howard, 151
Gully, William (1st Viscount Selby), 127

haemophiliacs, 2, 7, 349–50
Haggard, Sir (Henry) Rider, 140
Hailsham, 2nd Viscount, 225, 374
Haire, Norman, 230
Haiti, 2, 43
Halsbury, 1st Earl of, 134, 138–9, 200, 313
Halsbury, 3rd Earl of, 328, 367–73, 375
Hamilton, Sir Edward Walter, 129, 137
Hamilton, Lord George, 113–4
Hamilton and Brandon, 12th Duke of, 160
Hanley, James, 245, 248
Hannen, 1st Baron, 134–5, 185
Harberton, 7th Viscount, 140

Hardy, Thomas, 140, 332
Hare, Sir John, 314
Harman, Dr Nathaniel Bishop, 235, 245
Harris, Frank, 131–2
Harrison, Lawrence Whitaker, 180, 249–50, 252, 253, 261, 285
Harty, Russell, 340
Harvey, Gideon, 24–5
Hattersley, Roy, 225
Haweis, Revd Thomas, 38
Hawkesbury, Baron (*later* 2nd Earl of Liverpool), 86, 102
Hawkins, Sir Anthony Hope, 140
Health, Ministry of, 163, 199, 234, 237, 241–2, 250–3, 255, 257, 261–4, 266–9
Health Education Council (later Authority), 284, 351–2
Health and Social Security, Dept of, 351, 356–7
Heath, Sir Robert, 64
Helms, Jesse, 369
Helpmann, Sir Robert, 339
Henley, Joseph, 165
Henry VIII, King of England, 28–9, 32, 59, 60, 61, 132
Henry, Sir Edward, 241
Henry, Sir Thomas, 135
heroin, 340, 353, 361, 363–4
Higgins, Terrence, 331
Higton, Revd A. R., 377, 379
Hill, Sir Leonard, 238
Hill, Matthew Berkeley, 172, 185, 189–90
Hippocrates, 18, 23
Hitchin, Charles, 69
Hitler, Adolf, 225, 270
Hoffman, Erich, 193
Hogarth, William, 49–51
Holkar, Maharaja of, 113
Holloway, Robert, 75, 91, 100, 104
Home Office, 103, 143–5, 147, 225, 242, 270, 274–5, 293, 308, 317–8, 361–2
Home Security, Ministry of, 298
homosexuals, prosecuted, *see* prosecutions
Horder, 1st Baron, 185
hormone treatment, 293
Horsley, Canon J. W., 216, 218–9
Horsley, Sir Victor, 162, 184
hospitals,
  Bethlem, 116–8
  Birmingham General, 188

Birmingham Lock, 188
Bridewell Royal, 31
Bristol Lock, 188
Charing Cross, 251
Colchester, 187
for Diseases of the Throat, 188
East London, 238
Edinburgh Royal Infirmary, 251
for Epilepsy and Paralysis, 217
Glasgow Lock, 188
Guy's, 231
Hillingdon, 349
Hull General Infirmary, 187
Leeds Lock, 188
Liverpool, 187
Liverpool Lock, 188
London Lock, 35–8, 172, 188–9,
    196, 215, 251–4
Manchester Lock, 188
Maudsley, 217, 289, 295
Middlesex, 190, 195
Moorfields Ophthalmic, 188
Netley, 178
Newcastle Lock, 188
Nottingham, 188
Queen's Hospital, Birmingham, 188
Royal Free, 186–8, 196–7
St Bartholomew's, 30, 34, 187, 260,
    271
St George's, 186, 188
St Mary's, Paddington, 186, 272–3
St Thomas's, 34, 250, 252
Seaman's, 248
University College, 186, 187
West London, 342
Westminster, 255
Winchester, 187
Housman, A. E., 105
Housman, Laurence, 135
Howard League for Penal Reform, 309
Hudson, Rock, 9, 335
Hughes, Thomas, 167
Hunsdon, 2nd Baron, 60
Hunt, Violet, 190
Hunter, John, 25–6, 192
Huntingdon, Selina, Countess of, 34–5,
    38
Hurd, Douglas, 361, 377, 381–2
Hutten, Ulrich von, 24, 42
Hutton, Laura, 289–90

Ibsen, Henrik, 156
incest, 59, 365
Indecent Advertisements Act, 199–200
India, 113, 147, 167, 175–80, 191

Ingleby, 2nd Viscount, 373
Ingram, Kenneth, 121, 146, 292
Inskip, Sir Thomas (1st Viscount Calde-
    cote), 230
International Association for Planned
    Parenthood, 354
Iran, 300
Italy, 20–1

Jakobovits, Lord, 333, 376–7
James I and VI, King of England and
    Scotland, 61, 104
James IV, King of Scotland, 27–8
James, Henry, 68
James of Hereford, 1st Baron, 133
Jarman, Derek, 381
Jenny Lives With Eric and Martin, 368
Jersey, 4th Earl of, 69
Jews, 48, 120, 204
Jodhpur, Màharaja of, 113
Johnson, Sir William, 43
Johnstone, Sir Harcourt van den
    Bempde (1st Baron Derwent), 172
Jones, Sir David Brynmor, 215–6
journalists, 6–7, 9–10, 250–1, 266–7,
    336–40
Jowitt, 1st Earl, 297

Kellett-Bowman, Dame Elaine, 374
Kilmuir, 1st Earl of (*formerly* Sir David
    Maxwell-Fyfe), 304–5, 310, 312–13,
    322–3, 327
Kingsley, Charles, 167
Kimberley, 1st Earl of, 224
Kinnaird, 12th Baron, 254
Kinsey, Alfred, 274, 299–300
Kipling, Rudyard, 238
kissing, 71–2, 360, 366, 381
Kitchener of Khartoum, 1st Earl, 179–
    80
Knight, Dame Jill, 372, 374, 375
Korean War, 273

Labouchère, Henry, 130–6, 145, 149,
    153
Lads' Drill Association, 200
Lambert, E., 194
Lancaster, Sir Osbert, 325–6
Lancet, 139, 188, 212, 267
Lancisi, Giovanni Maria, 25
Lane, Dr James, 189–90
Lane, Dr James Ernest, 215
Lang, Cosmo, 1st Baron Lang of Lam-
    beth, Archbishop of Canterbury, 125,
    159, 249, 269

Index

Lankester, Sir Ray, 238
Latour, Terry, 374–5
lavatories, 86–7, 145, 146, 305
Lawrence, D. H., 225
Law Society, 319
League of Nations, 270–1
Lecky, W. E. H., 31–2, 46
Leeds, 5th Duke of, 83
Leeds, 8th Duke of, 5
Lee-Potter, Lynda, 7
Leitrim, 2nd Earl of, 50
Leitrim, Countess of (wife of 5th Earl), 254
Lennox, 3rd Duke of, 61
Lesbian and Gay Switchboard, 346, 371
lesbianism, 151–3
Lidgett, Revd J. Scott, 216, 218
Lilford, 4th Baron, 171, 174
Lincoln, John Jackson, Bishop of, 181
Liverpool, Bishop of (Albert David), 206, 207, 209
Liverpool, 2nd Earl of, see Hawkesbury
Lloyd, Sir Francis, 238
Local Government Board, 163, 222–3
Lockwood, Amelius, 1st Baron Lambourne, 143
Lombroso, Cesare, 119–20, 126, 300
London, Bishops of,
    Mandell Creighton, 216
    Beilby Porteus, xvii, 70
    Thomas Sherlock, 101
    Arthur Winnington-Ingram, 157–8, 210–11, 241
London County Council, 242, 253, 258–9, 260
London Lighthouse, 348
London Rubber Company, 278, 358
Long, 1st Viscount, 211
Long, Colonel Charles, 211
Longford, 7th Earl of, 322, 371
Lothian, 12th Marquess of, 319, 329
Loudoun, Countess of, 329
Low, Sir Sidney, 138
Lyster, Dr Robert, 271
Lyttelton, Revd Edward, 124, 208–9

Macaulay, 1st Baron, 139
McCardie, Sir Henry, 255
McCarthy, Senator Joseph, 301
MacDonald, Sir Hector, 113, 180
Machyn, Henry, 66
Mackay of Clashfern, Baron, 341
McKenna, Reginald, 143
Mackenzie, Sir Compton, 114, 316–7
Maclean, Donald, 300

McLean, Sir Kenneth, 302
MacLeod of Fuinary, Lord, 329
Macmillan, Alexander, 115
McNally, Edward, 303–4
McNalty, Sir Arthur, 261
MacQuisten, Frederick, 151–3
Madan, Revd Martin, 35–8
Magdalen homes, 36–7
Mallalieu, Francis, 171
Malmesbury, 4th Earl of, 177–8, 205
Malthusian League, 194, 240
Manchester, its chief constables, 13, 181
Manchester Guardian, 182, 322
Mao Tse-tung, 282
Marsh, Richard (Baron Marsh), 268, 280
Mars-Jones, Sir William, 366
Marston, John, 61
Martel de Janville, Comtesse de, 129
Marten, John, 39, 40, 47, 51, 52, 80, 82
masturbation, 110–1, 124, 175, 279, 355–8
Mates condoms, 231
Mathers, 1st Baron, 325
Mathew, Sir Theobald, 298–9, 303, 305, 327
Maude, Cyril, 314
Maudsley, Dr Henry, 14
Maugham, William Somerset, 122
Maupassant, Guy de, 333
Maurice, Frederick Denison, 94, 167
Maximilian I, Holy Roman Emperor, 26–7
Maxwell, Robert, 344
May, Dr Otto, 270–1
Meath, 12th Earl of, 199–200, 224
Medical Press, 289
Melly, George, 297
Mercantile and General Reinsurance, 342
mercury treatment, 40–3
Merrivale, 1st Baron, 249
Mersey, 1st Viscount, 214
Metchnikoff, Ilya, 192–4, 202, 223, 229
Mill, John Stuart, 115
Miller, Henry, xv
Millet, Kate, 380
Millington, Mary, 280
Mills, Ray, 336–7
Milner, 1st Viscount, 241
Milton, John, xv, 77
Minnes, Vice Admiral Sir John, 55

misogyny, 44–7, 53–4, 73–4, 100, 151–2, 198–9, 219, 255–9, 277, 280
Molson, Baron, 326
Mond, Sir Alfred (1st Baron Melchett), 242, 313
Montagu, 1st Duke of, 70
Montagu of Beaulieu, 3rd Baron, 303–4
Montesquieu, Charles Louis, Baron de la Brède et de, 8
Montgomery, 1st Earl of, 104
Montgomery of Alamein, 1st Viscount, 132
Moore, John, 364
More, Sir Thomas, 43
Morel, Benedict-Augustin, 119
Morley of Blackburn, 1st Viscount, 124, 164, 172, 174, 213–4, 221
Morning Chronicle, 49–50
Morning Herald, 98
Morning Post, 212, 214
Morris, Sir Malcolm, 6, 212–3, 215, 216, 221, 224, 229, 232, 234
Morrison, Dr George Ernest, 140
Morrison of Lambeth, Baron, 298, 300
Moses, 18
Mosher, Clelia, 197
Mott, Sir Frederick, 184, 215, 217, 223–4, 238
Moulton, Lord 229
Mullen, Revd Peter, 379–80
Murphy, Peter, 368

Napoleon Bonaparte, 101
National Council for Christian Standards in Society, 369
National Council for Combating Venereal Diseases, 216, 223, 230–43
National Council of Public Morals, 216, 221
National Liberal Federation, 175
National Secular Society, 281
National Vigilance Association, 212, 216
Neville-Rolfe, Sybil, 233, 261–2, 264
Nelson, 1st Viscount, 260
New York Native, 359
Newman, Sir George, 253
Newman, Cardinal John Henry, 269
News Chronicle, 300, 322
Newsholme, Sir Arthur, 215, 216, 222, 224
News of the World, 257, 295, 299, 338, 340, 341, 364, 366–71
Newton, Thomas, 91–2
New Zealand, 181

Nichols, Beverley, 141–2, 154–5
Nicolson, Sir Harold, 316
Niesser, Dr A., 192
Nightingale, Florence, 167
No Greater Sin, 229
Nordau, Max, 120–1, 126, 300
Northcliffe, 1st Viscount, 214
notification of diseases, 28, 182–3
Nott-Bower, Sir John, 304–5

O'Brien, William, 130–1
Observer, 322
Oldham, John, 34, 57, 65
Oliver, Sir Roland, 307–8
Onslow, 4th Earl of, 178
Osborne, Revd Lord Sydney Godolphin, 5
Osler, Sir William, 210

Paget, Lord Clarence, 167–8, 170
Paget, Dr Stephen, 190
Pall Mall Gazette, 212
Palmerston, 3rd Viscount, 170
Paracelsus (*nom de clinique* of Theophrastus Bombastus von Hohenheim), 24, 26, 45
Park, Fred ('Fanny'), 118
Parkinson, Cecil, 333
Pascal, Blaise, 16
Paton, J. L. A., 208–9
Paul, Saint, 12, 55, 246
Pavese, Cesare, xv, 330
Peacock, Sir Robert, 181
Pears, Sir Peter, 339
Peel, Arthur (1st Viscount Peel), 132
Peel, John, 282
Peel, Sir Robert, 97
Pellicci, Roger, 366
Pembroke and Montgomery, 4th Earl of, 104
penicillin, 271–3
Penzance, 1st Baron, 185
Pepys, Samuel, 34, 40, 55, 67
Peterborough and Monmouth, 3rd Earl of, 67
Petty, Sir William, 38, 185
physicians, 23–5, 30–1, 116–7, 119, 139, 159–61, 189–91, 234–5, 249–54, 347, 349
Pigg, Mrs Bonham, 271
pillory, 71, 94, 98–100
Pitt-Rivers, Michael, 303–4
Pius IX, Pope, 122

Index

police, 65, 91–2, 97, 145, 180, 284,
    298, 301, 306–7, 310–11, 319–20,
    346, 358, 360
Pollock, Sir Frederick, 59
Pollock, Sir John, 202
Pope, Alexander, 68
Porteus, Beilby, Bishop of London,
    xv, 70
Poyntz, Georgina (Lady John Town-
    shend), 69
Practitioner, 216
Praed, Winthrop Mackworth, 340
Priestley, J. B., 288
prisons, 9–10, 54, 91, 101–2, 292–4,
    361–3
Pritchett, Sir Victor, 37
privacy, 71–2, 326–7
projection, 3, 8, 100–2
prophylaxis, 51–2, 179, 181, 193–4,
    196–8, 202–3, 223–4, 226–9, 231–
    2, 234–8, 240–2, 335–7
prosecution of homosexuals, 58–65, 69,
    72–3, 75–6, 78–9, 82, 86–7, 92–100,
    102–3
    death penalty abolished, 96
    Labouchère's amendment, 130–35
    twentieth cent., earlier, 142–9,
        295–8, 302–11, 317
    twentieth cent., Wolfenden reforms,
        323–4, 328, 366
prostitutes, 49, 53–4, 166, 170–2, 176,
    194, 220, 227–8, 256–7, 312, 322
Proust, Marcel, 55
Punch, 284

quacks, 48–51, 229
Queensberry, 4th Duke of, 85
Queensberry, 9th Marquess of, 136–7
Queensborough, 1st Baron, 239
Quilter, Harry, 126–7, 139–40

Ranksborough, 1st Baron, 163, 183
Rees, J. Tudor, 300, 309, 320
Reid, Sir Archdall, 163, 196, 227, 233,
    238, 240, 241, 242, 244
rent boys, 136, 316, 333
Renton, Baron, 322
Reynolds, John, 303–4
Rhondda, 1st Viscount, 163
Richard III, King of England, 29
Richards, Revd Gregory, 10
Ricord, Philippe, 192
Ripon, Bishop of (David Young), 379
Ripon, 1st Marquess of, *see* de Grey
Robertson, Sir John, 196

Robinson, Sir Arthur, 241–2, 253, 262
Robson, Dr Henry, 202–3
Rochester, Bishops of
    Christopher Chavasse, 7, 320
    John Fisher, 29
Rochester, 2nd Earl of, 6, 16, 34, 46, 47,
    63, 65, 86
Rodney, Dr Jonathan, 370
Rosebery and Midlothian, 5th Earl of,
    136–8, 224, 398
Rothermere, 1st Viscount, 239, 267
Rothermere, 2nd Viscount, 299
Rout, Ettie, 198
Roux, Pierre, 192
Rowlandson, Thomas, 78
Roxburgh, J. F., 373
Royal Commission on Venereal Dis-
    eases, 211–24, 229, 243–4
Rubie, Revd George Crowhurst, 254
Rumbold, Angela, 372
Runcie, Robert, Archbishop of Canter-
    bury, 376, 380
Rupert, Prince, Duke of Cumberland,
    40
Rushdie, Salman, 225
Rutland, 1st Duke of, 63–4
Ryan, Michael, 343
Ryder, Sir Dudley, 76

sailors, 97–8, 103–4, 108, 167, 191,
    301–2
Saki (H. H. Munro), 55
Salisbury, 3rd Marquess of, 132, 136–9,
    211
Salvarsan, 195, 212, 222
Sandhurst, 1st Viscount, 202, 227
Santayana, George, 4
Sartre, Jean-Paul, 380
Saul, Jack, 146
Saunders, Dame Cicely, 342
Savage, Sir George, 116–18
Savage, Richard, 61
Scharlieb, Dame Mary, 195, 215, 216,
    220–1, 227, 232, 234, 240
Schaudinn, Fritz, 193
Schofield, Dr Michael, 294–5
schools, 61, 62, 76, 110–13, 143–4,
    367–73
Schopenhauer, Arthur, 45, 164, 330
Scott, C. P., 182
Scott, Revd Thomas, 38
Selwyn, George, 83, 85
Shakespeare, William, 21, 29, 42, 43–4,
    374
Shannon, Thomas, 144–5

Sharkey, Sir Seymour, 239
Shaw, George Bernard, 202, 207
Shelley, Percy Bysshe, 3
Sherlock, Thomas, Bishop of London, 101
Shiels, Sir Drummond, 272
Short, Clare, 381
Simpson, Revd Robert, 237–8
sin, 32, 38, 64–5, 125, 159, 165, 222, 235–6, 246, 320–1
Singleton, Sir John, 295–7
Skelmersdale, 7th Baron, 371, 373
Skipwith, Henry, 63
slicklegging, 78–9, 82, 294
Smith, F. E. (1st Earl of Birkenhead), 145, 153
Smith, George Joseph, 166
Smith, Revd Sidney, 71, 367
Smith, W. H. & Sons, 203
Smollett, Tobias, 53–4, 63, 88–90, 104
Snell, Alderman Leonard, 254
Snow, Lord, 326
Snowden, 1st Viscount, 215, 216
Society for Enforcing the King's Proclamation against Immorality and Profaneness, 70
Society for Preventing Venereal Diseases, 197, 238–43, 271
Society for Reformation of Manners, 69, 72
Society for Reformation of Vice, 71
soldiers, 146–9, 166–81, 210–11, 241, 302, 307, 359–60, 367
Solly, Samuel, 165–6
Somerset, 12th Duke of, 167
Somerset, 1st Earl of, 61
Somerset, Lord Arthur, 13, 134, 136, 137
Soper, Lord, 279
Soutar, William, 330
Spectator, 338, 345
Spencer, Herbert, 236
Spinke, John, 49
Stable, Sir Wintringham, 309
Stafford, Marchioness of (*formerly* Duchess of Sutherland), 69
Stafford-Clark, Dr David, 295
Stamp, 3rd Baron, 283, 328–9
Stapleton, Sir Thomas, 84
Star, 336
Stead, W. T., 129, 133, 149, 181–2
Steel, Sir Samuel Strang, 254
Stevens, Wallace, 286
Stevenson, London Constable, 92
Stirling, Sir Walter George, 182

Stone, Lawrence, 67, 73
Stopes, Marie, 220
Streatfield, Sir Geoffrey, 308
Summerskill, Baroness, 268
Sumner, 1st Viscount, 138, 154
Sun, 10, 333, 337–8, 339–40, 343, 379, 381
Sunday Correspondent, 363
Sunday Graphic, 322
Sunday Mirror, 10, 364
Sunday Pictorial, 308
Sunday Telegraph, 352, 364, 365, 367
Sunday Times, 322
Sutherland, Duchess of, 69
Swift, Graham, xv
Sydenham of Combe, 1st Baron, 214–7, 221, 223, 224, 229, 231, 232
Sydney, 2nd Viscount, 102
Symonds, Sir Charters, 231
Symonds, John Addington, 111–12, 127–8
syphilophobia, *see* worried well.

Tait, Andrew Wilson, 185
Tatchell, Peter, 359
Taylor, Teddy, 359
Temple, Frederick, Archbishop of Canterbury, 122
Temple, William, Archbishop of Canterbury, 14, 268–9
Tennant, Charles, 340
Tennant, Henry, 339–40
Tennyson, 1st Baron, 156, 169
Terrence Higgins Trust, 345, 350–3, 356
Texaco Oil Co., 347
Thatcher, Margaret, 333, 338, 362–3, 376
Thatcher, Mark, 333
Thompson, Sir Benjamin, Count von Rumford, 83–4
Thoresby, Ralph, 67
Times, The, 10, 178, 181, 186, 200, 214, 339, 358
Tiverton, Viscount, 373
Tocqueville, Alexis, Comte de, 265
Tomlin, 1st Baron, 242
Torbay Health Authority, 347
Torrella, Gasparo, 23
Traherne, Thomas, 66
Transport, Ministry of, 256
transvestites, 74, 78, 118
Treasury, 212
Tree, Sir Herbert Beerbohm, 314
Trevethin, 1st Baron, 242–3

Index

Trevor-Roper, Hugh (Lord Dacre of Glanton), 1
Trollope, Anthony, 159–60
Troup, Sir Edward, 143
Turner, Dr Edward, 234–6

Ulwar, Maharaja of, 113
USA, 265–6, 273–4, 299–301, 303, 350

Vallette, Marguerite, 129
Venereal Diseases, Royal Commission on, 211–24, 229, 243–4
Victoria, Queen of England, 126, 137, 181, 186, 200, 201
Vigilance Association for the Defence of Personal Rights, 183
Vigo, Joannes de, 24
Viguers, Joshua, 100
Vickers, Vincent, 238
Vincent, Sir Howard, 135
Vincent, John, 372

Wallace, William, 191
Warbeck, Perkin, 27–8
Walsingham, Sir Francis, 66
War Office, 147, 149, 170, 226, 228–9, 260, 270, 302
Wassermann, August von, 193, 212, 222, 265
Waterford and Lismore, Bishop of (John Atherton), 63
Watney, Simon, 383
Watters, David, 349
Waugh, Evelyn, 140
Wedgwood, 1st Baron, 153
Wellesley, 1st Marquess, 84
Wells, H. G., 140, 238
Wells, Richard, 348
Wesley, John, 35
West, Mae, 259
What's On, 284
White, Arnold, 148
White, Edmund, 180, 380
Whitefield, George, 34
Whitehead, Tony, 350
Whitehouse, Mary, 4

Wilberforce, Samuel, Bishop of Oxford and later Winchester, 181
Wild, Sir Ernest, 151–3, 297
Wilde, Oscar, 12, 63, 135–42, 145, 154, 314, 327, 362
  Dorian Gray, 14, 129
  Gay's the Word prosecution, 380
  on morality, 161, 210
  'sexual insanity', 120
  Stead's defence of, 133
  syphilis, 14, 190, 192
Wildeblood, Peter, 295, 302–4
Wilkes, John, 83–5
Wilks, Sir Samuel, 192
William III, King of England, 45
Williams, Tennessee, 380
Willis, London Constable, 92
Willis, W. N., 203–5
Willoughby de Broke, 19th Baron, 238, 241, 243
Windham, William ('Tricks and Fancies'), 76
Winnington-Ingram, Arthur, Bishop of London, 157–8, 210–11, 241
Winslow, Forbes, 158
Winster, 1st Baron 272
Winterton, 6th Earl, 313–4
Winterton, Nicholas, 331
Wiseman, Richard, 24–5, 40, 42
Wittkower, Dr E. D., 260
Wolfenden, Baron 286–7, 314–29, 373
Wollstonecraft, Mary, 76
Wolsey, Cardinal Thomas, 28–9
Woolf, Virginia, 232–3
Worden, Blair, 32
Workers' Liberty and Employment League, 239
World Health Organization, 2, 361
worried well, 39–40, 262, 281
Worsthorne, Peregrine, 365, 367
Wright, Thomas, 92
Wyatt of Weeford, Baron, 371–2

Yeats, W. B., 12

Zittman, Johann Friedrich, 43
Zola, Emile, 119, 161–2